Albert Gallatin

THE LIFE

OF

ALBERT GALLATIN.

BY

HENRY ADAMS.

───────

Reprinted under the auspices
of the
OUT-OF-PRINT BOOKS COMMITTEE
of the
AMERICAN LIBRARY ASSOCIATION

NEW YORK
PETER SMITH
1943

PREFACE.

A LARGE part of the following biography relates to a period of American history as yet unwritten, and is intended to supply historians with material which, except in such a form, would be little likely to see the light. The principal private source from which the author has drawn his information is of course the rich collection of papers which Albert Gallatin left behind him in the hands of his only now surviving son and literary executor, under whose direction these volumes are published. By the liberality and courtesy of Mr. Evarts, Secretary of State, and the active assistance of the admirable organization of the State Department, much material in the government archives at Washington has been made accessible, without which the story must have been little more than a fragment. The interesting series of letters addressed to Joseph H. Nicholson are drawn from the Nicholson MSS., which Judge Alexander B. Hagner kindly placed in the author's hands at a moment when he had abandoned the hope of tracing them. For other valuable papers and information he is indebted to Miss Sarah N. Randolph, of Edgehill, the representative of Mr. Jefferson, the Nicholases, and the Randolphs. The persevering inquiries of Mr. William Wirt Henry, of Richmond, have resulted in filling some serious gaps in the narrative, and the antiquarian research of Mr. James Veech, of Pittsburg, has been freely put at the author's service. Finally, he has to recognize the unfailing generosity with which his numerous and troublesome demands have been met by one whose path it is his utmost hope in some slight degree to have smoothed,—his friendly adviser, George Bancroft.

WASHINGTON, May, 1879.

TABLE OF CONTENTS.

(v)

LIFE OF ALBERT GALLATIN.

BOOK I.

YOUTH. 1761–1790.

JEAN DE GALLATIN, who, at the outbreak of the French revolution, was second in command of the regiment of Châteauvieux in the service of Louis XVI., and a devout believer in the antiquity of his family, maintained that the Gallatins were descended from A. Atilius Callatinus, consul in the years of Rome 494 and 498; in support of this article of faith he fought a duel with the Baron de Pappenheim, on horseback, with sabres, and, as a consequence, ever afterwards carried a sabre-cut across his face. His theory, even if held to be unshaken by the event of this wager of battle, is unlikely ever to become one of the demonstrable facts of genealogy, since a not unimportant gap of about fifteen hundred years elapsed between the last consulship of the Roman Gallatin and the earliest trace of the modern family, found in a receipt signed by the Abbess of Bellacomba for "quindecim libras Viennenses" bequeathed to her convent by "Dominus Fulcherius Gallatini, Miles," in the year 1258. Faulcher Gallatini left no other trace of his existence; but some sixty years later, in 1319, a certain Guillaume Gallatini, Chevalier, with his son Humbert Gallatini, Damoiseau, figured dimly in legal documents, and Humbert's grandson, Henri Gallatini, Seigneur de Granges, married Agnes de Lenthenay, whose will, dated 1397, creating her son Jean Gallatini her heir, fixes the local origin of the future Genevan family. Granges was an estate in Bugey, in the province of which Bellay was the capital, then a part of Savoy, but long since absorbed in France, and now embraced in the Département de l'Ain. It lay near the Rhone, some thirty or forty miles below Geneva, and about the same distance above Lyons. This Jean Gallatini, Seigneur de Granges and of many other manors, was an equerry of the Duke of Savoy, and a man of importance in his neighborhood. He too had a son Jean, who was also an equerry of the Duke of Savoy, and a man of gravity, conscientious in his opinions and serious in his acts. Not only Duke Philibert but even Pope Leo X. held him in esteem; the Duke made him his secretary with the title of Vice Comes, and the Pope clothed him with the dignity of Apostolic Judge, with the power to create one hundred and fifty notaries and public judges, and with the further somewhat invidious privilege of legitimatizing an equal number of bastards. Notwithstanding this mark of apostolic favor conferred on the "venerabilis vir dominus Johannes Gallatinus, civis Gebennensis" by a formal act dated at Salerno in 1522, Jean Gallatin was not an obedient son of the Church. For reasons no longer to be ascertained, he had in 1510 quitted his seigniories and his services in Savoy and caused himself to be enrolled as a citizen of Geneva. The significance of this act rests in the fact that the moment he chose for the change was that which immediately preceded the great revolution in Genevan history when the city tore itself away not only from Savoy but from the Church. Jean Gallatin was a man of too much consequence not to be welcomed at Geneva. He linked his fortunes with hers, became a member of the Council, and joined in the decree which, in 1535, deposed the Prince Bishop and abrogated the power of the Pope. He died in 1536, the year Calvin came to Geneva, and the Gallatins were so far among the close allies of the great reformer that a considerable number of his letters to them were still preserved by the family until stolen or destroyed by some of the wilder reformers who accompanied the revolutionary armies of France in 1794.[1]

After the elevation of Geneva to the rank of a sovereign republic in 1535, the history of the Gallatins is the history of the city. The family, if not the first in the state, was second

---

[1] A more detailed account of the Gallatin genealogy will be found in the Appendix to vol. iii. of Gallatin's Writings, p. 593.

to none. Government was aristocratic in this small republic, and of the eleven families into whose hands it fell at the time of the Reformation, the Gallatins furnished syndics and counsellors, with that regularity and frequency which characterized the mode of selection, in a more liberal measure than any of the other ten. Five Gallatins held the position of first syndic, and as such were the chief magistrates of the republic. Many were in the Church; some were professors and rectors of the University. They counted at least one political martyr among their number,—a Gallatin who, charged with the crime of being head of a party which aimed at popular reforms in the constitution, was seized and imprisoned in 1698, and died in 1719, after twenty-one years of close confinement. They overflowed into foreign countries. Pierre, the elder son of Jean, was the source of four distinct branches of the family, which spread and multiplied in every direction, although of them all no male representative now exists except among the descendants of Albert Gallatin. One was in the last century a celebrated physician in Paris, chief of the hospital established by Mme. Necker; another was Minister of Foreign Affairs to the Duke of Brunswick, who, when mortally wounded at the battle of Jena, in 1806, commended his minister to the King of Würtemberg as his best and dearest friend. The King respected this dying injunction, and Count Gallatin, in 1819, was, as will be seen, the Würtemberg minister at Paris.

That the Gallatins did not restrict their activity to civil life is a matter of course. There were few great battle-fields in Europe where some of them had not fought, and not very many where some of them had not fallen. Voltaire testifies to this fact in the following letter to Count d'Argental, which contains a half-serious, half-satirical account of their military career:

VOLTAIRE TO THE COUNT D'ARGENTAL.

9 février, 1761.

Voici la plus belle occasion, mon cher ange, d'exercer votre ministère céleste. Il s'agit du meilleur office que je puisse recevoir de vos bontés.

Je vous conjure, mon cher et respectable ami, d'employer tout
votre crédit auprès de M. le Duc de Choiseul; auprès de ses
amis; s'il le faut, auprès de sa maîtresse, &c., &c.   Et pourquoi
osé-je vous demander tant d'appui, tant de zèle, tant de vivacité,
et surtout un prompt succès?   Pour le bien du service, mon cher
ange; pour battre le Duc de Brunsvick.   M. Galatin, officier
aux gardes suisses, qui vous présentera ma très-humble requête,
est de la plus ancienne famille de Genève; ils se font tuer pour
nous de père en fils depuis Henri Quatre.   L'oncle de celui-ci a été
tué devant Ostende; son frère l'a été à la malheureuse et abominable journée de Rosbach, à ce que je crois; journée où les régi-
ments suisses firent seuls leur devoir.   Si ce n'est pas à Rosbach,
c'est ailleurs; le fait est qu'il a été tué; celui-ci a été blessé.   Il
sert depuis dix ans; il a été aide-major; il veut l'être.   Il faut
des aides-major qui parlent bien allemand, qui soient actifs, intel-
ligens; il est tout cela.   Enfin vous saurez de lui précisément ce
qu'il lui faut; c'est en général la permission d'aller vîte chercher
la mort à votre service.   Faites-lui cette grâce, et qu'il ne soit
point tué, car il est fort aimable et il est neveu de cette Mme.
Calendrin que vous avez vue étant enfant.   Mme. sa mère est
bien aussi aimable que Mme. Calendrin.

One Gallatin fell in 1602 at the Escalade, famous in Genevan
history; another at the siege of Ostend, in 1745; another at the
battle of Marburg, in 1760; another, the ninth of his name who
had served in the Swiss regiment of Aubonne, fell in 1788, acting as a volunteer at the siege of Octzakow; still another, in
1797, at the passage of the Rhine.   One commanded a battalion
under Rochambeau at the siege of Yorktown.   But while these
scattered members of the family were serving with credit and
success half the princes of Christendom, the main stock was
always Genevan to the core and pre-eminently distinguished in
civil life.

In any other European country a family like this would have
had a feudal organization, a recognized head, great entailed
estates, and all the titles of duke, marquis, count, and peer
which royal favor could confer or political and social influence
could command.   Geneva stood by herself.   Aristocratic as her

government was, it was still republican, and the parade of rank
or wealth was not one of its chief characteristics. All the honors
and dignities which the republic could give were bestowed on
the Gallatin family with a prodigal hand; but its members had
no hereditary title other than the quaint prefix of Noble, and the
right to the further prefix of *de*, which they rarely used; they had
no great family estate passing by the law of primogeniture, no
family organization centring in and dependent on a recognized
chief. Integrity, energy, courage, and intelligence were for the
most part the only family estates of this aristocracy, and these
were wealth enough to make of the little city of Geneva the
most intelligent and perhaps the purest society in Europe. The
austere morality and the masculine logic of Calvin were here
at home, and there was neither a great court near by, nor great
sources of wealth, to counteract or corrupt the tendencies of
Calvin's teachings. In the middle of the eighteenth century,
when Gallatins swarmed in every position of dignity or usefulness in their native state and in every service abroad, it does not
appear that any one of them ever attained very great wealth, or
asserted a claim of superior dignity over his cousins of the name.
Yet the name, although the strongest, was not their only common
tie. A certain François Gallatin, who died in 1699, left by
will a portion of his estate in trust, its income to be expended for
the aid or relief of members of the family. This trust, known
as the Bourse Gallatin, honestly and efficiently administered,
proved itself to be all that its founder could ever have desired.

One of the four branches of this extensive family was represented in the middle of the eighteenth century by Abraham
Gallatin, who lived on his estate at Pregny, one of the most
beautiful spots on the west shore of the lake, near Geneva, and
who is therefore known as Abraham Gallatin of Pregny. His
wife, whom he had married in 1732, was Susanne Vaudenet,
commonly addressed as Mme. Gallatin-Vaudenet. They were,
if not positively wealthy, at least sufficiently so to maintain their
position among the best of Genevese society, and Mme. Gallatin
appears to have been a woman of more than ordinary character,
intelligence, and ambition. The world knows almost every
detail about the society of Geneva at that time; for, apart from

a very distinguished circle of native Genevans, it was the society in which Voltaire lived, and to which the attention of much that was most cultivated in Europe was for that reason, if for no other, directed. Voltaire was a near neighbor of the Gallatins at Pregny. Notes and messages were constantly passing between the two houses. Dozens of these little billets in Voltaire's hand are still preserved. Some are written on the back of ordinary playing-cards. The deuce of clubs says:

"Nous sommes aux ordres de Mme. Galatin. Nous tâcherons d'employer ferblantier. Parlement Paris refuse tout édit et veut que le roi demande pardon à Parlement Bezançon. Anglais ont voulu rebombarder Hâvre. N'ont réussi. Carosse à une heure ½. Respects."

There is no date; but this is not necessary, for the contents seem to fix the date for the year 1756. A note endorsed "Des Délices" is in the same tone:

"Lorsque V. se présente chez sa voisine, il n'a d'autre affaire, d'autre but, que de lui faire sa cour. Nous attendons pour faire des répétitions le retour du Tyran qui a mal à la poitrine. S'il y a quelques nouvelles de Berlin, Mr. Gallatin est supplié d'en faire part. Mille respects."

Another, of the year 1759, is on business:

"Comment se porte notre malade, notre chère voisine, notre chère fille? J'ai été aux vignes, madame. Les guèpes mangent tout, et ce qu'elles ne mangent point est sec. Le vigneron de Mme. du Tremblay est venu me faire ses représentations. Mes tonneaux ne sont pas reliés, a-t-il dit; différez vendange. Relie tes tonneaux, ai-je dit. Vos raisins ne sont pas mûrs, a-t-il dit. Va les voir, ai-je dit. Il y a été; il a vu. Vendangez au plus vîte, a-t-il dit. Qu'ordonnez-vous, madame, au voisin V.?"

Another of the same year introduces Mme. Gallatin's figs, of which she seems to have been proud:

"Vos figues, madame, sont un présent d'autant plus beau que nous pouvons dire comme l'autre: *car ce n'était pas le temps des figues*. Nous n'en avons point aux Délices, mais nous aurons un théâtre à Tourney. Et nous partons dans une heure pour venir vous voir. Recevez vous et toute votre famille, madame, les tendres respects de V."

" Vous me donnez plus de figues, madame, qu'il n'y en a dans le pays de papimanie; et moi, madame, je suis comme le figuier de l'Évangile, sec et maudit. Ce n'est pas comme acteur, c'est comme très-attaché à toute votre famille que je m'intéresse bien vivement à la santé de Mme. Galatin-Rolaz. Nous répétons mardi en habits pontificaux. Ceux qui ont des billets viendront s'ils veulent. Je suis à vous, madame, pour ma vie. V."

Then follows a brief note dated "Ferney, 18e 7re," 1761 :

"Nous comptions revenir tous souper à Ferney après la comédie. Mr. le Duc de Villars nous retint; notre carosse se rompit ; nous essuyâmes tous les contretemps possibles; la vie en est semée; mais le plus grand de tous est de n'avoir pas eu l'honneur de souper avec vous."

One of the friends for whom Mme. Gallatin-Vaudenet seems to have felt the strongest attachment, and with whom she corresponded, was the Landgrave of Hesse-Cassel, a personage not favorably known in American history. The Landgrave, in 1776, sent Mme. Gallatin his portrait, and Mme. Gallatin persuaded Voltaire to write for her a copy of verses addressed to the Landgrave, in recognition of this honor. Here they are from the original draft :

> " J'ai baisé ce portrait charmant,
> Je vous l'avoûrai sans mystère.
> Mes filles en ont fait autant,
> Mais c'est un secret qu'il faut taire.
> Vous trouverez bon qu'une mère
> Vous parle un peu plus hardiment ;
> Et vous verrez qu'également
> En tous les temps vous savez plaire."[1]

The success of Mme. Gallatin in the matter of figs led Voltaire to beg of her some trees; but his fortune was not so good as hers.

"10e Auguste, 1768, à Ferney. Vous êtes bénie de Dieu, madame. Il y a six ans que je plante des figuiers, et pas un ne réussit. Ce serait bien là le cas de sécher mes figuiers. Mais si j'avais des miracles à faire, ce ne serait pas celui-là. Je me

---

[1] Printed in Voltaire's Works, xii. 371 (ed. 1819.)

borne à vous remercier, madame. Je crois qu'il n'y a que les vieux figuiers qui donnent. La vieillesse est encore bonne à quelque chose. J'ai comme vous des chevaux de trente ans; c'est ce qui fait que je les aime; il n'y a rien de tel que les vieux amis. Les jeunes pourtant ne sont pas à mépriser, mesdames. V."

One more letter by Voltaire is all that can find room here. The Landgrave seems to have sent by Mme. Gallatin some asparagus seed to Voltaire, which he acknowledged in these words:

VOLTAIRE TO THE LANDGRAVE OF HESSE.

Le 15e septembre, 1772, DE FERNEY.

Monseigneur,—Mme. Gallatin m'a fait voir la lettre où votre Altesse Sérénissime montre toute sa sagesse, sa bonté et son goût en parlant d'un jeune homme dont la raison est un peu égarée. Je vois que dans cette lettre elle m'accorde un bienfait très-signalé, qu'on doit rarement attendre des princes et même des médecins. Elle me donne un brevet de trois ans de vie, car il faut trois ans pour faire venir ces belles asperges dont vous me gratifiez. Agréez, monseigneur, mes très-humbles remerciements. J'ose espérer de vous les renouveler dans trois années; car enfin il faut bien que je me nourrisse d'espérance avant que de l'être de vos asperges. Que ne puis-je être en état de venir vous demander la permission de manger celles de vos jardins! La belle révolution de Suède opérée avec tant de fermeté et de prudence par le roi votre parent, donne envie de vivre. Ce prince est comme vous, il se fait aimer de ses sujets. C'est assurément de toutes les ambitions la plus belle. Tout le reste a je ne sais quoi de chimérique et souvent de très-funeste. Je souhaite à Votre Altesse Sérénissime de longues années. C'est le seul souhait que je puisse faire; vous avez tout le reste. Je suis, avec le plus profond respect, monseigneur, de Votre Altesse Sérénissime le très-humble et très-obéissant serviteur,

"Le vieux malade de Ferney,

"Voltaire."

The correspondence of his Most Serene Highness, who made himself thus loved by his subjects, cannot be said to sparkle like that of Voltaire; yet, although the Landgrave's French was little better than his principles, one of his letters to Mme. Gallatin may find a place here. The single line in regard to his troops returning from America gives it a certain degree of point which only Americans or Hessians are likely to appreciate at its full value.

THE LANDGRAVE OF HESSE TO Mᴿ. GALLATIN-VAUDENET.

MADAME!—Je vous accuse avec un plaisir infini la lettre que vous avez bien voulu m'écrire le 27 mars dernier, et je vous fais bien mes parfaits remercîmens de la part que vous continuez de prendre à ma santé, dont je suis, on ne peut pas plus, content. La vôtre m'intéresse trop pour ne pas souhaiter qu'elle soit également telle que vous la désirez. Puisse la belle saison qui vient de succéder enfin au tems rude qu'il a fait, la raffermir pour bien des années, et puissiez-vous jouir de tout le contentement que mes vœux empressés vous destinent.

Quoique la lettre dont vous avez chargé Mr. Cramer m'ait été rendue, j'ai bien du regret d'avoir été privé du plaisir de faire sa connaissance personnelle, puisqu'il ne s'est pas arrêté à Cassel, et n'a fait que passer. Le témoignage favorable que vous lui donnez ne peut que prévenir en sa faveur.

Au reste je suis sur le point d'entreprendre un petit voïage que j'ai médité depuis longtems pour changer d'air. Je serais déjà en route, sans mes Trouppes revenus de l'Amérique, que je suis bien aise de revoir avant mon départ, et dont les derniers régimens seront rendus à Cassel vers la fin du mois.

Continuez-moi en attendant votre cher souvenir, et, en faisant bien mes complimens à Mr. et à Mlle. Gallatin, persuadez-vous que rien n'est au-dessus des sentimens vrais et invariables avec lesquels je ne finirai d'être, madame, votre très-humble et très-obéissant serviteur.

FRÉDÉRIC L. D'HESSE.

CASSEL, le 25 mai, 1784.

Mme. Gallatin-Vaudenet had three children,—one son and two daughters. The son, who was named Jean Gallatin, was born in 1733, and in 1755 married Sophie Albertine Rolaz du Rosey of Rolle,—the Mme. Gallatin-Rolaz already mentioned in one of

Voltaire's notes. They had two children,—a boy, born on the 29th of January, 1761, in the city of Geneva, and baptized on the following 7th of February by the name of Abraham Alfonse Albert Gallatin ; and a girl about five years older.

Abraham Gallatin, the grandfather, was a merchant in partnership with his son Jean. Jean died, however, in the summer of 1765, and his wife, Mme. Gallatin-Rolaz, who had talent and great energy, undertook to carry on his share of the business in her own separate name. She died in March, 1770. The daughter had been sent to Montpellier for her health, which she never recovered, and died a few years after, in 1777. The boy, Albert, was left an orphan when nine years old, with a large circle of blood-relations ; the nearest of whom were his grandfather Abraham and his grandmother the friend of Voltaire and of Frederic of Hesse. The child would naturally have been taken to Pregny and brought up by his grandparents, but a different arrangement had been made during the lifetime of his mother, and was continued after her death. Mme. Gallatin-Rolaz had a most intimate friend, a distant relation of her husband, Catherine Pictet by name, unmarried, and at this time about forty years old. When Jean Gallatin died, in 1765, Mlle. Pictet, seeing the widow overwhelmed with the care of her invalid daughter and with the charge of her husband's business, insisted on taking the boy Albert under her own care, and accordingly, on the 8th of January, 1766, Albert, then five years old, went to live with her, and from that time became in a manner her child.

Besides his grandfather Abraham Gallatin at Pregny, and his other paternal relations, Albert had a large family connection on the mother's side, and more especially an uncle, Alphonse Rolaz of Rolle, kind-hearted, generous, and popular. Both on the father's and the mother's side Albert had a right to expect a sufficient fortune. His interests during his minority were well cared for, and nothing can show better the characteristic economy and carefulness of Genevan society than the mode of the boy's education. For seven years, till January, 1773, he lived with Mlle. Pictet, and his expenses did not exceed eighty dollars a year. Then he went to boarding-school, and in August, 1775,

to the college or academy, where he graduated in May, 1779.
During all this period his expenses slightly exceeded two hundred dollars a year. The Bourse Gallatin advanced a comparatively large sum for his education and for the expenses of
his sister's illness. " No necessary expense was spared for my
education," is his memorandum on the back of some old accounts of his guardian; " but such was the frugality observed
in other respects, and the good care taken of my property, that
in 1786, when I came of age, all the debts had been paid excepting two thousand four hundred francs lent by an unknown
person through Mr. Cramer, who died in 1778, and with him
the secret name of that friend, who never made himself known
or could be guessed." In such an atmosphere one might suppose that economists and financiers must grow without the need
of education. Yet the fact seems to have been otherwise, and
in Albert Gallatin's closest family connection, both his grandfather Abraham and his uncle Alphonse Rolaz ultimately died
insolvent, and instead of inheriting a fortune from them he was
left to pay their debts.

Of the nature of Albert's training the best idea can be got
from his own account of the Academy of Geneva, contained in
a letter written in 1847 and published among his works.[1] At
that time the academy represented all there was of education in
the little republic, and its influence was felt in every thought and
act of the citizens. " In its organization and general outlines
the academy had not, when I left Geneva in 1780, been mate-
rially altered from the original institutions of its founder. Whatever may have been his defects and erroneous views, Calvin had
at all events the learning of his age, and, however objectionable
some of his religious doctrines, he was a sincere and zealous
friend of knowledge and of its wide diffusion among the people.
Of this he laid the foundation by making the whole education
almost altogether gratuitous, from the A B C to the time when
the student had completed his theological or legal studies. But
there was nothing remarkable or new in the organization or
forms of the schools. These were on the same plan as colleges

---

[1] Letter to Eben Dodge, 21st January, 1847. Writings, vol. ii. p. 688.

were then, and generally continue to be in the old seminaries of learning. . . . In the first place, besides the academy proper, there was a preparatory department intimately connected with it and under its control. This in Geneva was called 'the College,' and consisted of nine classes, . . . the three lower of which, for reading, writing, and spelling, were not sufficient for the wants of the people, and had several *succursales* or substitutes in various parts of the city. But for that which was taught in the six upper classes (or in the academy), there were no other public schools but the college and the academy. In these six classes nothing whatever was taught but Latin and Greek,—Latin thoroughly, Greek much neglected. Professor de Saussure used his best endeavors about 1776, when rector of the academy, to improve the system of education in the college by adding some elementary instruction in history, geography, and natural science, but could not succeed, a great majority of his colleagues opposing him. . . .

"When not aided and stimulated by enlightened parents or friends, the students from the time when they entered the academy (on an average when about or rather more than fifteen years old) were left almost to themselves, and studied more or less as they pleased. But almost all had previously passed through at least the upper classes of the college. I was the only one of my class and of the two immediately preceding and following me who had been principally educated at home and had passed only through the first or upper class of the college. . . . In the years 1775–1779 the average number of the scholars in the four upper classes of the college was about one hundred, and that of the students in the four first years of the academical course, viz., the auditoires of belles-lettres and philosophy, about fifty, of whom not more than one or two had not passed through at least the three or four upper classes of the college. Very few mechanics, even the watchmakers, so numerous in Geneva and noted for their superior intelligence and knowledge, went beyond the fifth and sixth classes, which included about one hundred and twenty scholars. As to the lower or primary classes or schools, it would have been difficult to find a citizen *intra muros* who could not read and write. The peasantry or cultivators of the soil in the small Genevese territory were, indeed, far more intelligent than their Catholic neighbors, but still, as in the other continental parts of Europe, a distinct and inferior class, with some religious instruction, but speaking *patois* (the great obstacle to the diffusion of knowledge), and almost universally not knowing how to read or to write. The population *intra muros* was about 24,000 (in 1535, at the epoch of the Reformation and independence, about 13,000), of whom nearly one third not naturalized, chiefly Germans or Swiss, exercising what were considered as lower trades, tailors, shoemakers, &c., and including almost all the menial servants. I never knew or heard of a male citizen or native of Geneva serving as such. The number of citizens above twenty-five years of age, and having a right to vote, amounted, exclusively of those residing abroad, to 2000. . . .

"There was in Geneva neither nobility nor any hereditary privilege but that of citizenship; and the body of citizens assembled in Council General had preserved the power of laying taxes, enacting laws, and ratifying treaties. But they could originate nothing, and a species of artificial aristocracy, composed of the old families which happened to be at the head of affairs when independence was declared, and skilfully strengthened by the successive adoption of the most distinguished citizens and emigrants, had succeeded in engrossing the public employments and concentrating the real power in two self-elected councils of twenty-five and two hundred members respectively. But that power rested on a most frail foundation, since in a state which consists of a single city the majority of the inhabitants may in twenty-four hours overset the government. In order to preserve it, a moral, intellectual superiority was absolutely necessary. This could not be otherwise attained than by superior knowledge and education, and the consequence was that it became disgraceful for any young man of decent parentage to be an idler. All were bound to exercise their faculties to the utmost; and although there are always some incapable, yet the number is small of those who, if they persevere, may not by labor become, in some one branch, well-informed men. Nor was that love and habit of learning long confined to that self-created aristocracy.

A salutary competition in that respect took place between the two political parties, which had a most happy effect on the general diffusion of knowledge.

"During the sixteenth and the greater part of the seventeenth century the Genevese were the counterpart of the Puritans of Old and of the Pilgrims of New England,—the same doctrines, the same simplicity in the external forms of worship, the same austerity of morals and severity of manners, the same attention to schools and seminaries of learning, the same virtues, and the same defects,—exclusiveness and intolerance, equally banishing all those who differed on any point from the established creed, putting witches to death, &c., &c. And with the progress of knowledge both about at the same time became tolerant and liberal. But here the similitude ends. To the Pilgrims of New England, in common with the other English colonists, the most vast field of enterprise was opened which ever offered itself to civilized man. Their mission was to conquer the wilderness, to multiply indefinitely, to settle and inhabit a whole continent, and to carry their institutions and civilization from the Atlantic to the Pacific Ocean. With what energy and perseverance this has been performed we all know. But to those pursuits all the national energies were directed. Learning was not neglected; but its higher branches were a secondary object, and science was cultivated almost exclusively for practical purposes, and only as far as was requisite for supplying the community with the necessary number of clergymen and members of the other liberal professions. The situation of Geneva was precisely the reverse of this. Confined to a single city and without territory, its inhabitants did all that their position rendered practicable. They created the manufacture of watches, which gave employment to near a fourth part of the population, and carried on commerce to the fullest extent of which their geographical situation was susceptible. But the field of active enterprise was still the narrowest possible. To all those who were ambitious of renown, fame, consideration, scientific pursuits were the only road that could lead to distinction, and to these, or other literary branches, all those who had talent and energy devoted themselves.

" All could not be equally successful; few only could attain a distinguished eminence; but, as I have already observed, a far greater number of well educated and informed men were found in that small spot than in almost every other town of Europe which was not the metropolis of an extensive country. This had a most favorable influence on the tone of society, which was not light, frivolous, or insipid, but generally serious and instructive. I was surrounded by that influence from my earliest days, and, as far as I am concerned, derived more benefit from that source than from my attendance on academical lectures. A more general fact deserves notice. At all times, and within my knowledge in the years 1770–1780, a great many distinguished foreigners came to Geneva to finish their education, among whom were nobles and princes from Germany and other northern countries; there were also not a few lords and gentlemen from England; even the Duke of Cambridge, after he had completed his studies at Göttingen. Besides these there were some from America, amongst whom I may count before the American Revolution those South Carolinians, Mr. Kinloch, William Smith,— afterwards a distinguished member of Congress and minister to Portugal,—and Colonel Laurens, one of the last who fell in the war of independence. And when I departed from Geneva I left there, besides the two young Penns, proprietors of Pennsylvania, Franklin Bache, grandson of Dr. Franklin, —— Johannot, grandson of Dr. Cooper, of Boston, who died young. Now, amongst all those foreigners I never knew or heard of a single one who attended academical lectures. It was the Genevese society which they cultivated, aided by private teachers in every branch, with whom Geneva was abundantly supplied."

At the academy Albert Gallatin associated of course with all the young Genevese of his day. As most of these had no permanent influence on him, and maintained no permanent relations with him, it is needless to speak of them further. There were but two whose names will recur frequently hereafter. Neither of them was equal to Gallatin in abilities or social advantages, but in politics and philosophy all were evidently of one mind, and the fortunes of all were linked together. The name of one was Henri Serre, that of the other was Jean Badollet.

What kind of men they were will appear in the course of their adventures. A fourth, whose name is better known than those just mentioned, seems to have been a close friend of the other three, but differed from them by not coming to America. He was Étienne Dumont, afterwards the friend and interpreter of Bentham.

However enlightened the society of Pregny may have been under the influence of Voltaire and Frederic of Hesse, it is not to be supposed that Mme. Gallatin-Vaudenet or any other members of the Gallatin family were by tastes and interests likely to lean towards levelling principles in politics. Of all people in Geneva they were perhaps most interested in maintaining the old Genevese régime. The Gallatins were for the most part firm believers in aristocracy, and Albert certainly never found encouragement for liberal opinions in his own family, unless they may have crept in through the pathway of Voltairean philosophy as mere theory, the ultimate results of which were not foreseen. This makes more remarkable the fact that young Gallatin, who was himself a clear-headed, sober-minded, practical Genevan, should, by some bond of sympathy which can hardly have been anything more than the intellectual movement of his time, have affiliated with a knot of young men who, if not quite followers of Rousseau, were still essentially visionaries. They were dissatisfied with the order of things in Geneva. They believed in human nature, and believed that human nature when free from social trammels would display nobler qualities and achieve vaster results, not merely in the physical but also in the moral world. The American Revolutionary war was going on, and the American Declaration of Independence embodied, perhaps helped to originate, some of their thoughts.

With minds in this process of youthful fermentation, they finished their academical studies and came out into the world. Albert was graduated in May, 1779, first of his class in mathematics, natural philosophy, and Latin translation. Before this time, in April, 1778, he had returned to Mlle. Pictet, and his principal occupation for the year after graduating was as tutor to her nephew, Isaac Pictet. Both Gallatin and Badollet were students of English, and the instruction given to Isaac Pictet

seems to have been partly in English. Of course the serious
question before him was that of choosing a profession, and this
question was one in which his family were interested ; in which,
indeed, their advice would naturally carry decisive weight.   The
young man was much at Pregny with his grandparents, where,
during his childhood, he often visited Voltaire at Ferney.   His
grandmother had her own views as to his career.   She wished
him to take a commission of lieutenant-colonel in the military
service of her friend the Landgrave of Hesse, with whom her
interest was sufficient to insure for him a favorable reception and
a promising future.   At that moment, it is true, the military
prospects of the Landgrave's troops in the Jerseys were not peculiarly flattering, and the service can hardly have been popular with
such as might remember the dying words of Colonel Donop
at Red Bank ; but after all the opportunity was a sure one,
suitable for a gentleman of ancient family, according to the
ideas of the time, and flattering to the pride of Mme. Gallatin-
Vaudenet.   She spoke to her grandson on the subject, urging
her advice with all the weight she could give it.   He replied,
abruptly, that he would never serve a tyrant.   The reply was
hardly respectful, considering the friendship which he knew to
exist between his grandmother and the Landgrave, and it is not
altogether surprising that it should have provoked an outbreak
of temper on her part which took the shape of a box on the ear :
" she gave me a cuff," were Mr. Gallatin's own words in telling
the story to his daughter many years afterwards.   This " cuff "
had no small weight in determining the young man's course of
action.

Yet it would be unfair to infer from this box on the ear that
the family attempted to exercise any unreasonable control over
Albert's movements.   If any one in the transaction showed
himself unreasonable, it was the young man, not his relations.
They were ready to aid him to the full extent of their powers
in any respectable line of life which might please his fancy.
They would probably have preferred that he should choose a
mercantile rather than a military career.   They would have permitted, and perhaps encouraged, his travelling for a few years
to fit himself for that object.   It was no fault of theirs that he

suddenly took the whole question into his own hands, and, after making silent preparations and carrying with him such resources as he could then raise, on the 1st April, 1780, in company with his friend Serre, secretly and in defiance of his guardian and relations, bade a long farewell to Geneva and turned his back on the past.

The act was not a wise one. That future which the young Gallatin grasped so eagerly with outstretched arms had little in it that even to an ardent imagination at nineteen could compensate for the wanton sacrifice it involved. There is no reason to suppose that Albert Gallatin's career was more brilliant or more successful in America than with the same efforts and with equal sacrifices it might have been in Europe; for his character and abilities must have insured pre-eminence in whatever path he chose. Both the act of emigration and the manner of carrying it out were inconsiderate and unreasonable, as is clear from the arguments by which he excused them at the time. He wished to improve his fortune, he said, and to do this he was going, without capital, as his family pointed out, to a land already ruined by a long and still raging civil war, without a government and without trade. This was his ostensible reason; and his private one was no better,—that "daily dependence" on others, and particularly on Mlle. Pictet and his grandmother, which galled his pride. That he was discontented with Geneva and the Genevan political system was true; but to emigrate was not the way to mend it, and even in emigrating he did not pretend that his object in seeking America was to throw himself into the Revolutionary struggle. He felt a strong sympathy for the Americans and for the political liberty which was the motive of their contest; but this sympathy was rather a matter of reason than of passion. He always took care to correct the. idea, afterwards very commonly received, that he had run away from his family and friends in order to fight the British. So far as his political theories were concerned, aversion to Geneva had more to do with his action than any enthusiasm for war, and in the list of personal motives discontent with his dependent position at home had more influence over him than the desire for wealth. At this time, and long afterwards, he was proud and shy. His behavior for many years was controlled by these feelings, which only experience and success at last softened and overcame.

The manner of departure was justified by him on the ground that he feared forcible restraint should he attempt to act openly. The excuse was a weak one, and the weaker if a positive prohibition were really to be feared, which was probably not the case. No one had the power to restrain young Gallatin very long. He might have depended with confidence on having his own way had he chosen to insist. But the spirit of liberty at this time was rough in its methods. Albert Gallatin's contemporaries and friends were the men who carried the French Revolution through its many wild phases, and at nineteen men are governed by feeling rather than by common sense, even when they do not belong to a generation which sets the world in flames.

However severe the judgment of his act may be, there was nothing morally wrong in it; nothing which he had not a right to do if he chose. In judging it, too, the reader is affected by the fact that none of his letters in his own defence have been preserved, while all those addressed to him are still among his papers. These, too, are extremely creditable to his family, and show strong affection absolutely free from affectation, and the soundest good sense without a trace of narrowness. Among them all, one only can be given here. It is from Albert's guardian, a distant relative in an elder branch of the family.

P. M. GALLATIN TO ALBERT GALLATIN.

GENÈVE, 21e mai, 1780.

MONSIEUR,—Avant que de vous écrire j'ai voulu m'assurer d'une manière plus précise que je n'avais pu le faire les premiers jours de votre départ, et par vous-même, quels étaient vos projets, le but et le motif de votre voyage, les causes qui avaient fait naître une pareille idée dans votre esprit, vos sentimens passés et présens et vos désirs pour l'avenir. Il m'était difficile à tous ces égards de comprendre comment vous ne vous étiez ouvert ni à Mlle. Pictet qui, vous le savez bien, ne vous avait jamais aimé pour

elle-même mais pour vous seul, qui n'a jamais voulu que votre
plus grand bien, qui a pris de vous non-seulement les soins que vous
auriez pu attendre de madame votre mère avec laquelle elle s'était
individualisée à votre égard, mais même ceux que peu d'enfants
éprouvent de leurs pères ; ni à moi, qui jamais ne vous ai refusé
quoi que ce soit, parcequ'en effet les demandes en petit nombre
que vous m'aviez faites jusqu'à présent m'ont toujours paru sages
et raisonnables ; ni à aucun de vos parens, de qui vous n'avez reçu
que des douceurs dans tout le cours de votre vie.   C'est, je vous
l'avouerai, ce défaut de confiance, qui continue encore chez vous
à notre égard, qui m'afflige le plus vivement, voyant surtout qu'il
tourne contre vous au lieu de servir à votre avantage.   Croyez-
vous donc, monsieur, à votre âge, calculer mieux que les personnes
qui ont quelque expérience ? ou nous supposiez-vous assez dérai-
sonnables pour nous refuser à entrer dans des plans qui auraient
pu un jour vous conduire au bonheur que vous cherchez ? Il est
vrai qu'il n'est point de bonheur parfait en ce monde ; mais pensez-
vous que nous aurions été sourds ou insensibles à vos motifs les
plus secrets ? vous défiez-vous de notre discrétion pour nous refuser la confidence qui nous était due du développement successif
de vos sentimens ? est-ce la contrainte pour le choix d'un état,
sont-ce les lois que nous vous avons imposées pour quelque objet
que ce soit, qui nous ont enlevé votre confiance ? au contraire, ne
vous avons-nous pas déclaré en diverses occasions que nous vous
laissions cette liberté ? devions-nous et pouvions-nous nous attendre que vous l'interpréteriez en une indépendance absolue qui
ne reconnaîtrait pas non-seulement l'autorité légitime mais la
déférence naturelle et le besoin de direction et de conseils ?   Que
vos motifs fussent bons ou mauvais pour prendre le parti que
vous avez pris, je n'entre plus là-dedans.   La démarche est faite
et surtout la résolution est prise ; je ne chercherai point à vous
en détourner ; si vous ne réussissez pas, vous aurez été trompé
par de faux raisonnemens, comme vous le dites, et voilà tout.
Et quand ce projet nous aurait été communiqué avant son exécution, quand nous vous l'aurions représenté aussi extravagant qu'il
nous le paraît, quand nous vous aurions détaillé les inconvéniens,
si vous y aviez persisté, nous aurions dit Amen ; mais alors du
moins nous aurions pu d'avance en prévenir un grand nombre,

diminuer la grandeur de quelques autres, vous aider avec plus de
fruit pour le projet même, et avec moins d'inconvéniens en cas de
non-réussite; nous aurions préparé les voies autant qu'il nous
aurait été possible pour l'exécution et nous vous aurions facilité
le retour en fondant votre espérance d'un sort heureux si jamais
vous étiez forcé de revenir ici. Monsieur du Rosey votre oncle
vous avait fait entrevoir une situation aisée pour l'avenir; mais si
une honnête médiocrité n'eut pas satisfait vos désirs ambitieux,
ses offres généreuses ne devaient-elles pas lui ouvrir votre cœur
et vous déterminer à lui confier vos projets que (s'il n'eut pas pu
les anéantir par le raisonnement et la persuasion) il eut sans doute
favorisés? *Un ordre positif!* Avec quels yeux nous avez-vous
donc vus? Aujourd'hui croyez-vous cette défiance injuste que
vous nous avez montrée et par votre conduite et par vos lettres,
bien propre à le disposer en votre faveur? Soyez certain cependant, monsieur, que je vous aiderai autant que votre fortune
pourra le permettre sans déranger vos capitaux, dont je dois vous
rendre compte un jour et que vous me saurez peut-être gré de vous
avoir conservés; en attendant je suis obligé par un serment
solennel prêté en justice que j'observerai inviolablement jusques
à ce que j'en sois juridiquement dégagé; et vous refuser vos
capitaux pour un projet dont je ne saurais voir la fin, n'est ni
infamie ni dureté, mais prudence et sagesse.

Après ces observations, dont j'ai cru que vous aviez besoin,
permettez-moi quelques réflexions sur votre projet. D'abord j'ai
lieu de croire que la somme qui vous reste, ou qui vous restait,
n'est pas à beaucoup près de cent cinquante louis; secondement,
le gain que vous prétendez faire par le commerce d'armement
est très-incertain; il est en troisième lieu très-lent à se faire
apercevoir; en attendant il faut vivre; et comment vivrez-vous?
de leçons? quelle pitoyable ressource, pour être la dernière, dans
un pays surtout où les vivres sont si exorbitamment chers et où
tout le reste se paye si mal! Des terres incultes à acheter? avec
quoi? plus elles sont à bas prix, plus elles indiquent la cherté
des denrées; le grand nombre de terres incultes, le besoin qu'on
a de les défricher, sont deux preuves des sommes considérables
qu'il en coûte pour vivre. Vos réflexions sur le gain à faire sur
ces terres et sur le papier, supposent d'abord que vous aurez de

quoi en acheter beaucoup, supposition ridicule, et feraient croire
que vous vous êtes imaginé disposer des évènemens au gré de vos
souhaits et selon vos besoins. . . .

Mr. Franklin doit vous recommander à Philadelphie. Vous
y trouverez des ressources que bien d'autres n'auraient pas, mais
vous en aurez moins et vous les aurez plus tard que si nous
avions été prévenus à tems. Mr. Kenlock, connu de Mlle.
Beaulacre et de M. Muller, y est actuellement au Congrès; ne
faites pas difficulté de le voir; je ne saurais douter qu'il ne vous
aide de ses conseils et que vous ne trouviez auprès de lui des
directions convenables.

Malgré les choses désagréables que je puis vous avoir écrites
dans cette lettre, vous ne doutez pas, je l'espère, mon cher monsieur, du tendre intérêt que je prends à votre sort, qui me les a
dictées, et vous devez être persuadé des vœux sincères que je fais
pour l'accomplissement de vos désirs. Le jeune Serre est plus
fait que vous pour réussir; son imagination ardente lui fera
aisément trouver des ressources, et son courage actif lui fera
surmonter les obstacles; mais votre indolence naturelle en vous
livrant aux projets hardis de ce jeune homme vous a exposé sans
réflexion à des dangers que je redoute pour vous, et si vous
comptez sur l'amitié inviolable que vous vous êtes vouée l'un à
l'autre (dont à Dieu ne plaise que je vous invite à vous défier)
croyez-vous cependant qu'il soit bien délicat de se mettre dans le
cas d'attendre ses ressources pour vivre, uniquement de l'imagination et du courage d'autrui? Adieu, mon cher monsieur; ne
voyez encore une fois dans ce que je vous ai écrit que le sentiment
qui l'a dicté, et croyez-moi pour la vie, mon cher monsieur, votre
très-affectionné tuteur.

As has been said, none of Albert's letters to his family have
been preserved. Fortunately, however, his correspondence with
his friend Badollet has not been lost, and the first letter of this
series, written while he was still in the Loire, from on board the
American vessel, the Katty, in which the two travellers had
taken passage from Nantes to Boston, is the only vestige of
writing now to be found which gives a certain knowledge of the
writer's frame of mind at the moment of his departure.

GALLATIN TO BADOLLET.

PIMBEUF, 16 mai, 1780.
C'est un port de mer, 8 lieues
[au-dessous de Nantes. Nous]
nous y ennuyons beaucoup.

Mon cher ami, pourquoi ne m'as-tu point écrit? j'attendois pour t'écrire de savoir si tu étois à Clérac ou à Genève. J'espère que c'est à Clérac, mais si notre affaire t'a fait manquer ta place, j'espère, vu tout ce que je vois, que nous pourrons t'avoir cette année; j'aimerois cependant mieux que tu eusses quelqu'argent, parcequ'en achetant des marchandises tu gagnerois prodigieusement dessus. Si tu es à Clérac, c'est pour l'année prochaine. J'ai reçu des lettres fort tendres qui m'ont presqu'ébranlé et dans lesquelles on me promet en cas que je persiste, de l'argent et des recommandations. J'ai déjà reçu de celles-ci, et j'ai fait connoissance ici avec des Américains de distinction. En cas que tu sois à Clérac, je t'apprendrai que nous sommes venus à Nantes dans cinq jours fort heureusement, que nous avons trouvé un vaisseau pour Boston nommé la Katti, Cap. Loring, qui partoit le lendemain, mais nous avons été retenus ici depuis 15 jours par les vents contraires et nous irons à Lorient chercher un convoi. Mon adresse est à Monsieur Gallatin à Philadelphie, sous une enveloppe adressée: A Messieurs Struikmann & Meinier frères, à Nantes, le tout affranchi. Des détails sur ta place, je te prie. Nous ne craignons plus rien; on nous a promis de ne pas s'opposer à notre dessein si nous persistions. Hentsch s'est fort bien conduit. Adieu; la poste part, j'ai déjà écrit cinq lettres. Tout à toi.

Serre te fait ses complimens; il dort pour le moment.

The entire sum of money which the two young men brought with them from Geneva was one hundred and sixty-six and two-thirds louis-d'or, equal to four thousand livres tournois, reckoning twenty-four livres to the louis. One-half of this sum was expended in posting across France and paying their passage to Boston. Their capital for trading purposes was therefore about four hundred dollars, which, however, belonged entirely to Gallatin, as Serre had no means and paid no part of the expenses. For a long time to come they could expect no more supplies.

Meanwhile, the family at Geneva had moved heaven and earth to smooth their path, and had written or applied for letters of introduction in their behalf to every person who could be supposed to have influence. One of these persons was the Duc de la Rochefoucauld d'Enville, who wrote to Franklin a letter which may be found in Franklin's printed correspondence.[1] The letter tells no more than we know; but Franklin's reply is characteristic. It runs thus:

BENJ. FRANKLIN TO THE DUC DE LA ROCHEFOUCAULD D'ENVILLE.

PASSY, May 24, 1780.

DEAR SIR,—I enclose the letter you desired for the two young gentlemen of Geneva. But their friends would do well to prevent their voyage.

With sincere and great esteem, I am, dear sir, your most obedient and most humble servant,

B. FRANKLIN.

The letter enclosed was as follows:

PASSY, May 24, 1780.

DEAR SON,—Messrs. Gallatin and Serres, two young gentlemen of Geneva, of good families and very good characters, having an inclination to see America, if they should arrive in your city I recommend them to your civilities, counsel, and countenance.

I am ever your affectionate father,

B. FRANKLIN.

To RICHARD BACHE, Postmaster-General, Philadelphia.

Lady Juliana Penn, also, wrote to John Penn at Philadelphia in their favor. Mlle. Pictet wrote herself to Colonel Kinloch,

---

[1] Sparks's Franklin, viii. 454.

then a member of the Continental Congress from South Carolina. Her description of the young men is probably more accurate than any other: "Quoique je n'ai pas l'avantage d'être connue de vous, j'ai trop entendu parler de l'honnêteté et de la sensibilité de votre âme pour hésiter à vous demander un service absolument essentiel au bonheur de ma vie. Deux jeunes gens de ce pays, nommé Gallatin et Serre, n'étant pas contents de leur fortune, qui est effectivement médiocre, et s'étant échauffé l'imagination du désir de s'en faire une eux-mêmes, aidés d'un peu d'enthousiasme pour les Américains, prennent le parti de passer à Philadelphie. Ils sont tous deux pleins d'honneur, de bons sentiments, fort sages, et n'ont jamais donné le moindre sujet de plainte à leurs familles, qui ont le plus grand regret de leur départ. . . . Ils ont tous deux des talents et des connaissances; mais je crois qu'ils n'entendent rien au commerce et à la culture des terres qui sont les moyens de fortune qu'ils ont imaginés." . . .

With such introductions and such advantages, aided by the little fortune which Gallatin would inherit on coming of age in 1786, in his twenty-fifth year, the path was open to him. He had but to walk in it. Success, more or less brilliant, was as certain as anything in this world can be.

He preferred a different course. Instead of embracing his opportunities, he repelled them. Like many other brilliant men, he would not, and never did, learn to overcome some youthful prejudices; he disliked great cities and the strife of crowded social life; he never could quite bring himself to believe in their advantages and in the necessity of modern society to agglomerate in masses and either to solve the difficulties inherent in close organization or to perish under them. He preferred a wilderness in his youth, and, as will be seen, continued in theory to prefer it in his age. It was the instinct of his time and his associations; the atmosphere of Rousseau and Jefferson; pure theory, combined with shy pride. He seems never to have made use of his introductions unless when compelled by necessity, and refused to owe anything to his family. Not that even in this early stage of his career he ever assumed an exterior that was harsh or extravagant, or manners that were repulsive; but he chose to take the world from the side that least touched his pride, and, after cutting loose so roughly from the ties of home and family, he could not with self-respect return to follow their paths. His friends could do no more. He disappeared from their sight, and poor Mlle. Pictet could only fold her hands and wait. Adoring her with a warmth of regard which he never failed to express at every mention of her name, he almost broke her heart by the manner of his desertion, and, largely from unwillingness to tell his troubles, largely too, it must be acknowledged, from mere indolence, he left her sometimes for years without a letter or a sign of life. Like many another woman, she suffered acutely; and her letters are beyond words pathetic in their effort to conceal her suffering. Mr. Gallatin always bitterly regretted his fault: it was the only one in his domestic life.

His story must be told as far as possible in his own words; but there remain only his letters to Badollet to throw light on his manner of thinking and his motives of action at this time. In these there are serious gaps. He evidently did not care to tell all he had to endure; but with what shall be given it will be easy for the reader to divine the rest.

The two young men landed on Cape Ann on the 14th July, 1780. The war was still raging, and the result still uncertain. General Gates was beaten at Camden on the 16th August, and all the country south of Virginia lost. More than a year passed before the decisive success at Yorktown opened a prospect of peace. The travellers had no plans, and, if one may judge from their tone and behavior, were as helpless as two boys of nineteen would commonly be in a strange country, talking a language of which they could only stammer a few words, and trying to carry on mercantile operations without a market and with a currency at its last gasp. They had brought tea from Nantes as a speculation, and could only dispose of it by taking rum and miscellaneous articles in exchange. Their troubles were many, and it is clear that they were soon extremely homesick; for, after riding on horseback from Gloucester to Boston, they took refuge at a French coffee-house kept by a certain Tahon, and finding there a Genevan, whom chance threw in their way,

they clung to him with an almost pathetic persistence. On
September 4 they bought a horse and yellow chaise for eight
thousand three hundred and thirty-three dollars. Perhaps it
was in this chaise that they made an excursion to Wachusett
Hill, which they climbed. But their own letters will describe
them best.

GALLATIN TO BADOLLET.

No. 2.

BOSTON, 14 septembre, 1780.

Mon cher ami, je t'ai déjà écrit une lettre il y a quatre jours,
mais elle a bien des hazards à courir, ainsi je vais t'en récrire une
seconde par une autre occasion, et je vais commencer par un résumé
de ce que je te disais dans ma première.

Nous partîmes le 27e mai de Lorient, après avoir payé 60
louis pour notre voyage, les provisions comprises. Notre coquin
de capitaine, aussi frippon que bête et superstitieux, nous tint à
peu près tout le tems à viande salée et à eau pourrie. Le second
du vaisseau, plus frippon et plus hypocrite que le premier, nous
vola 6 guinées dans notre poche, plus la moitié de notre linge,
plus le 3½ pour 100 de fret de notre thé. (Il avait demandé
5 pr. cent. de fret pour du thé que nous embarquions, et il a
exigé 8½.) Au reste, point de tempête pour orner notre récit,
peu malades, beaucoup d'ennui, et souvent effrayés par des corsaires qui nous ont poursuivis. Enfin nous arrivâmes le 14e
juillet au Cap Anne à huit lieues de Boston où nous nous
rendîmes le lendemain à cheval.

———

Ce qui suit n'étoit pas dans [ma première lettre].

Boston est une ville d'environ 18 mille âmes, bâtie sur une
presqu'île plus longue que large. Je la crois plus grande que
Genève, mais il y a des jardins, des prairies, des vergers au milieu
de la ville et chaque famille a ordinairement sa maison. Ces
maisons ont rarement plus d'un étage ou deux. Elles sont de
briques ou de bois, couvertes de planches et d'ardoises, avec
des terrasses sur les toits et dans beaucoup d'endroits avec des
conducteurs qui ont presque tous trois pointes. Une ou deux

rues tirées au cordeau, point d'édifices publics remarquables, un hâvre très-vaste et défendu par des îles qui ne laissent que deux entrées très-étroites, une situation qui rendrait la ville imprenable si elle était fortifiée, voilà tout ce que j'ai à te dire de Boston. Les habitans n'ont ni délicatesse ni honneur ni instruction, et il n'y a rien de trop à l'égard de leur probité, non plus qu'à l'égard de celles des Français qui sont établis ici et qui sont fort haïs des naturels du pays.   On s'ennuye fort à Boston.   Il n'y a aucun amusement public et beaucoup de superstition, en sorte que l'on ne peut pas le dimanche chanter, jouer du violon, aux cartes, aux boules, &c.   Je t'assure que nous avons grand besoin de toi pour venir augmenter nos plaisirs.   En attendant, donne-nous de tes nouvelles et fais-nous un peu part de la politique de Genève.   Je vais te payer en te disant quelque chose de ce pays. . . .

Then follow four close pages of statistical information about the thirteen colonies, of the ordinary school-book type, which may be omitted without injury to the reader; at the end of which the letter proceeds :

On m'a dit beaucoup de mal de tous les habitans de la Nouvelle-Angleterre; du bien de ceux de la Pensilvanie, de la Virginie, du Maryland, et de la Caroline Septentrionale; et rien des autres.

J'en viens à l'Etat de Massachusetts, que je connais le mieux et que j'ai gardé pour le dernier.

Il est divisé en huit comtés et chaque comté en plusieurs villes. Car il n'y a point de bourgs.   Dès qu'un certain nombre de familles veulent s'aller établir dans un terrain en friche et qu'elles consentent à entretenir un ministre et deux maîtres d'école, on leur donne un espace de deux lieues en quarré nommé *township* et l'établissement obtient le nom de ville et en a tous les priviléges.   Les habitans de toutes les villes au-dessus de vingt-et-un ans et qui possèdent en Amérique un bien excédant trois livres sterling de revenu, s'assemblent une fois l'an pour élire un gouverneur et un sénat de la province, composé de six membres, dont on remplace deux membres par an.   On compte les suffrages dans chaque ville et ceux qui ont la pluralité des villes sont élus. Car les suffrages de chaque ville sont égaux. Boston n'a pas plus de droit qu'un village de deux cents hommes. Le sénat élit un conseil au gouverneur et chaque ville envoye le nombre de députés à Boston qu'elle veut. Cela forme la chambre des représentans et l'on prend toujours les suffrages par ville. Environ deux cents villes envoyent des députés et plus de cent ne sont pas assez riches pour en entretenir. Il faut le consentement de ces trois corps pour faire une loi, repartir les impôts (car c'est le Congrès Général qui les fixe sur chaque province, qui décide la paix ou la guerre, &c.), &c. Chaque ville élit les magistrats de police. Tout homme croyant un Dieu rémunérateur et une autre vie est toléré chez lui; et nombre de sectes ont des églises. Il y a cent ans qu'on y persécutait les Anglicans. Tel est le nouveau plan de gouvernement qui a eu l'approbation des villes après que deux autres ont été rejetés et qui sera en vigueur dans trois mois. Cette province est la plus commerçante de toutes et une des plus peuplées. Elle ne produit guère que du maïs, des patates, du poisson, du bois et des bestiaux. Ce sont actuellement ses corsaires qui la soutiennent. On fait ici d'excellent voiliers. Mais il n'y a aucune fabrique (excepté des toiles grossières). Il y a un collége et une académie et une bibliothèque à Cambridge, petite ville à une lieue de Boston. Je n'ai pas encore pu voir cela. Il n'y a aucune ville considérable excepté Boston dans cet état. A l'égard du comté de Main, les Anglais y ont un fort nommé Penobscot où les Américains se sont fait brûler 18 vaisseaux l'année dernière en voulant l'attaquer. Il est à peu près au milieu du comté. Au nord sont des tribus de sauvages; au nord-est, l'Acadie ou Nouvelle-Ecosse; et au nord-ouest, le Canada. Je te dirai plus de choses de ce pays dans peu de tems, car nous y allons faire un petit voyage pour commercer en pelleteries. Nous allons à Machias (on prononce Maitchais) qui est la dernière place au nord. Aye la bonté de t'informer de toutes les particularités que tu pourras apprendre sur les manufactures des environs de Bordeaux, sur la difficulté qu'il y aurait à en transporter des ouvriers ici, de même que des agriculteurs, sur le prix des marchandises qui doivent y être à bon compte tant parcequ'on les y fabrique que parcequ'elles y arrivent aisément, sur ce que coûtent les pendules de bois en particulier, &c. J'espère que nous te verrons dans peu auprès de nous. Cela se fera sur un vaisseau que nous pourrons t'indiquer. Nous aurons fait marché avec le capitaine et j'espère que tu pourras faire la traversée plus agréablement et économiquement que nous. Adieu, mon bon ami. Pense aussi souvent à nous que nous à toi et écris-nous longuement et très-souvent, car il y a bien des vaisseaux de pris.

"A MONSIEUR BADOLLET, Etudiant en Théologie."

Whoever gave the writer his information in regard to the Massachusetts constitution was remarkably ill informed. But this is a trifle. The next letter soon follows:

GALLATIN TO BADOLLET.

No. 3.

MACHIAS, 29 8re, 1780.

Mon cher ami, tu ne t'attendais sans doute pas à recevoir des lettres datées d'un nom aussi baroque, mais c'est celui que les sauvages y ont mis, et comme ils sont les premiers possesseurs du pays, il est juste de l'appeler comme eux. (On prononce Maitchais.) C'est ici que nous allons passer l'hiver. Nous avons préféré les glaces du nord au climat tempéré qu'habitent les Quakers, et si nous t'avions avec nous pour célébrer l'Escalade et pour vivre avec nous, je t'assure que nous serions fort contens de notre sort actuel. Car jusqu'à présent notre santé et nos affaires pécuniaires vont fort bien ; quand je dis fort bien, c'est qu'à l'égard du dernier article nous ne sommes pas trop ambitieux. Je vais te détailler tout l'état de nos affaires. Dans la maison où nous demeurions à Boston nous rencontrâmes une Suissesse qui avait épousé un Genevois nommé de Lesdernier de Russin et dont je crois t'avoir dit deux mots dans une de mes lettres précédentes. Il y avait trente ans qu'il était venu s'établir dans la Nouvelle-Ecosse. Tu sais que cette province et le Canada sont les seules qui soient restées sous le joug anglais. Une partie des habitans de la première essaya cependant de se révolter il y a deux ou trois ans. Mais n'ayant pas été soutenus ils furent obligés de s'enfuir dans la Nouvelle-Angleterre. Parmi eux était un des fils de de Lesdernier. Il

vint dans cette place où il fut fait lieutenant. Il fut ensuite
fait prisonnier et mené à Halifax (la capitale de la Nouvelle-
Ecosse). Son père l'alla voir en prison et la lui fit adoucir
jusqu'à ce qu'il fut échangé. Mais il essuya beaucoup de désa-
grémens de la part de ses amis qui lui reprochaient d'avoir un
fils parmi les rebelles. Il eut ensuite une partie de ses effets
pris par les Américains tandis qu'il les faisait transporter sur mer
d'une place à une autre où il allait s'établir. L'espérance de les
recouvrer s'il venait à Boston jointe au souvenir de l'affaire de
son fils l'engagea à quitter la Nouvelle-Ecosse avec un autre de
ses fils (trois autres sont au service du roi d'Angleterre) et sa
femme. Quand nous vinmes à Boston, n'ayant rien pu recouvrer, il était allé jusqu'à Baltimore dans le Maryland voir
s'il ne trouverait rien à faire ; et à l'arrivée de la flotte française
à Rhode Island, il y alla et y prit un Capucin pour servir de
missionnaire parmi les sauvages dans cette place. Car ils sont
tous catholiques et du parti des Français. Dans ce même temps
ayant de la peine à vendre notre thé et voyant beaucoup de
difficultés pour le commerce du côté de la Pensilvanie, nous
échangeâmes notre thé contre des marchandises des îles, et nous
résolûmes de venir ici acheter du poisson et faire la traite de la
pelleterie avec les sauvages. Machias est la dernière place au
nord-est de la Nouvelle-Angleterre, à environ cent lieues de
Boston, dans le comté de Main qui est annexé à l'état de Massachusetts Bay. Il n'y a que quinze ans qu'on y a formé un
établissement qui est fort pauvre à cause de la guerre et qui ne
consiste qu'en 150 familles dispersées dans un espace de 3 à 4
lieues. Nous sommes dans le chef-lieu, où est un fort, le colonel
Allan commandant de la place et surintendant de tous les
sauvages qui sont entre le Canada, la Nouvelle-Ecosse et la
Nouvelle-Angleterre, et tous les officiers. Lesdernier le fils,
chez qui nous logeons, est un très-joli garçon. Nous y passerons
l'hiver et probablement nous prendrons des terres le printems
prochain, non pas ici mais un peu plus au nord ou au sud où
elles sont meilleures. On les a pour rien, mais elles sont en
friche et assez difficiles à travailler. Ajoute à cela le manque
d'hommes. C'est pourquoi je te le répète, informe-toi des conditions auxquelles des paysans voudraient venir ici. Celles que

nous pourrions accorder à peu près seraient de les faire transporter gratis, de les entretenir la première année, après quoi la
moitié du revenu des terres qu'ils défricheraient en cas que ce
fussent des bleds, ou le quart si c'étaient des pâturages, leur
resteraient pendant dix, quinze ou vingt ans suivant les arrangemens (le plus longtems serait le mieux), et au bout de ce tems la
moitié ou le quart des terres leur appartiendrait à perpétuité sans
qu'ils fussent obligés de cultiver davantage l'autre moitié ou les
autres trois quarts.   En cas que tu en trouvasses, écris-nous le
avec les conditions, le nombre, &c.

Nous avons déjà vu plusieurs sauvages, tous presqu'aussi noirs
que des nègres, habillés presqu'à l'Européenne excepté les femmes
qui——Mais je veux te laisser un peu de curiosité sans la satisfaire, afin que tu ayes autant de motifs que possible pour venir
nous joindre au plus tôt.   Mais ne pars que quand nous te le
dirons, parcequ'en cas que tu ayes de l'argent, nous t'indiquerons
quelles marchandises tu dois acheter, et parceque nous tâcherons
de te procurer un embarquement agréable.   Dans notre passage
de Boston ici nous avons couru plus de risque qu'en venant
d'Europe.   Le second jour de notre voyage nous relâchâmes à
Newbury, jolie ville à dix lieues de Boston et nous y fûmes
retenus 5 à 6 jours par les vents contraires.   L'entrée du hâvre
est très-étroite et il y a un grand nombre de brisans, de manière
que quand les vents ont soufflé depuis le dehors pendant quelque
tems il y a des vagues prodigieuses qui pouvaient briser ou renverser le vaisseau quand nous voulûmes sortir.   Nous fûmes donc
obligés de rester encore quelques jours jusqu'à ce que la mer fût
calmée.   Enfin nous partîmes après nous être échoué 2 fois dans
le hâvre.   Après deux jours de navigation les vents contraires et
très-forts nous obligèrent d'entrer à Casco Bay, où est la ville
de Falmouth, une des premières victimes de cette guerre, car
elle a été presqu'entièrement brûlée par les Anglais en '79.   Le
lendemain nous en partîmes.   Bon vent tout le jour, la nuit et
le lendemain, mais un brouillard épais.   Le lendemain un coup
de vent déchira notre grande voile.   On la raccommoda tant
bien que mal, et à peine était-elle replacée que le vent augmenta
et un quart d'heure après on découvrit tout à coup la terre à
une portée-de-fusil à gauche.   Nous allions nord-est et le vent

était ouest, c'est à dire qu'il portait droit contre terre, et la
marée montait. L'on ne pouvait plus virer de bord et l'on fut
obligé d'aller autant contre le vent qu'on le pouvait (par un
angle de 80 degrés); malgré cela on approchait toujours de
terre, mais on en voyait le bout et heureusement elle tournait
moyennant quoi nous échappâmes, mais nous n'étions pas à deux
toises d'un roc qui était à l'avant de la terre quand nous la dé-
passâmes. Nous gagnâmes le large au plus vîte, et après avoir
été battus par la tempête toute la nuit, nous arrivâmes le lendemain ici.

Je n'ai pas besoin de te dire que ceci est écrit au nom de tous
les deux, et comme tu le vois le papier ne me permet pas de
causer plus longtems avec toi. Adieu, mon bon ami. Cette
lettre est achevée le 7e novembre. Je numérote mes lettres.
Fais-en autant et dis-moi quels numéros tu as reçus.

Tu ne recevras point de lettres de nous d'ici au printems, la
communication étant fermée.

En relisant ma lettre je vois que je ne t'ai rien dit de la
manière de vivre de ce pays. Le commerce consiste en poisson,
planches, mâtures, pelleteries, et il est fort avantageux. Avant la
guerre on ne faisait que couper des planches, depuis on a défriché
les terres; il n'y a encore que fort peu de bleds, mais des patates
et des racines de toute espèce en abondance, point de fruits, et du
bétail mais peu. Nous avons déjà une vache. C'est un commencement de métairie, comme tu vois. Trois rivières se jettent
dans le hâvre et c'est à deux lieues au-dessus de leur embouchure
que nous sommes à la jonction de deux d'entr'elles. Nous allons
en bâteaux de toute espèce et entr'autres sur des canots d'écorce,
dont tu seras enchanté, quelques fragiles qu'ils soient. Tout cela
gèle tout l'hyver et on peut faire dix lieues en patins. On va
sur la neige avec une sorte de machine qui s'attache aux pieds,
nommée raquettes, et avec laquelle on n'enfonce point, quelque
tendre qu'elle soit. On fait trente, quarante lieues à travers
les bois, les lacs, les rivières, en raquettes, en patins, en canots
d'écorce. Car on les porte sur son dos quand on arrive à un
endroit où il n'y a plus d'eau jusqu'au premier ruisseau, où l'on
se rembarque.

Dis-nous quelque chose de Genève; des affaires politiques, du

procès Rilliet, de ta manière de passer ton tems à présent, &c.
Adresse-nous tes lettres à Boston.

MONSIEUR JEAN BADOLLET,
Chez Monsieur le Chevalier de Vivens, à Clérac.

A letter from Serre, which was enclosed with the above long
despatch from Gallatin, throws some light on Serre's imaginative
and poetical character and his probable influence on the more
practical mind of his companion, although, to say the truth, his
idea of life and its responsibilities was simply that of the run-
away school-boy.

SERRE TO BADOLLET.

Mon cher ami Badollet, nous sommes ici dans un pays où je
crois que tu te plairais bien; nous demeurons au milieu d'une
forêt sur le bord d'une rivière; nous pouvons chasser, pêcher,
nous baigner, aller en patins quand bon nous semble. A présent nous nous chauffons gaillardement devant un bon feu, et ce
qu'il y a de mieux c'est que c'est nous-mêmes qui allons couper
le bois dans la forêt. Tu sais comme nous nous amusions à
Genève à nous promener en bâteau. Eh bien! je m'amuse encore
mieux ici à naviguer dans des canots de sauvages. Ils sont cons-
truits avec de l'écorce de bouleau et sont charmants pour aller
un ou deux dedans; on peut s'y coucher comme dans un lit, et
ramer tout à son aise; il n'y a pas de petit ruisseau qui n'ait assez
d'eau pour ces jolies voitures. Il y a quelque tems que je des-
cendis une petite rivière fort étroite; le tems était superbe; je
voyais des prairies à deux pas de moi; j'étais couché tout le long
du canot sur une couverture, et il y avait si peu d'eau qu'il me
semblait glisser sur les près et les gazons. Je tourne, je char-
pente, je dessine, je joue du violon; il n'y a pas diablerie que je
ne fasse pour m'amuser. Note avec cela que nous sommes ici en
compagnie de cinq bourgeois et bourgeoises de Genève. Il est
bien vrai qu'il y en a trois de nés en Amérique, mais ils n'en ont
pas moins conservé le sang républicain de leurs ancêtres, et M.
Lesdernier le fils, né dans ce continent d'un père genevois, est
celui de tous les Américains que j'ai vu encore le plus zélé et le
plus plein d'enthousiasme pour la liberté de son pays.

Adieu, mon cher ami.   J'espère que l'été prochain tu viendras
m'aider à *pagailler* (signifie *ramer*) dans un canot de sauvage.
Nous irons remonter la rivière St. Jean ou le fleuve St. Laurent
visiter le Canada.   Si tu pouvais trouver moyen de m'envoyer une
demi-douzaine de bouts de tubes capillaires pour thermomètre,
tu obligerais beaucoup ton affectionné ami.

P.S.—Nous allons bientôt faire un petit voyage pour voir une
habitation de sauvages.

A little more information is given by the fragment of another
letter, written nearly two years afterwards, but covering the same
ground.

GALLATIN TO BADOLLET.

CAMBRIDGE, 15 septembre, 1782.

Mon bon ami, je t'écris sans savoir où tu es, et sans savoir si
mes lettres te parviendront, ou si même tu te soucies d'en recevoir; car si je ne comptais pas autant sur ton amitié que je le
fais, je serais presque porté à croire que tu n'as répondu à aucune
des lettres que nous t'avons écrites, Serre et moi, depuis plus de
deux ans.   Cependant te jugeant par moi-même et surtout te
connaissant comme je fais, j'aime mieux penser que toutes nos
lettres ont été perdues, ou que toutes les tiennes ont subi ce sort.
Ainsi commençant par la deuxième supposition, je vais te faire
un court narré de nos aventures.

Notre voyage jusqu'en Amérique ne fut marqué par aucun
évènement remarquable excepté le vol que le second du vaisseau
nous fit de la moitié de notre linge et de quelqu'argent.   Nous
arrivâmes à Boston le 15 juillet, 1780, et nous y restâmes deux
mois avant de pouvoir nous défaire de quelques caisses de thé
que nous avions achetées avant de nous embarquer.   La difficulté
de se transporter à Philadelphie et le désir d'augmenter un peu
nos fonds avant d'y aller, nous détermina à passer dans le nord
de cet état dans le dernier établissement qu'aient les Américains
sur les frontières de la Nouvelle-Ecosse.   Cette place se nomme
Machias et est un port de mer situé sur la baye Funday, ou
Française, à cent lieues N.-E. de Boston.   Un Genevois nommé

Lesdernier, un bon paysan de Russin, qui après avoir fait de fort
bons établissements en Nouvelle-Ecosse, les avait perdus en partie
par sa faute, en partie par son attachement pour la cause des
Américains, et qui allait avec un capucin (destiné à prêcher des
sauvages) joindre son fils qui est lieutenant au service américain
à Machias,—ce Genevois, dis-je, fut un des motifs qui nous en-
traîna dans le nord, où notre curiosité ne demandait pas mieux
que de nous conduire.   Nous partîmes de Boston le 1er octobre,
1780, et après avoir relâché à Newbury et à Casco Bay (deux
ports de la Nouvelle-Angleterre, situés le premier à quinze lieues
et le second à quarante-cinq nord-est de Boston), et avoir pensé
nous perdre dans un brouillard contre un rocher, en grande partie
par l'ignorance de nos matelots, nous arrivâmes le 15e octobre
dans la rivière de Machias.   Te donner une idée de ce pays n'est
pas bien difficile; quatre ou cinq maisons ou plutôt cahutes de
bois éparses dans l'espace de deux lieues de côte que l'on dé-
couvre à la fois, deux ou trois arpens de terre défrichés autour
de chaque cahute, et quand je dis défrichés j'entends seulement
qu'on a coupé les arbres des alentours et que l'on a planté
quelques patates entre les souches, et au delà, de quel côté que
l'on se tourne, rien que des bois immenses qui bornent la vue de
tous côtés, voilà ce que le premier coup-d'œil présente.   Il ne
laisse cependant pas que d'y avoir quelques variétés dans cette
vue, quelqu'uniforme qu'elle soit naturellement.   Le port que la
rivière forme à son embouchure, port qui pour le dire en passant
est assez beau et très-sûr, est parsemé de quelques petites îles.
Les différentes réflexions du soleil sur les arbres de différentes
couleurs dont elles sont couvertes, sur les rocs escarpés qui en bor-
dent quelques-unes et sur les vagues qui se brisent à leur pied,
forment des contrastes assez agréables.   Ajoute à cela quelques
bâteaux à voiles ou à rames et quelques petits canots, les uns de
bois, les autres d'écorce d'arbre et faits par les sauvages, qui sont
menés par un ou deux hommes, souvent par quelques jolies jeunes
filles vêtues très-simplement mais proprement, armés chacun
d'une pagaye avec laquelle ils font voler leur fragile navire, et
tu auras une idée de la vue de toutes les côtes et bayes du nord de
la Nouvelle-Angleterre.   Cinq milles au-dessus de l'embouchure
de la rivière est le principal établissement, car il y a une vingt-

aine de maisons et un fort de terre et de bois défendu par sept pièces de canon, et par une garnison de 15 à 20 hommes. C'est un colonel nommé Allan qui est le commandeur de cette redoutable place, mais il a un emploi un peu plus important, celui de surintendant de tous les sauvages de cette partie. Je t'ai dit qu'un de nos motifs pour aller à Machias était d'augmenter un peu nos fonds; pour cela nous avions employé les deux mille livres argent de France qui formait notre capital, à acheter du rhum, du sucre et du tabac, que nous comptions vendre aux sauvages ou aux habitans; mais ces derniers n'ayant point d'argent, la saison du poisson salé qu'ils pêchent en assez grande quantité . . .

The remainder of this letter is lost, and the loss is the more unfortunate because the next movements of the two travellers are somewhat obscure. They appear to have wasted a year at Machias quite aimlessly, with possibly some advantage to their facility of talking, but at a serious cost to their slender resources. In the war, though they were on the frontier, and no doubt quite in the humor for excitement of the kind, they had little opportunity to take part. "I went twice as a volunteer," says Mr. Gallatin, in a letter written in 1846,[1] "to Passamaquoddy Bay, the first time in November, 1780, under Colonel Allen, who commanded at Machias and was superintendent of Indian affairs in that quarter. It was then and at Passamaquoddy that I was for a few days left accidentally in command of some militia, volunteers, and Indians, and of a small temporary work defended by one cannon and soon after abandoned. As I never met the enemy, I have not the slightest claim to military services." But what was of much more consequence, he advanced four hundred dollars in supplies to the garrison at Machias, for which he was ultimately paid by a Treasury warrant, which, as the Treasury was penniless, he was obliged to sell for what it would bring, namely, one hundred dollars. Nevertheless he found Machias and the Lesderniers so amusing, or perhaps he felt so little desire to throw himself again upon the world, that

---

[1] Letter to John Connor, 9th January, 1846. Writings, vol. ii. p. 621.

he remained all the following summer buried in this remote wilderness, cultivating that rude, free life which seems to have been Serre's ideal even more than his own. They came at length so near the end of their resources that they were forced to seek some new means of support. In October, 1781, therefore, they quitted Machias and returned to Boston, where Gallatin set himself to the task of obtaining pupils in French. None of his letters during this period have been preserved except the fragment already given, and the only light that can now be thrown on his situation at Boston is found in occasional references to his letters by his correspondents at home in their replies.

MLLE. PICTET TO GALLATIN.

No. 5.

GENÈVE, 5 février, 1782.

J'ai reçu, mon cher ami, ta lettre de Boston du 18e décembre, 1781, qui m'a fait grand plaisir. Je suis bien aise que vous ne soyez plus dans l'espèce de désert où vous avez passé l'hiver précédent et où je ne voyais rien à gagner pour vous mais beaucoup à perdre par la mauvaise compagnie à laquelle vous étiez réduit. Je suis content aussi de l'aveu naïf que tu fais de ton ennui; . . . vous n'êtes peut-être pas beaucoup mieux à Boston, n'y étant connu de personne; mais il n'est pas impossible de faire quelques bonnes connaissances si vous y passez quelque tems. Je t'y adressai une lettre le 6e janvier, 1782, No. 4, sous le couvert de M. le Docteur Samuel Cooper, à laquelle je joignis un mémoire pour lui demander à s'informer de vous à Machias, où je vous croyais encore, de vouloir bien vous protéger soit à Machias soit à Boston. Je lui contais votre histoire . . . et lui disais que M. Franklin, son ami, devait le charger de te remettre mille livres, . . . qu'on remettrait ici à M. Marignac, chez lequel M. Johannot son petit-fils est en pension. C'est ce jeune homme, que nous voyons souvent, qui voulut bien envoyer le tout dans une lettre de recommandation pour vous à son grand-père. . . . La lettre par laquelle M. Johannot te recommande à son ami et le charge de te payer mille livres . . . n'arrivera vraisemblablement qu'en même tems que celle-ci, ce dont je suis très-fâchée, ne doutant pas que tu n'aies grand besoin d'argent. J'ai peine à croire que les leçons de Français que vous donnez suffisent à vos besoins. . . . Si ton oncle le cadet consent, je t'enverrai à Philadelphie les 800 livres, . . . puisque tu dis que tu veux y aller au printems.

No. 8.
MLLE. PICTET TO GALLATIN.

14 novembre, 1782.

. . . Enfin le jeune Johannot vient de recevoir une lettre de M. son grand-père qui lui parle de toi ; il t'a fait obtenir une place de Professeur en langue française dans l'académie de Boston. . . .

No. 9.
MLLE. PICTET TO GALLATIN.

30 novembre, 1782.

Je reçois, mon cher ami, ta lettre du 5e septembre, 1782, No. 3. . . . Elle m'a fait d'autant plus de plaisir que je l'ai trouvée mieux que les précédentes ; elle est sensée et dépouillée d'enthousiasme ; il me semble que tu commences à voir les choses sous leur vrai point de vue. . . . Je vois avec grand plaisir que tu ne penses plus au commerce. . . . Je ne puis m'empêcher de te répéter que tu dois te défier de l'imagination et de la tête de Serre ; il l'a légère ; l'imagination a plus de part à ses projets que le raisonnement. . . .

No. 10.
MLLE. PICTET TO GALLATIN.

26 décembre, 1782.

. . . Tu me dis que ta santé est bonne ; je trouve que tu la mets à de terribles épreuves, et quoique ta vie soit moins pénible que quand tu étais coupeur de bois à Machias, la quantité de leçons que tu es obligé de donner me paraît une chose bien fatigante et bien ennuyeuse. J'espère que tu seras devenu un peu moins difficile et moins sujet à l'ennui. . . .

SERRE TO BADOLLET.

CAMBRIDGE, 13 décembre, 1782.

Mon cher ami, ma foi ! je perds patience et je n'ai pas tout à fait tort. Tu conviendras avec nous qu'après t'avoir écrit une douzaine de lettres sans recevoir aucune réponse, il nous est bien permis d'être un peu en colère. Au nom de Dieu, dis-nous où es-tu, que fais-tu, es-tu mort ou en vie? Comment serait-il possible que tu n'eusses reçu aucune de nos lettres, ou qu'en ayant reçu, tu te fusses si peu embarrassé de nous; toi sur qui nous comptions si fort! Non; j'aime mieux croire que tu te souviens encore de nous, et attribuer ta négligence apparente au mauvais sort de tes lettres.

Je ne vais point te faire ici le détail de toutes nos aventures dans ce pays, qui sont assez curieuses et intéressantes. Nous avons visité toute la côte septentrionale des États-Unis depuis Boston jusqu'à Pasmacadie, quelquefois séparés l'un de l'autre, mais le plus souvent ensemble; nous avons habité parmi les sauvages, voyagé avec eux, par tems dans leurs canots d'écorce, couché dans leurs cabanes et assisté à un de leurs festins; nous nous sommes trouvés rassemblés cinq Genevois à Machias pendant un hiver, au milieu des bois et des Indiens. Combien de fois nous avons pensé à toi alors; combien de fois nous t'avons désiré pour venir avec nous couper du bois le matin et le transporter dans notre chaumière pour nous en chauffer. Mr. Lesdernier avec qui nous demeurions a été fermier à Russin, et quoique depuis trente ans dans ce pays il a conservé en entier cette humeur joviale et franche et cet esprit libre qui caractérisent nos habitans de la campagne. La première fois que je le vis je me sentis ému de joie, j'aurais voulu lui sauter au cou et l'embrasser; je me crus à Genève parmi nos bons bourgeois de la campagne et il me semblait voir en lui un ancien ami.

Partout où nous avons été nous t'avons toujours regretté. De tous les jeunes gens de notre connoissance à qui nous avons pensé, tu es le seul que nous ayons toujours désiré pour compagnon de fortune et dont le caractère se plairoit le plus à notre genre de vie. Si tu pouvais t'imaginer la liberté dont nous jouissons et tous les avantages qui l'accompagnent, tu n'hésiterais pas un instant à venir la partager avec nous. Nous ne courons point après la Fortune. L'expérience nous a appris qu'elle court souvent après l'homme à qui elle crie: Arrête; mais son ardente ambition le rend sourd et la lui représente toujours comme fuyant devant lui. Alors croyant l'atteindre à force de courses et de fatigues, le malheureux s'en éloigne et lui échappe. De

quels regrets ne doit-il pas être consumé si après tant de peines
et de travaux il vient à connaître son erreur, misérable par sa
faute et trop faible pour retourner sur ses pas. Je ne m'éton-
nerais point que le désespoir de s'être si cruellement trompé, le
portât à se délivrer d'un reste d'existence que le souvenir de sa
faute et la pensée rongeante de son ambition déçue lui rendrait
insupportable. Ignorant donc si la fortune nous suit ou si elle
nous précède, nous ne risquerons point notre bonheur pour la
joindre, et nous aimons mieux un état qui procure une jouissance
modérée mais présente et continue, que celui qui demande des
souffrances préliminaires et n'offre en retour qu'un avenir plus
séduisant, il est vrai, mais éloigné et incertain. Et même en le
supposant certain, le grand avantage pour un homme qui a
employé toute sa jeunesse (c'est à dire toute la partie de sa vie
susceptible de jouissance) en veilles et en fatigues, de posséder
dans un âge avancé des richesses qui lui sont alors inutiles et
superflues! Ce n'est pas lorsqu'il est devenu incapable de sentir,
qu'il a perdu presque toute la vivacité de ses sens et de ses
passions, qu'il a besoin de l'instrument pour les satisfaire; le
plaisir le plus vif que ressent un vieillard est le ressouvenir de
ceux de la jeunesse, mais celui-ci n'aura que celui de ses peines
passées et cette réflexion le rendra triste et mélancolique.

Notre but donc, mon cher ami, est le plus tôt que nous pourrons
de nous procurer un fond de terre et de nous mettre fermiers;
ayant ainsi une ressource sûre pour vivre agréablement et indépendants, nous pourrons lorsque l'envie nous en prendra, aller de
tems en tems faire quelques excursions dans le dehors et courir
le pays, ce qui est un de nos plus grands plaisirs; or nous n'atten-
drons que toi pour accomplir notre projet; fais ton paquet, je t'en
prie, et hormis que tu ne sois dans des circonstances bien avantageuses, viens nous joindre tout de suite. Je ne saurais croire
avec quel plaisir je m'imagine quelquefois nous voir tous les
trois dans notre maison de campagne occupés des différents soins
de la campagne, puis de tems en tems pour varier, aller visiter
quelque nouvelle partie du monde; si la fortune se trouve en
passant, nous mettons la main dessus; si au contraire quelque
revers nous abat, nous nous en revenons vîte dans notre ferme,
où nous en sommes quittes pour couper notre bois nous-mêmes et

labourer notre champ; voilà notre pis-aller, et quel pis-aller! un de nos plus grands amusements!

Ah çà, nous t'attendons pour le plus tard le printems prochain. Pourvu que tu aies de quoi payer ton passage, ne t'inquiète pas du reste. Nous ignorons où nous serons positivement dans ce temps, mais dès le moment que tu seras arrivé, si c'est à Boston va loger chez Tahon qui tient une auberge française à l'enseigne de l'*alliance* dans la rue appelée Fore Street, prononcé Faure Strite. Si tu n'arrives pas à Boston, écris à Tahon, qui t'indiquera où nous sommes. Emporte avec toi tout ce que tu possèdes et tâche de te munir d'un ou deux bons baromètres et thermomètres et de tubes pour en faire, avec une longue vue.

Adieu, mon cher ami; je ne sais point à qui adresser cette lettre pour qu'elle te parvienne, car j'ignore totalement où est ta résidence actuelle. Gallatin t'écrit aussi, ainsi je ne te dis rien de lui.

It was the watchful care and forethought of Mlle. Pictet that enabled Gallatin to tide over the difficulties of these two years, by obtaining the countenance and aid of Dr. Cooper, which opened to him the doors of Harvard College. The following paper shows the position he occupied at the college, which has been sometimes dignified by the name of Professorship:

"At a meeting of the President and Fellows of Harvard College, July 2, 1782: Vote 5. That Mr. Gallatin, who has requested it, be permitted to instruct in the French language such of the students as desire it and who shall obtain permission from their parents or guardians in writing, signified under their hands to the President; which students shall be assessed in their quarter-bills the sums agreed for with Mr. Gallatin for their instruction; and that Mr. Gallatin be allowed the use of the library, a chamber in the college, and commons at the rate paid by the tutors, if he desire it.

"Copy. Attest,
"JOSEPH WILLARD, President."

The list of students who availed themselves of this privilege is still preserved, and contains a number of names then best known in Boston. The terms offered were: "Provided fifty students engage, the sum will be five dollars per quarter each, and provided sixty (not included Messrs. Oatis, Pyncheon, and Amory) have permits from their relations, the price will be four dollars each. They are under no obligation to engage more than by the quarter." The "Mr. Oatis" was apparently Harrison Gray Otis. About seventy appear to have taken lessons, which was, for that day, a considerable proportion of the whole number of students. Gallatin's earnings amounted to something less than three hundred dollars, and he seems to have found difficulty in procuring payment, for he intimates on a memorandum that this was the sum *paid*.

Of his life while in Boston and Cambridge almost nothing can be said. He was not fond of society, and there is no reason to suppose that he sought the society of Boston. The only American friend he made, of whose friendship any trace remains, was William Bentley, afterwards a clergyman long settled at Salem, then a fellow-tutor at Cambridge. When Gallatin left Cambridge after a year of residence, President Willard, Professor Wigglesworth, and Dr. Cooper, at his request, gave him a certificate that he had "acquitted himself in this department with great reputation. He appears to be well acquainted with letters, and has maintained an unblemished character in the University and in this part of the country." And Mr. Bentley, in whose hands he left a few small money settlements, wrote to him as follows, enclosing the testimonial:

WILLIAM BENTLEY TO GALLATIN.

HOLLIS HALL, CAMBRIDGE, August 20, 1783.

MR. GALLATIN,—I profess myself happy in your confidence. Your very reputable conduct in the University has obliged all its friends to afford you the most full testimony of their esteem and obligation, as the within testimonials witness. I should have answered your letter of July 11 sooner had not the call of a dissenting congregation at Salem obliged my absence at that time, and the immediately ensuing vacation prevented my attention to your business. . . . I expect soon to leave Cambridge, as the day appointed for my ordination at Salem is the 24th of September. In every situation of life I shall value your friendship and company, and subscribe myself your devoted and very humble servant.

N.B.—The tutors all expressed a readiness to subscribe to any recommendation or encomium which could serve Mr. Gallatin's interest in America; but our names would appear oddly on the list with the president, professors, and Dr. Cooper.

If Gallatin gained the esteem of so excellent a man as Bentley, there can be no doubt that he deserved it. In the small collegiate society of that day there was little opportunity to deceive, and Bentley and President Willard only repeat the same account of Gallatin's character and abilities which comes from all other sources. There is, too, an irresistible accent of truth in the quaint phraseology of Bentley's letter.

But he had no intention to stop here. In July, 1783, he took advantage of the summer vacation to travel.

GALLATIN TO SERRE.

NEW YORK, 22e juillet, 1783.

Mon bon ami, nous voici arrivés heureusement à New York après un passage plus long que nous n'avions compté. Nous laissâmes Providence jeudi passé, 17e courant, et arrivâmes le lendemain à Newport, où nous ne fîmes que dîner, et que j'ai trouvé mieux situé et plus agréable quoique moins bien bâti et moins commerçant que Providence. Apropos de cette dernière ville, j'ai été voir le collége, où il n'y a que 12 écoliers; je ne pus voir le président, mais le tutor, car il n'y en a qu'un, me parla de Poullin; il me dit qu'ils seraient très-charmés d'avoir un maître français; que le collége ni les écoliers ne pourraient lui donner que peu de chose, mais qu'il se trouverait dans la ville un nombre assez considérable d'écoliers pour l'occuper autant qu'il voudrait; qu'en cas qu'il s'en présentât un, le collége le ferait afficher sur la gazette afin qu'on ouvrît pour lui

une souscription dans la ville et qu'il sût sur quoi compter.
Pour revenir, nous laissâmes Newport vendredi à 2h. après
dîner, et ne sommes arrivés ici que hier, lundi, à la nuit. Nous
avons eu beau tems mais calme. Les bords de la Longue-Isle
près de New-York sont passables, mais ceux de l'île même où
est bâtie New-York sont couverts de campagnes charmantes au-
dessus de la ville. Le port paraît fort beau et il y a deux fois
autant de vaisseaux qu'à Boston. Ce que j'ai vu de la ville est
assez bien, mais il y fait horriblement chaud. Il y a comédie et
nous comptons y aller demain. Il y a aussi beaucoup de soldats,
de marins, et de réfugiés, les derniers très honnêtes et polis à ce
qu'on dit, mais les autres fort insolens. Nous comptons partir
après-demain pour Philadelphie, où j'espère trouver de tes nouvelles et de celles de N. W. Dans notre passage de Providence
nous avions pour compagnon de passage (parmi plusieurs autres)
un docteur français ou barbier, plus bavard que La Chapelle,
plus impudent que St. Pri et plus bête—ma foi, je ne sais à qui
le comparer pour cela; c'était un sot français au superlatif; il
a réussi à nous escroquer trois piastres, sans compter ce qu'il a
fait aux autres. Les filles ne sont pas si jolies ici qu'à Boston
et nous n'avons pas encore eu la moindre aventure galante dans
toute notre route. Au reste, comme tu es sans doute à présent
un grave maître d'école et que tu dois avoir pris toute la pédanterie
inséparable du métier, ce n'est plus à toi que j'oserais faire de
telles confidences. J'espère cependant que tu n'auras pas longtems à t'ennuyer à ce sot emploi et je t'écrirai tout ce que nous
avons à espérer dès que je serai à Philadelphie. Porte-toi bien.
Tout à toi.

Mr. Savary te fait bien des complimens. Notre autre compagnon de voyage n'est pas ici. Aussi je les supposerai en son
nom. Il est arrivé hier ici une frégate d'Angleterre qui a, dit-on,
apporté le traité définitif . . . traité de commerce de. . . .

The M. Savary mentioned here as Gallatin's fellow-traveller
from Boston was to have a great influence on his fortunes. M.
Savary de Valcoulon was from Lyons. Having claims against
the State of Virginia, he had undertaken himself to collect them,

and meeting Gallatin at Boston, they had become travelling companions. They went to Philadelphia together, where they remained till November. Serre rejoined them there; but Gallatin's means were now quite exhausted. Their combined expenses, since quitting Geneva, had been in three years about sixteen hundred dollars, including three hundred dollars lost by the Treasury warrant. Of this sum Gallatin had advanced about thirteen hundred dollars, Serre's father resolutely refusing to send his son any money at all or to honor his drafts. A settlement was now made. Serre gave to Gallatin his note for half the debt, about six hundred dollars, and, joining a countryman named Mussard, went to Jamaica, where he died, in 1784, of the West India fever. Fifty-three years afterwards his sister by will repaid the principal to Mr. Gallatin, who had, with great delicacy, declined to ask for payment. But when this separation between Gallatin and Serre took place, it was intended to be temporary only; Serre was to return and to rejoin his friend, who meanwhile was to carry out their scheme of retreat by a new emigration. The sea-coast was not yet far enough removed from civilization; they were bent upon putting another month's journey between themselves and Europe; the Ohio was now their aim. There may be a doubt whether they drew Savary in this direction, or whether Savary pointed out the path to them. In any case, Serre sailed for Jamaica in the middle of September, before the new plans were entirely settled, and nothing was ever heard from him again until repeated inquiries produced, in the autumn of 1786, a brief but apparently authentic report of his death two years before. Gallatin accepted Savary's offers, and went with him to Richmond to assist him in the settlement of his claims. But before they left Philadelphia a larger scheme was projected. Savary and Gallatin were to become partners in a purchase of one hundred and twenty thousand acres of land in Western Virginia, Gallatin's interest being one-fourth of the whole, and his share to be paid, until his majority, in the form of personal superintendence.

Meanwhile, a premonitory symptom of revolution had occurred in Geneva. The two parties had come to blows; blood was shed; the adjoining governments of Switzerland, France, and Savoy had interposed, and held the city in armed occupation. The Liberals were deeply disgusted at this treatment, and to those who had already left their country the temptation to return became smaller than ever.

PHILADELPHIE, ce 1er octobre, 1783.

Mon bon ami, je viens de recevoir ta lettre du 20 mars qui à quelques égards m'a fait le plus grand plaisir, mais qui en m'apprenant toutes les circonstances des troubles de notre malheureuse patrie a achevé de m'ôter toute espérance de jamais pouvoir m'y fixer. Non, mon ami, il est impossible à un homme de sens et vertueux, né citoyen d'un état libre, et qui est venu sucer encore l'amour de l'indépendance dans le pays le plus libre de l'univers; il est impossible, dis-je, à cet homme, quelques puissent avoir été les préjugés de son enfance, d'aller jouer nulle part le rôle de tyran ou d'esclave, et comme je ne vois pas qu'il y ait d'autre situation à choisir à Genève, je me vois forcé de renoncer pour toujours à ces murs chéris qui m'ont vu naître, à ma famille, à mes amis; à moins qu'une nouvelle révolution ne change beaucoup la situation des affaires. Tu vois par ce que je viens de te dire que la façon de penser de mes parens n'influe point sur la mienne et que j'en ai changé depuis mon départ d'Europe. Il est tout simple qu'étant entouré des gens qui pensent tous de la même manière, on s'habitue à penser comme eux; dès que l'on commence à être de leur parti, le préjugé a déjà pris possession de vous et à moins que par un heureux hasard la raison et le bon droit ne soient du côté que vous avez embrassé, vous tomberez d'écarts en écarts, de torts en torts, et vous ne verrez les excès auxquels vous vous serez abandonné que lorsque quelqu'évènement d'éclat vous aura ouvert les yeux. En voilà je crois assez pour me justifier d'avoir été Négatif à 19 ans lorsque j'abandonnai Genève. Mais à 1200 lieues de distance on juge bien plus sainement; le jugement n'étant plus embarrassé par les petites raisons, les petits préjugés, les petites vues et les petits intérêts de vos alentours, ne voit plus que le fond de la question, et peut décider hardiment. Si l'on se laisse gagner par un peu d'en-

thousiasme il y a mille à gager contre un que ce sera en faveur
de la bonne cause.   Voilà ce qui peu à peu produisit un grand
changement dans mon opinion après mon arrivée en Amérique.
Je fus bientôt convaincu par la comparaison des gouvernemens
américains avec celui de Genève que ce dernier était fondé sur de
mauvais principes; que le pouvoir judicatif tant au civil qu'au
criminel, le pouvoir exécutif en entier, et $\frac{2}{3}$ du pouvoir législatif
appartenant à deux corps qui se créaient presqu'entièrement eux-
mêmes, et dont les membres étaient élus à vie, il était presqu'impossible que cette formidable aristocratie ne rompît tôt ou tard
l'équilibre que l'on s'imaginait pouvoir subsister à Genève.   Je
compris que le droit d'élire la moitié des membres de l'un de ces
conseils sans avoir celui de les déplacer et le droit de déplacer
annuellement la 6me partie des membres de l'autre n'étaient que
de faibles barrières contre des hommes qui avaient la fortune et la
vie des citoyens entre les mains, le soin de la police de la manière
la plus étendue, deux négatifs sur toutes les volontés du peuple,
et dont les charges étaient à vie, pour ne pas dire héréditaires.
Quelle différence entre un tel gouvernement et celui d'un pays
où les différents conseils à qui sont confiés les pouvoirs législatifs
et exécutifs ne sont élus que pour une année, où les juges, qui ne
font qu'expliquer la loi, une fois élus ne sont plus sous l'influence
du souverain et ne peuvent être déplacés que juridiquement, où
enfin l'on est jugé non pas même par ces juges de nom, mais par
12 citoyens pris parmi les honnêtes gens et que les parties peuvent
récuser.   (Tu ne seras pas étonné, mon ami, après une telle comparaison, que je me sois décidé à me fixer ici.)   En voyant les
défauts du gouvernement genevois, je sentis qu'il était de l'intérêt des partisans de la liberté de veiller de près les aristocrates,
mais non pas de vouloir les combattre.   Le parti violent qu'ont
embrassé les représentans ne peut être justifié qu'en disant que
les circonstances les ont entraînés, car il était impossible de n'en
pas prévoir les conséquences et que la politique artificieuse des
négatifs en tireroit tout le parti possible; je n'ai rien à ajouter
à ce que tu dis sur la bassesse de ces derniers, et la faute des
citoyens produite par l'enthousiasme de liberté n'est que trop
sévèrement punie.

     La lettre que je viens de recevoir est la première qui nous soit parvenue de celles que tu nous annonces nous avoir écrites. J'ai quitté Cambridge en juillet de cette année et je suis venu ici où je n'ai encore rien trouvé à faire qui me convienne. Serre n'est pas ici ; je l'ai laissé à Boston d'où il est parti pour aller à . . . et d'où il ne reviendra que l'année prochaine. Ce n'est pas pour toi que je cache le lieu actuel de sa résidence, mais il a des raisons pour que d'autres l'ignorent et j'ai peur que cette lettre n'éprouve des accidents. J'irai en Virginie bientôt, mais écris-moi à Philadelphie : To Albert Gallatin, citizen of Geneva, Philadelphia. Ce n'est que de peur d'équivoque que je conserve le titre de *citizen of Geneva.* Ecris à Serre sous mon adresse. Tu ne saurais croire le plaisir que j'ai éprouvé en apprenant que tu étais agréablement et avantageusement placé, mais tu ne m'a pas donné assez de détails sur ce qui te concerne ; répare ta faute par ta première lettre.

Tu désires sans doute savoir quelles sont mes vues pour l'avenir ; les voici ! Ayant pour ainsi dire renoncé à Genève, je n'ai pas dû hésiter sur la choix de la patrie que je devais choisir, et l'Amérique m'a paru le pays le plus propre à me fixer par sa constitution, son climat, et les ressources que j'y pouvais trouver. Mais il serait bien dur pour moi de me voir séparé de tous mes amis et c'était sur toi que je comptais pour me faire passer une vie agréable. Dumont, dis-tu, te retient ; mais qu'est-ce qui retient Dumont ? Il ne doit pas douter de tout le plaisir que j'aurais à le voir. Si toi, lui, Serre et moi étions réunis, ne formerions-nous pas une société très-agréable ? Tu vois que je compte que vous seriez tous les deux aussi charmés d'être avec Serre et moi que nous deux d'être avec vous. Reste à proposer les moyens de pouvoir être passablement heureux quand nous serons réunis en ayant un honnête nécessaire et jouissant de cette médiocrité à laquelle je borne tous mes vœux. Comme la campagne est notre passion favorite, c'est de ce côté que se tournent entièrement mes projets. Dans l'espace situé entre les Apalaches et les Mississippi, sur les deux rives de l'Ohio se trouvent les meilleures terres de l'Amérique, et comme le climat en est tempéré je les préférerais à celles de Machias et de la Nouvelle-Angleterre. Celles au nord de l'Ohio appartiennent au Congrès, et celles du sud à la Virginie, aux Carolines et à la Georgie. Le

Congrès n'en a encore point vendu ou donné. C'est donc de celles de Virginie dont je vais parler, quoique ce que j'en dirai puisse s'appliquer au nord de l'Ohio si les achats quand ils se feront y étaient plus avantageux. Je rejette les deux Carolines et la Georgie comme malsaines et moins avantageuses. Les terres depuis le grand Canaway qui se jette dans l'Ohio 250 milles au-dessous du Fort Duquesne ou Fort Pitt ou Pittsburg, jusques tout près de l'endroit où l'Ohio se décharge dans le Mississippi, ont été achetées à très-bas prix par divers particuliers de l'État de Virginie, et c'est d'eux qu'il faudrait les racheter. Elles valent depuis 30 sols à 20 francs (argent de France) l'acre suivant leur qualité et surtout leur situation. Celles qui sont situées près de la chute de l'Ohio, le seul établissement qu'il y ait dans cet espace, sont les plus chères. On peut en avoir d'excellentes partout ailleurs pour 50 sols ou 3 francs. Je vais actuellement en Virginie et d'après mes informations j'en achèterai 2 à 3 mille acres dans une situation avantageuse. Si tu te détermines à venir te fixer avec moi, je tournerai sur-le-champ toutes mes vues de ce côté-là. Je ne te demanderais pas de quitter immédiatement la place avantageuse que tu as, mais seulement de me donner une réponse décisive. Aussitôt que ma majorité, qui sera le 29 janvier, 1786, sera arrivée, j'emploierai ma petite fortune à fixer un certain nombre de familles de fermiers irlandais, américains, &c., autour de moi, parcequ'ils m'enrichiront en se rendant heureux (enrichir veut dire une médiocrité aisée). Tu sens bien que si c'est mon avantage de faire des avances à des indifférents, ce sera me rendre service que de venir te joindre à nous, et que le peu que tu pourras apporter, joint à ce qu'il sera de mon propre intérêt de t'avancer, te mettra en état de te former une habitation par toi-même, car depuis ton paragraphe des deux louis je n'ose plus te dire que ce que j'ai t'appartient comme à moi-même. Quant à moi j'accepterais, je ne dis pas un prêt mais un don de toi comme si je prenais dans ma bourse, et je suis tellement identifié avec toi et Serre que toutes les fois que je dis *Je* en parlant ou en pensant à quelque plan de vie ou à quelque établissement, j'entends toujours *Badollet, Serre et Moi*. Je ne suis pas tout-à-fait aussi lié avec Dumont, mais je le suis autant avec lui qu'avec qui que ce soit excepté Serre et toi, et comme depuis mon départ de Genève je me suis beaucoup rapproché de sa façon de penser à bien des égards, comme il réunit les qualités du cœur et de l'esprit, il n'y a personne que je désirasse voir venir avec toi plus que lui, et à qui, si je le pouvais, je fusse de quelque utilité avec plus de plaisir. J'espère qu'en voilà assez pour l'engager à nous joindre s'il n'est pas retenu à Genève par des liens bien forts, et si ses goûts sont les mêmes que les nôtres. Je n'ai pas besoin de te dire qu'en s'établissant dans un bois loin des villes et n'ayant que peu d'habitans autour de soi, l'on doit s'attendre dans les commencements à bien des privations et surtout ne compter sur aucune des jouissances raffinées des villes. Je me sens assez de courage pour cela, mais je ne conseillerais à personne de prendre ce parti sans s'être bien consulté. Comme je suis très-gueux dans ce moment-ci, comme plus tu restes dans ta place actuelle et plus tu te prépares de moyens de réussite pour l'avenir, et comme il vaut mieux perdre un an que de s'apprêter des regrets, attends des nouvelles plus positives pour partir à moins que tu n'aies rien de mieux à faire. Mais surtout ne prends point d'engagemens en Europe qui pussent t'empêcher de venir nous joindre dans l'année prochaine ou au plus tard dans la suivante.

Si parmi les personnes que les malheurs de notre patrie en chassent, il s'en trouvait quelques-unes qui désirassent réunir leurs petites fortunes pour former un établissement un peu plus considérable, je désirerais que tu me le fisses savoir. Je pourrai depuis la Virginie leur proposer un plan plus déterminé et plus sûr. Je ne crois pas ce pays bien propre à établir des manufactures ; je ne parle que de petits capitalistes comme moi, et de fermiers ou ouvriers, ces derniers (les ouvriers) en petit nombre. S'il y avait un nombre suffisant de gens qui voulussent s'expatrier, peut-être le Congrès leur accorderait des terres. Je serais charmé de pouvoir être utile à tous ceux de mes compatriotes que leur amour pour la liberté a forcés de quitter Genève, et s'ils tournaient leur vue sur les États-Unis ils pourraient compter sur mon zèle à leur donner tous les renseignemens et à faire toutes les démarches qui pourraient leur être de quelque utilité. Les citoyens américains sont très-bien intentionnés à leur égard et il y a eu beaucoup de refroidissemens entre eux et les Français à leur sujet. Il y a environ un mois qu'un homme d'un rang et d'un mérite distingué de Philadelphie demandait à l'Ambassadeur français pourquoi sa Majesté Très-Chrétienne s'était mêlée des divisions des Genevois. C'était pour leur bien, répondit Mr. de Marbois, consul de France. J'espère, répliqua l'Américain, que le roi ne prendra jamais notre bien assez à cœur pour se mêler de nos brouilleries intestines. On ne lui fit aucune réponse. Quelque haine que je puisse avoir contre le Ministère français qui nous a perdus, elle ne s'étend point jusque sur toute leur nation ; je fais le plus grand cas d'un grand nombre de ses individus et il y en a quelques-uns à qui personnellement j'ai des obligations essentielles.

Je souhaiterais que cette lettre ne fût pas vue de mes parens à Génève, non pas que je veuille qu'ils ignorent ma façon de penser politique, ou que des vues intéressées me fassent désirer que mes oncles ne sussent pas que je veux me fixer en Amérique, ce qui est renoncer à toutes mes espérances de ce côté-là, mais parceque cette résolution, si elle était connue, ferait trop de peine à ma tendre mère Mlle. Pictet, qui est le seul chaînon subsistant des liens qui me retenaient à Genève. Je ne veux pas dire par là qu'elle soit la seule personne qui m'y attire ; j'y ai des amis et surtout une amie qu'il me serait bien dur de quitter ; mais tu me connais assez pour comprendre quels doivent être mes sentimens à l'égard de la personne à qui je dois tout et que j'ai bien mal récompensée de son amitié et de ses soins.

Mille amitiés à Dumont. Fais faire mes complimens à d'Ivernois ; la manière dont il s'est comporté lui fait beaucoup d'honneur. Ecris-moi promptement et longuement. Je te donnerai des nouvelles plus positives dans deux mois. Si tu changes de demeure, prie Mᵉ. de Vivens de t'envoyer les lettres qui te parviendront, et indique-moi ton adresse. J'espère que tu viendras bientôt tirer parti de ton Anglais. Tout homme qui a des terres ici devient citoyen et a droit de donner sa voix pour envoyer son représentant ou député à l'Assemblée Générale, et celui d'être élu soi-même s'il en est digne. Adieu, mon bon ami. Tout à toi.

Cette lettre est mise à bord du brig Le Comte du Duras, Capitaine Fournier, allant à Bordeaux, et adressée à Messrs. Archer, Baix & Cie.

12 novembre, 1783.

Mon bon ami, le sus-dit vaisseau a fait naufrage à l'entrée de la Delaware. L'équipage s'est sauvé et ma lettre m'est revenue. Je me porte toujours bien. Je pars demain matin pour Virginie d'où je reviendrai dans deux mois. Adresse toujours à Philadelphie. Je suis entré pour ¼ dans une spéculation de 120,000 acres de terre en Virginie. Cela de toi à moi. Tout à toi.

Clearly young Gallatin now thought that he had found the destiny so long imagined, and, modest as his sketch of their future prospects may appear, his acts show that the original scheme of bettering his fortune was by no means abandoned, but rather entertained on a vaster scale. He had solved the difficulty of speculating without capital and without debt; for certainly that modest retreat which he imagined for himself, Serre, and Badollet, did not require operations on the scale of a hundred thousand acres, and the element of speculation must have absorbed four-fifths of his thoughts. At this time, indeed, and for many years afterwards, all America was engaged in these speculations. General Washington was deep in them, and, as will be seen, jostled against Gallatin in the very act of opening up his lands. Robert Morris was a wild speculator, and closed his public career a bankrupt and in prison for that reason. Promising as the prospect was and certain as the ultimate profits seemed, it would be difficult to prove that any one was ever really enriched by these investments; certainly in Gallatin's case, as in the case of Washington and Robert Morris, the result was trouble, disappointment, and loss. It was for Gallatin something worse; it was another false start.

For the moment, however, he was with Savary at Richmond, attending to Savary's claims and making preparations for his Western expedition. No more complaints of ennui are heard. Richmond has far other fascinations than Boston. To the end of his life Mr. Gallatin always recalled with pleasure his experiences at this city, where he first began to feel his own powers and to see them recognized by the world. In a letter written in

1848, a few months before his death, to the Virginia Historical Society, he expressed this feeling with all the warmth that age gives to its recollections of youth.[1]

"I cannot complain of the world. I have been treated with kindness in every part of the United States where I have resided. But it was at Richmond, where I spent most of the winters between the years 1783 and 1789, that I was received with that old proverbial Virginia hospitality to which I know no parallel anywhere within the circle of my travels. It was not hospitality only that was shown to me. I do not know how it came to pass, but every one with whom I became acquainted appeared to take an interest in the young stranger. I was only the interpreter of a gentleman the agent of a foreign house that had a large claim for advances to the State; and this made me known to all the officers of government and some of the most prominent members of the Legislature. It gave me the first opportunity of showing some symptoms of talent, even as a speaker, of which I was not myself aware. Every one encouraged me and was disposed to promote my success in life. To name all those from whom I received offers of service would be to name all the most distinguished residents at that time at Richmond. I will only mention two: John Marshall, who, though but a young lawyer in 1783, was almost at the head of the bar in 1786, offered to take me in his office without a fee, and assured me that I would become a distinguished lawyer. Patrick Henry advised me to go to the West, where I might study law if I chose; but predicted that I was intended for a statesman, and told me that this was the career which should be my aim; he also rendered me several services on more than one occasion."

Gallatin remained in Richmond till the end of February, 1784, and then returned to Philadelphia, where he made the final preparations for his expedition to the West. None of his letters are preserved, but his movements may be followed with tolerable accuracy. He remained in Philadelphia during the month of March, then crossed the mountains to Pittsburg in April, went down the Ohio with his party, and passed the sum-

---

[1] See Writings, vol. ii., p. 659.

mer in the occupation of selecting and surveying the lands for which he and his associates had purchased warrants. These lands were in what was then part of Monongalia County, Virginia; but this county was in wealth and resources far behind the adjacent one of Fayette, in Pennsylvania, where no Indians had ever penetrated since its first settlement in 1769, whereas Monongalia had suffered severely from Indian depredations in the Revolution, a fact which decided Savary and Gallatin to fix upon a base of operations as near the Pennsylvania line as possible. They selected the farm of Thomas Clare, situated on the river Monongahela and George's Creek, about four miles north of the Virginia line, and here they established a store.

Gallatin seems to have been detained till late in the year by these occupations. They excluded all other thoughts from his mind. He wrote no letters; perhaps it would have been difficult, if not impossible, to find a conveyance if he had written them. There is but one fragment of his handwriting before the close of the year, and this only an unfinished draft of a letter to Badollet, which is worth inserting, not only because there is nothing else, but because it shows what was engaging his thoughts.

GALLATIN TO BADOLLET.

DES BORDS DE LA SUSQUEHANNA, 29 décembre, 1784.

Mon bon ami, retenu ici aujourd'hui par le mauvais temps dans une misérable auberge, je vais tâcher de passer quelques moments agréables en causant avec toi. Je laissai Boston en juillet, 1783, et vins à Philadelphie avec M. Savary de Valcoulon de Lyon, appelé par ses affaires en Amérique et qui n'entendant pas l'Anglais était bien aise d'avoir avec lui quelqu'un qui le sût; ou qui plutôt ayant pris de l'amitié pour moi et voyant que ma situation dans la Nouvelle-Angleterre était loin d'être gracieuse, crut qu'il me serait plus avantageux de changer de place et me promit de m'être aussi utile qu'il le pourrait. Il m'a bien tenu parole. Non-seulement il m'a aidé de sa bourse et de son crédit, mais il m'a mis à même d'espérer un jour de pouvoir jouir du plaisir de vivre heureux avec Serre et toi. Tu sens qu'un homme à qui j'ai consenti d'avoir des obligations doit

avoir un cœur digne d'être mon ami, et je crois te faire plaisir
en t'annonçant que ses plans sont les mêmes que les nôtres et que
probablement tu auras dans ce pays un ami de plus que tu
ne l'espérais.   Après avoir passé quatre mois à Philadelphie,
pendant lesquels Serre fut forcé par notre situation de passer à
la Jamaïque avec Mussard de Genève, M. Savary passa en Virginie pour des dettes que cet état avait contractées avec sa maison,
et je l'y accompagnai.   Ses plans de retraite étant les mêmes que
les miens, nous formions souvent ensemble des châteaux-en-
Espagne lorsque le hasard nous offrit une occasion qui nous fit
espérer que nous pourrions les réaliser.   L'état de Virginie est
borné au sud par la Caroline, à l'est par la mer, au nord par le
Maryland et la Pensilvanie, au nord-ouest et à l'ouest par la
rivière Ohio, ou Belle Rivière, et par le Mississippi.   Une
chaîne de montagnes nommées Apalaches ou Allegheny qui
courant sud-ouest et nord-est à environ 50 lieues de la mer
traverse tous les États-Unis de l'Amérique, sépare la Virginie
en deux parties, dont la plus petite comprise entre la mer et les
montagnes est sans comparaison la plus peuplée.   L'autre, in-
finiment plus grande, ne contient que deux établissements.   L'un
joignant les montagnes et le reste des anciens établissements
s'étend sur l'Ohio jusqu'à Fishing Creek 150 milles au-dessous
de Fort Pitt, et de là par une ligne parallèle à peu près aux
montagnes, formant au-delà de ces montagnes une lisière d'environ 10 à 20 lieues de largeur qui contient environ 500 familles.
Le second établissement qui est celui de Kentuckey, que tu écris
Quintoquay, est situé sur la rivière du même nom qui tombe
dans l'Ohio 700 milles au-dessous de Fort Pitt.   Il contient à
présent 20 à 30 mille âmes et est entouré et séparé de tous les
pays habités par des déserts. . . . .

There is, however, one proof that he was at George's Creek in
the month of September of this year.   Among Mr. John Russell
Bartlett's "Reminiscences of Mr. Gallatin" is the following anec-
dote, which can only refer to this time:

"Mr. Gallatin said he first met General Washington at the
office of a land agent near the Kenawha River, in North-Western
Virginia, where he (Mr. G.) had been engaged in surveying.

The office consisted of a log house fourteen feet square, in which was but one room.   In one corner of this was a bed for the use of the agent.   General Washington, who owned large tracts of land in this region, was then visiting them in company with his nephew, and at the same time examining the country with a view of opening a road across the Alleghanies.   Many of the settlers and hunters familiar with the country had been invited to meet the general at this place for the purpose of giving him such information as would enable him to select the most eligible pass for the contemplated road.   Mr. Gallatin felt a desire to meet this great man, and determined to await his arrival.

"On his arrival, General Washington took his seat at a pine table in the log cabin, or rather land agent's office, surrounded by the men who had come to meet him.   They all stood up, as there was no room for seats.   Some of the more fortunate, however, secured quarters on the bed.   They then underwent an examination by the general, who wrote down all the particulars stated by them.   He was very inquisitive, questioning one after the other and noting down all they said.   Mr. Gallatin stood among the others in the crowd, though quite near the table, and listened attentively to the numerous queries put by the general, and very soon discovered from the various relations which was the only practicable pass through which the road could be made. He felt uneasy at the indecision of the general, when the point was so evident to him, and without reflecting on the impropriety of it, suddenly interrupted him, saying, 'Oh, it is plain enough, such a place [a spot just mentioned by one of the settlers] is the most practicable.'   The good people stared at the young surveyor (for they only knew him as such) with surprise, wondering at his boldness in thrusting his opinion unasked upon the general.

"The interruption put a sudden stop to General Washington's inquiries.   He laid down his pen, raised his eyes from his paper, and cast a stern look at Mr. Gallatin, evidently offended at the intrusion of his opinion, but said not a word.   Resuming his former attitude, he continued his interrogations for a few minutes longer, when suddenly stopping, he threw down his pen, turned to Mr. Gallatin, and said, 'You are right, sir.'

" 'It was so on all occasions with General Washington,' re-marked Mr. Gallatin to me; 'he was slow in forming an opinion, and never decided until he knew he was right.'

" To continue the narrative: the general stayed here all night, occupying the bed alluded to, while his nephew, the land agent, and Mr. Gallatin rolled themselves in blankets and buffalo-skins and lay upon the bare floor.   After the examination mentioned, and when the party went out, General Washington inquired who the young man was who had interrupted him, made his acquaint-ance, and learned all the particulars of his history.   They occa-sionally met afterwards, and the general urged Mr. Gallatin to become his land agent; but as Mr. Gallatin was then, or in-tended soon to become, the owner of a large tract of land, he was compelled to decline the favorable offer made him by General Washington."

This is the story as told by Mr. Bartlett, and there can be no doubt of its essential correctness. But General Washington made only one journey to the West during which he could possibly have met Mr. Gallatin. This journey was in the month of September, 1784, and was not to the Kanawha, though origi-nally meant to be so. He went no farther than to George's Creek, and it so happens that he kept a diary of every day's work during this expedition. The diary has never been pub-lished; but it is among the archives in the State Department at Washington. In it are the following entries:

" September 23. Arrived at Colonel Phillips' about five o'clock in the afternoon, sixteen miles from Beason Town and near the mouth of Cheat River; . . . crossed no water of consequence except George's Creek. An apology made me from the court of Fayette (through Mr. Smith) for not addressing me, as they found my horses saddled and myself on the move. Finding by in-quiries that the Cheat River had been passed with canoes through those parts which had been represented as impassable, and that a Captain Hanway, the surveyor of Monongahela, lived within two or three miles of it, south side thereof, I resolved to pass it to obtain further information, and accordingly, accompanied by Colonel Phillips, set off in the morning of the

" 24th, and crossed it at the mouth. . . . From the fork to the surveyor's office, which is at the house of one Pierpont, is about eight miles along the dividing ridge. . . . Pursuing my inquiries respecting the navigation of the Western waters, Captain Hanway proposed, if I would stay all night, to send to Monongahela [Monongalia] court-house at Morgantown for Colonel Zach. Morgan and others who would have it in their power to give the best accounts that were to be obtained, which assenting to, they were sent for and came, and from them I received the following intelligence, viz.," &c.

No mention is made of Mr. Gallatin, nor indeed of any others besides Colonel Morgan, from whom the information was derived; but there can hardly be a doubt that this was the occasion of the meeting. The only possible importance of this district of country, in which both Washington and Gallatin had at times large interests, was derived from the fact that it lay between the head-waters of the Potomac and the nearest navigable branches of the Ohio.[1] The reason why Gallatin and Savary selected George's Creek for their base of operations was that in their opinion they thus held in their hands the best practicable connection between the Ohio and the Potomac which was their path to Richmond and a market. Probably this subject had engaged much of Gallatin's attention during a good part of this summer, and it is not unlikely that he had already arrived, from his own study, at the conclusion which he found Washington so slow to adopt.

The following winter was also passed in Richmond, where Savary ultimately built a brick house, long remembered for its tall, round chimneys. Gallatin was now established here so firmly that he regarded himself as a Virginian, and seems to have been regarded as such by his acquaintances, as the following paper testifies:

" The bearer hereof, Mr. Albert Gallatine, is going from this place to Greenbriar County, and from thence towards Monongalia and the Countys northwestward. His business is with the surveyors of some of these Countys, particularly with him of

---

[1] See map, p. 126.

Greenbriar. And I do request that from him in particular, as well as from all others, he may meet with particular attention and respect.

" I feel it my duty in a peculiar manner to give every possible facility to this gentleman, because his personal character, as well as his present designs, entitle him to the most cordial regards.

" Given under my hand at Richmond this 25th March, 1785.

"P. HENRY."

Governor Henry also intrusted Gallatin with the duty of locating two thousand acres of land in the Western country for Colonel James Le Maire, or of completing the title if the land were already located. This commission is dated March 29. On the 30th, Gallatin wrote to Badollet a letter, of which the following extract is all that has interest here. He at length tells Badollet to come over at once. His own position is sufficiently secure to warrant a decisive step of this kind. The next day began his second expedition to the West.

GALLATIN TO BADOLLET.

RICHMOND (EN VIRGINIE), ce 30 mars, 1785.

Mon bon ami, j'espère que tu as reçu la lettre que je t'ai écrite de Philadelphie en décembre dernier par laquelle je t'annonçais la réception de la tienne du 9e avril, 1784, et par laquelle je te renvoyais à ma première pour de plus grands détails sur ce qui me regardait. C'est avec le plus grand plaisir que je puis enfin te dire de partir par la première occasion pour venir me joindre; ce n'est qu'après m'être longtems consulté que j'ai pris ce parti, ayant toujours craint de te faire sacrifier un bien-être réel à des avantages incertains. Cependant, considérant ma position actuelle et voyant par tes lettres que ton attachement pour moi et ton goût pour la retraite sont toujours les mêmes, je crois que je puis accorder mon amitié et ton bonheur; du reste, voici l'état exact où je suis, tu jugeras par là s'il te convient de venir le partager.

J'ai fait connaissance avec M. Savary de Lyon, homme d'un rare mérite, et dont le cœur vaut mieux que l'esprit; après l'avoir aidé pendant quelque tems à suivre ses affaires, il m'a intéressé d'abord pour un quart et ensuite pour une moitié dans une spéculation de terres dans l'état de Virginie. Sans entrer dans tous les détails de cette affaire, dont la réussite est due en partie à mes soins pendant le voyage que j'ai fait l'été dernier dans les derrières de la Virginie, il te suffira de savoir que nous possédons actuellement plus de cent mille acres de terre sur les bords ou près de l'Ohio, 250 milles par eau au-dessous du Fort Pitt, autrefois Fort Duquesne, à 350 milles de Philadelphie et environ 300 de Baltimore. Elles sont situées entre le grand et le petit Kanhawa (ou Canhaway, ou Canway), deux rivières qui se jettent dans l'Ohio. C'est un pays montueux, très-coupé, mais fertile, propre surtout à la culture du bled et à élever du bétail. J'ai fait arpenter presque toutes ces terres l'année dernière ; je pars demain pour aller finir cet ouvrage et pour mener quelques familles afin de commencer un établissement. Nous avons au reste revendu quelques petites portions qui nous ont remboursé les trois quarts des premières avances. . . .

During this summer Gallatin kept a brief diary, so that it is possible to follow all his movements. Leaving Richmond on the 31st of March, alone, on horseback, he ascended James River, crossed the Blue Ridge near the Peaks of Otter, and arrived at the Court-House of Greenbrier County on the 18th April. Having seen the surveyor and attended to his locations of land, he started northwards on the 21st, and on the 29th reached his headquarters at Clare's on George's Creek. Here Savary joined him, and after making their preparations they set off on the 26th May, and descended the Ohio with their surveying party to the mouth of Little Sandy Creek, where from June 3 to July 1 they were engaged in surveying, varied by building a log cabin, clearing land, and occasionally killing a bear or a buffalo. On the 1st July, Gallatin, leaving Savary and four men at "Friends' Landing" to carry on the work, set off by water for the Grand Kanawha, and surveyed country about the head-waters of the Big Sandy and between the Elk and the Pocotaligo. On August 13 he descended the Pocotaligo, and on the 15th, striking across country to the southward, he reached "Meeting Camp," on the Elk, and received letters from Savary announcing that the

Indians had broken up his operations on the Ohio and compelled him to abandon the cabin and clearing.

This Indian outbreak deranged all their plans. It had been their intention to settle on these lands between the two Kanawhas, and for this purpose they had engaged men, built the log cabin, and cleared several acres on the banks of the Ohio adjoining the lands located by General Washington and known as " Washington's Bottom." They themselves, it is true, were not directly molested by the Indians, but boats had been captured and emigrants murdered a few miles from their settlement. They were obliged to abandon their plan and to return to Clare's. This wild attempt to make his home in an utter solitude one hundred and twenty miles beyond the last house then inhabited on the banks of the Ohio, was obviously impracticable even to Gallatin's mind, without incurring imminent danger of massacre.

The friends returned to George's Creek. It was then, at the October court of Monongalia County, Virginia, according to the record, that Gallatin at last "took the oath of allegiance and fidelity to the Commonwealth of Virginia." He had long considered himself an American citizen; this act merely fixed the place of citizenship. By the laws of his native country he was still a minor. He was actually residing in Pennsylvania. The old Confederation was still the only national government. Virginia was the State to which he was attached, and of Virginia he wished to be considered a citizen, so that even a year later he signed himself in legal documents " of Monongalia County, Virginia." He had fully determined to remain in the Western country, and he chose Monongalia County because his lands lay there; but the neighboring Pennsylvania county of Fayette was both by situation and resources a more convenient residence, and even so early as 1784, as has already been shown, Savary and he had established a store and made their base of operations in Fayette County. In November of this year 1785 they leased from Thomas Clare for five years a house and five acres of land at George's Creek, in Springhill Township, on the Monongahela: here they made their temporary residence, transferring their store to it, and placing in it several men who had been engaged as

settlers and had remained in their service.　After the joint establishment had been carried on for two or three years, Gallatin
bought a farm of four hundred acres about a mile higher up
the river, to which he transferred the establishment, and which
ultimately became his residence, under the name of Friendship
Hill, perhaps to commemorate the friendship of Serre, Savary,
and Badollet.

This then was the promised land, the "fond de terre" which
poor Serre had described, and to which Badollet was now on
his way.　In point of fact it suggested Switzerland.　No better
spot could have been found in the United States for men who had
passed their youth by the shore of Lake Geneva, overlooked by
the snow summit of Mont Blanc.　Friendship Hill rises abruptly from the Monongahela, and looks eastward to the Laurel
Ridge, picturesque as Serre could have imagined, remote as
Rousseau could have wished.　But as a place of permanent residence for men who were to earn their living according to the
Genevan theory, it had one disadvantage which is pointedly described by Gallatin himself in a letter to Badollet, written about
half a century afterwards.[1]　"Although I should have been contented to live and die amongst the Monongahela hills, it must
be acknowledged that, beyond the invaluable advantage of health,
they afforded either to you or me but few intellectual or physical
resources.　Indeed, I must say that I do not know in the United
States any spot which afforded less means to earn a bare subsistence for those who could not live by manual labor than the
sequestered corner in which accident had first placed us."

Thus much accomplished, Gallatin and Savary left George's
Creek on the 22d November, making their way to Cumberland on the Potomac, and so down the river to Richmond.
But in the following February he again returned to George's
Creek, and there he kept house for the future, having never less
than six persons and afterwards many more in his family.　Here
Badollet now came, in obedience to his friend's wishes.　With
him Gallatin buried himself in the wilderness, and his family
entreated for letters in vain.

---

[1] See below, p. 646.

ABRAHAM GALLATIN TO ALBERT GALLATIN.

PREGNY, ce 20 juin, 1785.

Quand une correspondance, mon cher fils, est aussi mal établie que la nôtre, on ne sait par où commencer. Je t'ai écrit quelques lettres dont j'ignore le sort; j'en ai reçu une de toi, il y a deux ou trois ans; si la date en était exacte, elle me fût rendue ici dans trente jours . . . d'où je conclus que nous étions assez voisins et qu'il ne tenait qu'à toi de nous donner plus souvent de tes nouvelles. Nous n'en avons eu que bien peu et la plupart indirectes. Mais enfin je ne te fais point de reproches; je sais que les jeunes gens s'occupent rarement de leurs vieux parents et que d'ailleurs j'ai cru entrevoir que tes occupations et tes divers déplacements ont dû avoir de longs momens inquiétans et pénibles. Il y a quelques mois qu'un Mr. Jennings qui a été ton ami et qui est parti pour l'île de Grenade, écrivit à Mlle. Pictet de Baltimore le 28e février qu'il avait été à Philadelphie où il avait compté de te trouver, mais que malheureusement pour lui tu en étais parti pour une province à 3 ou 400 lieues de là pour y faire arpenter un très-grand terrain inculte que tu avais acheté à vil prix. Il ajoutait ensuite que s'étant informé exactement de diverses personnes qui te connaissent, on avait fait de toi un très-bon rapport sur l'estime et le crédit que tu y avais acquis. . . . Tu n'as pas oublié sans doute que tu seras majeur dans le courant du mois de janvier prochain, 1786. . . .

MLLE. PICTET TO GALLATIN.

22 juillet, 1785.

Enfin j'ai reçu ta lettre du 29e mars. . . . J'ai peine à excuser ce long silence; je ne saurais même prendre pour bonnes les raisons que tu en donnes; il me paraît plus vraisemblable que l'amour-propre t'empêche d'écrire lorsque tu n'as rien à dire d'avantageux de ta situation. . . . Je me flatte que M. Savari a un mérite plus sûr que Serre et Badollet. Quant à Serre, je comprends qu'il y a quelques nuages entre vous. . . . Son goût sera toujours de courir des aventures. . . .

ANNE GALLATIN TO ALBERT GALLATIN.

6 mars, 1786.

Monsieur,—Je ne puis imaginer que vous soyez instruit que le bruit de votre mort est parvenu jusqu'à Genève comme la chose du monde la plus certaine et que vous ne vous soyez pas hâté de le détruire par vos lettres. . . .

MLLE. PICTET TO GALLATIN.

1 octobre, 1787.

. . . Monsieur Chaston . . . m'a parlé de toi; . . . il m'a dit que tu avais conservé ton ancienne indolence; que tu te souciais peu du monde, et que lorsque tu avais demeuré chez lui à Philadelphie il ne pouvait t'engager à voir le monde ni à t'habiller. Il dit que tu aimes toujours l'étude et la lecture. Voilà des goûts qui ne paraissent pas s'accorder avec tes grandes entreprises et pour lesquels une grande fortune est bien inutile, que tu aurais pu suivre sans quitter ton pays. . . .

So widely accredited was the rumor of his death that his family in Geneva made an application to Mr. Jefferson, then the United States minister at Paris, through the Genevan minister at that Court, who was a connection of the Gallatin family; and Mr. Jefferson on the 27th January, 1786, wrote to Mr. Jay on the subject a letter which will be found in his printed works. Mr. Jay replied on the 16th June, reassuring the family; but in the mean while letters had arrived from Gallatin himself. There were indeed other reasons than mere family affection which made correspondence at this moment peculiarly necessary. Gallatin reached his twenty-fifth year on the 29th January, when his little patrimony became his own to dispose of at his will; and without attributing to him an inordinate amount of self-interest, it would seem that he must certainly have been heard from at this time if at no other, seeing that he was pledged to undertakings which had been entered into on the strength of this expected capital. The family were not left long in doubt. Letters and drafts soon arrived, and Gallatin duly received through the firm of Robert

Morris about five thousand dollars,—the greatest part of his patrimony and all that could at once be remitted. This was the only capital he could as yet command or call his own. What he might further inherit was highly uncertain, and he seems to have taken unnecessary pains to avoid the appearance of courting a bequest. His grandfather's letter, just given, shows how little there was of the mercenary in the young man's relations with the wealthier members of his family, from whom he might originally have hoped, and in fact had reason to expect, an ultimate inheritance. In the course of time this expectation was realized. He was left heir to the estates of both his grandfather and his uncle, but the inheritance proved to be principally one of debts. After these had been discharged there remained of a fortune which should properly have exceeded one hundred thousand dollars only a sum of about twenty thousand dollars, which he practically sunk in Western lands and houses. But as yet his hopes from such investments were high, and he had no reason to be ashamed of his position.

Nevertheless, he was not yet quite firmly established in his American life. His existence at George's Creek was not all that imagination could paint; perhaps not all it once had painted. The business of store-keeping and land-clearing in a remote mountain valley had drawbacks which even the arrival of Badollet could not wholly compensate; and finally the death of Serre, learned only in the summer of 1786, was a severe blow, which made Gallatin's mind for a time turn sadly away from its occupations and again long for the sympathy and associations of the home they had both so contemptuously deserted.

There was indeed little at this time of his life, between 1786 and 1788, which could have been greatly enjoyable to him, or which can be entertaining to describe, in long residences at George's Creek, varied by journeys to Richmond, Philadelphia, and New York, land purchases and land sales, the one as unproductive as the other, house-building, store-keeping, incessant daily attention to the joint interests of the association while it lasted, endless trials of temper and patience in dealing with his associates, details of every description, since nothing could be trusted to others, and no pleasures that even to a mind naturally disposed, like his, to contentment under narrow circumstances, could compensate for its sacrifices.

In point of fact, too, nothing was gained by thus insisting upon taking life awry and throwing away the advantages of education, social position, and natural intelligence. All the elaborate calculations of fortune to result from purchases of land in Western Virginia were miscalculations. Forty years later, after Mr. Gallatin had made over to his sons all his Western lands, he summed up the result of his operations in a very few words: "It is a troublesome and unproductive property, which has plagued me all my life. I could not have vested my patrimony in a more unprofitable manner." It is, too, a mistake to suppose that he was essentially aided even in his political career by coming to a border settlement. There have been in American history three parallel instances of young men coming to this country from abroad and under great disadvantages achieving political distinction which culminated in the administration of the national Treasury. These were, in the order of seniority, Alexander Hamilton, Albert Gallatin, and A. J. Dallas, the latter of whom came to America in 1783 and was Gallatin's most intimate political friend and associate. Neither Hamilton nor Dallas found it necessary or advisable to retire into the wilderness, and political distinctions were conferred upon them quite as rapidly as was for their advantage. The truth is that in those days, except perhaps in New England, the eastern counties of Virginia and South Carolina, there was a serious want of men who possessed in any degree the rudimentary qualifications for political life. Even the press in the Middle States was almost wholly in the hands of foreign-born citizens. Had Gallatin gone at once to New York or Philadelphia and devoted himself to the law, for which he was admirably fitted by nature, had he invested his little patrimony in a city house, in public securities, in almost any property near at hand and easily convertible, there is every reason to suppose that he would have been, financially and politically, in a better position than ever was the case in fact. In following this course he would have had the advantage of treading the path which suited his true tastes and needs. This is proved by the whole experience of his life. In spite of himself, he was always more and more drawn back to the seaboard, until at length he gave up the struggle and became a resident of New York in fact, as he had long been in all essentials.

The time was, however, at hand in these years from 1786 to 1788 when, under the political activity roused by the creation of a new Constitution and the necessity of setting it in motion, a new generation of public men was called into being. The constitutional convention sat during the summer of 1787. The Pennsylvania convention, which ratified the Constitution, sat shortly afterwards in the same year. Their proceedings were of a nature to interest Gallatin deeply, as may be easily seen from the character of the letters already given. His first appearance in political life naturally followed and was immediately caused by the great constitutional controversy thus raised.

But before beginning upon the course of Mr. Gallatin's political and public career, which is to be best treated by itself and is the main object of this work, the story of his private life shall be carried a few steps further to a convenient halting-point.

In the winter of 1787–88, according to a brief diary, he made a rapid journey to Maine on business. He was at George's Creek a few days before Christmas. On Christmas-day occurs the following entry at Pittsburg: "Fait Noël avec Odrin (?) et Breckenridge chez Marie." Who these three persons were is not clear. Apparently, the Breckenridge mentioned was not Judge H. H. Brackenridge, who, in his "Incidents of the Insurrection," or whiskey rebellion, declares that his first conversation with Gallatin was in August, 1794. Marie was not a woman, but a Genevan emigrant.

January 5, 1788, he was in Philadelphia, where he remained till the 28th. On the 29th, his birthday, he was at Paulus Hook, now Jersey City. On the 2d February occurs the following entry at Hartford: "Depuis que je suis dans l'état de Connecticut, j'ai toujours voyagé avec des champs des deux côtés, et je n'ai rien vu en Amérique d'égal aux établissements sur la rivière Connecticut." On the 6th: "Déjeûné à Shrewsbury. Souvenirs en voyant Wachusett Hill. . . . Couché à Boston." On the 11th of February he started again for the

East by the stage: "Voyagé avec Dr. Daniel Kilham de Newbury Port, opposé à la Constitution. Vu mon bon ami Bentley
à Salem; il me croyait mort. Diné à Ipswich avec mes anciens
écoliers Amory et Stacey." On the 14th: "Loué Hailey et un
slay; descendu sur la glace partie d'Amoruscoguin [Androscoggin]
River et Merrymeeting Bay, et traversé Kennebeck, abordé à
Woolwich, traversé un Neck, puis sur la glace une cove de
Kennebeck, et allé par terre à Wiscasset Point sur Sheepscutt
River." Apparently at this time of his life Gallatin was proof
against hardship and fatigue. In returning he again crossed the
bay and ascended the Androscoggin on the ice: "Tout le jour
il a neigé; voyagé sur la glace sans voir le rivage; gouverné
notre course par la direction du vent." His return was much
retarded by snow, but he was again in Boston on the 27th, and
in New York on the 5th of March.

He passed the summer, apparently, in the West at his
George's Creek settlement, at least partially engaged in politics,
as will be shown hereafter. He passed also the winter here, and
it was not till the 12th March, 1789, that he set out on his usual
visit to Richmond, which he reached on the 1st April.

The following letter shows him occupied with a new interest.
Sophia Allegre was the daughter of William Allegre, of a
French Protestant family among the early settlers in this country. William Allegre married Jane Batersby, and died early,
leaving his widow with two daughters and a son. A young
Frenchman, Louis Pauly, who came to Virginia on some financial errand of his government, took lodgings with Mrs. Allegre,
fell in love with her daughter Jane, and married her against her
mother's consent. Young Gallatin also lodged under Mrs.
Allegre's roof, and fell in love with her other daughter, Sophia.

GALLATIN TO BADOLLET.

RICHMOND, 4 mai, 1789.

Mon bon ami, je suis arrivé ici le 1er avril et ai été jusques
à présent si occupé de mes amours que je n'ai eu la tête à rien
d'autre. Sophie était chez son beau-frère Pauli à New Kent.
J'y ai passé plus de 15 jours à deux fois différentes. Elle n'a

point fait la coquette avec moi, mais dès le second jour m'a
donné son plein consentement, m'a avoué qu'elle me l'aurait
donné à mon dernier voyage ou peut-être plus tôt si je le lui avais
demandé; avait toujours cru que je l'aimais, mais avait été surprise de n'avoir pas entendu parler de moi pendant plus d'un
an, ce qui avait causé sa réponse à Savary que tu m'apportas;
n'avait pas voulu s'ouvrir depuis à Savary parceque n'ayant pas
répondu à ma lettre, elle avait peur que je n'eusse changé et ne
voulait pas s'aventurer à faire une confidence inutile. Voilà le
bien; voici le mal. La mère, qui s'est bien doutée que je n'étais
pas à New Kent pour l'amour de Pauly, a ordonné à sa fille de
revenir, et je l'ai en effet amenée à Richmond. Je lui ai alors
demandé Sophie. Elle a été furieuse, m'a refusé de la manière
la plus brutale et m'a presque interdite sa maison. Elle ne veut
point que sa fille soit traînée sur les frontières de la Pensilvanie
par un homme sans agrémens, sans fortune, qui bredouille l'Anglais comme un Français et qui a été maître d'école à Cambridge.
J'ai ri de la plupart de ses objections, j'ai tâché de répondre aux
autres, mais je n'ai point pu lui faire entendre raison et elle
vient d'envoyer Sophie en campagne chez un de ses amis. C'est
une diablesse que sa fille craint horriblement, en sorte que j'aurai
de la peine à lui persuader de se passer du consentement ma-
ternel. Je crois pourtant que je réussirai, et c'est à quoi je vais
travailler malgré la difficulté que j'éprouve à la voir et à lui
parler. Dès que cette affaire sera décidée, je penserai à celles
d'intérêt. Je suis encore plus décidé que jamais à tout terminer
avec Savary, dont la conduite pendant mon absence a été presqu'
extravagante. Mais motus sur cet article. J'ai vu ici Perrin, qui
vient de repartir pour France, Savary ayant payé son passage.
Il a soutenu jusques au bout son digne caractère, ayant dit à
Mme. Allegre tout le mal possible de la Monongahela, tandis
qu'il savait par une lettre volée que j'aimais sa fille, et ayant fini
par mentir et tromper Savary qui est bien revenu sur son compte.
Tout le monde ici m'en a dit du mal.

Je crois que vu tout ce que j'ai à faire ici je ne pourrai guère
partir avant le mois prochain. Si je me marie, ce sera dans
environ 15 jours, et il faudra ensuite que je prenne des arrangemens avec Savary (quand je taxe sa conduite d'extravagante, ce

n'est que sa tête que je blâme; son cœur est toujours excellent
mais trop facile et il lui fait souvent faire des sottises); ainsi tu
ne dois m'attendre qu'au milieu de juin.   Tâche de faire planter
bien abondamment des patates, afin qu'il y en ait pour toi et pour
moi.   J'aurais bien à cœur que la maison se finît, mais si tu ne
veux pas t'en mêler, fais-moi le plaisir de prier Clare de pousser
Weibel.   Je ne te parle point de nos arrangemens futurs, parceque
je n'y vois encore rien de clair et qu'il faut que préalablement je
finisse avec Savary.   Rien de nouveau ici.   Tu auras sans doute
su que le roi d'Angleterre était devenu fou et que le Prince de
Galles avait été nommé Régent.   Par les dernières nouvelles il
est rétabli et va reprendre les rênes du gouvernement, à la grande
satisfaction de la nation, qui avec raison préfère Pitt à Fox.   Il
y a apparence que la guerre continuera en Europe et que la
Prusse prendra ouvertement le parti de la Suède contre le Dane-
mark.   Embrasse Peggy pour moi; je pense souvent à elle et
après ne l'avoir aimée pendant longtems que par rapport à toi, je
commence à l'aimer pour elle-même.   Je compte trouver Albert
sur ses jambes si je reste aussi longtems ici.   Fais mes complimens à Clare et à la famille Philips.   Dis à Pauly que son frère
se porte bien à un rhumatisme près; son frère Joseph va revenir pour le joindre et prendre la *tann-yard* que Maesh quittera.
Mme. Pauly, la sœur de Sophie, m'a aidé autant qu'elle a pu
auprès de sa mère, mais elle dissuade sa sœur d'un mariage
contre son consentement.   Au reste, la mère dit à tout le monde
qu'elle voit autant de mal qu'elle peut de moi et se fait par là
plus de tort qu'à moi-même.   Adieu, mon bon ami; je pense à
toi tout le tems que je ne suis pas occupé de Sophie; j'espère que
lorsque nous ne serons plus liés à un tiers, nos jours seront encore
heureux.   Crois mon pronostic et ne perds pas courage.   Tout
à toi.

The records of Henrico County Court contain the marriage
bond, dated May 14, 1789, declaring that "We, Albert Gallatin
and Savary de Valcoulon, are held and firmly bound unto Beverly Randolph, Esq., Governor of the Commonwealth of Virginia,
in the sum of fifty pounds, current money," the condition being
"a marriage shortly to be solemnized between the above-bound

Albert Gallatin and Sophia Allegre." In a little account-book of that date are some significant entries: "Ruban de queue, ⅙. Veste blanche 9/. Tailleur, £2.16. Souliers de satin, gants, bague, £1.11.6. License, ministre, £4.4. Perruquier, nègre, £0.2.0." Finally, many years afterwards, the following letter was printed as a historical curiosity in "The Staunton Vindicator":

SOPHIA ALLEGRE TO HER MOTHER.

New Kent, May 16, 1789.

MY DEAR MAMA,—Shall I venture to write you a few lines in apology for my late conduct? and dare I flatter myself that you will attend to them? If so, and you can feel a motherly tenderness for your child who never before wilfully offended you, forgive, dear mother, and generously accept again your poor Sophia, who feels for the uneasiness she is sure she has occasioned you. She deceived you, but it was for her own happiness. Could you then form a wish to destroy the future peace of your child and prevent her being united to the man of her choice? He is perhaps not a very handsome man, but he is possessed of more essential qualities, which I shall not pretend to enumerate; as coming from me, they might be supposed partial. If, mama, your heart is inclinable to forgive, or if it is not, let me beg you to write to me, as my only anxiety is to know whether I have lost your affection or not. Forgive me, dear mama, as it is all that is wanting to complete the happiness of her who wishes for your happiness and desires to be considered again your dutiful daughter,

SOPHIA.

No trace of Sophia Allegre now remains except this letter and a nameless gravestone within the grounds of Friendship Hill. Gallatin took her home with him to George's Creek; for a few months they were happy together, and then suddenly, in October, she died; no one knows, perhaps no one ever knew, the cause of her death, for medical science was not common at George's Creek. Gallatin himself left no account of it that has been preserved. He suffered intensely for the time; but he was fortunately still

young, and the only effect of his wretchedness was to drive him
headlong into politics for distraction.

PHILADELPHIA, 8 mars, 1790.

Mon cher Badollet . . . Tu sens sûrement comme moi que le
séjour du comté de Fayette ne peut pas m'être bien agréable, et
tu sais que je désirerais m'éloigner même de l'Amérique. J'ai
fait mes efforts pour réaliser ce projet, mais j'y trouve tous les
jours de nouvelles difficultés. Il m'est absolument impossible de
vendre mes terres de Virginie à quel prix que ce soit, et je ne sais
comment je trouverais à vivre à Genève. Sans parler de mon
âge et de mes habitudes et de ma paresse, qui seraient autant
d'obstacles aux occupations quelconques que je serais obligé d'embrasser en Europe, il s'en rencontre un autre dans les circonstances
actuelles de notre patrie. Les révolutions dans la politique et
surtout les finances de la France ont opéré si fortement sur
Genève que les marchands y sont sans crédit et sans affaires, les
artisans sans ouvrage et dans la misère, et tout le monde dans
l'embarras. Non-seulement les gazettes en ont fait mention,
mais j'en ai reçu quelques détails dans une lettre de M. Trembley,
qui quoiqu'antérieure aux derniers avis reçus par plusieurs Suisses
ici, et écrite dans un tems où les calamités publiques n'étaient pas
au point où elles sont à présent, m'apprenait que les difficultés et
les dangers étaient tels qu'il avait déposé le peu d'argent qu'il
avait à moi dans la caisse de l'hôpital. Tous les étrangers établis
ici s'accordent à dire que les ressources pour se tirer d'affaires en
Europe sont presqu'anéanties, au moins pour ceux qui n'en ont
d'autre que leur industrie, et ces faits sont confirmés par nombre
d'émigrants de toutes les nations et de tous les états. Dans ces
circonstances la petite rente que j'ai en France étant très-précaire
tant à cause de la tournure incertaine que prendront les affaires
que parcequ'elle est sur d'autres têtes et sur des têtes plus âgées
que la mienne, il est bien clair que je n'aurais d'autres ressources
que celles que je pourrais tirer des *dons* de ma famille, vu que
leurs efforts seraient probablement inutiles quant à me procurer
quelqu'occupation à laquelle je fusse propre. Cette circonstance

de recevoir serait non-seulement désagreable, mais l'espérance en serait fort incertaine; mon oncle Rolas, le cadet, le seul qui n'ait pas d'enfans, passe pour être généreux, mais il dépense beaucoup, plus, je crois, que ses revenus; sa fortune qui est en partie en France et en Hollande recevra probablement quelqu'échec dans ce moment de crise, et la seule occupation que je pourrais suivre en Europe serait celle de courtiser un héritage que je ne serais ni fâché ni honteux de recevoir s'il ne me coûtait aucunes bassesses, pour lequel je me serais cru peut-être obligé de faire quelques démarches si une épouse chérie avait vécu, mais qui dans mes circonstances actuelles ne saurait m'engager seul à retourner à Genève pour y vivre dans une totale indépendance. Ce que je dois à ma digne mère est la seule raison qui en pourrait contre-balancer d'aussi fortes; et si je puis entrevoir seulement la possi-bilité de vivre dans ma patrie pauvrement mais sans être à charge à personne, cette raison seule me décidera, mais jusqu'alors je ne vois que trop la nécessité de rester ici. Ce n'est pas que je me fasse illusion et que je crois pouvoir faire beaucoup mieux en Amérique, mais si j'y puis seulement vivre indépendant, c'est toujours plus que je ne peux espérer en Europe, du moins à pré-sent, et je crois qu'un an d'application à l'étude des lois me suffira non pas pour faire une fortune ou une figure brillante, mais pour m'assurer du pain quelques puissent être les évènemens. Je t'ai parlé bien longuement de moi seul, et la seule apologie que je te donnerai c'est de ne l'avoir pas fait plus tôt. Ne crois pas cepen-dant que dans mes incertitudes et les différentes idées qui m'ont agité, je n'aie pas pensé à toi. Je te déclarerai d'abord franche-ment que je n'aurais pas balancé entre Mlle. Pictet et toi, et que si je voyais possibilité d'aller la joindre, elle l'emporterait sûre-ment; l'idée de devoir et de reconnaissance est si intimement liée chez moi avec l'affection que j'ai pour cette respectable personne que quelques regrets que j'eusse de te quitter, j'éprouverais même du plaisir en le faisant dans l'intention de contribuer à son bon-heur; mais ce seul objet excepté, il n'y a rien que je ne te sacri-fiasse; je ne te sacrifierais même rien en te préférant au reste de mes amis et parens à Genève, et si le temps pouvait effacer le souvenir de mes chagrins, j'aimerais mieux vivre près de toi en Amérique que sans toi dans ma patrie, et même dans ce moment je sens combien de consolations je recevrais du seul ami qui ait connu mon aimable Sophie ; en un mot je n'ai pas besoin de te dire que si je reste ici, mon sort doit être intimement lié avec le tien. Mais à l'égard de la manière, du lieu futur de notre séjour, je ne puis encore former d'opinion vu l'arrivée de ton frère. . . . Quelque parti que nous puissions prendre pour l'avenir, je désire aussi fortement que toi que nous soyons indépendants l'un et l'autre, quant à notre manière de vivre. Si tu crois que nous ne quittions pas Fayette, ne néglige pas l'ouvrage que tu avais commencé pour vivre chez toi en préparant une cabane joignant le champ de Robert. Si tu supposes qu'il soit probable que nous changions de demeure, attends jusques à l'arrivée de ton frère pour faire une dépense qui n'augmenterait pas la valeur de la terre. . . . Voilà, je crois, tout ce que j'ai à te dire pour le présent ; si je ne peux pas vendre cette semaine une traite, je serai dans 15 à 20 jours avec toi. . . .

Every letter received by Gallatin from Geneva between 1780 and 1790 had, in one form or another, urged his return or expressed discontent at his situation. But the storm of the French revolution had at last fairly begun, and Geneva felt it severely and early. Not till the 7th of April, 1790, did Gallatin overcome his repugnance to writing in regard to his wife's death to Mlle. Pictet, and he then expressed to her his wish to return for her sake. At this critical moment of his life the feelings of his family had begun to change. They no longer looked upon him as a subject of pity. "L'état précaire de la France" is mentioned by Mlle. Pictet in June and July, 1790, as a subject of anxiety ; "nous ignorons encore quel il sera, notre gouvernement ;" "quant aux conseils que tu me demandes par rapport à ton retour, et aux ressources que tu pourrais trouver dans notre pays, je suis bien embarrassée à te répondre." It was too late. Indeed, it may be doubted whether this idea of returning to Geneva for the sake of Mlle. Pictet was really more than the momentary sickness at heart consequent on a great shock, which in any case could not have lasted long. Gallatin's career already lay open before him. His misfortunes only precipitated the result.

BOOK II.

THE Federal Constitution of 1787, accepted only a few years later by all parties and by the whole people as the last word of political wisdom, was at its birth greatly admired by no one. The public mind was divided between two classes of axioms and theories, each embodying sound reasoning and honest conviction, but resting at bottom upon divergent habits of life and forms of industry. Among the commercial and professional citizens of the sea-board towns a strong government was thought necessary to protect their trade and their peace; but there was a wide latitude of opinion in regard to the degree of strength required for their purpose, and while a few of the ablest and most determined leaders would have frankly accepted the whole theory of the English constitution and as much of its machinery as possible, the mass even of their own followers instinctively preferred a federative and democratic system. Among the agricultural and scattered population of the country, where the necessity of police and authority was little felt, and where a strong government was an object of terror and hatred, the more ignorant and the more violent class might perhaps honestly deny the necessity for any national government at all; with the great majority, however, it was somewhat unwillingly conceded that national government was a necessary evil, and that some concessions of power must be made to it; their object was to reduce these concessions to the lowest possible point. No one can doubt where Mr. Gallatin's sympathies would lie as between the two great social and political theories. The reaction against strong governments and their corruptions had a great part in that general feeling of restlessness and revolt which drew him from the centre of civilization to its outskirts. There could be no question of

76

the "awful squinting towards monarchy" in portions of the proposed constitution, more especially in the office of President, and
no one pretended that the instrument as it stood contained sufficient safeguards against abuse of public or of private liberties.
It could expect little real sympathy among the western counties
of Pennsylvania.

Nevertheless, in the convention, which was immediately called
to ratify the Constitution on the part of the State, there was a
majority in its favor of nearly two to one; a majority so large
and so earnest that extremely little respect was paid to the
minority and its modest proposals of amendments, the vote of
ratification being at last carried against a helpless opposition by a
species of force.   Of this convention Mr. Gallatin was not a
member; but when the action of other States, and notably
of Massachusetts, Virginia, and New York, in recommending
amendments at the moment of ratification, gave to the opposition new hopes of yet carrying some of their points, the party
made a last effort in Pennsylvania, which resulted in calling
a conference at Harrisburg on the 3d September, 1788.   There
thirty-three gentlemen assembled, of whom Mr. Gallatin was
one; Blair McClanachan was chosen chairman; "free discussion
and mature deliberation" followed, and a report, or declaration
of opinion, was formally adopted.   Two drafts of this document are among Mr. Gallatin's papers, both written in his own
hand, one of them, much amended and interlined, obviously a
first sketch, used probably in committee as the ground-work of
the adopted instrument.   It is only a natural inference that he
was the draughtsman.

There can be no doubt that Mr. Gallatin was one of those
persons who thought the new Constitution went much too far.
He would, doubtless, have preferred that all the great departments—executive, legislative, and judicial—should have been
more closely restricted in their exercise of power, and, indeed,
he would probably have thought it better still that the President
should be reduced to a cipher, the legislature limited to functions
little more than executive, and the judiciary restricted to admiralty and inter-state jurisdiction, with no other court than the
Supreme Court, and without appellate jurisdiction other than

by writ of error from the State courts. This would best have suited his early theories and prejudices. This rough draft, therefore, has some interest as showing how far he was disposed to carry his opposition to the Constitution, and it seems to show that he was inclined to go considerable lengths. The resolutions as there drafted read as follows:

"1st. Resolved, that in order to prevent a dissolution of the Union, and to secure our liberties and those of our posterity, it is necessary that a revision of the Federal Constitution be obtained in the most speedy manner.

"2d. That the safest manner to obtain such a revision will be, in conformity to the request of the State of New York, to use our endeavors to have a convention called as soon as possible;

"Resolved, therefore, that the Assembly of this State be petitioned to take the earliest opportunity to make an application for that purpose to the new Congress.

"3d. That in order that the friends to amendments of the Federal Constitution who are inhabitants of this State may act in concert, it is necessary, and it is hereby recommended to the several counties in the State, to appoint committees, who may correspond one with the other and with such similar committees as may be formed in other States.

"4th. That the friends to amendments to the Federal Constitution in the several States be invited to meet in a general conference, to be held at   , on   , and that   members be elected by this conference, who, or any   of them, shall meet at said place and time, in order to devise, in concert with such other delegates from the several States as may come under similar appointments, on such amendments to the Federal Constitution as to them may seem most necessary, and on the most likely way to carry them into effect."

But it seems that the tendency of opinion in the meeting was towards a less energetic policy. The first resolution was transformed into a shape which falls little short of tameness, and has none of the simple directness of Gallatin's style and thought:

"1st. Resolved, that it be recommended to the people of this State to acquiesce in the organization of the said government.

But although we thus accord in its organization, we by no means lose sight of the grand object of obtaining very considerable amendments and alterations which we consider essential to preserve the peace and harmony of the Union and those invaluable privileges for which so much blood and treasure have been recently expended.

"2d. Resolved, that it is necessary to obtain a speedy revision of said Constitution by a general convention.

" 3d. Resolved that, therefore, in order to effect this desirable end, a petition be presented to the Legislature of the State requesting that honorable body to take the earliest opportunity to make application for that purpose to the new Congress."

Thus it appears that if Mr. Gallatin went to this conference with the object indicated in his first draft, he abandoned the scheme of a national organization for a reform of the Constitution, and greatly modified his attitude towards the Constitution itself before the conference adjourned.   The petition, with which the report closed, recommended twelve amendments, drawn from among those previously recommended by Massachusetts, Virginia, New York, and other States, and containing little more than repetitions of language already familiar.   How far Mr. Gallatin led or resisted this acquiescent policy is unknown; at all events, it was the policy henceforth adopted by the opposition, which readily accepted Mr. Madison's very mild amendments and rapidly transformed itself into a party organization with hands stretched out to seize for itself these dangerous governmental powers.   But Mr. Gallatin never changed his opinion that the President was too powerful; even in his most mature age he would probably have preferred a system more nearly resembling some of the present colonial governments of Great Britain.

In the course of the next year the Legislature of Pennsylvania summoned a convention to revise the State constitution.   There was perhaps some ground for doubting the legality of this step, for the existing constitution of 1776 gave to the Council of Censors the power to devise and propose amendments and to call a convention, and the Assembly had properly nothing to do with the subject.   Mr. Gallatin held strong opinions upon the impropriety of obtaining the desired amendments by a process which was itself unconstitutional, and he even attempted to organize an opposition in the western counties, and to persuade the voters of each election district to adopt resolutions denouncing the proceeding as unconstitutional, unnecessary, and highly improper, and refusing to elect delegates. Early in October, 1789, he wrote to this effect to the leading politicians of Washington and Alleghany Counties, and, among the rest, to Alexander Addison, who was a candidate for the convention, and whom he urged to withdraw. A part of this letter, dated October 7, ran as follows:

"Alterations in government are always dangerous, and no legislator ever did think of putting, in such an easy manner, the power in a mere majority to introduce them whenever they pleased. Such a doctrine once admitted would enable not only the Legislature but a majority of the more popular house, were two established, to make another appeal to the people on the first occasion, and instead of establishing on solid foundations a new government, would open the door to perpetual changes and destroy that stability so essential to the welfare of a nation ; as no constitution acquires the permanent affection of the people but in proportion to its duration and age. Finally, those changes would, sooner or later, conclude in an appeal to arms,—the true meaning of those words so popular and so dangerous, *An appeal to the People.*"

Mr. Gallatin's opposition came too late. His correspondents wrote back to the effect that combined action was impossible, and a few days later he was himself chosen a delegate from Fayette County to this same convention which he had felt himself bound in conscience to oppose. This was in accordance with all his future political practice, for Mr. Gallatin very rarely persisted in following his own judgment after it had been overruled, but in this instance his course was perhaps decisively affected by the sudden death of his wife, which occurred at this moment and made any escape from his habitual mode of life seem a relief and an object of desire.

The convention sat from November 24, 1789, till February 26, 1790, and was Gallatin's apprenticeship in the public service. Among his papers are a number of memoranda, some of them indicating much elaboration, of speeches made or intended to be made in this body; one is an argument in favor of enlarging the number of Representatives in the House; another, against James Ross's plan of choosing Senators by electors; another, on the liberty of the press, with "quotations from Roman code, supplied by Duponceau." There is further a memorandum of his motion in regard to the right of suffrage, by virtue of which every "freeman who has attained the age of twenty-one years and been a resident and inhabitant during one year next before the days of election;" every naturalized freeholder, every naturalized citizen who had been assessed for State or county taxes for two years before election day, or who had resided ten years successively in the State, should be entitled 'to the suffrage, paupers and vagabonds only being excluded. Gallatin seems also to have been interested, both at this time and subsequently, in an attempt to lessen the difficulties growing from the separation of law and equity. On this subject he wrote early to John Marshall for advice, and although the reply has no very wide popular interest, yet, in the absence of any collection of Marshall's writings, this letter may claim a place here, illustrating, as it does, not only the views of the future chief justice, but the interests and situation of Mr. Gallatin:

JOHN MARSHALL TO GALLATIN.

RICHMOND, January 3, 1790.

DEAR SIR,—I have received yours of the 23d of December, and wish it was in my power to answer satisfactorily your questions concerning our judiciary system, but I was myself in the army during that period concerning the transactions of which you inquire, and have not since informed myself of the reasons which governed in making those changes which took place before the establishment of that system which I found on my coming to the bar. Under the colonial establishment the judges of common law were also judges of chancery; at the Revolution these powers were placed in different persons. I have not understood that there was any considerable opposition to this division of jurisdiction. Some of the reasons leading to it, I presume, were that the same person could not appropriate a sufficiency of time to each court to perform the public business with requisite despatch; that the principles of adjudication being different in the two courts, it was scarcely to be expected that eminence in each could be attained by the same man; that there was an apparent absurdity in seeing the same men revise in the characters of chancellors the judgments they had themselves rendered as common-law judges. There are, however, many who think that the chancery and common-law jurisdiction ought to be united in the same persons. They are actually united in our inferior courts; and I have never heard it suggested that this union is otherwise inconvenient than as it produces delay to the chancery docket. I never heard it proposed to give the judges of the general court chancery jurisdiction. When the district system was introduced in '82, it was designed to give the district judges the powers of chancellors, but the act did not then pass, though the part concerning the court of chancery formed no objection to the bill. When again introduced it assumed a different form, nor has the idea ever been revived.

The first act constituting a high court of chancery annexed a jury for the trial of all important facts in the cause. To this, I presume, we were led by that strong partiality which the citizens of America have for that mode of trial. It was soon parted with, and the facts submitted to the judge, with a power to direct an issue wherever the fact was doubtful. In most chancery cases the law and fact are so blended together that if a jury was impanelled of course the whole must be submitted to them, or every case must assume the form of a special verdict, which would produce inconvenience and delay.

The delays of the court of chancery have been immense, and those delays are inseparable from the court if the practice of England be observed. But that practice is not necessary. 'Tis greatly abridged in Virginia by an Act passed in 1787, and great advantages result from the reform. There have been instances of suits depending for twenty years, but under our present regulations a decision would be had in that court as soon as any other in which there were an equal number of weighty causes. The parties may almost immediately set about collecting their proofs, and so soon as they have collected them they may set the cause on the court docket for a hearing.

It has never been proposed to blend the principles of common law and chancery so as for each to operate at the same time in the same cause; and I own it would seem to me to be very difficult to effect such a scheme, but at the same time it must be admitted that could it be effected it would save considerable sums of money to the litigant parties.

I enclose you a copy of the act you request. I most sincerely condole with you on your heavy loss. Time only, aided by the efforts of philosophy, can restore you to yourself.

I am, dear sir, with much esteem, your obedient servant,

J. MARSHALL.

In a letter written in 1838, when the constitution was revised, Mr. Gallatin gave an account of the convention of 1789, which was, he said, "the first public body to which I was elected, and I took but a subordinate share in its debates. It was one of the ablest bodies of which I was a member and with which I was acquainted. Indeed, could I except two names, Madison and Marshall, I would say that it embraced as much talent and knowledge as any Congress from 1795 to 1812, beyond which my personal knowledge does not extend. But the distinguishing feature of the convention was that, owing perhaps to more favorable times, it was less affected by party feelings than any other public body that I have known. The points of difference were almost exclusively on general and abstract propositions; there was less prejudice and more sincerity in the discussions than usual, and throughout a desire to conciliate opposite opinions by mutual concessions. The consequence was that, though not formally submitted to the ratification of the people, no public act was ever more universally approved than the constitution of Pennsylvania at the time when it was promulgated."[1]

The next year, in October, 1790, Mr. Gallatin was elected to the State Legislature, to which he was re-elected in 1791 and 1792. In 1790 there was a contest, and he had a majority of

---

[1] Writings, ii. 523.

about two-thirds of the votes. Afterwards he was returned
without opposition.

The details of State politics are not a subject of great interest
to the general public, even in their freshest condition, and the
local politics of Pennsylvania in 1790 are no exception to this
law. They are here of importance only so far as they are a
part of Mr. Gallatin's life, and the medium through which he
rose to notice. He has left a memorandum, which is complete
in itself, in regard to his three years' service in the State
Legislature:

"I acquired an extraordinary influence in that body (the
Pennsylvania House of Representatives),—the more remarkable,
as I was always in a *party* minority. I was indebted for it to
my great industry and to the facility with which I could understand and carry on the current business. The laboring oar was
left almost exclusively to me. In the session of 1791–1792 I
was put on thirty-five committees, prepared all their reports, and
drew all their bills. Absorbed by those details, my attention
was turned exclusively to administrative laws, and not to legislation properly so called. The great reforms of the penal code,
which, to the lasting honor of Pennsylvania, originated in that
State, had already been carried into effect, principally under the
auspices of William Bradford. Not being a professional lawyer,
I was conscious of my incapacity for digesting any practicable
and useful improvement in our civil jurisprudence. I proposed
that the subject should be referred to a commission, and Judge
Wilson was accordingly appointed for that purpose. He did
nothing, and the plan died away. It would have been better
to appoint the chief justice and the attorney-general of the State
(McKean and Bradford), and, in the first instance at least, to
have confined them to a revision of the statute law, whether
colonial, State, or British, still in force.

"I failed, though the bill I had introduced passed the House,
in my efforts to lay the foundation for a better system of education. Primary education was almost universal in Pennsylvania,
but very bad, and the bulk of schoolmasters incompetent, miserably paid, and held in no consideration. It appeared to me that
in order to create a sufficient number of competent teachers, and

to raise the standard of general education, intermediate academical education was an indispensable preliminary step; and the object of the bill was to establish in each county an academy, allowing to each out of the treasury a sum equal to that raised by taxation in the county for its support.   But there was at that time in Pennsylvania a Quaker and a German opposition to every plan of general education.

"The spirit of internal improvements had not yet been awakened.   Still, the first turnpike-road in the United States was that from Philadelphia to Lancaster, which met with considerable opposition.   This, as well as every temporary improvement in our communications (roads and rivers) and preliminary surveys, met, of course, with my warm support.   But it was in the fiscal department that I was particularly employed, and the circumstances of the times favored the restoration of the finances of the State.

"The report of the Committee of Ways and Means of the session 1790–1791 (presented by Gurney, chairman) was entirely prepared by me, known to be so, and laid the foundation of my reputation.   I was quite astonished at the general encomiums bestowed upon it, and was not at all aware that I had done so well.   It was perspicuous and comprehensive; but I am confident that its true merit, and that which gained me the general confidence, was its being founded in strict justice, without the slightest regard to party feelings or popular prejudices.   The principles assumed, and which were carried into effect, were the immediate reimbursement and extinction of the State paper money, the immediate payment in specie of all the current expenses or warrants on the treasury (the postponement and uncertainty of which had given rise to shameful and corrupt speculations), and provision for discharging without defalcation every debt and engagement previously recognized by the State. In conformity with this the State paid to its creditors the difference between the nominal amount of the State debt assumed by the United States and the rate at which it was funded by the Act of Congress.

"The proceeds of the public lands, together with the arrears, were the fund which not only discharged all the public debts but left a large surplus. The apprehension that this would be squandered by the Legislature was the principal inducement for chartering the Bank of Pennsylvania with a capital of two millions of dollars, of which the State subscribed one-half. This and similar subsequent investments enabled Pennsylvania to defray out of the dividends all the expenses of government without any direct tax during the forty ensuing years, and till the adoption of the system of internal improvement, which required new resources.

"It was my constant assiduity to business and the assistance derived from it by many members which enabled the Republican party in the Legislature, then a minority on a joint ballot, to elect me, and no other but me of that party, Senator of the United States."

Among the reports enumerated by Mr. Gallatin as those of which he was the author is the following, made by a committee on the 22d March, 1793:

"That they . . . are of opinion that slavery is inconsistent with every principle of humanity, justice, and right, and repugnant to the spirit and express letter of the constitution of this Commonwealth; therefore submit the following resolution, viz.:

"Resolved, that slavery be abolished in this Commonwealth, and that a committee be appointed to bring in a bill for that purpose."

A certificate dated "Philadelphia, 3d month, 25th, 1793," signed by James Pemberton, President, records that Albert Gallatin "is a member of the Pennsylvania Society for promoting the abolition of slavery, the relief of free negroes unlawfully held in bondage, and for improving the condition of the African race."

Party spirit was not violent in Pennsylvania during these few years of Washington's first Administration. As yet Mr. Madison was a good Federalist; Mr. Jefferson, as Secretary of State, was the champion of his country against Genet and French aggression; Governor Mifflin was elected without opposition from the Republican interest; Alexander J. Dallas was appointed by him Secretary of State for Pennsylvania; and Albert Gallatin was elected Senator by a Federalist Legislature. Gallatin,

who at every period of his life required the spur of sincere conviction to act a partisan part, found in this condition of things
precisely the atmosphere most agreeable to his tastes; but there
was one political issue which had already risen, and which, while
tending to hasten the rapid growth of parties, threatened also to
wreck his entire career.   This was the excise.

So far as Mr. Gallatin himself was concerned, the tax on
whiskey-stills could hardly have been a matter of serious importance, and he must have seen that as a political issue it was not
less dangerous to his own party than to the Administration; but
he was the representative of a remote border county, beyond the
mountains, where the excise was really oppressive and worked
injustice, and where the spirit of liberty ran high.   Opposition
to the tax was a simple matter to Republicans elsewhere; they
had merely to vote and to argue, and make what political advantage they might from this unpopular measure into which
the Administration was dragged in attempting to follow out the
policy of Mr. Hamilton; but the case was very different with
Mr. Gallatin.   He had not only to lead the attack on Mr. Hamilton, but to restrain his own followers from fatal blunders to which
they were only too well disposed; over these followers, at least
outside his own county, he had absolutely no authority and very
little influence.   From the first it became a mere question of
policy how far he could go with his western friends.   The
answer was simple, and left a very narrow margin of uncertainty: Mr. Gallatin, like any other political leader, could go
to the limits of the law in opposition to the tax, and no further.
His political existence depended on his nerve in applying this
rule at the moment of exigency.

The excise on domestic spirits was a part of Mr. Hamilton's
broad financial scheme, and the necessary consequence of the
assumption of the State debts.   To this whole scheme, and to all
Mr. Hamilton's measures, the Republican party, and Gallatin
among them, were strongly opposed.   In the original opposition,
however, Gallatin had no public share; he began to take a part
only when his position as a Representative required him to do so.

The very first legislative paper which he is believed to have
drafted is a series of resolutions on the excise, introduced into

the Pennsylvania Legislature, by Francis Gurney, on the 14th January, 1791, and intended to affect the bill then before Congress.   These resolutions were very strong, and intimated a distinct opinion that the excise bill, as it stood, was "subversive of the peace, liberty, and rights of the citizen," and "exhibited the singular spectacle of a nation resolutely opposing the oppression of others in order to enslave itself."   Strong as they were, however, the House of Representatives adopted them by a vote of 40 to 16.

The reasons of the peculiar hostility of the western counties to the whiskey tax are clearly given in the petition which Gallatin drafted in 1792 for presentation to Congress on the part of the inhabitants of that country:

"Our peculiar situation renders this duty still more unequal and oppressive to us.   Distant from a permanent market and separate from the eastern coast by mountains, which render the communication difficult and almost impracticable, we have no means of bringing the produce of our lands to sale either in grain or in meal.   We are therefore distillers through necessity, not choice, that we may comprehend the greatest value in the smallest size and weight.   The inhabitants of the eastern side of the mountains can dispose of their grain without the additional labor of distillation at a higher price than we can after we have bestowed that labor upon it.   Yet with this additional labor we must also pay a high duty, from which they are exempted, because we have no means of selling our surplus produce but in a distilled state.

"Another circumstance which renders this duty ruinous to us is our scarcity of cash.   Our commerce is not, as on the eastern coast, carried on so much by absolute sale as by barter, and we believe it to be a fact that there is not among us a quantity of circulating cash sufficient for the payment of this duty alone. We are not accustomed to complain without reason; we have punctually and cheerfully paid former taxes on our estates and possessions because they were proportioned to our real wealth. We believe this to be founded on no such equitable principles, and are persuaded that your honorable House will find on investigation that its amount, if duly collected, will be four times as large as any taxes which we have hitherto paid on the whole of our lands and other property."

The excise law was passed in 1791, and in that year a public meeting was held in the town of Washington, and adopted resolutions, one of which brought the remonstrants to the extreme verge of lawful opposition. They agreed to hold no communication with, and to treat with contempt, such men as accepted offices under the law. Mr. Gallatin was not present at this meeting, which was held while he was attending to his duties as a member of the State Legislature.

Few of his letters at this period have been preserved, and of these none have any public interest. During the session of 1792 the following extracts from letters to Badollet are all that have the smallest political importance:

GALLATIN TO BADOLLET.

PHILADELPHIA, 7th January, 1792

. . . We have yet done nothing very material, and Congress do not seem to be over-anxious to shorten their sitting, if at least we can form any judgment from the slowness of their proceedings. As to that part of their laws which concerns us more immediately,—I mean the excise and the expected amendments, —all the papers relative to it, petitions, &c., have been referred to the Secretary of the Treasury, Mr. Hamilton, by the House of Representatives. That officer has not yet reported, nor can we guess at what will probably be the outlines of his report, although I am apt to think the amendments he will propose will fall short of our wishes and expectations. As to a repeal, it is altogether out of the question.

But the event which now mostly engrosses the public attention, and almost exclusively claims ours, is the fatal defeat of St. Clair's army. Our frontiers are naked; the Indians must be encouraged by their success; the preparations of the United States must take some time before they are completed, and our present protection must rest chiefly on the security we may derive from the season of the year and on the exertions of the people and of the State government. . . .

GALLATIN TO BADOLLET.

PHILADELPHIA, February 22, 1792.

DEAR FRIEND,— . . . You must observe, on the whole, that for this year past we have not gone backwards, as we had the five preceding, and that being the most difficult part of anything we might undertake, we may hope that, better taught by experience, we will in future be more successful. It is true the part of the country where we have fixed our residence does not afford much room for the exercise of the talents we may possess; but, on the other hand, we enjoy the advantage in our poverty not to be trampled upon or even hurt by the ostentatious display of wealth. The American seaports exhibit now such a scene of speculation and excessive fortunes, acquired not by the most deserving members of the community, as must make any person who has yet some principles left, and is not altogether corrupted or dazzled by the prospect, desirous of withdrawing himself from these parts, and happy to think he has a retreat, be it ever so poor, that he may call his own. Do not think, however, from what I now say that I am dissatisfied at my being here; I should not wish to reside at Philadelphia, but feel very happy to stay in it a few months in the station I am now in, and nothing would be wanted to render this kind of life perfectly satisfactory to me except seeing you happy, and finding a home and a family of my own when I return to Fayette. . . .

As to ourselves we have yet done but little, and have a great deal to do. We will this session pay the principal of all our debts, and remain rich enough to go on three or four years without taxes. We have a plan before us, which I brought forward, to establish a school and library in each county; each county to receive £1000 for buildings and beginning a library, and from £75 to £150 a year, according to its size, to pay at least in part a teacher of the English language and one of the elements of mathematics, geography, and history. I do not know whether it will succeed; it is meant as a preparatory step to township schools, which we are not yet rich enough to establish. I had the plan by me, but your letter, in which you mention the

want of more rational teachers, &c., spurred me in attempting
to carry it this session. I have also brought forward a new plan
of county taxation, but am not very satisfied with it myself.
We are trying to get the land office open upon generous terms
to actual settlers; if we succeed, we will have a settlement at
Presqu' Isle, on Lake Erie, within two years, if the Indians
permit us. But the illiberality of some members of the lower
counties throws every possible objection and delay in the way
of anything which may be of advantage to the western country.
Some, however, now join us for fear that the other States should
become more populous, and of course have a larger representation in Congress than Pennsylvania. We have thrown out a
chancery bill a few days ago, and are now attempting to engraft
in our common law the beneficial alterations adopted by the
courts of equity in England, without their delays, proceedings
and double jurisdiction, so as to have but one code. But I
much doubt our ability to carry it into execution; the thing is
difficult in itself, and our lawyers either unwilling or not capable
to give us the requisite assistance. . . .

Modifications of the excise law were made on the recommendation of Mr. Hamilton, but without pacifying the opposition, and
on the 21st August, 1792, another meeting was held, this time at
Pittsburg, and of this meeting John Canon 'was chairman and
Albert Gallatin clerk.   Among those present were David Bradford, James Marshall, John Smilie, and John Badollet.   The
meeting appointed David Bradford, James Marshall, Albert
Gallatin, and others to draw up a remonstrance to Congress.
They appointed also a committee of correspondence, and closed
by reiterating the resolution adopted by the Washington meeting
of 1791.   This resolution is as follows :

" Whereas, some men may be found among us so far lost to
every sense of virtue and feeling for the distresses of this country
as to accept offices for the collection of the duty,

" Resolved, therefore, that in future we will consider such
persons as unworthy of our friendship, have no intercourse or
dealings with them, withdraw from them every assistance and
withhold all the comforts of life which depend upon those duties

that as men and fellow-citizens we owe to each other, and upon all occasions treat them with that contempt they deserve, and that it be and it is hereby most earnestly recommended to the people at large to follow the same line of conduct towards them."

To these resolutions Mr. Gallatin's name is appended as clerk of the meeting. It is needless to say that he considered them unwise, and that they were adopted against his judgment; but he did not attempt to throw off his responsibility for them on that score. In his speech on the insurrection, delivered in the Pennsylvania House of Representatives in January, 1795, he took quite a different ground. "I was," said he, "one of the persons who composed the Pittsburg meeting, and I gave my assent to the resolutions. It might perhaps be said that the principle of those resolutions was not new, as it was at least partially adopted on a former period by a respectable society in this city,—a society that was established during the late war in order to obtain a change of the former constitution of Pennsylvania, and whose members, if I am accurately informed, agreed to accept no offices under the then existing government, and to dissuade others from accepting them. I might say that those resolutions did not originate at Pittsburg, as they were almost a transcript of the resolutions adopted at Washington the preceding year; and I might even add that they were not introduced by me at the meeting. But I wish not to exculpate myself where I feel I have been to blame. The sentiments thus expressed were not illegal or criminal; yet I will freely acknowledge that they were violent, intemperate, and reprehensible. For by attempting to render the office contemptible, they tended to diminish that respect for the execution of the laws which is essential to the maintenance of a free government; but whilst I feel regret at the remembrance, though no hesitation in this open confession of that *my only political sin*, let me add that the blame ought to fall where it is deserved," that is to say, on the individuals who composed the meeting, not on the people at large.

Who, then, was the person who introduced these violent resolutions? This is nowhere told, either by Gallatin, Findley, or Brackenridge in their several accounts of the troubles. Perhaps a guess may be hazarded that David Bradford had something to do with them. Bradford was a lawyer with political aspirations, and had seized on the excise agitation as a means of riding into power; as will be seen, he was jealous of Gallatin,—a jealousy requited by contempt. He was this year returned by Washington County as a member of the House of Representatives of the State, and went up to Philadelphia with other delegates.

GALLATIN TO THOMAS CLARE.

PHILADELPHIA, December 18, 1792.

DEAR SIR,—We arrived here, Bradford, Smilie, Torrence, Jackson, and myself, the first Sunday of this month, all in good health, and have found our friends as kind and even our opponents as polite as ever, so that the apprehensions of some of our fearful friends to the westward who, from the President's proclamation and other circumstances, thought it was almost dangerous for us to be here, were altogether groundless.   True it is that our meeting at Pittsburg hurt our general interest throughout the State, and has rather defeated the object we had in view, to wit, to obtain a repeal of the excise law, as that law is now more popular than it was before our proceedings were known.   To everybody I say what I think on the subject, to wit, that our resolutions were perhaps too violent, and undoubtedly highly impolitic, but in my opinion contained nothing illegal.   Indeed, it seems that last opinion generally prevails, and no bills having been even found at York against the members of the committee must convince everybody that our measures were innocent, and that the great noise that was made about them was chiefly, if not merely, to carry on electioneering plans. In this, however, the views of the high-fliers have been so completely defeated, and the election of Smilie has disappointed them to such a degree, that I believe they rather choose to be silent on the subject, and are now very willing to give us districts for the next election.   I must add that the conduct of Clymer has rendered him obnoxious to many of his own friends and ridiculous to everybody. He has published a very foolish piece on the occasion, to which Wm. Findley has answered under the signature of Monongahela; as the pieces were published before my coming to town, I have not got the newspapers in which they were published, but I suppose they have been reprinted in the Pittsburg Gazette. . . .

GALLATIN TO BADOLLET.

PHILADELPHIA, December 18 1792.

MY DEAR FRIEND,—I found on my arrival here a letter from Geneva, dated the last spring, which announced to me the death of my grandfather, which has happened more than one year ago, and which was followed a short time after by that of my aunt,—his only daughter. My grandmother, worn out by age and disorders, had, happily perhaps for herself, fell in a state of insensibility bordering upon childhood, which rendered those losses less painful to her and my presence altogether useless to her, as she would not be able to derive much comfort from it and had preserved but very faint ideas of me. Yet it may perhaps be necessary that in order finally to settle my business I should go over there, but I have resolved not to go the ensuing summer, so that I will have time to speak to you more largely on the subject. My grandfather has left but a small landed estate, much encumbered with debts. That and the settlement of what may be my share of the West India inheritance of my Amsterdam relation would be the reasons that might oblige me to go; the pleasure to see once more my respectable mother would perhaps be sufficient to induce me to take that trip, was it not that I think she would grieve more at seeing me setting off again for this country than she possibly can now at my absence. . . .

We have not yet done any business here; we are generally blamed, by even our friends, for the violence of our resolutions at Pittsburg, and they have undoubtedly tended to render the excise law more popular than it was before. It is not perhaps a bad sign on the whole in a free country that the laws should be so much respected as to render even the appearance of an illegal opposition to a bad law obnoxious to the people at large, although I am still fully convinced that there was nothing illegal in our measures, and that the whole that can be said of them is that they were violent and impolitic. Two bills have been found in the federal court against Alexander Beer and —— Carr, of

the town of Washington, as connected with the riot there. I
believe them to be innocent, and I think the precedent a very
dangerous one to drag people at such a distance in order to be
tried on governmental prosecutions.   I wish, therefore, they may
keep out of the way and not be found when the marshal will go
to serve the writ; but, at all events, I hope the people will not
suffer themselves to be so far governed by their passions as to
offer any insult to the officer, as nothing could be more hurtful
to our cause, and indeed to the cause of liberty in general.   It
must also be remembered that he is a man who did not accept
the office with a view of hurting our western country, but that
mere accident obliges him to go there in the discharge of the
duties of his office. . . .

GALLATIN TO THOMAS CLARE.

PHILADELPHIA, March 9, 1793.

MY DEAR SIR,— . . . I have attended but very little to the
land or other business I was intrusted with, owing to the great
attention I have been obliged to pay, much against my inclination you may easily guess, to our business both in the House and
in committees, owing to the very great indolence of most of our
members this year.   I have not, however, neglected your bill for
Dublin, which I got at par.   We have now got to work in
earnest, and I believe three weeks will finish the whole of our
business, but I will be obliged to stay some time longer in order
to complete the private business of other people.   You will see
by the enclosed papers that the whole world is in a flame,—England ready to make war against France, Ireland ready to assert
her own rights, &c.   As to our private news, I can tell you that
three commissioners are appointed to treat with the Indians,—
General Lincoln, Tim. Pickering, and Beverly Randolph; what
they can possibly do nobody pretends to say, but every person
seems tired of Indian wars; about twelve hundred thousand
dollars a year might be better employed; but I do not like the
idea of a disgraceful peace.

You will see by the papers that I am elected one of the Senators to represent this State in the Senate of the United States,

an appointment which has exceedingly mortified the high-fliers, but which, notwithstanding its importance, I sincerely wish had not taken place for more reasons than I can write at present, but Gappen may give you some details relative to that point until I have the pleasure to see you myself. It will be enough to say that none of my friends wished it, and that they at last consented to take me up because it was nearly impossible to carry any other person of truly Republican principles. The votes were, for myself, 45; for Henry Miller, of York, 35; for General Irvine, 1; and for General St. Clair, 1; absent members, 5.

. . . Congress died away last Sunday; our friends will have a majority of ten or fifteen votes in the next, so that if the Indian war is at an end, I am not without hopes to see the excise law repealed. . . . Poor Bradford makes but a poor figure in our Legislature. Tenth-rate lawyers are the most unfit people to send there. He has done nothing but drafting a fee bill, which is not worth a farthing as far as I am able to judge. . . .

GALLATIN TO BADOLLET.

PHILADELPHIA, 9th March, 1793.

MY DEAR FRIEND,—I thank you for your letter, which has pleased me exceedingly, on account both of the sentiments it contains and of the situation of mind it seems to show you are in. May you long remain so, and enjoy that happiness which depends more upon ourselves than we are commonly aware of. I wrote you, I believe, that I had some thoughts of going to Geneva this summer, in order to try to settle finally my business there; but I can assure you nothing was more remote from my mind than finally to fix there. Your supposing that if a change of government was to take place there I might be of use, shows your good opinion of me, but not your knowledge of men; for you may rely upon it that opportunity and circumstances will have more influence towards giving weight to a man, and of course rendering him useful, than his talents alone; and, granting I have some in politics, I think at Geneva they would be of no use, as prejudices would there strongly operate against me. A complete revolution, however, has taken place there.

Hardly had the Swiss troops left Geneva, in conformity with the agreement made with France, when the looks, the discourse, and the rising commotions of the mass of the people began to fore-tell a storm. The magistrates for once were wise enough to avert it by yielding before it was too late. An almost unanimous vote of the three councils has extended the right of citizenship to every native, and has given a representation to the people, who are now acting under the name of Genevan Assembly. I believe that fear of the people joining France has been the real motive which has induced their proud aristocracy at last to bend their necks.

I have found myself, however, obliged to lay aside my plan of an European trip. The two Houses of Assembly having at last agreed to choose a Senator of the United States by joint vote, I have been elected from necessity rather than from the wishes of our friends, and although there is yet a doubt whether I will take my seat there, I cannot run the risk of being absent at the next meeting of Congress. . . . Your Bradford is an empty drum, as ignorant, indolent, and insignificant as he is haughty and pompous. I do not think he'll wish himself to come another year, for his vanity must be mortified on account of the poor figure he has been cutting here. . . .

We have before us a militia law, a fee bill, a law to reduce the price of improved lands, a new system of county taxation, where I have introduced trustees yearly elected, one to each township, without whose consent no tax is to be raised, nor any above one per cent. on the value of lands, &c., which I hope, if carried, will, by uniting the people, tend to crush the aris-tocracy of every petty town in the State; also, a plan for schools, &c. . . .

GALLATIN TO THOMAS CLARE.

PHILADELPHIA, 3d May, 1793.

. . . You must have heard that I cannot go home this sum-mer; the reason is that Mr. Nicholson, the comptroller-general, having been impeached by the House for misdemeanor in office, it was thought proper to appoint a committee of three members to investigate all his official accounts and transactions during the recess, and to report to the House at their next meeting, which will be the 27th of August. I am one of the committee, and the business we are to report on is so complex and extensive, that it will take us the whole of the recess to do it even in an imperfect manner.

As these letters show, Mr. Gallatin left the western country at the beginning of December, 1792, passed his winter in Philadelphia, laboring over legislation of an almost entirely nonpartisan character, and was still detained in Philadelphia by public business during the summer of 1793. From the time of his leaving home, in December, 1792, till the time of his next return there, in May, 1794, his mind was occupied in matters much more attractive than the tax on whiskey ever could have been.

In fact, his opposition to the excise and his strong republican sympathies did not prevent his election to the Senate of the United States by a Federalist Legislature, notwithstanding the fact that he did not seek the post and his closer friends did not seek it for him. At the caucus held to select a candidate for Senator, when his name was proposed, he made a short speech to the effect that there were many other persons more proper to fill the office, and indeed that it was a question whether he was eligible, owing to the doubt whether he had been nine years a citizen. His reasons for not wishing the election are nowhere given, but doubtless one of the strongest was that the distinction was invidious and that it was likely to make him more enemies than friends. His objection as to citizenship was overruled by the caucus at its next meeting. He was accordingly chosen Senator on the 28th February, under circumstances peculiarly honorable to him, by a vote of 45 to 37; yet one member of his party—a member, too, from the county of Washington—refused to support him, and threw away his vote on General Irvine. This was David Bradford, who from the beginning of Mr. Gallatin's political career was uniformly, openly, and personally hostile to him, from motives, as the latter believed, of mere envy and vanity; such at least is the statement made by Mr. Gallatin himself in a note written on the margin of p. 104 in Brackenridge's "Incidents of the Insurrection."

Other matters, however, soon began to engage Mr. Gallatin's thoughts, and made even the Senatorship and politics less interesting than heretofore. Immediately after the Legislature adjourned he joined his friends Mr. and Mrs. Dallas on an excursion to Albany.

GALLATIN TO BADOLLET.

PHILADELPHIA, 30th July, 1793.

. . . And so you have a *woman-like* curiosity to know what took me to Albany. Instinct (I beg your pardon) dictated that expression to you, for there was a woman in the way, or rather she fell in the way. I went merely upon an excursion of pleasure, in order to get a little diversion and to recover my health, which so long confinement and so strict an attention to business had rather impaired. Dallas, his wife and another friend, and myself went together to Passyack Falls, in New Jersey, to New York, and thence by water up to Albany, looked at the Mohock Falls, and returned, highly delighted with our journey, which took us near four weeks. I recovered my health, and have not felt myself better these many years. But at New York I got acquainted with some ladies, friends of Mrs. Dallas, who were prevailed upon to go along with us to Albany; and amongst them there was one who made such an impression on me that after my arrival here I could not stay long without returning to New York, from whence I have been back only a few days. I believe the business to be fixed, and (but for some reasons this must remain a secret to anybody but Savary, Clare, and yourself) I know you will be happy in hearing that I am contracted with a girl about twenty-five years old, who is neither handsome nor rich, but sensible, well-informed, good-natured, and belonging to a respectable and very amiable family, who, I believe, are satisfied with the intended match. However, for some reasons of convenience, it will not take place till next winter. . . .

The young lady in question was Hannah Nicholson, and the

characteristic self-restraint of Mr. Gallatin's language in describing her to his friend is in striking contrast with the warmth of affection which he then felt, and ever retained, towards one whose affection and devotion to him during more than half a century were unbounded. Of Mr. Gallatin's domestic life from this time forward little need be said. His temper, his tastes, and his moral convictions combined to make him thoroughly dependent on his wife and his children. He was never happy when separated from them, and he received from them in return an unlimited and unqualified regard.

Hannah Nicholson was the daughter of Commodore James Nicholson, born in 1737 at Chester Town, on the Eastern Shore of Maryland, of a respectable family in that province. He chose to follow the sea for a profession, and did so with enough success to cause Congress in 1775, at the outbreak of the Revolutionary war, to place him at the head of the list of captains. In 1778 he took command of the Trumbull, a frigate of thirty-two guns, and fought in her an action with the British ship-of-war Wyatt, which, next to that of Paul Jones with the Serapis, is supposed to have been the most desperate of the war. After a three hours' engagement both ships were obliged to draw off and make port as best they could. On a subsequent cruise Commodore Nicholson had another engagement of the same severe character, which ended in the approach of a second English cruiser, and after the loss of three lieutenants and a third of her crew the Trumbull was towed a prize into New York harbor without a mast standing. In 1793, Commodore Nicholson was living in New York, a respectable, somewhat choleric, retired naval captain, with a large family, and in good circumstances. He had two brothers, Samuel and John, both captains in the naval service during the Revolution. Samuel was a lieutenant with Paul Jones on the Bon Homme Richard, and died at the head of the service in 1811; he had four sons in the navy, and his brother John had three. Eighteen members of this family have served in the navy of the United States, three of whom actually wore broad pennants, and a fourth died just as he was appointed to one.[1]

---

[1] Cooper's Naval History, vol. i. p. 226.

One brother, Joseph, resided in Baltimore, and among his children was Joseph H. Nicholson, of whom more will be said hereafter.

Commodore Nicholson married Frances Witter, of New York, and their second child, Hannah, was born there on the 11th September, 1766. The next daughter was Catherine, who married Colonel Few, the first Senator from Georgia. A third, Frances, married Joshua Seney, a member of Congress from Maryland. Maria, the youngest, in 1793 an attractive and ambitious girl, ultimately married John Montgomery, a member of Congress from Maryland and mayor of Baltimore. Thus Mr. Gallatin's marriage prodigiously increased his political connection. Commodore Nicholson was an active Republican politician in the city of New York, and his house was a head-quarters for the men of his way of thinking. The young ladies' letters are full of allusions to the New York society of that day, and to calls from Aaron Burr, the Livingstons, the Clintons, and many others, accompanied by allusions anything but friendly to Alexander Hamilton. Another man still more famous in some respects was a frequent visitor at their house. It is now almost forgotten that Thomas Paine, down to the time of his departure for Europe in 1787, was a fashionable member of society, admired and courted as the greatest literary genius of his day. His aberrations had not then entirely sunk him in public esteem. Here is a little autograph, found among the papers of Mrs. Gallatin; its address is to

Miss Hannah Nicholson

at

The Lord knows where.

You Mrs. Hannah, if you don't come home, I'll come and fetch you.

T. PAINE.

But both Mrs. Nicholson and the Commodore were religious people, in the American sense as well as in the broader meaning of the term. They were actively as well as passively religious, and their relations with Paine, after his return to America in 1802, were those of compassion only, for his intemperate and offensive habits, as well as his avowed opinions, made intimacy impossible. When confined to his bed with his last illness he sent for Mrs. Few, who came to see him, and when they parted she spoke some words of comfort and religious hope. Poor Paine only turned his face to the wall and kept silence.

When Mr. Gallatin came into the family Paine was in Europe. Party spirit had not yet been strained to fury by the French excesses and by Jay's treaty. In this short interval fortune smiled on the young man as it never had smiled before. He had at length and literally found his way out of the woods in which he had buried himself with so much care; he was popular; a United States Senator at the age of thirty-three; adopted into a new family that received him with unreserved cordiality and attached him by connection and interest to the active intellectual movement of a great city. Revelling in these new sensations, he thought little about Geneva or about Fayette, and let his correspondence, except with Miss Nicholson, more than ever take care of itself.

The meeting of the Pennsylvania Legislature, of which he was still a member, recalled him to business; but his story may now be best gathered from his letters to his future wife:

GALLATIN TO MISS NICHOLSON.

PHILADELPHIA, 25th July, 1793.

. . . For four years I have led a life very different indeed from what I was wont to follow. Looking with equal indifference upon every pleasure of life, upon every object that can render life worth enjoying, and, of course, upon every woman, lost in a total apathy for everything which related to myself, alive only to politics (for an active mind must exert itself in some shape or another), I had become perfectly careless of my own business or my private fortune. . . . Of course I led the most active life as a public man, the most indolent as an individual.

27th August, 1793.

. . . And yet you think that I can improve you. Except
some information upon a few useful subjects which you have not
perhaps turned your attention to, I will be but a poor instructor.
Women are said generally to receive from a familiar intercourse
with men several advantages, one of the most conspicuous of
which I have often heard asserted to be the acquirement of a
greater knowledge of the world, in which they are supposed to
live less than our bustling sex. There, however, I am but a
child, and will have to receive instruction from you, for most of
my life has been spent very far indeed from anything like the
polite part of the world. I had but left college when I left
Geneva, and the greatest part of the time I have spent in America
has been very far from society, at least from that society I would
have relished. Thence, although I feel no embarrassment with
men, I never yet was able to divest myself of that anti-Ches-
terfieldan awkwardness in mixed companies which will forever
prevent a man from becoming a party in the societies where he
mixes. It is true the four last years, on account of my residence
in Philadelphia, I might have improved, but I felt no wish of
doing it; so that whilst I will teach you either history, French,
or anything else I can teach or you wish to learn, I will have to
receive far more important instructions from you. You must
polish my manners, teach me how to talk to people I do not
know, and how to render myself agreeable to strangers,—I was
going to say, to ladies,—but as I pleased you without any instructions, I have become very vain on that head. . . .

25th August, 1793.

. . . Well, my charming patriot, why do you write me about
politics? . . . I believe that, except a very few intemperate, un-
thinking, or wicked men, no American wishes to see his country
involved in war. As to myself, I think every war except a
defensive one to be unjustifiable. We are not attacked by any
nation, and unless we were actually so, or had undeniable proofs
that we should be in a very short time, we should be guilty of a
political and moral crime were we to commence a war or to behave
so as to justify any nation in attacking us. As to the present

cause of France, although I think that they have been guilty of
many excesses, that they have many men amongst them who are
greedy of power for themselves and not of liberty for the nation,
and that in their present temper they are not likely to have a
very good government within any short time, yet I firmly believe
their cause to be that of mankind against tyrants, and, at all
events, that no foreign nation has a right to dictate a government
to them.   So far I think we are interested in their success ; and
as to our political situation, they are certainly the only real allies
we have yet had.   I wish Great Britain and Spain may both
change their conduct towards us and show that they mean to be
our friends, but till then no event could be more unfavorable to
our national independence than the annihilation of the power
of France or her becoming dependent upon either of those two
powers.   Yet, considering our not being attacked and our weakness in anything but self-defence, I conceive we should be satisfied
with a strict adherence to all our treaties whether with France or
with other powers.   That is certainly the object of the President,
and the only difficulty that has arisen between him and Mr. Genet
is upon the construction of some articles of the treaty with France.
So far as I am able to judge, it seems to me that the interpretation given by the President is the right one, and I guess that
although Mr. Genet is a man of abilities and of firmness, he is
not endowed with that prudence and command of his temper
which might have enabled him to change the opinion of our
Executive in those points where they might be in the wrong.
I have, however, strong reasons to believe that Messrs. Jay and
King were misinformed in the point on which they gave their
certificate.   Upon the whole, I think that unless France or England attack us we shall have no war, and of either of them doing
it I have no apprehension. . . . Please to remember that my
politics are only for you.   Except in my public character I do
not like to speak on the subject, although I believe you will agree
with me that I need not be ashamed of my sentiments ; but
moderation is not fashionable just now. . . . This city is now
violently alarmed, more indeed than they should, on account of
some putrid fevers which have made their appearance in Water
Street.   I mention this because I suppose you will read it in the

newspapers, and I want to inform you that I live in the most healthy part of the city, and the most distant from the infection.

29th August, 1793.

. . . The alarm is greater than I could have conceived it to be, and although there is surely so far this foundation for it, that a very malignant and, to all appearances, infectious fever has carried away about forty persons in a week, yet, when we consider the great population of this city and that the disease is yet local, I believe that with proper care it might be checked, whilst, on the other hand, the fears of people will undoubtedly tend to spread it. Our Legislature are very much alarmed. I believe that if it was not for the comptroller's impeachment they would adjourn at once; and as it is, they may possibly remove to Germantown. . . .

2d September, 1793.

I feel, my beloved friend, very much depressed this evening. My worthy friend Dr. Hutchinson lies now dangerously ill with the malignant fever that prevails here, and it is said the crisis of this night must decide his fate. He was the boldest physician in this city, and from his unremitted attention to the duties of his profession, both as physician of the port and as practitioner, he has caught the infection, and such is the nature of that fatal disorder that his best friends, except his family and the necessary attendants, cannot go near him. His death would be a grievous stroke to his family, who are supported altogether by his industry, to his friends, to whom he was endeared by every social virtue, and, indeed, to his country, who had not a better nor more active friend. From his extensive information I had many times derived the greatest assistance, and his principles, his integrity, and the warmth of his affection for me had attached me to him more than to any other man in Philadelphia. . . . The disorder, although it has not yet attacked those who use proper cautions, is rather increasing in the poorer class of people, who are obliged to follow their daily industry in every part of the town, who are less cautious and perhaps less cleanly than others, and who cannot use bark, wine, and other preventives, whose price is above their faculties. The corporation have, however, taken precautions to prevent their spreading the disorder and to provide for their being properly attended. Hamilton's house at Bush Hill is converted into an hospital for that purpose. The members of the Legislature are so much alarmed and so unfit to attend to business that I believe it is not improbable they will adjourn this week, and the time of the election being so very near, they will, I guess, adjourn *sine die.* If that happens, my intention is to go immediately to New York. . . . I will not dissemble that, although I feel it was of some importance that some public business should have been finished whilst I was in the Legislature (I write to you what I would say to no other person), and although it is not impossible that by using proper exertions the Assembly might have been prevented from breaking up, I have felt more alarmed than I thought myself liable to, as much indeed as most of my fellow-members, and have not attempted anything to inspire the members with a courage I did not feel myself. Can you guess at the reason? Yet I trust that if I thought it an absolute *duty* to stay I should not suffer even love to get the better of *that.* Indeed, I know you would not like me the better for making myself unworthy of you, and if there is any hesitation or any division upon the subject, I think, unless some new argument prevails with me, that I will vote against the adjournment, but if everybody agrees it is best to go, I will throw no objection in the way. So much for my fortitude, which you see is not greater than it ought to be. . . .

4th September, 1793.

. . . Yesterday I was appointed a member of a committee to confer with a committee of the Senate upon the expediency of an adjournment, so that I had to take an active part upon that very subject which of all I wished to be decided by others. Will it please you to hear that I urged every reason against an adjournment that I could think of? If that does not afford you much satisfaction, it will perhaps relieve you to know that at the same time I was almost wishing that my arguments might have no effect. Whether it arose from that cause or not I do not know, but my eloquence was thrown away upon the Senate, and they immediately after resolved that they would adjourn to-day.

Of that resolution, however, we have in our hou
notice; but this afternoon the Senate have resolv
would not try the comptroller's impeachment this se
they are the only judges of that point, inasmuch a
oblige them to fix any earlier period, and as that w
business of sufficient importance to detain us, I ra............ .... believe
that our house will agree to adjourn to-morrow, as the whole
blame of it, if any, will fall upon the Senate. If that takes
place, you will easily believe that I do not mean to stay long
here. . . . I feel much happier than I did two days ago. Dr.
Hutchinson is much better, though not yet out of danger.[1] . . .
The symptoms of the raging fever are said to be milder than at
first. Several have escaped or are in a fair way of recovering
who had been attacked, although there was no instance a few
days ago of any person once infected being saved. The number
of sick and that of deaths are still considerable, but although the
first has not diminished, the last, I believe, has; and there is less
alarm amongst the citizens than there was a few days ago. . . .

GALLATIN TO BADOLLET.

PHILADELPHIA, 1st February, 1794.

MY DEAR FRIEND,—I was deprived of the pleasure of writing
you sooner by Major Heaton not calling on me, nor giving me
notice of the time of his departure; I hope, however, that notwithstanding your complaints, you know me too well to have
ascribed my silence to forgetfulness or want of friendship; but,
without any further apologies, let me proceed to answering your
letter, which, by the by, is the only one I have received of you
since I let you know, in last August, that I was in expectation
of getting married after a while. Now for my history since
that time. The dreadful calamity which has afflicted this city
had spread such an alarm at the time when the Assembly met,
that our August session was a mere scene of confusion, and we
adjourned the 6th of September. The next day I set off for
New York, according to contract; it was agreed that I should

---

[1] Dr. Hutchinson died on the 6th.

go and spend a week there, and from thence go to Fayette
County, where I was to remain till December, and then upon
my return here we were to fix the time of our union. As I
expected to be only a week absent, I left all my papers, clothes,
patents, money, &c., in Philadelphia; but on my arrival at New
York, and after I had been there a few days, the disorder increased to such a degree in Philadelphia, it became so difficult
to leave that city if you were once in it, and the terrors were so
much greater at a distance, that I was easily prevailed upon not
to return here, although I was wishing to go nevertheless to
Fayette, which I could have done, as I had left my horse in
Bucks County. Three weeks, however, elapsed without my
perceiving time was running away, and I was in earnest preparing to set off, when I fell sick, a violent headache, fever, &c.;
the symptoms would have put me on the list of the yellow fever
sick had I been in Philadelphia, and although I had been absent
three weeks from thence, the alarm had increased so much at
New York, that it was thought that, if the people knew of my
disorder, they might insist on my being carried to a temporary
hospital erected on one of the islands of the harbor, which was
far from being a comfortable place. Under those circumstances
Commodore Nicholson (at present my father-in-law) would have
me to be removed to his house, where I was most tenderly
attended and nursed, and very soon recovered. It was then too
late to think of going home before the meeting of Congress, and
being under the same roof we agreed to complete our union, and
were accordingly married on the 11th of November. And now
I suppose you want to know what kind of a wife I have got.
Having been married near three months, my description will not
be as romantic as it would have been last fall; but I do not
know but what it may still be partial, if we feel so in favor of
those we love. Her person is, in my opinion, far less attractive
than either her mind or her heart, and yet I do not wish her to
have any other but that she has got, for I think I can read in
her face the expression of her soul; and as to her shape and
size you know my taste, and she is exactly formed on that scale.
She was twenty-six when I married her. She is possessed of
the most gentle disposition, and has an excellent heart. Her

understanding is good; she is as well informed as most young ladies; she is perfectly simple and unaffected; she loves me, and she is a pretty good democrat (and so, by the by, are all her relations). But, then, is there no reverse to that medal? Yes, indeed, one, and a pretty sad one. She is what you will call a city belle. She never in her life lived out of a city, and there she has always lived in a sphere where she has contracted or should have contracted habits not very well adapted to a country life, and specially to a Fayette County life. This I knew before marriage, and my situation she also knew. Nevertheless, we have concluded that we would be happier united than separated, and this spring you will see us in Fayette, where you will be able to judge for yourself. As to fortune, she is, by her grandfather's will, entitled to one-sixth part of his estate at her mother's death (and what that is I do not know); but at present she receives only three hundred pounds, New York money. To return, I attended Congress at their meeting, and upon Mr. and Mrs. Dallas's invitation I brought Mrs. Gallatin to this place about the latter end of December, and have remained at their house ever since. I believe I wrote you, at the time of my being elected a Senator, that the election would probably be disputed. This has, agreeable to my expectation, taken place, which arises from my having expressed doubts, prior to my election, whether I had been a citizen nine years. The point as a legal one is a nice and difficult one, and I believe it will be decided as party may happen to carry. On that ground it is likely I may lose my seat, as in Senate the majority is against us in general.

I believe I have told you now everything of any importance relative to myself. By the enclosed you will see that your brother is safe at Jeremie, which is now in the possession of the British. Who has been right or in the wrong in the lamentable scene of Hispaniola nobody can tell; but to view the subject independent of the motives and conduct of the agent who may have brought on the present crisis, I see nothing but the natural consequence of slavery. For the whites to expect mercy either from mulattoes or negroes is absurd, and whilst we may pity the misfortune of the present generation of the whites of that island, in which, undoubtedly, many innocent victims have been involved, can we help acknowledging that calamity to be the just punishment of the crimes of so many generations of slave-traders and slave-holders? As to our general politics, I send you, by Jackson, the correspondence between our government and the French and British ministers, which will give you a better idea of our situation in regard to those two countries than either newspapers or anything I could write. The Spanish correspondence and that relative to the Algerian business were communicated by the President "in confidence," and therefore are not printed. If there be another campaign, as there is little doubt of at present, our situation next summer will be truly critical. France, at present, offers a spectacle unheard of at any other period. Enthusiasm there produces an energy equally terrible and sublime. All those virtues which depend upon social or family affections, all those amiable weaknesses which our natural feelings teach us to love or respect, have disappeared before the stronger, the only, at present, powerful passion the *Amor Patriæ*. I must confess my soul is not enough steeled not sometimes to shrink at the dreadful executions which have restored at least apparent internal tranquillity to that republic. Yet, upon the whole, as long as the combined despots press upon every frontier and employ every engine to destroy and distress the interior parts, I think they and they alone are answerable for every act of severity or injustice, for every excess, nay, for every crime which either of the contending parties in France may have committed.

The above letter to Badollet runs somewhat in advance of the story, which is resumed in the letters to his wife. After their marriage on the 11th November, he remained with her till the close of the month, when he was obliged to take his seat in the Senate.

GALLATIN TO HIS WIFE.

PHILADELPHIA, 2d December, 1793.

I have just time to let you know that I arrived safe to this place; indeed, it is not an hour since I am landed, and we must meet an hour hence. . . .

3d December, 1793.

. . . We made a house the first day we met, and have had
this day the President's speech. The very day we met, a petition
was sent to our house signed by nineteen individuals of Yorktown objecting to my election, and stating that I have not been
nine years a citizen of the United States. It lies on the table,
and has not yet been taken up. Mr. Morris told me it was first
given to him by a member of the Legislature for the county of
York, but that he declined presenting it, and that he meant to
be perfectly neutral on the occasion. . . .

6th December, 1793.

. . . Till now we have had nothing to do but reading long
correspondences and no real business to apply to. Whilst I am
on that subject I must add that from all the correspondence of
the French minister, I am fully confirmed in the opinion I had
formed, that he is a man totally unfit for the place he fills. His
abilities are but slender; he possesses some declamatory powers,
but not the least shadow of judgment. Violent and self-conceited,
he has hurted the cause of his country here more than all her
enemies could have done. I think that the convention will recall
him agreeable to the request of the President, and that if they
do not he will be sent away. . . . I met here with my friend
Smilie and some more, who brought me letters from my, shall I
say from our, home. They do not know what has become of
me, are afraid I have died of the yellow fever, scold me in case
I am alive for having neglected to write, and tell me that neither
my barn, my meadow, nor my house are finished. I write back
and insist on this last at least being finished this winter. . . .

11th December, 1793.

. . . The situation of America (I know my love is not
indifferent to her country's fate) is the most critical she has
experienced since the conclusion of the war that secured her independence. On the one hand, the steps taken by the Executive
to obtain the recall of Genet, the intemperance of that minister,
and the difficulty of forming any rational conjecture of the part
the national convention may take, give us sufficient grounds of

alarms, whilst, on the other, the declared intentions (declared to us officially) of Great Britain to break through every rule of neutrality and to take our vessels, laden with provisions, the hostility of the Indians and of the Algerines, and our own weakness render it equally difficult to bear so many insults with temper and to save the dignity of the nation. I guess the first step must be to establish some kind of naval force, but I have as yet formed no fixed opinion of my own, nor do I know what is the general intention. . . .

15th December, 1793.

I was indeed sadly disappointed, my dearest love, on receiving your letter of the 12th. Whether it was wiser or not that you should not come here till after the decision of my election I will not pretend to say. To myself that decision will not be very material. As I used no intrigue in order to be elected, as I was indeed so rather against my own inclination, and as I was undoubtedly fairly elected, since the members voted *viva voce*, I will be liable to none of those reflections which sometimes fall upon a man whose election is set aside, and my feelings cannot be much hurt by an unfavorable decision, since having been elected is an equal proof of the confidence the Legislature of Pennsylvania reposed in me, and not being qualified, if it is so decided, cannot be imputed to me as a fault. . . . I hope that a decision will take place this week, and if it does, I will go to New York next Saturday, and once more enjoy the society of my Hannah, either there or here. I think the probability is that it will be there, as the committee (to wit : Livermore, Cabot, Mitchell, Ellsworth, and Rutherford) are undoubtedly the worst for me that could have been chosen, and they do not seem to me to be favorably disposed ; this, however, between you and me, as I should not be hasty in forming a judgment, or at least in communicating it. . . . I am happy to see that you are a tolerable democrat, and, at the same time, a moderate one. I trust that our parties at this critical juncture will as far as possible forget old animosities, and show at least to the foreign powers who hate us that we will be unanimous whenever the protection and defence of our country require it. None but such as are entirely blinded by self-interest or their passions, and such as wish us to be only an appendage of some foreign power, can try to increase our weakness by dividing us. I hope that the public measures will show firmness tempered with moderation, but if France is annihilated, as seems to be the desire of the combined powers, sad indeed will the consequences be for America. They talk of fortifying some of the principal seaports and of building a few frigates. Both measures may probably be adopted. . . .

18th December, 1793.

. . . I really enjoy no kind of pleasure in this city, and if the committee delay their report much longer I believe I may be tempted to run away and let them decide just as they please. I know, or rather I have the best grounds to believe, that they mean to report unanimously against me, and if their report, as it is most likely, is adopted by the Senate, what will my girl say to my dividing our winter into three parts?—the best, the longest, and the most agreeable part to be spent in New York; a fortnight in Philadelphia, with our friends Mr. and Mrs. Dallas, and by myself, four weeks to go, stay, and return from Fayette. . . . You must be sensible, my dearest friend, that it will also be necessary for me this winter to take such arrangements as will enable me to follow some kind of business besides attending my farm. What that will be I cannot yet tell, but it either will be in some mercantile line, but to a very limited and moderate extent, or in some land speculation, those being indeed the two only kinds of business I do understand. As I mentioned that it would be only to a limited amount that I would follow any kind of mercantile business, I think I will have a portion of time left, which I may devote possibly to the study of law, the principles of which I am already acquainted with, and in which some people try to persuade me I could succeed. My only apprehension is that I am too old, at least my memory is far from being equal to what it was ten years ago. Upon the whole I do not know but what, although perhaps less pleasing, it may not turn out to be more advantageous for me (and of course for my love) to be obliged to abandon those political pursuits in which I trust I have been more useful to the public than to myself. . . .

20th December, 1793.

. . . This committee business is protracted farther than I had expected, and had I nothing but a personal concern in it, I would really leave them to themselves; but as the question seems to be whether Pennsylvania will have one or two Senators (for there is no law to fill the vacancy if I am declared ineligible), and as I owe some regard to the proof of confidence given to me by the Legislature, I am obliged to appear as a party and to support what I conceive to be right as well as I can. I was in hopes they would have reported to-day; now I doubt whether they will do it before Tuesday or Thursday next. . . . 11 o'clock. Notwithstanding what I wrote you this morning, it is not impossible that I may get off to-morrow for New York, in which case I mean that we should return together on Monday evening to this place, as I could not be absent any longer time. The reason of this change of opinion since this morning is that by the turn which this business takes in the committee, it will not come, I believe, to a conclusion for a fortnight or three weeks, and to be so long absent is too much. . . .

Mr. Gallatin was a member of the Senate only a few weeks, from December 2, 1793, till February 28, 1794, during which time he was, of course, principally occupied with the matter of his own election. There was, however, one point to which he paid immediate attention. Being above all things a practical business man, he had very strict ideas as to the manner in which business should be performed, and the Department of the Treasury was, therefore, in his eyes the most important point to watch. That Department, organized a few years before by Mr. Hamilton, had not yet quite succeeded in finding its permanent place in the political system, owing perhaps partially to the fact that Mr. Hamilton may have, in this respect as in others, adopted in advance some theoretical views drawn from the working of the British system, but also owing to the fact that there had not yet been time to learn the most convenient rules for governing the relations of the Departments to the Legislature. Even the law requiring an annual report from the Secretary of the Treasury was not enacted till the year 1800. In the interval Congress knew of the proceedings of the Treasury only what the Secretary from time to time might please to tell them, or what they themselves might please to call for. The Department was organized on the assumption that Congress would require no more than what the Secretary would naturally and of his own accord supply; any unusual call for additional information deranged the whole machinery of the Treasury and called forth the most energetic complaints of its officers.[1] Such calls, too, were always somewhat invidious and implied a reflection on the Department; they were therefore not likely to proceed from the friends of the government, and the opposition was not strong in financial ability. The appearance of Mr. Gallatin in the Senate, with already a high reputation as a financier, boded ill for the comfort of the Treasury, and it is difficult to see how a leader of the opposition under the circumstances could possibly have performed his duty without giving trouble. One of Mr. Gallatin's financial axioms was that the Treasury should be made to account specifically for every appropriation; a rule undoubtedly correct, but very difficult to apply. On the 8th of January, 1794, he moved in the Senate that the Secretary of the Treasury be called upon for certain elaborate statements: 1st, a statement of the domestic debt under six specific heads; 2d, of the redeemed domestic debt under specific heads; 3d, of the foreign debt in a like manner; 4th, a specific account of application of foreign loans in like manner; and finally a summary statement, for each year since 1789, of actual receipts and expenditures, distinguishing the receipts according to the branch of revenue, and the expenditures according to the specific appropriations, and stating the balances remaining unexpended either in the Treasury or in the hands of its agents.

This was a searching inquiry, and one that might give some trouble, unless the books of the Treasury were kept in precisely such a manner as to supply the information at once; probably, too, a portion of the knowledge might have been obtained from previous statements already supplied; but the demand was, from

---

[1] See Hamilton's letter to the Senate of 6th February, 1794, State Papers, vii. 274.

the legislative point of view, not unreasonable, and the resolutions were accordingly adopted, without a division, on the 20th January.

The exclusion of Mr. Gallatin from the Senate on the 28th February put an end to his inquiries, and the only answer he ever got to them came in the shape of an indirect allusion contained in a letter from Secretary Hamilton to the Senate on another subject, dated 22d February, 1794. This letter, which seems never to have been printed, offers an example in some respects so amusing and in some so striking of the political ideas of that day, and of the species of discipline in which Mr. Hamilton trained his majority in Congress, that it must be introduced as an essential element in any account of Mr. Gallatin's political education.[1]

---

[1] Endorsed by Mr. Gallatin in a later hand,—"complains of *unnecessary* calls, alluding indirectly to certain resolutions, founded on my motion, calling for explanatory financial statements which were never furnished."

ALEXANDER HAMILTON TO THE UNITED STATES SENATE.

TREASURY DEPARTMENT, February 22, 1794.

SIR,—I have received a late order of the Senate on the subject of a petition of Arthur Hughes. Diligent search has been made for such a petition, and it has not been found. Neither have I now a distinct recollection of ever having seen it. Whether, therefore, it may not have originally failed in the transmission to me, or may have become mislaid by a temporary displacement of the papers of my immediate office, occasioned by a fire which consumed a part of the building in the use of the Treasury, or by some of those accidents which in an extensive scene of business will sometimes attend papers, especially those of inferior importance, is equally open to conjecture. There is no record in the office of its having been received, nor does any of my clerks remember to have seen it. A search in the auditor's office has brought up the enclosed paper, which it is presumed relates to the object of the petition; but this paper, it will appear from the memorandum accompanying it, was placed in that office prior to the reference of the petition.

The auditor of the Treasury is of opinion, though his recollection is not positive, that the claim had relation to the services of John Hughes as forage-master. Two objections opposed its admission: 1, the not being presented in time; 2, the name of John Hughes in the capacity in which he claimed not appearing upon any return in the Treasury.

If these be the circumstances, I should be of opinion that it would not be

" The occupations necessarily and permanently incident to the office [of Secretary of the Treasury]," said Mr. Hamilton, " are at least sufficient fully to occupy the time and faculties of one man. The burden is seriously increased by the numerous private cases, remnants of the late war, which every session are objects of particular reference by the two Houses of Congress.

---

advisable by a special legislative interposition to except the case out of the operation of the acts of limitation.

The second order of the Senate on the subject of this petition leads to the following reflections:

Does this hitherto unusual proceeding (in a case of no public and no peculiar private importance) imply a supposition that there has been undue delay or negligence on the part of the Secretary of the Treasury?

If it does, the supposition is unmerited; not merely from the circumstances of the paper, which have been stated, but from the known situation of the officer. The occupations necessarily and permanently incident to the office are at least sufficient fully to occupy the time and faculties of one man. The burden is seriously increased by the numerous private cases, remnants of the late war, which every session are objects of particular reference by the two Houses of Congress. These accumulated occupations, again, have been interrupted in their due course by unexpected, desultory, and distressing calls for lengthy and complicated statements, sometimes with a view to general information, sometimes for the explanation of points which certain leading facts, witnessed by the provisions of the laws and by information previously communicated, might have explained without those statements, or which were of a nature that did not seem to have demanded a laborious, critical, and suspicious investigation, unless the officer was understood to have forfeited his title to a reasonable and common degree of confidence. Added to these things, it is known that the affairs of the country in its external relations have for some time past been so circumstanced as unavoidably to have thrown additional avocations on all the branches of the Executive Department, and that a late peculiar calamity in the city of Philadelphia has had consequences that cannot have failed to derange more or less the course of public business.

In such a situation was it not the duty of the officer to postpone matters of mere individual concern to objects of public and general concern, to the preservation of the essential order of the department committed to his care? Or is it extraordinary that in relation to cases of the first description there should have been a considerable degree of procrastination? Might not an officer who is conscious that public observation and opinion, whatever deficiencies they may impute to him, will not rank among them want of attention and industry, have hoped to escape censure, expressed or implied, on that score?

I will only add that the consciousness of devoting myself to the public service to the utmost extent of my faculties, and to the injury of my health,

These accumulated occupations, again, have been interrupted in their due course by unexpected, desultory, and distressing calls for lengthy and complicated statements, sometimes with a view to general information, sometimes for the explanation of points which certain leading facts, witnessed by the provisions of the laws and by information previously communicated, might have explained without those statements, or which were of a nature that did not seem to have demanded a laborious, critical, and suspicious investigation, unless the officer was understood to have forfeited his title to a reasonable and common degree of confidence. . . . I will only add that the consciousness of devoting myself to the public service to the utmost extent of my faculties, and to the injury of my health, is a tranquillizing consolation of which I cannot be deprived by any supposition to the contrary."

A country which can read expressions like this with feelings only of surprise or amusement must have greatly changed its character. Only in a simple and uncorrupted stage of society would such a letter be possible, and the time has long passed when a Secretary of the Treasury, in reply to a request for financial details, would venture to say in an official communication to the Senate of the United States : "The consciousness of devoting myself to the public service to the utmost extent of my faculties, and to the injury of my health, is a tranquillizing consolation of which I cannot be deprived by any supposition to the contrary." Nevertheless, this was all the information which Mr. Gallatin obtained as to the condition of the Treasury in response to his inquiries, and he resigned himself the more readily to accepting assurances of the Secretary's injured health as an equivalent for a statement of receipts and expenditures, for the reason that the

---

is a tranquillizing consolation of which I cannot be deprived by any supposition to the contrary.

With perfect respect, I have the honor to be, sir, your most obedient servant,

Signed   ALEXANDER HAMILTON,
Secretary of the Treasury.

THE VICE-PRESIDENT OF THE UNITED STATES
AND PRESIDENT OF THE SENATE.

True copy.   Attest :   SAMUEL A. OTIS, S. Secretary.

Senate, on this strong hint from the Treasury, proceeded at once to cut short the thread of his own official existence.

The doubt which Mr. Gallatin had expressed in caucus as to his eligibility to the Senate was highly indiscreet; had he held his tongue, the idea could hardly have occurred to any one, for he was completely identified with America, and he had been a resident since a time antecedent to both the Federal Constitutions; but Article I. Sect. 3, of the new Constitution declared that, "No person shall be a Senator who shall not have attained to the age of thirty years, and been nine years a citizen of the United States, and who shall not, when elected, be an inhabitant of that State for which he shall be chosen." Mr. Gallatin had come to America, as a minor, in May, 1780, before the adoption of the old Articles of Confederation which created citizenship of the United States. That citizenship was first defined by the fourth of these Articles of Confederation adopted in March, 1781, according to which " the free inhabitants," not therefore the citizens merely, " of each of these States, paupers, vagabonds, and fugitives from justice excepted, shall be entitled to all privileges and immunities of free citizens in the several States." Mr. Gallatin had certainly been an inhabitant of Massachusetts from July, 1780.

Moreover, the fact of Mr. Gallatin's citizenship was established by the oath which he had taken as a citizen of Virginia, in October, 1785. Whatever doubt might attach to his previous citizenship, this act had certainly conferred on him *all* the privileges of free citizens in the several States, and without the most incontrovertible evidence it was not to be assumed that the new Constitution, subsequently adopted, was intended to violate this compact by depriving him, and through him his State, of any portion of those privileges. Equity rather required that the clause of the Constitution which prescribed nine years' citizenship should be interpreted as prospective, and as intended to refer only to persons naturalized subsequently to the adoption of the Constitution. If it were objected that such an interpretation, applied to the Presidency, would have made any foreigner naturalized in 1788 immediately eligible to the chief magistracy of the Union, a result quite opposed to the constitutional doctrine in regard to foreign-born citizens, a mere reference to Article II., Section 1, showed that this was actually the fact: "No person except a natural-born citizen, or a citizen of the United States at the time of the adoption of this Constitution, shall be eligible to the office of President." There never was a doubt that Mr. Gallatin was eligible to the Presidency. That a reasonable interpretation of Article I., Section 3, must have made him equally eligible to the Senate is also evident from the fact that a strict interpretation of that clause, if attempted in 1789 when Congress first met, must have either admitted him or vacated the seat of every other Senator, seeing that technically no human being had been a citizen of the United States for nine years; national citizenship had existed in law only since and by virtue of the adoption of the Articles of Confederation in 1781, before which time State citizenship was the only defined political status.

Opposed to this view stood the letter of the Constitution. We now know, too, through Mr. Madison's Notes, that when the question of eligibility to the House of Representatives came before the Convention on August 13, 1788, both Mr. Hamilton and Gouverneur Morris tried to obtain an express admission of the self-evident rights of actual citizens. For unknown reasons Mr. Morris's motion was defeated by a vote of 6 States to 5. Failing here, he seems to have succeeded in regard to the Presidency by inserting his proviso in committee, and no one in the Convention subsequently raised even a question against its propriety. Of course the Senate was at liberty now to put its own interpretation on this obvious inconsistency, and the Senate was so divided that one member might have given Mr. Gallatin his seat. The vote was 14 to 12, with Vice-President John Adams in his favor had there been a tie. There was no tie, and Mr. Gallatin was thrown out. He always believed that his opponents made a political blunder, and that the result was beneficial to himself and injurious to them.

GALLATIN TO THOMAS CLARE.

PHILADELPHIA, 5th March, 1794.

. . . I have nothing else to say in addition to what I wrote you by my last but what Mr. Badollet can tell you. He will inform you of what passed on the subject of my seat in the Senate, and that I have lost it by a majority of 14 to 12.   One vote more would have secured it, as the Vice-President would have voted in my favor; but heaven and earth were moved in order to gain that point by the party who were determined to preserve their influence and majority in the Senate.   The whole will soon be published, and I will send it to you.   As far as relates to myself I have rather gained credit than otherwise, and I have likewise secured many staunch friends throughout the Union.   All my friends wish me to come to the Assembly next year. . . .

After this rebuff, Mr. Gallatin, being thrown entirely out of politics for the time, began to pay a little more attention to his private affairs.   He could not at this season of the year set out for Fayette, and accordingly returned to New York, where he left his wife with her family, while he himself went back to Philadelphia to make the necessary preparations for their western journey and future residence.   Here he sold a portion of his western lands to Robert Morris, who was then, like the rest of the world, speculating in every species of dangerous venture. Like everything else connected with land, the transaction was an unlucky one for Mr. Gallatin.

GALLATIN TO HIS WIFE.

PHILADELPHIA, 7th April, 1794.

We arrived here, my dearest friend, on Saturday last. . . . No news here.   You will see by the newspapers the motion of Mr. Clark to stop all intercourse with Great Britain.   I believe it is likely to be supported by our friends.   Dayton is quite warm.   The other day, when it was observed in Congress by Tracy that every person who would vote for this motion of sequestering the British debts must be an enemy to morality and common honesty, 'I might,' replied Dayton,—'I might with equal propriety call every person who will refuse to vote for that motion a slave of Great Britain and an enemy to his country; but if it is the intention of those gentlemen to submit to every insult and patiently to bear every indignity, I wish (pointing to the eastern members, with whom he used to vote),—*I wish to separate myself from the herd.*'

The majority of the Assembly of Pennsylvania had several votes, previous to the election of a Senator in my place, to agree upon the man. Sitgreaves, a certain Coleman, of Lancaster County, a fool and a tool, and James Ross, were proposed and balloted for. Ross had but seven votes, on account of his being a western man and a man of talents, who upon great many questions would judge for himself. They divided almost equally between Sitgreaves and Coleman, and at last agreed to take up Coleman, in order to please the counties of Lancaster and York. Our friends, who were the minority, had no meeting, and waited to see what would be the decision of the other party, in hopes that they might divide amongst themselves. As soon as they saw Coleman taken up they united in favor of Ross as the best man they had any chance of carrying, and they were joined by a sufficient number of the disappointed ones of the other party to be able to carry him at the first vote. As he comes chiefly upon our interest, I hope he will behave tolerably well, and, upon the whole, although it puts any chance of my being again elected a member of that body beyond possibility itself, I am better pleased with the fate of the election than most of our adversaries. . . .

PHILADELPHIA, 19th April, 1794.

. . . I have concluded this day with Mr. Robert Morris, who, in fact, is the only man who buys. I give him the whole of my claims, but without warranting any title, for £4000, Pennsylvania currency, one-third payable this summer, one-third in one year, and one-third in two years. That sum therefore, my dearest, together with our farm and five or six hundred pounds cash, makes the whole of our little fortune. Laid out in cultivated lands in our neighborhood it will provide us amply with all the necessaries of life, to which you may add that, as property is gradually increasing in value there, should in future any circumstances induce us to change our place of abode, we may always sell to advantage. . . .

Early in May Mr. and Mrs. Gallatin set out for Fayette. His

mind was at this time much occupied with his private affairs and private anxieties. His sale of lands to Robert Morris had, as he hoped, relieved him of a serious burden; but he was again trying the experiment of taking an Eastern wife to a frontier home, and he was again driven by the necessities and responsibilities of a family to devise some occupation that would secure him an income. The farm on George's Creek was no doubt security against positive want, but in itself or in its surroundings offered little prospect of a fortune for him, and still less for his children.

He had barely reached home, and his wife had not yet time to set her house in order and to get the first idea of her future duties in this wholly strange condition of life, when a new complication threatened them with dangers greater than any which their imaginations could have reasonably painted. They suddenly found themselves in the midst of violent political disturbance, organized insurrection and war, an army on either side.

For eighteen months Mr. Gallatin had almost lost sight of the excise agitation, and possibly had not been sorry to do so. Throughout his political life he followed the sound rule of identifying himself with his friends and of accepting the full responsibility, except in one or two extreme cases, even for measures which were not of his own choice. But under the moderation of his expressions in regard to the Pittsburg resolutions of 1792 it seems possible to detect a certain amount of personal annoyance at the load he was thus forced to carry, and a determination to keep himself clear from such complications in future. The year had been rather favorable than otherwise to the operation of the excise law. To use his own language in his speech of January, 1795: "It is even acknowledged that the law gained ground during the year 1793. With the events subsequent to that meeting [at Pittsburg] I am but imperfectly acquainted. I came to Philadelphia a short time after it, and continued absent from the western country upon public business for eighteen months. Neither during that period of absence, nor after my return to the western country in June last, until the riots had begun, had I the slightest conversation that I can recollect, much less any deliberate conference or correspondence, either directly or indirectly, with any of its inhabitants on the subject of the excise law. I became first acquainted with almost every act of violence committed either before or since the meeting at Pittsburg upon reading the report of the Secretary of the Treasury."

Occasional acts of violence were committed from time to time by unknown or irresponsible persons with intent to obstruct the collection of the tax, but no opposition of any consequence had as yet been offered to the ordinary processes of the courts; not only the rioters, wherever known, but also the delinquent distillers, were prosecuted in all the regular forms of law, both in the State and the Federal courts. The great popular grievance had been that the distillers were obliged to enter appearance at Philadelphia, which was in itself equivalent to a serious pecuniary fine, owing to the distance and difficulty of communication. In modern times it would probably be a much smaller hardship to require that similar offenders in California and Texas should stand their trial at Washington. This grievance had, however, been remedied by an Act of Congress approved June 5, 1794, by which concurrent jurisdiction in excise cases was given to the State courts. Unluckily, this law was held not to apply to distillers who had previously to its enactment incurred a penalty, and early in July the marshal set out to the western country to serve a quantity of writs issued on May 31 and returnable before the Federal court in Philadelphia. All those in Fayette County were served without trouble, and the distillers subsequently held a meeting at Uniontown about the 20th July, after the riots had begun elsewhere and the news had spread to Fayette; a meeting which Mr. Gallatin attended, and at which it was unanimously agreed to obey the law, and either abandon their stills or enter them. In fact, there never was any resistance or trouble in Fayette County except in a part the most remote from Mr. Gallatin's residence.

But the marshal was not so fortunate elsewhere. He went on to serve his writs in Alleghany County, and after serving the last he was followed by some men and a gun was fired. General Neville, the inspector, was with him, and the next day, July 16,

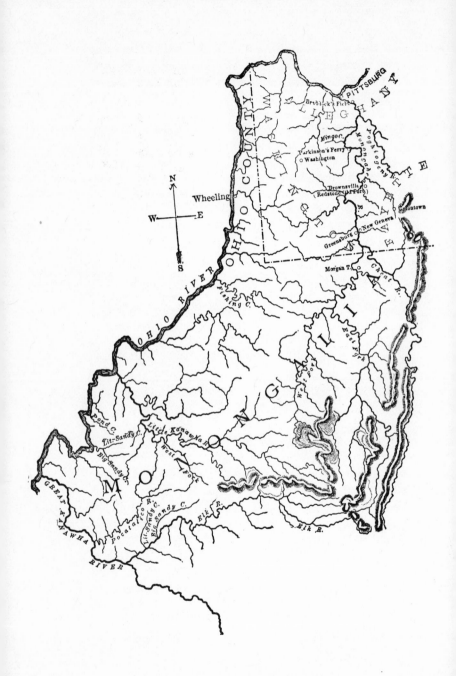

General Neville's house was approached by a body of men, who demanded that he should surrender his commission. They were fired upon and driven away, with six of their number wounded and one killed. Then the smouldering flame burst out. The whole discontented portion of the country rose in armed rebellion, and the well-disposed, although probably a majority, were taken completely by surprise and were for the moment helpless. The next day Neville's house was again attacked and burned, though held by Major Kirkpatrick and a few soldiers from the Pittsburg garrison. The leader of the attacking party was killed.

The whole duration of the famous whiskey rebellion was precisely six weeks, from the outbreak on the 15th July to the substantial submission at Redstone Old Fort on the 29th August. This is in itself evidence enough of the rapidity with which the various actors moved. From the first, two parties were apparent, those in favor of violence and those against it. The violent party had the advantage in the very suddenness of their movement. The moderates were obliged to organize their force at first in the districts where their strength lay, before it became possible to act in combination against the disturbers of the peace. Of course an armed collision was of all things to be avoided by the moderates, at least until the national government could have time to act; in such a collision the more peaceable part of the community was certain to be worsted.

Mr. Gallatin, far away from the scene of disturbance, did not at first understand the full meaning of what had happened. He and his friend Smilie attended the meeting of distillers at Uniontown, and, although news of the riots had been received there, they found no difficulty in persuading the distillers to submit. He therefore felt no occasion for further personal interference until subsequent events showed him that there was a general combination to expel the government officers.[1] But events moved fast. On the 21st July, the leaders in the attack on Neville's house called a meeting at Mingo Creek meeting-house for the 23d, which was attended by a number of leading men, among whom were Judge Brackenridge and David Bradford.

---

[1] Gallatin's Deposition in Brackenridge's Incidents, vol. ii. p. 186.

Judge Brackenridge, then a prominent lawyer of Pittsburg, was a humorist and a scholar, constitutionally nervous and timid, as he himself explains,[1] the last man to meet an emergency such as was now before him, and furthermore greatly inclined to run away, if he could, and leave the rebels to their own devices; he did nevertheless make a fairly courageous stand at the Mingo Creek meeting, and disconcerted the movements of the insurgents for the time. Had others done their duty as well as he, the organization of the insurgents would have ended then and there, but Brackenridge was deserted by the two men who should have supported him. James Marshall and David Bradford had gone over to the insurgents, and by their accession the violent party was enabled to carry on its operations. The Mingo Creek meeting ended in a formal though unsigned invitation to the townships of the four western counties of Pennsylvania and the adjoining counties of Virginia to send representatives on the 14th August to a meeting at Parkinson's Ferry on the Monongahela.

Had this measure been left to itself it is probable that it would have answered sufficiently well the purposes of the peace party, since it allowed them time for consultation and organization, which was all they really required. Bradford and his friends knew this, and were bent on forcing the country into their own support; Bradford therefore conceived the ingenious idea of stopping the mail and seizing the letters which might have been written from Pittsburg and Washington to Philadelphia. This was done on the 26th by a cousin of Bradford, who stopped the post near Greensburg, about thirty miles east of Pittsburg, and took out the two packages. In the Pittsburg package were found several letters from Pittsburg people, the publication of which roused great offence against them, and, what was of more consequence, carried consternation among the timid. It was the beginning of a system of terror.

Certainly Bradford showed energy and ability in conducting his campaign, at least as considered from Brackenridge's point of view. His stroke at the peace party through the mail-rob-

---

[1] Incidents, vol. ii. p. 68.

bery was instantly followed up by another, much more serious and thoroughly effective.   On the 28th July he with six others, among whom was James Marshall, issued a circular letter, in which, after announcing that the intercepted letters contained secrets hostile to their interest, they declared that things had now "come to that crisis that every citizen must express his sentiments, not by his words but by his actions."   This letter, directed to the officers of the militia, was in the form of an order to march on the 1st August, with as many of their command as possible, fully armed and equipped, with four days' provision, to the usual rendezvous of the militia at Braddock's Field.

This was levying war on a complete scale, but it was well understood that the chief object was to overawe opposition, more especially in Pittsburg, although the Federal garrison and stores in that city were also aimed at.   The order met with strong resistance, and under the earnest remonstrances of James Ross and other prominent men, in a meeting at Washington, even Marshall was compelled to retract and assent to a countermand.   But, notwithstanding their opposition, the popular vehemence in Washington County was such that it was decided to go forward, and, after a moment's wavering, Bradford became again the loudest of the insurgent leaders.

On the 1st August, accordingly, several thousand people assembled at Braddock's Field, about eight miles from Pittsburg. Of these some fifteen hundred or two thousand were armed militia, all from the counties of Washington, Alleghany, and Westmoreland ; there were not more than a dozen men present from Fayette.   Brackenridge has given a lively description of this meeting, which he attended as a delegate from Pittsburg, in the hope of saving the town, if possible, from the expected sack.   Undoubtedly a portion of the armed militia might easily have been induced to attack the garrison, which would have led to the plundering of the town, but either Bradford wanted the courage to fight or he found opposition among his own followers. He abandoned the idea of assailing the garrison, and this formidable assemblage of armed men, after much vague discussion, ended by insisting only upon marching through the town, which was done on the 2d of August, without other violence than the burning of Major Kirkpatrick's barn. A lively sense of the meaning of excise to the western people is conveyed by the casual statement that this march cost Judge Brackenridge alone four barrels of his old whiskey, gratuitously distributed to appease the thirst of the crowd; how much whiskey the western gentleman usually kept in his house nowhere appears, but it is not surprising under such circumstances that the march should have thoroughly terrified the citizens of Pittsburg and quenched all thirst for opposition in that quarter.

Mr. Gallatin did not attend the meeting at Braddock's Field; it was not till after that meeting that the serious nature of the disturbances first became evident to him. What had been riot was now become rebellion. He rapidly woke to the gravity of the occasion when disorder spread on every side and even Fayette was invaded by riotous parties of armed men. A liberty-pole was raised, and when he asked its meaning he was told it was to show they were for liberty; he replied by expressing the wish that they would not behave like a mob, and was met by the pointed inquiry whether he had heard of the resolves in Westmoreland that if any one called the people a mob he should be tarred and feathered.[1] Unlike many of the friends of order, he felt no doubts in regard to the propriety of sending delegates to the coming assembly at Parkinson's Ferry, and, feeling that Fayette would inevitably be drawn into the general flame unless measures were promptly taken to prevent it, he offered to serve as a delegate himself, and was elected. All the friends of order did not act with the same decision. The meeting at Braddock's Field was intended to control the elections to the meeting at Parkinson's Ferry, and to a considerable extent it really had this effect. The peace party was overawed by it. The rioters extended their operations; chose delegates from all townships where they were a majority, and from a number where they were not, and made an appearance of election in some places where no election was held. The peace party hesitated to the last whether to send delegates at all.

When the 14th of August came, all the principal actors were

---

[1] Gallatin's Deposition.

on the spot,—Bradford, Marshall, Brackenridge, Findley, and
Gallatin,—226 delegates in all, of whom 93 from Washington,
43 from Alleghany, 49 from Westmoreland, and 33 from Fayette, 2 from Bedford, 5 from Ohio County in Virginia, and about
the same number of spectators. They were assembled in a grove
overlooking the Monongahela. Marshall came to Gallatin before
the meeting was organized, and showed him the resolutions which
he intended to move, intimating at the same time that he wished
Mr. Gallatin to act as secretary. Mr. Gallatin told him that he
highly disapproved the resolutions, and had come to oppose both
him and Bradford, therefore did not wish to serve. Marshall
seemed to waver; but soon the people met, and Edward Cook,
who had presided at Braddock's Field, was chosen chairman,
with Gallatin for secretary.

Bradford opened the debate by a speech in which, beginning
with a history of the movement, he read the original intercepted
letters, and stated the object of the present meeting as being
to deliberate on the mode in which the common cause was to
be effectuated; he closed by pronouncing the terms of his own
policy, which were to purchase or procure arms and ammunition,
to subscribe money, to raise volunteers or draft militia, and to
appoint committees to have the superintendence of those departments. Marshall supported Bradford, and moved his resolutions,
which were at once taken into consideration. The first denounced
the practice of taking citizens to great distances for trial, and this
resolution was put to vote and carried without opposition. The
second appointed a committee of public safety "to call forth the
resources of the western country to repel any hostile attempt that
may be made against the rights of the citizens or of the body of the
people." It was dexterously drawn. It did not call for a direct
approval of the previous acts of rebellion, but, by assuming their
legality and organizing resistance to the government on that
assumption, it committed the meeting to an act of treason.[1]

Mr. Gallatin immediately rose, and, throwing aside all tactical
manœuvres, met the issue flatly in face. "What reason," said he,

---

[1] See the resolutions as proposed and as ultimately adopted, in Appendix
to Gallatin's speech on the insurrection. Writings, iii. 56.

"have we to suppose that hostile attempts will be made against our rights? and why, therefore, prepare to resist them? Riots have taken place which may be the subject of judicial cognizance, but we are not to suppose hostility on the part of the general government; the exertions of government on the citizens in support of the laws are coercion and not hostility; it is not understood that a regular army is coming, and militia of the United States cannot be supposed hostile to the western country."[1] He closed by moving that the resolutions should be referred to a committee, and that nothing should be done before it was known what the government would do.

Mr. Gallatin's speech met the assumption that resistance to the excise was legal by a contrary assumption, without argument, that it was illegal, and thus threatened to force a discussion of the point of which both sides were afraid. Mr. Gallatin himself believed that the resolutions would then have been adopted if put to a vote; the majority, even if disposed to peace, had not the courage to act. Now was the time for Brackenridge to have thrown off his elaborate web of double-dealing and with his utmost strength to have supported Gallatin's lead; but Brackenridge's nerves failed him. "I respected the courage of the secretary in meeting the resolution," he says,[2] "but I was alarmed at the idea of any discussion of the principle." "I affected to oppose the secretary, and thought it might not be amiss to have the resolution, though softened in terms." Nevertheless, the essential point was carried; Marshall withdrew the resolution, and a compromise was made by referring everything to a committee of sixty, with power to call a new meeting of the people.

The third and fourth resolutions required no special opposition. The fifth pledged the people to the support of the laws, except the excise law and the taking citizens out of their counties for trial. Gallatin attacked this exception, and succeeded in having it expunged. A debate then followed on the adoption of the amended resolution, which was supported by both Bracken-

---

[1] Brackenridge, Incidents, vol. i. p. 90; Findley, p. 144; Gallatin's Deposition.

[2] Incidents, vol. i. p. 90.

ridge and Gallatin, and an incident said to have occurred in the course of the latter's speech is thus related by Mr. Brackenridge:[1]

"Mr. Gallatin supported the necessity of the resolution, with a view to the establishment of the laws and the conservation of the peace. Though he did not venture to touch on the resistance to the marshal or the expulsion of the proscribed, yet he strongly arraigned the destruction of property; the burning of the barn of Kirkpatrick, for instance. 'What!' said a fiery fellow in the committee, 'do you blame that?' The secretary found himself embarrassed; he paused for a moment. 'If you had burned him in it,' said he, 'it might have been something; but the barn had done no harm.' 'Ay, ay,' said the man, 'that is right enough.' I admired the presence of mind of Gallatin, and give the incident as a proof of the delicacy necessary to manage the people on that occasion."

Opposite this passage on the margin of the page, in Mr. Gallatin's copy of this book, is written in pencil the following note, in his hand:

"Totally false. It is what B. would have said in my place. The fellow said, 'It was well done.' I replied instantly, 'No; it was not well done,' and I continued to deprecate in the most forcible terms every act of violence. For I had quoted the burning of this house as one of the worst."

The result of the first day's deliberation was therefore a substantial success for the peace party, not so much from what they succeeded in effecting as from the fact that they had obtained energetic leadership and the efficiency which comes from confidence in themselves. The resolutions were finally referred to a committee of four,—Gallatin, Bradford, Herman Husbands, and Brackenridge; a curious party in which Brackenridge must have had a chance to lay up much material for future humor, Bradford being an utterly hollow demagogue, Husbands a religious lunatic, and Brackenridge himself a professional jester.[2]

---

[1] Incidents, vol. i. p. 91.

[2] Badollet, who was at the same time a terribly severe critic of himself and of others, had little patience with Judge Brackenridge, who was perhaps the first, and not far from being the best, of American humorists. Badollet's own sense of humor seems not to have been acute, to judge

This committee, or rather Gallatin and Bradford, the next morning remodelled the resolutions. The only point on which Bradford insisted was that the standing committee to which all business was now to be committed should have power, "in case of any sudden emergency, to take such temporary measures as they may think necessary."

The next point with Gallatin was to get the meeting dissolved. The Peace commissioners were expected soon to arrive on the opposite bank of the river, and President Washington's proclamation calling out the militia to suppress the insurrection had already been received. In the general tendency of things the army could hardly fail to decide the contest in favor of the peace party by the mere moral effect of its advance; but at the moment the news excited and exasperated the violent, who were a very large proportion, if not a majority, of the meeting. The committee of sixty was chosen, one from each township, from whom another committee of twelve was selected to confer with the Federal and State commissioners. The final struggle came upon the question whether the meeting should be now dissolved, or should wait for a report from their committee of twelve after

---

from the following extract from one of his letters to Gallatin, dated 13th February, 1790:

"J'ai vu Brakenridge à Cat-fish où j'ai été à l'occasion d'Archey, et je puis déclarer en conscience que de mes jours je n'ai vu un si complet impertinent fat. Peut-être ne seras-tu pas fâché de lire une partie d'une conversation qu'il eut devant moi. Un inconnu (à moi du moins) voulant le faire parler, à ce que je suppose, lui adresse ainsi la parole:

"N. I think, Mr. Brakenridge, you are one of the happiest men in the world.

"B. Yes, sir; nothing disturbs me. I can declare that I never feel a single moment of discontent, but laugh at everything.

"N. I believe so, sir; but your humor . . .

"B. Oh, sir, truly inexhaustible; yes, truly inexhaustible,—et tout en disant ces mots avec complaisance il tirait ses manchettes et son jabot, caressait son visage de sa main, et souriait en Narcisse,—truly inexhaustible. Sir, I could set down and write a piece of humor for fifty seven years without being the least exhausted. I have just now two compositions agoing. . . .

"N. Happy turn of mind!

"B. You may say that, sir. I enjoy a truly inexhaustible richness and strength of mind, &c., &c."

a conference with the commissioners of the government. Both Gallatin and Brackenridge exerted themselves very much in carrying this point, and after great difficulty succeeded in getting a dissolution.[1]

The result of the Parkinson's Ferry meeting was practically to break the power of the insurrectionary party. Bradford and his friends, instead of carrying the whole country with them, were checked, outmanoeuvred, and lost their prestige at the moment when the calling out of a Federal army made their cause quite desperate; nevertheless, owing to the fact that the committee of sixty was chosen by the meeting, and therefore was of doubtful complexion, much remained to be done in order to bring about complete submission; above all, time was needed, and the government could not allow time, owing to the military necessity of immediate action.

On the 20th August the committee of twelve held their conference with the government commissioners at Pittsburg. All except Bradford favored submission and acceptance of the very liberal terms offered by the government. The committee of sixty was called together at Redstone Old Fort (Brownsville) on the 28th. It was a nervous moment. The committee itself was in doubt, and the desperate party was encouraged by the accidental presence of sixty or seventy riflemen, whose threatening attitude very nearly put Brackenridge's nerves to a fatal test; the simple candor with which he relates how Gallatin held him up and carried him through the trial is very honorable to his character.[2] The committee met; Bradford attempted to drive it into an immediate decision and rejection of the terms, and it was with difficulty that a postponement till the next day was obtained. Such was the alarm among the twelve conferees that Gallatin's determination to make the effort, cost what it might, seems to have been the final reason which decided them to support their

---

[1] " In the report of the commissioners of the United States to the Presi dent, it was most erroneously stated that I wanted the committee, viz., the Parkinson's Ferry members, to remain till the twelve commissioners or conferees should report. The reverse was the fact." Marginal note by Mr. Gallatin on pp. 98–99 of Brackenridge's Incidents.

[2] Incidents, vol. i. p. 111.

own report;[1] even then they only ventured to propose half of it; they made their struggle on the question of accepting the government proposals, not on that of submission. The next morning Gallatin took the lead; no one else had the courage. "The committee having convened, with a formidable gallery, as the day before, Gallatin addressed the chair in a speech of some hours. It was a piece of perfect eloquence, and was heard with attention and without disturbance."[2] This is all that is known of what was, perhaps, Mr. Gallatin's greatest effort. Brackenridge followed, and this time spoke with decision, notwithstanding his alarm. Then Bradford rose and vehemently challenged the full force of the alternative which Gallatin and Brackenridge had described; he advocated the creation of an independent government and war on the United States. James Edgar followed, with a strong appeal in favor of the report. William Findley, who should have been a good judge, says, "I had never heard speeches that I more ardently desired to see in print than those delivered on this occasion. They would not only be valuable on account of the oratory and information displayed in all the three, and especially in Gallatin's, who opened the way, but they would also have been the best history of the spirit and the mistakes which then actuated men's minds. But copies of them could not be procured. They were delivered without any previous preparation other than a complete knowledge of the actual state of things and of human nature when in similar circumstances. This knowledge, and the importance of the occasion on which it was exhibited, produced such ingenuity of reasoning and energy of expression as never perhaps had been exhibited by the same orators before."

Bradford's power was not yet quite broken; even on the frontiers human nature is timid, and a generation which was shuddering at the atrocities of Robespierre might not unreasonably shrink from the possibilities of David Bradford. Gallatin pressed a vote, but could not induce the committee to take it;

---

[1] Findley, History of the Insurrection, p. 122; Brackenridge, Incidents, vol. i. p. 111.

[2] Brackenridge, Incidents, vol. i. p. 112.

the twelve conferees alone supported him.   He then proposed
an informal vote, and still the sixty hesitated.   At last a member
suggested that Mr. Gallatin, as secretary, should write the words
" yea" and " nay" on sixty scraps of paper, and, after distrib-
uting them among the members, should collect the votes in a
hat.   This expedient was, of course, highly satisfactory to Gallatin, and Bradford could not openly oppose.   It was adopted,
and, with these precautions, the vote was taken, each man, of his
own accord, carefully concealing his ballot and destroying that
part of the paper on which was the yea or nay not voted.

The tickets were taken out of the hat and counted ; there
were 34 yeas and 23 nays ; Gallatin had won the battle.   The
galleries grumbled ; the minority were enraged ; Bradford's face
fell and his courage sank.   Outwardly the public expressed
dissatisfaction at the result.   Brackenridge's terrors became more
acute than ever, and not without reason, for had Bradford chosen
now to appeal to force, he might have cost the majority their
lives ; men enough were at the meeting ready to follow him
blindly, but either his nerves failed him or he had sense to see
the folly of the act ; he allowed the meeting to adjourn, and he
himself went home, leaving his party without a head and dissolved into mere individual grumblers.

Throughout this meeting, Mr. Gallatin was in personal danger
and knew it.   Any irresponsible, drunken frontiersman held the
lives of his opponents in his hands ; a word from Bradford, the
old, personal enemy of Gallatin, would have sent scores of bullets
at his rival.   Doubtless Mr. Gallatin believed David Bradford
to be "an empty drum," deficient in courage as in understanding,
and on that belief he risked his whole venture ; but it was a
critical experiment, not so much for the western country, which
had now little to fear from violence, but for the obnoxious
leader, who, by common consent, was held by friends and enemies
responsible for the submission of the people to the law.

From the time of this meeting, and the vote of 34 to 23 at
Redstone Old Fort, the situation entirely changed and a new class
of difficulties and dangers arose ; it was no longer the insurgents
who were alarming, but the government.   As Bradford on one
side was formally giving in his submission, and, on finding that

his speech at Redstone had put him outside the amnesty, made a rapid and narrow escape down the Ohio to Louisiana, on the other side an army of fifteen thousand men was approaching, and the conditions of proffered amnesty could not be fulfilled for lack of time. Before the terms were fixed between the committee of twelve and the government commissioners, three days had passed; to print and prepare the forms of submission to be signed by the people took two days more. The 4th September arrived before these preliminaries were completed; the 11th September was the day on which the people were to sign. No extension of time was possible. In consequence there was only a partial adhesion to the amnesty, and among those excluded were large numbers of persons who refused or neglected to sign on the ground that they had been in no way concerned in the insurrection and needed no pardon.

Gallatin was active in procuring the adhesion of the citizens of Fayette, and the address he then drafted for a meeting on September 10 of the township committees of that county is to be found in his printed works.[1] There, indeed, the danger was slight, because of all the western counties Fayette had been the least disturbed; yet there, too, numbers were technically at the mercy of the army and the law. Mr. Gallatin was, therefore, of opinion that as the rebellion was completely broken, and the submissions made on the 11th September, if not universal, were so general and had been followed by such prostration among the violent party as to preclude the chance of resistance, a further advance of the army was inadvisable. He drafted a letter on the part of the Fayette townships committee to the governor, on the 17th September, representing this view of the case.[2] The President, however, acting on the report of the government commissioners, decided otherwise, and the order for marching was issued on the 25th September.

The news of the riots and disturbances of July had caused prompt action on the part of the general government for the restoration of order, and on the 7th August, President Washington had issued a proclamation calling out the militia of Pennsylvania,

---

[1] Writings, vol. i. p. 4.   [2] Ibid, p. 9.

New Jersey, Maryland, and Virginia.   The 1st September
was the time fixed for the insurgents to disperse, and active
preparations were made for moving the militia when ordered.
Naturally the feeling predominant in the army was one of
violent irritation, and, as strict discipline was hardly to be expected in a hastily-raised militia force, there was reason to fear
that the western country would suffer more severely from the
army than from the rebels.   The arrival of the President and
of Secretary Hamilton, however, and their persistent efforts to
repress this feeling and to maintain strict discipline among the
troops, greatly diminished the danger, and the army ultimately
completed its march, occupied Pittsburg, and effected a number
of arrests without seriously harassing the inhabitants.   Nevertheless there was, perhaps inevitably, more or less injustice done
to individuals, and, as is usual in such cases, the feeling of the
army ran highest against the least offending parties.   Mr. Gallatin
was one of the most obnoxious, on the ground that he had been a
prominent leader of opposition to the excise law and responsible
for the violence resulting from that opposition.   In this there
was nothing surprising; Gallatin was unknown to the great
mass of the troops, and the victorious party in politics cannot
be expected to do entire justice to its opponents.   So far as
the President was concerned, no one has ever found the smallest
matter to blame in his bearing; the only prominent person connected with the government whose conduct roused any bitterness
of feeling was the Secretary of the Treasury.   It was asserted,
and may be believed, that Mr. Hamilton, who in Pittsburg
and other places conducted the examination into the conduct
of individuals, showed a marked desire to find evidence in-
criminating Gallatin.   In what official character Mr. Hamilton
assumed the duty of examiner, which seems to have properly
belonged to the judicial authorities, does not appear; Findley,
however, asserts that certain gentlemen, whose names he gives,
were strictly examined as witnesses against Gallatin, urged to
testify that Gallatin had expressed himself in a treasonable manner at Parkinson's Ferry, and when they denied having heard

---

[1] Findley, History, &c., p. 240.

such expressions, the Secretary asserted that he had sufficient proofs of them already. It is not impossible that Mr. Hamilton really suspected Mr. Gallatin of tampering with the insurgents, and really said that " he was a foreigner, and therefore not to be trusted;"[1] it is not impossible that he thought himself in any case called upon to probe the matter to the bottom; and finally, it is not impossible that he foresaw the advantages his party would gain by overthrowing Mr. Gallatin's popularity. However this may be, the Secretary gave no public expression to his suspicions or his thoughts, and Gallatin was in no way molested or annoyed.

The regular autumnal election took place in Pennsylvania on the 14th October. The army had not then arrived, but there was no longer any idea of resistance or any sign of organization against the enforcement of all the laws. More than a month had passed since order had been restored; even Bradford had submitted, and he and the other most deeply implicated insurgents were now flying for their lives. On the 2d October another meeting of the committee had been held at Parkinson's Ferry, and unanimously agreed to resolutions affirming the general submission and explaining why the signatures of submission had not been universal; on the day of election itself written assurances of submission were universally signed throughout the country; but the most remarkable proof of the complete triumph of the peace party was found in the elections themselves.

Members of Congress were to be chosen, as well as members of the State Legislature. Mr. Gallatin was, as a matter of course, sent back to his old seat in the Assembly from his own county of Fayette. In the neighboring Congressional district, comprising the counties of Washington and Alleghany and the whole country from Lake Erie to the Virginia line, there was some difficulty and perhaps some misunderstanding in regard to the selection of a candidate. Very suddenly, and without previous consultation, indeed without even his own knowledge, and only about three days before election, Mr. Gallatin's name was introduced. The result was that he was chosen over Judge Brackenridge, who stood second on the poll, while the candi-

---

[1] Findley, p. 243.

date of the insurgents, who had received Bradford's support, was lowest among four. By a curious reverse of fortune Mr. Gallatin suddenly became the representative not of his own county of Fayette, but of that very county of Washington whose citizens, only a few weeks before, had been to all appearance violently hostile to him and to his whole course of action. This spontaneous popular choice was owing to the fact that Mr. Gallatin was considered by friend and foe as the embodiment of the principle of law and order, and, rightly or wrongly, it was believed that to his courage and character the preservation of peace was due. It was one more evidence that the true majority had at last found its tongue.

This restoration of Mr. Gallatin to Congress was by no means pleasing to Mr. Hamilton, who, as already mentioned, on his arrival soon afterwards at Pittsburg expressed himself in strong terms in regard to the choice. From the party point of view it was, in fact, a very undesirable result of the insurrection, but there is no reason to suppose that the people in making it cast away a single thought on the question of party. They chose Mr. Gallatin because he represented order.

The 1st November, 1794, had already arrived before the military movements were quite completed. The army had then reached Fayette, and Mr. Gallatin, after having done all in his power to convince the government that the advance was unnecessary, set off with his wife to New York, and, leaving her with her family, returned to take his seat in the Assembly at Philadelphia. Here again he had to meet a contested election. A petition from citizens of Washington County was presented, averring that they had deemed it impossible to vote, and had not voted, at the late election, owing to the state of the country, and praying that the county be declared to have been in insurrection at the time, and the election void. The debate on this subject lasted till January 9, 1795, when a resolution was adopted to the desired effect. In the course of this debate Mr. Gallatin made the first speech he had yet printed, which will be found in his collected works.[1] Like all his writings, it is a plain, concise, clear statement of facts and argument, extremely well done, but not remarkable for rhetorical show, and effective merely because, or so far as, it convinces. He rarely used hard language under any provocation, and this speech, like all his other speeches, is quite free from invective and personality; but, although his method was one of persuasion rather than of compulsion, he always spoke with boldness, and some of the passages in this argument grated harshly on Federalist ears.

The decision of the Pennsylvania Legislature, "that the elections held during the late insurrection . . . were unconstitutional, and are hereby declared void," was always regarded by him as itself in clear violation of the constitution, but for his personal interests a most fortunate circumstance. His opponents were, in fact, by these tactics giving him a prodigious hold upon his party; he had the unusual good fortune of being twice made the martyr of a mere political persecution. This second attempt obviously foreshadowed a third, for if the election to the State Legislature was unconstitutional, that to Congress was equally so, and there was no object in breaking one without breaking the other; but the action of the western country rendered the folly of such a decision too obvious for imitation. All the ejected members except one, who declined, were re-elected, and Mr. Gallatin took his seat a second time on the 14th February, 1795, not to be again disturbed. During this second part of the session he seems to have been chiefly occupied with his bill in regard to the school system; but he closed his service in the State Legislature on the 12th of March, when other matters pressed on his attention.

GALLATIN TO HIS WIFE.

PHILADELPHIA, 3d December, 1794.

. . . I arrived here without any accident and have already seen several of my friends. The Assembly met yesterday, but my colleague having neglected to take down the return of our election we must wait as spectators till it comes, which will not be before a fortnight, I believe. . . . I saw Dallas yesterday. Poor fellow had a most disagreeable campaign of it. He says the spirits, I call it the madness, of the Philadelphia Gentlemen

Corps was beyond conception before the arrival of the President. He saw a list (handed about through the army by officers, nay, by a general officer) of the names of those persons who were to be destroyed at all events, and you may easily guess my own was one of the most conspicuous. Being one day at table with sundry officers, and having expressed his opinion that the army were going only to support the civil authority and not to do any military execution, one of them (Dallas did not tell me his name, but I am told it was one Ross, of Lancaster, aide-de-camp to Mifflin) half drew a dagger he wore instead of a sword, and swore any man who uttered such sentiments ought to be dagged. The President, however, on his arrival, and afterwards Hamilton, took uncommon pains to change the sentiments, and at last it became fashionable to adopt, or at least to express, sentiments similar to those inculcated by them. . . .

7th December, 1794.

. . . You want me to leave politics, but I guess I need not take much pains to attain that object, for politics seem disposed to leave me. A very serious attempt is made to deprive me of my seat in next Congress. The intention is to try to induce the Legislature of this State either to vacate the seats of the members for the counties of Alleghany and Washington, or to pass a law to declare the whole election both for Congress and Assembly in that district to be null and void, and to appoint another day for holding the same. If they fail in that they will pursue the thing before Congress. A petition was accordingly presented to the Legislature last Friday, signed by thirty-four persons, calling themselves peaceable inhabitants of Washington County, and requesting the Assembly to declare the district to have been in a state of insurrection at the time of the election, and to vacate the same. John Hoge, who, however, has not signed it, is the ostensible character who has offered it to be signed, but he did not draw it, and I know the business originated in the army. It is couched in the most indecent language against all the members elect from that district. Did those poor people know how little they torment me by tormenting themselves, I guess they would not be so anxious to raise a second persecution against me.

GALLATIN TO BADOLLET, Greensburg, Washington Co.

PHILADELPHIA, 10th January, 1795.

. . . Savary writes you on the fate of our elections. One thing only I wish and I must insist upon. If the same members are not re-elected, the people here will undoubtedly say that our last elections were not fair and that the people were in a state of insurrection. The only danger I can foresee arises from your district. You have been ill-treated; you have no member now, and every engine will now be set at work to mislead you by your very opponents. Fall not in the snare; take up nobody from your own district; re-elect unanimously the same members, whether they be your favorites or not. It is necessary for the sake of our general character. . . .

Meanwhile, a new scheme was brought to Mr. Gallatin's attention. The French revolution produced a convulsion in Geneva. Large numbers of the Genevese emigrated or thought of emigration. Mr. Gallatin was consulted and made a plan for a joint-stock company, to form a settlement by immigration from Geneva. The expected immigration never came, but this scheme ended in an unforeseen way; Mr. Gallatin joined one or two of the originators of the plan in creating another joint-stock company, and his mind was long busied with its affairs.

GALLATIN TO BADOLLET.

PHILADELPHIA, 29th December, 1794.

Mon bon ami, si je t'écris cette lettre en français ce n'est pas qu'elle contienne des secrets d'état, car je n'en ai point à te dire, mais c'est qu'elle renferme plusieurs choses particulières et qui jusqu'à nouvel ordre doivent rester entre toi et moi absolument. . . . Le retour de mon élection est ou perdu ou n'a jamais été envoyé, en sorte que je n'ai pas encore pu prendre siège dans l'Assemblée, et demain l'on va décider si l'élection de nos quatre comtés sera cassée ou non, sans que je puisse prendre part aux débats. . . . Ci-inclus tu trouveras un abrégé de la dernière révolution de Genève, écrit par D'Yvernois qui est à Londres.

Genève est dans la situation la plus triste. Affamé également par les Français et par les Suisses, déchiré par des convulsions sanguinaires auxquelles l'esprit national paraissait si opposé, une grande partie de ses habitants cherchent, et beaucoup sont obligés de quitter ses murs. Plusieurs tournent leurs yeux vers l'Amérique et quelques-uns sont déjà arrivés. D'Yvernois avait formé le plan de transplanter toute l'université de Genève ici, et il m'a écrit sur cet objet ainsi qu'à Mr. Jefferson et à Mr. Adams; mais il supposait qu'on pourrait obtenir des États-Unis pour cet objet 15,000 dollars de revenu, ce qui est impraticable; et il comptait associer à ce projet une compagnie de terres par actions avec un capital de 3 a 400,000 piastres. D'un autre côté les Genevois arrivés ici cherchaient tant pour eux que pour ceux qui devaient les suivre quelque manière de s'établir, de devenir fermiers, &c. Ils se sont adressés à moi, et d'après les lettres de D'Yvernois et les conversations que les nouveaux arrivés et moi avons eues ensemble, nous avons formé un plan d'établissement et une société dans laquelle je t'ai réservé une part. En voici les fondements. . . . Tu sais bien que je n'ai jamais encouragé personne excepté toi à venir en Amérique de peur qu'ils n'y trouvassent des regrets, mais les temps ont changé. Il faut que beaucoup de Genevois émigrent et un grand nombre vont venir en Amérique. J'ai trouvé autant de plaisir que c'était de mon devoir de tâcher de leur offrir le plan qui m'a paru devoir leur convenir le mieux en arrivant. En 1er lieu j'ai cru qu'il serait essentiel qu'ils fussent réunis, non-seulement pour pouvoir s'entr'aider, mais aussi afin d'être à même de retrouver leurs mœurs, leurs habitudes et même leurs amusements de Genève. 2e, que, comme il y aurait parmi les émigrants bien des artisans, hommes de lettres, &c., et qu'il était bon d'ailleurs d'avoir plus d'une ressource, il conviendrait de former une ville ou village dans le centre d'un corps de terres qu'on achèterait pour cela, en sorte qu'on pût exercer une industrie de ville ou de campagne suivant les goûts et les talents. Ci-inclus tu trouveras deux papiers que je viens de retrouver et qui renferment une esquisse des premières idées que j'avais jetées sur les papiers sur ce sujet, et le brouillon de notre plan d'association qui consiste de 150 actions de 800 piastres chacune, dont nous Genevois ici, savoir Odier, Fazzi, deux Cazenove, Cheriot, Bourdillon, Duby, Couronne, toi et moi avons pris 25; nous en offrons 25 autres ici à des Américains et je les ai déjà presque toutes distribuées; je crois même que je pourrais distribuer cent de plus ici sur-le-champ si je voulais; et nous avons envoyé les cent autres à Genève, en Suisse, et à D'Yvernois pour les Genevois qui voudront y prendre part. . . . En attendant une réponse de Genève nous comptons examiner les terres et peut-être même en acheter, si nous le croyons nécessaire. Il est entendu que c'est à toi et à moi à faire cet examen, car c'est surtout à nous que s'en rapportent tant les émigrés que ceux qui doivent les suivre. J'ai jeté les yeux en général sur la partie nord-est de la Pennsilvanie ou sur la partie de New York qui la joint. Jette les yeux sur la carte et trouve Stockport sur la Delaware et Harmony tout près de là, sur la Susquehannah joignant presque l'état de New York. Des gens qui veulent s'intéresser à la chose m'offrent le corps de terres compris entre le Big Bend de la Susquehannah joignant Harmony et la ligne de New York; mais il faut d'abord examiner. Si on casse nos élections, j'emploierai à ce travail cet hiver; sinon, c'est sur toi que nous comptons, bien entendu que quoique ce ne fût pas aussi nécessaire, il me serait bien plus agréable que tu pusses aller avec moi si j'allais moi-même. . . .

In April, 1795, he made an expedition through New York to examine lands with a view to purchase for the projected Geneva settlement. This expedition brought him at last to Philadelphia, where he was detained till August by the trials of the insurgents and by the business of his various joint-stock schemes.

GALLATIN TO HIS WIFE.

CATSKILL LANDING, 22d April, 1795.

. . . The more I see of this State the better I like Pennsylvania. It may be prejudice, or habit, or whatever you please, but there are some things in the western country which contribute to my happiness, and which I do not find here. Amongst other things which displease me here I may mention, in the first place, *family influence.* In Pennsylvania not only we have neither Livingstones nor Rensselaers, but from the suburbs of Philadelphia to the banks of the Ohio I do not know a single family that has any extensive influence. An equal distribution of property has rendered every individual independent, and there is amongst us true and real equality. In the next place, the lands on the western side of the river are far inferior in quality to those of Pennsylvania, and in the third place, provisions bear the same price as they do in New York, whence arises a real disadvantage for persons wishing to buy land; for the farmers will sell the land in proportion to the price they can get for their produce, and that price being at present quite extravagant and above the average and common one, the consequence is that the supposed value of land is also much greater. In a word, as I am lazy I like a country where living is cheap, and as I am poor I like a country where no person is very rich. . . .

PHILADELPHIA, May 6, 1795.

. . . I arrived here yesterday, pretty much jolted by the wagon, and went to bed in the afternoon, so that I saw nobody till this morning. . . . Hardly had I walked ten minutes in the streets this morning before I was summoned as a witness before the grand jury on the part of government, and must appear there in a few minutes. . . .

8th May, 1795.

. . . I wrote you that I was summoned on behalf of government. I am obliged to attend every day at court, but have not yet been called upon. I am told the bill upon which I am to be examined is not yet filled. I guess it is against Colonel Gaddis; but I have, so far as I can recollect, nothing to say which in my opinion can hurt him. You remember that Gaddis is the man who gave an affidavit to Lee against me. He came yesterday to me to inform me that he meant to have me summoned in his favor, as he thought my testimony must get him discharged. I did not speak to him about his affidavit, nor he to me, but he had a guilty look. I guess the man was frightened, and now feels disappointed in his hope that his accusing me would discharge him. The petty jury consists of twelve from each of the counties of Fayette, Washington, and Alleghany, and twelve from Northumberland, but none from West-

moreland.   Your friend Sproat is one of them, Hoge another.
All from Fayette supposed to have been always friendly to the
excise, but I think in general good characters.   All those of
any note known to have been in general of different politics
with us. . . .

12th May, 1795.

. . . The two bills for treason against Mr. Corbly and Mr.
Gaddis have been returned *ignoramus* by the grand jury; but
there are two bills found against them for misdemeanor,—against
the first for some expressions, against the last for having been
concerned in raising the liberty-pole in Union town.   I am a
witness in both cases,—in the case of Mr. Corbly altogether in
his favor; in the other case my evidence will about balance
itself. . . .   The grand jury have not yet finished their inquiry,
but will conclude it this morning.   They have found twenty-
two bills for treason.   Some of those against whom bills were
found are not here; but I believe fourteen are in jail and will
be tried.   I do not know one of them.   John Hamilton, Sedgwick, and Crawford, whom Judge Peters would not admit to
bail, and who were released little before we left town, after
having been dragged three hundred miles and being in jail
three months, are altogether cleared, the grand jury not having
even found bills for misdemeanor against them.   After the
strictest inquiry the attorney-general could send to the grand
jury bills only against two inhabitants of Fayette, to wit, Gaddis
and one Mounts; he sent two against each of them, one for
treason and one for misdemeanor.   In the case of Mounts, who
has been in jail more than five months, and who was not admitted to give bail, although the best security was offered, not a
shadow of proof appeared, although the county was ransacked
for witnesses, and both bills were found *ignoramus*.   And it is
proper to observe that the grand jury, who are respectable, were,
however, all taken from Philadelphia and its neighborhood, and,
with only one or two exceptions, out of one party, so that they
cannot be suspected of partiality.   In the case of Gaddis the
bill for treason was returned *ignoramus;* the bill for misdemeanor was found.   So that the whole insurrection of Fayette
County amounts to one man accused of misdemeanor for raising

a pole. I can form no guess as to the fate of the prisoners who are to be tried for treason, and whether, in case any are found guilty, government mean to put any to death. There is not a single man of influence or consequence amongst them, which makes me hope they may be pardoned. There is one, however, who is said to be Tom the Tinker; he is a New England man, who was concerned in Shay's insurrection, but it is asserted that he signed the amnesty. I have had nothing but that business in my head since I have been here, and can write about nothing else. . . .

25th May, 1795.

I believe, my dear little wife, that I will not be able to see thee till next week, for the trials go on but very slowly; there has been but one since my last letter, and there are nine more for high treason, besides misdemeanors. I am sorry to add that the man who was tried was found guilty of high treason. He had a very good and favorable jury, six of them from Fayette; for, although he is from Westmoreland County, the fact was committed in Fayette. . . . There is no doubt of the man [Philip Vigel] being guilty in a legal sense of levying war against the United States, which was the crime charged to him. But he is certainly an object of pity more than of punishment, at least when we consider that death is the punishment, for he is a rough, ignorant German, who knew very well he was committing a riot, and he ought to have been punished for it, but who had certainly no idea that it amounted to levying war and high treason. . . .

1st June, 1795.

. . . Those trials go still very slowly, only two since I wrote to you; the men called Curtis and Barnet, both indicted for the attack upon and burning Nevil's house, and both acquitted; the first without much hesitation, as there was at least a strong presumption that he went there either to prevent mischief or at most only as a spectator. The second was as guilty as Mitchell, who has been condemned, but there were not sufficient legal proofs against either. The difference in the verdict arises from the difference of counsel employed in their respective defences, and chiefly from a different choice of jury. Mitchell was very poorly defended by Thomas, the member of Senate, who is young, unexperienced, impudent, and self-conceited. He challenged (that is to say, rejected, for, you know, the accused person has a right to reject thirty-five of the jury without assigning any reason) every inhabitant of Alleghany, and left the case to twelve Quakers (many of them probably old Tories), on the supposition that Quakers would condemn no person to death; but he was utterly mistaken. Lewis defended Barnet, made a very good defence, and got a jury of a different complexion; the consequence of which was that, although the evidence, pleadings, and charge took up from eleven o'clock in the forenoon till three o'clock the next morning, the jury were but fifteen minutes out before they brought in a verdict of not guilty. Brackenridge says that he would always choose a jury of Quakers, or at least Episcopalians, in all common cases, such as murder, rape, etc., but in every possible case of insurrection, rebellion, and treason, give him Presbyterians on the jury by all means. I believe there is at least as much truth as wit in the saying. . . . I have drawn, at the request of the jury who convicted Philip Vigel, a petition to the President recommending him as a proper object of mercy; they have all signed it, but what effect it will have I do not know, and indeed nobody can form any conjecture whether the persons convicted will be pardoned or not. It rests solely with the President. . . .

GALLATIN TO BADOLLET.

PHILADELPHIA, 20th May, 1795.

I am sorry, my dear friend, that I cannot go and meet you, agreeable to our appointment; but I am detained here as an evidence in the case of Corbly, and of two more in behalf of the United States, although I know nothing about any of them except Corbly. I lend my horse to Cazenove, who goes in my room, and who will tell you what little has passed since I saw you on the subject of our plan. Upon the whole, I conceive that further emigrations from Geneva will not take place at present, and that our plan will not be accepted in Europe. We must therefore depend merely on our own present number and strength, and this you should keep in view in the course of the examination you are now making. Our own convenience and the interest of those few Genevans who now are here must alone be consulted, and it may be a question whether under those circumstances it will be worth while for you and me to abandon our present situation, and for them to encounter the hardships and hazards of a new settlement in the rough country you are now exploring; whether, on the contrary, it would not be more advantageous for them to fix either in the more populous parts of the State, or even in our own neighborhood, where they might perhaps find resources sufficient for a few and enjoy all the advantages resulting from our neighborhood, experience, and influence.

GALLATIN TO HIS WIFE.

PHILADELPHIA, 29th June, 1795.

. . . You will see in this day's Philadelphia paper an abstract of the treaty; it is pretty accurate, for I read the treaty itself yesterday. I believe it will be printed at large within a day or two. It exceeds everything I expected. . . . As to the form of ratification I have not seen it, but from the best information I could collect it is different from what has been printed in some papers. It is, I think, nearly as followeth: The Senate consent to and advise the President to ratify the treaty upon condition that an additional article be added to the same suspending the operation of, or explaining (I do not know which), the 12th Article, so far as relates to the intercourse with the West India Islands. If that information is accurate, it follows that the treaty is not ratified, because the intended additional article, if adopted by Great Britain, is not valid until ratified by the Senate, and unless that further ratification takes place the whole treaty falls through. You know the vote, and that Gunn is the man who has joined the ratifying party. I am told that Burr made a most excellent speech. . . . I think fortitude is a quality which depends very much upon ourselves, and which we lose more and more for want of exercising it. Indeed, I want it now myself more than you. I have just received a letter from one of my uncles, under date 23d January, which informs me that Miss Pictet is dangerously ill and very little hope of her recovering. She had not yet received my and your letter. I hope she may, for I know how much consolation it would give her; but I have not behaved well. . . .

Gallatin remained in Philadelphia till July 31, to form a new company, dissolving the old one, and joining with Bourdillon, Cazenove, Badollet, and his brother-in-law, James W. Nicholson, in a concern with nine or ten thousand dollars capital, the business being "to purchase lots at the mouth of George's Creek," "a mill or two" in the neighborhood, keeping a retail store and perhaps two (the main business), and land speculations on their own account and on commission. After settling the partnership he remained to buy supplies and to get money from Morris, who at last paid him eight hundred dollars cash and gave a note at ninety days for a thousand. On July 31 he started for Fayette.

GALLATIN TO HIS WIFE.

PHILADELPHIA, 31st July, 1795.

. . . After being detained here two days by the rain, we finally go this moment. . . . I have settled with Mr. Morris. . . . I have balanced all my accounts, and find that we are just worth 7000 dollars. . . . In addition to that, we have our plantation, Mr. Morris's note for 3500 dollars, due next May, and about 25,000 acres waste lands. . . .

FAYETTE COUNTY, September 6, 1795.

. . . Upon a further examination of Wilson's estate I have purchased it at £3000, which is a high price, but then we have the town seat (which is the nearest portage from the western waters to the Potowmack and the Federal city, and as near as any to Philadelphia and Baltimore) and three mill seats, one built, another building, and the third, which is the most valuable, will be on the river-bank, so that we will be able to load boats for New Orleans from the mill-door, and they stand upon one of the best, if not the very best, stream of the whole country. The boat-yards fall also within our purchase, so that, with a good store, we will, in a great degree, command the trade of this part of the country. I have also purchased, for about £300, all the lots that remained unsold in the little village of Greensburgh, on the other side of the river, opposite to our large purchase, and 20 acres of the bottom-land adjoining it. It will become necessary, of course, for us to increase our capital. . . . As to politics, I have thought but little about them since I have been here. I wish the ratification of the treaty may not involve us in a more serious situation than we have yet been in. May I be mistaken in my fears and everything be for the best! I would not heretofore write to you on the subject of the dispute between your father and Hamilton, as I knew you were not acquainted with it. I feel indeed exceedingly happy that it has terminated so, but I beg of you not to express your sentiments of the treatment I have received with as much warmth as you usually do, for it may tend to inflame the passions of your friends and lead to consequences you would forever regret. It has indeed required all my coolness and temper, and I might perhaps add, all my love for you, not to involve myself in some quarrel with that gentleman or some other of that description; but, however sure you may be that I will not myself, others may, so that I trust that my good girl will be more cautious hereafter. . . .

PHILADELPHIA, 29th September, 1795.

. . . I arrived here pretty late last night. . . . Since I wrote to you I received the account which I expected, that of the death of my second mother. I trust, I hope at least, the comfort she must have experienced from hearing she had not been altogether disappointed in the hopes she had formed of me, and in the cares she had bestowed on my youth, will in some degree have made amends for my unpardonable neglect in writing so seldom to her. . . . I expect to set off to-morrow.

The dispute between Commodore Nicholson and Mr. Hamilton, to which allusion is made above, was a private one, which, of course, had its source in politics. For a time the commodore expected a duel, and it may well be imagined that to a gentleman of his fighting temperament a duel was not altogether without its charm. Mr. Hamilton, however, had too much good sense to seek this species of distinction. The dispute was amicably settled, and probably no one was better pleased at the settlement than Mr. Gallatin, although he had nothing to do with the quarrel.

Mr. Gallatin's career as a member of Congress now began, and lasted till 1801, when he became Secretary of the Treasury. In some respects it was without a parallel in our history. That a young foreigner, speaking with a foreign accent, laboring under all the odium of the western insurrection, surrounded by friendly rivals like Madison, John Nicholas, W. B. Giles, John Randolph, and Edward Livingston; confronted by opponents like Fisher Ames, Judge Sewall, Harrison Gray Otis, Roger Griswold, James A. Bayard, R. G. Harper, W. L. Smith, of South Carolina, Samuel Dana, of Connecticut, and even John Marshall,—that such a man under such circumstances should have at once seized the leadership of his party, and retained it with firmer and firmer grasp down to the last moment of his service; that he should have done this by the sheer force of ability and character, without ostentation and without the tricks of popularity; that he should have had his leadership admitted without a dispute, and should have held it without a contest, made a curious combination of triumphs. Many of the great parliamentary leaders in America, John Randolph, Henry Clay, Thaddeus Stevens, have maintained their supremacy by their dogmatic and overbearing temper and their powers of sarcasm or invective. Mr. Gallatin seldom indulged in personalities. His temper was under almost perfect control. His power lay in courage, honesty of purpose, and thoroughness of study. Undoubtedly his mind was one of rare power, perhaps for this especial purpose the most apt that America has ever seen; a mind for which no principle was too broad and no detail too delicate; but it was essentially a scientific and not a political mind. Mr. Gallatin always tended to think with an entire disregard of the emotions; he could only with an effort refrain from balancing the opposing sides of a political question. His good fortune threw him into public life at a time when both parties believed that principles were at stake, and when the struggle between those who would bar the progress of democracy and those who led that progress allowed little latitude for doubt on either side in regard to the necessity of their acts. While this condition of things lasted, and it lasted throughout Mr. Gallatin's stormy Congressional career, he was an ideal party leader, uniting boldness with caution, good temper with earnestness, exact modes of thought with laborious investigation, to a degree that has no parallel in American experience. Perhaps the only famous leader of the House of Representatives who could stand comparison with Mr. Gallatin for the combination of capacities, each carried to uniform excellence, was Mr. Madison; and it was precisely Mr. Madison whom Gallatin supplanted.

On the subject of his Congressional service Mr. Gallatin left two fragmentary memoranda, which may best find place here:

"As both that body [Congress] and the State Legislature sat in Philadelphia, owing also to my short attendance in the United States Senate and my defence of my seat, I was as well known to the members of Congress as their own colleagues, and at once took my stand in that Assembly. The first great debate in which we were engaged was that on the British treaty; and my speech, or rather two speeches, on the constitutional powers of the House, miserably reported and curtailed by B. F. Bache, were, whether I was right or wrong, universally considered as the best on either side. I think that of Mr. Madison superior and more comprehensive, but for this very reason (comprehensiveness) less impressive than mine. Griswold's reply was thought the best; in my opinion it was that of Goodrich, though this was deficient in perspicuity. Both, however, were secondrate. The most brilliant and eloquent speech was undoubtedly that of Mr. Ames; but it was delivered in reference to the expediency of making the appropriations, and treated but incidentally of the constitutional question. I may here say that though there were, during my six years of Congressional service, many clever men in the Federal party in the House (Griswold, Bayard, Harper, Otis, Smith of South Carolina, Dana, Tracy, Hillhouse, Sitgreaves, &c.), I met with but two superior men, Ames, who sat only during the session of 1795–1796, and John

Marshall, who sat only in the session of 1799–1800, and who took an active part in the debates only two or three times, but always with great effect. On our side we were much stronger in the Congress of 1795–1797. But Mr. Madison and Giles (an able commonplace debater) having withdrawn, and Richard Brent become hypochondriac, we were reduced during the important Congress of 1797–1799 to Ed. Livingston, John Nicholas, and myself, whilst the Federalists received the accession of Bayard and Otis. John Marshall came in addition for the Congress of 1799–1801, and we were recruited by John Randolph and Joseph Nicholson."

" The ground which I occupied in that body [Congress] is well known, and I need not dwell on the share I took in all the important debates and on the great questions which during that period (1795–1801) agitated the public mind, in 1796 the British treaty, in 1798–1800 the hostilities with France and the various unnecessary and obnoxious measures by which the Federal party destroyed itself. It is certainly a subject of self-gratulation that I should have been allowed to take the lead with such coadjutors as Madison, Giles, Livingston, and Nicholas, and that when deprived of the powerful assistance of the two first, who had both withdrawn in 1798, I was able to contend on equal terms with the host of talents collected in the Federal party,—Griswold, Bayard, Harper, Goodrich, Otis, Smith, Sitgreaves, Dana, and even J. Marshall. Yet I was destitute of eloquence, and had to surmount the great obstacle of speaking in a foreign language, with a very bad pronunciation. My advantages consisted in laborious investigation, habits of analysis, thorough knowledge of the subjects under discussion, and more extensive general information, due to an excellent early education, to which I think I may add quickness of apprehension and a sound judgment.

" A member of the opposition during the whole period, it could not have been expected that many important measures should have been successfully introduced by me. Yet an impulse was given in some respects which had a powerful influence on the spirit and leading principles of subsequent Administrations. The principal questions in which I was engaged related to constitutional construction or to the finances. Though not quite so orthodox on the first subject as my Virginia friends (witness the United States Bank and internal improvements), I was opposed to any usurpation of powers by the general government. But I was specially jealous of Executive encroachments, and to keep that branch within the strict limits of Constitution and of law, allowing no more discretion than what appeared strictly necessary, was my constant effort.

"The financial department in the House was quite vacant, so far at least as the opposition was concerned; and having made myself complete master of the subject and occupied that field almost exclusively, it is not astonishing that my views should have been adopted by the Republican party and been acted upon when they came into power. My first step was to have a standing committee of ways and means appointed. That this should not have been sooner done proves the existing bias in favor of increasing as far as possible the power of the Executive branch. The next thing was to demonstrate that the expenditure had till then exceeded the income: the remedy proposed was economy. Economy means order and skill; and after having determined the proper and necessary objects of expense, the Legislature cannot enforce true economy otherwise than by making *specific* appropriations. Even these must be made with due knowledge of the subject, since, if carried too far by too many subdivisions, they become injurious, if not impracticable. This subject has ever been a bone of contention between the legislative and executive branches in every representative government, and it is in reality the only proper and efficient legislative check on executive prodigality.

"Respecting the objects of expenditure, there was not, apart from that connected with the French hostilities, any other subject of division but that of the navy. And the true question was whether the creation of an efficient navy should be postponed to the payment of the public debt." . . .

During Mr. Gallatin's maiden session of Congress, the exciting winter of 1795–96, when the first of our great party contests took place, not even a private letter seems to have been written by him that throws light on his acts or thoughts. His wife was with him in Philadelphia. If he wrote confidentially to **any** other person, his letters are now lost. The only material for his biography is in the Annals of Congress and in his speeches, with the replies they provoked; a material long since worn threadbare by biographers and historians.

Of all portions of our national history none has been more often or more carefully described and discussed than the struggle over Mr. Jay's treaty. No candid man can deny that there was at the time ample room for honest difference of opinion in regard to the national policy. That Mr. Jay's treaty was a bad one few persons even then ventured to dispute; no one would venture on its merits to defend it now. There has been no moment since 1810 when the United States would have hesitated to prefer war rather than peace on such terms. No excuse in the temporary advantages which the treaty gained can wholly palliate the concessions of principle which it yielded, and no considerations of a possible war with England averted or postponed can blind history to the fact that this blessing of peace was obtained by the sacrifice of national consistency and by the violation of neutrality towards France. The treaty recognized the right of Great Britain to capture French property in American vessels, whilst British property in the same situation was protected from capture by our previous treaty with France; and, what was yet worse, the acknowledgment that provisions might be treated as contraband not only contradicted all our principles, but subjected the United States government to the charge of a mean connivance in the British effort to famish France, while securing America from pecuniary loss.

Nevertheless, for good and solid reasons, the Senate at the time approved, and President Washington, after long deliberation, signed, the treaty. The fear of a war with Great Britain, the desire to gain possession of the Western posts, and the commercial interests involved in a neutral trade daily becoming more lucrative, were the chief motives to this course. So far as Mr. Gallatin's private opinions were concerned, it is probable that no one felt much more aversion to the treaty than he did; but before he took his seat in Congress the Senate had approved and the President had signed it; a strong feeling in its favor existed among his own constituents, always in dread of Indian difficulties ; the treaty, in short, was law, and the House had only to consider the legislation necessary to carry it into effect

Bad as the treaty was, both in its omissions and in its admissions, as a matter of foreign relations, these defects were almost trifles when compared with its mischievous results at home. It thrust a sword into the body politic. So far as it went, and it went no small distance, it tended to overturn the established balance of our neutrality and to throw the country into the arms of England. Nothing could have so effectually arrayed the two great domestic parties in sharply defined opposition to each other, and nothing could have aroused more bitterness of personal feeling. In recent times there has been a general disposition to explain away and to soften down the opinions and passions of that day ; to throw a veil over their violence ; to imagine a possible middle ground, from which the acts and motives of all parties will appear patriotic and wise, and their extravagance a mere misunderstanding. Such treatment of history makes both parties ridiculous. The two brilliant men who led the two great divisons of national thought were not mere declaimers ; they never for a moment misunderstood each other ; they were in deadly earnest, and no compromise between them ever was or ever will be possible. Mr. Jefferson meant that the American system should be a democracy, and he would rather have let the world perish than that this principle, which to him represented all that man was worth, should fail. Mr. Hamilton considered democracy a fatal curse, and meant to stop its progress. The partial truce which the first Administration of Washington had imposed on both parties, although really closed by the retirement of Mr. Jefferson from the Cabinet, was finally broken only by the arrival of Mr. Jay's treaty. From that moment repose was impossible until one party or the other had triumphed beyond hope of resistance ; and it was easy to see which of the two parties must triumph in the end.

One of the immediate and most dangerous results of the British treaty was to put the new Constitution to a very serious test. The theory which divides our government into departments, executive, legislative, and judicial, and which makes each department supreme in its own sphere, could not be worked out with even theoretical perfection; the framers of the Constitution were themselves obliged to admit exceptions in this arrangement of powers, and one of the most serious exceptions related to treaties. The Constitution begins by saying, " *All* legislative powers herein granted shall be vested in a Congress of the United States, which shall consist of a Senate and House of Representatives," and proceeds to give Congress the express power " to make *all* laws which shall be necessary and proper for carrying into execution the foregoing powers, and all other powers vested by this Constitution in the government of the United States or in any department or officer thereof." But on the other hand the Constitution also says that the President " shall have power, by and with the advice and consent of the Senate, to make treaties," and finally it declares that " this Constitution, and the laws of the United States which shall be made in pursuance thereof, and *all* treaties made, or which shall be made, under the authority of the United States shall be the supreme law of the land," State laws or constitutions to the contrary notwithstanding.

Here was an obvious conflict of powers resulting from an equally obvious divergence of theory. Congress possessed *all* legislative powers. The President and Senate possessed the power to make treaties, which were, like the Constitution and the laws of Congress, the supreme law of the land. Congress, then, did not possess *all* legislative powers. The President alone, with two-thirds of the Senate, could legislate.

The British treaty contained provisions which could only be carried into execution by act of Congress; it was, therefore, within the power of the House of Representatives to refuse legislation and thus practically break the treaty. The House was so evenly divided that no one could foresee the result, when Edward Livingston began this famous debate by moving to call on the President for papers, in order that the House might deliberate with official knowledge of the conditions under which the treaty was negotiated.

The Federalists met this motion by asserting that under the Constitution the House had no right to the papers, no right to deliberate on the merits of the treaty, no right to refuse legislation. In Mr. Griswold's words, " The House of Representatives have nothing to do with the treaty but provide for its execution." Untenable as this ground obviously was, and one which no respectable legislative body could possibly accept, it was boldly taken by the Federalists, who plunged into the contest with their characteristic audacity and indomitable courage, traits that compel respect even for their blunders.

The debate began on March 7, 1796, and on the 10th Mr. Gallatin spoke, attacking the constitutional doctrine of the Federalists and laying down his own. He claimed for the House, not a power to make treaties, but a check upon the treaty-making power when clashing with the special powers expressly vested in Congress by the Constitution; he showed the existence of this check in the British constitution, and he showed its necessity in our own, for, "if the treaty-making power is not limited by existing laws, or if it repeals the laws that clash with it, or if the Legislature is obliged to repeal the laws so clashing, then the legislative power in fact resides in the President and Senate, and they can, by employing an Indian tribe, pass any law under the color of treaty."

The argument was irresistible; it was never answered; and indeed the mere statement is enough to leave only a sense of surprise that the Federalists should have hazarded themselves on such preposterous ground. Some seventy years later, when the purchase of Alaska brought this subject again before the House on the question of appropriating the purchase-money stipulated by the treaty, the Administration abandoned the old Federalist position; the right of the House to call for papers, to deliberate on the merits of the treaty, even to refuse appropriations if the treaty was inconsistent with the Constitution or with the established policy of the country, was fully conceded. The Administration only made the reasonable claim that if, upon just consideration, a treaty was found to be clearly within the constitutional powers of the government, and consistent with the national policy, then it was the duty of each co-ordinate branch of the government to shape its action accordingly.[1] This claim

---

[1] See the Speech of N. P. Banks, of June 30, 1868, Cong. Globe, vol. lxxv., Appendix, p. 385.

was recognized; the House voted the money, and the controversy may be considered at an end. In 1796, on the contrary, Mr. Griswold, whose reply to Mr. Gallatin's argument was considered the most effective, and who never shrank from a logical conclusion however extreme, admitted and asserted that the legislative power did reside in the President and Senate to the exclusion of the House, and added, "Allowing this to be the case, what follows?—that the people have clothed the President and Senate with a very important power."

On this theme the debate was continued for several weeks; but the Federalists were in a false position, and were consequently overmatched in argument. Madison, W. C. Nicholas, Edward Livingston, and many other members of the opposition, in speeches of marked ability, supported the claim of their House. The speakers on the other side were obliged to take the attitude of betraying the rights of their own body in order to exaggerate the powers of the Executive, and as this practice was entirely in accordance with the aristocratic theory of government, they subjected themselves to the suspicion at least of acting with ulterior motives.

On the 23d March, Mr. Gallatin closed the debate for his side of the House by a second speech, in which he took more advanced ground. He had before devoted his strength to overthrowing the constitutional theory of his opponents; he now undertook the far more difficult task of establishing one of his own. The Federalist side of the House was not the temperate side in this debate, and Mr. Gallatin had more than one personal attack to complain of, but he paid no attention to personalities, and went on to complete his argument. Inasmuch as the Federalists characterized their opponents on this question as disorganizers, disunionists, and traitors, and even to this day numbers of intelligent persons still labor under strong prejudice against the Republican opposition to Washington's Administration, a few sentences from Mr. Gallatin's second speech shall be inserted here to show precisely how far he and his party did in fact go:

"The power claimed by the House is not that of negotiating and proposing treaties; it is not an active and operative power of making and repealing treaties; it is not a power which absorbs and destroys the constitutional right of the President and Senate to make treaties; it is only a negative, a restraining power on those subjects over which Congress has the right to legislate. On the contrary, the power claimed for the President and Senate is that, under color of making treaties, of proposing and originating laws; it is an active and operative power of making laws and of repealing laws; it is a power which supersedes and annihilates the constitutional powers vested in Congress.

" If it is asked, in what situation a treaty is which has been made by the President and Senate, but which contains stipulations on legislative objects, until Congress has carried them into effect? whether it is the law of the land and binding upon the two nations? I might answer that such a treaty is precisely in the same situation with a similar one concluded by Great Britain before Parliament has carried it into effect.

" But if a direct answer is insisted on, I would say that it is in some respects an inchoate act. It is the law of the land and binding upon the American nation in all its parts, except so far as relates to those stipulations. Its final fate, in case of refusal on the part of Congress to carry those stipulations into effect, would depend on the will of the other nation."

The Federalists had in this debate failed to hold well together; the ground assumed by Mr. Griswold was too extreme for some even among the leaders, and concessions were made on that side which fatally shook their position; but among the Republicans there was concurrence almost, if not quite, universal in the statements of the argument by Mr. Madison and Mr. Gallatin, and this closing authoritative position of Mr. Gallatin was on the same day adopted by the House on a vote of 62 to 37, only five members not voting.

The Administration might perhaps have contented itself with refusing the papers called for by the House, and left the matter as it stood, seeing that the resolution calling for the papers said not a word about the treaty-making power, and the journals of the House contained no allusion to the subject; or the President might have contented himself with simply asserting his own powers and the rights of his own Department; but, as has been already seen, there was at this time an absence of fixed precedent which occasionally led executive officers to take liberties with the Legislature such as would never afterwards have been tolerated. The President sent a message to the House which was far from calculated to soothe angry feeling. Two passages were especially invidious. In one the President adverted to the debates held in the House. In the other he assumed a position in curious contrast to his generally cautious tone: "Having been a member of the general convention, and knowing the principles on which the Constitution was formed, I have, &c., &c." For the President of the United States on such an occasion to appeal to his personal knowledge of the intentions of a body of men who gave him no authority for that purpose, and whose intentions were not a matter of paramount importance, seeing that by universal consent it was not their intentions which interpreted the Constitution, but the intentions of the people who adopted it; and for him to use this language to a body of which Mr. Madison was leader, and which had adopted Mr. Madison's views, was a step not likely to diminish the perils of the situation. Had the President been any other than Washington, or perhaps had the House been led by another than Madison, the opportunity for a ferocious retort would probably have been irresistible. As it was, the House acted with great forbearance; it left unnoticed this very vulnerable part of the message, and in reply to the implication that the House claimed to make its assent "necessary to the validity of a treaty," it contented itself with passing a resolution defining its own precise claim. On this resolution Mr. Madison spoke at some length and with perfect temper in reply to what could only be considered as the personal challenge contained in the message, while Mr. Gallatin did not speak at all. The resolutions were adopted by 57 to 35, and the House then turned to the merits of the treaty.

On this subject Mr. Gallatin spoke at considerable length on the 26th April, a few days before the close of the debate. The situation was extremely difficult. In the country at large opinion was as closely divided as it was in the House itself. Even at the present moment it is not easy to decide in favor of either party. Nothing but the personal authority of General Washington carried the hesitating assent of great masses of Federalists. Nothing but fear of war made approval even remotely possible. Whether the danger of war was really so great as the friends of the treaty averred may be doubted. No Federalist Administration would have made war on England, for it was a cardinal principle with the Hamiltonian wing of the party that only through peace with England could their ascendency be preserved, while war with England avowedly meant a dissolution of the Union by their own act.[1] The Republicans wanted no war with England, as they afterwards proved by enduring insults that would in our day rouse to madness every intelligent human being within the national borders. Nevertheless war appeared or was represented as inevitable in 1796; the eloquent speech of Fisher Ames contained no other argument of any weight; it was abject fear to which he appealed: "You are a father: the blood of your sons shall fatten your corn-field. You are a mother: the war-whoop shall wake the sleep of the cradle."

It was the truth of this reproach on the weakness of the argument for the treaty that made the sting of Mr. Gallatin's closing remarks:

"I cannot help considering the cry of war, the threats of a dissolution of government, and the present alarm, as designed for the same purpose, that of making an impression on the fears of this House. It was through the fear of being involved in a war that the negotiation with Great Britain originated; under the impression of fear the treaty has been negotiated and signed; a fear of the same danger, that of war, promoted its ratification: and now every imaginary mischief which can alarm our fears is conjured up, in order to deprive us of that discretion which this House thinks it has a right to exercise, and in order to force us to carry the treaty into effect."

Nevertheless Mr. Gallatin carefully abstained from advocating a refusal to carry the treaty into effect. With his usual caution he held his party back from any violent step; he even went so far as to avow his wish that the treaty might not now be defeated:

"The further detention of our posts, the national stain that would result from receiving no reparation for the spoliations on

---

[1] See, among other expressions to this effect, Lodge's Cabot, pp. 342, 345.

our trade, and the uncertainty of a final adjustment of our differences with Great Britain, are the three evils which strike me as resulting from a rejection of the treaty; and when to these considerations I add that of the present situation of the country, of the agitation of the public mind, and of the advantages that would arise from a union of sentiments; however injurious and unequal I conceive the treaty to be, however repugnant it may be to my feelings and, perhaps, to my prejudices, I feel induced to vote for it, and will not give my assent to any proposition which would imply its rejection."

He also carefully avoided taking the ground which was undoubtedly first in his anxieties, that of the bearing which the treaty would have on our relations with France. This was a subject which his semi-Gallican origin debarred him from dwelling upon. The position he took was a new one, and for his party perfectly safe and proper; it was that, in view of the conduct of Great Britain since the treaty was signed, her impressment of our seamen, her uninterrupted spoliations on our trade, especially in the seizure of provision vessels, "a proceeding which they might perhaps justify by one of the articles of the treaty," a postponement of action was advisable until assurances were received from Great Britain that she meant in future to conduct herself as a friend.

This was the ground on which the party recorded their vote against the resolution declaring it expedient to make appropriations for carrying the treaty into effect. In committee the division was 49 to 49,—Muhlenberg, the chairman, throwing his vote in favor of the resolution, and thus carrying it to the House. There the appropriation was voted by 51 to 48.

Perhaps the only individual in any branch of the government who was immediately and greatly benefited by the British treaty was Mr. Gallatin; he had by common consent distinguished himself in debate and in counsel; bolder and more active than Mr. Madison, he was followed by his party with instinctive confidence; henceforth his leadership was recognized by the entire country.

Absorbing as the treaty debate was, it did not prevent other and very weighty legislation. One Act, adopted in the midst of the excitement of the treaty, was peculiarly important, and, although the idea itself was not new, Mr. Gallatin was the first to embody it in law, so far as any single individual can lay claim to that distinction. This Act created the land-system of the United States government; it applied only to lands north-west of the Ohio River, in which the Indian titles had been extinguished, and it provided for laying these out in townships, six miles square, and for selling the land in sections, under certain reservations. This land-system, always a subject of special interest to Mr. Gallatin, and owing its existence primarily to his efforts while a legislator, took afterwards an immense development in his hands while he was Secretary of the Treasury, and, had he been allowed to carry out his schemes, would probably have been made by him the foundation of a magnificent system of internal improvement. Circumstances prevented him from realizing his plan; only the land-system itself and the Cumberland Road remained to testify the breadth and accuracy of his views; but even these were achievements of the highest national importance.

Deeply as these two subjects interested him, his permanent and peculiar task was a different one. To Mr. Gallatin finance was an instinct. He knew well, as Mr. Hamilton had equally clearly understood before him, that the heart of the government was the Treasury; like many another man of high financial reputation, he had little talent for money-making, and never was, or cared to be, rich; but he had one great advantage over most Americans of his time, even over Mr. Hamilton and Mr. Jefferson; he was an economist as well as a statesman; he was exact not merely in the details but in the morality of affairs; he held debt in horror; punctilious exactness in avoiding debt was his final axiom in finance; the discharge of debt was his first principle in statesmanship; searching and rigid economy was his invariable demand whether in or out of office, and he made this demand imperative upon himself as upon others.

Mr. Hamilton, to whom the organization of the financial system was due, and who left public life just as Gallatin began his Congressional career, had belonged to a different school and had acted on different principles. Adhering more or less closely to the

English financial and economical theories then in vogue, he had intentionally constructed a somewhat elaborate fabric, of which a considerable national debt was the foundation. Had Mr. Hamilton foreseen in 1790 the course public affairs would take during the next ten years, he would perhaps have modified his plan and would have guarded more carefully against overloading the Treasury; but at that moment it was not unreasonable to suppose that what the country wanted was centralization, and that a national debt was one means of consolidating divergent local interests. Mr. Hamilton, therefore, accepted as much debt as he thought the country could reasonably bear, and allowed the rest to be expunged. In forming this debt he had at least in one respect permitted an unnecessary and very mischievous addition to be made to the acknowledged and existing national burden. In order to settle the accounts between the States, he had permitted Congress—perhaps forced Congress—to assume a large proportion of the State debts. The balance to be adjusted by payment of the debtor to the creditor States was ultimately ascertained to be a little more than $8,000,000. To settle this account as nearly as it was settled in fact, required an assumption of State debts to the amount of $11,609,000; but, instead of waiting for a settlement of accounts, Congress had, in 1790, voted to assume a certain amount of State debts at once and to charge each State in the ultimate settlement with the amount assumed on her account. A sum of over $18,000,000 was thus funded, and so much debt transferred from the States to the national government. In addition to this sum a further amount of about $3,500,000 was funded in order to get rid of the balances in favor of the creditor States. Altogether, including back interest from 1790 to 1795, a debt of $22,500,000 was imposed on the new government, where half that sum would have answered the purpose, and of this about $2,000,000 was actually new debt, created for the occasion.

The entire amount of the national debt when fairly funded was about $78,000,000. Had no political complications in its foreign relations embarrassed the government, this burden might have been easily carried in spite of Indian wars and even in spite of the whiskey rebellion, though these troubles steadily tended to increase the sum. The annual charge was in 1796 nearly $4,000,000, but after the year 1800 an additional charge of $1,100,000 on deferred stock was to be provided for by taxation, and this future addition to the annual charge hung over the government during all these years as a perpetual anxiety. The population of the country in 1791 was not quite 4,000,000 souls, of whom 700,000 were slaves. The expenditures, including the charge on the debt, amounted in 1796 to about $7,000,000 a year, and the receipts nearly balanced the expenditures. Considering the poverty of the country, taxation was high; so high as to make any increase dangerous. Thus the new government was not in a condition to hazard experiments, and needed five or ten years of careful management in order to give the country time for expansion.

In the middle of this state of affairs, while the Treasury was wrestling with the problems of Indian wars and domestic revolt, came the ominous signs of foreign aggression. War was thought to be imminent, either with France or England, from 1795 to 1800, and the government was in great straits to provide for it. The time now came when the Federalists would probably have been delighted to recover the ten millions which had been unnecessarily assumed, and the theory of a national debt must have taken a different aspect in their eyes. Mr. Hamilton had not calculated on this emergency; his system had rested on the assumption that the old situation was to be permanent. The question was forced upon the country whether it should increase its debt or neglect its defences.

Here was the point where the theories of Mr. Hamilton and of Mr. Gallatin sharply diverged. The Federalists in a body demanded an army and navy, with an indefinite increase of debt. Mr. Gallatin and his party demanded that both army and navy should be postponed until they could be created without increase of debt. The question as a matter of statesmanship was extremely difficult. In a country like America any really efficient defence, either by land or sea, was out of the question except at an appalling cost, yet to be quite defenceless was to tempt aggression. Deeper feelings, too, were involved in the dispute. An army and a navy might be used for domestic as well as foreign purposes; to use the words of Fisher Ames in private consultation with the Secretary of the Treasury in 1800, when the situation was most critical: "a few thousand, or even a few hundred, regular troops, well officered, would give the first advantages to government in every contest;"[1] and this idea was always foremost in the minds of the extreme Federalists as it was among the extreme Republicans. To crush democracy by force was the ultimate resource of Hamilton. To crush that force was the determined intention of Jefferson.

Mr. Gallatin's policy was early, openly, and vigorously avowed and persistently maintained. In this session of 1795–96, when appropriations for finishing three frigates were demanded, he said in a few words what he continued to say to the end of his service: "I am sensible that an opinion of our strength will operate to a certain degree on other nations; but I think a real addition of strength will go farther in defending us than mere opinion. If the sums to be expended to build and maintain the frigates were applied to paying a part of our national debt, the payment would make us more respectable in the eyes of foreign nations than all the frigates we can build. To spend money unnecessarily at present will diminish our future resources, and instead of enabling us will perhaps render it more difficult for us to build a navy some years hence." "Perhaps I may be asked if we are then to be left without protection. I think there are means of protection which arise from our peculiar situation, and that we ought not to borrow institutions from other nations, for which we are not fit. If our commerce has increased, notwithstanding its want of protection; if we have a greater number of seamen than any other nation except England, this, I think, points out the way in which commerce ought to be protected. The fact is, that our only mode of warfare against European nations at sea is by putting our seamen on board privateers and covering the sea with them; these would annoy their trade and distress them more than any other mode of defence we can adopt."[2]

---

[1] Gibbs's Administrations of Washington and Adams, ii. p. 320.
[2] Annals of Congress, February 10, 1797.

Yet government has to deal with beings ruled not only by reason but by feeling, and its success depends on the degree to which it can satisfy or at least compromise between the double standard of criticism.   Mr. Gallatin habitually made too little allowance for the force and complexity of human passions and instincts. Self-contained and self-reliant himself, and, like most close reasoners, distrustful of everything that had a mere feeling for its justification, he held government down to an exact observance of rules that made no allowance for national pride. The three frigates whose construction he so pertinaciously resisted were the Constitution, the Constellation, and the United States. The time came, after Mr. Gallatin and his party had for nearly twelve years carried out their own theories with almost absolute power, when the American people, bankrupt and disgraced on land, turned with a frenzy of enthusiasm towards the three flags which these frigates were carrying on the ocean, and, with little regard to party differences, would have seen the national debt and no small part of the national life expunged rather than have parted with the glories of these ships; when the broadsides of the Constitution and United States, to use the words of George Canning in the British Parliament, "produced a sensation in England scarcely to be equalled by the most violent convulsion of nature;" and when Mr. Gallatin himself, exhausting every resource of diplomacy in half the courts of Europe, found that his country had no national dignity abroad except what these frigates had conquered.

Notwithstanding all this, and with every motive to recognize in the fullest extent the honors won by the American navy, the cool and candid decision of history should be that Mr. Gallatin was essentially in the right. A few years of care and economy were alone necessary in order to secure the certainty of national power, and that power would be so safe in its isolation as to be able to dispense with great armies and navies. The real injury suffered by Great Britain in the war of 1812 was not in the loss of half a dozen vessels of war out of her eight hundred in commission, but in the ravages of our privateers on her commercial marine. As a matter of fact the United States have continued to act on Mr. Gallatin's theory ; government has never pretended to protect the national commerce by a powerful navy; no navy, not even that of Great Britain, could protect it in case of war. That commerce has continued to flourish without such protection. Every one concedes that it would be the wildest folly even now, with forty millions of people and a continent to protect, for America to establish a proportionate navy. Every smatterer in finance knows that, inefficient as the existing navy is, hundreds of millions have been uselessly expended upon it. There could be no more instructive thesis proposed to future Secretaries of the Treasury than to ask themselves on entering into office, " What would Mr. Gallatin wish to do with the navy were he now in my place?"

But opposition to a navy was only a detail in Mr. Gallatin's theory of American finance, and his plans extended over a far wider range than could be comprehended within the limits of one or many speeches. The debate on the British treaty had, no doubt, won him a large share of attention, but the essentials of power in a deliberative body are only to be secured by labor and activity and by mastery of the business in hand. Mr. Gallatin knew perfectly well what was to be done, and lost no time in acting. Before the House had been ten days in session, on the 17th December, 1795, he brought forward a resolution for the appointment of " a committee to superintend the general operations of finance. No subject," said he, " more requires a system, and great advantages will be derived from it." This is the origin of the standing Committee of Ways and Means, the want of which hitherto he ascribed, it seems, to Mr. Hamilton's jealousy of legislative supervision. On the 21st December the resolution was adopted and a committee of fourteen appointed, Mr. William Smith, of South Carolina, being chairman, supported by Theodore Sedgwick, Madison, Gallatin, and other important members of the House.

The British treaty consumed most of this session, and until that question was settled the regular business was much neglected; but Mr. Gallatin did not wait till then in order to begin his attack. As early as April 12, 1796, a somewhat warm debate arose in the House on the subject of the debt, and he undertook, with an elaborate comparison of receipts and expenditures, to analyze the financial situation and to show that the revenue was steadily running behindhand. The true situation of the government was a point not altogether easy to ascertain. One of several English ideas adopted by Mr. Hamilton from Mr. Pitt was a sinking fund apparatus. Even at that time of Mr. Pitt's supreme authority it can hardly be conceived that any one really believed a sinking fund to be effective so long as the government's expenditure exceeded its income; it was, however, certainly the fashion to affect a belief in its efficacy at all times, and although, if Mr. Pitt and Mr. Hamilton had been pressed on the subject, they might perhaps have agreed that a sinking fund was always expensive and never efficient except when there was a surplus, they would in the end have fallen back on the theory that it inspired confidence in ultimate payment of the debt. Their opponents would not unnaturally consider it to be a mere fraud designed to cover and conceal the true situation.

Apart, however, from every question of the operation of the sinking fund, there were intrinsic difficulties in ascertaining the facts. The question was, as in such cases it is apt to be, in a great degree one of accounts. The immediate matter in dispute was a sum of $3,800,000 advanced by the bank in anticipation of revenue. Mr. Sedgwick and the Administration wished to fund it, and made considerable effort to prove that the debt would not only be unaffected thereby, but that, as a matter of fact, the debt had been diminished. Mr. Gallatin opposed the funding, and insisted that provision should be made for its payment, and he undertook to prove by a comparison of receipts and expenditures that the debt had been increased $2,800,000 down to the 1st January, 1796. It was felt to be a crucial point, and Mr. Gallatin was not allowed to go unanswered. On the last day of the session Mr. William Smith replied to him, elaborately proving that so far from there being a total increase of $5,000,000 in the debt, as he had undertaken to show, there was an actual excess of over $2,000,000 in favor of the government. To this Mr. Gallatin made an immediate reply, Mr. Smith rejoined, and the session ended.

Of course each party adhered to its own view, which was a

matter of very little consequence so long as Mr. Gallatin gained his point of fixing public attention upon the subject; his aim was to educate his own party and to plant his own principles deep in popular convictions. After the adjournment he wrote a book for this purpose called "A Sketch of the Finances of the United States," which was in fact a text-book, and answered its purpose admirably. In two hundred pages, with a few tabular statements appended, he discussed the revenues, expenditures, and debt of the United States with his usual clearness, and, while avoiding all apparent party feeling, he freely criticised the financial measures of the government. The duty of preventing increase of debt, of discharging the principal as soon as possible, was the foundation of the work; criticisms of the cases in which the burden had been unnecessarily increased were interwoven in the statement, which concluded with suggestions of additional sources of revenue.[1]

Thus already in the first year of his Congressional service Mr. Gallatin had sketched out and begun to infuse into his party those financial schemes and theories that were ultimately to be realized when they came into power. That these ideas, as forming a single complete body of finance, were essentially new, has already been remarked. In theory Mr. Hamilton also was in favor of discharging the debt, and originated the machinery for doing so; that is to say, he originated the sinking fund machinery, or rather borrowed it from Mr. Pitt, although this financial juggle has now become, both in England and America, a monument of folly rather than of wisdom; while a much more effectual step was taken in the last year of his service, when he recommended the conversion of the six per cents. into an eight per cent. annuity for twenty-three years, which was equivalent to an annual appropriation of about $800,000 a year for the payment of the principal. This, however, was not the real point of difference between the systems of Mr. Gallatin and Mr. Hamilton. Laying entirely aside the general proposition that the Hamiltonian Federalists considered a national debt as in itself a desirable institution, and conceding

---

[1] This essay is republished in his Writings, vol. iii. p. 70.

that the Federalists would themselves have ultimately reduced or discharged it, there still remains the fact that the Federalists made the debt a subordinate, Mr. Gallatin made it a paramount, consideration in politics. The one believed that if debt was not a positive good, it was a far smaller evil than the growth of French democracy; the other, that debt was the most potent source of all political evils and the most active centre of every social corruption. The Hamiltonian doctrine was that the United States should be a strong government, ready and able to maintain its dignity abroad and its authority at home by arms. Mr. Gallatin maintained that its dignity would protect itself if its resources were carefully used for self-development, while its domestic authority should rest only on consent.

Which of these views was correct is quite another matter. Certain it is that the system so long and ably maintained by Mr. Gallatin was rudely overthrown by the war of 1812, and overthrew Mr. Gallatin with it. Equally certain it is that the United States naturally and safely gravitated back to Mr. Gallatin's system after the war of 1812, and has consistently followed it to the present time. The debt has been repeatedly discharged. Neither army nor navy has been increased over the proportions fixed by Mr. Gallatin and Mr. Jefferson. Commerce protects itself not by arms nor even by the fear of arms, but by the interests it creates. America has pursued in fact an American system,—the system of Mr. Gallatin.

True it also is that this result does not settle the question as between Mr. Hamilton and Mr. Gallatin, for there were special circumstances which then made the situation exceptional. As has been said, the war of 1812 was a practical demonstration of at least the momentary failure of Mr. Gallatin's principle, and the failure occurred in dealing with precisely those difficulties which the Federalists had foreseen and tried to provide for. The question therefore recurs, whether the Federalist policy would have resulted better, and this is one of those inquiries which lose themselves in speculation. There is no answer to so large a problem.

Congress rose on the 1st June, 1796, and Mr. and Mrs. Gallatin passed the summer in New York. Meanwhile, the co-partnership in which he had engaged had resulted in establishing on

George's Creek a little settlement named New Geneva, and here were carried on various kinds of business, the most important and profitable of which was that of glass-making, begun during Mr. Gallatin's absence in the spring of 1797.

Leaving his wife in New York, Mr. Gallatin went to New Geneva for a few weeks in the autumn of 1796.

GALLATIN TO HIS WIFE.

PHILADELPHIA, 26th September, 1796.

. . . I arrived here last Saturday. . . . I have received pretty positive and certain information that Findley will be re-elected unanimously in our district, my name not being mentioned there, and that I will be superseded in Washington and Alleghany by Thomas Stokeley. This I have from Woods's friends, who seem to be equally sure that neither he nor myself are to be elected. The Republicans despair to be able to carry me, not, by the by, so much on account of the treaty question as because I do not reside in the district and have not been this summer in the western country, and they hesitate whether they will support Edgar or Brackenridge. At all events, I think I will be gently dropped without the parade of a resignation. The other party will call it a victory, but it will do neither me nor our friends any harm. I think, indeed, it will not be any disadvantage to the Republican interest that my name should be out of the way, at least for a while. . . .

SHIPPENSBURG, 3d October, 1796.

. . . The farther I go from you the more I feel how hateful absence is, and the stronger my resolution is not to be persuaded to continue in public life. Indeed, we must be settled and give up journeying. This design gives me but one regret, it is to part you and to part myself from your family; they are the only beings I will feel sorry to leave behind, but I will feel the want of them more than I can express. . . .

NEW GENEVA, 12th October, 1796.

. . . I arrived here last Friday without any accident. . . . As to politics, the four or five last newspapers are filled with the most scurrilous and abusive electioneering pieces for and against myself and Thomas Stokeley. This has raised the contention so high in the counties of Alleghany and Washington that my old friends have again taken me up very warmly, and I came too late to prevent it. There is, however, the highest probability that I will not be elected. The election took place yesterday, but we do not know the result. In this and Westmoreland County James Findlay, who was a great admirer of the treaty, has been prevailed upon by Addison & Co. to oppose William Findley, whom we have been supporting, notwithstanding all his weaknesses, because it became a treaty question, and I expect he must be elected by a majority of two to one. . . .

NEW GENEVA, 16th October, 1796.

. . . No, my Hannah, we shall not, so far as it can depend upon ourselves,—we shall not hereafter put such a distance between us. It is perfectly uncertain whether I am elected in Congress or not; but if I am, that shall not prevent the execution of our plans, and I will undoubtedly resign a seat which in every point of view is perfectly indifferent to me, and which is certainly prejudicial to my interest if it does interfere with the happiness of our lives. . . . Ambition, love of power, I never felt, and if vanity ever made one of the ingredients which impelled me to take an active part in public life, it has for many years altogether vanished away. . . .

NEW GENEVA, November 9, 1796.

. . . I will not put your patience and good nature to a much longer trial, and I know you will be glad to hear that this is the last letter I mean to write you from this place, and that next Tuesday, the 15th inst., is the day I have fixed for my departure. I have been tolerably industrious since I have been here, settling accounts, arranging some matters relative to the concerns of the copartnership, getting some essential improvements on our farm, getting rid of my tenants, and electioneering for electors of the President. Our endeavors to induce the people to turn out on that day have not been as successful as I might have wished. In this county our ticket got 406 votes, and Adams's had 66. What the general result will be you will know before I do. . . .

The Presidential election of 1796, which was to decide the succession to Washington, ended in the choice of John Adams over Thomas Jefferson and in a very evenly balanced condition of parties. The constitutional arrangement by which the President was not chosen by the people, but by electors themselves chosen by Legislatures, makes it impossible to decide where the popular majority lay; and the rule that the person having the highest number of electoral votes should be President, without regard to the intentions of the electors, at once began to throw discord into the ranks of both parties. John Adams thought with reason that he had been nearly made the victim of an intrigue to elect Thomas Pinckney; and Aaron Burr, the Republican leader in the North, as Jefferson was in the South, with equal reason believed himself to have been sacrificed as a candidate for the Vice-Presidency by the jealousy of Virginia. Both these suspicions, deeply rooted in sectional feeling, bore fruit during the next few years.

Mr. Gallatin, contrary to his expectation, was re-elected to the House of Representatives by the district which had chosen him two years before, although his long absences from the western country and his opposition to the British treaty threatened to destroy his popularity. After six weeks' absence at New Geneva during the elections, he returned to Philadelphia to take part in the coming session.

The times were stormy. President Washington, whose personal weight had thus far to a great extent overawed the opposition, was about to leave office, and his successor could hope for little personal consideration. The British treaty and the policy which dictated it had been warmly resented by France. The government of that country was in a state of wild confusion, and its acts were regulated by no steadiness of policy and by little purity of principle. Without actually declaring war, it insulted our agents and plundered our commerce. Its course was damaging in the extreme to the opposition party in America; it strengthened and consolidated the Federalists, and left the Republicans only the alternative of silence or of apology more fatal than silence. Mr. Monroe, our minister to France, recalled by President Washington for too great subservience to

French influence, adopted the course of apologizing for France, and was supported by most of his party.   Mr. Gallatin wisely preferred silence.   The economical condition of the country was equally unsatisfactory.   Speculation had exhausted itself and had broken down.   Robert Morris was one of the victims, and Mr. Gallatin began to despair of recovering his debt.   Things were in this situation when Congress met, and Gallatin, leaving his wife in New York, took his seat, December 5, 1796.

GALLATIN TO HIS WIFE.

PHILADELPHIA, 14th December, 1796.

. . . Every day in this city increases the distress for money, and you may rely upon it that the time is not far when a general and heavy shock will be felt in all the commercial cities of America.   This opinion is not grounded upon a slight or partial view of the present situation of affairs.   Many will be much injured by it, and frugality is the only remedy I see to the evil. As to ourselves, I look upon Morris's debt as being in a very precarious situation.   He has told me that he could not make any payment to me until he had satisfied the judgments against him.   We must do as well as we can, and, although I had rather it was otherwise, it is not one of those circumstances which will make me lose a single hour of rest. . . . As to politics, we are getting to-day upon the answer to the President's address.   The one reported by the committee is as poor a piece of stuff, as full of adulation and void of taste and elegance, as anything I ever saw.   The return of Greene County did not come; but Mr. Miles voted for Jefferson and Pinckney, which made the general vote what you have seen. . . .

After remaining a fortnight in Philadelphia he took leave of absence and went to New York, where he remained till the 1st January.   His eldest child, James, was born on the 18th December, 1796, a circumstance which not a little contributed to turn his attention away from politics and to disgust him with the annoying interruptions of domestic life then inseparable from a political career.   From this time forward his letters to his wife are chiefly about herself and the child, but here and there come glimpses of public characters and affairs. Party feeling was now running extremely high, and Mr. Gallatin was a party leader, thoroughly convinced of the justice of his views, smarting under bitter and often brutal attacks, which he never returned in kind, and imbued with the conviction that the intentions of a large portion of his political opponents were deeply hostile to the welfare of his country and the interests of mankind. In his letters to his wife he sometimes expresses these feelings in a personal form. It will be seen that he felt strongly; but the worst he said was mildness in comparison to what he had daily to hear.

So far as his Congressional work was concerned he confined himself closely to finance, and, although taking a very considerable share in debate, he avoided as much as possible the discussion of foreign affairs. His most strenuous efforts were devoted to cutting down the estimates, preventing an increase, and, if possible, diminishing the force of the army and navy, and insisting upon the rule of specific appropriations. He had begun to apply this rule more stringently in the appropriation bills of the preceding session, and how necessary the application was is shown by a letter now written by the Secretary of the Treasury, saying that "it is well known to have been a rule since the establishment of the government that the appropriations for the military establishment were considered as general grants of money, liable to be issued to any of the objects included under that Department." It was only with considerable difficulty that he carried this year his restriction of specific appropriations against the resistance of the Administration party.

In his efforts this year and in subsequent years to cut down appropriations for the army, navy, and civil service, he was rarely successful, and earned much ill-will as an obstructionist. Acting as he did on a view of the duties of government quite antagonistic to those of his adversaries, it was inevitable that he should arouse hostile feeling. Whether his proposed reductions were always wise or not depends of course on the correctness of his or his opponents' theories; but the point is of little importance to his character as a leader of opposition. The duty of an opposition is to compel government to prove the propriety of its measures, and Mr. Gallatin's incessant watchfulness gave the party in power a corresponding sense of responsibility.

Mr. Gallatin, too, did his utmost to carry the imposition of a direct tax, in view of the increasing burden of expenditure and of debt. The additional annual expense of $1,100,000 to be met in 1800 weighed not only on his mind but on that of Secretary Wolcott; they agreed that a direct tax was the best resource, and, unless advocated in principle at once, would stand no chance of adoption, but on this point they had both parties against them, and for the present failed.

The session of Congress ended with the 3d March, but a new session was called to meet on May 13, to consider our relations with France. Of this new Congress Mr. Madison was not a member, and Mr. Gallatin more and more assumed the leadership of the party. On questions of foreign policy he left the debate, for the most part, to others, and confined himself to limiting the appropriations and resisting all measures which directly tended to war.

GALLATIN TO HIS WIFE.

11th January, 1797.

. . . And have you really set aside a mother's partiality and then decided that our boy was a lovely child? You may rely upon it that *I* shall not appeal from your decision, whether impartial or not; but I feel every day a stronger desire to see him and to judge for myself. Yet I must not begin to fret, for fear you may catch the infection, and the 5th of March is not so far distant but what you, with the comfort you receive from your boy, and I, with my head, though not my heart, full of politics, may wait at least with resignation if not without reluctance. . . .

17th January, 1797.

. . . I pay no visits; I see nobody; I never dine out; I sit up late, and sleep regularly till nine in the morning; I hardly speak in Congress, and, when I do, a great deal worse than I used formerly; I neither write nor think, only read some miscellaneous works; I am in fact good for nothing when I am not with you. . . .

Most charming nurse of the loveliest and most thoughtful-looking babe of his age (I mean of the age he lives in), your husband is as worthless as ever. Instead of writing to you last night, he sat up two hours examining Judge Symmes's contract for lands on the Miami, which is now before Congress, and instead of devoting part of this morning to you, he remained in bed till nine o'clock, as usual, and hardly had he done breakfast, dressing, etc., when he was obliged to go to Mr. Wolcott, with whom he has been agreeably employed for more than one hour on the entertaining subject of direct taxes. . . . It seems to me that I have just now mentioned dressing. Yet it is necessary that you should know that I have not exhibited my new, or rather my only good coat, my new jacket, and my pair of black silk inexpressibles more than once, to wit, last Thursday at the President's, where I dined and saw him for the first time this year. He looked, I thought, more than usually grave, cool, and reserved. Mrs. W. inquired about you, so that you may suppose yourself still in the good graces of our most gracious queen, who, by the by, continues to be a very good-natured and amiable woman. Not so her husband, in your husband's humble opinion; but that between you and me, for I hate treason, and you know that it would be less sacrilegious to carry arms against our country than to refuse singing to the tune of the best and greatest of men. . . .

. . . Your husband was not formed for the bustles of a political life in a stormy season. Conscious of the purity of my motives and (shall I add when I write to my bosom friend?) conscious of my own strength, I may resist the tempest with becoming firmness, but happinesss dwells not there. I feel the truth of that observation more forcibly this winter than ever I did before. I feel disgusted at the mean artifices which have so long been successfully employed in order to pervert public opinion, and I anticipate with gloomy apprehension the fatal consequences to our independence as a nation and to our internal union which must follow the folly or wickedness of those who have directed

our public measures. Nor are my depressed spirits enlivened
by the pleasures of society; I can relish none at a distance from
you, and was I to continue much longer my present mode of life
I would become a secluded and morose hermit. . . . Perhaps,
however, am I myself to blame, and a more intense application
to business might have contributed to render this session less
tiresome, but . . . disgust at the symptoms of the prevailing influence of prejudice in the public mind have rendered me far
more indolent than usual. The latter part of this session will,
however, give me more employment than its beginning, as many
money questions must necessarily compel me to take an active
share. . . .

26th February, 1797.

. . . I never, I believe, write you anything about our politics
and on what takes place in Congress. But we have had nothing
very interesting, being employed only in the details of administration. And then you see the substance in the newspapers,
though not very correct, as to our speeches and debates. The
little anecdotes I reserve for the happy time when we shall meet,
and in the mean while I am sufficiently engaged in the scene
without spending the moments I correspond with you in thinking
on the dry subject. . . .

GALLATIN TO JAMES NICHOLSON.

PHILADELPHIA, 26th May, 1797.

DEAR SIR,—I received your political letter, and am not surprised at seeing your irritation upon the perusal of Mr. Adams's
speech. I have felt less because I was not much disappointed.
I mean in a pretty long letter to give you a better idea of our
present situation than you can possibly derive from a view of our
debates. These give only the *apparent* state of the business, and
at this time it is very different from the real one. For the present, as I have not time to enter into details, I will only mention
that the complexion of affairs is much less gloomy now than at
the beginning of the session, that although the other party have
rather a majority in this Congress, and although from party pride,
and indeed for the sake of supporting their party through the

United States, they may be induced to negative any proposition coming from us, yet there are but few of that party who do not feel and acknowledge in conversation the propriety of treating with France upon the terms we mention. They add, indeed, that it is necessary to obtain at the same time a compensation for the spoliations upon our trade. Upon the whole, I believe that we will not adopt a single hostile measure, and that we will evince such a spirit as will induce Mr. Adams to negotiate on the very ground we propose. I am of opinion that Wolcott, Pickering, Wm. Smith, Fisher Ames, and perhaps a few more were disposed to go to war, and had conceived hopes to overawe us by a clamor of foreign influence and to carry their own party any lengths they pleased. They are disappointed in both points, for we have assumed a higher tone than ever we did before, and their own people will not follow them the distance they expected. . . .

GALLATIN TO HIS WIFE.

PHILADELPHIA, 14th June, 1797.

. . . As to our debates, they are tedious beyond measure, and we are beating and beaten by turns, although, by the by, our defeats are usually owing to the mistakes of some of our friends, who do not always perceive the remote consequences of every object which comes under consideration. . . . Your papa has not yet answered my last political letter. I am afraid he thinks me too moderate and believes I am going to trim. But moderation and firmness have ever been and ever will be my motto. . . .

PHILADELPHIA, 19th June, 1797.

. . . I cannot yet form any very accurate opinion as to the time of our adjournment, although I think it probable that it will be some time next week. William Smith & Co. wish to detain us as long as they can, from a hope, which is not altogether groundless, that some of our members will abandon the field, return to their homes, and leave them an undisputed majority at the end of the session. My own endeavors and those of most of our friends are now applied to despatching with as little debate as possible the most important business which remains to be decided.   I brought a motion to adjourn on next Saturday, but I must modify it to this day week; whether it will pass is yet uncertain. . . . I dine next Thursday at court.   Courtland, dining there the other day, heard *her* majesty, as she was asking the names of the different members of Congress to Hindman, and being told that of some one of the aristocratic party, say, 'Ah, that is one of *our* people.'   So that she is Mrs. President not of the United States, but of a faction. . . . But it is not right.   Indeed, my beloved, you are infinitely more lovely than politics.

PHILADELPHIA, 21st June, 1797.

. . . Mr. Gerry is nominated envoy to France instead of Mr. Dana, who has declined, but it is doubtful whether the aristocratic party in Senate will appoint him.   We are very still just now waiting for European intelligence.   May it bring us the tidings of general peace!   But many doubt it. . . .

23d June, 1797.

. . . The Senate approved yesterday Mr. Gerry's nomination, with six dissentient voices, to wit, Sedgwick, Tracy, Reed, Goodhue, Ross, and Marshall.   The real reason of the opposition was that Gerry is a doubtful character, not British enough; but the ostensible pretence was that he was so obstinate that he would not make sufficient concessions. . . .

26th June, 1797.

. . . A vessel has arrived at New York, but we have not yet got the news, although I am sorry to say that from present appearances it seems to be the intention of France to prosecute the war against Great Britain.   The aristocrats here give up the point as to that kingdom, and acknowledge that she is gone beyond recovery.   The situation of their bank and finances and the mutiny of the fleet seem to have worked a rather late conviction upon their minds.   Had they been something less prejudiced in favor of the perpetual power of that country, ours would be in a better situation now.   I dined at the President. . . . Blair McClanachan dined there, and told the President that by G—— he had rather see a world annihilated than this country united with Great Britain; that there would not remain a single king in Europe within six months, &c., &c. All that in the loudest and most decisive tone. It did not look at all like Presidential conversation. . . .

28th June, 1797.

. . . Mr. Monroe arrived last night. . . . I spent two hours with him, during which he gave us (Jefferson and Burr, who is also in town) much interesting information, chiefly in relation to his own conduct and to that of the Administration respecting himself and France. It appears that he was desirous, as soon as the treaty had been concluded by Jay, that it should be communicated to him, in order that he might lay it with candor and at once before the Committee of Public Safety; and he apprehends that if that mode had been adopted, France, under the then circumstances, would have been satisfied, would have accepted some verbal explanations, and would not have taken any further steps about it.[1] But he never got the treaty until it appeared in the newspapers in August, 1795 (it was signed in November, 1794). The French government received it, of course, indirectly and without any previous preparations having been made to soften them. Yet did Mr. Monroe, unsupported by the Administration here, without having any but irritating letters to show, for seven months stop their proceedings, giving thereby full time to our Administration to send powers or any conciliatory propositions which might promote an accommodation. But the precious time was lost, and worse than lost; and it is indeed doubtful whether for a certain length of time it will be possible to make *any* accommodation. The time they chose to recall Monroe was when from his correspondence they had reason to believe that he had succeeded in allaying the resentment of the French. Then, thinking they had nothing to fear from France, and that they had used Monroe so as to obtain every service that he could render, they recalled him, with the double view of giving to another person the merit of

---

[1] This statement should be compared with Mr. Monroe's published account of this transaction (View of the Conduct of the Executive, pp. xix.–xxii.), in order to gather the sense in which Mr. Monroe probably meant it to be understood.

terminating the differences and of throwing upon him (Monroe) the blame of any that had existed before.   They were, however, deceived as to the fact, for, in spite of his honest endeavors, as soon as the final vote of the House of Representatives in favor of the treaty was known in France (and long before the letters of recall had reached that country) the die was cast.   Upon the whole, I am happy to tell you that from my conversation with Monroe, from his manner and everything about him (things which are more easily felt than expressed), I have the strongest impression upon my mind that he is possessed of integrity superior to all the attacks of malignity, and that he had conducted with irreproachable honor and the most dignified sense of duty. Sorry am I to be obliged to add that I am also pretty well convinced that the American Administration have acted with a degree of meanness only exceeded by their folly, and that they have degraded the American name throughout Europe.   If you want more politics, read Bache, where you will find a letter from Thomas Paine.   I have marked it with his name. . . . The second mutiny on board the British fleet still subsists, and is considered as being of very serious nature.   Adams says that England is done over, and I am told that France will not make peace with that country, but mean to land there.

30th June, 1797.

. . . We give to-morrow a splendid dinner to Monroe at Oeller's hotel, in order to testify our approbation of his conduct and our opinion of his integrity.   Jefferson, Judge McKean, the governor, and about fifty members of Congress will be there; for which I expect the Administration, Porcupine & Co. will soundly abuse us. . . .

Congress adjourned on July 10, and Gallatin at once went to New Geneva with his wife.

On the 20th November he was again in Philadelphia, writing to his wife at her father's in New York.

PHILADELPHIA, 1st December, 1797.

. . . Do you not admire our unanimity and good nature? Yet it is difficult to say whether it is the calm that follows or that which precedes a storm. On the subject of the address, it seems to have been agreed on all hands that something general and inoffensive was the best answer that could be given to the wise speech of our President. He was highly delighted to find that we were so polite, and in return treated us with cake and wine when we carried him the answer. . . .

19th December, 1797.

. . . Our Speaker has made Harper chairman of several committees, amongst others of that of Ways and Means, and he is as great a bungler as ever I knew, very good-hearted, and not deficient in talents, exclusively of that of speaking, which he certainly possesses to a high degree ; but his vanity destroys him. Dana is the most eloquent man in Congress. Sewall is the first man of that party ; but, upon the whole, I think this Congress weaker than the last or any former one. The other party have a small majority, and our members do not attend well as usual. Add to that that we are extremely deficient on our side in speakers. Swanwick is sick and quite cast down. I do not believe from his statement, which he has published, that he will be able to pay above twelve shillings in the pound. It is extremely unfortunate for us that he and B. McClanachan have been chosen by our party. Yet, notwithstanding all that, I think that unless the French government shall treat our commissioners very ill, this session will pass on quietly and without much mischief being done. We will attack the mint and the whole establishment of foreign ministers, and will push them extremely close on both points. Even if we do not succeed in destroying those useless expenses, we may check the increase of the evil. I have read Fauchet's pamphlet on the subject of our dispute with France. There is but one copy, which is in the hands of Administration, and I only could obtain a reading in the House. It is candid, argumentative, well written, and not in the least tainted with the fashionable French declamation. After a pretty full refutation of Pickering's arguments on many points, blaming, however, the Directory in many things, he strongly advises a reconciliation. . . .

PHILADELPHIA, 2d January, 1798.

. . . "According to custom, I have been monstrously lazy ever since I have been here, have seen nobody, not even . . . Mr. Jefferson, to whom I owe a visit this fortnight past. I mean, however, within a short time to make a powerful effort and to pay half a dozen of visits in one morning. . . . My greatest leisure time is while Congress sits, for we have nothing of any real importance before us. . . .

11th January, 1798.

. . . You wonder at our doing nothing, but you must know that, generally speaking, our government always fails by doing or attempting to do and to govern too much, and that things never go better than when we are doing very little. Upon the whole, we remain in suspense in relation to the most important subject that can attract our attention, the success of our negotiation with France, and till we know its fate we will not, I believe, enter into any business with much spirit.

19th January, 1798.

. . . Our situation grows critical; it will require great firmness to prevent this country being involved in a war should our negotiations with France meet with great delay or any serious interruption. We must expect to be branded with the usual epithets of Jacobins and tools of foreign influence. We must have fortitude enough to despise the calumnies of the war-faction and to do our duty, notwithstanding the situation in which we have been dragged by the weakness and party spirit of our Administration and by the haughtiness of France. We must preserve self-dignity, not suffer our country to be debased, and yet preserve our Constitution and our fellow-citizens from the fatal effects of war. The task is difficult, and will be impracticable unless we are supported by the body of the American people. You know that I am not deficient in political fortitude, and I feel therefore perfectly disposed to do my duty to its full extent and under every possible circumstance. We have made a violent attack upon our foreign intercourse, as it relates to the increase of ministers abroad, of ministerial influence, &c., and we have made it violent because it is of importance that we should begin to assume that high tone which we must necessarily support in case of worse news from France, and because there is no other way to make any important impression upon public opinion. . . .

30th January, 1798.

Indeed I am to blame. I should have written to you two days earlier, and it is no sufficient justification that I have been interrupted every moment I had set aside to converse with you. My mind has, it is true, been uncommonly taken up and agitated by the question now before Congress. The ground is so extensive, the views and principles of the two parties so fully displayed in the debate, so much yet remains to be said and ideas upon that subject crowd so much upon my mind, that I think it important to speak again, and feel afraid that it will not be in my power to do justice to my own feelings and to the cause in which we are engaged. The subject has the same effect upon many others; it keeps Nicholas and Dr. Jones almost in a fever, and it has actually made Brent very sick. It is not that we expect at present to carry the question; it stands so much on party grounds that we cannot expect at once to break upon their well-organized phalanx; but we must lay the foundation in the minds of the disinterested and moderate part of their own side of the House of a change as to the general policy of our affairs. We must show to the President and his counsellors that we understand fully their principles, and we must publish and expose to the people of America the true grounds upon which both parties act in and out of Congress. . . .

3d February, 1798.

. . . Although I had intended not to write till to-morrow, when I will have time to converse more amply with you, yet having a few minutes to spare this morning I thought you would be glad to hear something of myself and of our Congressional dispute which has interrupted our debates on the foreign ministers. As to myself, I am very well and feel in pretty good spirits. I have been so long used to personal abuse from party that I hardly knew I had lately received any till your letter informed me that you had felt on the occasion; but, upon the whole, that circumstance cannot make me unhappy. We have a new acquisition in our family, Mr. and Mrs. Law (she was, you know, Miss Custis), both very agreeable, and I feel quite rejoiced that there should be some female in our circle in order to soften our manners; indeed, the dispute between Griswold and Lyon shows you what asperity has taken place between members of Congress. The facts you now know from the accounts in the papers, the report of the committee, and Lyon's defence in this morning's Aurora. I must only add that there is but little delicacy in the usual conversation of most Connecticut gentlemen; that they have contracted a habit of saying very hard things, and that considering Lyon as a low-life fellow they were under no restraint in regard to him. No man can blame Lyon for having resented the insult. All must agree in reprobating the mode he selected to show his resentment, and the place where the act was committed. As two-thirds are necessary to expel, he will not, I believe, be expelled, but probably be reprimanded at the bar by the Speaker. . . .

The once famous affair of Lyon and Griswold is narrated in every history or memoir that deals with the time, and the facts are given at large in the Annals of Congress. Mr. Gallatin's comment on Connecticut manners is supported by ample evidence, among which the contemporaneous remarks of the Duc de Rochefoucauld-Liancourt may be consulted with advantage, himself one of the very few thorough gentlemen in feeling who have ever criticised America. General Samuel Smith, of Maryland, whose evidence may be supposed impartial, since his party character was at this time not strongly marked, told the story of Griswold and Lyon to the committee; after narrating a bantering conversation which had been going on in the rear of the House between Matthew Lyon, of Vermont, Roger Griswold, of Connecticut, the Speaker (Dayton, of New Jersey), and others, General Smith continued:

" Mr. Griswold had removed outside of the bar to where Mr. Lyon stood. At this time, having left my seat with intention to leave the House, I leaned on the bar next to Mr. Lyon and fronting Mr. Griswold. Mr. Lyon having observed (still directing himself to the Speaker) that could he have the same opportunity

of explanation that he had in his own district, he did not doubt
he could change the opinion of the people in Connecticut. Mr.
Griswold then said, ' If you, Mr. Lyon, should go into Connecticut, you could not change the opinion of the meanest hostler in
the State.' To which Mr. Lyon then said, ' That may be your
opinion, but I think differently, and if I was to go into Connecticut, I am sure I could produce the effect I have mentioned.'
Mr. Griswold then said, 'Colonel Lyon, when you go into Connecticut you had better take with you the wooden sword that
was attached to you at the camp at ——.'   On which Mr. Lyon
spit in Mr. Griswold's face, who coolly took his handkerchief out
of his pocket and wiped his face."

Some days afterwards, while Lyon was sitting at his desk just
before the House was called to order, Griswold walked across
the House and beat him over the head and shoulders "with all
his force" with "a large yellow hickory cane."   Lyon disengaged
himself from his desk, got hold of the Congressional tongs, and
attempted to try their power on the head of the Connecticut
member, whereupon Mr. Griswold closed with him and they both
rolled on the floor, various members pulling them apart by the
legs, while the Speaker, justly indignant, cried, " What! take
hold of a man by the legs! that is no way to take hold of him !"
Being, however, pulled apart by this irregular process, they went
on to endanger the personal safety of members by striking at
each other with sticks in the lobbies and about the House at
intervals through the day, until at last Mr. H. G. Otis succeeded
in procuring the intervention of the House to compel a suspension of hostilities.   Lyon, though a very rough specimen of
democracy, was by no means a contemptible man, and, politics
aside, showed energy and character in his subsequent career.
Mr. Griswold was one of the ablest and most prominent members
of the Federal party, and also one of the most violent in his
political orthodoxy then and afterwards.

GALLATIN TO HIS WIFE.

8th February, 1798.

. . . We are still hunting the Lyon, and it is indeed the
most unpleasant and unprofitable business that ever a respect-

able representative body did pursue. Enough on that subject, for I hear too much of it every day. . . . I am good for nothing without you. I think and I smoke and I fret and I sleep and I eat, but that is really the sum total of the enjoyments both of my body and soul. I walk not, I visit not, I read not, and, you know, alas, I write not. . . .

13th February, 1798.

. . . Are you as tired of modern Congressional debates as I am? I suspect you wish your husband had no share in them, and was in New York instead of attending the farcical exhibition which has taken place here this last week; and indeed my beloved Hannah is not mistaken. I feel as I always do when absent from her, more anxious to be with her than about anything else; but in addition to that general feeling I am really disgusted at the turn of public debates, and if nothing but such subjects was to attract our attention it must be the desire of every man of sense to be out of such a body. The affectation of delicacy, the horror expressed against illiberal imputations and vulgar language in the mouth of an Otis or a Brooks, were sufficiently ridiculous; but when I saw the most modest, the most decent, the most delicate man, I will not say in Congress, but that I ever met in private conversation, when I saw Mr. Nicholas alone dare to extenuate the indecency of the act committed by Lyon, and when I saw at the same time Colonel Parker, tremblingly alive to the least indelicate and vulgar expression of the Vermonteer, vote in favor of his expulsion, I thought the business went beyond forbearance, and the whole of the proceeding to be nothing more than an affected cant of pretended delicacy or the offspring of bitter party spirit. And after all that, the question recurs, When shall I go and visit New York? Alas, my love, I do not know it. I am bound here the slave of my constituents and the slave of my political friends. We do not know which day may bring the most important business before us. Every vote is important, and our side of the House is so extremely weak in speakers and in men of business that it is expected that at least Nicholas and myself must stay, and at all events be ready to give our support on the floor to those measures upon which the political salvation of the

Union may perhaps eventually depend. I feel it, therefore, a matter of duty now to stay. . . .

23d February, 1798.

. . . Do you want to know the fashionable news of the day? The President of the United States has written, in answer to the managers of the ball in honor of G. Washington's birthday, that he took the earliest opportunity of informing them that he *declined* going. The court is in a prodigious uproar about that important event. The ministers and their wives do not know how to act upon the occasion; the friends of the old court say it is dreadful, a monstrous insult to the late President; the officers and office-seekers try to apologize for Mr. Adams by insisting that he feels conscientious scruples against going to places of that description, but it is proven against him that he used to go when Vice-President. How they will finally settle it I do not know; but to come to my own share of the business. A most powerful battery was opened against me to induce me to go to the said ball; it would be remarked; it would look well; it would show that we democrats, and I specially, felt no reluctance in showing my respect to the person of Mr. Washington, but that our objections to levees and to birthday balls applied only to its being a Presidential, anti-republican establishment, and that we were only afraid of its being made a precedent; and then it would mortify Mr. Adams and please Mr. Washington. All those arguments will appear very weak to you when on paper, but they were urged by a fine lady, by Mrs. Law, and when supported by her handsome black eyes they appeared very formidable. Yet I resisted and came off conqueror, although I was, as a reward, to lead her in the room, to dance with her, &c.; all which, by the by, were additional reasons for my staying at home. Our club have given me great credit for my firmness, and we have agreed that two or three of us who are accustomed to go to these places, Langdon, Brent, &c., will go this time to please the Law family. . . .

27th February, 1798.

. . . We are pretty quiet at present; G. and L. business at an end. The other party found that L. could not be expelled, on account of the assault committed on him, and the question as to his first misbehavior was already decided in the negative. They concluded, therefore, not to expel G., and we generally joined them on the same principle upon which we had acted in respect to L., and we then proposed to reprimand both; but their anxiety to shelter G. from any kind of censure induced them to reject that proposal—48 to 47—through the means of the previous question. . . .

2d March, 1798.

. . . I spoke yesterday three hours and a quarter on the foreign intercourse bill, and my friends, who want the speech to be circulated, mean to have it printed in pamphlets, and have laid upon me the heavy tax of writing it. I wish you were here to assist me and correct. Alas, I wish you upon every possible account. . . .

6th March, 1798.

. . . The task imposed upon me by my friends to write my speech, of which they are going to print two thousand copies, leaves me no time to converse with you. I had rather speak forty than write one speech. I have received your letter, and will expect you anxiously; the roads are very deep, but the weather delightful. . . . You will receive by this day's post the papers containing the French intended decree. It will, I am afraid, put us in a still more critical situation. They behave still worse than I was afraid from their haughtiness they would. May God save us from a war! Adieu. . . .

13th March, 1798.

. . . I feel now as desirous that you should not be on the road during this boisterous, damp weather as I was anxious last week to see you arrived. . . . I cannot form any conjecture of the plans of our statesmen; they have got a majority, and if they are unanimous among themselves they may do what they please. So far as I can judge and hear, it seems that the other despatches of our commissioners at Paris will not be communicated to us, under the plea that they contain details which might injure their personal safety there; but it is whispered that the true reason is because their contents might injure the party, either because they declare that their powers were not sufficient, or because they intimate that France has no objection to treat with the United States, but has some personal objections to the individuals appointed for that purpose.   This last reason, if true, appears to me a very bad plea on the part of France, who have nothing to do, that I can see, with the personal character or politics of the envoys our government may think fit to appoint.   But it is perhaps apprehended by our Administration that a knowledge of the fact would injure their own character here by evincing a want of sincerity or of wisdom.   I rather think, although it is extremely doubtful, that the arming merchantmen will not take place; but it is probable that the frigates will be armed and a dozen of vessels that may carry from fourteen to twenty guns be purchased, and both placed in the hands of the President to act as convoys and to protect the coast (by coast I mean not only our harbors, but to the extent of one or two hundred miles off) against the privateers, who may be expected to come on a spring cruise to take British goods in our vessels.   All this will be very expensive, of little real utility, and may involve us still deeper.   It seems to me that it would be wiser to wait at all events, to bear with the loss of a few more captures, and to see whether peace will not be concluded this spring between France and England, an event which to me appears highly probable, and if it does not, what will be the result of the intended invasion.   May God preserve to us the blessings of peace, and may they soon be restored to all the European nations! . . .

GALLATIN TO MARIA NICHOLSON.

PHILADELPHIA, 10th July, 1798.

. . . I see the prosecutions of printers are going on.   I do not admire much the manner in which the new editor of the Time-Piece conducts his paper.   Cool discussion and fair statements of facts are the only proper modes of conveying truth and disseminating sound principles.   Let squibs and virulent paragraphs be the exclusive privilege of Fenno, Porcupine & Co., and let those papers which really are intended to support Republicanism unite candor and moderation to unconquerable firmness.   Pieces may be written in an animated style without offending decency. This is the more necessary at a time when the period of persecution is beginning, and at this peculiar crisis prudence might enforce what propriety at all times should dictate. . . .

The Time-Piece was a newspaper originally edited by Freneau, the poet, who soon associated Matthew L. Davis in the direction. After a few months of editorship, Freneau seems to have retired, and in March, 1798, Davis became the sole responsible editor. The Time-Piece was short-lived, and expired about six weeks after Mr. Gallatin's letter was written.

The speech on Foreign Intercourse, made on the 1st March, 1798, was that in which Mr. Gallatin rose to a freer and more rhetorical treatment of his subject than had yet been his custom. The motion was to cut off the appropriations for our ministers in Berlin and Holland, which would have limited our diplomatic service to Great Britain, France, and Spain. Mr. Gallatin began by proving, against the Federalist arguments, that the House might lawfully refuse appropriations, and then proceeded to attack the whole system of diplomatic connections and commercial treaties, asking whether, as a matter of fact, we had derived any commercial advantages from the commercial treaties we had made, and entering into an eloquent discussion of the dangers attending increase of executive patronage and influence. " What has become of the Cortes of Spain? Of the States-General of France? Of the Diets of Denmark? Everywhere we find the executive in the possession of legislative, of absolute powers. The glimmerings of liberty which for a moment shone in Europe were owing to the decay of the feudal system." To Mr. Bayard, who had argued that the executive was the weakest branch of the government and most in danger of encroachment, he replied: " To such doctrines avowed on this floor, to such systems as the plan of government which the late Secretary of the Treasury (Mr. Hamilton) proposed in the convention, may perhaps be ascribed that belief in a part of the community, the belief, which was yesterday represented as highly criminal, that there exists in America a monarchico-aristocratic faction who would wish to impose upon us the substance of the

British government. I have allowed myself to make this last observation only in reply to the gentleman who read the paper I alluded to.[1]   It is painful to recriminate; I wish denunciations to be avoided, and I am not in the habit of ascribing improper motives to gentlemen on the other side of the question. Never shall I erect myself into a high-priest of the Constitution, assuming the keys of political salvation and damning without mercy whosoever differs with me in opinion. But what tone is assumed to us by some gentlemen on this floor? If we complain of the prodigality of a branch of the Administration or wish to control it by refusing to appropriate all the money which is asked, we are stigmatized as disorganizers; if we oppose the growth of systems of taxation, we are charged with a design of subverting the Constitution and of making a revolution; if we attempt to check the extension of our political connections with European nations, we are branded with the epithet of Jacobins. Revolutions and Jacobinism do not flow from that line of policy we wish to see adopted. They belong, they exclusively belong to the system we resist; they are its last stage, the last page in the book of the history of governments under its influence."

The speech, which was in effect a vigorous and eloquent defence of Mr. Jefferson's Mazzei letter, although that letter was barely mentioned in its course, is probably the best ever made on the opposition side in the Federalist days, and ranks with that of Fisher Ames on the British treaty, as representing the highest point respectively attained by the representative orators of the two parties.   Doubtless Mr. Gallatin saw reason in his maturer age to modify his opinions of commercial treaties, for a large part of the twelve best years of his life was subsequently passed in negotiations for commercial treaties with England, France, and the Netherlands; possibly, too, he modified his hostility to diplomatic connections with Europe, for bitter experience taught him that too little diplomatic connection might produce worse evils than too much; but he never overcame his jealousy of executive power, and never doubted the propriety of his course in 1798.   Whether the time is to come when Mr. Gallatin's views

---

[1] Mr. Coit, of Connecticut, had read Mr. Jefferson's Mazzei letter.

in regard to the diplomatic service will be universally adopted
may remain a matter for dispute; the essential point to be remembered is that in 1798 the majority in Congress made a deliberate and persistent attempt to place extraordinary powers in
the hands of the President, with a view to the possible necessity
for the use of such powers in case of domestic difficulties then
fully expected to occur.   The extreme Federalists hoped that a
timely exercise of force on their side might decide the contest
permanently in their favor.   They were probably mistaken, for,
as their correspondence shows,[1] there never was a time when
the political formulas of Hamilton, George Cabot, Fisher Ames,
Gouverneur Morris, and Rufus Griswold could have been
applied even in New England with a chance of success; but it
is none the less certain that a small knot of such men, with no
resources other than their own energy and will, practically created
the Constitution, administered the government under it for ten
years, and at last very nearly overthrew it rather than surrender
their power.   Fisher Ames, one of their ablest chiefs, thought in
1806 that there were hardly five hundred who fully shared his
opinions.[2]   It was against the theoretical doctrines and ulterior
aims of this political school that Mr. Gallatin was now waging
active war.

The difficulties with France were on the point of a tremendous
explosion, but he avoided so far as possible every public reference
to the subject.   As a native of Geneva he had no reason to love
France.   Unfortunately, the distinction between Geneva and
France was not one to which his opponents or the public were
likely to pay attention; to them he was essentially a Frenchman,
and he could not expect to be heard with patience.   Nevertheless, he was not absolutely silent.   As the conduct of the French
Directory pushed our government nearer and nearer to war, he
recognized the fact and accepted it, but urged that if war was
necessary the House should at least avow the fact, and not be
drawn into it by the pretence that it already existed by the act

---

[1] See especially George Cabot to Pickering, 14th February, 1804. Lodge's
Cabot, p. 341.
[2] See Works of Fisher Ames, ii. 354.

of France. On the 27th March, Mr. Gallatin spoke on a resolution then before the House in committee, "that under existing circumstances it is not expedient for the United States to resort to war against the French republic," and after recapitulating the steps of both governments and the last decree of France, he said, "I differ in opinion from the gentleman last up (Mr. Sewall, of Massachusetts) that this is a declaration of war. I allow it would be justifiable cause for war for this country, and that on this account it is necessary to agree to or reject the present proposition, in order to determine the ground intended to be taken. For, though there may be justifiable cause for war, if it is not our interest to go to war the resolution will be adopted. . . . The conduct of France must tend to destroy that influence which gentlemen have so often complained of as existing in this country. Indeed, I am convinced that at the commencement of her revolution there was a great enthusiasm amongst our citizens in favor of her cause, which naturally arose from their having been engaged in a similar contest; but I believe these feelings have been greatly diminished by her late conduct towards this country. I think, therefore, that whether we engage in war or remain in a state of peace, much need not be apprehended from the influence of France in our councils."

A few days afterwards, on the 3d April, the President sent to Congress the famous X.Y.Z. despatches, which set the country in a flame, and for a time swept away all effective resistance to the war policy. These despatches were discussed by the House in secret session, and there are no letters or memoranda of Mr. Gallatin which reflect his feelings in regard to them. His policy, however, is clearly foreshadowed by his course before, as it was consistently carried out by his course after, the excitement. Believing, as he did, that America had nothing to fear but foreign war, he preferred enduring almost any injuries rather than resort to that measure. His conviction that war was the most dangerous possible course which the United States could adopt was founded on sound reason, and was in reality shared by a vast majority of his fellow-citizens, who were divided in principle rather by the question whether war could be avoided and whether resistance was not the means best calculated to prevent it. He took clear ground on this subject in a speech made on April 19 in the discussion on war measures :

"The committee is told by the gentleman from South Carolina (Mr. Harper) that if we do not resist, France will go on step by step in her course of aggressions against this country. This is mere matter of speculation. It is possible France may go on in this way. If she goes on to make war upon us, then let our vessels be used in their full power. Let us not, however, act on speculative grounds, but examine our present situation, and, if better than war, let us keep it. The committee has been told that this doctrine is a doctrine of submission. The gentleman calls war by the name of resistance, and they give the appellation of abject submission to a continuance of forbearance under our present losses and captures. I affix a different idea to the word submission. I would call it submission to purchase peace with money. I would call it submission to accept of ignominious terms of peace. I would call it submission to make any acknowledgments unworthy of an independent country. I would call it submission to give up by treaty any right which we possess. I would call it submission to recognize by treaty any claim contrary to the laws of nations. But there is a great difference between surrendering by treaty our rights and independence as a nation, and saying, 'We have met with captures and losses from the present European war ; but, as it is coming to a close, it is not our interest to enter into it, but rather to go on as we have done.' This I think would be a wise course, and extremely different from a state of submission."

For these remarks Mr. Gallatin was violently assailed, the Speaker (Dayton) leading the attack. Perhaps the sting lay, however, not so much in what the Speaker called its "tame and submissive language," as in its implied suggestion that Mr. Jay's treaty, not a merely passive attitude of protest, was the real act of submission. Whether his policy was correct or not is a matter of judgment in regard to which enough has already been said ; but there would seem to have been nothing in his language or in his sentiments that justified the savageness with which he was assailed. In truth, after the X.Y.Z. storm burst, Gallatin was left to bear its brunt alone in Congress, and the forbearance which he exercised in regard to personalities was not imitated by his opponents; Mr. R. G. Harper, then of South Carolina, Mr. H. G. Otis, of Massachusetts, and Speaker Dayton, to say nothing of the Connecticut gentlemen, were as much attached to this kind of political warfare as Mr. Gallatin was averse to it, and, the majority having now fairly settled to their side, they could afford to resort freely to the weapons of majorities everywhere. There was, too, some excuse for the violence of their attacks, for Mr. Gallatin exhibited very extraordinary powers during the remainder of this excessively difficult session. Party feeling never ran so high; he stood exposed to its full force, and by his incessant activity in opposition concentrated all its energy upon himself, until to break him down became a very desirable object, for, though always outvoted on war measures, his influence was still very troublesome to the Administration. On the 5th April of this year, Secretary Wolcott wrote to Hamilton: "The management of the Treasury becomes more and more difficult. The Legislature will not pass laws in gross. Their appropriations are minute; Gallatin, to whom they yield, is evidently intending to break down this Department by charging it with an impracticable detail."[1] Three weeks later, on the 26th April, Mr. Jefferson wrote from Washington to Mr. Madison: "The provisional army of 20,000 men will meet some difficulty. It would surely be rejected if our members were all here. Giles, Clopton, Cabell, and Nicholas have gone, and Clay goes to-morrow. . . . Parker has completely gone over to the war party. In this state of things they will carry what they please. One of the war party, in a fit of unguarded passion, declared some time ago they would pass a citizen bill, an alien bill, and a sedition bill; accordingly, some days ago Coit laid a motion on the table of the House of Representatives for modifying the citizen law. Their threats pointed at Gallatin, and it is believed they will endeavor to reach him by this bill."[2] The citizen's bill broke down so far as it was aimed at Mr. Gallatin, the Constitution standing in the way; but the feeling behind it

---

[1] Gibbs's Administrations, &c., ii. 45.
[2] Jefferson's Works, iv. 237.

was so strong that a serious attempt was made to amend the
Constitution itself. Long afterwards Mr. Gallatin recurred to
this scheme in a letter to Samuel Breck, dated 20th June, 1843.[1]
He said, in reply to an inquiry made by Mr. Breck, " I believe
the 'black cockade' of 1798 to have been worn exclusively by
members of the Federal party, but certainly not by all of them.
Many did object to such external badge; to what extent it was
adopted I really cannot say, as I have but a general and vague
recollection of that slight incident. In some other respects my
impaired memory is more retentive, and I have not forgotten
acts of kindness. Your mention of Mr. Hare reminds me, and
I do recollect with feelings of gratitude, that his father was the
principal agent in arresting in Pennsylvania an amendment to
the Constitution of the United States, proposed and adopted by
the New England States, which was personally directed against
me. And I may add that, notwithstanding the heat of party
feelings, I was always treated with personal kindness and consideration by Mr. Hare's father and by his connections,—the
Willing, Bingham, and Powell families. It is well known that
I think the general policy of the Federal party at that time to
have been erroneous; but independent of this, which is a matter
of opinion, it certainly became intoxicated. The black cockade
was a petty act of folly that did not originate with the leaders;
but they committed a series of blunders sufficient alone to have
given the ascendency to their opponents, and which at this time
appears almost incredible."

Mr. Gallatin made no blunders. He led his party into no
untenable positions. He offered no merely factious or dilatory
opposition. Beaten at one point he turned to another, accepting
the last decision as final and contesting the next step with equal
energy. The Federalists, on their part, gave him incessant occupation. Feeling that the country was with them and that for
once there was no hindrance to their giving to government all
the "energy" it required in order to accord with their theories,
the Administration party in the Legislature, without waiting even
for a request from the President, proceeded to enact bill after bill

---

[1] Gallatin's Writings, vol. ii. p. 604.

into law, conferring enlarged or doubtful powers on the Executive. Two of these, the most famous, are mentioned in Mr. Jefferson's letter above quoted,—the alien and sedition laws.

There were in fact two alien laws: one relating to alien enemies, which was permanent in its nature and applied only during periods of declared foreign war; the other relating to alien friends, and limited in operation to two years. This last was the subject of hot opposition and almost hotter advocacy. As enacted, it empowered the President, without process of law, to order out of the country any alien whatever whom " he shall judge dangerous" or " shall have reasonable grounds to suspect" to be dangerous to the public peace and safety; and in case of disobedience to the order the alien "shall, on conviction thereof, be imprisoned for a term not exceeding three years" and be denied the right to become a citizen.

The sedition law, as enacted, was also limited to two years, and expired on the 3d March, 1801. Its first section was calculated to annoy Mr. Gallatin, who had always maintained, in opposition to his opponents, that the famous Pittsburg resolutions of 1792 were not illegal, however ill-advised. These resolutions had been flung in his face during every exciting debate since he had entered Congress. The sedition law enacted, first, that any persons who " shall unlawfully combine with intent to oppose" any measure of government, or to impede the operation of any law, or to prevent any officer from doing his duty, or who shall attempt to procure any unlawful combination, shall be guilty of a misdemeanor and punished by fine and imprisonment. Whether the Pittsburg meeting came within the terms of this law was, however, a matter of mere personal interest, about which Mr. Gallatin did not trouble himself, but devoted all his labor to the second section of the bill.

This was certainly vulnerable enough. It enacted that " if any person shall write, print, utter, or publish," or aid in so doing, any scandal against the government, or either House, or the President, with intent to defame, or to excite hatred or unlawful combinations against the laws, he shall be punished by fine and imprisonment.

The alien law came first under consideration, and Mr. Gallatin took the ground that under the Constitution Congress had no power to restrain the residence of alien friends, this power being among those reserved to the States; and after arguing this point he turned to the clause in the Constitution which debarred Congress from prohibiting "the emigration *or* importation of such persons as any of the States shall think proper to admit," and maintained that this provision, so far as it related to immigrants, would be defeated by the law, which gave the President the right to remove such persons even though the States might admit them. His third position was that the law suspended the right of habeas corpus guaranteed by the Constitution except in cases of rebellion and insurrection, and that it violated the clause that "no person shall be deprived of life, liberty, or property without due process of law."

The friends of the bill, Sewall and Otis, of Massachusetts, Bayard, of Delaware, and Dana, of Connecticut, replied to the constitutional objections by deriving the authority of Congress from the power to regulate commerce; from that to lay and collect taxes, to provide for the common defence and general welfare; and ultimately from the essential right of every government to protect itself. Mr. Gallatin made a rejoinder on each of these heads, and reinforced his own arguments by attacking the alleged necessity of the measure and dwelling on the conflict it tended to excite between the general and the State governments. In the debate that followed, Mr. Harper adverted to the plot which he asserted to exist, and of which he intimated that the opposition to this bill was a part, aiming at the betrayal of the country to a French invading army. To this insinuation Mr. Gallatin replied with an exhibition of warmth quite unusual with him; he turned sharply upon Mr. Harper with the question, "Might I not, if I chose to preserve as little regard to decency as that gentleman, charge him at once with a wilful intention to break the Constitution and an actual violation of the oath he has taken to support it?" Mr. Harper's retort shows the spirit of the majority, of which he was now the acknowledged leader. He neither apologized nor disavowed: " When a gentleman, who is generally so very cool, should all at once assume such a tone of passion as to forget all decorum of language, it would seem as if the observation had been properly applied to that gentleman." Obviously Mr. Gallatin was driven to the wall; the majority had no idea of sparing him if he laid himself open to their attacks, and indeed, at this moment, to crush Mr. Gallatin would have been to crush almost the last remnant of parliamentary opposition. Mr. Jefferson has himself described the situation at this time in language which, if somewhat exaggerated, is, as regards Mr. Gallatin, essentially exact.[1] "The Federalists' usurpations and violations of the Constitution at that period, and their majority in both Houses of Congress, were so great, so decided, and so daring, that, after combating their aggressions inch by inch without being able in the least to check their career, the Republican leaders thought it would be best for them to give up their useless efforts there, go home, get into their respective Legislatures, embody whatever of resistance they could be formed into, and, if ineffectual, to perish there as in the last ditch. All therefore retired, leaving Mr. Gallatin alone in the House of Representatives and myself in the Senate, where I then presided as Vice-President. . . . No one who was not a witness to the scenes of that gloomy period can form any idea of the afflicting persecutions and personal indignities we had to brook." Then it was that the Federalist majority, on the 18th May, 1798, amended the standing rules by providing that no member should speak more than once on any question, either in the House or in committee of the whole, an amendment intended to silence Mr. Gallatin. He laughed at it, and, the House very soon becoming convinced of its uselessness, the rule was repealed.

The alien bill passed, after a warm but a short debate, by a vote of 46 to 40, and on the 5th July, ten days before the session closed, the sedition bill came down from the Senate. As the bill then stood, it contained a clause enacting that " if any person shall, by writing, printing, or speaking, threaten" an officer of the government " with any damage to his character, person, or estate," he shall be deemed guilty of a high misdemeanor and be punished by fine and imprisonment.

Edward Livingston immediately moved that the bill be re-

---

[1] Works, vol. ix. p. 507.

jected. In opposition to this motion, and in order to prove the necessity of such extravagant legislation, Mr. Allen, of Connecticut, made an elaborate speech, which is still entertaining and instructive reading. He arraigned the newspapers, and asserted that they showed the existence of a dangerous combination to overturn the government; to this combination Mr. Edward Livingston was a party, as shown by an extract from his speech on the alien bill; the New York Time-Piece was one of its organs, as shown by a tirade against the President; the Aurora, of Philadelphia, was another organ, "the great engine of all these treasonable combinations." These quotations now read tamely, and it requires a considerable exercise of the imagination to understand how America could ever have had a society to which such writings should have seemed dangerous. Mr. Harper himself, the author of "The Plot," was obliged to concede that he did not give much weight to the newspapers; in his eyes Mr. Edward Livingston was the real offender, and speeches made in that House were the real objects which the bill aimed to suppress. Mr. Livingston had in fact announced that the people would oppose and the States would not submit to the alien act, and added, in imitation of Lord Chatham's famous declaration, "They ought not to acquiesce, and I pray to God they never may." The debate went on in this style, with criminations and recriminations, until Mr. Gallatin rose. He took the ground—the only ground indeed which he could take in the present stage of the bill—that necessity alone could warrant its passage; that the proof of that necessity must be furnished by its supporters; that the proof thus far furnished was by no means sufficient; that the newspaper paragraphs cited by Mr. Allen were not of a nature to require such a measure of coercion; that the expressions used by members in debate could not be reached by the bill; that the bill itself as it then stood was in part useless, in part dependent on the proof of necessity, and had best be rejected.

The House, by a vote of 47 to 36, refused to reject the bill, but when, a few days afterwards, they entered on the discussion of its sections, even Mr. Harper took the lead in advocating considerable amendments. By his assistance and that of Mr.

Bayard the bill was remodelled, and especially a clause was inserted allowing evidence of the truth to be given in justification of the matter contained in the libel, and another giving to the jury the right to determine the law and the fact. On the bill as thus amended one day of final debate took place, closed on the part of the opposition by Mr. Gallatin, and by Mr. Harper on behalf of the majority.

Mr. Gallatin's speech as reported is quite short, and mostly devoted to the constitutionality of the measure. He first answered Mr. Otis, who had argued that Congress had the power to punish libel, because the men who framed the Constitution were familiar with the common law and had given the judiciary a common-law jurisdiction, and that this power was not taken away by the amendment to the Constitution securing the freedom of speech and of the press. The argument indeed answered itself to a great degree, for if the Federal courts had this common law jurisdiction, why enact this measure which had no other object than to confer it on them? But the courts had no such jurisdiction, and Congress had no power to give it, because it was conceded that no such power was specifically given, and yet the Constitution and the laws hitherto made in pursuance thereof had actually specified the offences for which Congress might define the punishment. They must therefore fall back on the " necessary and proper" clause; but, as this was to be used only to carry the specific powers into effect, it could not apply here: "they must show which of those constitutional powers it was which could not be carried into effect unless this law was passed;" and finally the amendment which secured the liberty of speech and of the press had been proposed and adopted precisely to guard against an apprehended perversion of this " necessary and proper" clause. This outline was filled up with concise argument, and comparatively little was said on the merits of the bill, although it was pointed out that the mere expression of an opinion was made punishable by it, and how could the truth of an opinion be proven by evidence? The writing of a paper which might be adjudged a libel was punishable, even though not communicated to any one, and this was the rule under which Sidney suffered. In Pennsylvania the marshal would summon the juries, and the marshal was the President's creature. To this and the other arguments in opposition Mr. Harper replied, and the bill then passed by a vote of 44 to 41. A week later Congress rose.

So much has already been said of this memorable session that it would utterly exhaust the patience of readers to give any completer sketch of Mr. Gallatin's activity in legislation on other subjects. His share in measures of finance and in opposition to the abrogation of the French treaties, as well as to the other war measures, may be passed over; but one word must be said on another point.

In March of this year, 1798, a bill for the erection of a government in the Mississippi Territory being before the House, Mr. Thacher, of Massachusetts, moved an amendment that would have excluded slavery forever from all the then existing territory west of Georgia. This amendment was strongly supported by Mr. Gallatin, on the ground that, if it were rejected, Congress really established slavery in that country for all time, but he found only ten members in the House to support Mr. Thacher and himself.

The session of 1798 closed on the 16th July, and Mr. Gallatin returned with his wife to New Geneva. Hard as his position was in public life, it was becoming yet more alarming in his private affairs. The joint-stock company which he had formed, and in which all his available capital was invested, had been obliged to act independently, owing to his long absences, and had been largely controlled by a Genevese named Bourdillon, a man of ability, but more fond of speculation than Mr. Gallatin ever could have been. He had adopted a system of buying and selling on credit, which he carried further than Mr. Gallatin approved, and the company had also entered into the manufacture of glass, an undertaking which promised well, but which required a considerable expenditure of borrowed money at the outset. Meanwhile, the country was still suffering from the collapse of speculation. Robert Morris was quite bankrupt, and Gallatin could recover neither land nor money. Among the Gallatin papers is an autograph which tells its own story in this relation:

DEAR SIR,—Asking you to come here is not inviting you as I wish to a pleasant place, but, as I want an opportunity of conversing with you a few minutes, I hope you will give me a call as soon as your convenience will permit.

I am your obedient servant,

ROBERT MORRIS.

Monday morning, 10th Dec., 1798.

Hon'ble ALBERT GALLATIN.

This note is endorsed in Mr. Gallatin's hand, " Written from city gaol."

To anxiety in connection with his private affairs was added a certain degree of embarrassment arising from his political situation as representative of a district which was not his residence and to which he was almost a total stranger. It is an extraordinary proof of his importance to his party that he should have been three times re-elected to Congress over all local opposition. This year he went so far as to decline a re-election, and in June sent early notice of his intention to Judge Brackenridge, in order that he might take advantage of it if he chose; but Mr. Brackenridge absolutely rejected all idea of coming forward, and united with others in urging Mr. Gallatin to remain. No steps were taken to provide a new candidate, and when, late in September, a letter was at last received from Mr. Gallatin containing the bare consent to serve if re-elected, the season was already so far advanced that a new candidate could hardly have been put in the field. In spite of his private interests and of what was more important still, the wishes of his wife, who was cruelly situated during these long separations, Mr. Gallatin was in a manner compelled to remain in public life. Beyond a doubt all his true interests lay there, and he knew it, yet these complications, resulting from the theories of his boyhood and their conflict with all the facts of his character, continued to embarrass his situation during his whole public career.

A few weeks at New Geneva were all the vacation he could obtain, and these in the turmoil of an election. The war fever against France had been employed by the Federalists to strengthen the hands of government, and no one now denies that the Federalists carried this process too far; the alien and sedition laws were unwise; the greatest of all the Federalists, next to Washington, John Marshall, of Virginia, did not hesitate to avow this opinion at the time, though at the risk of being ruled out of the party by his New England allies; but a more curious example of Federalist temper is furnished by the constitutional amendment proposed by Massachusetts:

COMMONWEALTH OF MASSACHUSETTS.

In the House of Representatives, June 28, 1798.

. . . It is the wish and opinion of this Legislature that any amendment which may be agreed upon should exclude at all events from a seat in either branch of Congress any person who shall not have been actually naturalized at the time of making this amendment, and have been admitted a citizen of the United States fourteen years at least at the time of such election.

This amendment was universally understood to be aimed at Mr. Gallatin, yet it is not easy to see how its supporters could have expected its adoption unless they looked forward to a development of party power as a result of the war fever, and a substantial eradication of the Republicans, such as would leave no bounds to their own sway. On the other hand, the Republicans were not behindhand in their acts of defence. They believed, not without ground,[1] that the Federalists aimed at a war with France and an alliance with England for the purpose of creating an army and navy to be used to check the spread of democracy in America; already the army had been voted and Hamilton had been made its commander, in fact if not in name. A collision between the two parties was imminent, and Virginia prepared for it on her side as the Federalists were doing on theirs. She armed her militia and made ready to seize the government arsenals. Her Legislature and that of Kentucky took in advance the ground that was to sustain their acts, and Mr. Madison him-

---

[1] See the letters of Wolcott to Ames, 29th December, 1799, and Ames to Wolcott, 12th January, 1800. Gibbs's Administrations, &c., ii. 313–321

self drew the famous nullification resolves of Virginia, in which he declared that Virginia was "in duty bound to interpose for arresting the progress of the evil," and did "hereby declare" the alien and sedition laws "unconstitutional *and not law, but utterly null, void, and of no force or effect.*" It is true that the words italicized were struck out by the Legislature; but the principle remained.   What Mr. Gallatin thought of these measures nowhere appears, but there is among his papers a copy of the Virginia resolutions as adopted, which was endorsed by him at a much later period : "Moved by Taylor, of Caroline.   Mr. Madison was not member of Legislature at that session.   At the ensuing session he drew the report justifying the resolutions as well as he could."   Mr. Madison continued all his life to justify these resolutions "as well as he could," but the only justification they were susceptible of receiving was one of history and not of law.   They formed a foundation for revolution, if revolution proved unavoidable.

The session of 1798–99 opened in the midst of a highly-excited political feeling.   The two parties were face to face, and the Union was in the utmost peril; all that was needed to insure collision was war with France, for in that case the repressive measures adopted or contemplated by the Hamiltonian Federalists must have been put in force, and both parties were well aware what would result.   Meanwhile, Mr. Gallatin, aided only by John Nicholas, of Virginia, carried on the opposition as he best could.   Cautious as ever, he rarely risked himself in a position he could not maintain, and his boldest sallies were apt to be made in order to cover the retreat of less cautious friends, like Edward Livingston, who were perpetually quitting the lines to fight in advance of their leader.   How Mr. Gallatin was then regarded by his party is best seen in the letters of Curtius, which had a great vogue during this winter and were reprinted in Bache's paper, afterwards the Aurora.   Their author, John Thompson, was looked upon as a most brilliant young man, and, since his age was but twenty-three, it is probable that he might have one day worked through the stilted and artificial style and thought of this early production and developed into something ripe and strong, although it must be confessed that the reader who now runs his eye over these pages of ponderous invective addressed to John Marshall is strongly inclined to smile at the expressions as well as at the thought.   At all events, they serve to show how Mr. Gallatin was regarded by at least one young Virginian of unusual promise, whose language was an echo of party feeling, however florid in expression.

"Mr. Gallatin has been persecuted with all the detestable rancor of envy and malice.   The accuracy of his information, the extent of his knowledge, the perspicuity of his style, the moderation of his temper, and the irresistible energy of his reasoning powers render him the ablest advocate that ever appeared in the cause of truth and liberty.   Patient and persevering, temperate and firm, no error escapes his vigilance, no calumny provokes his passions.   To expose the blunders and absurdities of his adversaries is the only revenge which he will condescend to take for their insolent invectives.   Serene in the midst of clamors, he exhibits the arguments of his opponents in their genuine colors, he divests them of the tinsel of declamation and the cobwebs of sophistry, he detects the most plausible errors, he exposes the most latent absurdities, he holds the mirror up to folly, and reasons upon every subject with the readiness of intuition and the certainty of demonstration.   Elevated above the intrigues of parties and the weaknesses of the passions, he is never transported into any excess by the zeal of his friends or the virulence of his enemies.   His object is the happiness of the people; his means, economy, liberty, and peace; his guide, the Constitution.   The sympathies which fascinate the heart and mislead the understanding have never allured him from the arduous pursuit of truth through her most intricate mazes. Never animated by the impetuous and turbulent feelings which agitate popular assemblies, he preserves in the midst of contending factions that coolness of temper and that accuracy of thought which philosophy has hitherto claimed as the peculiar attribute of her closest meditations.   He unites to the energy of eloquence and the confidence of integrity the precision of mathematics, the method of logic, and the treasures of experience.   His opponents slander him and admire him; they assail him with ignorant impertinence and pitiless malice, and yet they feel that he is the darling of philosophy, the apostle of truth, and the favorite votary of liberty. . . . The men who are supported by a foreign faction have the effrontery to vilify him because he is a foreigner. . . . This foreigner has defended the Constitution against the attacks of native Americans, and has displayed a noble ardor in the defence of his adopted country." . . .

Critical as the situation was, and trying to the temper and courage of a party leader, it had nevertheless some conspicuous advantages for Gallatin. He had nothing to gain by deserting his post and retiring to the safe shelter of a State Legislature. The nullification of an Act of Congress had no fascinations for him. Like other foreign-born citizens, in this respect like Mr. Hamilton himself, Gallatin felt the force of his larger allegiance to the Union more strongly than men like Jefferson and Madison, Fisher Ames or Roger Griswold, whose heartiest attachments were to their States, and who were never quite at their ease except on the soil and in the society of their birthplace. Gallatin was equally at home in Virginia, in Pennsylvania, and in New York. It is curious to observe that even in argument he rarely attempted to entrench himself behind States' rights without a perceptible betrayal of discomfort and a still more evident want of success. His triumphs must necessarily be those of a national leader upon national ground, and these triumphs were helped rather than hurt by that defection among his friends which left him to sustain the contest alone. There was no one to control his freedom of action, and there was little danger that his party would refuse to follow where he led, when they had no other leader. Moreover, even in that day, when party feeling ran higher than ever since, there was no such party tyranny as grew up afterwards in American politics. During the six turbulent years of Gallatin's Congressional service there were but two meetings of his party associates in Congress called to deliberate on their political action : the first was after the House had asserted its abstract right to decide on the propriety of making appropriations necessary to carry a treaty into effect, whether such appropriations should be made with respect to the British treaty; the other was in this year, 1798, to decide upon the course to be pursued after the hostile and scandalous conduct of the French Directory. On

both occasions the party was divided, and the minority were left
to vote as they pleased without being considered as abandoning
their party principles.[1] Under such circumstances an honest
man might belong to a party, and a leader might remain an
honest man; his action was not impeded by the dictation of a
caucus, and his personal authority and influence were irresistible.

If the discipline and unanimity of his own party were in his
favor, on the other hand the strength of his opponents was more
apparent than real. In the face of a foreign war the Federalists
were in equal peril whether they advanced or whether they receded. The Hamiltonian Federalists were ardent for war, for
an army, and for coercive measures against domestic opposition;[2]
the moderate Federalists, probably a large majority of the party
with the President at their head, would have been glad to
recede with credit. Under these circumstances Mr. Gallatin
adopted the only safe and sensible line of conduct open to
him; leaving the field of foreign relations entirely alone, and
abandoning every attempt to stand between the exasperated
majority and the corrupt French Directory, he turned his attention exclusively to domestic affairs, to the necessity for economy,
to the alien and sedition laws, and to Executive encroachments.
Within these limits he was ready and able to carry on a vigorous and effective campaign, and accordingly he reappeared at the
opening of the session of 1798–99 with as little hope of a majority
as ever, but determined to maintain his position and to assert his
strength. At the very outset this determination brought him
sharply in contact with his old antagonist, Harper, of South
Carolina, in debate on the principle of " Logan's Act," by which
it was made a high misdemeanor for any man to carry on " directly or indirectly any verbal or written correspondence or intercourse with any foreign government" or its officers with intent
to influence its measures in any dispute with the United States.
Dr. Logan, of Philadelphia, had constituted himself a negotiator
with the French nation, and his conduct gave rise to the Act.

---

[1] See Gallatin's Writings, iii. 553.

[2] See the letter of George Cabot to Wolcott of 6th October, 1798. Lodge's
Cabot, p. 168. The letter is printed in Gibbs's Administrations, &c., as of
25th October, vol. ii. p. 109.

Mr. Gallatin opposed the resolution which directed a committee to report such a bill, and he concluded a speech by threatening retaliation on those who imputed motives to him and his party after the manner which Mr. Harper greatly affected:

" I should have been glad to have avoided any insinuations of party motives; but if motions are laid upon the table to bring about again and again declamations such as have been heard, full of the grossest insinuations, all I can say is that I shall be ready to repel them. If it is the intention of gentlemen constantly to make it appear we are a divided people, I am not willing to stand mute as a mark to be shot at. I shall attack them in my turn as to their motives and principles; I will carry war into their own territory and oppose them on their own ground."

Mr. Harper responded to this challenge with a defiance that carried an innuendo with it, the meaning of which, whether public or private in its direction, was not and is not obvious:

" Whom does the gentleman expect to frighten by this menace? Let me remind him, before he begins, of an old proverb on which he will do well seriously to reflect: ' A man living in a glass house should never throw stones at his neighbors.' The gentleman's own habitation is exceedingly brittle. A small pebble will be sufficient to demolish it. Let him therefore beware how he rashly provokes a retort."

And Mr. Harper followed up this defiance by charging Mr. Gallatin himself with gross offences on the score of personality and insinuations. To this Mr. Gallatin at once replied, and his reply is characteristic:

" Notwithstanding what the gentleman from South Carolina has insinuated to the contrary, I believe it will be allowed that the manner in which I argue upon any proposition is as unexceptionable as that of any other member. It is not my custom to depart from a question under discussion; still less have I done it, and that times without number, as that gentleman has done, for the purpose of introducing declamation on the conduct and motives, not of one man, but of all who differ from him in opinion with respect to his favorite measures. By ' offensive war' I did not mean personal attack, but a retaliation of that kind of attack which the gentleman from South Carolina himself made. If that member thinks proper to misrepresent the motives of the party opposed to him, I will myself retaliate, not by personality nor by vague assertions, but by bringing forth facts to show the true motives of the party to which that gentleman belongs. As to the personal attacks which he says I have made upon him. what are they? That I charged that gentleman two years ago with not understanding the subject of revenue. Is this personality? Certainly not. How could I resist an argument on the subject of revenue, made by that gentleman, better than by showing that he does not understand the subject, if that is true? And I think, indeed, the gentleman ought to be obliged to me for having told him so; because it led him to attend to the subject, and I believe he understands it much better now than he did then. Unconscious as I am of having made any personal attack upon the gentleman from South Carolina, I shall not be deterred on a proper occasion from carrying into effect that kind of offensive war I alluded to, from that investigation of the true motives of that gentleman's party, by any threats of personal retaliation, especially from that gentleman. Of whatever materials my house may be composed, it is at least proof against any pebble which that gentleman may cast against it. I believe that both my private and political character, when compared with that of that member, are not in much danger of being hurt by any insinuations coming from that quarter."

This was perhaps the sharpest thrust that Mr. Gallatin ever allowed himself to make in debate, and its full force could only be appreciated on the spot, where both men were best known.

During the session he resumed his attacks on the navy, which it was proposed to augment by building six seventy-fours. The President in his speech and the committee in their report had dwelt upon the effect of the naval force already created, in reducing the dangers of capture and the rates of insurance. Mr. Gallatin criticised this argument at some length, and then proceeded to impress the necessity of economy, fortifying himself by a statement which showed that the expense of the permanent establishment, as it now stood, exceeded the revenue by half a million dollars, to which it was proposed to add the cost of a navy. In a second and more elaborate speech, a few days later,

he returned to the general question of the advantages of a navy
and the unsoundness of the proposition that commerce required
one for its protection, or that the commerce of any European
state had in fact been protected by her ships of war. England
alone had required a naval force for reasons which did not exist
in the United States. Commerce depended on wealth and industry, not on a navy; the expense of a naval establishment bore
with disproportionate weight on domestic industry. "We have
had no navy, no protection to our commerce. During the course
of the present war we have been plundered by both parties in a
most shameful manner. . . . Yet year after year our exports and
imports have increased in value." He then discussed the question of increasing the national burdens for the purpose of creating a navy. Mr. Harper had taken the ground that this increase
was not to be feared; that the national means increased more
rapidly than the national burdens; that we paid less taxes than
other nations and could bear an increase of them. "I am not
surprised," said Mr. Gallatin, "that we should at this time pay
less taxes than Great Britain, Holland, and France; but paying
what we do at present, if we follow their steps, as we are now
proposing to do, by building a navy and increasing our debt,
it cannot be doubted that before our system has been as long
in existence as theirs have been we shall pay as much as they
do. What do we pay now? To the general government ten
millions of dollars. How much do we pay to the State governments? How much for poor-rates, county taxes, &c.? Suppose these do not exceed two millions of dollars; that will
make twelve millions of dollars to be paid by four millions
of white people,—about three dollars a head annually. I do
not think this is a very low tax." And he closed by recurring
to his favorite proposition that the effect of a navy would be
merely to draw us into the political movement of Europe. "I
know not," said he, "whether I have heretofore been indulging
myself in a visionary dream, but I had conceived, when con-
templating the situation of America, that our distance from the
European world might have prevented our being involved in
the mischievous politics of Europe, and that we might have
lived in peace without armies and navies and without being

deeply involved in debt. It is true in this dream I had conceived it would have been our object to have become a happy and not a powerful nation, or at least no way powerful except for self-defence."

The navy having been provided for, the House fell into a dispute on the reference of certain petitions against the alien and sedition laws. Matthew Lyon, the member from Vermont, had been, during the summer, prosecuted, convicted, and imprisoned under the sedition law. There was great vehemence of feeling on both sides regarding this law, and the majority in the House were unwilling even to hear it discussed. Mr. Gallatin took the occasion to disavow all idea of encouraging resistance to it. "I do not expect the alien law to be repealed, though I have hopes that the sedition law may be repealed; and though I do not believe the alien law to be supported by the Constitution, yet I wish the people to submit to it. So far from desiring to inflame the public opinion on account of it or anything else, I would endeavor to calm the minds of the people, because I know that whenever anarchy shall be produced in any part of the country it will ruin the cause which I wish to support, and tend only to give additional power to the Executive department of the government, which, in my opinion, already possesses too much." A few days afterwards occurred the curious scene mentioned by Mr. Jefferson in his letter of 26th February, 1799, to Mr. Madison: "Yesterday witnessed a scandalous scene in the House of Representatives. It was the day for taking up the report of their committee against the alien and sedition laws, &c. They held a caucus and determined that not a word should be spoken on their side in answer to anything which should be said on the other. Gallatin took up the alien and Nicholas the sedition law; but after a little while of common silence they began to enter into loud conversations, laugh, cough, &c., so that for the last hour of these gentlemen's speaking they must have had the lungs of a vendue master to have been heard. Livingston, however, attempted to speak. But after a few sentences the Speaker called him to order and told him what he was saying was not to the question. It was impossible to proceed. The question was taken and carried in favor of the report, fifty-two to forty-eight; the real strength of the two parties is fifty-six to fifty. But two of the latter have not attended this session."

These two speeches of Mr. Gallatin and Mr. Nicholas were published in pamplet form and widely circulated. That of Mr. Gallatin was devoted to answering the report of the committee, and followed closely the arguments of that paper; he urged that the doctrine of constructive powers, on which Congress rested its belief of the necessity and propriety of this Act, " substituted in that clause of the Constitution a supposed usefulness or propriety for the necessity expressed and contemplated by the instrument, and would, in fact destroy every limitation of the powers of Congress. It will follow that instead of being bound by any positive rule laid down by their charter, the discretion of Congress, a discretion to be governed by suspicions, alarms, popular clamor, private ambition, and by the views of fluctuating factions, will justify any measure they may choose to adopt." There was no good answer to this objection, and none has ever been made, but nevertheless it is quite clear that Congress alone can decide upon the necessity and propriety of any Act intended to carry its powers into effect, and that there exists no force in the government which can control its decision. The "necessary and proper" clause, dangerous as it was and is, did not become less dangerous by the defeat of the Federalists and their expulsion from power. The time came when Mr. Gallatin and his present opponents stood in positions precisely reversed, and when he was compelled by the force of circumstances to ask for powers quite as dangerous as those he was now arguing against. Congress granted them, and he exercised them, greatly against his will and amid the denunciations of his Federalist enemies. The logic of events not infrequently proved, in Mr. Gallatin's experience, more effective than all his theoretical opinions.

Already, however, a week before this speech was delivered, an event had occurred which entirely changed the situation of affairs and made Mr. Gallatin's position comparatively easy. The President suddenly intervened between the two excited parties, and, taking the matter into his own hands, without consulting his Cabinet, without the knowledge of any of his friends, on the 19th February, 1799, sent to the Senate the nomination of William Vans Murray as minister to the French republic. This nomination fell like a thunder-bolt between the conflicting forces. At first its full consequences were not understood; only by slow degrees did it become clear that it meant the expulsion from power of the Hamiltonian wing of the party and the end of their whole system of politics. Their war with France, their army, their navy, their repressive legislation, all fell together. The immediate dangers, which had threatened civil war, disappeared. A violent schism in the Federal ranks immediately followed, and the overthrow of that party in the next election became almost inevitable.

Before these startling changes were fully understood by either party, the Fifth Congress came to its end, on the 4th March, 1799, and Mr. Gallatin at once set out for Fayette to rejoin his wife and struggle with the financial difficulties that now perplexed his mind. After long hesitation, he had taken on the part of his firm a contract for supplying arms to the State of Pennsylvania. Like most of his financial undertakings, this became a source of loss rather than of profit, and it was probably fortunate that his acceptance of the Treasury Department in 1801 obliged him to dissolve his partnership and wind up its affairs.

GALLATIN TO HIS WIFE.

PHILADELPHIA, 7th December, 1798.

. . . Once more I am fixed at Marache's, and write you from the fire-corner in my old front room. I wrote you a few lines from Lancaster, which I hope you have received. I could not make my letter any longer, and it was with difficulty I could even write at all. I arrived there after dark, mistook the tavern I intended to have lodged at, and took my lodgings at an old German Tory who happened to know me. He was a little tipsy, followed me to my room where I was writing, in order to have some political conversation with me, and was, at the time whilst I was writing my letter to you, reading me a lecture to prove to me that the Hessian fly was improperly so called, that Porcupine had proven it to be of French extraction, and that it was a just cause of war against that nation. Saturday night I lodged comfortably at Downingstown, where many kind inquiries were made about you. The weather changed during the night, and Sunday we had almost all day a cold, chilling rain. William Findley joined me in the morning at Downing's, and we made shift to go that evening as far as Buck. Monday was a fine day, and at nine o'clock I was at breakfast in Marache's parlor with Mr. Langdon, who arrived a few minutes after me. Havens joined us the same day, as did Elmendorf the following and Nicholas yesterday. Dr. Jones is not yet in town. . . . The account of my business in Europe is as followeth: 1st. They have sold my grandfather's estate and paid all his debts, which (on account of losses of rents, &c.) amounted to about 200 dollars more than what they sold the estate for. The price it sold for is less than one-half of what it was worth before the French revolution. But my orders were positive to sell and to pay all the debts, although they amounted to more than the proceeds of the estate, in order to do full honor to the memory of my parents. Thus their inheritance has cost me 200 dollars, instead of leaving me 6000 as they expected, but I could not have reconciled it to my feelings that any individual had lost a single half-penny either by me or by them. 2d. My annuities in France, amounting to about 3000 livres a year (555 dollars), have in four years produced 369 livres cash (not quite 80 dollars), and the principal, which at the beginning of the revolution was worth about 5000 dollars, has been paid off in various species of paper which are worth now exactly 300 dollars cash. 3d. My share of the Dutch inheritance consists of 15,000 guilders (6000 dollars) in the Dutch public funds, 333 pounds sterling in the English South Sea stock, and one-sixth undivided part of a sugar plantation in Surinam. The effect of the French and Dutch revolutions on the Dutch funds has been to sink them 60 per cent., so that my 6000 dollars there are worth only 2000. You may see by that that the French revolution has cost me exactly 16,000 dollars, to wit: 6000 loss on my grandfather's inheritance, 6000 on the interest and principal of my annuities in France, and 4000 on the Dutch stock. Yet the Federals call me a Frenchman, in the French interest and forsooth in the French pay. Let them clamor. I want no reward but self-approbation,—and yours, my beloved, too.

. . . On the other hand, my friends' letters are as affectionate and tender as I could expect, and more than from my long neglect I deserved. Many things for you. They say that at a former period they would have insisted on my bringing you to Europe, but think that Providence has placed us in a better situation. And so do I. . . . As to politics, you know the destruction of the French fleet in Egypt. The news of peace being made by them at Radstat with the Empire and Emperor is generally believed. That they have found it their interest to change their measures with all neutrals, and that an honorable accommodation is in the power of our Administration is, in my opinion, a certain fact. We are to have the speech only to-morrow (Saturday). I expect it will be extremely violent against an insidious enemy and a domestic faction. They (the Federals) avow a design of keeping up a standing army for *domestic* purposes, for since the French fleet is destroyed they cannot even affect to believe that there is any danger of French invasion. General Washington, Hamilton, Pinckney, are still in town. In their presence and at the table of Governor Mifflin, Hamilton declared that a standing army was necessary, that the aspect of Virginia was threatening, and that he had the most correct and authentic information that the ferment in the western counties of Pennsylvania was greater than previous to the insurrection of 1794. You know this to be an abominable lie. But I suppose that Addison & Co. have informed him that the people turning out on an election day was a symptom of insurrection. Pickering says that militia are good for nothing unless they have 50,000 men of regular troops around which to rally. When John Adams was informed that the Batavian republic had offered their mediation to accommodate the disputes between this country and France, he answered, " I do not want any mediation." . . .

14th December, 1798.

. . . The papers will show you the speech of the President more moderate than we expected. For by offering terms of peace in case France shall send an ambassador, and I believe they will do it, he has left an opening to negotiation which was not perhaps desired by all his faction. If we consider that at the same time he openly disclaims any idea of alliance with any nation, and if it is also remembered that from the wisdom of our conduct all our trade now centres in Great Britain, and that this last nation, being also now the most favored here, derives in fact greater benefit from our continuing to act in the same manner we have lately done than from our becoming actually parties to the war; it will not appear improbable that a refusal on the part of England to enter into an alliance with us except on such terms as even our Administration would not or dared not accept, is the true occasion of the apparent change. I do not enclose the debates, since Bache has reprinted them from Claypoole. We have thought better to let the answer to the address go without debate, as we mean, if possible, to avoid fighting on foreign ground. Their clamor about foreign influence is the only thing we have to fear, and on domestic affairs exclusively we must resist them. . . .

21st December, 1798.

. . . Here government proceeds slowly. We have not yet received the promised communication of French affairs; we understand that the object of the Executive party will be to obtain from us the building of six 74-gun ships and something that may increase the number of Federal volunteers and convert a greater part of the militia into an army. As to ourselves, we will avoid French questions and foreign ground, and, when our House is full, make an attempt against the sedition and alien bills. Resolutions to declare them unconstitutional, *null* and *void*, are now before the Legislature of Virginia, and will probably be carried by a large majority. The amendment to the Constitution (to exclude *me*) proposed by Massachusetts has also been recommended by the four other New England States and rejected by Maryland. It will, I believe, be recommended by Pennsylvania, as the party have got a majority in both Houses. All that is very ridiculous, for they have nothing to do with it unless two-thirds of both Houses of Congress shall *first* recommend it, and then three-fourths of the States must again take it into consideration and ratify it. I do not believe it will even be taken under consideration by Congress, and if it is, it will be rejected. Poor, weak Governor Henry recommended its adoption to the Legislature

of Maryland in his last speech.   They rejected it almost unanimously.   The poor old gentleman is since dead. . . .

4th January, 1799.

. . . Another year has revolved over our heads, and on a retrospect (how shall I ever dare to accuse you with want of fortitude
or resignation?) I mark it as one of those in which I have experienced most unhappiness.   Take notice, however, that I do
not set it down as one of those in which I have been least happy.
. . . I think that no man ever felt less uneasiness from a mere
loss of money than I do.   The folly of applying a part of our
property to the building of houses, &c., the bad sale of my lands
to Mr. Morris, the final loss of the balance of 3000 dollars he
owed me, the eventual loss of the 1000 dollars I had lent to Badollet in our company's business and which he has consumed, the
almost total destruction of what I might have called a handsome
estate, I mean my property in Europe, and I may add of my
future prospects there,—all these, although they are losses incurred since our union, have never had the least effect on my
spirits or happiness.   To be in debt was at all times viewed by
me with a kind of horror, and that feeling has become so much
the habit of my mind that it has perhaps disarmed me from that
fortitude which is necessary in order to meet any of the accidents
of life; at least I am sure that I cannot exercise it in that particular instance.   Hence the egregious folly, knowing myself as
I did, ever to have entered in business with anybody, so as to
put it in the power of any person to involve me in a situation in
which no possible consideration would have induced me voluntarily to fall.   A folly still more aggravated by the knowledge I
had that I could not personally attend myself, and that the business would be chiefly conducted by a man whose disposition and
turn of mind were unknown to me. . . . From all these considerations arises that fluctuation of mind which you cannot but have
observed in my correspondence on the subject of the contract for
arms. . . . Should I agree to that contract, and should we fail
in the execution from any accident whatever, it is a risk of
26,000 dollars, that is to say, more than we as a company, and
I as an individual, are worth. . . .

18th January, 1799.

. . . I begin to think that one of the causes of my opposition to a ' great extension of Executive power is that constitutional indolence which, notwithstanding some share of activity of mind, makes me more fit to think than to act. I believe that I am well calculated to judge and to determine what course ought to be followed either in private or public business. But I must have executive officers who will consult me and act for me. In that point of view my connection with Bourdillon was unfortunate. . . . My eyes are no better. I neither read nor write after dark, and I go to bed earlier. But every morning when I rise, almost an hour elapses before I can read without feeling something like fatigue. In the evening I might read if I chose; it is only out of caution that I have given it up. Hence I have but very little time to do anything whatever. For rising at 9, attending Congress from 11 till 3, and, it being dark almost immediately after dinner, I have literally but one hour, from 10 to 11, to read or write anything whatever. I have made this year no statement and have prepared myself for no business in Congress. As to Congress, we stand on higher ground than during last session, and can feel that a change of public opinion in the people and of confidence in the Executive party has taken place. . . .

25th January, 1799.

. . . I have this day, upon mature consideration, taken the contract for arms in my own name (this last was necessary, as the application had been made and reported upon by the quartermaster-general of Pennsylvania in my name), and have only got inserted as a proviso that I might deliver the arms either in the western country or in Philadelphia, so that if any unforeseen accident should prevent a completion of the contract at home I might be enabled to transfer it to some one person here, and not run the risk to which I had alluded in my gloomy letter to you. . . .

1st February, 1799.

. . . I have very much recovered my spirits, and feel ready to continue my exertions to extricate ourselves. I think we have well-grounded hopes to do it within a reasonable time, and your last letter on the success of the last blast, although it does not dazzle me, induces me to believe that we may not finally be losers by those glass-works which have caused me so much anxiety and have so much contributed to involving us in our difficulties. You ask, " Who *is* Curtius ?" Poor fellow ! I am afraid by this time I can only inform you who he *was*. For by the last post from Petersburg, in Virginia, we hear that he was on the point of death by a pleurisy, and no hopes left of his recovery. His name was John Thompson, his age only twenty-three, too young to be Giles's successor in the ensuing Congress, but would have undoubtedly been elected in the following one. One of the brightest geniuses of Virginia and the United States ; spoke with as much eloquence as he wrote, and remarkable for extensive information and immense assiduity. His loss will be as severe to the Republican interest as any we have yet felt. I never saw him, and he knew me only from report and from my political conduct. . . .

1st March, 1799.

. . . I have been overwhelmed with business since my last to you. I have been obliged to correct for the press two speeches on the navy, which I enclose ; you will find, however, that they are not *written* by me but by Gales, and although correct in point of sense are not so as to style. I have also written one on the subject of the alien bill, and in addition to that I have had our goods to select and sundry political meetings to attend on the subject of our next election for governor. Thos. McKean is to be our man, and James Ross the other. . . . Do you want a dish of politics till I see you ? The President nominated Mr. Murray minister to France with powers to treat, with instructions that he should not go from Holland to Paris until he should have received assurances of being met by a similar envoy ; and he sent along with it a letter from Talleyrand to the secretary of the French legation at the Hague, in which, referring to some former conversations of the secretary with Murray, he added that they would lead to a treaty, and that the French government were ready to admit any American envoy as the representative of a free, great, and independent nation. Murray, I guess, wanted to make himself a greater man than he is by going to

France and treating, and wrote privately, it is said, to the President on the subject. The President, without consulting any of his Secretaries, made the nomination. The whole party were prodigiously alarmed. Porcupine and Fenno abused the old gentleman. The nomination instead of being approved was in the Senate committed to a select committee. They then attacked so warmly the President that he sent a new nomination of Ellsworth, P. Henry, and Murray, and none of them to go until assurances are received *here* that France will appoint a similar envoy. Which will postpone the whole business six months at least. . . .

The summer and autumn of 1799 were passed at New Geneva, and when Mr. Gallatin returned to Philadelphia for the session of 1799–1800, he brought his wife with him, and they kept house in Philadelphia till the spring. There were therefore no domestic letters written during this season, and his repugnance to writing was such that even the letters he received were chiefly filled with grumbling at his silence. There seems at no time before 1800 to have been much communication by writing between Mr. Gallatin and the other Republicans. One or two unimportant letters from Edward Livingston, Matthew L. Davis, Walter Jones, or Tench Coxe, are all that remain on Mr. Gallatin's files. The long series of Mr. Jefferson's notes or letters, most carefully preserved, begin only in March, 1801. The same is true of Mr. Madison's and Mr. Monroe's. Mr. Gallatin had no large constituency of highly-educated people to correspond with him; he was greatly occupied with current business; his own State of Pennsylvania was the seat of government, and its affairs were carried on directly by word of mouth. Mr. Jefferson, the leader of the party, did attempt by correspondence and by personal influence to produce some sort of combination in its movements, but sharp experience taught him to remain as quiet as possible, and his relations were chiefly with his confidential Virginia friends. In this respect the Federalists were much better organized than their rivals.

It is unfortunate, too, that the debates of the Sixth Congress, from December, 1799, to March, 1801, should have been very poorly reported; indeed, hardly reported at all.   Yet the winter of 1799–1800 was so much less important than those which preceded and followed it, that the loss may not be very serious. The death of General Washington a few days after Congress met had a certain momentary effect in diverting the current of public thought.   The attitude of the President occupied the attention of his own party, and the probability, which approached a certainty, of peace with France, paralyzed the armaments. Mr. Gallatin himself was not disposed to press his economies too strongly.   "I was averse," he said in debate, "to the general system of hostility adopted by this country; but once adopted, it is my duty to support it until negotiation shall have restored us to our former situation or some cogent circumstances shall compel a change.   At present I think it proper that the system of hostility and resistance should continue, and I would vote against any motion to change that system.   At the same time I am of opinion that a naval establishment is too expensive for this country, but, as we have assumed an attitude of resistance, it would be wrong to change it at present."   His opinion was that a reduction should be made in the army to the extent of $2,500,000, which would, he thought, still leave a deficiency of an equal amount to be provided for by a loan.

It was in connection with this motion to reduce the army that Mr. Harper made a speech, of which the following passage is a portion:

. . . "Sir, we never need be, and I am persuaded never shall be, taxed as the English are.   A very great portion of their permanent burdens arises from the interest of a debt which the government most unwisely suffered to accumulate almost a century, without one serious effort or systematic plan for its reduction. Her present minister, at the commencement of his administration in 1783, established a permanent sinking fund, which now produces very great effects; he also introduced a maxim of infinite importance in finance which he has steadily adhered to, that whenever a new loan is made the means shall be provided not only of paying the interest but of effecting a gradual extinction of the principal.   Had these two ideas been adopted and practised upon at the beginning of the century which we have' just seen close, England might have expended as much money as she has expended and not owed at this moment a shilling of debt, except that contracted in the present war. These ideas, profiting by the example of England, we have adopted and are now practising on. We have provided a fund which is now in constant operation for the extinguishment of our debt. This fund will extinguish the foreign debt in nine years from now, and the six per cent., a large part of our domestic debt, in eighteen years. I trust we shall adhere to this plan, and whenever we are compelled by the exigency of our affairs to make a loan, by providing also for its timely extinguishment, we may always avoid an inconvenient or burdensome accumulation of debt. We may gather all the roses of the funding system without its thorns."

This was the theory of the English financiers, of William Pitt and his scholars, which held possession of the English exchequer throughout the French war and was only exploded in 1813 by a pamphlet written by a Scotchman named Hamilton.[1] Mr. Gallatin, however, was never its dupe. He answered Mr. Harper on the spot; and short as his reply was, it gave in perfectly clear language the substance of all that fourteen years later was supposed to be a new discovery in English finance:

. . . "I know but one way that a nation has of paying her debts, and that is precisely the same which individuals practise. 'Spend *less* than you receive,' and you may then apply the surplus of your receipts to the discharge of your debts. But if you spend *more* than you receive, you may have recourse to sinking funds, you may modify them as you please, you may render your accounts extremely complex, you may give a scientific appearance to additions and subtractions, you must still necessarily increase your debt. If you spend more than you receive, the difference must be supplied by loans; and if out of these receipts you have set a sum apart to pay your debts, if you have so mortgaged or disposed of that sum that you cannot apply it to your

---

[1] Inquiry concerning the Rise and Progress, the Redemption and Present State, and the Management of the National Debt of Great Britain. By Robert Hamilton, LL.D. Edinburgh, 1813. Reprinted at Philadelphia in 1816, and by Lord Overstone in his collection of Financial Tracts, 1856–1859.

useful expenditure, you must borrow so much more in order to meet your expenditure. If your revenue is nine millions of dollars and your expenditure fourteen, you must borrow, you must create a new debt of five millions. But if two millions of that revenue are, under the name of sinking fund, applicable to the payment of the principal of an old debt, and pledged for it, then the portion of your revenue applicable to discharging your current expenditures of fourteen millions is reduced to seven millions; and instead of borrowing five millions you must borrow seven; you create a new debt of seven millions, and you pay an old debt of two. It is still the same increase of five millions of debt. The only difference that is produced arises from the relative price you give for the old debt and rate of interest you pay for the new. At present we pay yearly a part of a domestic debt bearing six per cent. interest, and of a foreign debt bearing four or five per cent. interest; and we may pay both of them at par. At the same time we are obliged to borrow at the rate of eight per cent. At present, therefore, that nominal sinking fund increases our debt, or at least the annual interest payable on our debt." . . .

The two speeches made by Mr. Harper and Mr. Gallatin on this occasion, the 10th January, 1800, were very able, and are even now interesting reading; but they find their proper place in the Annals of Congress, and the question of the reduction of the army was to be settled by other events. A matter of a very different nature absorbed the attention of Congress during the months of February and March. This was the once famous case of Jonathan Robbins, a British sailor claiming to be an American citizen, who, having committed a murder on board the British ship-of-war Hermione, on the high seas, had escaped to Charleston, and under the 27th article of the British treaty had been delivered up by the United States government. At that time extradition was a novelty in our international relations. The President was violently attacked for the surrender, and a long debate ensued in Congress. Mr. Gallatin spoke at considerable length, but his speech is not reported, and although voluminous notes, made by him in preparing it, are among his papers, it is impossible to say what portion of these notes was actually used in the speech. The triumphs of the contest, however, did not fall to him or to his associates, but to John Marshall, who followed him, and who, in a speech that still stands without a parallel in our Congressional debates, replied to him and to them. There is a tradition in Virginia that after Marshall concluded his speech, the Republican members pressed round Gallatin, urging with great earnestness that it should be answered at once, and that Gallatin replied in his foreign accent, "Gentlemen, answer it yourselves; for my part I think it unanswerable," laying the stress on the antepenultimate syllable. The story is probably true. At all events, Mr. Gallatin made no answer, and Mr. Marshall's argument settled the dispute by an overwhelming vote.

But the coming Presidential election, one of the most interesting in our history, now cast its shadow in advance over the whole political field. The two parties were so equally divided that the vote of New York City would probably decide the result, and for this reason the city election of May, 1800, was the turning-point of American political history in that generation. There the two party champions, Hamilton and Burr, were pitted against each other. Commodore Nicholson was hotly engaged, and Edward Livingston, Matthew L. Davis, and the other Republican politicians of New York became persons of uncommon interest. Mr. Gallatin, as leader of the Republican party in Congress and as closely connected by marriage with the Republican interests of New York City, was kept accurately informed of every step in the political campaign. He himself was in constant communication with Matthew L. Davis, who was Burr's most active friend then and ever afterwards. Davis's letters are now of historical importance, and may be compared with the narrative in his subsequent Life of Burr:

MATTHEW L. DAVIS TO GALLATIN.

NEW YORK, March 29, 1800.

DEAR SIR,—I yesterday saw a family letter of yours developing the views of the Federal party; with many of the facts contained in that letter I was previously acquainted, but I was in some measure at a loss to account for certain proceedings of the supreme Legislature; this letter completely unmasks the party. Your opinion respecting the importance of our election for members of Assembly in this city is the prevailing opinion among our Republican friends. You ask, "What are your prospects?" All things considered, they are favorable. We have been so much deceived already that a prudent man perhaps will not hazard an opinion but with extreme diffidence. At the request of Mr. Nicholson, I shall briefly state the leading features of our plan.

You are already acquainted with the circumstances which so much operated against us at the last election: the tale of the ship Ocean, Captain Kemp; the Manhattan Company; the contemplated French invasion; the youth of many of our candidates, &c., &c. These things, united with bank influence and bank jealousy, had a most astonishing effect. The bank influence is now totally destroyed; the Manhattan Company will in all probability operate much in our favor; and it is hoped the crew of the Ocean will not *again* be murdered; but this is not all: a variety of trifling acts passed during the session of the former Legislature were also brought forward and adapted to the purposes of the party. Menaces from the Federal party had also a great influence. I think they will not dare to use them at the approaching election.

The Federalists have had a meeting and determined on their Senators; they have also appointed a committee to nominate suitable characters for the Assembly. Out of the thirteen that now represent the city, eleven decline standing again. They are much perplexed to find men. Mr. Hamilton is very busy, more so than usual, and no exertions will be wanting on his part. Fortunately, Mr. Hamilton will have at this election a most powerful opponent in Colonel Burr. This gentleman is extremely active; it is his opinion that the Republicans had better not publish a ticket or call a meeting until the Federalists have completed theirs. Mr. Burr is arranging matters in such a way as to bring into operation all the Republican interest. He is not to be on our nomination, but is to represent one of the country counties. At our first meeting he has pledged himself to come forward and address the people in firm and manly language on the importance of the election and the momentous crisis at which we have arrived. This he has never done at any former election, and I anticipate great advantages from the effect it will produce.

In addition to this, he has taken great trouble to ascertain what characters will be most likely to run well, and by his address has procured the assent of eleven or twelve of our most influential friends to stand as candidates. Among the number are:

George Clinton (late governor).	Philip J. Arcularius.
Henry Rutgers (colonel).	Thos. Storm.
Sam. Osgood.	Ezek. Robbins.
Jno. Broome.	Sam. L. Mitchill.
Geo. Warner, Sen.	Jno. Swartwout.
Elias Nexsen.	

On the whole, I believe we shall offer to our fellow-citizens the most formidable list ever offered them by any party in point of morality, public and private virtue, local and general influence, &c., &c. From this ticket and the exertions that indisputably will be made we have a right to expect much, and I trust we shall be triumphant. If we carry this election, it may be ascribed principally to Colonel Burr's management and perseverance. Hamilton fears his influence; the party seem in a state of consternation, while ours possess more than usual spirits. Such are our prospects. We shall open the campaign under the most favorable impressions, and headed by a man whose intrigue and management is most astonishing, and who is more dreaded by his enemies than any other character in our [   ]. Excuse, sir, this hasty scrawl; I have no time to copy. . . .

MATTHEW L. DAVIS TO GALLATIN.

New York, April 15, 1800.
Tuesday night, 11 o'clock.

DEAR SIR,—Well knowing the importance of the approaching election in this city, and consequently the anxiety which you and every friend to our country must experience on the subject, I am highly gratified in affording you such information on the occasion as will be interesting and pleasing. The eyes of our friends and of our enemies are turned towards us; all unite in the opinion that if the city and county of New York elect Republicans they will most assuredly have it in their power to appoint Republican electors for President and Vice-President. The counties of Westchester and Orange have selected the most respectable and influential advocates for the rights of the people their respective towns afforded. But of our adversaries in this city. This evening, agreeably to public notice, a meeting was held; the assembly was small, and not attended by either Colonels Hamilton or Troup, two gentlemen who are generally most officious on these occasions. I have already stated to you in a former letter that jealousies and schisms existed among them. This fact has not only been evinced in their numerous caucuses, but they have been doomed to the mortification of bringing the matter this night before the public. A few of their most active men had determined on Philip Brazier as a candidate for the Assembly. Mr. Brazier is a man of very little influence and very limited understanding; he is, however, a Republican, but composed of such pliable materials as will enable his leaders to mould him to almost any form. A large majority of the Federal committee were opposed to him, but his adherents possessing stronger lungs and being vociferous at one of their caucuses, he was carried.

A division took place in the same committee on another subject, viz., who was the most proper candidate for Congress. Some supported Colonel J. Morton, while others as furiously supported William W. Woolsey; both gentlemen consented to stand; as the committee could not agree owing to their divisions, it was resolved to report both candidates to the meeting and let them make their election. Accordingly the two names were publicly brought forward this night, and after much confusion and litigation it was determined by a majority of only 15 or 20 that Jacob Morton should be the candidate for Congress, while the adherents of Mr. Woolsey bawled aloud, "Morton shall not be the man." Next came the Assembly ticket. It was agreed to without opposition, excepting in the case of Mr. Brazier. He was again violently opposed, and a large majority appeared against him; yet the chairman being a military commander (Brigadier-General Jared Hughes), he decided that it was carried in favor of Mr. Brazier. In this temper the meeting separated. So much for the friends of good order and regular government.

FEDERAL TICKET.

For Congress.

Jacob Morton, Esq

For Assemblymen.

Peter Schermerhorn, ship-chandler.

Jno. Bogert, baker.

Gabriel Furman, nothing. The man who whipped the ferryman in Bridewell, and on account of whom Kettletas was imprisoned.

John Croleus, Jun., potter.

Philip Ten Eyck, bookseller, late clerk, present partner of Hugh Gaine.

Isaac Burr, grocer.

Samuel Ward, a bankrupt endeavoring to settle his affairs by paying 000 in the pound.

C. D. Colden, assistant attorney-general.

James Tyler, shoemaker.

Philip Brazier, lawyer.

N. Evertson, lawyer.

Isaac Sebring, grocer, one of the firm Sebring & Van Wyck.

Abraham Russel, mason.

A private meeting of our friends was held this evening at the house of Mr. Brockholst Livingston; about forty attended; we determined on calling the Republicans together on Thursday evening next, and for that purpose sent advertisements to the different printers. The prevailing opinion was that we should appoint a committee at that meeting to withdraw for half an hour, form a ticket, and return and report, so that on Friday morning we shall most probably publish. Never have I observed such an union of sentiment, so much zeal, and so general a determination to be active. Indeed, on presenting the Federal ticket to our meeting (for we had friends who attended theirs) all was joy and enthusiasm. Our ticket is complete, and stands as follows:

Congress.

Dr. Samuel L. Mitchill.

Assembly.

Geo. Clinton.
Horatio Gates.
Henry Rutgers.
Thomas Storm.
Samuel Osgood.
Geo. Warner, Senior.
John Broome.
Philip J. Arcularius.
Ezekiel Robins.
Brockholst Livingston.
John Swartwout.
James Hunt.
Elias Nexsen.

The late hour at which I write this will be a sufficient apology for the scrawl. . . .

MATTHEW L. DAVIS TO GALLATIN.

Thursday night, 12 o'clock.
May 1, 1800.

REPUBLICANISM TRIUMPHANT.

DEAR SIR,—It affords me the highest gratification to assure you of the complete success of the Republican Assembly ticket in this city. This day the election closed, and several of the wards have been canvassed for Congress; the result as follows:

	For Mitchill.	For Morton.
First Ward, majority,	...	76
Second do., do.,	...	258
Third do., not canvassed.		
Probable majority,	...	250
Fourth do., canvassed majority,	72	...
Fifth do., not canvassed.		
Probable majority,	100	...
Sixth do., canvassed majority,	432	...
	604	584

Seventh do. do. do.

For Van Cortlandt, 312.

Thus, sir, it is probable Mr. Mitchill is elected a member of Congress, and no doubt can remain but our whole Assembly ticket is elected by a majority of three hundred and fifty votes. To Colonel Burr we are indebted for everything. This day has he remained at the poll of the Seventh Ward ten hours without intermission. Pardon this hasty scrawl; I have not ate for fifteen hours.

With the highest respect, &c.

P.S.—Since writing the above I learn from undoubted authority that Mr. Mitchill is elected by upwards of one hundred majority.

MATTHEW L. DAVIS TO GALLATIN.

NEW YORK, May 5, 1800.

DEAR SIR,—I have already informed you of the complete triumph which we have obtained in this city,—a triumph which I trust will have some influence in promoting the rights of the people and establishing their liberties on a permanent basis. Our country has arrived at an awful crisis. The approaching election for President and Vice-President will decide in some measure on our future destiny. The result will clearly evince whether a republican form of government is worth contending for. On this account the eyes of all America have been turned towards

the city and county of New York.   The management and industry of Colonel Burr has effected all that the friends of civil
liberty could possibly desire.

Having accomplished the task assigned us, we in return feel
a degree of anxiety as to the characters who will probably be
candidates for those two important offices.   I believe it is pretty
generally understood that Mr. Jefferson is contemplated for
President.   But who is to fill the Vice-President's chair?   I
should be highly gratified in hearing your opinion on this subject; if secrecy is necessary, you may rely on it; and, sir, as I
have no personal views, you will readily excuse my stating the
present apparent wishes and feelings of the Republican party in
this city.

It is generally expected that the Vice-President will be selected from the State of New York.   Three characters only can
be contemplated, viz., Geo. Clinton, Chancellor Livingston, and
Colonel Burr.

The first seems averse to public life, and is desirous of retiring
from all its cares and toils.   It was therefore with great difficulty he was persuaded to stand as candidate for the State Legislature.   A personal interview at some future period will make
you better acquainted with this transaction.   In addition to this,
Mr. Clinton grows old and infirm.

To Mr. Livingston there are objections more weighty.   The
family attachment and connection; the prejudices which exist
not only in this State, but throughout the United States, against
the name; but, above all, the doubts which are entertained of
his firmness and decision in trying periods.   You are well acquainted with certain circumstances that occurred on the important question of carrying the British treaty into effect.   On
that occasion Mr. L. exhibited a timidity that never can be
forgotten.   Indeed, it had its effect when he was a candidate for
governor, though it was not generally known.

Colonel Burr is therefore the most eligible character, and on
him the eyes of our friends in this State are fixed as if by sympathy for that office.   Whether he would consent to stand I am
totally ignorant, and indeed I pretend not to judge of the policy
farther than it respects this State.   If he is elected to the office

of V. P., it would awaken so much of the zeal and pride of our friends in this State as to secure us a Republican governor at the next election (April, 1801). If he is not nominated, many of us will experience much chagrin and disappointment. If, sir, you do not consider it improper, please inform me by post the probable arrangement on this subject. I feel very anxious. Any information you may wish relative to our election I will at all times cheerfully communicate.

With sentiments of respect, &c.

GALLATIN TO HIS WIFE.

PHILADELPHIA, 6th May, 1800.

. . . The New York election has engrossed the whole attention of all of us, meaning by us Congress and the whole city. Exultation on our side is high; the other party are in low spirits. Senate could not do any business on Saturday morning when the intelligence was received, and adjourned before twelve. As to the probabilities of election, they stand as followeth:

	Adams.	Doubtful.	Jefferson.
New Hampshire	6	...	...
Massachusetts	14	2	...
Connecticut	9	...	...
Rhode Island	4	...	...
Vermont	4	...	...
New York	...	...	12
New Jersey	...	7	...
Pennsylvania	...	...	...
Delaware	...	3	...
Maryland	3	5	2
Virginia	...	...	21
Kentucky	...	...	4
N. Carolina	2	4	6
S. Carolina	...	...	8
Tennessee	...	...	3
Georgia	...	...	4
	42	21	60

There are 123 electors, supposing Pennsylvania to have no vote. Of these, 62 make a majority. We count 60 for Jefferson certain. If we therefore get only 2 out of the 21 doubtful votes, he must be elected. Probabilities are therefore highly in our favor. Last Saturday evening the Federal members of Congress had a large meeting, in which it was agreed that there was no chance of carrying Mr. Adams, but that he must still be supported ostensibly in order to carry still the votes in New England, but that the only chance was to take up ostensibly as Vice-President, but really as President, a man from South Carolina, who, being carried everywhere except in his own State along with Adams, and getting the votes of his own State with Jefferson, would then be elected. And for that purpose, abandoning Thomas Pinckney, they have selected General Charles Cotesworth Pinckney. I think they will succeed neither in S. Carolina in getting the votes for him, nor in New England in making the people jilt Adams. Who is to be our Vice-President, Clinton or Burr? This is a serious question which I am delegated to make, and to which I must have an answer by Friday next. Remember this is important, and I have engaged to procure correct information of the wishes of the New York Republicans. . . .

JAMES NICHOLSON TO GALLATIN.

May 6, 1800.

DEAR SIR,—My situation and health did not permit my writing you during our election, but supposed you received information from Mr. Warner, who I requested would take the task off my hands. That business has been conducted and brought to issue in so miraculous a manner that I cannot account for it but from the intervention of a Supreme Power and our friend Burr the agent. The particulars I have since the election understood, and which justifies my suspicion. His generalship, perseverance, industry, and execution exceeds all description, so that I think I can say he deserves anything and everything of his country; but he has done it at the risk of his life. This I will explain to you when I have the pleasure of seeing you. I am informed he is coming on to you. Perhaps

he will be the bearer of this. I shall conclude by recommending him as a general far superior to your Hambletons ;[1] as much
so as a man is to a boy ; and I have but little doubt this State,
through his means and planning, will be as Republican in the
appointment of electors as the State of Virginia.

I have not been able since my being here before to-day to
visit my friend and neighbor, Governor Clinton. I understand
his health and spirits are both returning. His name at the head
of our ticket had a most powerful effect. I cannot inform you
what either Burr's or his expectations are, but will write you
more particularly about the governor after my visit. . . .

JAMES NICHOLSON TO GALLATIN.

GREENWICH LANE, May the 7th, 1800.

DEAR SIR,—I have conversed with the two gentlemen mentioned in your letter. George Clinton, with whom I first spoke,
declined. His age, his infirmities, his habits and attachment to
retired life, in his opinion, exempt him from active life. He
(Governor Clinton) thinks Colonel Burr is the most suitable
person and perhaps the only man. Such is also the opinion of
all the Republicans in this quarter that I have conversed with ;
their confidence in A. B. is universal and unbounded. Mr. Burr,
however, appeared averse to be the candidate. He seemed to
think that no arrangement could be made which would be
observed to the southward ; alluding, as I understood, to the
last election, in which he was certainly ill used by Virginia and
North Carolina.

I believe he may be induced to stand if assurances can be
given that the Southern States will act fairly.

Colonel Burr may certainly be governor of this State at the
next election if he pleases, and a number of his friends are very
unwilling that he should be taken off for Vice-President, thinking the other the most important office. Upon the whole, however, we think he ought to be the man for V. P., if there is a
moral certainty of success. But his name must not be played
the fool with. I confidently hope you will be able to smooth

---

[1] Sic.

over the business of the last election, and if Colonel Burr is
properly applied to, I think he will be induced to stand.　At
any rate we, the Republicans, will make him.

MRS. GALLATIN TO HER HUSBAND.

7th May, 1800.

. . . Papa has answered your question about the candidate
for Vice-President.　Burr says he has no confidence in the
Virginians; they once deceived him, and they are not to be
trusted. . . .

GALLATIN TO HIS WIFE.

12th May, 1800.

. . . We do not adjourn to-day, but certainly shall to-morrow.
. . . We had last night a very large meeting of Republicans,
in which it was unanimously agreed to support Burr for Vice-
President. . . .

Between the adjournment of Congress in May and his departure for the western country in July, Mr. Gallatin prepared and
published another pamphlet on the national finances, which was
his contribution to the canvass for the Presidential election of that
year.　Mr. Wolcott, the Secretary of the Treasury, in a letter to
the Committee of Ways and Means, dated January 22, 1800,
had expressed the opinion that the principal of the debt had increased $1,516,338 since the establishment of the government in
1789.　A committee of the House, on the other hand, had on
May 8 reported that the debt had been diminished $1,092,841
during the same period.　Mr. Gallatin entered into a critical examination of the methods by which these results were obtained,
and then proceeded to test them by applying his own method of
comparing the receipts and expenditures.　His conclusion was
that the nominal debt had been increased by $9,462,264.　Two
millions of this increase, however, was caused by unnecessary
assumption of State debts.　But allowing for funds actually acquired by government and susceptible of being applied to reduction of debt, the nominal increase reduced itself to $6,657,319.

And since all these results were more or less nominal, he devoted the larger part of his work to an elaborate and searching investigation into the actual receipts and expenditures of the past ten years.

The summer of 1800 was again passed in the western country ; the last summer which Mr. Gallatin was to pass there for more than twenty years. With the autumn came the Presidential election, and the dreaded complication occurred by which Mr. Jefferson and Mr. Burr, having received an equal number of electoral votes, became rival candidates for the choice of the House of Representatives. The session of 1800–1801 was almost wholly occupied in settling this dispute. The whole Federalist party insisted upon voting for Burr, and, although not able to elect him, they were able to delay for several days the election of Mr. Jefferson. Mr. Gallatin's position as leader of the Republicans in the House, and in a manner responsible for the selection of Mr. Burr as candidate for the Vice-Presidency, was one of controlling influence and authority. His letters to his wife give a clear picture of the scene at Washington as he saw it from day to day, but there are one or two points on which some further light is thrown by his papers.

He rarely expressed his opinions of the men with whom he acted. He never expressed any opinion about Colonel Burr. Yet he knew that the Virginians distrusted Burr, and even in his own family, where Colonel Burr was probably warmly admired, there were moments when their faith was shaken. The following letter is an example:

MARIA NICHOLSON TO MRS. GALLATIN.

New York, February 5, 1801.

. . . As I know you are interested for Theodosia Burr, I must tell you that Mr. Alston has returned from Carolina, it is said, to be married to her this month. She accompanied her father to Albany, where the Legislature are sitting ; he followed them the next day. I am sorry to hear these accounts. Report does not speak well of him ; it says that he is rich, but he is a great dasher, dissipated, ill-tempered, vain, and silly.

I know that he is ugly and of unprepossessing manners.   Can it be that the father has sacrificed a daughter so lovely to affluence and influential connections?   They say that it was Mr. A. who gained him the 8 votes in Carolina at the present election, and that he is not yet relieved from pecuniary embarrassments.   Is this the man, think ye?   Has Mr. G. a favorable opinion of this man of talents, or not?   He loves his child. Is he so devoted to the customs of the world as to encourage such a match? . . .

Colonel Burr himself overacted his part.   For some private reason Mr. Gallatin was unable to take his seat when Congress met, and it was not till January 12, 1801, that he at last appeared in Washington, to which place the government had been transferred during the summer.   The contest, which was to decide the election, took place a month later.   Colonel Burr was at New York, about to go up to Albany to perform his duties as member of the Legislature.   He felt the necessity of reassuring the minds of his friends at Washington, and he did so from time to time with a degree of off-hand simplicity very suggestive of ulterior thoughts.   His first letter to Gallatin is as follows:

AARON BURR TO GALLATIN.

NEW YORK, 16th January, 1801.

DEAR SIR,—I am heartily glad of your arrival at your post. You were never more wanted, for it was absolutely vacant.

Livingston will tell you my sentiments on the proposed usurpation, and indeed of all the other occurrences and projects of the day.

The short letter of business which I wrote you may be answered to Dallas; anything you may wish to communicate to me may be addressed this city.   Our postmaster and that at Albany are "honorable men."

Yours, A. B.

The next is written from Albany, in reply to a letter from Mr. Gallatin, which has not been preserved:

AARON BURR TO GALLATIN.

ALBANY, 12th February, 1801.

DEAR SIR,—My letters for ten days past had assured me that all was settled and that no doubt remained but that J. would have 10 or 11 votes on the first trial; I am, therefore, utterly surprised by the contents of yours of the 3d. In case of usurpation, by law, by President of Senate pro tem., or in any other way, my opinion is definitively made up, and it is known to S. S. and E. L. On that opinion I shall act in defiance of all timid, temporizing projects.

On the 21st I shall be in New York, and in Washington the 3d March at the utmost; sooner if the intelligence which I may receive at New York shall be such as to require my earlier presence.

Mr. Montfort was strongly recommended to me by General Gates and Colonel Griffin. At their request I undertook to direct his studies in pursuit of the law. He left New York suddenly and apparently in some agitation, without assigning to me any cause and without disclosing to me his intentions or views, or even whither he was going, except that he proposed to pass through Washington. Nor had I any reason to believe that I should ever see him again. You may communicate this to Mr. J., who has also written me something about him.

Yours, A. B.

Mr. Gallatin in the last years of his life came upon this letter, and endorsed on it, in a hand trembling with age, the following words with a significant mark of interrogation:

"had thought that Jefferson would be elected on first ballot by 10 or 11 votes (out of 16)?"

Burr's last letter in this connection was written from Philadelphia after the result was decided:

BURR TO GALLATIN.

PHILADELPHIA, February 25, 1801.

DEAR SIR,—The four last letters of your very amusing history of balloting met me at New York on Saturday evening. I thank you much for the obliging attention, and I join my hearty congratulations on the auspicious events of the 17th. As to the infamous slanders which have been so industriously circulated, they are now of little consequence, and those who have believed them will doubtless blush at their own weakness.

The Feds boast aloud that they have compromised with Jefferson, particularly as to the retaining certain persons in office. Without the assurance contained in your letter, this would gain no manner of credit with me. Yet in spite of my endeavors it has excited some anxiety among our friends in New York. I hope to be with you on the 1st or 2d March.

Adieu.

These letters from Mr. Burr suggest much more than they intentionally express; for if they show that Burr still felt the weight of that Virginia mistrust which had four years previously cost him his place as next in succession to Mr. Jefferson, they show, too, that his confidence in Virginia was scarcely greater than when in May, 1800, he told Commodore Nicholson that the Virginians had once deceived him and were not to be trusted. There was a sting in his remark about the anxiety among his friends in New York. In spite of his efforts to the contrary, they still thought that Mr. Jefferson might have made a bargain with the Federalists. The letters also show that Mr. Gallatin at the very moment denied the existence of any such bargain; with his usual disposition to conciliate, he seems to have coupled together the charges against both candidates as equal slanders. Whether Mr. Gallatin was admitted so far into the confidence of his chief as to know all that was said and done in reference to this election in February, 1801, is a question that may remain open; but that something passed between Mr. Jefferson and General Smith which was regarded by the Federalists as a bargain, is not to be denied. Fortunately, Mr. Gallatin lived to hear all the discussions which rose long afterwards on this subject, and almost the last letter he ever wrote was written to record his understanding of the matter:

GALLATIN TO HENRY A. MUHLENBERG.

NEW YORK, May 8, 1848.

DEAR SIR,—A severe cold, which rendered me incapable of attending to any business, has prevented an earlier answer to your letter of the 12th of April.

Although I was at the time probably better acquainted with all the circumstances attending Mr. Jefferson's election than any other person, and I am now the only surviving witness, I could not, without bestowing more time than I can spare, give a satisfactory account of that ancient transaction. A few observations must suffice.

The only cause of real apprehension was that Congress should adjourn without making a decision, but without usurping any powers. It was in order to provide against that contingency that I prepared myself a plan which did meet with the approbation of our party. No appeal whatever to physical force was contemplated, nor did it contain a single particle of revolutionary spirit. In framing this plan Mr. Jefferson had not been consulted, but it was communicated to him, and he fully approved it.

But it was threatened by some persons of the Federal party to provide by law that, if no election should take place, the executive power should be placed in the hands of some public officer. This was considered as a revolutionary act of usurpation, and would, I believe, have been put down by force if necessary. But there was not the slightest intention or suggestion to call a convention to reorganize the government and to amend the Constitution. That such a measure floated in the mind of Mr. Jefferson is clear from his letters of February 15 and 18, 1801, to Mr. Monroe and Mr. Madison. He may have wished for such measure, or thought that the Federalists might be frightened by the threat.

Although I was lodging in the same house with him, he never mentioned it to me. I did not hear it even suggested by any one. That Mr. Jefferson had ever thought of such plan was never known to me till after the publication of his correspondence, and I may aver that under no circumstances would that plan have been resorted to or approved by the Republican party. Anti-federalism had long been dead, and the Republicans were the most sincere and zealous supporters of the Constitution. It was that which constituted their real strength.

I always thought that the threatened attempt to make a President by law was impracticable. I do not believe that, if a motion had been made to that effect, there would have been twenty votes for it in the House. It was only intended to frighten us, but it produced an excitement out-of-doors in which some of our members participated. It was threatened that if any man should be thus appointed President by law and accept the office, he would instantaneously be put to death. It was rumored, and though I did not know it from my own knowledge I believe it was true, that a number of men from Maryland and Virginia, amounting, it was said, to fifteen hundred (a number undoubtedly greatly exaggerated), had determined to repair to Washington on the 4th of March for the purpose of putting to death the usurping pretended President.

It was under those circumstances that it was deemed proper to communicate all the facts to Governor McKean, and to submit to him the propriety of having in readiness a body of militia, who might, if necessary, be in Washington on the 3d of March for the purpose not of promoting, but of preventing civil war and the shedding of a single drop of blood. No person could be better trusted on such a delicate subject than Governor McKean. For he was energetic, patriotic, and at the same time a most steady, stern, and fearless supporter of law and order. It appears from your communication that he must have consulted General Peter Muhlenberg on that subject. But subsequent circumstances, which occurred about three weeks before the 4th of March, rendered it altogether unnecessary to act upon the subject.

There was but one man whom I can positively assert to have been decidedly in favor of the attempt to make a President by law. This was General Henry Lee, of Virginia, who, as you know, was a desperate character and held in no public estimation. I fear from the general tenor of his conduct that Mr. Griswold, of Connecticut, in other respects a very worthy man, was so warm and infatuated a partisan that he might have run the risk of a civil war rather than to see Mr. Jefferson elected. Some weak and inconsiderate members of the House might have voted for the measure, but I could not designate any one.

On the day on which we began balloting for President we knew positively that Mr. Baer, of Maryland, was determined to cast his vote for Mr. Jefferson rather than that there should be no election; and his vote was sufficient to give us that of Maryland and decide the election. I was certain from personal intercourse with him that Mr. Morris, of Vermont, would do the same, and thus give us also the vote of that State. There were others equally prepared, but not known to us at the time. Still, all those gentlemen, unwilling to break up their party, united in the attempt, by repeatedly voting for Mr. Burr, to frighten or induce some of us to vote for Mr. Burr rather than to have no election. This balloting was continued several days for another reason. The attempt was made to extort concessions and promises from Mr. Jefferson as the conditions on which he might be elected. One of our friends, who was very erroneously and improperly afraid of a defection on the part of some of our members, undertook to act as an intermediary, and confounding his own opinions and wishes with those of Mr. Jefferson, reported the result in such a manner as gave subsequently occasion for very unfounded surmises.

It is due to the memory of James Bayard, of Delaware, to say that although he was one of the principal and warmest leaders of the Federal party and had a personal dislike for Mr. Jefferson, it was he who took the lead and from pure patriotism directed all those movements of the sounder and wiser part of the Federal party which terminated in the peaceable election of Mr. Jefferson.

Mr. Jefferson's letter to Mr. Monroe dated February 15, 1801, at the very moment when the attempts were making to obtain promises from him, proves decisively that he made no concessions whatever. But both this letter, that to Mr. Madison of the 18th of February, and some others of preceding dates afford an instance of that credulity, so common to warm partisans, which makes them ascribe the worst motives, and occasionally acts of which they are altogether guiltless, to their opponents. There was not the slightest foundation for suspecting the fidelity of the post. . . .

This interesting letter also suggests something more than appears on its surface.   Evidently Mr. Gallatin meant to intimate, with as much distinctness as was decent, his opinion that it was not Mr. Jefferson who guided or controlled the result of this election, and that altogether too much importance was attached to what Mr. Jefferson did and said.   The election belonged to the House of Representatives, where not Mr. Jefferson but Mr. Gallatin was leader of the party and directed the strategy.   The allusion to General Samuel Smith's intervention is very significant.   Evidently Mr. Gallatin considered General Smith to have been guilty of what was little better than an impertinence in having intruded between the House and Mr. Jefferson with "erroneous and improper" fears of the action of men for whom Mr. Gallatin himself was responsible.   This was the first occasion on which the Smiths crossed Gallatin's path, and when he looked back upon it at the end of fifty years it seemed an omen.

Mr. Gallatin considered himself to be, and doubtless was, the effective leader in this struggle.   He marshalled the forces; he fought the battle; he made the plans, and in making them he did not even consult Mr. Jefferson, but simply obtained his assent to what had already received the assent of his followers in the House.   These plans, alluded to in the Muhlenberg letter, are printed in Mr. Gallatin's Writings.[1]   They were framed to cover every emergency.   If the Federalists, acting on the assumption of a vacancy in the Presidential office, undertook to fill that vacancy by law, the Republicans were to refuse recognition of such a President and to agree on a uniform mode of not obeying the orders of the usurper, and of discriminating between those and the laws which should be suffered to continue in operation. In case only a new election were the object desired, without usurpation of power in the mean while, submission was on the whole preferable to resistance.   An assumption of executive

---

[1] Vol. i. pp. 18–23.

power by the Republicans in any mode not recognized by the Constitution was discouraged, and a reliance on the next Congress was preferred in any case short of actual usurpation. The idea of a convention to reorganize the government was not even suggested.

The crisis lasted until the 17th February, when the Federalists gave way and Mr. Jefferson's election was quietly effected. With this event Mr. Gallatin's career in Congress closed.

GALLATIN TO HIS WIFE.

WASHINGTON CITY, 15th January, 1801.

. . . I arrived here only on Saturday last. The weather was intensely cold the Saturday I crossed the Alleghany Mountains, and afterwards I was detained one day and half by rain and snow. . . . Our local situation is far from being pleasant or even convenient. Around the Capitol are seven or eight boarding-houses, one tailor, one shoemaker, one printer, a washing-woman, a grocery shop, a pamphlets and stationery shop, a small dry-goods shop, and an oyster house. This makes the whole of the Federal city as connected with the Capitol. At the distance of three-fourths of a mile, on or near the Eastern Branch, lie scattered the habitations of Mr. Law and of Mr. Carroll, the principal proprietaries of the ground, half a dozen houses, a very large but perfectly empty warehouse, and a wharf graced by not a single vessel. And this makes the whole intended commercial part of the city, unless we include in it what is called the Twenty Buildings, being so many unfinished houses commenced by Morris and Nicholson, and perhaps as many undertaken by Greenleaf, both which groups lie, at the distance of half-mile from each other, near the mouth of the Eastern Branch and the Potowmack, and are divided by a large swamp from the Capitol Hill and the little village connected with it. Taking a contrary direction from the Capitol towards the President's house, the same swamp intervenes, and a straight causeway, which measures one mile and half and seventeen perches, forms the communication between the two buildings. A small stream, about the size of the largest of the two runs between Clare's and our house,

and decorated with the pompous appellation of "Tyber," feeds
without draining the swamps, and along that causeway (called
the Pennsylvania Avenue), between the Capitol and President's
House, not a single house intervenes or can intervene without
devoting its wretched tenant to perpetual fevers. From the
President's House to Georgetown the distance is not quite a
mile and a half; the ground is high and level; the public offices
and from fifty to one hundred good houses are finished; the
President's House is a very elegant building, and this part of the
city on account of its natural situation, of its vicinity to Georgetown, with which It communicates over Rock Creek by two
bridges, and by the concourse of people drawn by having business with the public offices, will improve considerably and may
within a short time form a town equal in size and population to
Lancaster or Annapolis. But *we* are not there; the distance is
too great for convenience from thence to the Capitol; six or seven
of the members have taken lodgings at Georgetown, three near
the President's House, and all the others are crowded in the
eight boarding-houses near the Capitol. I am at Conrad &
McMunn's, where I share the room of Mr. Varnum, and pay at
the rate, I think, including attendance, wood, candles, and liquors,
of 15 dollars per week. At table, I believe, we are from twenty-
four to thirty, and, was it not for the presence of Mrs. Bailey
and Mrs. Brown, would look like a refectory of monks. The
two Nicholas, Mr. Langdon, Mr. Jefferson, General Smith, Mr.
Baldwin, &c., &c., make part of our mess. The company is
good enough, but it is always the same, and, unless in my own
family, I had rather now and then see some other persons. Our
not being able to have a room each is a greater inconvenience. As
to our fare, we have hardly any vegetables, the people being
obliged to resort to Alexandria for supplies; our beef is not
very good; mutton and poultry good; the price of provisions
and wood about the same as in Philadelphia. As to rents, I
have not yet been able to ascertain anything precise, but, upon
the whole, living must be somewhat dearer here than either in
Philadelphia or New York. As to public news, the subject
which engrosses almost the whole attention of every one is the
equality of votes between Mr. Jefferson and Mr. Burr. The

most desperate of the Federalists wish to take advantage of this by preventing an election altogether, which they may do either by dividing the votes of the States where they have majorities or by still persevering in voting for Burr whilst we should persevere in voting for Jefferson; and the next object they would then propose would be to pass a law by which they would vest the Presidential power in the hands of some man of their party. I believe that such a plan if adopted would be considered as an act of usurpation, and would accordingly be resisted by the people; and I think that partly from fear and partly from principle the plan will not be adopted by a majority. But a more considerable number will try actually to make Burr President. He has *sincerely* opposed the design, and will go *any lengths* to prevent its execution. Hamilton, the Willing and Bingham connection, almost every leading Federalist out of Congress in Maryland and Virginia, have openly declared against the project and recommend an acquiescence in Mr. Jefferson's election. Maryland, which if decided in our favor would at once make Mr. J. President (for we have eight States sure,—New York, New Jersey, Pennsylvania, Virginia, North Carolina, Tennessee, Kentucky, and Georgia), is afraid about the fate of the Federal city, which is hated by every member of Congress without exception of persons or parties; and I know that if a vote was to take place to-day we would obtain the vote of that State. Even Bayard from Delaware and Morris from Vermont (this last I suspect under the influence of Gouv. Morris) are inclined the same way. The vote of either is sufficient to decide in our favor. And from all those circumstances I infer that there will be an election, and that in favor of Mr. Jefferson. If not, there will be either an interregnum until the new Congress shall meet and then a choice made in favor of him also, or in case of usurpation by the present Congress (which of all suppositions is the most improbable), either a dissolution of the Union if that usurpation shall be supported by New England, or a punishment of the usurpers if they shall not be supported by New England. In every possible case I think we have nothing to fear. The next important object is the convention with France, which hangs in the Senate. The mercantile interest, Mr. Adams and Mr. Ham-

ilton are in favor of its ratification. Yet I think it rather probable that either a decision will be postponed or that it shall be
clogged by the rejection or modification of some articles, an event
which might endanger the whole. I understand that Great
Britain does not take any offence at the treaty itself, and that
being the case, although I dislike myself several parts of the instrument, I see no sufficient reason why we should not agree to
it. . . .

22d January, 1801.

. . . As to politics, you may suppose that being all thrown
together in a few boarding-houses, without hardly any other
society than ourselves, we are not likely to be either very moderate politicians or to think of anything but politics. A few,
indeed, drink, and some gamble, but the majority drink naught
but politics, and by not mixing with men of different or more
moderate sentiments, they inflame one another. On that account, principally, I see some danger in the fate of the election
which I had not before contemplated. I do not know precisely
what are the plans of the New England and other violent Federals, nor, indeed, that they have formed any final plan; but I
am certain that if they can prevail on three or four men who
hold the balance, they will attempt to defeat the election under
pretence of voting for Burr. At present it is certain that our
friends will not vote for him, and as we cannot make nine States
without the assistance of some Federal, it is as certain that, if
all the Federal will vote for him, there will be no choice of the
House. In that case what will be the plans of the Federalists,
having, as they have, a majority in both Houses? Will they
usurp at once the Presidential powers? An attempt of that
kind will most certainly be resisted. Will they only pass a law
providing for a new election? This mode, as being the most
plausible, may, perhaps, be the one they will adopt. And in
that case, as no State has provided for an election in such cases;
as the concurrence of the Legislature of any one State will be
necessary to pass a law providing for the same; as in the five
New England States, Jersey, and Delaware (which give 49 Federal votes), both branches of the Legislature are Federal, whilst
in New York, Pennsylvania, Maryland, and South Carolina,

where we have a majority, the State Senates are against us; the consequence might be that the Senates of these four last States refusing to act, the 49 votes of New England, Jersey, and Delaware would outweigh the 44 votes of Virginia, North Carolina, Georgia, Kentucky, and Tennessee; and they would thus, by in fact disfranchising four States and annulling the last election, perpetuate themselves in power, whilst they would in appearance violate none of the forms of our Constitution. If they shall act so, shall we submit? And if we do not submit, in what manner shall we act ourselves? These are important questions, and not yet finally decided. At all events, no appeal shall be made to the physical strength of the country except in self-defence, and as that strength is with us, I am not afraid of an attack on their part. Thus I am confident that we will have no civil war, and the love of union and order is so general that I hope that in every possible case we shall preserve both. My opinion is, however, decided that we must consider the election as completed, and under no possible circumstance consent to a new election. In that I may be overruled by our friends, but I think it a miserable policy, and calculated to break for a length of time the Republican spirit, should we at present yield one inch of ground to the Federal faction, when we are supported by the Constitution and by the people. I will every mail let you know the prospect. At present it is still considered as probable that Maryland will unite in the vote in favor of Mr. Jefferson. . . .

29th January, 1801.

. . . Here the approaching 11th February engrosses all our attention. And opinions vary and fluctuate so much every day, that I will confine myself to a few general observations in communicating to you what I know you must be very anxious of understanding as fully as the nature of the case will admit. If a choice is not made by the House, either the next House must choose between Jefferson and Burr or a new election must take place. Which mode would be most constitutional is doubtful with many. I think the first to be the only truly constitutional way of acting. But whatever mode be adopted, we are sure of success, provided the election be fair. The next House will give us a majority of nine States, and, counting members individually, of more than twenty votes. That House must be in session at all events before a new election can be completed in order to count the votes. That House may therefore adopt either the mode I think right, by choosing between J. and B., or acquiesce in a new election if it has been fair (that is to say, if the Senates of Pennsylvania, New York, Maryland, and South Carolina shall have permitted those States to vote). But if through trick or obstinacy the election has been unfair, that House will not acquiesce. That being an indubitable position, what interest can the Federalists have in defeating an election? None, unless they mean to usurp government. And if they do make the attempt, is it possible they would run the immense risk attending the attempt merely for the sake of keeping government in their hands till December next, with the certainty of losing it then and the probability of being punished, at all events annihilated as a party on account of the attempt? Hence I conclude that if they are in earnest they must mean something more than a temporary usurpation. The intention of the desperate leaders must be absolute usurpation and the overthrow of our Constitution. But although this may be the object of a few individuals actuated by pride and ambition, it cannot be the true object of a majority of the Federal men. Many may not indeed see and calculate all the consequences of their defeating an election. But I am confident that the true motive of action, which may possibly induce at first a sufficient number to vote against Mr. J., is an opinion of our imbecility and a supposition that we will yield ourselves rather than to run any risk. This is the only rational way to account for their conduct. It is yet extremely doubtful whether we will not on the first ballot carry Mr. J.; but if we do not, I am firmly of opinion that by persevering we will compel a sufficient number of Federals to yield. Should, however, the election be defeated, I apprehend no very dangerous consequences. Usurpation will undoubtedly be resisted in a legal and constitutional way by several of the largest and most populous States, and I much doubt whether they would find any man bold enough to place himself in front as an usurper. If, what I think much more probable, there is no usurpation, we

would acquiesce in a kind of interregnum until the meeting of
next Congress, which in that case would probably be hastened.
I conclude on that subject by observing that there is no appearance of any of our friends seceding. If any do secede, B. may
be elected; if not, I think it is one hundred to one that Jef.
will. . . . Lucius H. Stockton (the indicter of Baldwin) was
nominated Secretary of War. The Senate suspended the appointment and gave him time to decline. His brother, your
friend's husband, writes on this occasion that although it might
be well for Mr. A. to reward those who had written in his favor,
yet he should take care not to offer them appointments which
must render them ridiculous. And to-day Griswold, of our
House, has been nominated for the same Department. He has
too much sense not to be mortified at being rendered ridiculous
by that nomination, and I am sure will not accept. Mr. Marshall is Chief Justice. His Department (Secretary of State) is
not yet filled, so that Dexter is pro temp. Secretary in chief of
all the Departments. He is rather unfortunate; the auditor's
office and all the papers therein were burnt. Malice ascribes
the fire to design, and party will believe it. But I do not.
What renders the thing unlucky is that the very books which
had been, through the infidelity of a clerk, in Duane's hands
are burnt. Hence it will be extremely difficult to remove the
suspicion from the minds of many. The French convention, as
I had foretold, has been rejected by the Senate. But they have
contrived to agree that it was not a final determination, and they
are now negotiating amongst themselves on the subject. The
merchants are in favor of the convention; the Senators who
voted against it are rather afraid of the unpopularity of the
measure, and some of them are willing to come in and approve,
provided they may have a decent cover for changing their vote.
So that it is not improbable that on the next trial the convention
may be adopted with some immaterial modifications; but it is
far from certain.

I believe I have given you every political and private information that I can trust to a letter. Much will remain for me to
tell when we meet. Yet, as the newspapers have made me Secretary of the Treasury, hereafter, that is to say, I may tell you

that I have received no hint of that kind from Mr. J.   Indeed, I do not suppose that it would be proper in him to say anything on the subject of appointments until he knows whether he shall be elected.   The Republicans may wish me to be appointed, but there exist two strong doubts in my mind on the subject, 1st, whether the Senate would confirm; 2d, what you have already heard me express, whether my abilities are equal to the office. . . .

5th February, 1801.

. . . Indeed, I feel more forcibly than ever I did before that you cannot, that you must not be left alone in that country.   The habits of the people and state of society create difficulties and inconveniences which you cannot overcome.   And it is to similar circumstances that we are to ascribe the establishment and introduction of slavery in the Middle States.   Under my and your peculiar situation and place of abode, it has required no uncommon exertion to resist the temptation.   And should imperious circumstances compel a longer residence in the western country than we now contemplate, some method must be taken to obviate the inconvenience.   At all events, if through any means I can subsist and be independent on this side the mountains I will attempt it, for from experience I am fully convinced that you cannot live happy where you are. . . . I have had a cold since my last, and nursed myself; have been out but once to dine at Georgetown with some of our members who lodge there.   I mean to go and stay there all night this evening in order to have a more full conversation with Dallas in relation to myself and future plans than can be done by letter.

The Federal party in Senate got frightened at their having rejected the French treaty, which is certainly extremely popular. And they offered to recant provided they were afforded a decent cover.   To this our friends agreed, and the treaty was two days ago ratified, with the exception of the 2d Article (which was a mere matter of form and introduced at the request of our own commissioners), and a limitation for eight years.   From thence I am inclined to think that the party will also want perseverance in the execution of the other plan, that of defeating the election. A variety of circumstances induce me to believe that either the

plan is abandoned or that they know that it will fail. Bayard
has proposed, and a committee of sixteen members, one from
each State, have agreed, that on the 11th February, the day fixed
by law for counting the votes, if it shall appear, as is expected,
that the two persons highest in vote (Jef. and Burr) have an
equality, the House shall immediately proceed (in their own
chamber) to choose by ballot the President, and *shall not adjourn until a choice is made.* I do not know whether the House
will agree; but if they do, and the two parties are obstinate in
adhering, the one to B., the other to Jef., we will have for the
last three weeks of the session to sleep on blankets in the Capitol, and also to eat and drink there. For the idea is that of a
permanent sitting, without doing any other business whatever
until we have chosen. But this evidently shows that they mean
to choose. For if no choice was made, they could neither pass
a law for a new election or usurpation, nor indeed for any object
whatever; and there is as yet no appropriation law passed;
which would leave us on 3d March without any government.
I believe I told you before that we had expectations of Bayard
and Morris joining us on this question. Mr. Adams has very
improperly called Senate for the 4th of March next, at which
time the three new Republican Senators from Kentucky, Georgia,
and South Carolina cannot, from their distance, be here; the new
Republican Senator from Pennsylvania instead of Bingham will
not be appointed, our thirteen Senators refusing to agree; the
same with a new Senator from Maryland; Charles Pinckney
has also dislocated his shoulder. The fact is that in December
next the Senate will be 16 to 16, or at worst 15 to 17. And on
4th March only 8 or 9 Republicans against 17 or 18. The
secretaries may and probably will all resign on that day, and
the Senate being in session, that will compel Mr. J. to appoint
immediately and submit his appointments to that *Rump* Senate.
The object is undoubtedly to embarrass him by crippling his
intended Administration. . . .

12th February, 1801.

. . . Yesterday, on counting the votes, Burr and Jefferson had
73 votes each, as was already known. At one o'clock in the
afternoon we returned to our chamber and kept balloting till

eight o'clock this morning without making a choice. We balloted 27 times, and on each ballot the result was the same; eight States for Jefferson, six for Burr, two divided. At eight o'clock we agreed (without adjourning the House) to suspend the further balloting till twelve o'clock, and during that time I went to sleep. We have just returned and balloted once more, when, the result being still the same, we have just now agreed to suspend the balloting till to-morrow at eleven o'clock. Still the House is not adjourned, and we consider this as a permanent sitting; but by mutual agreement it is a virtual adjournment, as we shall not meet nor do any business till to-morrow. I must write to Philadelphia, Lancaster, and New York, to keep them acquainted of our situation, and I want to return to bed, which must be my apology, with my love, for this short letter. Our hopes of a change on their part are exclusively with Maryland, but everything on that subject is conjecture. . . .

GALLATIN TO JAMES NICHOLSON, NEW YORK.

CITY OF WASHINGTON, 14th February, 1801.
3 o'clock, afternoon.

DEAR SIR,—Nothing new to-day; 3 ballots, making in all 33, result the same. We have postponed balloting till Monday, twelve o'clock.

That day will, I think, show something more decisive, either yielding on their part or an attempt to put an end to balloting in order to legislate. We will be ready at all points, and rest assured that *we* will not yield. It is the most impudent thing that they, with only six States and two half States, represented on this floor only by 39 members, should expect that a majority of eight States and two half States, represented on this floor by 67 members, should give up to the minority, and that, too, against the decided opinion of an immense majority of the people.

Federal instructions are pouring from this vicinity on Thomas, the representative of this district, to induce him to make an election by voting for Mr. Jefferson, but I do not know what effect they may have.

Mr. Joseph Nicholson has been very unwell, but would not desert his post. A bed was fixed for him in the committee-room, and he lay there and voted all night the 11th to 12th. He has also attended every day since, and has recovered amazingly, notwithstanding the risk he ran in exposing himself to cold.

GALLATIN TO JAMES NICHOLSON, NEW YORK.

CITY OF WASHINGTON, 16th February, 1801.

DEAR SIR,—I am sorry that I cannot yet relieve you from the present general anxiety. We have balloted for the 34th time this morning, and the result is still the same.

Mr. Bayard had positively declared on Saturday to some of his own party that he would this day put an end to the business by voting for Mr. Jefferson. He has acted otherwise. But it is supposed that the cause of the delay is an attempt on his part and some others to prevail on the whole Federal party to come over.

We have agreed to suspend the ballot till to-morrow, twelve o'clock.

GALLATIN TO HIS WIFE.

17th February, 1801

. . . We have this day, after 36 ballots, chosen Mr. Jefferson President. Morris, of Vermont, withdrew; Craik, Dennis, Thomas, and Baer put in blank votes; this gives us ten States. The four New England States voted to the last for Mr. Burr. South Carolina and Delaware put in blank ballots in the general ballot-box; that is to say, they did not vote. Thus has ended the most wicked and absurd attempt ever tried by the Federalists. . . .

19th February, 1801.

. . . My last letter informed you of our final success in electing Mr. Jefferson. The Republicans are allowed, even by their opponents, to have acted on that occasion with a cool firmness which, before the first day of the contest was over, convinced the wisest of that party that we would never yield, that we had well ascertained the ground on which we stood, and that a determination thus formed was not likely to be changed from fear or intrigue. They were much at a loss how to act; unsupported even by their party out-of-doors, terrified at the prospect of their own attempt, convinced that they must give up their untenable ground, their unsubdued pride stood in the way of any dignified way of acting on their part. They had but one proper mode to pursue, and that was for the whole party to come over; instead of which they contrived merely to suffer Mr. Jefferson to be chosen without a single man of theirs voting for him. This is construed by some as a symptom of a general hostility hereafter by an unbroken phalanx. But in this I do not agree, and I have no doubt of our making an impression on them and effectually breaking up the party, provided we have patience and discretion. At present, however, they are decidedly hostile, and as the Senate has, very improperly indeed, been called by Mr. Adams to meet on the 4th March next, when three of the newly-elected Republican Senators cannot attend, and the expected Republican Senator from Maryland is not yet elected, they will, it is expected, evince that hostility by thwarting Mr. Jefferson's nominations. Amongst those nominations which, as communicated yesterday to me by Mr. Jefferson, are intended to be made, the most obnoxious to the other party, and the only one which I think will be rejected, is that of a certain friend of yours. That *he* should be fixed at the seat of government and should hold one of the great offices is pressed on *him* in such manner and considered as so extremely important by several of our friends, that *he* will do whatever is ordered. But I will not be sorry nor hurt in my feelings if his nomination should be rejected, for exclusively of the immense responsibility, labor, &c., &c., attached to the intended office, another plan which would be much more agreeable to him and to you has been suggested not by his political friends, but by his New York friends. I will be more explicit when we meet. . . .

23d February, 1801.

. . . From every present appearance I am led to think that it will be necessary for us (by *us* I mean you, the children, and me) to remove to this city about 1st May next; but then there is a chance that we may leave it next fall if the Senate shall then refuse to confirm. At all events, I conclude that, however inconvenient that arrangement may be in other respects, it will be agreeable to you. But I must state one thing. Remember that whatever may be our station this side the mountains, it will be essentially necessary that we should be extremely humble in our expenses. This I know will be found by you a little harder than you expect, for the style of living here is Maryland-like, and it requires more fortitude to live here in a humble way than it did in Philadelphia; but I repeat it, it will be strictly necessary, and on that you must resolve before you conclude to leave our present home. . . .

26th February, 1801.

. . . I still calculate upon leaving this city Friday week, 6th of March; at all events, not before the Thursday. Wednesday, 4th, is the inauguration day of our new President. I want to stay on that day at least, and so long as to ascertain how far the Senate will approve or reject the nominations submitted to them for the intended future Administration. These will be but few in number and decided on Wednesday or Thursday at farthest. As I had foreseen, the greatest exertions are made to defeat the appointment of a Secretary of the Treasury, and I am still of opinion that if presented the 4th of March it will be rejected. If not presented, and an appointment by the President without Senate should afterwards take place, it must be confirmed in December next, and although it is probable, yet it is not certain, that it would then be ratified. This would be a serious inconvenience. To have removed to this place at considerable expense, made, as must necessarily be the case, some sacrifices in order to close the business at home, and in winter to be obliged to move again, would not be pleasing nor advantageous. Indeed, on the whole, a positive refusal to come in on any terms but a previous confirmation by Senate was at first given; but subsequent circumstances, which I cannot trust to a letter, but will mention at large when we meet, induced a compliance with the general wish of all our political friends. The Federal Senators generally continue very hostile. They have brought in a bill to prevent the Secretary of the Navy from being concerned in trade, which is aimed at General S. Smith, and is the more indecent on their part, as Stoddart has always been in trade himself. Bingham is quite sincere in his exertions in support of the intended nomination of Secretary of the Treasury, but in favor of the bill intended on the subject of the Secretary of the Navy. I speak to you more on that than on any other subject because I know you feel more interested in it. . . .

5th March, 1801.

. . . The President was inaugurated yesterday, and this day has nominated Messrs. Madison, Dearborn, Lincoln, and Robert R. Livingston for Secretaries of State and War, Attorney-General and minister to France, respectively, all of which have been approved of by the Senate. A majority of that body would, it is supposed, have rejected a nomination for a new Secretary of the Treasury; whether that be true or not I cannot tell, but as I could not at any event have accepted immediately, no nomination was made. Mr. Dexter has with great civility to the President agreed to stay until a successor shall have been appointed. Both Smith and Langdon decline. Mrs. Smith is here and hates this place. But to come to the point: Mr. Jefferson requested that I should stay three days longer in order to see Mr. Madison and that I should be able to understand the general outlines which are contemplated or may be agreed on as the leading principles of the new Administration. As it was for my convenience that the appointment was delayed, I could not, even had I thought my presence useless, have objected to his wish. . . . Mr. Adams left the city yesterday at four o'clock in the morning. You can have no idea of the meanness, indecency, almost insanity, of his conduct, specially of late. But he is fallen and not dangerous. Let him be forgotten. The Federal phalanx in Senate is more to be feared. Yet with the people on our side and the purity of our intentions, I hope we will be able to go on. But indeed, my dear, this is an arduous and momentous undertaking in which I am called to take a share. . . .

The struggle was completely over. All the dangers, real and imaginary, had vanished. The great Federal party which had created, organized, and for twelve years administered the government, and whose chief now handed it, safe and undisturbed, to Mr. Jefferson and his friends, was prostrate, broken and torn by dying convulsions. The new political force of which Mr. Jefferson was the guide had no word of sympathy for the vanquished. Full of hope and self-confidence, he took the helm and promised that "now the ship was put on her Republican tack she would show by the beauty of her motion the skill of her builders." Even Mr. Gallatin's cooler head felt the power of the strong wine, success. He too believed that human nature was to show itself in new aspects, and that the failures of the past were due to the faults of the past. "Every man, from John Adams to John Hewitt, who undertakes to do what he does not understand deserves a whipping," he wrote to his wife a year later, when his tailor had spoiled a coat for him. He had yet to pass through his twelve years of struggle and disappointment in order to learn how his own followers and his own President were to answer his ideal, when the same insolence of foreign dictation and the same violence of a recalcitrant party presented to their and to his own lips the cup of which John Adams was now draining the dregs.

BOOK III.

In governments, as in households, he who holds the purse holds the power. The Treasury is the natural point of control to be occupied by any statesman who aims at organization or reform, and conversely no organization or reform is likely to succeed that does not begin with and is not guided by the Treasury. The highest type of practical statesmanship must always take this direction. Washington and Jefferson doubtless stand pre-eminent as the representatives of what is best in our national character or its aspirations, but Washington depended mainly upon Hamilton, and without Gallatin Mr. Jefferson would have been helpless. The mere financial duties of the Treasury, serious as they are, were the least of the burdens these men had to carry ; their keenest anxieties were not connected most nearly with their own department, but resulted from that effort to control the whole machinery and policy of government which is necessarily forced upon the holder of the purse. Possibly it may be said with truth that a majority of financial ministers have not so understood their duties, but, on the other hand, the ministers who composed this majority have hardly left great reputations behind them. Perhaps, too, the very magnitude and overshadowing influence of the Treasury have tended to rouse a certain jealousy in the minds of successive Presidents, and have worked to dwarf an authority legitimate in itself, but certainly dangerous to the Executive head. Be this as it may, there are, to the present time, in all American history only two examples of practical statesmanship which can serve as perfect models, not perhaps in all respects for imitation, but for study, to persons who wish to understand what practical statesmanship has been under an American system. Public men in considerable numbers

267

and of high merit have run their careers in national politics, but only two have had at once the breadth of mind to grapple with the machine of government as a whole, and the authority necessary to make it work efficiently for a given object; the practical knowledge of affairs and of politics that enabled them to foresee every movement; the long apprenticeship which had allowed them to educate and discipline their parties; and finally, the good fortune to enjoy power when government was still plastic and capable of receiving a new impulse. The conditions of the highest practical statesmanship require that its models should be financiers; the conditions of our history have hitherto limited their appearance and activity to its earlier days.

The vigor and capacity of Hamilton's mind are seen at their best not in his organization of the Treasury Department, which was a task within the powers of a moderate intellect, nor yet in the essays which, under the name of reports, instilled much sound knowledge, besides some that was not so sound, into the minds of legislature and people; still less are they shown in the arts of political management,—a field into which his admirers can follow him only with regret and some sense of shame. The true ground of Hamilton's great reputation is to be found in the mass and variety of legislation and organization which characterized the first Administration of Washington, and which were permeated and controlled by Hamilton's spirit. That this work was not wholly his own is of small consequence. Whoever did it was acting under his leadership, was guided consciously or unconsciously by his influence, was inspired by the activity which centred in his department, and sooner or later the work was subject to his approval. The results—legislative and administrative —were stupendous and can never be repeated. A government is organized once for all, and until that of the United States fairly goes to pieces no man can do more than alter or improve the work accomplished by Hamilton and his party.

What Hamilton was to Washington, Gallatin was to Jefferson, with only such difference as circumstances required. It is true that the powerful influence of Mr. Madison entered largely into the plan of Jefferson's Administration, uniting and modifying its other elements, and that this was an influence the want of which was painfully felt by Washington and caused his most serious difficulties; it is true, too, that Mr. Jefferson reserved to himself a far more active initiative than had been in Washington's character, and that Mr. Gallatin asserted his own individuality much less conspicuously than was done by Mr. Hamilton; but the parallel is nevertheless sufficiently exact to convey a true idea of Mr. Gallatin's position. The government was in fact a triumvirate almost as clearly defined as any triumvirate of Rome. During eight years the country was governed by these three men, —Jefferson, Madison, and Gallatin,—among whom Gallatin not only represented the whole political influence of the great Middle States, not only held and effectively wielded the power of the purse, but also was avowedly charged with the task of carrying into effect the main principles on which the party had sought and attained power.

In so far as Mr. Jefferson's Administration was a mere protest against the conduct of his predecessor, the object desired was attained by the election itself. In so far as it represented a change of system, its positive characteristics were financial. The philanthropic or humanitarian doctrines which had been the theme of Mr. Jefferson's philosophy, and which, in a somewhat more tangible form, had been put into shape by Mr. Gallatin in his great speech on foreign intercourse and in his other writings, when reduced to their simplest elements amount merely to this: that America, standing outside the political movement of Europe, could afford to follow a political development of her own; that she might safely disregard remote dangers; that her armaments might be reduced to a point little above mere police necessities; that she might rely on natural self-interest for her foreign commerce; that she might depend on average common sense for her internal prosperity and order; and that her capital was safest in the hands of her own citizens. To establish these doctrines beyond the chance of overthrow was to make democratic government a success, while to defer the establishment of these doctrines was to incur the risk, if not the certainty, of following the career of England in "debt, corruption, and rottenness."

In this political scheme, whatever its merits or its originality, everything was made to depend upon financial management, and, since the temptation to borrow money was the great danger, payment of the debt was the great dogma of the Democratic principle. " The discharge of the debt is vital to the destinies of our government," wrote Mr. Jefferson to Mr. Gallatin in October, 1809, when the latter was desperately struggling to maintain his grasp on the Administration; " we shall never see another President and Secretary of the Treasury *making all other objects subordinate to this.*" And Mr. Gallatin replied: " The reduction of the debt was certainly the principal object in bringing me into office." With the reduction of debt, by parity of reasoning, reduction of taxation went hand in hand. On this subject Mr. Gallatin's own words at the outset of his term of office give the clearest idea of his views. On the 16th November, 1801, he wrote to Mr. Jefferson:

" If we cannot, with the probable amount of impost and sale of lands, pay the debt at the rate proposed and support the establishments on the proposed plans, one of three things must be done; either to continue the internal taxes, or to reduce the expenditure still more, or to discharge the debt with less rapidity. The last recourse to me is the most objectionable, not only because I am firmly of opinion that if the present Administration and Congress do not take the most effective measures for that object, the debt will be entailed on us and the ensuing generations, together with all the systems which support it and which it supports, but also, any sinking fund operating in an increased ratio as it progresses, a very small deduction from an appropriation for that object would make a considerable difference in the ultimate term of redemption which, provided we can in some shape manage the three per cents. without redeeming them at their nominal value, I think may be paid at fourteen or fifteen years.

" On the other hand, if this Administration shall not reduce taxes, they never will be permanently reduced. To strike at the root of the evil and avert the danger of increasing taxes, encroaching government, temptations to offensive wars, &c., nothing can be more effectual than a repeal of *all* internal taxes; but let them all go and not one remain on which sister taxes máy be hereafter engrafted. I agree most fully with you that pretended tax-preparations, treasure-preparations, and army-preparations against contingent wars tend only to encourage wars. If the United States shall unavoidably be drawn into a war, the people will submit to any necessary tax, and the system of internal taxation which then shall be thought best adapted to the then situation of the country may be created instead of engrafted on the old or present plan. If there shall be no real necessity for them, their abolition by this Administration will most powerfully deter any other from reviving them."

To these purposes, in the words of Mr. Jefferson, all other objects were made subordinate, and to carry these purposes into effect was the peculiar task of Mr. Gallatin. No one else appears even to have been thought of; no one else possessed any of the requisites for the place in such a degree as made him even a possible rival. The whole political situation dictated the selection of Mr. Gallatin for the Treasury as distinctly as it did that of Mr. Jefferson for the Presidency.

But the condition on which alone the principles of the Republicans could be carried out was that of peace. To use again Mr. Gallatin's own words, written in 1835: "No nation can, any more than any individual, pay its debts unless its annual receipts exceed its expenditures, and the two necessary ingredients for that purpose, which are common to all nations, are frugality and peace. The United States have enjoyed the last blessing in a far greater degree than any of the great European powers. And they have had another peculiar advantage, that of an unexampled increase of population and corresponding wealth. We are indebted almost exclusively for both to our geographical and internal situation, the only share which any Administration or individual can claim being its efforts to preserve peace and to check expenses either improper in themselves or of subordinate importance to the payment of the public debt. In that respect I may be entitled to some public credit, as nearly the whole of my public life, from 1795, when I took my seat in Congress, till 1812, when the war took place, was almost exclusively devoted with entire singleness of purpose to those objects."[1]

To preserve peace, therefore, in order that the beneficent in-

---

[1] Letter to Gales & Seaton, 5th February, 1835, Writings, ii. 535.

fluence of an enlightened internal policy might have free course, was the special task of Mr. Madison. How much Mr. Gallatin's active counsel and assistance had to do with the foreign policy of the government will be seen in the narrative. Here, however, lay the danger, and here came the ultimate shipwreck. It is obvious at the outset that the weak point of what may be called the Jeffersonian system lay in its rigidity of rule. That system was, it must be confessed, a system of doctrinaires, and had the virtues and faults of *a priori* reasoning. Far in advance, as it was, of any other political effort of its time, and representing, as it doubtless did, all that was most philanthropic and all that most boldly appealed to the best instincts of mankind, it made too little allowance for human passions and vices; it relied too absolutely on the power of interest and reason as opposed to prejudice and habit; it proclaimed too openly to the world that the sword was not one of its arguments, and that peace was essential to its existence. When narrowed down to a precise issue, and after eliminating from the problem the mere dogmas of the extreme Hamiltonian Federalists, the real difference between Mr. Jefferson and moderate Federalists like Rufus King, who represented four-fifths of the Federal party, lay in the question how far a government could safely disregard the use of force as an element in politics. Mr. Jefferson and Mr. Gallatin maintained that every interest should be subordinated to the necessity of fixing beyond peradventure the cardinal principles of true republican government in the public mind, and that after this was accomplished, a result to be marked by extinction of the debt, the task of government would be changed and a new class of duties would arise. Mr. King maintained that republican principles would take care of themselves, and that the government could only escape war and ruin by holding ever the drawn sword in its hand. Mr. Gallatin, his eyes fixed on the country of his adoption, and loathing the violence, the extravagance, and the corruption of Europe, clung with what in a less calm mind would seem passionate vehemence to the ideal he had formed of a great and pure society in the New World, which was to offer to the human race the first example of man in his best condition, free from all the evils which infected

Europe, and intent only on his own improvement.   To realize this ideal might well, even to men of a coarser fibre than Mr. Gallatin, compensate for many insults and much wrong, borne with dignity and calm remonstrance.   True, Mr. Gallatin always looked forward to the time when the American people might safely increase its armaments; but he well knew that, as the time approached, the need would in all probability diminish: meanwhile, he would gladly have turned his back on all the politics of Europe, and have found compensation for foreign outrage in domestic prosperity.   The interests of the United States were too serious to be put to the hazard of war; government must be ruled by principles; to which the Federalists answered that government must be ruled by circumstances.

The moment when Mr. Jefferson assumed power was peculiarly favorable for the trial of his experiment.   Whatever the original faults and vices of his party might have been, ten years of incessant schooling and education had corrected many of its failings and supplied most of its deficiencies.   It was thoroughly trained, obedient, and settled in its party doctrines.   And while the new administration thus profited by the experience of its adversity, it was still more happy in the inheritance it received from its predecessor.   Whatever faults the Federalists may have committed, and no one now disputes that their faults and blunders were many, they had at least the merit of success; their processes may have been clumsy, their tempers were under decidedly too little control, and their philosophy of government was both defective and inconsistent; but it is an indisputable fact, for which they have a right to receive full credit, that when they surrendered the government to Mr. Jefferson in March, 1801, they surrendered it in excellent condition.   The ground was clear for Mr. Jefferson to build upon.   Friendly relations had been restored with France without offending England; for the first time since the government existed there was not a serious difficulty in all our foreign relations, the chronic question of impressment alone excepted; the army and navy were already reduced to the lowest possible point; the civil service had never been increased beyond very humble proportions; the debt, it is true, had been somewhat increased, but in nothing like propor tion to the increase of population and wealth; and through all their troubles the Federalists had so carefully managed taxation that there was absolutely nothing for Mr. Gallatin to do, and he attempted nothing, in regard to the tariff of impost duties, which were uniformly moderate and unexceptionable, while even in regard to the excise and other internal taxes he hesitated to interfere. This almost entire absence of grievances to correct extended even to purely political legislation. The alien and sedition laws expired by limitation before the accession of Mr. Jefferson, and only the new organization of the judiciary offered material for legislative attack. Add to all this that Europe was again about to recover peace.

On the other hand, the difficulties with which Mr. Jefferson had to deal were no greater than always must exist under any condition of party politics. From the Federalists he had nothing to fear; they were divided and helpless. The prejudices and discords of his own followers were his only real danger, and principally the pressure for office which threatened to blind the party to the higher importance of its principles. In proportion as he could maintain some efficient barrier against this and similar excesses and fix the attention of his followers on points of high policy, his Administration could rise to the level of purity which was undoubtedly his ideal. What influence was exerted by Mr. Gallatin in this respect will be shown in the course of the narrative.

The assertion that Jefferson, Madison, and Gallatin were a triumvirate which governed the country during eight years takes no account of the other members of Mr. Jefferson's Cabinet, but in point of fact the other members added little to its strength. The War Department was given to General Dearborn, while Levi Lincoln became Attorney-General; both were from Massachusetts, men of good character and fair though not pre-eminent abilities. Mr. Gallatin described them very correctly in a letter written at the time:

GALLATIN TO MARIA NICHOLSON.

CITY OF WASHINGTON, 12th March, 1801.

MY DEAR SISTER,—I think I am going to reform; for I feel a kind of shame at having left your friendly letters so long unanswered. How it happens that I often have and still now do apparently neglect, at least in the epistolary way, those persons who are dearest to me, must be unaccountable to you. I think it is owing to an indulgence of indolent habits and to want of regularity in the distribution of my time. In both a thorough reformation has become necessary, and as that necessity is the result of new and arduous duties, I do not know myself, or I will succeed in accomplishing it. You will easily understand that I allude to the office to which I am to be appointed. This has been decided for some time, and has been the cause of my remaining here a few days longer than I expected or wished. To-morrow morning I leave this place, and expect to return about the first day of May with my wife and family. Poor Hannah has been and is so forlorn during my absence, and she meets with so many difficulties in that western country, for which she is not fit and which is not fit for her, that I will at least feel no reluctance in leaving it. Yet were my wishes alone to be consulted I would have preferred my former plan with all its difficulties, that of studying law and removing to New York. As a political situation the place of Secretary of the Treasury is doubtless more eligible and congenial to my habits, but it is more laborious and responsible than any other, and the same industry which will be necessary to fulfil its duties, applied to another object, would at the end of two years have left me in the possession of a profession which I might have exercised either in Philadelphia or New York. But our plans are all liable to uncertainty, and I must now cheerfully undertake that which had never been the object of my ambition or wishes, though Hannah had always said that it should be offered to me in case of a change of Administration.

. . . As to our new Administration, the appearances are favorable, but storms must be expected. The party out of power had it so long, loved it so well, struggled so hard to the very last to preserve it, that it cannot be expected that the leaders will rest contented after their defeat. They mean to rally and to improve every opportunity which our errors, our faults, or events not under our control may afford them. As to ourselves, Mr. Jefferson's and Mr. Madison's characters are well known to you.

General Dearborn is a man of strong sense, great practical information on all the subjects connected with his Department, and what is called a man of business. He is not, I believe, a scholar, but I think he will make the best Secretary of War we [have] as yet had. Mr. Lincoln is a good lawyer, a fine scholar, a man of great discretion and sound judgment, and of the mildest and most amiable manners. He has never, I should think from his manners, been out of his own State or mixed much with the world except on business. Both are men of 1776, sound and decided Republicans; both are men of the strictest integrity; and both, but Mr. L. principally, have a great weight of character to the Eastward with both parties. We have as yet no Secretary of the Navy, nor do I know on whom the choice of the President may fall, if S. Smith shall persist in refusing. . . .

The Navy Department in a manner went begging. General Smith was strongly pressed to take it, and did in fact perform its duties for several weeks. Had he consented to accept the post he would have added to the weight of the government, for General Smith was a man of force and ability; but he persisted in refusing, and ultimately his brother, Robert Smith, was appointed, an amiable and respectable person, but not one of much weight except through his connections by blood or marriage.

The first act of the new Cabinet was to reach a general understanding in regard to the objects of the Administration. These appear to have been two only in number: reduction of debt and reduction of taxes, and the relation to be preserved between them. On the 14th March, Mr. Gallatin wrote a letter to Mr. Jefferson, discussing the subject at some length;[1] immediately afterwards he set out for New Geneva to arrange his affairs there and to bring his wife and family to Washington. His sharp experience of repeated exclusion from office by legislative bodies made him nervous in regard to confirmation by the Senate, and Mr. Jefferson therefore postponed the appointment until after

---

[1] Writings, vol. i. p. 24.

the Senate had adjourned. These fears of factious opposition were natural enough, but seem to have been unfounded. Samuel Dexter, the Secretary of the Treasury under President Adams, consented to hold over until Mr. Gallatin was ready. Mr. Stoddart, President Adams's Secretary of the Navy, was equally courteous. If the story, told in some of Mr. Jefferson's biographies, be true, that Mr. Marshall, while still acting as Secretary of State, was turned out of his office by Mr. Lincoln, under the orders of Mr. Jefferson, at midnight on the 3d of March,[1] it must be confessed that, so far as courtesy was concerned, the Federalists were decidedly better bred than their rivals. The new Administration was in no way hampered or impeded by the old one, and Mr. Gallatin himself was perhaps of the whole Administration the one who suffered least from Federal attacks; henceforward his enemies came principally from his own camp. This result was natural and inevitable; it came from his own character, and was a simple consequence of his principles; but, since this internal dissension forced itself at once on the Administration and became to some extent its crucial test in the matter of removals from office for party reasons, the whole story may best be told here before proceeding with the higher subjects of state policy.

Among Mr. Gallatin's papers is a sort of pamphlet in manuscript, stitched together, and headed in ornamental letters: "CITIZEN 𝔚. 𝔇𝔲𝔞𝔫𝔢." It is endorsed in Mr. Gallatin's hand: "1801. Clerks in offices; given by W. Duane." It contains a list of all the Department clerks, after the following style:

	Offices.	Names.	Remarks.
Secretary of State's Office.	1400	Jacob Wagner.	Complete picaroon.
	600	Steph. Pleasanton.	Nothingarian.
	800	—— Brent.	Nincumpoop.

Some of Duane's remarks are still more pointed:

---

[1] See Miss Randolph's Domestic Life of Thomas Jefferson, pp. 307–308, and Parton's Jefferson, pp. 585–586.

Offices.	Names.	Remarks.
1500	John Newman.	Democratic executioner.
800	—— Golding.	Adamite.
600	Israel Loring.	Assistant throat-cutter.
1000	Charles W. Goldsborough.	Damned Reps.
1000	Jeremiah Nicolls.	
1700	A. Bradley, Jr., A.P.M.	Three execrable aristocrats.
1200	Robt. T. Howe.	
800	Tunis Craven.	
1200	E. Jones.	A notorious villain.
1200	David Sheldon.	Wolcott's *dear nephew*.
1200	Jos. Dawson.	Hell-hot.

The pressure for sweeping removals was very great. From the first, Mr. Gallatin set his face against them, and although apparently yielding adhesion to Mr. Jefferson's famous New Haven letter of July 12, in which it was attempted to justify the principle and regulate the proportion of removals, he urged Mr. Jefferson to authorize the issue of a circular to collectors which would have practically made the New Haven letter a nullity. On the 25th July he sent to the President a draft of this circular:

CIRCULAR TO COLLECTORS.

The law having given to the collectors the appointment of a number of inferior officers subject to my approbation, there is on that subject on which we must act in concert, but one sentiment that I wish to communicate; it is that the door of office be no longer shut against any man merely on account of his political opinions, but that whether he shall differ or not from those avowed either by you or by myself, integrity and capacity suitable to the station be the only qualifications that shall direct our choice.

Permit me, since I have touched this topic, to add that whilst freedom of opinion and freedom of suffrage at public elections are considered by the President as imprescriptible rights which, possessing as citizens, you cannot have lost by becoming public officers, he will regard any exercise of official influence to restrain

or control the same rights in others as injurious to that part of
the public administration which is confided to your care, and
practically destructive of the fundamental principles of a republican Constitution.

In his letter to Mr. Jefferson of the same date he said, "It is
supposed that there is no danger in avowing the sentiment that
even at present, so far as respects subordinate officers, talent and
integrity are to be the only qualifications for office. In the second
paragraph, the idea intended to be conveyed is that an electioneering collector is commonly a bad officer as it relates to his official
duties (which I do sincerely believe to be true), and that the
principle of a corrupting official influence is rejected by the present
Administration in its own support and will not be forgiven when
exercised against itself."

Mr. Jefferson and Mr. Madison thought this declaration premature, and the circular was not issued. The time never came
when they thought it had reached maturity; nevertheless Mr.
Jefferson wrote back: "I approve so entirely of the two paragraphs on the participation of office and electioneering activity
that on the latter subject I proposed very early to issue a proclamation, but was restrained by some particular considerations;
with respect to the former, we both thought it better to be kept
back till the New Haven remonstrance and answer have got into
possession of the public, and then that it should go further and
require an equilibrium to be first produced by exchanging one-
half of their subordinates, after which talents and worth alone to
be inquired into in the case of new vacancies."

Mr. Gallatin, however, soon returned to his remonstrances:

GALLATIN TO JEFFERSON.

10th August, 1801.

. . . The answer to New Haven seems to have had a greater
effect than had been calculated upon. The Republicans hope for
a greater number of removals; the Federals also expect it. I
have already received several letters from Philadelphia applying
for the offices of customs, upon the ground that it is generally
understood that the officers there are to be removed.

There is no doubt that the Federal leaders are making a powerful effort to rally their party on the same ground. Although some mistakes may have been made as to the proper objects both of removal and appointment, it does not appear that less than what has been done could have been done without injustice to the Republicans.

But ought much more to be done? It is so important for the permanent establishment of those republican principles of limitation of power and public economy for which we have so successfully contended, that they should rest on the broad basis of the people, and not on a fluctuating party majority, that it would be better to displease many of our political friends than to give an opportunity to the irreconcilable enemies of a free government of inducing the mass of the Federal citizens to make a common cause with them. The sooner we can stop the ferment the better, and, at all events, it is not desirable that it should affect the eastern and southern parts of the Union. I fear less from the importunity of obtaining offices than from the arts of those men whose political existence depends on that of party. Office-hunters cannot have much influence; but the other class may easily persuade the warmest of our friends that more ought to be done for them. Upon the whole, although a few more changes may be necessary, I hope there will be but a few. The number of removals is not great, but in importance they are beyond their number. The supervisors of all the violent party States embrace all the collectors. Add to that the intended change in the post-office, and you have in fact every man in office out of the seaports. . . .

JEFFERSON TO GALLATIN.

MONTICELLO, August 14, 1801.

. . . The answer to New Haven does not work harder than I expected; it gives mortal offence to the Monarchical Federalists who were mortally offended before. I do not believe it is thought unreasonable by the Republican Federalists. In one point the effect is not exactly what I expected. It has given more expectation to the sweeping Republicans than I think its terms justify;

to the moderate and genuine Republicans it seems to have given perfect satisfaction.   I am satisfied it was indispensably necessary in order to rally round one point all the shades of Republicanism and Federalism, exclusive of the monarchical; and I am in hopes it will do it.   At any event, while we push the patience of our friends to the utmost it will bear, in order that we may gather into the same fold all the Republican Federalists possible, we must not even for this object absolutely revolt our tried friends. It would be a poor manœuvre to exchange them for new converts. . . .

GALLATIN TO JEFFERSON.

17th August, 1801.

. . . You will find by the other letter that the Republicans expect a change in Philadelphia; this expectation is owing partly to the removal of the collector of New York and partly to the answer to New Haven, which, as I mentioned before, has had a greater if not a better effect than was expected. . . . Upon the whole . . . it is much better to wait the meeting of Congress. Dallas, who was here, agrees with me.   Yet it must be allowed that the warm Republicans will be displeased; it is the same in New York in regard to Rogers, who though the most capable was the most obnoxious to the zealous Republicans.   Duane has been here, and I have taken an opportunity of showing the impropriety of numerous removals.   He may think the reasons good, but his feelings will be at war with any argument on the subject. . . .

With regard to Duane, he was quite right.   The course of Mr. Gallatin and Mr. Dallas in resisting the sweeping removals urged by the Aurora forfeited Duane's confidence.   Perhaps Mr. Gallatin, who had yet to learn something about the depths of human nature, expected that at least Duane would give him the credit of honest intention; perhaps he thought the Aurora itself might be disregarded if the public were satisfied; possibly he foresaw all the consequences of making Duane an enemy, and accepted them; certain it is that the party schisms in Pennsylvania began here, and that in the long list of enmities which were at last to coalesce for Mr. Gallatin's overthrow, this of Duane stands first in importance and in date.

Years, however, were to pass before the full effects of this difference showed themselves; meanwhile the removals were checked, and Duane pacified at least in some degree, but it is a curious fact that the cause which interposed the first obstacle to these wholesale removals was another party schism, of which New York was the field and Aaron Burr the victim; and in this case it appears that Mr. Gallatin favored removal rather than otherwise, while it was Mr. Jefferson who, out of distrust to Burr, maintained the Federal incumbent in office. The story is curious and interesting.

The naval officer in New York was one Rogers, said to have been a Tory of the Revolution. The candidate for his place was Matthew L. Davis, Burr's right-hand man, and supported by Burr with all his energy. The great mass of New York Republicans, outside of the Livingston and Clinton interests, were attached to Burr and pressed Davis for office. Commodore Nicholson was hot about it. "It is rumored," he wrote to Gallatin on the 10th August, "that Mr. Harrison in the State government and Mr. Rogers in the general one are to be continued. Should that be the determination, a petition should go on to both governments pointing out the consequences. I can with truth declare I have no doubt it will bring the Republican interest in this city (if not the State) in the minority; and as it applies to the President himself, I am of opinion that he ought to be made acquainted with it. There is no truth more confirmed in my mind of the badness of the policy than keeping their political enemies in office to trample upon us; after which, if he perseveres, I am bold to say if I live to see another election I shall think it my duty to use my interest against his re-election." The commodore was a great admirer of Burr, but a month later the commodore himself, much against Mr. Gallatin's wishes, applied for and obtained the post of loan-officer in New York, under a recommendation of De Witt Clinton, and his mouth was henceforth closed. The share which Mr. Gallatin took in the New York contest is shown in the following letters:

BURR TO GALLATIN.

NEW YORK, June 8, 1801.

DEAR SIR,—I have seen with pain a paragraph in the Citizen of Friday respecting removals from office. Pray tell the President, notwithstanding any ebullitions of this kind, he may be confidently assured that the great mass of Republicans in this State are determined that he shall do things at his own time and in his own manner, and that they will justify his measures without inquiring into his reasons. I think you will not see any more paragraphs in the style of that referred to. . . .

BURR TO GALLATIN.

NEW YORK, June 23, 1801.

DEAR SIR,— . . . Strange reports are here in circulation respecting secret machinations against Davis. The arrangement having been made public by E. L., the character of Mr. D. is, in some measure, at stake on the event. He has already waived a very lucrative employment in expectation of this appointment. I am more and more confirmed in the opinion that his talents for that office are superior to those of any other person who can be thought of, and that his appointment will be the most popular. The opposition to him, if any is made, must proceed from improper motives, as no man dare openly avow an opinion hostile to the measure. This thing has, in my opinion, gone too far to be now defeated. Two men from the country, both very inferior to Mr. Davis in talents and pretensions, are spoken of as candidates,—I hope not seriously thought of. Any man from the country would be offensive,—either of these would be absurd, and Davis is too important to be trifled with.

You say nothing of the sinking fund.

Affectionately yours.

If you will show to the President what of the above relates to the naval office, you will save me the trouble of writing and him that of reading a longer letter to him on the subject.

BURR TO GALLATIN.

New York, September 8, 1801.

Dear Sir,—Mr. Davis is on his way to Monticello on the business too often talked of and too long left in suspense. I was surprised to learn from Mr. Jefferson that nothing had been said to him on this subject since a meeting had with his ministers early in May. About that period I wrote you a letter which I desired you to show him. Such requests are, however, always an appeal to discretion. The matter is now arrived at a crisis which calls for your opinion. This, I presume, you will give in unqualified terms. In the letter you may write by Davis I beg you also to inform Mr. J. of the characters of the gentlemen whose letters will be shown you, and I do entreat that there may now be a determination of some kind, for it has become a matter of too much speculation here why R. is kept in and why D. is not appointed.

Bradley will resign in the course of this month; you will have due notice. The next time you send a *verbal* message on business, I will thank you to commit it to writing.

God bless you!

Mr. D. has been goaded into this journey by the instances of an hundred friends, of whom I am not one. Yet I have not opposed it, and am rather gratified that he undertakes it.

GALLATIN TO JEFFERSON.

Washington, September 12, 1801.

Dear Sir,—This will be handed by M. L. Davis, of New York, the candidate for the naval office. I used my endeavors to prevent his proceeding to Monticello, but he has left New York with that intention, and is not easily diverted from his purpose. The reason he gives for his anxiety is that, immediately after the adjournment of Congress, E. Livingston and others mentioned to him that a positive arrangement was made by the Administration by which he was to be appointed to that office; that he was so perfectly confident, till some time in June, that such was the fact as to refuse advantageous proposals of a permanent establishment, and the general belief on that subject has placed him in a very awkward situation in New York.

He presses me much, on the ground of my personal knowledge both of him and of the local politics of New York, to give you my opinion in a decided manner on that subject, which to him I declined, both because in one respect it was not made up, and because my own opinion, even if decided, neither ought nor would decide yours. The propriety of removing Rogers remains with me the doubtful point; after Fish's removal and that of others, they in New York seem to suppose that the removal of Rogers is, on account of ante-revolutionary adherence to enemies, unavoidable; the answer to New Haven appears to have left no doubt on their minds on that subject, and I apprehend that the numerous removals already made by you there, and the almost general sweep by their State government, have only increased the anxiety and expectations of a total change. In relation to Rogers himself, though he is a good officer, I would feel but little regret at his being dismissed, because he has no claim detached from having fulfilled his official duties, has made an independent fortune by that office, and, having no personal popularity, cannot lose us one friend nor make us one enemy. But I feel a great reluctance in yielding to that general spirit of persecution, which, in that State particularly, disgraces our cause and sinks us on a level with our predecessors.

Whether policy must yield to principle by going further into those removals than justice to our political friends and the public welfare seem to require, is a question on which I do not feel myself at present capable of deciding.

I have used the word "persecution," and I think with propriety, for the council of appointments have extended their removals to almost every auctioneer, and that not being a political office the two parties ought certainly to have an equal chance in such appointments.

As to the other point, if Rogers shall be removed, I have no hesitation in saying that I do not know a man whom I would prefer to Mr. Davis for that office.

This may, however, be owing to my knowing him better than

I do others who may be equally well qualified. I believe Davis to be a man of talent, particularly quickness and correctness, suited for the office, of strict integrity, untainted reputation, and pure Republican principles. Nor am I deterred from saying so far in his favor on account of any personal connection with any other individuals; because I am convinced that his political principles stand not on the frail basis of persons, but are exclusively bottomed on conviction of their truth and will ever govern his political conduct. So far as I think a prejudice against him in that respect existed, I consider myself in justice to him bound to declare as my sincere opinion. Farther I cannot go. . . .

GALLATIN TO JEFFERSON.

WASHINGTON, 14th September, 1801.

. . . This is, however, only a trifling *family* controversy, and will not be attended with any other effect abroad except giving some temporary offence to Duane, Beckley, Israel, and some other very hot-headed but, I believe, honest Republicans. This leads me to a more important subject. Pennsylvania is, I think, fixed. Although we have there amongst our friends several office-hunters, Republicanism rests there on principle pretty generally, and it rests on the people at large, there not being in the whole State a single individual whose influence could command even now one county, or whose defection could lose us one hundred voters at an election.

It is ardently to be wished that the situation of New York was as favorable; but so much seems to depend in that State on certain individuals, the influence of a few is so great, and the majority in the city of New York, on which, unfortunately, the majority in the State actually depends (that city making one-eighth of the whole), is so artificial, that I much fear that we will eventually lose that State before next election of President.

The most favorable event would certainly be the division of every State into districts for the election of electors; with that single point and only common sense in the Administration, Republicanism would be established for one generation at least beyond controversy; but if not attainable as a general constitu-

tional provision, I think that our friends, whilst they can, ought
to introduce it immediately in New York. Davis's visit to Monticello has led me to that conclusion by drawing my attention
to that subject.

There are also two points connected with this, on which I wish
the Republicans throughout the Union would make up their
mind. Do they eventually mean not to support Burr as your
successor, when you shall think fit to retire? Do they mean
not to support him at next election for Vice-President? These
are serious questions, for although with Pennsylvania and Maryland we can fear nothing so long as you will remain the object
of contention with the Federalists, yet the danger would be
great should any unfortunate event deprive the people of your
services. Where is the man we could support with any reasonable prospect of success? Mr. Madison is the only one, and his
being a Virginian would be a considerable objection. But if,
without thinking of events more distant or merely contingent,
we confine ourselves to the next election, which is near enough,
the embarrassment is not less, for even Mr. Madison cannot on
that occasion be supported with you, and it seems to me that
there are but two ways: either to support Burr once more or to
give only one vote for President, scattering our other votes for
the other person to be voted for. If we do the first, we run, on
the one hand, the risk of the Federal party making Burr President, and we seem, on the other, to give him an additional pledge
of being eventually supported hereafter by the Republicans for
that office. If we embrace the last party, we not only lose the
Vice-President, but pave the way for the Federal successful candidate to that office to become President. All this would be
remedied by the amendment of distinguishing the votes for the
two offices, and by that of dividing the States into districts; but,
as it is extremely uncertain whether such amendments will succeed, we must act on the ground of elections going on as heretofore. And here I see the danger, but cannot discover the remedy.
It is indeed but with reluctance that I can ever think of the
policy necessary to counteract intrigues and personal views, and
wiser men than myself must devise the means. Yet had I felt
the same diffidence, I mean total want of confidence, which

during the course of last winter I discovered in a large majority
of the Republicans towards Burr, I would have been wise enough
never to give my consent in favor of his being supported last
election as Vice-President.   In this our party, those at least who
never could be reconciled to having him hereafter as President,
have made a capital fault, for which there was no necessity at the
time, and which has produced and will produce us much embarrassment.   I need not add that so far as your Administration can
influence anything of that kind, it is impossible for us to act
correctly unless the ultimate object is ascertained.   Yet I do not
believe that we can do much, for I dislike much the idea of supporting a section of Republicans in New York and mistrusting
the great majority because that section is supposed to be hostile
to Burr and he is considered as the leader of that majority.   A
great reason against such policy is that the reputed leaders of that
section, I mean the Livingstons generally, and some broken remnants of the Clintonian party, who hate Burr (for Governor
Clinton is out of question and will not act), are so selfish and so
uninfluential that they never can obtain their great object, the
State government, without the assistance of what is called Burr's
party, and will not hesitate a moment to bargain for that object
with him and his friends, granting in exchange their support
for anything he or they may want out of the State.   I do not
include in that number the Chancellor nor Mr. Armstrong, but
the first is in that State only a name, and there is something
which will forever prevent the last having any direct influence
with the people.   I said before that I was led to that train of
ideas by Davis's personal application, for, although in writing to
you by him I said, as I sincerely believe it, that he never would
nor could be influenced by B. or any other person to do an improper act or anything which could hurt the general Republican
principle, yet it is not to be doubted that, after all that has been
said on the subject, his refusal will by Burr be considered as a
declaration of war.   The Federals have been busy on the occasion.
Tillotson also has said many things which might not have been said
with equal propriety, and I do not know that there is hardly a
man who meddles with politics in New York who does not believe
that Davis's rejection is owing to Burr's recommendation. . . .

To all this Mr. Jefferson merely replied in a letter of 18th September, written from Monticello: "Mr. Davis is now with me. He has not opened himself. When he does, I shall inform him that nothing is decided, nor can be till we get together at Washington."

The appointment was not made. Rogers was retained in office until May 10, 1803, when he was removed and Samuel Osgood appointed in his place. Burr's last appeal is dated March 25, 1802, after the matter had been a year in debate. It is actually pathetic:

BURR TO GALLATIN.

March 25.

DEAR SIR,—. . . As to Davis, it is a small, very small favor to ask a *determination*. That "nothing is determined" is so commonplace that I should prefer any other answer to this only *request* which I have ever made.

I shall be abroad this evening, which I mention lest you might meditate a visit.

Yours.

These letters need no comment. Be the merits of the ultimate rupture between Jefferson and Burr what they may, the position of Mr. Gallatin is clear enough. He did not want that rupture. He had no affection for the great New York families which were the alternative to Burr; he regretted that deep-set distrust of the Vice-President which had always existed among the Virginians; his own relations with Burr and his friends were never otherwise than agreeable, and he could have no motive for expelling them from the party and driving them to desperation. On the other hand, Burr never included Mr. Gallatin in that exasperated vindictiveness of feeling which he entertained towards Mr. Jefferson himself and the southern Republicans; long afterwards, in conversation with Etienne Dumont in London, he expressed the opinion that Gallatin was the best head in the United States.[1] Yet, little as Mr. Gallatin was inclined to join in the persecution of Burr, he could not be

---

[1] See Parton's Burr, ii. 69.

blind to the fact that the large majority of Republicans felt no confidence in him; and time showed that this distrust was deserved. Mr. Jefferson followed quietly his own course of silent ostracism as regarded the Vice-President, and retained Rogers in office, so far as can be seen, solely to destroy Burr's influence, in the teeth of the reflection curtly expressed by Commodore Nicholson in the concluding sentence of the letter above quoted: "I would have Mr. Jefferson reflect, before I conclude, what will be said of his conduct in displacing officers who served in our revolution, and retaining a British tory, to say the least of Rogers." Whatever may have been Mr. Gallatin's own wishes, further intervention on his part was neither judicious nor likely to be successful.

Under the influence of these jealousies, Burr was rapidly forced into opposition, and New York politics became more than ever chaotic. Whether the Administration ultimately derived any advantage from pulling down Burr in order to set up George Clinton and General Armstrong is a matter in regard to which the opinion of Mr. Madison in 1812 would be worth knowing. The slight personal hold which Mr. Gallatin might have retained upon New York through the agency of his old friend Edward Livingston, who had received the appointment of district attorney, was destroyed in 1803 by Livingston's defalcation and removal to New Orleans. As these events occurred, and as they were rapidly followed by the Pennsylvania schism, in which Mr. Jefferson carefully balanced between the two parties, Mr. Gallatin, more and more disgusted at the revelations of moral depravity which forced themselves under his eyes, drew away from local and personal politics as far as he could, and became to a considerable degree isolated in regard to the two great States which he represented in the Cabinet. Disregarding, perhaps, too much the controversies which, however contemptible, necessarily involved his political influence, he devoted his attention to the loftier interests of national policy.

The summer and autumn of 1801 were consumed in mastering the details of Treasury business, in filling appointments to office, and in settling the scale of future expenditure in the different Departments. But when the time came for the preparation of the President's message at the meeting of Congress in December, Mr. Gallatin had not yet succeeded in reaching a decision on the questions of the internal revenue and of the debt. He had the support of the Cabinet on the main point, that payment of the debt should take precedence of reduction in the taxes, but reduction in the taxes was dependent on the amount of economy that could be effected in the navy, and the Secretary of the Navy resisted with considerable tenacity the disposition to reduce expenditures.

What Mr. Gallatin would have done with the navy, had he been left to deal with it in his own way, nowhere appears. He had opposed its construction, and would not have considered it a misfortune if Congress had swept it away; but he seems never to have interfered with it, after coming into office, further than to insist that the amount required for its support should be fixed at the lowest sum deemed proper by the head of that Department. In fact, Mr. Jefferson's Administration disappointed both friends and enemies in its management of the navy. The furious outcry which the Federalists raised against it on that account was quite unjust. Considering the persistent opposition which the Republican party had offered to the construction of the frigates, there can be no better example of the real conservatism of this Administration than the care which it took of the service, and even Mr. Gallatin, who honestly believed that the money would be better employed in reducing debt, grumbled not so much at the amount of the appropriations as at the want of good management in its expenditure. He thought that more should have been got for the money; but so far as the force was concerned, the last Administration had itself fixed the amount of reduction, and the new one only acted under that law, using the discretion given by it. That this is not a mere partisan apology is proved by the effective condition of our little navy in 1812; but the facts in regard to the subject are well known and fully stated in the histories of that branch of the service,—works in which there was no motive for political misrepresentation.[1]

---

[1] See Cooper's Naval History, i. 192–194.

Mr. Jefferson was in the habit of communicating the draft of his annual message to each head of department and requesting them to furnish him with their comments in writing. On these occasions Mr. Gallatin's notes were always elaborate and interesting. In his remarks in November, 1801, on the first annual message he gave a rough sketch of the financial situation, and at this time it appears that he hoped to cut down the army and navy estimates to $930,000 and $670,000 respectively. His financial scheme then stood as follows:

REVENUE.		EXPENDITURE.	
Impost,	$9,500,000	Interest, &c.,	$7,200,000
Lands and postage,	300,000	Civil expend.,	1,000,000
	$9,800,000	Military "	930,000
		Naval "	670,000
			$9,800,000

He calculated that the annual application of $7,200,000 to the payment of interest and principal would pay off about thirty-eight millions of the debt in eight years, and, fixing this as his standard, he proposed to make the other departments content themselves with whatever they could get as the difference between $7,200,000 and the revenue estimated at $9,800,000. On these terms alone he would consent to part with the internal revenue, which produced about $650,000.

This, however, seems to have been beyond his power. Few finance ministers have ever pressed their economies with more perseverance or authority than Mr. Gallatin, but he never succeeded in carrying on the government with so much frugality as this, and the sketch seems to indicate what the Administration would have liked to do, rather than what it did. The report of the Secretary of the Treasury a month later shows that he had been obliged to modify his plan. As officially announced, it was as follows:

REVENUE.		EXPENDITURE.	
Impost, &c.,	$9,500,000	Interest, &c.,	$7,100,000
Lands and postage,	450,000	Civil expend.,	980,000
	$9,950,000	Military "	1,420,000
Internal revenue,	650,000	Navy "	1,100,000
Total,	$10,600,000		$10,600,000

The problem of repealing the internal taxes was therefore not yet settled, and it is not very clear on the face of the estimates how it would be possible to effect this object. Mr. Gallatin expected to do it by economies in the military and naval establishments by which he should save the necessary $650,000. It is worth while to look forward over his administration and to see how far this expectation was justified, in order to understand precisely what his methods were.

His first step, as already noticed, was to fix the rate at which the debt should be discharged. This rate was ultimately represented by an annual appropriation of $7,300,000, which at the end of eight years, according to his first report, would pay off $32,289,000, and leave $45,592,000 of the national debt, and within the year 1817 would extinguish that debt entirely. This sum of $7,300,000 was therefore to be set aside out of the revenue as the permanent provision for paying the principal and interest of the debt.

Of the residue of income, which, without the internal taxes, was estimated at about $2,700,000, the civil expenditure was to require one million, the army and navy the remainder. But the tables of actual expenditure show a very different result:

	Civil.	Military.	Naval.	Total.
1802	$1,462,928	$1,358,988	$915,561	$3,737,477
1803	1,841,634	944,957	1,215,230	4,001,821
1804	2,191,008	1,072,015	1,189,832	4,452,855
1805	3,768,597	991,135	1,597,500	6,357,232
1806	2,890,136	1,540,420	1,649,641	6,080,197
1807	1.697,896	1,564,610	1,722,064	4,984,570
1808	1,423,283	3,196,985	1,884,067	6,504,335
1809	1,195,803	3,761,108	2,427,758	7,384,669
1810	1.101,144	2,555,692	1,654,244	5,311,080
1811	1,367,290	2,259,746	1,965,566	5,592,602
Total.	$18,939,719	$19,245,656	$16,221,463	$54,406,838

From these figures it appears that Mr. Gallatin's proposed economies were never realized, and that his results must have been attained by other means. The average expenditure on the navy during these ten years was $1,600,000 a year. Instead of establishments costing $2,700,000, the average annual expenditure reached $5,400,000, or precisely double the amount named. As a matter of fact, notwithstanding the frugality of Mr. Gallatin and the complaints of parsimony made by the Federalists, it is difficult to see how Mr. Jefferson's Administration was in essentials more economical than its predecessors, and this seems to have been Mr. Gallatin's own opinion at least so far as concerned the Navy Department. On the 18th January, 1803, he wrote a long letter to Mr. Jefferson on the navy estimates, closing with a strong remonstrance: "I cannot discover any approach towards reform in that department, and I hope that you will pardon my stating my opinion on that subject when you recollect with what zeal and perseverance I opposed for a number of years, whilst in Congress, similar loose demands for money. My opinions on that subject have been confirmed since you have called me in the Administration, and although I am sensible that in the opinion of many wise and good men my ideas of expenditure are considered as too contracted, I feel a strong confidence that on this particular point I am right." Again, on the 20th May, 1805, he renewed his complaint: "It is proper that I should state that the War Department has assisted us in that respect [economy] much better than the Navy Department. . . . As I know that there was an equal wish in both departments to aid in this juncture, it must be concluded either that the War is better organized than the Navy Department, or that naval business cannot be conducted on reasonable terms. Whatever the cause may be, I dare predict that whilst that state of things continues we will have no navy nor shall progress towards having one. As a citizen of the United States it is an event that I will not deprecate, but I think it due to the credit of your Administration that, after so much has been expended on that account, you should leave an increase of, rather than an impaired fleet. On this subject, the expense of the navy greater than the object seemed to require, and a merely nominal accountability, I have, for the sake of preserving perfect harmony in your councils, however grating to my feelings, been almost uniformly silent, and I beg that you will ascribe what I now say to a sense of duty and to the grateful attachment I feel for you."

Nevertheless, the internal duties were abolished as one of the

first acts of Mr. Jefferson's Administration, and at the same time
Congress adopted Mr. Gallatin's scheme of regulating the discharge of the public debt. The truth appears to be that the repeal
of these taxes was a party necessity, and that under the pressure
of that necessity both the Secretary of War and the Secretary of
the Navy were induced to lower their estimates to a point at which
Mr. Gallatin would consent to part with the tax. Mr. Gallatin
never did officially recommend the repeal. This measure was
founded on a report of John Randolph for the Committee of
Ways and Means, and Mr. Randolph's recommendation rested
on letters of the War and Navy Secretaries promising an economy
of $600,000 in their combined departments. These economies
never could be effected. The resource which for the time carried
Mr. Gallatin successfully over his difficulties was simply the
fact that he had taken the precaution to estimate the revenue
very low, and that there was uniformly a considerable excess in
the receipts over the previous estimate; but even this good fortune was not enough to save Mr. Gallatin's plan from failure.
The war with Tripoli had already begun, and further economies
in the navy were out of the question. Government attempted
for two years to persevere in its scheme, but it soon became evident that, even with the increased production of the import duties,
the expense of that war could not be met without recovering the
income sacrificed by the repeal of the internal taxes in 1802.
Accordingly an addition of 2½ per cent. was imposed on all im-
ported articles which paid duty *ad valorem*. The result of the
whole transaction, therefore, amounted only to a shifting of the
mode of collection, or, in other words, instead of raising a million
dollars from whiskey, stamps, &c., the million was raised on
articles of foreign produce or manufacture. This extra tax was
called the Mediterranean Fund, and was supposed to be a temporary resource for the Tripolitan war.

The final adjustment of this difficulty, therefore, took a simple
shape. Mr. Gallatin obtained his fund of $7,300,000 for dis-
charging principal and interest of the debt. This was what
he afterwards called his "fundamental substantial measure,"
which was intended to affirm and fix upon the government the
principle of paying its debt and of thus separating itself at

once from the whole class of corruptions and political theories
which were considered as the accompaniment of debt and which
were at that time identified with English and monarchical principles. To obtain the surplus necessary for maintaining this
fund he relied at first on frugality, and, finding that circumstances offered too great a resistance in this direction, he resorted
to taxation in the most economical form he could devise. In
regard to mere machinery he made every effort to simplify rather
than to complicate it. In his own words: "As to the forms
adopted for attaining that object [payment of the debt], they
are of a quite subordinate importance. Mr. Hamilton adopted
those which had been introduced in England by Mr. Pitt, the
apparatus of commissioners of the sinking fund, in whom were
vested the redeemed portions of the debt, which I considered as
entirely useless, but could not as Secretary of the Treasury
attack in front, as they were viewed as a check on that officer,
and because, owing to the prejudices of the time, the attempt
would have been represented as impairing the plan already
adopted for the payment of the debt. I only tried to simplify
the forms, and this was the object of my letter [of March 31,
1802] to the Committee of Ways and Means. The injury which
Mr. Pitt's plan did was to divert the public attention from the
only possible mode of paying a debt, viz., a surplus of receipts
over expenditures, and to inspire the absurd belief that there
was some mysterious property attached to a sinking fund which
would enable a nation to pay a debt without the *sine qua non*
condition of a surplus. . . . But the only injury done here by
the provisions respecting the commissioners of the sinking fund,
and by certain specific appropriations connected with the subject,
was to render it more complex, and the accounts of the public
debt less perspicuous and intelligible. Substantially they did
neither good nor harm. The payments for the public debt and
its redemption were not in the slightest degree affected, either
one way or the other, by the existence of the commissioners of
the sinking fund or by the repeal of the laws in reference to
them. The laws making permanent appropriations were much
more important. Even with respect to these it is obvious that
they must also have become nugatory whenever the expenditure

exceeded the income. Still they were undoubtedly useful by their tendency to check the public expenses."

The letter on the management of the sinking fund, mentioned in the above extract, will be found in the American State Papers[1] by readers who care to study the details of American finance. These details have a very subordinate importance; the essential points in Mr. Gallatin's history are the rules he caused to be adopted in regard to the payment of the debt, and the measures he took to secure revenue with which to make that payment. The rule adopted at his instance secured the ultimate extinction of the debt within the year 1817, provided he could maintain the necessary surplus revenue. The story of Mr. Gallatin's career as Secretary of the Treasury relates henceforward principally to the means he used or wished to use in order to defend or recover this surplus, and the interest of that career rests mainly in the obstructions which he met and the defeat which he finally sustained.

Nevertheless, it would be very unjust to Mr. Gallatin to imagine that his interest in the government was limited to payment of debt or to details of financial management. He was no doubt a careful, economical, and laborious financier, and this must be understood as the special field of his duty, but he was also a man of large and active mind, and his Department was charged with interests that were by no means exclusively financial. One of these interests related to the public lands.

As has been already seen, the public land system was organized under the previous Administrations, but it took shape and found its great development in Mr. Gallatin's hands. When the Administration of Mr. Jefferson came into power there were sixteen States in the Union, all of them, except Kentucky and Tennessee, lying on or near the Atlantic seaboard; at that time the Mississippi River bounded our territory to the westward, and the 31st parallel, which is still the northern line of portions of the States of Florida and Louisiana, was our southern boundary until it met the Mississippi. The public lands lay therefore in two great masses, divided by the States of Kentucky and Ten-

---

[1] Finance, vol. i. p. 746.

nessee; one of these masses was north of the Ohio River, extending to the lakes, the other west of Georgia, and both extended to the Mississippi. As yet the Indian titles had been extinguished over comparatively small portions of these territories, and in the process of managing her part of the lands the State of Georgia had succeeded in creating an entanglement so complicated as to defy all ordinary means of extrication. One of the first duties thrown upon Mr. Gallatin was that of acting, together with Mr. Madison and Mr. Lincoln, as commissioner on the part of the United States, to effect a compromise with the State of Georgia in regard to the boundary of that State and the settlement of the various claims already existing under different titles. Mr. Gallatin assumed the principal burden of the work, and the settlement effected by him closed this fruitful source of annoyances, fixed the western boundary of Georgia, and opened the way to the gradual development of the land system in the Alabama region. This settlement was the work of two years, but it was so deeply complicated with the famous Yazoo corruptions that fully ten years passed before the subject ceased to disturb politics.

At the same time he took in hand the affairs of the North-Western Territory. The more eastern portion of this vast domain had already a population sufficient to entitle it to admission as a State, and the subject came before Congress on the petition of its inhabitants. It was referred to a select committee, of which Mr. William B. Giles was chairman, and this committee in February, 1802, made a report based upon and accompanied by a letter from Mr. Gallatin.[1] The only difficulty presented in this case was that "of making some effectual provisions which may secure to the United States the proceeds of the sales of the western lands, so far at least as the same may be necessary to discharge the public debt for which they are solemnly pledged." To secure this result Mr. Gallatin proposed to insert in the act of admission a clause to that effect, but in order to obtain its acceptance by the State convention he suggested that an equivalent should be offered, which consisted in the reservation of one section in each

---

[1] Gallatin to W. B. Giles, 14th Feb., 1802, Writings, vol. i. p. 76.

township for the use of schools, in the grant of the Scioto salt springs, and in the reservation of one-tenth of the net proceeds of the land, to be applied to the building of roads from the Atlantic coast across Ohio. Congress reduced this reservation one-half, so that one-twentieth instead of one-tenth was reserved for roads ; but, with this exception, all Mr. Gallatin's ideas were embodied in a law passed on the 30th April, 1802, under which Ohio entered the Union. This was the origin of the once famous National Road, and the first step in the system of internal improvements, of which more will be said hereafter.

The details of organization of the land system belong more properly to the history of the new Territories and States than to a biography.[1] They implied much labor and minute attention, but they are not interesting, and they may be omitted here. There remains but one subject which Mr. Gallatin had much at heart, and which he earnestly pressed both upon the Administration and upon Congress. This was his old legislative doctrine of specific appropriations, which he caused Mr. Jefferson to introduce into his first message, and which he then seems to have persuaded his friend Joseph H. Nicholson to take in charge as the chairman of a special committee. At the request of this committee, Mr. Gallatin made a statement at considerable length on the 1st March, 1802.[2] The burden of this document was that too much arbitrary power had been left to the Secretary of the Treasury to put his own construction on the appropriation laws, and that no proper check existed over the War and Navy Departments ; the remedies suggested were specific appropriations and direct accountability of the War and Navy Departments to the Treasury officers. Mr. Nicholson accordingly introduced a bill for these purposes on April 8, 1802, but it was never debated, and it went over as unfinished business. Probably the resistance of the Navy Department prevented its adoption, for the letters of Mr. Gallatin to Mr. Jefferson, quoted above, show how utterly Mr. Gallatin failed in securing the exactness

---

[1] See Mr. Gallatin's " Introduction to the Collection of Land Laws, &c.," reprinted in his Writings, vol. iii.

[2] Printed in American State Papers, Finance, i. p. 755.

and accountability in that Department which he had so persistently demanded. Nor was this all. Probably nothing was farther from Mr. Gallatin's mind than to make of this effort a party demonstration. He was quite in earnest and quite right in saying that the practice had hitherto been loose and that it should be reformed, but his interest lay not in attacking the late Administration so much as in reforming his own. Unfortunately, the charge of loose practices under the former Administrations, unavoidable though it was, and indubitably correct, roused a storm of party feeling and even called out a pamphlet from the late Secretary of the Treasury, Wolcott. Mr. Gallatin therefore not only was charged with slandering the late Administration, but was obliged to submit to see the very vices which he complained of in it perpetuated in his own.

These were the great points of public policy on which Mr. Gallatin's mind was engaged during his first year of office, and it is evident that they were enough to absorb his entire attention. The mass of details to be studied and of operations to be learned or watched completely weighed him down, and caused him ever to look back upon this year as the most laborious of his life. The mere recollection of this labor afterwards made him shrink from the idea of returning to the Treasury when it was again pressed upon him in later years: "To fill that office in the manner I did, and as it ought to be filled, is a most laborious task and labor of the most tedious kind. To fit myself for it, to be able to understand thoroughly, to embrace and to control all its details, took from me, during the two first years I held it, every hour of the day and many of the night, and had nearly brought a pulmonary complaint."[1] Fortunately, his mind was not, in these early days of power, greatly agitated by anxieties or complications in public affairs. The whole struggle which had tortured the two previous Administrations both abroad and at home, the internecine contest between France and her enemies, was for a time at an end; Mr. Madison had nothing on his hands but the vexatious troubles with the Algerine powers, in regard to which there was no serious difference of opinion in

---

[1] See infra, p. 607.

America; Congress was mainly occupied with the repeal of the judiciary bill, a subject which did not closely touch Mr. Gallatin's interests otherwise than as a measure of economy; Mr. Jefferson's keenest anxieties, as shown in his correspondence of this year, seem to have regarded the distribution of offices and the management of party schisms. After the tempestuous violence of the two last Administrations the country was glad of repose, and its economical interests assumed almost exclusive importance for a time.

It was at this period of his life that Gilbert Stuart painted the portrait, an engraving of which faces the title-page of this volume. Mrs. Gallatin always complained that her husband's features were softened and enfeebled in this painting until their character was lost. Softened though they be, enough is left to show the shape and the poise of the head, the outlines of the features, and the expression of the eyes. Set side by side with the heads of Jefferson and Madison, this portrait suggests curious contrasts and analogies, but, looked at in whatever light one will, there is in it a sense of repose, an absence of nervous restlessness, mental or physical, unusual in American politicians; and, unless Stuart's hand for once forgot its cunning, he saw in Mr. Gallatin's face a capacity for abstraction and self-absorption often, if not always, associated with very high mental power; an habitual concentration within himself, which was liable to be interpreted as a sense of personal superiority, however carefully concealed or controlled, and a habit of judging men with judgments the more absolute because very rarely expressed. The faculty of reticence is stamped on the canvas, although the keen observation and the shrewd, habitual caution, so marked in the long, prominent nose, are lost in the feebleness of the mouth, which never existed in the original. Mr. Gallatin lived to have two excellent portraits taken by the daguerreotype process. Students of character will find amusement in comparing these with Stuart's painting. Age had brought out in strong relief the shrewd and slightly humorous expression of the mouth; the most fluent and agreeable talker of his time was still the most laborious analyzer and silent observer; the consciousness of personal superiority was more strongly apparent than ever;

but the man had lost his control over events and his confidence in results; he had become a critic, and, however genial and conscientious his criticism might be, he had a deeper sense of isolation than fifty years before.

In person he was rather tall than short, about five feet nine or ten inches high, with a compact figure, and a weight of about one hundred and fifty pounds. His complexion was dark; his hair black; but when Stuart painted him he was already decidedly bald. His eyes were hazel, and, if one may judge from the painting, they were the best feature in his face.

Of his social life, his private impressions, and his intimate conversation with the persons most in his confidence at this time, not a trace can now be recovered. Rarely separated from his wife and children, except for short intervals in summer, he had no occasion to write domestic letters, and his correspondence, even with Mr. Jefferson, was for the most part engrossed by office-seeking and office-giving. After some intermediate experiment he at last took a house on Capitol Hill, where he remained through his whole term of office. When the British army entered Washington in 1814, a shot fired from this house at their general caused the troops to attack and destroy it, and even its site is now lost, owing to the extension of the Capitol grounds on that side. It stood north-east of the Capitol, on the Bladensburg Road, and its close neighborhood to the Houses of Congress brought Mr. Gallatin into intimate social relations with the members. The principal adherents of the Administration in Congress were always on terms of intimacy in Mr. Gallatin's house, and much of the confidential communication between Mr. Jefferson and his party in the Legislature passed through this channel. Nathaniel Macon, the Speaker; John Randolph, the leader of the House; Joseph H. Nicholson, one of its most active members; Wilson Cary Nicholas, Senator from Virginia; Abraham Baldwin, Senator from Georgia, and numbers of less influential leaders, were constantly here, and Mr. Gallatin's long service in Congress and his great influence there continued for some years to operate in his favor. But the communication was almost entirely oral, and hardly a trace of it has been preserved either in the writings of Mr. Gallatin or in those of his contemporaries. For several years the government worked smoothly; no man appeared among the Republicans with either the disposition or the courage to oppose Mr. Jefferson, and every moment of Mr. Gallatin's time was absorbed in attention to the duties of his Department, on which the principal weight of responsibility fell.

The adjournment of Congress on May 3, 1802, left the Administration at leisure to carry on the business of government without interruption. Mr. Gallatin immediately afterwards took his wife and family to New York, where, as now became their custom, they passed the summer with Commodore Nicholson, and where Mr. Gallatin himself was in the habit of joining them during the unhealthy season of the Washington climate, when the Administration usually broke up. "Grumble who will," wrote Mr. Jefferson, "I will never pass those months on tidewater." Leaving his wife in New York, Mr. Gallatin returned to his work at Washington. On these journeys he usually stopped at Baltimore to visit the Nicholsons, and at Philadelphia to see Mr. and Mrs. Dallas. The society of Washington was small and intimate, but seems to have had no very strong hold over him. He was much in the habit, when left alone there, of dining informally with Mr. Jefferson and Mr. Madison. General Dearborn's family was in close relations with his, and the Laws, who were now at Mount Vernon, were leaders of fashionable society. But his residence at Washington was saddened in the month of April of this year, by the loss of an infant daughter, a misfortune followed in 1805 and 1808 by two others almost precisely similar, which tended to throw a dark shadow over the Washington life and to make society distasteful. His close attention to business seems at this time to have affected his health, and the absence of his family still more affected his spirits. He worked persistently to get the business of his office into a condition that would enable him to rejoin his wife for a time, and almost the only glimpse of society his letters furnish is contained in the following extract, which has a certain interest as characteristic of his political feelings:

WASHINGTON, 7th July, 1802.

. . . Monday all the city, ladies and gentlemen, dined in a tent near the navy yard; we were about 150 in company. I suppose every one enjoyed it as his spirits permitted; to me it looked very sober and dull. Indeed, dinners of a political cast cannot, in the present state of parties, be very cheerful unless confined to one party. It is unfortunate, but it is true. I had another cause which damped my spirits. We were in an enclosure formed with sails stretched about six feet high, and some marines were placed as sentries to prevent intrusion; for the arrangements had been made by Burrows and Tingey. The very sight of a bayonet to preserve order amongst citizens rouses my indignation, and you may judge of my feelings when I tell you that one of the sentries actually stabbed a mechanic who abused him because he had been ordered away. The bayonet went six inches in his body and close to his heart. He is not dead, but still in great danger, and the marine in jail. Such are the effects of what is called discipline in times of peace. The distribution of our little army to distant garrisons where hardly any other inhabitant is to be found is the most eligible arrangement of that perhaps necessary evil that can be contrived. But I never want to see the face of one in our cities and intermixed with the people. The mammoth cheese was cut on Monday; it is said to be good; I found it detestable.

At length he succeeded in getting away, but was obliged to return in August, and his letters became wails of despair, in which there was always a little mingling of humor. The following is a specimen:

WASHINGTON, August 17, 1802.

. . . As to myself I cannot complain, but yet am as low-spirited as before; it will never do for me to keep house apart from you and in this hateful place. I am told that even within five or six miles from this place, and off the waters, intermittent and bilious complaints are unknown. . . . I am good for nothing during your absence; the servants do what they please; everything goes as it pleases. I smoke and sleep; mind nothing,—neither chairs, bedstead, or house,—ten to one whether I will call on Mrs. Carroll till your return. All those concerns you must mind. I grow more indolent and unsociable every day. If I have not you, and the children, and the sisters in a very short time, I cannot tell what will become of me. I have not called on Mrs. Law, though she sent a message to know when you and Maria were expected. How is Maria? as prudish as ever? I wish she was in love. You do not perceive the connection, perhaps, but I do. Tell her, ugly as I am, I love her dearly, that is to say, as much as my apathy will permit. . . . I have been so gloomy this summer that I mean to frolic all next winter with the girls,—assemblies, dinners, card-parties, abroad and at home. You, my dear, will stay home to nurse the children and entertain political visitors. . . .

24th August, 1802.

. . . Nothing but the hope of seeing you soon has kept in any degree my spirits from sinking. Whether in the plains or over the hills, whether in city or in retreat, I cannot live without you. It is trifling with that share of happiness which Providence permits us to enjoy to be forever again and again parted. I am now good for nothing but for you, and good for nothing without you; you will say that anyhow I am not good for much; that may be, but such as I am, you are mine, and you are my comfort, my joy, and the darling of my soul. Now do not go and show this to Maria; not that I am ashamed of it, for I glory in my love for you; but she will think my expressing myself that way very foolish, and I am afraid of her.

Early in October, 1802, they were again in Washington, and Mr. Gallatin resumed work with more philosophy. The rest of the Cabinet gradually assembled. When the time came for the Secretary of the Treasury to make his annual report to Congress, he was able to say, as the result of his first year's administration, that the revenue from import duties, instead of $9,500,000 as he had estimated, had produced $12,280,000, a sum which exceeded "by $1,200,000 the aggregate heretofore collected in any one year, on account of both the import and the internal duties repealed by an Act of last session." The report, however, was still cautious in its estimates for the future; in the face of possible losses in revenue, arising from peace in Europe, it adhered closely to last year's estimates, and in the face of navy deficits for 1801 and 1802 still maintained $1,700,000 as the total appropriation for army and navy combined. The receipts and expenditures were still to be $10,000,000, and last year's excess was to be held as a protection against a possible falling off in the revenue.

In his notes on the draft of Mr. Jefferson's annual message, Mr. Gallatin's criticisms this year seem to express the satisfaction he doubtless felt at the success they had met. Mr. Jefferson's weakest side was his want of a sense of humor and his consequent blind exposure to ridicule. Mr. Gallatin himself now and then ventured to indulge a little of his own sense of humor at the cost of his chief, as, for instance, when he criticised the first paragraph of this message as follows: "As to style, I am a bad judge; but I do not like in the first paragraph the idea of limiting the *quantum* of thankfulness due to the Supreme Being, and there is also, it seems, too much said of the Indians in the enumerations of our blessings in the next sentence." But occasionally he flatly opposed Mr. Jefferson's favorite schemes, and it is curious to notice the results in some of these cases. This year, in regard to Mr. Jefferson's famous recommendation of dry-docks at Washington, Mr. Gallatin's note said: "I am *in toto* against this recommendation, 1st, because, so long as the Mediterranean war lasts, we will not have any money to spare for the navy; and 2d, because, if dry-docks are necessary, so long as we have six navy-yards, it seems to me that a general recommendation would be sufficient, leaving the Legislature free either to designate the place or to trust the Executive with the selection." This was certainly travelling out of his own department into the bounds of another, and Mr. Jefferson adhered to his dry-docks in spite of Mr. Gallatin, who told him that the scheme would not command thirty votes in Congress; and this turned out to be the case.

But the Mediterranean war was Mr. Gallatin's great annoyance at present. His letters to Mr. Jefferson show how persistently he pressed his wish for peace. In one, dated August 16, 1802, he said : "I sincerely wish you could reconcile it to yourself to empower our negotiators to give, if necessary for peace [with Tunis, Tripoli, and Morocco], an annuity to Tripoli. I consider it no greater disgrace to pay them than Algiers. And, indeed, we share the dishonor of paying those barbarians with so many nations as powerful and interested as ourselves, that, in our present situation, I consider it a mere matter of calculation whether the purchase of peace is not cheaper than the expense of a war, which shall not even give us the free use of the Mediterranean trade. . . . Eight years hence we shall, I trust, be able to assume a different tone ; but our exertions at present consume the seeds of our greatness and retard to an indefinite time the epoch of our strength."

But the Tripolitan war and the difficulties with Morocco were soon thrown into the shade by events of a much more serious kind, which threatened to break down Mr. Gallatin's arrangements in a summary way. In the course of the summer of 1802 it had become known that France, by a secret treaty, had acquired Louisiana from Spain, and had determined to take possession of that province. While our minister in Paris was reporting the progress of the movements which were to place a French army across the stream of the lower Mississippi, our government received information in October that the Spanish intendant at New Orleans had interdicted the right of deposit for merchandise which had hitherto been enjoyed there by our citizens. Kentucky and Tennessee were exasperated at this step, and there was some danger that they might begin a war on their own account. The Administration at once took measures to guard against these perils, so far as was possible. A confidential message was sent to the Senate on January 11, containing the nomination of Mr. Monroe to act with Mr. Livingston, then minister in Paris, as special commissioners for the purchase of the eastern bank of the Mississippi. Another confidential message had been previously sent to the House, which debated upon it in secret session. What passed there is briefly mentioned by Mr. Galla-

tin in a note of the 3d December, 1805: "A public resolution
. . . was moved by Randolph and adopted by the House. A
committee in the mean while brought in a confidential report to
support and justify the President in the purchase he was going
to attempt, and to this an appropriation law in general terms was
added."

After a few months of anxiety and silent preparation, the
Administration had the profound satisfaction to see this storm
disappear as suddenly as it had risen. The renewal of war
between England and France led the First Consul not to accept
the American offer to purchase Louisiana from the Mississippi
to Pensacola, but to propose the sale of all Louisiana, which
then embraced the whole western bank of the Mississippi from
its source to the Gulf of Mexico. This idea was naturally
accepted with eagerness by the Administration, and even Mr.
Gallatin seems to have felt for once no hesitation about increasing the national debt, a necessary consequence of the
purchase.

The session, however, did not pass away without producing
an attack upon Mr. Gallatin's management of the Treasury.
This attack was not a very serious one, nor is it one that either
then or now could be made interesting. The Federal party,
which had created the United States Bank, viewed with jealousy
the course pursued by the Administration towards that institution. Mr. Jefferson's letters, in fact, show a deep and not very
intelligent hostility to the bank. On the 7th October, 1802, he
wrote to Mr. Gallatin that he should make a judicious distribution of his favors among all the banks, since the stock of the
United States Bank was held largely by foreigners, and "were
the Bank of the United States to swallow up the others and
monopolize the whole banking business of the United States,
which the demands we furnish them with tend shortly to favor,
we might, on a misunderstanding with a foreign power, be immensely embarrassed by any disaffection in that bank." On
the 12th July, 1803, he renewed this proposition from another
stand-point: "I am decidedly in favor of making all the banks
republican by sharing deposits among them in proportion to the
dispositions they show. If the law now forbids it, we should

not permit another session of Congress to pass without amending it. It is material to the safety of Republicanism to detach the mercantile interest from its enemies and incorporate them into the body of its friends. A merchant is naturally a Republican, and can be otherwise only from a vitiated state of things."[1] Mr. Gallatin gently put aside these demonstrations of Mr. Jefferson,[2] and administered his Department on business principles, with as little regard to political influence as possible. He looked on the bank as an instrument that could not be safely thrown away; without it his financial operations would be much more slow, more costly, more hazardous, and more troublesome than with it; indeed, he was quite aware that its fall would necessarily be followed by much financial confusion, and he had no mind to let such experiments in finance come between him and his great administrative objects. He was, therefore, by necessity a friend and protector of the bank.

The Federalists did not yet fully understand this fact, and they were disturbed at learning that Mr. Gallatin had sold, on account of the sinking fund, a certain number of bank shares in order to pay the Dutch debt. The shares were purchased by Alexander Baring under very favorable conditions, and the Federalists showed that they expected little from their motion by making it only on the last day of the session. At the same time Mr. Griswold, in an elaborate speech made on March 2, attacked the accounts of the sinking fund. The only result of these combined attacks was to call out replies from the Administration speakers and a long letter from Mr. Gallatin himself on the operations of the sinking fund. This letter, replying to Mr. Griswold's attack, was written in response to a resolution of the House, and was completed in time to be presented, before the close of the session, on the night of the 3d March. It appears to have met all Mr. Griswold's criticisms. At all

---

[1] See also his letter to Mr. Gallatin of 13th December, 1803, Jefferson's Works, iv. 518.

[2] See his letter to Mr. Jefferson of 13th December, 1803, Writings, vol. i. p. 171.

[3] This paper is printed in the Annals of Congress, 7th Cong., 2d Sess., p. 690; also in American State Papers, Finance, vol. ii. p. 87.

events, the attack seems to have made no impression, and in all probability the Federalists themselves intended only to punish Mr. Gallatin for the trouble he had so often in a similar manner inflicted upon them.

The adjournment of Congress closed the second year of Mr. Jefferson's Administration. With the exception of that Louisiana anxiety, which another month was to clear away, these two years had been marked by complete success. Never before had the country enjoyed so much peace, contentment, and prosperity. Mr. Gallatin himself had in these two years succeeded in making himself master of the situation; he was more powerful and more indispensable than ever; his financial policy was firmly established; his hold, both in Cabinet and in Congress, was undisputed; every day brought his projects nearer to realization, and every day relieved him from the absorbing labor which had made his first two years of office so burdensome.

Nevertheless there was cause enough for anxiety. The approaching storm in Europe, which was to shake Louisiana into the President's lap, brought with it dangers in regard to which the experience of Washington and John Adams would have been valuable to Mr. Jefferson had he only been willing to profit by it; but, over-confident in the virtue of his theories, he, as his correspondence shows, was firmly convinced that he could balance himself between the two mighty powers which had dealt so rudely with his predecessors, and it was a cardinal principle with the Republican party that our foreign relations were endangered only by the faults of Federalism, and were safe only in Republican hands. "I do not believe," wrote Mr. Jefferson on July 11, 1803, "we shall have as much to swallow from them as our predecessors had." "We think," he wrote on the next day, "that peaceable means may be devised of keeping nations in the path of justice towards us, by making justice their interest, and injuries to react on themselves." This was the very point to be proved, and on the result of this theoretical doctrine was to depend the fate of Mr. Jefferson's Administration and of Mr. Gallatin's financial hopes.

Besides this grave danger, which was destined steadily to take more and more serious proportions, there were smaller political difficulties, which in their nature must increase in importance with every embarrassment that the future had in store. The party schism led by Vice-President Burr was now beginning to rage with fury and to do infinite mischief in New York. In Pennsylvania matters were still worse, at least for Mr. Gallatin, whose political interests lay in that State. The very completeness of the Republican triumph in Pennsylvania was fatal to the party. The extremists, led by Duane and his friend Michael Leib, began a schism of their own, the more dangerous because they avoided the mistake of Burr and declared no war on Mr. Jefferson. Indeed, they followed the very opposite policy, and, sheltering themselves under the cover of their pure Republicanism with Mr. Jefferson for their peculiar patron, they declared war upon Mr. Jefferson's Cabinet. On the 10th May, 1803, Joseph H. Nicholson warned Mr. Gallatin of what was to happen: "I have enclosed the President a letter from Captain Jones to me, which you can see if you please. He says that Duane and his coadjutors meditate an attack upon Mr. Madison and yourself for setting your faces against the office-hunters." Mr. Jefferson on this occasion did not treat Duane as he had treated Burr; he attempted to intervene and soothe the susceptibilities of his over-zealous partisans. He consulted Mr. Gallatin on the subject, and sent him the draft of a letter to Duane. Mr. Gallatin, on the 13th August, 1803, returned the draft and attempted to dissuade the President from sending the proposed letter: "Either a schism will take place, in which case the leaders of those men would divide from us, or time and the good sense of the people will of themselves cure the evil. I have reason to believe that the last will happen, and that the number of malcontents is not very considerable and will diminish. . . . It is highly probable that Duane, who may be misled by vanity and by his associates, but whose sincere Republicanism I cannot permit myself to doubt, will adhere to us when his best friends shall have taken a decided part. . . . If a letter shall be written, I think that, if possible, it should be much shorter than your draft, and have perhaps less the appearance of apology. The irresistible argument to men disposed to listen to argument appears to me to be the perfect approbation given by the Republicans to all the leading measures of government, and the inference that men who are disposed under those circumstances to asperse Administration seem to avow that the hard struggle of so many years was not for the purpose of securing our republican institutions and of giving a proper direction to the operations of government, but for the sake of a few paltry offices,—offices not of a political and discretionary nature, but mere inferior administrative offices of profit."

Mr. Jefferson seems to have followed this advice and to have suppressed the proposed letter.[1]　Duane continued his attacks on the moderate wing of the Republican party, and Mr. Gallatin's hopes that he would find no following were soon disappointed. A complete separation took place between him and Governor McKean.　Perhaps the existence of this schism had something to do with the offer, which Mr. Dallas was now commissioned to make, of putting Governor McKean in nomination for the Vice-Presidency in the general election of 1804.　The offer was declined, and George Clinton was substituted in his place, but Governor McKean's letter of declination is so characteristic as to be worth publication.

THOMAS McKEAN TO ALEXANDER J. DALLAS.

LANCASTER, 16th October, 1808.

DEAR SIR,—Your friendly letter of the 14th has been read with pleasure.　I am much obliged to the kind sentiments of my friends in thinking me a suitable character to be proposed as a candidate for the dignified station of Vice-President of the United States, but must absolutely decline that honor.　The office of Governor of Pennsylvania satisfies my ambition, and it has been conferred in such a manner, at two elections, that the people are endeared to me; indeed, it appears to me that I am engaged to continue in this distinguished character the constitutional term, if it shall be the desire of my fellow-citizens.　I am now descending in the vale of years, and am satisfied with my share of honors; that of President of the United States in Con-

---

[1] This letter will be found in Gallatin's Writings, vol. i. p. 130.

gress assembled in the year 1781 (a proud year for Americans) equalled any merit or pretensions of mine, and cannot now be increased by the office of Vice-President. But, all personal considerations waived, what would be the probable result of my acceptance of the proposed post? Little, very little benefit to the people of America, but at least a doubtful situation to my fellow-citizens of Pennsylvania. What would be the fate of my friends, of those I have placed in office, and of the liberty of the State at this most critical period, were I to resign the office? Who is there to control the wanton passions of men in general respectable, suddenly raised to power and frisking in the pasture of true liberty, yet not sufficiently secured by proper barriers? But I must say no more on this head, even to a friend; it savors so much of vanity. In brief, who will be my successor, possessing the same advantages from nativity in the State, education, experience, and from long public services in the most influential stations and employments; who can or will take the same liberty in vetoes of legislative acts, or otherwise, as I have done? I confess I am at a loss to name him, and yet, when I must resign by death or otherwise, I trust the world will go on as well as it has done, if not better, though I never had existed.

Be so good as to pay my most respectful compliments to the President, to Messrs. Madison, Gallatin, Dearborn, Granger, etc., and compliments to all mine and your friends. Farewell and prosper. Adieu.

Mr. Jefferson's party required very delicate handling. Embracing, as it did, materials of the most discordant kind, schism was its normal condition. Between the purity of Madison and Gallatin and the selfishness and prejudice of the local politicians, Mr. Jefferson was obliged to make what compromise he could; but while with quiet determination he drove Burr out of the party, he tolerated Duane and Leib with extraordinary patience. There were very strong reasons which justified or excused his treatment of Burr; particularly the position of heir-apparent, which the Vice-President occupied, made it necessary either to recognize or reject his claims, and Mr. Jefferson did not hesitate to reject them. Whether his treatment of Duane was to be equally defensible became more and more a subject of vital consequence to Mr. Gallatin.

So long as Virginia remained steady the Administration had little to fear, and as yet there was no sign of schism in the Virginia ranks. Of all the Virginia members John Randolph was the most prominent, and his support was firm. Mr. Gallatin and he were on the most intimate terms, and since Gallatin's letters to him are lost, some of his letters to Gallatin may be worth inserting, to show their relations together:

JOHN RANDOLPH TO GALLATIN.

BIZARRE, 9th April (27th year), 1803.

DEAR SIR,—When your letter arrived I was from home, and, ours being a weekly post, my reply is necessarily delayed longer than I could wish.

Mr. Griswold's first objections to the report of the commissioners of the sinking fund are (if in existence, which I very much doubt) among other loose papers which I left in Georgetown. The paragraph which you enclose differs from most which have appeared of late in a certain description of prints, in this, that it contains *some truth*. But, as it is resorted to only to serve as the vehicle of much falsehood, it is proper that a correct statement should go forth to the public of this singular transaction.

If I mistake not, the printing of the report of the sinking fund was considerably delayed. Be that as it may, when Mr. Griswold moved to commit it to the Ways and Means he specified no objection; he barely said that there were some parts which required explanation; but, as all documents of that sort are of course committed to that committee, there was no occasion for any reasoning to induce the House to agree to such a motion. The resolution which he afterwards drafted, and which he showed to me, was, I believe, couched in the very terms of that which was passed by the House, the words "in fact" excepted, which at my suggestion he expunged, since he declared that he had no intention to criminate the Treasury and doubted not that everything could and would be satisfactorily explained. I then proposed to him to reduce his objections to writing. They con-

sisted of a denial of the soundness of the construction given by
the Treasury to the law of 1802 making provision for the redemption of the whole public debt, which was the object embraced by the resolution; and an inquiry into the variance
between the report of the Secretary of the Treasury of December, 1801, and the report of the sinking fund, in respect to the
amount of interest of the public debt and the instalments of the
Dutch debt due in 1802. There may have been some items
which I do not recollect. But I perfectly remember what they
did not contain. There was not a syllable about the unaccounted
balance of 114,000 dollars, nor of the detailed accounts in relation to the remittances on account of the foreign debt, contained
in the 4th, 7th, and part of the 3d queries in my official letter to
you (A. 1). The first intelligence which I had of this unaccounted balance was from yourself. It made its appearance in
a pamphlet ascribed to Stanley and addressed to his constituents.
So careful were the friends of this little work that it should not
get abroad, that by mere accident a single copy fell into the hands
of Alston on the day before Mr. Griswold brought forward his
motion. Huger, who let Alston have it, enjoined him not to let
it go out of his hands. He on the contrary carried it to you, and
during the short time that it was in your possession I accidentally
stepped in whilst you were looking over it, and this was the first
notice which I received of Mr. Griswold's redoubtable attack on
that point. It may be proper to add that when he put into my
hands the paper containing the first objections to the report, I
offered to transmit them to you, provided he would move it in
committee; and the committee were actually convened for that
purpose, but he did not attend. He declined also a proposition
of waiting on you in person when I offered to accompany him.
The committee taking no order on his objections, they were submitted to you by me, and so long a time elapsed that I really
conceived he had abandoned his project. On our return home
Alston told me that Huger was very much irritated against him,
and those in his quarter of the House mortified and astonished,
when I mentioned the coincidence between Griswold's speech and
Stanley's letter.

And now, dismissing this miserable race of cavillers and

equivocators, let me beg you to have a reverend care of your
health, and to assure Mrs. G. (*not* Griswold) and her sisters of
my best wishes for their health and happiness. Mr. Nym and
the young secretary will participate my friendly inquiries. I do
not ask you to continue to write to me, because I know the
demands upon your time both by health and business. But a
line of how and where you all are will always be acceptable to
one who interests himself in everything relating to you.

My health is fluctuating; the weather is raw and the spring a
month behindhand. Moreover, we have had but one rain, and
that moderate, since the last snow on the 8th March. Of course
I am vaporish and gouty. Adieu.

Yours truly.

P.S.—Smith should make a statement "by authority" in his
paper conformably with the within.

At an election at Charlotte C. H. on Monday last, J. Randolph had 717 votes, C. Carrington 2.

JOHN RANDOLPH TO GALLATIN.

BIZARRE, 4th June, 27th year [1803].

DEAR SIR,—Having sustained an injury in my hand, I have
been for some time debarred the use of my pen. The first exercise
of my recovered right shall be to thank you for your last very
friendly and acceptable letter.

Nothing can be more clear and satisfactory than Bayard's
answer to himself, according to your statement of it. But I
cannot help suspecting a difference between the printed speech
and the original, not at all to the advantage of the latter. I
am unwilling to believe that he was guilty of so gross an absurdity (in debate), because I am unwilling to believe that we
were guilty of yet grosser stupidity, even after making every
allowance for being worried down with fatigue. Such a thing
might have escaped me, and perhaps Nicholson; but that General Smith should fail to detect it appears incredible. So far,
however, from overdosing me with the bank stock, as you seem
to apprehend, it is evident you have not given me quantum
suff.

You have seen the result of our elections. Federal exultation has, however, received a severe check in those of New York. Indeed, I do not conceive the event here to be indicative of any change in the public sentiment. The elections, with a single exception, have been conducted on personal rather than on party motives. Brent completely defeated himself, and, although I love the man, I cannot very heartily lament his ill success. By the way, I think you wise men at the seat of government have much to answer for in respect to the temper prevailing around you. By their fruit shall ye know them. Is there something more of system yet introduced among you? or are you still in chaos, without form and void? Should you have leisure, give me a hint of the first news from Mr. Monroe. After all the vaporing, I have no expectation of a serious war. Tant pis pour nous.

You ask if I have seen Rennell's new map of North Africa? forgetting that I live out of the light of anything but the sun; and he has not condescended to shine, but at short intervals, for a fortnight. I suppose it is the map which he compiled from Parke's Travels. Do you recollect my suggesting to you, soon after the work came out, a suspicion that the Niger was the true Nile? and your determining that he should be swallowed up in the sands of the desert, which we carried into instant execution.

Present me most sincerely, and permit me to add, affectionately, to Mrs. Gallatin, and believe me, dear sir, most truly yours.

P.S.—I address this to Washington, where it will be put in train to reach you. I sincerely hope it will find you much recruited by the wise step which you have taken.

The Louisiana treaty threw on Mr. Gallatin a new class of duties. He had to make all the arrangements not only for payment of the purchase-money to France, but for the modifications of his financial system which so large and so sudden an emergency required. Fortunately, Alexander Baring was the person with whom he had principally to deal in regard to payments, and his relations with Mr. Baring were very friendly; so friendly, indeed, as to have a decisive influence, some ten years later, in a most serious crisis of Mr. Gallatin's life and of our national history. With Mr. Baring's assistance the business details were successfully arranged, and it only remained to adjust the new burden of debt to the national resources.

Congress was called together in October on account of the Louisiana business. It is curious to notice how, in his comments on this year's message, Mr. Gallatin gently held the President back from every appearance of hostility to England and of overwarm demonstrations towards Bonaparte, and how he still talked of economies in the Navy Department to supply some of his financial deficiencies, though this resource was already mentioned only as a desirable possibility. In fact, Congress was about to abandon the attempt at further economy in that Department, and in order to relieve the Treasury the Mediterranean fund was now created for naval expenses. Mr. Gallatin had to look for his resources elsewhere.

The financial problem was to provide for the new purchase and its consequent expenditure without imposing new taxes. The point was a delicate one, and was managed by Mr. Gallatin as follows:

The purchase-money for Louisiana was $15,000,000. Of this sum, $11,250,000 was paid in new six per cent. stock. There was specie enough in the Treasury to pay $2,000,000 more; and Mr. Gallatin requested authority to borrow the remaining $1,750,000 at six per cent.

The consequent increase of annual interest on the debt, including commissions and exchange, he estimated at $800,000. To provide this he counted on an increase of revenue from imposts and lands, as indicated by the returns for the past year, equal to $600,000, and an income of $200,000 from Louisiana.

An annual appropriation of $700,000 was to be set aside for the interest on the $11,250,000 new stock, and added to the permanent appropriation of $7,300,000; so that in future $8,000,000 should be annually applied to payment of interest and principal of the debt, thus preserving the ratio of reduction already established.

Perhaps as a matter of fact the success of Mr. Gallatin in avoiding new taxes was rather apparent than real. Had he been able to carry out his economies in the navy, he might indeed have avoided taxation, but this was fairly proved impossible, and the confession of a failure here was only evaded by the fiction of creating a temporary fund for extraordinary naval purposes, which allowed the supposed regular naval expenditure to be estimated at Mr. Gallatin's figures. This was obviously in the nature of a compromise between the Treasury and the Navy, but it was not the less a real increase of taxation, and, as events proved, a permanent increase. The capture of the frigate Philadelphia by the Tripolitans was, it is true, the immediate occasion for this tax, but not its cause; this lay much deeper, and, as Mr. Gallatin's letters clearly show, was the result of a failure in the attempt at economy in the navy.

Even at the last hour, however, the Administration was alarmed by the fear that Louisiana might after all be lost; the protest of Spain against the sale gave reason to doubt whether she would consent to surrender the province. Here again Mr. Gallatin of his own accord urged increased expenditure, and actively pressed the collection and movement of troops to take possession by force if the Spanish government should resist. Fortunately, the alarm proved to be unnecessary: Louisiana was promptly handed over to the French official appointed for the purpose, and by him to General Wilkinson and Governor Claiborne; the troops were stopped on their march from Tennessee and ordered home, and all that remained to be done was to incorporate the new territory in the old, and to settle its boundaries with Spain.

The process of incorporation, however, brought into prominence a very serious constitutional question, which had already been elaborately argued in the Cabinet. Had the Constitution given to the President and Congress the right to do an act of this transcendent importance, an act which could not but result in immense and incalculable changes in the relations between the States who were the original parties to the constitutional compact; an act which could only rest on a prodigious extension of the treaty-making power, such as would legalize the annexation of Mexico or of Europe itself? Mr. Jefferson was very strongly of opinion that an amendment to the Constitution could alone legalize the act, and this opinion seems to have been shared by Mr. Madison and by the Attorney-General. The tenor of Mr. Gallatin's reasoning as a member of Congress in opposition certainly leads to the inference that he would take the same side. His speeches on the alien bill had carried the doctrine of strict construction to the verge of extravagance. Nevertheless, Mr. Gallatin did not properly belong to the Virginia school of strict constructionists, and although, as a member of Congress, he earnestly resisted the growth of Executive power, he assumed with difficulty and with a certain awkwardness the tone of States' rights. In this Louisiana case he wrote on the 13th January, 1803, a letter to Mr. Jefferson, which might have been written, without a syllable of change, by Alexander Hamilton to General Washington ten years before:

"To me it would appear, 1st. That the United States as a nation have an inherent right to acquire territory.

"2d. That whenever that acquisition is by treaty, the same constituted authorities in whom the treaty-making power is vested have a constitutional right to sanction the acquisition.

"3d. That whenever the territory has been acquired, Congress have the power either of admitting into the Union as a new State, or of annexing to a State with the consent of that State, or of making regulations for the government of such territory.

"The only possible objection must be derived from the 12th amendment, which declares that powers not delegated to the United States nor prohibited by it to the States are reserved to the States or to the people. As the States are expressly prohibited from making treaties, it is evident that if the power of acquiring territory by treaty is not considered within the meaning of the amendment as delegated to the United States, it must be reserved to the people. If that be the true construction of the Constitution, it substantially amounts to this, that the United States are precluded from and renounce altogether the enlargement of territory; a provision sufficiently important and singular to have deserved to be expressly enacted. Is it not a more natural construction to say that the power of acquiring territory is delegated to the United States by the several provisions which authorize the several branches of government to make war, to make treaties, and to govern the territory of the Union?"[1]

Mr. Jefferson, it is needless to say, was not convinced by this reasoning. He mildly replied: "I think it will be safer not to permit the enlargement of the Union but by amendment of the Constitution."[2] But the heresy spread into his own Virginia church, and his friend and confidant Wilson Cary Nicholas became infected by it. In reply to him Mr. Jefferson wrote a passionate appeal: "Our peculiar security is in the possession of a written Constitution; let us not make it a blank paper by construction." For a time he adhered to this view, and framed an amendment to answer his purpose, but at length he resigned himself to committing the whole responsibility to Congress, and held his peace. Mr. Gallatin's opinion became the accepted principle of the party and the ground on which their legislation was made to rest.

The same fate attended Mr. Jefferson's vehement remonstrances against the establishment of a branch bank of the United States at New Orleans, an object which Mr. Gallatin considered as of the highest importance and one which he was actively engaged in carrying into effect. Mr. Jefferson, however, wrote to him on the 13th December, 1803, in the strongest language against this plan: "This institution is one of the most deadly hostility existing against the principles and form of our Constitution. . . . What an obstruction could not this bank of the United States, with all its branch banks, be in time of war? It might dictate to us the peace we should accept, or withdraw its aids. Ought we then to give further growth to an institution so powerful, so hostile?" And he went on to give his own views as to the proper course for government to follow, which was in fact very nearly the plan ultimately realized in the form of a subtreasury. Mr. Gallatin, however, attached no great weight to these arguments; he wrote back on the same day: "I am extremely anxious to see a bank at New Orleans; considering the distance of that place, our own security and even that of the

---

collector will be eminently promoted, and the transmission of moneys arising both from the impost and sales of lands in the Mississippi Territory would without it be a very difficult and sometimes dangerous operation.   Against this there are none but political objections, and those will lose much of their force when the little injury they can do us and the dependence in which they are on government are duly estimated.   They may vote as they please and take their own papers, but they are formidable only as individuals and not as bankers.   Whenever they shall appear to be really dangerous, they are completely in our power and may be crushed."

Mr. Jefferson again yielded, and Mr. Gallatin procured the passage of an Act of Congress authorizing the establishment of a branch bank at New Orleans.   Meanwhile Governor Claiborne had undertaken to establish a bank there by his own authority. When the news of this proceeding reached Mr. Gallatin he was very angry, and wrote to Mr. Jefferson at once on April 12, 1804, sharply condemning Governor Claiborne for this unauthorized act, which, he added, " will probably defeat the establishment of a branch bank which *we* considered of great importance to the safety of the revenue and as a bond of union between the Atlantic and Mississippi interests."   Apparently, therefore, Mr. Gallatin believed that he had entirely converted his chief; in reality the conversion was only one more example of that capacity for yielding his own prejudices to the weight of his advisers, which made Mr. Jefferson so often disappoint his enemies and preserve the harmony of his party.

On the whole, this third year of the Administration closed not less satisfactorily than its predecessors, and Congress adjourned without anxiety after carrying into effect all the measures which Mr. Gallatin had at heart.   So far as he was concerned, hardly a lisp of discontent was heard, except, perhaps, among the followers of Duane and Leib.   By them he was accused of wishing to build up a third party by the patronage of the Treasury, a charge which meant only that he had refused to put his patronage at their disposal.

The summer again found Mr. Gallatin at Washington, alone, discontented, and occupied only with the details of Treasury

work.   One pleasure indeed he had, and as his acquaintance
with Alexander Baring was destined to have no little value to
him in future life, so his acquaintance of this summer with
Alexander von Humboldt was turned to good account in after-
years.   In a letter to his wife he gave an amusing account of
his first impressions of Humboldt.   Among his correspondents
of this year there are none whose letters seem to have any permanent value, unless one by John Randolph be an exception.
In this there are curious suggestions of restlessness under the
sense of political inferiority.   It would be interesting to know
what that opinion of Mr. Gallatin's was which could induce
Randolph to concur with it so far as to favor the creation of a
navy to blow the British cruisers out of water.

GALLATIN TO HIS WIFE.

WASHINGTON, 6th June, 1804.

. . . I have received an exquisite intellectual treat from Baron
Humboldt, the Prussian traveller, who is on his return from
Peru and Mexico, where he travelled five years, and from which
he has brought a mass of natural, philosophical, and political
information which will render the geography, productions, and
statistics of that country better known than those of most European countries.   We all consider him as a very extraordinary
man, and his travels, which he intends publishing on his return
to Europe, will, I think, rank above any other production of
the kind.   I am not apt to be easily pleased, and he was not
particularly prepossessing to my taste, for he speaks more than
Lucas, Finley, and myself put together, and twice as fast as
anybody I know, German, French, Spanish, and English, all
together.   But I was really delighted, and swallowed more information of various kinds in less than two hours than I had
for two years past in all I had read or heard.   He does not
seem much above thirty, gives you no trouble in talking yourself, for he catches with perfect precision the idea you mean to
convey before you have uttered the third word of your sentence,
and, exclusively of his travelled acquirements, the extent of his
reading and scientific knowledge is astonishing.   I must ac-

knowledge, in order to account for my enthusiasm, that he was surrounded with maps, statements, &c., all new to me, and several of which he has liberally permitted us to transcribe.

JOHN RANDOLPH TO GALLATIN.

BIZARRE, 14th October, 1804.   29th Ind.

On my return from Fredericksburg after a racing campaign, I was very agreeably accosted by your truly welcome letter; to thank you for which, and not because I have anything (stable news excepted) to communicate, I now take up the pen. It is some satisfaction to me, who have been pestered with inquiries that I could not answer on the subject of public affairs, to find that the Chancellor of the Exchequer and First Lord of the Treasury is in as comfortable a state of ignorance as myself. Pope says of governments, that is best which is best administered. What idea, then, could he have of a government which was not administered at all? The longer I live, the more do I incline to somebody's opinion, that there is in the affairs of this world a mechanism of which the very agents themselves are ignorant, and which, of course, they can neither calculate nor control. As much free will as you please in everything else, but in politics I must ever be a necessitarian. And this comfortable doctrine saves me a deal of trouble and many a twinge of conscience for my heedless indolence. I therefore leave Major Jackson and his Ex. of Casa Yrujo to give each other the lie in Anglo-American or Castilian fashions, just as it suits them, and when people resort to me for intelligence, instead of playing the owl and putting on a face of solemn nonsense, I very fairly tell them with perfect nonchalance that I know nothing of the matter,—from which, if they have any discernment, they may infer that I care as little about it,—and then change the subject as quickly as I can to horses, dogs, the plough, or some other upon which I feel myself competent to converse. In short, I like originality too well to be a second-hand politician when I can help it. It is enough to live upon the broken victuals and be tricked out in the cast-off finery of you first-rate statesmen all the winter. When I cross the Potomac, I leave behind me all the scraps, shreds, and patches of politics which I collect during the session, and put on the plain homespun, or (as we say) the "Virginia cloth," of a planter, which is clean, whole, and comfortable, even if it be homely.   Nevertheless, I have patriotism enough left to congratulate you on the fulness of the public purse, and cannot help wishing that its situation could be concealed from our Sangrados in politics, with whom depletion is the order of the day.   On the subject of a navy you know my opinion concurs with yours.   I really feel ashamed for my country, that, whilst she is hectoring before the petty corsairs of the coast of Barbary, she should truckle to the great pirate of the German Ocean; and I would freely vote a naval force that should blow the Cambrian and Leander out of water. Indeed, I wish Barron's squadron had been employed on that service.   I am perfectly aware of the importance of peace to us, particularly with Great Britain, but I know it to be equally necessary to her; and, in short, if we have any honor as a nation to lose, which is problematical, I am unwilling to surrender it.

On the subject of Louisiana you are also apprised that my sentiments coincide with your own; and it is principally because of that coincidence that I rely upon their correctness. But as we have the misfortune to differ from that great political luminary, Mr. Matthew Lyon, on this as well as on most other points, I doubt whether we shall not be overpowered.   If Spain be "fallen from her old Castilian *faith, candor*, and *dignity*," it must be allowed that we have been judicious in our choice of a minister to negotiate with her; and Louisiana, it being presumable, partaking something of the character which distinguished her late sovereign when she acquired that territory, the selection of a *pompous nothing* for a governor will be admitted to have been happy.   At least, if the appointment be not defensible upon this principle, I am at a loss to discover any other tenable point. In answer to your question I would advise the printing of . . . thousand copies of Tom Paine's answer to their remonstrance and transmitting them by as many thousand troops, who can speak a language perfectly intelligible to the people of Louisiana, whatever that of their governor may be.   It is, to be sure, a little awkward, except in addresses and answers where each party is previously well apprised of what the other has to say, that whilst the eyes and ears of the admiring Louisianians are filled with the majestic person and sonorous periods of their chief magistrate, their understandings should be utterly vacant. If, however, they were aware that, even if they understood English, it might be no better, they would perhaps be more reconciled to their situation.   You really must send something better than this mere ape of greatness to those Hispano-Gaulo. He would make a portly figure delivering to "my lords and gentlemen" a speech which Pitt had previously taught him; but we want an *automaton*, and a *puppet* will not supply his place.

Pray look to the "ways and means" of entertainment for man and horse against the assembling of our annual mob.   Here we have no bilious fevers, and although I shall enjoy your geographical treat I shall require more substantial food.

Because I had nothing to say, I have prattled through four pages; like a quondam fellow-laborer of ours, who seemed to speak not to express his ideas, but to gain time to acquire some.

The general election of November, 1804, proved the strength of the Administration in a more emphatic manner than even its friends had counted upon.   Mr. Jefferson received an almost unanimous electoral vote.   In Pennsylvania, however, there was little satisfaction over the result; the schism there became more and more serious, and on the 16th October, 1804, Mr. Dallas could only write to Mr. Gallatin: "Thank Heaven, our election is over!   The violence of Duane has produced a fatal division. He seems determined to destroy the Republican standing and usefulness of every man who does not bend to his will.   He has attacked me as the author of an address which I never saw till it was in the press.   He menaces the governor.   You have already felt his lash.   And I think there is reason for Mr. Jefferson himself to apprehend that the spirit of Callender survives."

Again Congress came together, and for the fourth time the President was able to draw a picture of the political situation which had few shadows and broad light.   For the fourth time Mr. Gallatin sent in a report which announced a steadily increasing revenue, if not a reduced expenditure.   He had not yet made use of his authority to borrow the additional $1,750,000 of the Louisiana purchase, and hoped for a surplus that would render this loan unnecessary.   For the coming year he estimated an expenditure of $11,540,000, and a revenue of $11,750,000.

The usual reaction which follows general elections followed that of 1804, and the Administration escaped attack in the following session of 1804-05, which was chiefly devoted to the trial of Judge Chase.   Whether Mr. Gallatin had anything to do with influencing the result of this trial is unknown.   A curious mystery has always hung and probably always will hang over the share which Mr. Jefferson's Administration had in affecting the decision of the Senate by which Judge Chase was acquitted. Probably, however, the schism which was taking place in Pennsylvania on this same point of impeachments had an immediate effect on the party at Washington and cooled its eagerness for conviction.   Perhaps Mr. Gallatin's feelings may be partly reflected in a letter from his friend Mr. Dallas, who was now acting as counsel for the impeached Pennsylvania judges.   This letter, it will be noticed, was written while the trial of Judge Chase was going on, and only a few days before Mr. Dallas was called to Washington to give his testimony before the Senate.

A. J. DALLAS TO GALLATIN.

LANCASTER, 16th January, 1805.

MY DEAR SIR,—I thank you for your friendly letter, but I regret that it expresses a depression on public business which I have long felt.   It is obvious to me that unless our Administration take decisive measures to discountenance the factious spirit that has appeared, unless some principle of political cohesion can be introduced into our public councils as well as at our elections, and unless men of character and talents can be drawn from professional and private pursuits into the legislative bodies of our governments, federal and State, the empire of Republicanism will moulder into anarchy, and the labor and hope of our lives will terminate in disappointment and wretchedness. Perhaps the crisis is arrived when some attempt should be made to rally the genuine Republicans round the standard of reason, order, and law. At present we are the slaves of men whose passions are the origin and whose interests are the object of all their actions,—I mean your Duanes, Cheethams, Leibs, &c. They have the press in their power, and, though we may have virtue to assert the liberty of the press, it is too plain that we have not spirit enough to resist the tyranny of the printers. We will talk of this matter when we meet.

. . . The argument on our impeachment will close to-day, and the decision will probably be given to-morrow or Monday. The Aurora man has been here during the trial, with all his audacity, intrigue, and malevolence. I think, however, he will fail. A cause more deserving of success than that of the judges never was discussed, and I am confident that there will be an acquittal. . . .

The letter in which Mr. Gallatin expressed his depression is lost, but there was more than one cause to justify it. However annoying the condition of Pennsylvania politics might be, the greatest actual danger to be feared from it was that it might spread into national politics and find leaders in Congress. The conduct of John Randolph already suggested an alliance between him and Duane that might paralyze the Administration and ruin the Republican party. This alliance was foreshadowed not only by the fact that Randolph led the impeachment of Judge Chase in the spirit of Duane, but also by another still more extravagant display of Randolph's temper which touched Mr. Gallatin personally. When the public lands came under Mr. Gallatin's direction in 1801, he had been obliged to disentangle the State of Georgia, as well as he could, from a complication which she had herself created. One element in this tangle consisted in the corrupt sale by Georgia of certain lands, and her subsequent annulling these sales on the ground of her own corruption. The purchasers pressed their claims, and Mr. Gallatin with his fellow-commissioners, Madison and Lincoln, recommended a compromise by which five million acres were to be reserved in order to make a reasonable compensation for all claims, these as well as others; a proposition which was embodied by Congress in a law. To carry this compromise into effect was the work of ten years, during which time the subject was incessantly before Congress. When it came up in January, 1805, John Randolph astounded the House by a series of speeches violent beyond all precedent, outrageously and vindictively slanderous, and fatal to the harmony of the party and to all effective legislation. With the malignity of a bully he attacked Gideon Granger, the Post-master-General, who could not answer him, and he only met his match in Matthew Lyon, whose old experience now, to the delight of the Federalists, enabled him to meet Randolph with a torrent of personal abuse, and to tell him that he was a jackal and a madman with the face of a monkey. All this was doubt-less vexatious enough to Mr. Gallatin, who knew well that it boded no good to the Administration; but Randolph could not even stop here. He made a very serious reflection upon Mr. Gallatin himself and the report of the commissioners. "When I first read their report," said he, "I was filled with unutterable astonishment; finding men in whom I had and still have the highest confidence, recommend a measure which all the facts and all the reasons which they had collected opposed and unequivo-cally condemned." This speech was made on February 3, 1805, and the course taken by Randolph was warmly applauded by Duane.

Mr. Gallatin remained impassive and his relations with Ran-dolph were undisturbed. Randolph himself either had no clear idea what he was doing, or was indifferent to its consequences. One of his letters to Mr. Gallatin, written in October, 1805, is so judicial in its tone and expresses such proper sentiments about divisions in the party as to appear quite out of keeping with its writer and to suggest dissimulation, which was not at all in his character. But on one point the two men had strong sympathies: their concurrence of opinion on the management of the navy was a bond of union.

The summer of 1805 brought matters to a crisis. Duane and his friends set up an opposition candidate to Governor McKean in the person of Simon Snyder, Speaker of the House, and car-ried the bulk of the party with them. Mr. Dallas and the conservative element were obliged to depend upon Federalist aid in order to carry the election of McKean. Mr. Jefferson and the Administration refrained from interference, and the result was to isolate Mr. Gallatin and to deprive him of that support in his own State, without which the position of a public man must always be precarious. The elements of future trouble were gathering into alarming consistency and needed only some national crisis to concentrate all their force against Mr. Gallatin.

A. J. DALLAS TO GALLATIN.

4th April, 1805.

. . . The political part of your letter corresponds precisely with the ideas I entertain and have uniformly inculcated on the subject. The Aurora perverts everything, however, that can be said or done. The Legislature adjourns to-day. You have read the report; but I fear it will be followed by some wild, irregular step after the adjournment, aimed against the Governor as well as the Constitution. The evil of the day has obviously proceeded from the neglect of Dr. Leib's official pretensions; and Duane's assertions that he possesses the confidence and acts at the instance of the President will buoy him up on the surface for some time longer. While he has influence, the State, the United States, will never enjoy quiet. I hope therefore, and there is every reason to expect, that his present machinations will be exposed and defeated as a prelude to his fall. . . .

JOHN RANDOLPH TO GALLATIN.

BIZARRE, June 28, 1805.

. . . I do not understand your manœuvres at headquarters, nor should I be surprised to see the Navy Department abolished, or, in more appropriate phrase, swept by the board, at the next session of Congress. The nation has had the most conclusive proof that a *head* is no necessary appendage to the establishment. . . .

GALLATIN TO BADOLLET.

WASHINGTON, 25th October, 1805.

. . . Whilst the Republicans opposed the Federalists the necessity of union induced a general sacrifice of private views and personal objects; and the opposition was generally grounded on the purest motives and conducted in the most honorable manner. Complete success has awakened all those passions which only slumbered. In Pennsylvania particularly the thirst for offices, too much encouraged by Governor McKean's first measures, created a schism in Philadelphia as early as 1802. Leib, ambitious, avaricious, envious, and disappointed, blew up the flame, and watched the first opportunity to make *his* cause a general one. The vanity, the nepotism, and the indiscretion of Governor McKean afforded the opportunity. Want of mutual forbearance amongst the best intentioned and most respectable Republicans has completed the schism. Duane, intoxicated by the persuasion that he alone had overthrown Federalism, thought himself neither sufficiently rewarded nor respected, and, possessed of an engine which gives him an irresistible control over public opinion, he easily gained the victory for his friends. I call it victory, for the number of Republicans who have opposed him rather than supported McKean does not exceed one-fourth, or at most one-third, of the whole; and McKean owes his re-election to the Federalists. What will be the consequence I cannot even conjecture. My ardent wishes are for mutual forgiveness and a reunion of the Republican interest; but I hardly think it probable. McKean and Duane will be both implacable and immovable, and the acts of the first and the continued proscriptions of the last will most probably and unfortunately defeat every attempt to reconcile. Yet I do not foresee any permanent evil beyond what arises from perpetual agitation and from that party spirit which encourages personal hatred; but the intolerance and persecution which we abhorred in Federalism will be pursued by the prevailing party till the people, who do not love injustice, once more put it down.

JOHN RANDOLPH TO GALLATIN.

BIZARRE, October 25, 1805.

DEAR SIR,—Your very acceptable letter reached me this morning, and I hasten to return you my thanks for it and to answer your very friendly inquiries after my health. It is much better than it has been for some months; so much so that I propose braving another winter at Washington. I do assure you, however, that I look forward to the ensuing session of Congress with no very pleasant feelings. To say nothing of the disadvantages of the place, natural as well as acquired, I anticipate a plentiful harvest of bickering and blunders; of which, however, I hope to be a quiet, if not an unconcerned, spectator.

It is a great comfort to me to find that we entirely agree as to the causes of disunion in Pennsylvania. I have no interest in their local squabbles, except so far as they may affect the Union at large. In that point of view I have regretted the divisions of the Republican party in that great and leading State, well knowing that whichever side prevailed, Federalism must thereby acquire a formidable accession of strength. It now remains to be seen whether there is temper and good sense enough left among them to heal their animosities, or whether, as to Pennsylvania at present and speedily throughout the Union, we must acknowledge the humiliating position of our adversaries, "that the Republicans do not possess virtue and understanding enough to administer the government." Perhaps the reconciliation which I speak of is more to be desired than hoped. Wiser heads and those better acquainted with the particular circumstances of the case than mine must determine whether this is to be effected by an act of mutual amnesty and oblivion, or by expelling in the first instance the rogues on both sides. That such there are is self-evident; though who they are is a much more difficult question. Unconnected as I am in that quarter, yourself excepted, it appears from what I can gather that there has been no want of indiscretion, intemperance, and rashness on either side. If the vanquished party have exceeded in these, it has been amply counterbalanced by dereliction of principle in the victors. I speak of chieftains. As to the body of the people, their intentions are always good, *since it can never be their interest to do wrong*. Whilst you in Pennsylvania have been tearing each other to pieces about a governor, we in Virginia, who can hardly find any one to accept our throne of the Mahrattas, have been quietly taking the goods the gods have provided us; enjoying the sports of the turf and the field. Which has the better bargain, think you?

. . . I regret exceedingly Mr. Jefferson's resolution to retire, and almost as much the premature annunciation of that determination. It almost precludes a revision of his purpose, to say nothing of the intrigues which it will set on foot. If I were sure that Monroe would succeed him, my regret would be very much diminished. Here, you see, the Virginian breaks out; but, like the Prussian cadet, " I must request you not to make this known to the Secretary of the Treasury."

A. J. DALLAS TO GALLATIN.

21st December, 1805.

MY DEAR SIR,—In perfect confidence I tell you that Governor McK. has pressed me to accept the office of chief justice. This I have peremptorily declined. But I believe he means to appoint the present Attorney-General to that office; and I am again pressed to say whether I will accept the commission of Attorney-General. It is an office more lucrative, less troublesome, and infinitely less responsible than the one I hold. There are considerations, however, that make me pause. I am disgusted with the fluctuation of our politics, with the emptiness of party friendships, and with the influence of desperate and violent men upon our popular and legislative movements in the State business. I had determined never to think of State dependence. At this time, too, when the thunders of the Aurora are daily rolling over my head; when it is publicly asserted that I have lost the personal and political confidence of the Administration; a resignation would be perverted into a dismissal, and my succession to the office of Attorney-General would increase the clamors against Governor McKean. In this dilemma I repose myself on your friendship for information and advice. I do not want either office, but I am shocked at the idea of incurring the least disgrace under the sanction of an Administration which has had all my attachment and all my services. Tell me, therefore, what I ought to do by the return of the post. I do not wish you to enter into any detail of the grounds of your opinion, but let the opinion be explicit, and, if you please, let it be the result of a consultation with our friend Robert Smith.

Meanwhile, the fate of the Administration became every day more visibly involved in the management of foreign affairs. Mr. Jefferson's theory, that the belligerents would not make him swallow so much as they had forced down the throats of his predecessors, was rapidly becoming more than questionable. England blockaded our ports and impressed our seamen; Spain refused to carry out her pledges of indemnification for illegal seizures of our ships, insisted upon limiting our Louisiana purchase to a mere strip of territory on the west bank of the Mississippi, and was supported by France in doing so. Mr. Jefferson was at this time impressed with the idea that he could balance one belligerent against another and could force Spain to recede by throwing himself into the arms of England.

Under these circumstances, on the 7th August, 1805, he called upon the members of his Cabinet for their written opinions on the course to be pursued towards Spain. Mr. Gallatin's reply, dated September 12,[1] is a very interesting paper, covering the whole ground of discussion, and composed in a spirit of judicial fairness towards Spain very unusual in American state papers. Acting on his invariable theory of American interests, he dissuaded from war, and urged continued negotiation even if it only resulted in postponing a rupture. To gain time was with him to gain everything; after the year 1809 the redemption of debt would have gone so far that $3,500,000 would be annually available, out of the $8,000,000 fund, for other purposes; adding the savings and preparations of these three years and the intermediate growth of the country, there was no difficulty in showing the importance of preserving peace. But perhaps the most curious part of this paper is that in which Mr. Gallatin accepts the doctrine of a navy; after explaining that he could count on a probable annual surplus of $2,000,000, he went on to deal with its application:

"It is probable that the greater part of that surplus will be applied to the formation of a navy; and if Congress shall decide in favor of that measure, I would suggest that the mode best calculated, in my opinion, to effect it, and so impress other

---

[1] Gallatin's Writings, vol. i. p. 241.

nations that we are in earnest about it, would be a distinct Act enacted for that sole purpose, appropriating for a fixed number of years (or for as many years as would be sufficient to build a determinate number of ships of the line) a fixed sum of money, say one million of dollars annually, . . . the money to be exclusively applied to the building of ships of the line, for there would still be a sufficient surplus to add immediately a few frigates to our navy. . . . Whether the creation of an efficient navy may not, by encouraging wars and drawing us in the usual vortex of expenses and foreign relations, be the cause of greater evils than those it is intended to prevent, is not the question which I mean to discuss. This is to be decided by the representatives of the nation, and although I have been desirous that the measure might at least be postponed, I have had no doubt for a long time that the United States would ultimately have a navy. It is certain that, so long as we have none, we must perpetually be liable to injuries and insults, particularly from the belligerent powers when there is a war in Europe; and in deciding for or against the measure Congress will fairly decide the question, whether they think it more for the interest of the United States to preserve a pacific and temporizing system, and to tolerate those injuries and insults to a great extent, than to be prepared, like the great European nations, to repel every injury by the sword."

This seems to have been sound Federalist doctrine so far as it went. Time and the growth of natural resources were gradually bringing Mr. Gallatin to a point not much behind the last Administration; had the Navy been in the hands of a stronger man it is not unlikely that the appropriation offered by Mr. Gallatin might now have been carried through Congress, but even in making the proposition Mr. Gallatin showed his sense of Mr. Robert Smith's capacity by insisting that the money should be placed in the hands of commissioners. To judge from John Randolph's expressions, he was at this time of the same opinion with Mr. Gallatin, both in regard to the navy and its Secretary.

But Mr. Jefferson's views, never heartily turned towards strong measures, soon changed. On the 23d October, 1805, he wrote to Mr. Gallatin that there was no longer any occasion for a hasty decision; the European war was certain to continue. "We may make another effort for a peaceable accommodation with Spain without the danger of being left alone to cope with both France and Spain." And he closed by propounding an entirely new proposition: "Our question now is in what way to give Spain another opportunity of arrangement. Is not Paris the place? France the agent? The purchase of the Floridas the means?"

If there was anything in this rapid change of front on the part of Mr. Jefferson that argued vacillation of mind, it still amounted to the adoption of Mr. Gallatin's views, and he seems to have so regarded it. Unfortunately, when Mr. Jefferson undertook to carry out his new policy he attempted the difficult task of concealing it under the cover of the old one; he wished, in other words, to combine the advantages of a war policy with those of a peace policy, and to escape the consequences of both, so far as risks were concerned. The success of the Louisiana purchase, two years before, now led him to repeat the experiment; the scheme in his mind was intended to be a close imitation of the course which had resulted in obtaining Louisiana; Spain was partly to be frightened, partly to be bribed, into the sale of Florida.

Mr. Gallatin's notes on the message of this year seem to indicate that it showed in the original draft more inconsistency than in its ultimate form. Mr. Jefferson spoke of war as probable, and recommended preparation for it,—organization of the militia, gun-boats, and land-batteries; he even gave a strong hint that he was ready to build ships of the line; yet at the same time he recommended the abandonment of the Mediterranean Fund which, as Mr. Gallatin pointed out, was necessary to provide for the purchase of Florida on their own scheme, or to impose upon Spain a sense of their being in earnest about war.[1] After thorough revision the message was at last made to suit its double purpose, and was sent in.

This, however, was only the beginning. The plan of operations was intended to be an exact repetition of that which had been followed in the Louisiana case,—a public message to be

[1] Gallatin's Writings, vol. i. p. 263.

followed by a secret one, public resolutions to be adopted by the House, and a confidential report and appropriation.   Mr. Gallatin advised this course as the one already settled by precedent, and Mr. Jefferson set to work drafting the public resolutions which were to be adopted by the House and to impose upon Spain.

The President's first draft[1] met with little success; indeed, it was open to ridicule, and both Mr. Gallatin and Mr. Joseph H. Nicholson remonstrated.   Mr. Jefferson accordingly made what he called a revised edition;[2] but there was a serious difficulty in the task itself, as Mr. Gallatin wrote on December 3, 1805, to Mr. Jefferson: "The apparent difficulty in framing the resolutions arises from the attempt to blend the three objects together.   The same reasons which have induced the President to send two distinct messages, render it necessary that the public resolutions of Congress should be distinct from the private ones; those which relate to the war-posture of the Spanish affairs, which are intended to express the national sense on that subject, and to enable the President to take the steps which appear immediately necessary on the frontier, should not be mixed with those proceedings calculated only to effect an accommodation."

There was, however, a more serious difficulty, on which Mr. Gallatin did not dwell; the Administration was not in earnest. He had himself already pointed out what should be done if war were really contemplated.   Half a dozen ships of the line, a few more frigates, and some regiments for the regular army were the only measures which Spain would respect.   It is true that this policy would have been merely a repetition of that pursued by the last Administration towards France, but that policy had at least not been feeble.   Mr. Jefferson should not have taken a "war posture" unless he was ready to do so with vigor.

The confidential message was sent in on the 6th December, 1805, three days after the annual message.   Its object as understood by Mr. Gallatin was " to inform Congress that France being disposed to favor an arrangement, the present moment should not be lost, but that the means must be supplied by Congress.   It is also intended to say that in the mean while, and in

---

[1] Gallatin's Writings, vol. i. p. 277.   [2] Ibid., p. 281.

order to promote an arrangement, force should be interposed to a certain degree. . . . To the tenor of the message itself I have but one objection: that it does not explicitly declare the object in view, and may hereafter be cavilled at as having induced Congress into a mistaken opinion of that object. For although the latter end of the third paragraph is expressed in comprehensive terms, yet the omission of the word Florida may lead to error; nor does the message convey the idea that in order to effect an accommodation a much larger sum of money will probably be requisite than had been contemplated."

The President had now carried out his part of the project. Both the public and secret messages were before the House; it remained for the House to echo back the wishes of the Administration, and on this score Mr. Jefferson seems to have felt no alarm, for he supposed himself to be asking merely an exact repetition of action taken only two years before in the Louisiana case. John Randolph had done then precisely what he was expected to do now. Mr. Gallatin, on the 7th December, wrote a note to Mr. Nicholson, and put the matter of the President's resolutions in his hands. John Randolph called on the President the same day and made an appointment with him for a conversation the next morning. He has himself given an account of this interview. Full explanations were made to him, and Mr. Jefferson seems to have told him with perfect frankness all the views of the Administration. There was in fact, so far as Congress was concerned, nothing to conceal.

"He then learned," according to his account published under the signature of Decius, in the Richmond Enquirer, the following August, "not without some surprise, that an appropriation of two millions was wanted to purchase Florida. He told the President without reserve that he would never agree to such a measure, because the money had not been asked for in the message; that he could not consent to shift upon his own shoulders or those of the House the proper responsibility of the Executive; but that even if the money had been explicitly demanded he should have been averse to granting it, because, after the total failure of every attempt at negotiation, such a step would disgrace us forever."

This opposition of Mr. Randolph endangered the whole scheme. Mr. Nicholson, who was second on the committee, was a close friend of Randolph, and more or less influenced by him, while the other members friendly to the Administration wanted the weight necessary to overbalance the chairman. Nevertheless it was impossible to recede. After waiting till the 21st December for Randolph to act, Mr. Nicholson seems to have interposed and in a manner obliged him to meet the committee. "As they were about to assemble," says Decius, "the chairman (Randolph) was called aside by the Secretary of the Treasury, with whom he retired, and who put into his hands a paper headed ' Provision for the purchase of Florida.' As soon as he had cast his eyes on the title the chairman declared that he would not vote a shilling. The Secretary interrupted him by observing, with his characteristic caution, that he did not mean to be understood as recommending the measure, but, if the committee should deem it advisable, he had devised a plan for raising the necessary supplies, as he had been requested or directed in that case to do. The chairman expressed himself disgusted with the whole of the proceeding, which he could not but consider as highly disingenuous."

Not until January 3, 1806, did the committee report, and then its report provided only for a " war posture," and not for purchase. The House now proceeded in secret session to debate the message, and then at last Mr. Randolph flung his bomb into the midst of his friends and followers. Seizing with considerable dexterity, but with extravagant violence, the really weak point in Mr. Jefferson's message, he assailed the Administration, or at least its foreign policy, with the fury of a madman. The whole Administration phalanx was thrown into disorder and embittered to exasperation; the whole effect proposed from the negotiation was destroyed in advance; but the government was obliged to go on, and at last its propositions, in spite of Randolph, were carried through Congress.

Although the actual struggle took place in secret session, Randolph lost no time in making his attack public, and it very soon became evident that the true object of his hostility was Mr. Madison. On the 5th March, in debating the non-importation policy, he began a violent assault by asserting that he had asked the Administration, "What is the opinion of the Cabinet? . . . My answer was (and from a Cabinet minister, too), ' *There is no longer any Cabinet.*' " On the 15th, he developed this suggestion into a rhetorical panegyric upon Mr. Gallatin at the expense of Mr. Madison; he told how certain despatches from Europe had arrived at the State Department in December, and how Mr. Gallatin, in reply to an inquiry, had told him at a later time that the contents of these despatches had not yet been communicated to the Cabinet: "It was when I discovered that the head of the second department under the government did not know they were in existence, much less that his opinion on them had not been consulted, that I declared what I repeat, that there is no Cabinet. You have no Cabinet! What, the head of the Treasury Department,—a vigorous and commanding statesman, a practical statesman, the benefit of whose wisdom and experience the nation fondly believes it always obtained before the great measures of the government are taken,—unacquainted with and unconsulted on important despatches,—and yet talk of a Cabinet! Not merely unconsulted, but ignorant of the documents. . . . I have no hesitation in saying, *there is no Cabinet,* when I see a man second to none for vigorous understanding and practical good sense ousted from it."

The movement was an insidious one, calculated to sow distrust between Mr. Gallatin and Mr. Madison; but to judge from the tone of Mr. Randolph's letters, even as far back as June, 1803, it was an understood fact with him and with Mr. Gallatin that the Administration wanted cohesion and co-operation, and it appears clearly enough that at least so far as the Navy Department was concerned, Mr. Gallatin made this a subject of repeated remonstrance to the President himself, although he never made complaint against Mr. Madison, and, as his correspondence shows, he was fully in harmony with the foreign policy pursued.[1] That he agreed with Randolph in considering the President too lax in discipline seems certain.

Mr. Gallatin did what he could to correct the impression thus

---

[1] Cf. Jefferson to Wirt, 3d May, 1811. Jefferson's Writings, vol. v. p. 593.

given, and Randolph was obliged ultimately to withdraw his assertion, or at least essentially to qualify it; but this seems to have irritated him into making another similar attack on the 7th April, immediately after withdrawing the former one: "I wish," said he, "the heads of departments had seats on this floor. Were this the case, to one of them I would immediately propound this question: Did you or did you not, in your capacity of a public functionary, tell me, in my capacity of a public functionary, that France would not suffer Spain to settle her differences with us, that she wanted money, that we must give her money or take a Spanish or French war? . . . I would put this question to another head of department: Was or was not an application made to you for money to be conveyed to Europe to carry on any species of diplomatic negotiation there? I would listen to his answer, and if he put his hand on his heart and like a man of honor said, No! I would believe him, though it would require a great stretch of credulity. I would call into my aid faith, not reason, and believe where I was not convinced."

At the moment this was said, Mr. Gallatin was on the floor of the House, and Mr. Jackson, of Virginia, at once asked him whether it was true that such an application was made. He replied that it was not, and explained how the mistake arose. Mr. Jackson immediately took the floor and repeated his words, characterizing the charge that Mr. Madison had attempted to draw money out of the Treasury without the authority of law, as "destitute of truth and foundation,—mark the expression; I say it is destitute of truth," evidently courting a quarrel. He took care, however, to relieve Mr. Gallatin of responsibility for these words, while, in order to establish the fact of denial, he caused a resolution of inquiry to be adopted by the House, which produced a categorical reply from Mr. Gallatin, "that no 'application has been made to draw money from the Treasury before an appropriation made by law for that purpose.' The circumstances which may have produced an impression that such an application had been made, being unconnected with any matter pertaining to the duties of the office of Secretary of the Treasury, are not presumed to come within the scope of the information required from this Department by the House."

Meanwhile Mr. Gallatin had already taken measures to correct at its source the error to which Mr. Randolph was giving currency.[1] It appears that in explaining the wishes of the government to two New York members, George Clinton, Jr., and Josiah Masters, Mr. Gallatin had found them sceptical in regard to the propriety of the proposed action of Congress, and, in order to convince them that the President and Cabinet were in earnest and really anxious for the appropriation, he said that so anxious were they as to have actually had a discussion in Cabinet, before Congress met, whether they might not promise in the negotiation to pay a sum down without waiting for action from Congress; so anxious were they that Mr. Madison, although the bill was not yet fairly passed, though certain to pass within less than a week, had already requested Mr. Gallatin to buy exchange.[2] This conversation, repeated by Mr. Masters, and coming to the ears of John Randolph, produced his solemn inquiry meant to imply that Mr. Madison had approached Mr. Gallatin with a proposition to take money illegally from the Treasury, and that Mr. Gallatin had repelled the idea. What made this notion more absurd was that the first proposition was not Mr. Madison's, but came from Mr. Jefferson; only by jumbling the two facts together and recklessly disregarding every means of better informing himself, had Randolph succeeded in dragging Mr. Madison into the field at all.

This official denial and private correction of the story, afterwards made public in the shape of a letter from the New York member to his constituents, seem to be sufficient for the satisfaction of all parties. Still, the innuendo of Randolph was compromising to Mr. Gallatin, and was made the theme of long-continued attacks upon him. Five years afterwards, when Mr. Madison was President and Gallatin was in sore need of support, Mr. Jefferson wrote to William Wirt a letter warmly defending him in this matter as in others. He said, in taking up one by one the charges that Mr. Gallatin had been a party

---

[1] Letter to George Clinton, Jr., dated 5th April, 1806. Writings, vol. i. p. 295.

[2] Gallatin's Writings, Endorsement on letter of G. Clinton, Jr., vol. i. p. 298.

to Randolph's opposition: " But the story of the two millions; Mr. Gallatin satisfied us that this affirmation of J. R. was as unauthorized as the fact itself was false. It resolves itself, therefore, into his inexplicit letter to a committee of Congress. As to this, my own surmise was that Mr. Gallatin might have used some hypothetical expression in conversing on that subject, which J. R. made a positive one, and he being a duellist, and Mr. Gallatin with a wife and children depending on him for their daily subsistence, the latter might wish to avoid collision and insult from such a man."

There are occasions when defence is worse than attack. If Mr. Jefferson thought that his Secretary of the Treasury wanted the moral courage to speak out at the risk of personal danger, there is no more to be said so far as concerns Mr. Jefferson; but in regard to Mr. Gallatin the suggestion seems to be completely set aside by two considerations: in the first place, the question put by Randolph was not founded, nor even alleged to be founded, on his own conversations with Mr. Gallatin,[1] and therefore not he, but Mr. Masters alone, had the right to call Mr. Gallatin to account; in the second place, Mr. Gallatin's letter was very explicit on one point, and that to a duellist the essential one; it flatly and categorically contradicted Randolph's charge, and there seems to be no reason why Mr. Randolph might not have founded a challenge on that contradiction as well as on any other had he felt that the occasion warranted a duel.

The truth is that Mr. Randolph at this time might have fought as many duels as there were days, had he wished to do so. Bitter as his tongue was, there were men enough who were not afraid either of it or of his pistols. Mr. Gallatin, on the other hand, was anxious that, if possible, Randolph should not be outlawed. Until March, 1807, at all events, he was chairman of the Ways and Means, and Mr. Gallatin's relations with him must be maintained. More than this, there was absolutely no other member on the Administration side of the House who

---

[1] See " Decius, II.," Richmond Enquirer, November, 1806, republished in the Aurora for 25th November, 1806.

had the capacity to take the place of leader. Even in October, 1807, when Randolph was at last dethroned, it was, as will be seen, much against Mr. Gallatin's will, and, as he well knew, much to the risk of public interest and his own comfort. He would rather have continued to tolerate Randolph than to trust the leadership of the House in the hands of incompetent men.

Nevertheless, this conduct of Mr. Randolph necessarily broke up the confidence existing between him and Mr. Gallatin, and although Randolph was never one of Mr. Gallatin's declared enemies, but, on the contrary, always spoke of him as "that great man,—for great let *me* call him,"[1] their intimacy ceased from this time. In July, 1807, Randolph wrote to Joseph H. Nicholson: "I have no communication with the great folks. Gallatin used formerly to write to me, but of late our intercourse has dropped. I think it is more than two years since I was in his house. How this has happened I can't tell, or rather I *can*, for I have not been invited there." The loss was all the more serious to Mr. Gallatin, because at this same moment Joseph H. Nicholson left the House to accept a seat on the bench, and thus the two members on whom he had most depended were beyond his reach. A corresponding loss of personal influence was inevitable; but this was not all; the Aurora, while shrewdly avoiding direct support of Randolph's defection, made use of Randolph's assertions to charge Mr. Gallatin with what amounted to treason against Mr. Jefferson, and at last Mr. Jefferson himself had to interpose to reassure his Secretary of the Treasury in the following letter:

JEFFERSON TO GALLATIN.

WASHINGTON, October 12, 1806.

DEAR SIR,—You witnessed in the earlier part of the Administration the malignant and long-continued efforts which the Federalists exerted in their newspapers to produce misunderstanding between Mr. Madison and myself. These failed completely. A like attempt was afterwards made through other

---

[1] See Randolph's speeches in Congress of May 26, 1812, and 15th April, 1824.

channels to effect a similar purpose between General Dearborn and myself, but with no more success. The machinations of the last session to put you at cross-questions with us all were so obvious as to be seen at the first glance of every eye. In order to destroy one member of the Administration, the whole were to be set to loggerheads to destroy one another. I observe in the papers lately new attempts to revive this stale artifice, and that they squint more directly towards you and myself. I cannot, therefore, be satisfied till I declare to you explicitly that my affection and confidence in you are nothing impaired, and that they cannot be impaired by means so unworthy the notice of candid and honorable minds. I make the declaration that no doubts or jealousies, which often beget the facts they fear, may find a moment's harbor in either of our minds. I have so much reliance on the superior good sense and candor of all those associated with me as to be satisfied they will not suffer either friend or foe to sow tares among us. Our Administration now drawing towards a close, I have a sublime pleasure in believing it will be distinguished as much by having placed itself above all the passions which could disturb its harmony, as by the great operations by which it will have advanced the well-being of the nation.

Accept my affectionate salutations and assurances of my constant and unalterable respect and attachment.

GALLATIN TO JEFFERSON.

WASHINGTON, 13th October, 1806.

DEAR SIR,—In minds solely employed in honest efforts to promote the welfare of a free people there is but little room left for the operation of those passions which engender doubts and jealousies. That you entertained none against me I had the most perfect conviction before I received your note of yesterday. Of your candor and indulgence I have experienced repeated proofs; the freedom with which my opinions have been delivered has been always acceptable and approved, even when they may have happened not precisely to coincide with your own view of the subject and you have thought them erroneous. But I am not the less sensible of your kindness in repeating at this juncture the expression of your confidence. If amongst the authors of the animadversions to which you allude there be any who believe that in my long and confidential intercourse with Republican members of Congress, that particularly in my free communications of facts and opinions to Mr. Randolph, I have gone beyond what prudence might have suggested, the occasion necessarily required, or my official situation strictly permitted, those who are impressed with such belief must be allowed to reprove the indiscretion, and may perhaps honestly suspect its motive. For those having charged me with any equivocation, evasion, or the least deviation from truth in any shape whatever, I cannot even frame an apology. And, without cherishing resentment, I have not the charity to ascribe to purity of intention the Philadelphia attacks, which indeed I expect to see renewed with additional virulence and a total disregard for truth. I am, however, but a secondary object, and you are not less aware than myself that the next Presidential election lurks at the bottom of those writings and of the Congressional dissensions. [To you my wish may be expressed that whenever you shall be permitted to withdraw, the choice may fall on Mr. Madison, as the most worthy and the most capable. But I know that on that point, as well as on all others which relate to elections, no Executive officer ought to interfere].[1]

Much more, however, do I lament the injury which the Republican cause may receive from the divisions amongst its friends in so many different quarters. Sacrificing the public good and their avowed principles to personal views, to pride and resentment, they afford abundant matter of triumph to our opponents; they discredit at all events, and may ultimately ruin, the cause itself. But if we are unable to control the conflicting passions and jarring interests which surround us, they will not at least affect our conduct. The Administration has no path to pursue but to continue their unremitted attention to the high duties entrusted to their care, and to persevere in their efforts to preserve peace abroad, and at home to improve and invigorate our repub-

---

[1] Omitted in final draft.

lican institutions. The most important object at present is to arrange on equitable terms our differences with Spain. That point once accomplished, your task shall have been satisfactorily completed, and those you have associated in your labors will be amply rewarded by sharing in the success of your Administration. From no other source can any of them expect to derive any degree of reputation.

With sincere respect and grateful attachment.

GALLATIN TO MARIA NICHOLSON.

WASHINGTON, October 27, 1806.

. . . I had seen the piece in the " Enquirer" to which you allude before I left New York. To be abused and misunderstood by political friends of worth is not pleasant, but the great question in all those things is : Did you perform your duty, and did you, as far as you were able, promote the public good ? For, worldly as you think me, rest assured that, however I may prize public opinion, it is not there that I seek for a reward. I suspect—but that is solely between ourselves—that some friends of John Randolph, mortified at his conduct and still more at its effect on his consequence, would wish to throw the blame of his excesses on me; and that, on the other hand, a weak friend of the President has felt hurt that my opinions had not in every particular coincided with the President's. To those joint causes I ascribe the Virginia attack. Mr. Jefferson, thinking that I might be hurt by it, wrote me the enclosed letter. . . . It affords additional proof of the goodness of his heart, and shows that he is much above all those little squabbles. . . .

In order to follow out to its conclusion this long story of John Randolph's schism, it has been necessary to leave the larger questions of public interest far behind. Whatever misstatements of fact Randolph may have made, his opinion on one point was indubitably correct : Mr. Jefferson's Spanish policy in 1805–6 was feeble, and it was a failure. It was feeble not because it proposed the purchase of Florida from France or from Spain, but because it threatened war without backing its threats by real force. The situation in regard to England was no better. To the very serious questions of impressments, of the annual blockade of New York, and of the lawless proceedings of the British ships of war, was now added the settled determination on the part of England to stop the prodigious increase of American commerce which threatened to ruin the shipping interests of Great Britain. For this purpose an old rule of the war of 1756 was revived, and the American shipping engaged in the hitherto legal trade of carrying West India produce from the United States to Europe was suddenly swept into British ports and condemned. All the resistance that Mr. Madison could offer was a pamphlet,—convincing enough as to the right, but not equally so as to the power, of the United States. Congress, however, reinforced it by a non-importation act, and Mr. Monroe and William Pinkney were appointed a special commission to negotiate.

Meanwhile, the affairs of Mr. Gallatin's own Department had suffered no check or misfortune. His report of December, 1805, showed that the revenue had risen high above its highest previous mark, to $12,672,000, which, with the produce of the Mediterranean Fund and of the land sales, carried the receipts of the government nearly to $14,000,000. The surplus in the Treasury, after meeting all the regular expenditures and navy deficiencies, French claims, and the $1,750,000 of the Louisiana purchase, for which a loan had been authorized, would still exceed one million dollars on a reasonable estimate. The reduction of debt had already reached that point at which Mr. Gallatin was obliged to pause and impress upon Congress the idea that a new class of duties lay before them; four years more of the application of his system would pay off all the debt that was susceptible of immediate payment; the rest could be redeemed only by purchase, or by waiting until the law permitted its redemption. "Should circumstances render it eligible, a considerable portion of the revenue now appropriated for that purpose [payment of debt] may then, in conformity with existing provisions, be applied to other objects."

The following year, 1806, was still more prosperous. The regular revenue exceeded $13,000,000; the receipts altogether

had reached the sum of $14,500,000; the two millions appro-
priated for purchasing Florida had been supplied out of surplus
and sent abroad; the Tripolitan war was over; a surplus of
$4,000,000 was left in the Treasury; and only three years
remained before the day when some disposition must be made
of the excess of revenue.

So far as the mere financial arrangements for this event were
concerned, Mr. Gallatin took them himself in charge.   He abandoned at once the salt tax, which produced about $500,000, and
he proposed to continue the Mediterranean Fund only one year
longer.   At the same time he procured the passage of an Act
authorizing him to convert the unredeemed amount of the old
six per cent. deferred stock, representing a capital of about
$32,000,000, and the three per cents. (about $19,000,000), into
a six per cent. stock, redeemable at six months' notice.   The
inducements offered to the holders are explained in Mr. Gallatin's letter of 20th January, 1806,[1] to John Randolph, chairman
of the Ways and Means Committee.

The greater measures of public policy which were to crown
the edifice of republican government, and to realize all those
ideal benefits to humanity which Mr. Jefferson and his friends
aimed at, fell of necessity and properly to the President's charge.
Nowhere in all the long course of Mr. Jefferson's great career
did he appear to better advantage than when in his message of
1806 he held out to the country and the world that view of his
ultimate hopes and aspirations for national development, which
was, as he then trusted, to be his last bequest to mankind.
Having now reached the moment when he must formally announce to Congress that the great end of relieving the nation
from debt was at length within reach, and with it the duty of
establishing true republican government was fulfilled, he paused
to ask what use was to be made of the splendid future thus
displayed before them.   Should they do away with the taxes?
Should they apply them to the building up of armies and navies?
Both relief from taxation and the means of defence might be
sufficiently obtained without exhausting their resources, and still

---

[1] State Papers, Finance, ii. p. 212.

the great interests of humanity might be secured. These great interests were economical and moral; to supply the one, a system of internal improvement should be created commensurate with the magnitude of the country; " by these operations new channels of communication will be opened between the States, the lines of separation will disappear, their interests will be identified, and their union cemented by new and indissoluble ties." To provide for the other, the higher education should be placed among the objects of public care; "a public institution can alone supply those sciences which, though rarely called for, are yet necessary to complete the circle, all the parts of which contribute to the improvement of the country and some of them to its preservation." A national university and a national system of internal improvement were an essential part, and indeed the realization and fruit, of the republican theories which Mr. Jefferson and his associates put in practice as their ideal of government.

In this path Mr. Jefferson and Mr. Gallatin went hand in hand. The former, indeed, thought an amendment of the Constitution necessary in order to bring these objects within the enumerated powers of the government, while Mr. Gallatin, here, as in regard to the bank and the Louisiana purchase, found no difficulty on that score; but Mr. Jefferson looked forward to the adoption of such an amendment before the three years' interval had elapsed, and in the mean while Mr. Gallatin was actually putting his schemes into operation. The first report of the commissioners appointed to lay out the Cumberland Road, from the Potomac to the Ohio, was laid before Congress in January, 1807. A month later Congress passed the act under which the coast survey was authorized, and appropriated $50,000 to carry it into effect. A few weeks afterwards, Senator Worthington, of Ohio, one of Mr. Gallatin's closest friends, caused a resolution to be adopted directing the Secretary of the Treasury to prepare and report to the Senate a general scheme of internal improvement.

Few persons have now any conception of the magnitude of the scheme thus originated. The university was but a trifle, which Mr. Gallatin was ready to take upon his shoulders at once without waiting for other resources than he already had. He seemed to have a passion for organization. The land system, the sinking fund system, the Cumberland Road, the coast survey, were all in his hands, and were, if not exclusively yet essentially, organized by him. He now turned his attention to the creation of a new scheme, in comparison with which all the others were only fragments and playthings. His report on internal improvements was sent in to the Senate on the 12th of April, 1808, after a year's preparation. It presented a plan the mere outlines of which can alone find place here.

According to this sketch, the projected improvements were classified under the following heads:

I. Those parallel with the sea-coast, viz., canals cutting Cape Cod, New Jersey, Delaware, and North Carolina, so as to make continuous inland navigation along the coast to Cape Fear, at an estimated cost of $3,000,000; and a great turnpike road from Maine to Georgia, at an estimated cost of $4,800,000.

II. Those that were to run east and west, viz., improvement of the navigation of four Atlantic rivers, the Susquehanna, the Potomac, the James, and the Santee, and of four corresponding western rivers, the Alleghany, the Monongahela, the Kanawha, and the Tennessee, to the highest practicable points, at an estimated cost of $1,500,000; and the connection of these highest points of navigation by four roads across the Appalachian range, at an estimated cost of $2,800,000; and finally, a canal at the falls of the Ohio, $300,000, and improvement of roads to Detroit, St. Louis, and New Orleans, $200,000.

III. Those that were to run north and northwest to the lakes, viz., to connect the Hudson River with Lake Champlain, $800,000; to connect the Hudson River with Lake Ontario at Oswego by canal, $2,200,000; a canal round Niagara Falls, $1,000,000.

IV. Local improvements, $3,400,000.

The entire estimated expense was $20,000,000; by an appropriation of $2,000,000 a year the whole might be accomplished in ten years; by a system of selling to private parties the stock thus created by the government for turnpikes and canals, the fund might be made itself a permanent resource for further improvements.

Naturally the improvements thus contemplated were so laid out as to combine and satisfy local interests. The advantage which Mr. Gallatin proposed to gain was that of combining these interests in advance, so that they should co-operate in one great system instead of wasting the public resources in isolated efforts. He wished to fix the policy of government for at least ten years, and probably for an indefinite time, on the whole subject of internal improvements, as he had already succeeded in fixing it in regard to the payment of debt. By thus establishing a complete national system to be executed by degrees, the whole business of annual chaffering and log-rolling for local appropriations in Congress, and all its consequent corruptions and inconsistencies, were to be avoided.

Nor did Mr. Gallatin in making these propositions overlook the pressing necessity of providing for the national defence. His anticipated surplus exceeded five millions of dollars, and he intended that while two millions were annually set aside for internal improvements, the other three millions should be applied simultaneously for arsenals, magazines, and fortifications, or, if desired, for building a navy, while even from a military point of view the proposed roads and canals were as essential as arms, forts, or ships to national defence. In one respect, however, Mr. Gallatin differed rather widely from Mr. Jefferson, and this difference of opinion concerned a cardinal point of the President's policy. The famous gun-boat scheme, which seems to have been the creation of Mr. Jefferson and Mr. Robert Smith, took shape during the winter of 1806-7, in a special message, dated February 10, which recommended the immediate building of two hundred gun-boats. When the draft of this message was sent to Mr. Gallatin for his criticisms, he wrote that he was " clearly of opinion" there was no necessity for building so many of these vessels, and he urged that the seventy-three already in course of construction were more than enough in a time of peace. "Of all the species of force which war may require,—armies, ships of war, fortifications, and gun-boats,—there is none which can be obtained in a shorter notice than gun-boats, and none therefore that it is less necessary to provide beforehand. I think that within sixty days, perhaps half the time, each of the seaports of Boston, New York, Philadelphia, and Baltimore might build and fit out thirty, and the smaller ports together as many, especially if the timber was prepared beforehand. But beyond that preparation I would not go, for exclusively of the first expense of building and the interest of the capital thus laid out, I apprehend that, notwithstanding the care which may be taken, they will infallibly decay in a given number of years, and will be a perpetual bill of costs for repairs and maintenance."[1]

Mr. Jefferson's reply to this argument will be found in his letter of February 9, 1807, to Mr. Gallatin. When he fairly mounted a hobby-horse he rode it over all opposition, and, of all hobby-horses, gun-boats happened at this time to be his favorite. He insisted that the whole two hundred must be built, for five reasons: 1. Because they could not be built in two, or even in six, months. 2. Because, in case of war, the enemy would destroy them on the stocks in New York, Boston, Norfolk, or any seaport. 3. "The first operation of war by an enterprising enemy would be to sweep all our seaports of their vessels at least." 4. The expense of their preservation would be nothing. 5. The expense of construction would be less than supposed.[2]

Mr. Jefferson was a great man, and like other great men he occasionally committed great follies, yet it may be doubted whether in the whole course of his life he ever wrote anything much more absurd than this letter. When war came, each of his three former reasons was shown to be an error, and long before the war arrived, his two concluding reasons were contradicted by facts. These letters were written in February, 1807. In June, 1809, barely two years later, the then Secretary of the Navy, Paul Hamilton, reported that 176 gun-boats had been built, of which 24 only were in actual service. The aggregate expense to that date had been $1,700,000, or about $725,000 a year; while the reader will remember that the whole navy expenditure for 1807 was $1,722,000, and in 1808 nearly $1,900,000, against the modest $650,000 which had been agreed upon at the beginning of Mr. Jefferson's Administration. Any one who is curious to see how far Mr. Gallatin's opinion as to

---

[1] Gallatin's Writings, i. 330.   [2] Jefferson's Writings, v. 42.

the "perpetual bill of costs for repairs" was correct, may refer to Paul Hamilton's letter of June 6, 1809, to the Senate committee.[1] Had all this expenditure improved the national defences, the waste of money would have seemed less outrageous even to Mr. Gallatin, who was its chief victim; but, as most naval officers expected, the gun-boats were in some respects positively mischievous, in others of very little use, and they were easily destroyed by the enemy whenever found. At the end of the war such of them as were not already captured, burned, wrecked, or decayed were quietly broken up or sold.[2]

Friends and enemies have long since agreed that Mr. Jefferson's gun-boats were a grievous mistake. How decidedly Mr. Gallatin remonstrated against the development given to this policy, may be seen in the letter of which a portion has been quoted. He strongly urged that no more gun-boats should be built till they were wanted, and he begged Mr. Jefferson to let Congress decide whether they were wanted or not. Mr. Jefferson did not take the advice, and, as usual, Mr. Gallatin was the one to suffer for the mistakes of his chief; the gun-boats lasted long enough to give him great trouble and to be one of the principal means of bankrupting the Treasury even before the war; unfortunately, he had exhausted his strength in complaints of the Navy Department; he had spoken again and again in language which for him was without an example; in the present instance he had Mr. Jefferson himself for his strongest opponent, and there was nothing to be done but to submit.

With this exception, one merely of detail and judgment, Mr. Gallatin seems to have cordially supported the comprehensive scheme which the Administration of Mr. Jefferson pointed out to Congress as the goal of its long pilgrimage. Six years of frugality and patience had, as it conceived, fixed beyond question the republicanism of national character, established a political system purely American, and sealed this result by reducing the national debt until its ultimate extinction was in full view. To fix the future course of the republican system thus established

---

[1] State Papers, xiv. 194.

[2] Under the Act of Congress of February 27, 1815.

was a matter of not less importance, was perhaps a matter of much greater difficulty, than the task already accomplished. To make one comprehensive, permanent provision for the moral and economical development of the people, to mark out the path of progress with precision and to enter upon it at least so far as to make subsequent advance easy and certain, this was the highest statesmanship, the broadest practical philanthropy. For this result Mr. Gallatin, in the ripened wisdom of his full manhood, might fairly say that his life had been well spent.

For a time he saw the prize within his grasp; then almost in an instant it was dashed away, and the whole fabric he had so laboriously constructed fell in ruins before his eyes. That such a disaster should have overwhelmed him at last was neither his fault nor that of Mr. Jefferson; it was the result of forces which neither he nor any other man or combination of men, neither his policy nor any other policy or resource of human wisdom, could control. In the midst of the great crash with which the whole structure of Mr. Jefferson's Administration toppled over and broke to pieces in its last days, there is ample room to criticise and condemn the theories on which he acted and the measures which he used, but few critics would now be bold enough to say that any policy or any measure could have prevented that disaster.

The story is soon told. Mr. Monroe and Mr. William Pinkney, appointed as a special commission to negotiate with the government of Great Britain, began their labors in July, 1806. They were fortunate enough to find the British government in friendly hands, for they happened to fall upon the short administration of Mr. Fox. With much difficulty they negotiated a treaty which was signed on the last day of the year. This treaty was doubtless a bad treaty; not so bad as that of Mr. Jay, but still very unsatisfactory, and, what was worse, the British government, by a formal note appended to it, reserved the right to render it entirely nugatory if the United States did not satisfy Great Britain that she would resist the maritime decrees of France. Whether, under these circumstances, the treaty was worth accepting, is doubtful; whether Mr. Jefferson erred in insisting upon modifications of it, may be a question. Certain it is that the Administration concurred in sending it back to England for essential changes, and that Mr. Jefferson, undaunted by his previous failure to influence France by fear of his alliance with England, now expected to control England by fear of his alliance with France. "It is all-important that we should stand on terms of the strictest cordiality" with France, he wrote to Paris in announcing his treatment of the British treaty; but this cordiality was to go no further than friendly favors. "I verily believe," he wrote at the same time,[1] "that it will ever be in our power to keep so even a stand between England and France as to inspire a wish in neither to throw us into the scale of his adversary."

Never did a man deceive himself more miserably, for even while he wrote these lines the government of England was reverting to its policy of crushing the commercial growth of America. Mr. Fox was dead; a new Administration had come into power, strongly retrograde in policy, and with George Canning for its soul. Whatever the errors or faults of Mr. Canning may have been, timidity was not one of them, and the diplomatic ingenuity of Mr. Jefferson, with its feeble attempts to play off France against England and England against France, was the last policy he was likely to respect. Even the American who reads the history of the year 1807, seeing the brutal directness with which Mr. Canning kicked Mr. Jefferson's diplomacy out of his path, cannot but feel a certain respect for the Englishman mingled with wrath at his insolent sarcasm. From the moment Mr. Canning and his party assumed power, the fate of Mr. Jefferson's Administration was sealed; nothing he could do or could have done could avert it; England was determined to recover her commerce and to take back her seamen, and America could not retain either by any means whatever; she had no alternative but submission or war, and either submission or war was equally fatal to Mr. Jefferson's Administration. Mr. Canning cared little which course she took, but he believed she would submit.

The first intimation of the new state of affairs came in an unexpected and almost accidental shape. The winter of 1806–7 had passed, and, so far as Congress was concerned, it had passed without serious conflicts. Burr's wild expedition had startled

---

[1] To Tench Coxe, 27th March, 1807.

and excited the country, but this episode had no special connection with anything actual; it was rather a sporadic exhibition of the personal peculiarities of Mr. Burr and his lurid imagination. Congress adjourned on the 3d March, 1807; as the summer advanced, Mr. Gallatin went with his family to New York; on the 25th June he was suddenly summoned back to Washington by a brief note from Mr. Jefferson announcing the capture of the American frigate Chesapeake by the British ship-of-war Leopard.

The story of this famous event, which more than any other single cause tended to exasperate national jealousies and to make England and America permanently hostile, is told in every American school history, and will probably be familiar to every schoolboy in the United States for generations yet to come. Even time is slow in erasing the memory of these national humiliations, and the singular spectacle has been long presented of a great nation preserving the living memory of a wrong that the offending nation hardly noticed at the time and almost immediately forgot. The reason was that in this instance the wrong was a cruel and cynical commentary on all the mistakes of our national policy; it gave the sentence of death to the favorite dogmas and doctrines of the American Administration, and it was a practical demonstration of their absurdity, the more mortifying because of its incontestable completeness.

Mr. Gallatin hastened to Washington, sickened by anxiety and responsibility; his state of mind and that of his political friends may be shown by a few extracts from his papers:

GALLATIN TO HIS WIFE.

WASHINGTON, 10th July, 1807.

. . . I am afraid that in common with many more your feelings prevent your taking a correct view of our political situation. To spurn at negotiation and to tremble for the fate of New York are not very consistent. But every person not blinded by passion and totally ignorant of the laws and usages of civilized nations knows that, whenever injuries are received from subordinate officers, satisfaction is demanded from the government itself before reprisals are made; and that time to receive our property from abroad and to secure our harbors as well as we can is of importance to us, can any one doubt in New York? It is our duty to ask for reparation, to avert war if it can be done honorably, and in the mean while not to lose an instant in preparing for war. On the last point I doubt, between ourselves, whether everything shall be done which ought to be done. And for that reason alone I wish that Congress may be called somewhat earlier than is now intended. The President wishes the call for the last of October. I had at first proposed the middle, but from various circumstances I now want an immediate call. The principal objection will not be openly avowed, but it is the unhealthiness of this city. I am glad to see the spirit of the people, but I place but a moderate degree of confidence on those first declarations in which many act from the first impulse of their feelings, more from sympathy or fear, and only a few from a calm view of the subject. I think that I have taken such a view, probed the extent of the dangers and evils of a war, and, though fully aware of both, will perhaps persevere longer under privations and evils than many others. Our commerce will be destroyed and our revenue nearly annihilated. That we must encounter; but our resources in money and men will be sufficient considerably to distress the enemy and to defend ourselves everywhere but at sea. I have, in a national point of view, but one subject of considerable uneasiness, and that is New York, which is now entirely defenceless, and from its situation nearly indefensible. This last idea I keep altogether to myself. I think that I increased my sickness by intensity of thinking and not sleeping at nights. I certainly grew better as soon as my plans were digested, and, except as to New York, I feel now very easy, provided that our resources shall be applied with ability and in the proper direction. In the mean while the ships on our coast may accelerate hostilities. This we will try to avoid, and so will Mr. Erskine, who, having neither orders nor advice from his government on this subject, cannot be very easy and will not be very influential. (Admiral Berkeley's order is, very curiously, drawn and dated as far back as 1st June.) But I think that these hostilities will be confined to blockade and captures till they receive new instructions, and that New York has no immediate danger to apprehend. At all events, against such a force it may be defended. The difficulty is in case a fleet of ten ships of the line shall attack it. . . .

14th July, 1807.

. . . Of our public affairs I have nothing new to say. It is probable that the attack on our frigate was not directly authorized by the British government; it is certain that the subsequent acts of the commodore in the vicinity of Norfolk were without any order even from his admiral. But from the character and former orders of the last-mentioned (Berkeley) it is probable that, considering the proclamation as hostile, he will order all merchant vessels on our coast to be taken and the Chesapeake to be blockaded. They will not venture on any hostilities on shore until they receive orders from Great Britain; for their naval arrogance induces them to make unfounded distinctions between what is legal on land or on water even within our jurisdiction, and they have not really sense or knowledge enough to feel that their present conduct within the Chesapeake is as much an actual invasion as if an army was actually landed. Upon the whole, you will, I am persuaded, have time to do whatever is practicable for the defence of New York. I have seen Mr. Erskine, whom I treated with more civility than cordiality; but I could not help it. I believe that he is much embarrassed between what is right and his fear of the naval officers and of his own government.

NATHANIEL MACON TO GALLATIN.

BUCK SPRING, 12th July, 1807.

SIR,—The attack of the British on the Chesapeake and their subsequent conduct near Norfolk has much irritated every one here, and all are anxious to learn what the President intends to do. From the tenor of his proclamation I suppose he intends to have a representation made to the British government, and, in case that does not produce the desired effect, to order our ministers home, and in the mean time to have all the preparations for war he can ready. I also suppose from the proclamation that Congress will not be called until he hears from London, unless there should be a change in the state of affairs. . . .

If war must be, we ought to prosecute it with the same zeal that we have endeavored to preserve peace, and by great exertions convince the enemy that it is not from fear or cowardice that we dread it. But peace, if we can have it, is always best for us, and if the Executive can get justice done and preserve it, that Executive will deserve the thanks of every democrat in the Union.

JOSEPH H. NICHOLSON TO GALLATIN.

CHESTERFIELD, 14th July, 1807.

DEAR SIR,—. . . We are looking with great anxiety towards Washington for the measures to be adopted by the government. For myself I consider a war inevitable, and almost wish for it. An unqualified submission to Britain would not be more degrading than forbearance now. The Ministry may probably, and I think will, disavow the late act of their officer; but there are insults and injuries for which neither an individual nor a nation can accept an apology. I had hoped, therefore, that Mr. Erskine would have been ordered home and our own envoys recalled. Nothing is now left to negotiate on. No man ever saved his honor who opened a negotiation for it. It is no subject of barter. If Tarquin had begged pardon of Collatinus for ravishing his wife, I think it would not have been granted. At all events we cannot, or at least ought not, negotiate till our seamen are restored. In 1764, when France took possession of Turk's Island, her minister at the Court of London proposed to negotiate for some claims that his master had upon it. George Grenville told him, "We will not hear you; we will listen to nothing while the island is in your possession. Restore it, and we will then hear what you have to say." It was instantaneously given up. I wish Mr. Jefferson would read the history of that transaction, and also Lord Chatham's celebrated speech on the business of Falkland Islands. Each furnishes an admirable lesson for the present moment. But one feeling pervades the nation. All distinctions of federalism and democracy are vanished. The people are ready to submit to any deprivation, and if we withdraw ourselves within our own shell, and turn loose some thousands of privateers, we shall obtain in a little time an absolute renunciation of the right of search for the purposes of impressment. A parley will prove fatal, for the merchants will begin to calculate. They rule us, and we should take them before their resentment is superseded by considerations of profit and loss. I trust in God the Revenge is going out to bring Monroe and Pinkney home.

GALLATIN TO JOSEPH H. NICHOLSON.

WASHINGTON, 17th July, 1807.

DEAR SIR,—. . . With you I believe that war is inevitable, and there can be but one opinion on the question whether the claims of the parties prior to the attack on the Chesapeake should be a subject of discussion. There were but two courses to be taken : either to consider the attack as war and retaliate accordingly, or, on the supposition that that act might be that of an unauthorized officer, to ask simply, and without discussion, disavowal, satisfaction, and security against a recurrence of outrages. The result will in my opinion be the same, for Great Britain will not, I am confident, give either satisfaction or security ; but the latter mode, which, as you may have perceived by the President's proclamation and his answer to military corps, has been adopted, was recommended not only by the nature of our Constitution, which does not make the President arbiter of war, but also by the practice of civilized nations ; and the cases of Turk's Island, Falkland Islands, Nootka Sound, etc., are in point in that respect. Add to this that the dissatisfaction caused by that course operates only against the Administration, and that the other will produce an unanimity in support of the war which would not otherwise have existed. It will also make our cause completely popular with the Baltic powers, and may create new enemies to Britain in that quarter. Finally, four months were of importance to us, both by diminishing the losses of our merchants and for preparations of defence and attack.

I will, however, acknowledge that on that particular point I have not bestowed much thought ; for, having considered from the first moment war was a necessary result, and the preliminaries appearing to me but matters of form, my faculties have been exclusively applied to the preparations necessary to meet the times; and although I am not very sanguine as to the brilliancy of our exploits, the field where we can act without a navy being very limited, and perfectly aware that a war in a great degree passive and consisting of privations will become very irksome to the people, I feel no apprehension of the immediate result. We will be poorer both as a nation and as a government; our debt and taxes will increase, and our progress in every respect be interrupted. But all those evils are not only not to be put in competition with the independence and honor of the nation, they are, moreover, temporary, and very few years of peace will obliterate their effects. Nor do I know whether the awakening of nobler feelings and habits than avarice and luxury might not be necessary to prevent our degenerating, like the Hollanders, into a nation of mere calculators. In fact, the greatest mischiefs which I apprehend from the war are the necessary increase of Executive power and influence, the speculation of contractors and jobbers, and the introduction of permanent military and naval establishments. . . .

NATHANIEL MACON TO GALLATIN.

ROCK SPRING, 2d August, 1807.

. . . Peace is everything to us, especially in this part of the Union. Here the three last crops have been uncommonly short, and the last the shortest of the three. These bad crops have compelled many, who were both careful and industrious, to go in debt for bread and to leave their merchant account unpaid. If the Executive shall put a satisfactory end to the fracas with Great Britain, it will add as much to his reputation as the purchase of Louisiana. But if this cannot be done, we must try which can do the other the most harm.

I suppose while I am thinking what effect the war may have on my neighbors and countrymen, you are engaged in calculating its effects on the payment of the national debt.

I still wish peace, but if this be denied to us I am for strong measures against the enemy.

Until it was quite certain whether the attack on the Chesapeake was an authorized act, government could only prepare for war. Mr. Jefferson called upon his Cabinet for written opinions, and Mr. Gallatin prepared an elaborate paper containing a general view of the defensive and offensive measures which war would require.[1] This done, and temporary arrangements made, the Cabinet again separated, and Mr. Gallatin returned to New York.

Congress was called for the 26th October, 1807, and the Administration came together a few weeks earlier to prepare for the meeting. When Mr. Jefferson sent as usual the draft of his message for revision, Mr. Gallatin found that it was drawn up " rather in the shape of a manifesto issued against Great Britain on the eve of a war, than such as the existing, undecided state of affairs seems to require." He remonstrated in a letter, too long to quote, but of much historical interest.[2] The conclusion was that " in every view of the subject I feel strongly impressed with the propriety of preparing to the utmost for war and carrying it with vigor if it cannot be ultimately avoided, but in the mean while persevering in that caution of language and action which may give us some more time and is best calculated to preserve the remaining chance of peace, and most consistent with the general system of your Administration." Mr. Jefferson at once acceded to this view.

GALLATIN TO HIS WIFE.

WASHINGTON, 30th October, 1807.

. . . Varnum has, much against my wishes, removed Randolph from the Ways and Means and appointed Campbell, of Tennessee. It was improper as related to the public business, and will give me additional labor. Vanzandt has missed the clerkship of the House, and lost his place, from Mr. Randolph's declaration that he had listened to and reported secret debates. The punishment, considering its consequences on his future prospects, is rather hard. (The President's speech was origi-

---

[1] See Writings, vol. i. p. 341.   [2] Ibid., p. 358, 21st October, 1807.

nally more warlike than was necessary, but I succeeded in getting it neutralized; this between us; but it was lucky; for) Congress is certainly peaceably disposed. . . .

The British government, however, had no intention of making a war out of the Chesapeake affair. With much dexterity Mr. Canning used this accident for his own purposes. He applied the curb and spur at the same moment with marvellous audacity; disavowing the acts of the British naval officers, he evaded the demand of our government for satisfaction, and, while thus showing how sternly he meant to repress what he chose to consider our insolence, he sent Mr. Rose to Washington to amuse Mr. Jefferson with negotiations, while at the same time he himself carried out his fixed policy, with which the affair of the Chesapeake had no other than a general and accidental connection. Contemptuously refusing to renew negotiations over Mr. Monroe's treaty, at the very moment of Mr. Rose's departure to Washington he issued his famous orders in council of November 11, 1807, by which the chief part of the trade of America with the continent of Europe was, with one stroke of the pen, suppressed.

As there was no pretence of law or principle under which this act could be justified, Mr. Canning put it upon the ground of retaliation for the equally outrageous decrees of France; but in fact he cared very little what ground it was placed upon. The act was in its nature one of war, and, as a war measure for the protection of British commercial shipping rapidly disappearing before French regulations and American competition, this act was no more violent than any other act of war. Its true foundation was a not unwarranted contempt for American national character. As Lord Sidmouth, who disapproved the orders in council, wrote in 1807 : " It is in vain to speculate on the result when we have to bear with a country in which there is little authority in the rulers, and as little public spirit and virtue in the people. America is no longer a bugbear; there is no terror in her threats."[1] America had her redress if she chose

---

[1] Diary and Correspondence of Lord Colchester, ii. 132.

to take it; if she did not choose to take it, as Mr. Canning would probably have argued, it could only be because, after all, it was against her interest to do so, which to Mr. Canning was the demonstration of his own problem.[1]

---

[1] The actual author of the orders in council of November 11, 1807, was Spencer Perceval, then Attorney-General. The objects he had in view are very clearly given in a letter written by him towards the end of that month to Charles Abbot, then Speaker of the House of Commons, afterwards Lord Colchester:

SPENCER PERCEVAL TO SPEAKER ABBOT.

. . . The business of recasting the law of trade and navigation, as far as belligerent principles are concerned, for the whole world, has occupied me very unremittingly for a long time; and the subject is so extensive, and the combinations so various, that, even supposing our principles to be right, I cannot hope that the execution of the principle must not in many respects be defective; and I have no doubt we shall have to watch it with new provisions and regulations for some time.

The short principle is that trade in British produce and manufactures, and trade either from a British port or with a British destination, is to be protected as much as possible. For this purpose all the countries where French influence prevails to exclude the British flag shall have no trade but to or from this country or from its allies. All other countries, the few that remain strictly neutral (with the exception of the colonial trade, which backwards and forwards direct they may carry on), cannot trade but through this being done as an ally with any of the countries connected with France. If, therefore, we can accomplish our purposes, it will come to this, that either those countries will have no trade, or they must be content to accept it through us.

This is a formidable and tremendous state of the world; but all the part of it which is particularly harassing to English interests was existing through the new severity with which Buonaparte's decrees of exclusion against our trade were called into action.

Our proceeding does not aggravate our distress from it. If he can keep out our trade he will, and he would do so if he could, independent of our orders. Our orders only add this circumstance: they say to the enemy, if you will not have *our* trade, as far as we can help it you shall have *none*. And as to so much of any trade as you can carry on yourselves, or others carry on with you through us, if you admit it you shall pay for it. The only trade, cheap and untaxed, which you shall have shall be either direct from us, in our own produce and manufactures, or from our allies, whose increased prosperity will be an advantage to us. . . .

Diary and Correspondence of Lord Colchester, vol. ii. p. 134. See also the Life of Spencer Perceval, by Spencer Walpole, vol. i. p. 263 ff., for the further history and Cabinet discussions of this subject.

The certain news of the orders in council of November 11 reached Washington on December 18, together with threatening news from France. A Cabinet council was instantly held, and the confidential friends of the Administration consulted. The situation was clear. In the face of the orders in council our commerce must be kept at home, at least until further measures could be taken. Whether as a war or as a peace measure, an embargo was inevitable, and, unwilling as all parties were to be driven into it, there was no alternative. A much more difficult question was whether the embargo should be made a temporary measure; in other words, whether war, after a certain date, should be the policy of the government.

Mr. Gallatin's opinions on these points are fortunately preserved. He wrote to Mr. Jefferson, apparently after a Cabinet council, on the 18th December as follows:

GALLATIN TO JEFFERSON.

TREASURY DEPARTMENT, 18th December, 1807.

DEAR SIR,—Reflecting on the proposed embargo and all its bearings, I think it essential that foreign vessels may be excepted so far at least as to be permitted to depart in ballast or with such cargoes as they may have on board at this moment. They are so few as to be no object to us, and we may thereby prevent a similar detention of our vessels abroad, or at least a pretence for it. Such a seizure of our property and seamen in foreign ports would be far greater than any possible loss at sea for six months to come. I wish to know the name of the member to whom Mr. Rodney sent the sketch of a resolution, in order to mention the subject to him, and also, if you approve, that you would suggest it to such as you may see. I also think that an embargo for a limited time will at this moment be preferable in itself, and less objectionable in Congress. In every point of view, privations, sufferings, revenue, effect on the enemy, politics at home, &c., I prefer war to a permanent embargo. Governmental prohibitions do always more mischief than had been calculated; and it is not without much hesitation that a statesman should hazard to regulate the concerns of individuals as if he could do it better than themselves.

The measure being of a doubtful policy, and hastily adopted on the first view of our foreign intelligence, I think that we had better recommend it with modifications, and at first for such a limited time as will afford us all time for reconsideration, and, if we think proper, for an alteration in our course without appearing to retract.   As to the hope that it may have an effect on the negotiation with Mr. Rose, or induce England to treat us better, I think it entirely groundless.

Respectfully, your obedient servant.

Mr. Jefferson wrote back approving the first suggestion, and it was inserted in the bill, but on the other point Mr. Gallatin was overruled.   Mr. Jefferson and most of the Southern leaders of his party had a strong faith in the efficacy of commercial regulations; they believed that as the commerce of America was very valuable to England and France, therefore England and France might be forced to do our will by depriving them of that commerce; and perhaps they were in the right, within certain limits, for, other agencies being disregarded and the influences of commerce being left to act through periods of years, nations will ultimately be controlled by them; England herself was ultimately compelled by the policy of commercial restrictions to revoke her orders in council, but only after five years of experiment and too late to prevent war.

Meanwhile, the effect of a permanent embargo was to carry out by the machinery of the United States government precisely the policy which Mr. Canning had adopted for his own.   American shipping ceased to exist; American commerce was annihilated; American seamen were forced to seek employment under the British flag, and British ships and British commerce alone occupied the ocean.   The strangest and saddest spectacle of all was to see Mr. Jefferson and Mr. Gallatin, after seven years of patient labor in constructing their political system, forced to turn their backs upon that future which only a few weeks before had been so brilliant, and, with infinitely more labor and trouble than they had used in building their edifice up, now toil to pull it down.

Mr. Gallatin had no faith in the embargo as a measure of constraint upon the belligerent powers; he characterized as "utterly groundless" the idea that it would have any effect on negotiation or induce England to treat us better; but he accepted it as the policy fixed by his party and by Congress, for the adoption of which Congress was primarily responsible, and for the execution of which he had himself to answer; he accepted it also as the only apparent alternative to war, but not as a permanent alternative.

Mr. Jefferson went much farther. Without at this time avowing a belief that the embargo would force England and France to recede, he was warm in the determination that its power should be tried. "I place immense value in the experiment being fully made how far an embargo may be an effectual weapon in future as on this occasion," he wrote to Mr. Gallatin.[1] Elsewhere he repeated the same earnest wish to test the powers of this "engine for national purposes," as he called it. He was restive and even intolerant of opposition on this subject. The embargo as a coercive measure against England and France was in fact the only policy upon which a fair degree of unanimity in the party was attainable, or which their political education had prescribed. No spectacle could be more lamentable and ludicrous than the Congressional proceedings of this session; under the relentless grasp of Mr. Canning, the American Congress threw itself into contortions such as could not but be in the highest degree amusing to him, and when watched as a mere spectacle of powerless rage may have been even instructive. There was but one respectable policy,—war, immediate and irrespective of cost or risk; but of war all parties stood in dread, and as between England and France it was difficult to choose an opponent. Even for war some preparation was necessary, but when Congress attempted to consider preparations, some members wished for militia, some for regular troops, some for a navy, some for fortifications, some for gun-boats, and there were convincing reasons to prove that each of these resources was useless by itself, and that taken

---

[1] On the 15th May, 1808.

together they were not only far beyond the national means, but quite opposed to American theories. Nevertheless, a good deal of money was appropriated in an unsystematic manner among these various objects, and Mr. Gallatin's surplus soon began to dwindle away.

On the embargo alone some degree of unanimity could be attained. The omnipotent influence with which Mr. Jefferson had begun his Administration, although steadily diminishing with the advent of a new generation and the apparent accomplishment of the great objects for which the party had been educated, was still capable of revival in its full strength to give effect to the old party dogma of commercial regulations. Every one was earnestly impressed with what Mr. Jefferson called "our extreme anxiety to give a full effect to the important experiment of the embargo at any expense within the bounds of reason." The first embargo law of December 22, 1807, was a mere temporary measure of precaution; in order to carry out the policy with effect, a completer system had to be framed, and Mr. Gallatin was obliged himself to draft the bill which was to beggar the Treasury; but no ordinary grant of powers would answer a purpose which consisted in stopping the whole action and industry of all the great cities and much of the rural population; thus the astonishing spectacle was presented of Mr. Jefferson, Mr. Madison, and Mr. Gallatin, the apostles of strict construction, of narrow grants, the men who of all others were the incarnation of that theory which represented mankind as too much governed, and who, according to Mr. Jefferson, would have had government occupy itself exclusively with foreign affairs and leave the individual absolutely alone to manage his own concerns in his own way,—of these men demanding, obtaining, and using powers practically unlimited so far as private property was concerned; powers in comparison with which the alien and sedition laws were narrow and jealous in their grants; powers which placed the fortunes of at least half the community directly under their control; which made them no more nor less than despots; which gave Mr. Jefferson the right to say: "we may fairly require positive proof that the individual of a town tainted with a general spirit of disobedience has never said or done anything himself to countenance that spirit;"[1] and which dictated his letter to the Governor of Massachusetts, then among the proudest, the wealthiest, and the most populous States in the Union, that the President had permitted her to have sixty thousand barrels of flour; that this was enough, and she must have no more.[2]

Congress conferred on the President the enormous grants of power which he asked for, and Mr. Gallatin proceeded to execute the law; the result was what he had predicted when he said that government prohibitions do always more harm than was calculated. The law was first evaded, then resisted; then came the ominous demand for troops, gun-boats, and frigates to use against our own citizens, and to be used by Mr. Gallatin, who, of all men, held military force so applied in horror; then came the announcement of insurrection, in August, from the Governor of New York, an insurrection which became chronic along the northern frontier, from Passamaquoddy to Niagara. All along the coast the United States navy was spread out to destroy that commerce which it had been built to protect, and the officers of our ships of war, frantic to revenge upon the British cruisers their disgrace in the Chesapeake, were compelled to assist these very cruisers to plunder their own countrymen.

The struggle between government and citizens was violent and prolonged. Mr. Gallatin's letters at this time to Mr. Jefferson are curious reading. He set himself with his usual determination to the task of carrying out his duty; his agents and instruments broke down in every direction; his annoyances were innumerable and his efforts only partially successful. The powers he had demanded and received, immense as they were, proved insufficient, and he demanded more. Already in July, 1808, he had reached this point. On the 29th of that month he wrote to Mr. Jefferson from New York: "I am perfectly satisfied that if the embargo must be persisted in any longer, two principles must necessarily be adopted in order to make it sufficient: 1st. That not a single vessel shall be permitted to move without the special

---

[1] To Gallatin, 13th November, 1808. Jefferson's Writings, v. 385.

[2] To Governor Sullivan, 12th August, 1808. Jefferson's Writings, v. 340.

permission of the Executive. 2d. That the collectors be invested
with the general power of seizing property anywhere, and taking
the rudders or otherwise effectually preventing the departure of
any vessel in harbor, though ostensibly intended to remain there;
and that without being liable to personal suits. I am sensible that
such arbitrary powers are equally dangerous and odious. But
a restrictive measure of the nature of the embargo applied to a
nation under such circumstances as the United States cannot be
enforced without the assistance of means as strong as the measure
itself. To that legal authority to prevent, seize, and detain, must
be added a sufficient physical force to carry it into effect; and,
although I believe that in our seaports little difficulty would be
encountered, we must have a little army along the lakes and
British lines generally. With that result we should not perhaps
be much astonished, for the Federalists having at least prevented
the embargo from becoming a measure generally popular, and
the people being distracted by the complexity of the subject,—
orders of council, decrees, embargoes,—and wanting a single
object which might rouse their patriotism and unite their passions and affections, selfishness has assumed the reins in several
quarters, and the people are now there altogether against the
law. In such quarters the same thing happens which has taken
place everywhere else, and even under the strongest governments, under similar circumstances. The navy of Great Britain
is hardly sufficient to prevent smuggling, and you recollect,
doubtless, the army of employees and the sanguinary code of
France, hardly adequate to guard their land frontiers.

"That in the present situation of the world every effort should
be attempted to preserve the peace of this nation cannot be
doubted. But if the criminal party rage of Federalists and
Tories shall have so far succeeded as to defeat our endeavors to
obtain that object by the only measure that could possibly have
effected it, we must submit and prepare for war. I am so much
overwhelmed even here with business and interruptions that I
have not time to write correctly or even with sufficient perspicuity;
but you will guess at my meaning where it is not sufficiently clear.
I mean generally to express an opinion founded on the experience
of this summer, that Congress must either invest the Executive

with the most arbitrary powers and sufficient force to carry the embargo into effect, or give it up altogether. And in this last case I must confess that, unless a change takes place in the measures of the European powers, I see no alternative but war. But with whom? This is a tremendous question if tested only by policy, and so extraordinary in our situation that it is equally difficult to decide it on the ground of justice, the only one by which I wish the United States to be governed. At all events, I think it the duty of the Executive to contemplate that result as probable, and to be prepared accordingly."

There can be no more painful task to a man of high principles than to do what Mr. Gallatin was now doing. Not only was he obliged to abandon the fruit of his long labors, and to see even those results that had seemed already gained suddenly cast in doubt, but he was obliged to do this himself by means which he abhorred, and which he did not hesitate to characterize, even to Mr. Jefferson, as "equally dangerous and odious," "most arbitrary powers," such as his whole life had offered one long protest against. On this score he had no defence against the ferocity of party assaults; he disdained to attempt a defence; all that could reasonably be said was true, and he felt the consequences more keenly than any one; he uttered no complaints, but accepted the responsibility and kept silence. Others were less discreet.

A. J. DALLAS TO GALLATIN.

30th July, 1808.

. . . The Spanish affairs have an obvious effect upon our political and territorial position. I do not know the measures or the designs of the government, and of course I cannot say what ought to be done as to foreign nations. As to ourselves, I will candidly tell you that almost everything that is done seems to excite disgust. I lament the state of things, but I verily believe one year more of writing, speaking, and appointing would render Mr. Jefferson a more odious President, even to the Democrats, than John Adams. My only hope is that Mr. Madison's election may not be affected, nor his administration perplexed, in consequence of the growing dissatisfaction among

the reputable members of the Republican party. But I have
abandoned politics, and hasten to assure you of the constant love
and esteem of all my family for all yours.

ROBERT SMITH TO GALLATIN.

BALTIMORE, August 1, 1808.

DEAR SIR,—Your favor of the 29th, with the enclosures, I
have received. The letters of General Dearborn and Lincoln
I have forwarded to the President. The requisite orders will
go without delay to the commanders of the Chesapeake, the
Wasp, and the Argus. Most fervently ought we to pray to
be relieved from the various embarrassments of this said embargo. Upon it there will in some of the States, in the course
of the next two months, assuredly be engendered monsters.
Would that we could be placed upon proper ground for calling
in this mischief-making busybody.

Even in his own family Mr. Gallatin maintained perfect
silence on this point. The use of arbitrary, odious, and dangerous means having been decided upon by his party and by
Congress, and he being the instrument to employ these means,
he did employ them as conscientiously as he had formerly opposed them, not because they were his own choice, but because
he could see no alternative. Not even war was clearly open to
him, for it was impossible to say which of the two belligerents
he ought to make responsible for the situation. How obnoxious
the embargo was to him can only be seen in his allusions to its
effects: "From present appearances," he wrote to his wife on
June 29, 1808, "the Federalists will turn us out by 4th March
next;" and on the 8th July, "As to my Presidential fears, they
arise from the pressure of the embargo and divisions of the
Republicans. I think that Vermont is lost; New Hampshire
is in a bad neighborhood, and Pennsylvania is extremely doubtful. But I would not even suggest such ideas so that they
should go abroad." But he suggested them to the President on
the 6th August: "I deeply regret to see my incessant efforts in
every direction to carry the law into effect defeated in so many

quarters, and that we will probably produce, at least on the British, but an inconsiderable effect by a measure which at the same time threatens to destroy the Republican interest. For there is almost an equal chance that if propositions from Great Britain, or other events, do not put it in our power to raise the embargo before the 1st of October, we will lose the Presidential election. I think that at this moment the Western States, Virginia, South Carolina, and perhaps Georgia, are the only sound States, and that we will have a doubtful contest in every other. The consciousness of having done what was right in itself is doubtless sufficient; but for the inefficacy of the measure on the lakes and to the northward there is no consolation; and that circumstance is the strongest argument that can be brought against the measure itself."

These fears proved ungrounded; Mr. Madison was elected by a large majority, and only the New England States reverted to opposition; but New England was on the verge of adopting the ground taken by Mr. Jefferson and Mr. Madison ten years before, and declaring the embargo, as they had declared the sedition law, unconstitutional, null, and void. Mr. Canning treated the embargo with sarcastic and patronizing contempt as a foolish policy, which he regretted because it was very inconvenient to the Americans. As an "engine for national purposes" it had utterly failed, but no one was agreed what to do next.

GALLATIN TO HIS WIFE.

WASHINGTON, July, 1808.

I enclose a National Intelligencer, one paragraph of which, together with the Bayonne decree, contains *the substance* of the intelligence. The last we have not officially. I think the aspect of affairs unfavorable. England seems to rely on our own divisions and on the aggressions of France as sufficient to force us into a change of measures, perhaps war with France, without any previous reparation or relaxation on her part. Of the real views of the French Emperor nothing more is known than what appears on the face of his decrees and in his acts; and these manifest, in my opinion, either a deep resentment because we would not make war against England, or a wish to seek a quarrel with us. Between the two our situation is extremely critical, and I believe that poor, limited human wisdom can do and will do but little to extricate us. Yet I do not feel despondent, for so long as we adhere strictly to justice towards all, I have a perfect reliance on the continued protection of that Providence which has raised us and blessed us as a nation. But we have been too happy and too prosperous, and we consider as great misfortunes some privations and a share in the general calamities of the world. Compared with other nations, our share is indeed very small. . . .

GALLATIN TO JOSEPH H. NICHOLSON.

WASHINGTON, 18th October, 1808.

. . . Your political questions are of no easy solution. We cannot yet conjecture whether the belligerent powers will alter their orders and decrees, and if they do not, what is to be done? I am as much at a loss what answer to make as yourself. The embargo, having been adopted, ought, if there was virtue enough in the Eastern people, to be continued. But without the support and the full support of the people, such a strong coercive measure cannot be fairly executed. If the embargo is taken off, I do not perceive yet any medium between absolute subjection or war. Perhaps, however, some substitute may be devised. A non-importation act is the only one which has been suggested; and that would not answer entirely the object which had been intended by the embargo, which was to avoid war without submitting to the decrees of either nation. . . .

GALLATIN TO CHARLES PINCKNEY, GOVERNOR OF SOUTH CAROLINA.

24th October, 1808.

. . . On the subject of the embargo, and particularly of what you should communicate to the Legislature, I must refer you to the President, who can alone judge of the propriety and extent of communications prior to the meeting of Congress. As an individual, but this is conjecture and not fact, I believe that the

British ministry is either unwilling, if they can avoid it, to repeal their orders in any event whatever, or that they wait for the result of their intrigues and of the exertions of their friends here, with hopes of producing irresistible dissatisfaction to the embargo, and a change of measures and of men. I trust that if this be their object they will be disappointed, and of the steadiness and patriotism of South Carolina I never entertained any doubt. On an alteration in the measures of the French Emperor I place no more confidence, perhaps even less, than on Great Britain. The only difference in his favor, and it arises probably from inability alone, is that he interferes not with our domestic concerns. But let those nations pursue what course they please, I feel a perfect confidence that America will never adopt a policy which would render her subservient to either, and that, after twenty-five years of peace and unparalleled prosperity, she will meet with fortitude the crisis, be it what it will, which may result from the difficult situation in which she is for the first time placed since the treaty of 1783.

Mr. Gallatin, to judge from these last words, which he repeated in "Campbell's Report," seems to have considered the situation as infinitely more difficult than it had been in 1798 or in 1794. In one respect at least he was certainly right. Mr. Jefferson's hope of having to swallow less foreign insolence than his predecessors was by this time thoroughly dispelled. There seems to have been no form of insult, simple or aggravated, which Mr. Jefferson and his Administration did not swallow; between the exquisitely exasperating satire of Mr. Canning and the peremptory brutality of Bonaparte, he was absolutely extinguished; he abandoned his hope of balancing one belligerent against another, and his expectation of guiding them by their interests; he abandoned even the embargo; he laid down the sceptre of party leadership; he had no longer a party; Virginia herself ceased to be guided by his opinion; his most intimate friend, Mr. Wilson Cary Nicholas, favored war; Mr. William B. Giles was of the same mode of thinking; Mr. Jefferson, overwhelmed by all these difficulties, longed for the moment of his retreat: "Never did a prisoner, released from his chains, feel such relief as I shall

on shaking off the shackles of power."[1] So cowed was he as
to do what no President had ever done before, or has ever done
since, and what no President has a constitutional right to do :
he abdicated the duties of his office, and no entreaty could
induce him to resume them. So soon as the election was decided,
he hastened to throw upon his successor the burden of responsibility and withdrew himself from all but the formalities of
administration : " I have thought it right," he wrote on December 27, 1808, " to take no part myself in proposing measures,
the execution of which will devolve on my successor. I am therefore chiefly an unmeddling listener to what others say."[2] " Our
situation is truly difficult. We have been pressed by the belligerents to the very wall, and all further retreat is impracticable."

The duty of providing a policy fell of necessity upon Mr.
Madison and Mr. Gallatin, although they could not act effectively
without the President's power. Under these circumstances, on
the 7th November, 1808, Congress met. The President's message, in conformity with his determination to decline any expression of opinion,[3] proposed nothing in regard to the embargo,
and this silence necessarily threw the party into still greater disorder, until Mr. Madison and Mr. Gallatin were driven to make
a combined attempt to recall Mr. Jefferson to his duties.

GALLATIN TO JEFFERSON.

DEPARTMENT OF TREASURY, 15th November, 1808.

DEAR SIR,—Both Mr. Madison and myself concur in opinion
that, considering the temper of the Legislature, or rather of its
members, it would be eligible to point out to them some precise
and distinct course.

As to what that should be we may not all perfectly agree, and
perhaps the knowledge of the various feelings of the members
and of the apparent public opinion may on consideration induce

---

[1] To Dupont de Nemours, 2d March, 1809. Writings, v. 432.

[2] To Dr. Logan. Jefferson's Writings, v. 404. Letter to Lieutenant-
Governor Lincoln, 13th November, 1808, v. 387.

[3] Letter to Mr. Gallatin of October 30, 1808. Gallatin's Writings, vol. i.
p. 420.

a revision of our own. I feel myself nearly as undetermined between enforcing the embargo or war as I was on our last meetings. But I think that we must (or rather you must) decide the question absolutely, so that we may point out a decisive course either way to our friends. Mr. Madison, being unwell, proposed that I should call on you and suggest our wish that we might with the other gentlemen be called by you on that subject. Should you think that course proper, the sooner the better. The current business has prevented my waiting on you personally in the course of the morning.

Mr. Jefferson, however, as appears from his letter to Dr. Logan of December 27, quoted above, persisted in declining responsibility. Mr. Madison and Mr. Gallatin were obliged to follow another course. Mr. Gallatin drafted a report for the Committee of Foreign Relations, which was, on the 22d November, 1808, presented to the House by Mr. G. W. Campbell for the committee, and which has been always known under the name of Campbell's Report. This paper is probably the best statement ever made of the American argument against the British government and the orders in council; it certainly disposed of the pretence that those orders were justifiable either on the ground of retaliation upon France or on that of American acquiescence in French infractions of international law; but its chief object was to unite the Republican party on common ground and to serve as the foundation of a policy; for this purpose it concluded by recommending the adoption of three resolutions, the first of which pledged the nation not to submit to the edicts of Great Britain and France; the second pledged them to exclude the commerce and productions of those countries from our ports; and the third, to take immediate measures to put the United States in a better condition of defence. These resolutions were debated nearly a month, and finally adopted by large majorities.

In the mean time Mr. Gallatin asked for the extension which he needed of powers to carry out the embargo law, and the force to back these powers. A bill to that effect was soon reported, and was rapidly passed, a bill famous in history as the Enforcement Act. It was a terrible measure, and in comparison with its sweeping grants of arbitrary power, all previous enactments of the United States Congress sank into comparative insignificance. How it could be defended under any conceivable theory of the Republican party, and how it could receive the support of any Republican whose memory extended ten years back, are questions which would be difficult to answer if the Annals of Congress were not at hand to explain. The two parties had completely changed their position, and while the Republicans stood on the ground once occupied by the Federalists, the Federalists were seeking safety under the States' rights doctrines formerly avowed by the Virginia and Kentucky Republicans.

As a result of eight years' conscientious and painful effort, the situation was calculated to sober and sadden the most sanguine Democrat. The idea was at last impressed with unmistakable emphasis upon every honest and reflecting mind in the Republican party that the failures of the past were not due to the faults of the past only, and that circumstances must by their nature be stronger and more permanent than men. Brought at last face to face with this new political fact which gave the lie to all his theories and hopes, even the sanguine and supple Jefferson felt the solid earth reel under him,[1] and his courage fled; it was long before he recovered his old confidence, and he never could speak of the embargo and the last year of his Presidency without showing traces of the mental shock he had suffered.

Mr. Gallatin was made of different stuff. In his youth almost as sanguine as Mr. Jefferson, he knew better how to accept defeat and adapt himself to circumstances, how to abandon theory and to move with his generation; but it needed all and more than all the toughness of Mr. Gallatin's character to support his courage in this emergency. He knew, quite as well as John Randolph or as any Federalist, how far he had drifted from his true course, and how arbitrary, odious, and dangerous was the course he had to pursue; but he at least now learned to recognize in the fullest extent the omnipotence of circumstance. He had no longer a principle to guide him. Except, somewhere far in the background, a general theory

---

[1] Letter to Cabell, 2d February, 1816. Writings, vi. 540.

that peace was better than war, not a shred was left of Republican principles. Facts, not theories, were all that survived in the wreck of Mr. Jefferson's Administration, and the solitary fact which asserted itself prominently above all others, was that the United States could only be likened to an unfortunate rat worried by two terrier bull-dogs; whether it fought or whether it fled, its destiny was to be eaten up. The only choice was one of evils; that of the manner of extinction. The country had selected the manner of its own free will, not under any urgency from Mr. Gallatin; but when it was tried, it was found to be suicide by suffocation. New England, hostile to the government, and dependent more immediately on commerce than her neighbors, resisted, revolted, and gasped convulsively for life and air. Her struggle saved her; necessity taught new modes of existence and made her at length almost independent of the sea. Virginia, however, friendly to the government and herself responsible for the choice, submitted with hardly a murmur, and never recovered from the shock; her ruin was accelerated with frightful rapidity because she made no struggle for life.

Mr. Gallatin saw the situation as clearly as most men of his time, and at this moment, when New England was struggling most wildly, he was obliged to say whether in his opinion the policy of government should be changed or not. How slowly and doubtfully he came to his decision has been seen in his letters, and was inevitable from his character. As he said on December 18, 1807, to Mr. Jefferson, he preferred war in every point of view to a permanent embargo; but the embargo had been adopted as a policy; it had been maintained at a fearful cost; the injury it could inflict was for the most part accomplished; the difficulties of enforcing it were overcome; its effect on England was only beginning to be felt; so far as New England was concerned, the danger was less imminent than it appeared to be, and the task of carrying that part of the country into armed rebellion was by no means an easy one; to abandon the embargo now was to exhibit the government in the light of a vacillating and feeble guide, to destroy all popular faith in its wisdom and courage, to shake the supports and undermine the authority of the new Administration, and to encourage every element of faction. Abroad the effect of this feebleness would be fatal. In the face of opponents like Canning and Bonaparte, weakness of will was the only unpardonable and irrevocable crime.

Another motive which probably decided Mr. Madison and Mr. Gallatin was one they could not use for an argument. Mr. Erskine, the British minister at Washington, was a young man of liberal politics and with an American wife; he was honestly anxious to restore friendly relations between the two governments, and he was stimulated by the idea of winning distinction. It appears from his letters that as early as the end of November, 1808, the moment the election was fairly decided and Mr. Jefferson had in effect surrendered the Presidency to Mr. Madison, the idea had begun to work in his mind that the time for attempting a reconciliation had come. What Mr. Canning had refused to concede to Mr. Jefferson, the friend of France, he might be willing to offer to Mr. Madison, whose sympathies were rather English than French. Mr. Erskine lost no time in sounding the members of the new Administration, and he found them one and all disposed to encourage him. He talked long and earnestly with Mr. Gallatin, "whose character," he wrote to Mr. Canning on December 4, 1808, "must be well known to you to be held in the greatest respect in this country for his unrivalled talents as a financier and a statesman." Mr. Gallatin flattered and encouraged him. "At the close of my interview with Mr. Gallatin, he said, in a familiar way, 'You see, sir, we could settle a treaty in my private room in two hours which might perhaps be found to be as lasting as if it was bound up in all the formalities of a regular system.'" He hinted to Mr. Gallatin his theory that Mr. Jefferson had acted with partiality to France, at which Mr. Gallatin "seemed to check himself," and turned the conversation immediately upon the character of Mr. Madison, saying "that *he* could not be accused of having such a bias towards France," whereat the young diplomatist, instead of inferring that Mr. Gallatin saw through him and all his little motives and meant to let them work undisturbed, drew only the inference that Mr. Gallatin thought as he did about Mr. Jefferson, but dared not say so.

Acting under these impressions, Mr. Erskine early in December, 1808, wrote a series of despatches to Mr. Canning, suggesting that this favorable moment should be used. While waiting for the necessary instructions, he continued his friendly relations with the Cabinet, and the Cabinet, not a little pleased at discovering at length one example of a friendly Englishman, cultivated these relations with cordiality.

The policy adopted by Mr. Madison and Mr. Gallatin is to be found in scattered pieces of evidence. Mr. Gallatin's letter of 15th November, 1808, to Mr. Jefferson seems to prove that he was still on that day not quite decided; but his annual report, dated December 10, which was clearly intended to supply to some extent the want of distinctness in the President's message, shows that in the interval the course had been marked out which the new Administration meant to pursue.

This report began, as usual, with a sketch of the financial situation. The receipts of the Treasury during the year ending September 30, 1808, had been $17,952,000, a sum greater than the receipts of any preceding year, but principally consisting of revenue accrued during 1807. On January 1, 1809, the Treasury would have a sum of $16,000,000 on hand, of which Mr. Gallatin estimated that the expenses of 1809 would consume $13,000,000, leaving a surplus of only $3,000,000 to be disposed of.

Thus the government could look forward with confidence to the 1st January, 1810, and if extraordinary preparations for war were necessary, it could, by stopping the redemption of debt, provide some $5,000,000 additional for the year without recurring to loans.

After thus describing the resources of the government, the Secretary proceeded to discuss its probable expenses under the four contingencies among which he supposed the choice of Congress to lie. Two of these were merely forms of submission to Great Britain and France, and, as in this case resistance would not be contemplated, no provision beyond an immediate reduction of expenses was required. The other two were forms of resistance; embargo, or war.

The embargo considered as a temporary measure, which would ultimately be superseded by war, was, financially, to be considered as a war measure, and preparations made accordingly; while if the embargo were adopted as a permanent system, coterminous with the belligerent edicts, it was a peace measure, and needed no other provision than economy at least for the next two years.

War must be carried on principally by loans, and the embargo had produced a situation most favorable for effecting loans.   No internal taxes of any description need be imposed.   All that the Treasury required, besides economy, was to double the import duties; to limit the system of drawbacks; either to repeal or to complete the partial non-intercourse law, and to reform the system of accountability in the Army and Navy Departments.

The report was decidedly warlike; clearly, if war was to come, Mr. Gallatin wished it to be begun within another year. His policy, therefore, is evident; he would have had Congress take a strong tone; continue the embargo for a given time until the results of Mr. Erskine's representations should be known; and let it be clearly understood that the embargo was to give place to war.   He would have had Congress apply six or eight millions to the purchase of arms and stores, to the building of forts or of ships, and to the organization of the militia; and with a firm party behind him and such measures of preparation, he would have spoken to Mr. Canning and to Napoleon with as much authority as it was in his power to command.   He would boldly have retaliated upon both.

This was the plan adopted for the new Administration and earnestly pressed by the Secretary of the Treasury whom the President elect then looked upon as his future Secretary of State. Mr. Jefferson's theory that his successor was responsible for the government after his election was decided, utterly untenable and mischievous as it was, compelled Mr. Madison to act through Mr. Gallatin.   The whole future of his Administration turned on his success in holding the party together on this line of policy, and Mr. Gallatin labored night and day to effect this object.

WASHINGTON, December 4, 1808.

. . . The war men in the House of Representatives are, I conceive, gaining strength, and I should not be much surprised if we should be at war with both Great Britain and France before the 4th of March. Gallatin is most decidedly for war, and I think that the Vice-President and W. C. Nicholas are of the same opinion. It is said that the President gives no opinion as to the measures that ought to be adopted. It is not known whether he be for war or peace. It is reported that Mr. Madison is for the plan which I have submitted, with the addition of high protecting duties to encourage the manufacturers of the United States. I am as much against war as Gallatin is in favor of it. Thus I have continued in Congress till there is not one of my old fellow-laborers that agrees with me in opinion. I do not know what plan Randolph will pursue. He is against continuing the embargo. I wish he would lay some plan before the House. It grieves me to the heart to be compelled from a sense of right and duty to oppose him. I am not consulted, as you seem to suppose, about anything, nor do I consult any one. I am about as much out of fashion as our grandmothers' ruffle cuffs, and I do not believe that I shall be in fashion as soon as they will.

GALLATIN TO JOSEPH H. NICHOLSON.

WASHINGTON, 29th December, 1808.

. . . Never was I so overwhelmed with public business. That would be nothing if we went right. But a great confusion and perplexity reign in Congress. Mr. Madison is, as I always knew him, slow in taking his ground, but firm when the storm arises. What I had foreseen has taken place. A majority will not adhere to the embargo much longer, and if war be not speedily determined on, submission will soon ensue. This entirely between us. When will you be here? We expect you, and the sooner the better. Exclusively of the pleasure we always have in seeing you, rely upon it that your presence will at this crisis be useful. I actually want time to give you more details, but I will only state that it is intended by the Essex Junto to prevail on the Massachusetts Legislature, who meet in two or three weeks, to call a convention of the five New England States, to which they will try to add New York; and that something must be done to anticipate and defeat that nefarious plan.

Mr. Jefferson's private letters tell the story of Mr. Madison's failure to control his party, and of the collapse of his war policy. On the 19th January, 1809, he wrote to Thomas Lomax :[1] " I think Congress, although they have not passed any bill indicative of their intentions, except the new embargo law, have evidently made up their minds to let that continue only till their meeting in May, and then to issue letters of marque and reprisal against such powers as shall not then have repealed their illegal decrees. Some circumstances have taken place which render it very possible that Great Britain may revoke her orders of council. This will be known before May." Two days later, Mr. Jefferson wrote to Mr. Leiper :[2] " The House of Representatives passed last night a bill for the meeting of Congress on the 22d of May. This substantially decides the course they mean to pursue,—that is, to let the embargo continue till then, when it will cease, and letters of marque and reprisal be issued against such nations as shall not then have repealed their obnoxious edicts. The great majority seem to have made up their minds on this, while there is considerable diversity of opinion on the details of preparation, to wit : naval force, volunteers, army, non-intercourse, &c." But on the 7th February Mr. Jefferson wrote :[3] " I thought Congress had taken their ground firmly for continuing their embargo till June, and then war. But a sudden and unaccountable revolution of opinion took place the last week, chiefly among the New England and New York members, and in a kind of panic they voted the 4th of March for removing the embargo, and by such a majority as gave all reason to believe they would not agree either to

[1] Jefferson MSS.   [2] Jefferson's Writings, v. 417.
[3] To T. M. Randolph. Writings, v. 424.

war or non-intercourse. This, too, was after we had become satisfied that the Essex Junto had found their expectation desperate of inducing the people there to either separation or forcible opposition. The majority of Congress, however, has now rallied to removing the embargo on the 4th of March, non-intercourse with France and Great Britain, trade everywhere else, and continuing war preparations." The defeat of the Administration on the crucial point of fixing the 1st June, 1809, for removing the embargo, took place on February 2, by a vote of 73 to 40. The substitution of March 4 was carried on February 3, by a vote of 70, no ayes and noes having been taken on either side. The new Administration had already met with a serious if not fatal check. As Mr. Gallatin said in a note to Mr. Jefferson of February 4, the day after the disaster: "As far as my information goes, everything grows more quiet in Massachusetts and Maine. All would be well if our friends remained firm here."

The votes of February 2 and February 4, 1809, carried a deeper significance to Mr. Gallatin than to any one else, for they did not stand alone. Congress had already shown that it meant to accept his control no longer, and this was no mere panic and no result of New England defection. He had at last to meet the experience of defeat where he had supposed himself strongest. As has been seen, the administration of naval affairs had always been repugnant to Mr. Gallatin's wishes; the time when he had opposed a moderate navy had long passed, and, as Secretary of the Treasury, he had never wished to diminish the efficiency or lessen the force of the few frigates we had; but he conceived that the management of the Department under Mr. Robert Smith was wasteful and inefficient. Very large sums of money had been spent, for which there was little to show except one hundred and seventy gun-boats, which had cost on an average $9000 each to build and would cost $11,500 a year in actual service. At the beginning of the session it had been distinctly intimated by the Executive that no present increase of force was required; but suddenly, on the 4th January, 1809, the Senate adopted a bill which directed that all the frigates and other armed vessels of the United States, including the gun-boats, should be immediately fitted out, officered, manned, and employed. The law was mandatory; it required the immediate employment of some six thousand seamen and the appropriation of some six million dollars, and this excessive expenditure on the part of the navy was not accompanied by any corresponding measures for shore armaments and defences. If war did not take place the expense was entirely lost. Had these six millions been expended in buying arms, constructing fortifications and putting them in readiness for war, or in organizing and arming the militia, or in building frigates and ships of the line, the government would have had something to show for them; but to waste the small national treasure before war began; to support thousands of seamen in absolute idleness, with almost a certainty that the moment a British frigate came within sight they would have to run ashore for safety, seemed insane extravagance. Yet when the Senate's amendment came before the House it was adopted on the 10th January by a vote of 64 to 59, in the teeth of Mr. Gallatin's warm remonstrances. Among his papers is the following curious analysis of this vote.

THE NAVY COALITION OF 1809.

By whom were sacrificed

Forty Republican members, nine Republican States,

The Republican cause itself, and the people of the United States,

To a system of

Favoritism, extravagance, parade, and folly.

---

1. *Smith Faction, or Ruling Party.*

File Leader, W. C. Nicholas, E. W.; Assistants, Dawson, J. G.
    Jackson, McCreery, Montgomery, Newton 6

2. *Federalists, Old and New.*

Dana, Elliot, Goldsborough, Harris, Kay, Lewis, Livermore,
    Lyon, Masters, Mosely, Pitkin, Russel, Sloan, Stedman,
    Sturges, Van Dyke, Van Rensselaer 17

3. *Quids.*

Cook, Findley, Gardner, Van Horn 4

4. *New York Malcontents.*

Mumford, Swart, Thompson, Van Cortland, Wilson, Riker . 6

27*

5. *Scared Yankees.*   33

Bacon, Barker, Durell, Illsley, Storer 5

6. *Republicans.*

Virginia.	N. York.	N. England.	N. Jersey.	Other States.
Basset.	Blake.	Cutts.	Helms.	Kenan.
Clay.	Humphreys.	Deane.	Lambert.	N. Moore.
Clopton.	Kirkpatrick.	Fisk.	Newbold.	Smelt.
Gholson.	Van Allan.	Green.		Troup.
Holmes.	Verplanck.	Seaver.		
Smith.		Smith.		
		Wilbour.		

25

7. *Sui Generis.*

Jones 1

—

64

—

* 27

—

Friendly only 37

The meaning of all this confusion was soon made clear to Gallatin. A web of curious intrigue spun itself over the chair which Mr. Madison now left empty in the Department of State; there was no agreement upon the person who was to fill it, and who would, perhaps, be made thereby the most prominent candidate for succession to the throne itself. Not until his inauguration approached did Mr. Madison distinctly give it to be understood that he intended to make Mr. Gallatin his Secretary of State. This intention roused vehement opposition among Senators. Leib and the Aurora influence were of course hostile to Gallatin, and Leib now found a formidable ally in William B. Giles, Senator from Virginia. Giles made no concealment of his opposition. "From the first," wrote Mr. Wilson Cary Nicholas, "Mr. Giles declared his determination to vote against Gallatin. I repeatedly urged and entreated him not to do it; for several days it was a subject of discussion between us. There was no way which our long and intimate friendship would justify, consistent with my respect for him, in which I did not assail him. To all my arguments he replied that his duty to his country was to him paramount to every other consideration, and that he could not justify to himself permitting Gallatin to be Secretary of State if his vote would prevent it." "The objection to him that I understood had the most weight, and that was most pressed in conversation, was that he was a foreigner. I thought it was too late to make that objection. He had for eight years been in an office of equal dignity and of greater trust and importance."

But Leib and Giles, separate or combined, were not strong enough to effect this object; they needed more powerful allies, and they found such in the Navy influence, represented in the Senate chiefly by General Smith, Senator from Maryland, brother of the Secretary of the Navy, and brother-in-law of Wilson Cary Nicholas. General Smith joined the opposition to Gallatin. An effort appears to have been made to buy off the vote of General Smith; it is said that he was willing to compromise if his brother were transferred to Mr. Gallatin's place in the Treasury, and that Mr. Madison acquiesced in this arrangement, but Gallatin dryly remarked that he could not undertake to carry on both Departments at once, and requested Mr. Madison to leave him where he was. Mr. Madison then yielded, and Robert Smith was appointed Secretary of State.

Mr. J. Q. Adams, who at just this moment was rejected as minister to Russia by the same combination, has left an unpublished account of this affair:

MADISON AND GALLATIN. 1809.

"In the very last days of his [Jefferson's] Administration there appeared in the Republican portion of the Senate a disposition to control him in the exercise of his power. This was the more remarkable, because until then nothing of that character had appeared in the proceedings of the Senate during his Administration. The experience of Mr. Burr and of John Randolph had given a warning which had quieted the aspirings of others, and, with the exception of an ineffectual effort to reject the nomination of John Armstrong as minister to France, there was scarcely an attempt made in the Senate for seven years to oppose anything that he desired. But in the summer of 1808, after the peace of Tilsit, the Emperor Alexander of Russia had caused it to be signified to Mr. Jefferson that an exchange of ministers plenipotentiary between him and the United States would be very agreeable to him, and that he waited only for the appointment of one from the United States to appoint one in return. Mr. Jefferson accordingly appointed an old friend and pupil of his, Mr. William Short, during the recess of the Senate, and Mr. Short, being furnished with his commission, credentials, and instructions, proceeded on his mission as far as Paris. Towards the close of the session of Congress he nominated Mr. Short to the Senate, by whom the nomination was rejected. This event occasioned no small surprise. It indicated the termination of that individual personal influence which Mr. Jefferson had erected on the party division of Whig and Tory. It was also the precursor of a far more extensive scheme of operations which was to commence, and actually did commence, with the Administration of Mr. Madison.

" He had wished and intended to appoint Mr. Gallatin, who had been Secretary of the Treasury during the whole of Mr. Jefferson's Administration, to succeed himself in the Department of State, and Mr. Robert Smith, who had been Secretary of the Navy, he proposed to transfer to the Treasury Department. He was not permitted to make this arrangement. Mr. Robert Smith had a brother in the Senate. It was the wish of the individuals who had effected the rejection of Mr. Short that Mr. Robert Smith should be Secretary of State, and Mr. Madison was given explicitly to understand that if he should nominate Mr. Gallatin he would be rejected by the Senate.

" Mr. Robert Smith was appointed. This dictation to Mr. Madison, effected by a very small knot of association in the Senate, operating by influence over that body chiefly when in secret session, bears a strong resemblance to that which was exercised over the same body in 1798 and 1799, with this difference, that the prime agents of the faction were not then members of the body, and now they were.

" In both instances it was directly contrary to the spirit of the Constitution, and was followed by unfortunate consequences. In the first it terminated by the overthrow of the Administration and by a general exclusion from public life of nearly every man concerned in it. In the second its effect was to place in the Department of State, at a most critical period of foreign affairs and against the will of the President, a person incompetent, to the exclusion of a man eminently qualified for the office. Had Mr. Gallatin been then appointed Secretary of State, it is highly probable that the war with Great Britain would not have taken place. As Providence shapes all for the best, that war was the means of introducing great improvements in the practice of the government and of redeeming the national character from some unjust reproaches, and of strongly cementing the Union. But if the people of the United States could have realized that a little cluster of Senators, by caballing in secret session, would place a sleepy Palinurus at the helm even in the fury of the tempest, they must almost have believed in predestination to expect that their vessel of state would escape shipwreck. This same Senatorial faction continued to harass and perplex the Administration of Mr. Madison during the war with Great Britain, till it became perceptible to the people, and the prime movers losing their popularity were compelled to retire from the Senate. They left behind them, however, practices in the Senate and a disposition in that body to usurp unconstitutional control, which have already effected much evil and threaten much more."

Thus the Administration of Mr. Jefferson, whose advent had been hailed eight years before by a majority of the nation as the harbinger of a new era on earth; the Administration which, alone among all that had preceded or were to follow it, was freighted with hopes and aspirations and with a sincere popular faith that could never be revived, and a freshness, almost a simplicity of thought that must always give to its history a certain indefinable popular charm like old-fashioned music; this Administration, into which Mr. Gallatin had woven the very web of his life, now expired, and its old champion, John Randolph, was left to chant a palinode over its grave: "Never has there been any Administration which went out of office and left the nation in a state so deplorable and calamitous."

Under such conditions, with such followers and such advisers,

Mr. Madison patched up his broken Cabinet and his shattered policy; broken before it was complete, and shattered before it was launched. He had to save what he could, and by rallying all his strength in Congress he succeeded in preserving a tolerable appearance of energy towards the belligerent nations; but in fact the war-policy was defeated, and a small knot of men in the Senate were more powerful than the President himself. The Cabinet was an element not of strength but of weakness, for whatever might be Mr. Smith's disposition he could not but become the representative of the group in the Senate which had forced him into prominence. Under such circumstances, until then without a parallel in our history, government, in the sense hitherto understood, became impossible.

Had Mr. Gallatin followed his own impulses, he would now have resigned his seat in the Cabinet and returned to his old place in Congress. That course, as the event proved, would have been the wisest for him, but his ultimate decision to remain in the Treasury was nevertheless correct. He had at least an even chance of regaining his ground and carrying out those ideas to which his life had been devoted; the belligerents might return to reason; the war in Europe could not last forever; the country might unite in support of a practicable policy; at all events there was no immediate danger that the government would go to pieces, and heroic remedies were not to be used but as a last resort. So far as Mr. Madison was concerned, the question was not whether he was to be deserted, but in what capacity Mr. Gallatin could render him the most efficient support.

Suddenly the skies seemed to clear, and the new Administration for a brief moment flattered itself that its difficulties were at an end. Mr. Erskine received the reply of Mr. Canning to his letters of December 3 and 4, and this reply declared in substance that if the United States would of her own accord abandon the colonial trade and allow the British fleet to enforce that abandonment, England would withdraw her orders in council. This was, it is true, a matter of course. Mr. Canning's object in imposing the orders in council, though nominally retaliatory upon France, had been really to counteract Napo-

leon's Continental policy and to save British shipping and commerce from American competition, and his condition of withdrawing the orders could only be that America should abandon her
shipping and employ British ships of war in destroying her own
trade.   Mr. Erskine, however, conceived that a loose interpretation might be put on these conditions.   After communicating
their substance to the Secretary of State and receiving the reply
that they were inadmissible, he " considered that it would be in
vain to lay before the government of the United States the despatch in question, which I was *at liberty* to have done in extenso
had I thought proper."[1]   He therefore set aside his instructions
and proceeded to act in what he conceived to be their spirit.   A
hint thrown out by Mr. Gallatin that the substitution of non-
intercourse for embargo had so altered the situation as to put
England in a more favorable position with reference to France,
served as the ground for Mr. Erskine's propositions; but these
propositions, in fact, rested on no solid ground whatever, for in
them Mr. Erskine entirely omitted all reference to an abandonment of the colonial trade, and while the American government
professed its readiness to abandon that trade so far as it was
direct from the West Indies to Europe, this was all the foundation Mr. Erskine had for considering as fulfilled that condition
of his instructions by which America was to abjure all colonial
trade, direct and indirect, and allow the British fleet to enforce
this abjuration.

On this slender basis, and without communicating his authority,
Mr. Erskine, early in April, 1809, made a provisional arrangement with the Secretary of State by which the outrage on the
Chesapeake was atoned for, and the orders in council withdrawn.   The President instantly issued a proclamation bearing
date the 19th April, 1809, declaring the trade with Great Britain
renewed.   Great was the joy throughout America; so great as
for the moment almost to obliterate party distinctions.   When
Congress met on May 22, for that session which had been called
to provide for war, all was peace and harmony ; John Randolph
was loudest in singing praises of the new President, and no

---

[1] Erskine to Robert Smith, 14th August, 1809.

one ventured to gainsay him.   The Federalists exulted in the demonstration of their political creed that Mr. Jefferson had been the wicked author of all mischief, and that the British government was all that was moderate, just, and injured.

The feelings of Mr. Canning on receiving the news were not of the same nature.   The absurd and ridiculous side of things was commonly uppermost in his mind, and in the whole course of his stormy career there was probably no one event more utterly absurd than this.   His policy in regard to the United States was simple even to crudeness ; he meant that her neutral commerce, gained from England and France, should be taken away, and that, if possible, she should not be allowed to fight for it.   In carrying out this policy he never wavered, and he was completely successful ; even an American can now admire the clearness and energy of his course, though perhaps it has been a costly one in its legacy of hate.   That one of his subordinates should undertake to break down his policy and give back to the United States her commerce, and that the United States should run wild with delight at this evidence of Mr. Canning's defeat and the success of her own miserable embargo, was an event in which the ludicrous predominated over the tragic.   Mr. Canning made very short work of poor Mr. Erskine ; he instantly recalled that gentleman and disavowed his arrangement ; but in order to prevent war he announced that a new minister would be immediately sent out.   Even this civility, however, was conceded with very little pretence of a disposition to conciliate, and the minister chosen for the purpose was calculated rather to inspire terror than good-will.   Mr. Rose had at least borne an exterior of civility, and had affected a decent though patronizing benevolence.   Mr. Jackson made no such pretensions.   His feelings and the object of his mission were odious enough at the time, and, now that his private correspondence has been published,[1] it can hardly be said that, however insolent the American government may have thought him, he was in the least degree more insolent than his chief intended him to be.

---

[1] Bath Archives.   Diaries and Letters of Sir George Jackson.   See, among other instances, Second Series, i. 109.

The news of Mr. Canning's disavowal reached America in July, and spread consternation and despair. Mr. Gallatin found himself involved in a sort of controversy with Mr. Erskine, resulting from the publication of Erskine's despatches in England, and, although he extricated himself with skill, the result could at best be only an escape. The non-intercourse had to be renewed by proclamation, and the Administration could only look about and ask itself in blank dismay what it could do next.

GALLATIN TO JOSEPH H. NICHOLSON.

WASHINGTON, 20th April, 1809.

DEAR SIR,—I do not perceive, unless the President shall otherwise direct, anything that can now prevent my leaving this on Sunday for Baltimore. I fear that Mrs. Gallatin will not go; she is afraid to leave the children, who have all had slight indispositions. Yet she would, I think, be the better for a friendly visit to Mrs. Nicholson and croaking with you. As you belong to that tribe, I presume that, although you found fault yesterday with Mr. Madison because he did not make peace, you will now blame him for his anxiety to accommodate on any terms. Be that as it may, I hope that you will get 1 dollar and $\frac{60}{100}$ for your wheat. And still you may say that you expected two dollars. Present my best respects to Mrs. Nicholson.

Yours truly.

Eustis may have his faults, but I will be disappointed if he is not honorable and disinterested.

GALLATIN TO JOHN MONTGOMERY.

WASHINGTON, 27th July, 1809.

. . . The late news from England has deranged our plans, public and private. I was obliged to give up my trip to Belair, have also postponed our Virginia journey, and have written to Mr. Madison that I thought it necessary that he should return here immediately. We have not yet received any letters from Mr. Pinckney nor any other official information on the subject.

Even Mr. Erskine, who is, however, expected every moment, has not written. I will not waste time in conjectures respecting the true cause of the conduct of the British government, nor can we, until we are better informed, lay any permanent plan of conduct for ourselves. I will only observe that we are not so well prepared for resistance as we were one year ago. All or almost all our mercantile wealth was safe at home, our resources entire, and our finances sufficient to carry us through during the first year of the contest. Our property is now all afloat; England relieved by our relaxations might stand two years of privations with ease; we have wasted our resources without any national utility; and, our Treasury being exhausted, we must begin our plan of resistance with considerable and therefore unpopular loans. All these considerations are, however, for Congress; and at this moment the first question is, what ought the Executive to do? It appears to me from the laws and the President's proclamation, that as he had no authority but that of proclaiming a certain fact on which alone rested the restoration of intercourse, and that fact not having taken place, the prohibitions of the Non-Intercourse Act necessarily revive in relation to England, and that a proclamation to that effect should be the first act of the Executive. If we do not adopt that mode, our intercourse with England must continue until the meeting of Congress, whilst her orders remain unrepealed and our intercourse with France is interdicted by our own laws. This would be so unequal, so partial to England and contrary to every principle of justice, policy, and national honor, that I hope the Attorney-General will accede to my construction and the President act accordingly.

The next question for the Executive is how we shall treat Mr. Jackson; whether and how we will treat with him. That must, it is true, depend in part on what he may have to say. But I have no confidence in Canning & Co., and if we are too weak or too prudent to resist England in the direct and proper manner, I hope at least that we will not make a single voluntary concession inconsistent with our rights and interest. If Mr. Jackson has any compromise to offer which would not be burthened with such, I will be very agreeably disappointed. But, judging by what is said to have been the substance of Mr. Erskine's instructions, what can we expect but dishonorable and inadmissible proposals? He is probably sent out, like Mr. Rose, to amuse and to divide, and we will, I trust, by coming at once to the point, bring his negotiation to an immediate close. . . .

One may reasonably doubt whether during the entire history of the United States government the difficulties of administration have ever been so great as during the years 1809–11. Peace usually allows great latitude of action and of opinion without endangering the national existence. War at least compels some kind of unity; the path of government is then clear. Even in 1814 and in 1861 the country responded to a call; but in 1809 and 1810 the situation was one of utter helplessness. The session of 1808–9 had proved two facts: one, that the nation would not stand the embargo; the other, that it could not be brought to the point of war. So far as Mr. Madison and his Administration are concerned, it is safe to say that they would at any time have accepted any policy, short of self-degradation, which would have united the country behind them. As for Mr. Gallatin, he had yielded to the embargo because it had the support of a great majority of Congress; he had done his utmost to support the only logical consequence of the embargo, which was war. Congress had rejected both embargo and war, and had in complete helplessness fallen back on a system of non-intercourse which had most of the evils of embargo, much of the expense of war, and all the practical disgrace of submission. He could do nothing else than make the best of this also. The country had lost its headway and was thoroughly at the mercy of events.

When studied as a mere matter of political philosophy, it is clear enough that this painful period of paralysis was an inevitable stage in the national development. The party which had come into power in 1801 held theories inconsistent with thorough nationality, and, as a consequence, with a firm foreign policy. The terrible treatment which the government received, while in its hands, from the great military powers of Europe came upon the Republican party before it had outgrown its theories, and necessarily disorganized that party, leaving the old States-rights, anti-nationalizing element where it stood, and forcing the more malleable element forward into a situation inconsistent with the party tenets. Another result was to give the mere camp-followers and mercenaries of both parties an almost unlimited power of mischief. Finally, the Federalist opposition, affected in the same manner by the same causes, also rapidly resolved itself into three similar elements, one of which seriously meditated treason, while the more liberal one maintained a national character. It was clear, therefore, or rather it is now clear, that until the sentiment of nationality became strong enough to override resistance and to carry the Administration on its shoulders, no effective direction could be given to government.

That Mr. Gallatin consciously and decidedly followed either direction, it would be a mistake to suppose. He too, like his party, was torn by conflicting influences. A man already fifty years old, whose life has been earnestly and arduously devoted to certain well-defined objects that have always in his eyes stood for moral principles, cannot throw those objects away without feeling that his life goes with them. So long as a reasonable hope was left of attaining the results he had aimed at, or of preventing the dangers he dreaded, it was natural that Mr. Gallatin should cling to it and fight for it; but, on the other hand, he was a man of very sound understanding, and little, if at all, affected by mere local prejudices; his ideal government was one which should be free from corruption and violence; which should interfere little with the individual; which should have neither debt, nor army, nor navy, nor taxes, beyond what its simplest wants required; and which should wish " to become a happy, and not a powerful, nation, or at least no way powerful except for self-defence." On this side he was in sympathy with all moderate and sensible men in both parties, and was more naturally impelled to act with them than with his old allies, who were chiefly jealous of national power because it diminished the sovereignty of Virginia or South Carolina.

To one standing, therefore, as Mr. Gallatin was now standing, on the verge of several years' inaction, out of which the nation could rescue itself only by a slow process of growth, the ends to be attained and the dangers to be feared would arrange them-

selves almost axiomatically. War was out of the question, not
only because both parties had united against it, but because the
Treasury was very rapidly losing its war fund and would soon
be unable to promise resources. If peace, therefore, were to be
preserved, the policy of commercial restrictions was the only
form of protest practicable, and it must again become the task
of diplomacy to re-establish the old Jeffersonian "balance" between the belligerents. In other words, diplomacy had become
more important than finance.

Candid criticism certainly tends to show that the only national
policy which had a chance of success was also the only one
which had not a chance of adoption. A sudden, concentrated,
and determined attack upon Bonaparte would, in all human
probability, have been successful; the Emperor would have
given way, and in this case England must also have receded;
but this would have been a mere repetition of the Federalist
policy of 1798, and the Republican party had no fancy for
Federalist precedents. The behavior of Canning had roused so
bitter a feeling as to paralyze measures against Bonaparte, while
the Republican party was as little competent to imitate the dash
and stubborn intensity of the Federalists as the calm temperament of Mr. Madison to lash itself into the fiery impetuosity of
John Adams. Nothing remained but to settle the nature and
extent of the mild protest which was to be maintained against
the armed violence of the two belligerents, and, now that the
doors of the State Department were closed in Mr. Gallatin's
face, his only hope was to create a new financial system that
would serve to meet the wants of the new political situation as
Congress might ultimately give it shape. Throwing behind
him, therefore, all his old hopes and ambitions, all schemes for
discharging debt and creating canals, roads, and universities, he
turned his energies to the single point of defending the Treasury
and resisting follies. He regarded the habit of borrowing money
with horror; this was a resource to be reserved for war, when
national life depended upon it; until that time came he insisted
that the expenditure should not exceed the revenue. The experience of only last winter had shown how readily Congress
wasted its resources: although Mr. Gallatin had succeeded in

partially checking the navy appropriations, nearly three millions were voted, and two and a half millions were actually spent on the navy in 1809, without increasing its force or effecting the smallest good; and meanwhile the surplus upon which Mr. Gallatin had relied to carry on the first year of war was rapidly vanishing, while the militia were not organized, the forts were not completed, arms were not on hand, and military roads were wholly wanting.

To raise by taxation, so long as peace lasted, all the money to be spent by Congress, was the rule which Mr. Gallatin was now struggling to enforce. If Congress appropriated money, Congress must lay taxes. To maintain this ground required a firm, almost a rough hand, and unless both the Cabinet and the Senate were ready to support the Secretary of the Treasury in his effort, his position was untenable, and resignation must follow of course.

The question whether the Cabinet and Senate would support Mr. Gallatin was, therefore, the necessary point to decide in advance. In the Cabinet, Mr. Robert Smith was the dangerous element. In the Senate, General Samuel Smith and his friend Mr. Giles were the chief disturbing forces, since without them the fulminations of Leib and the Aurora offered, after all, no very serious danger. Unfortunately, a circumstance had now occurred which seriously embittered the relations between Mr. Gallatin and the Smiths. The failure and disappearance of the navy agent at Leghorn disclosed a somewhat loose way of managing business in the Navy Department, which had bought exchange on Leghorn, largely in bills on Samuel Smith and his relations, in excess of its wants, while at the same time it had neglected to make its naval officers draw on Leghorn, so that they had drawn on London at considerable extra expense. Thus, at the close of the Tripoli war a large balance had remained in the hands of the navy agent at Leghorn, which was partly sent back in specie to America by a ship of war, and partly carried off by the navy agent to Paris, where he was arrested by the interposition of our minister, General Armstrong, and compelled to disgorge. In all this there was enough to irritate Mr. Gallatin, who had for eight years endured, with such patience as he could command, the loose and extravagant habits of the Navy Department, and who was now making a new effort to enforce a thorough system of accountability in that department. But there appeared at first sight to be something still more objectionable in this transaction. Mr. Robert Smith, as Secretary of the Navy, had bought bills of exchange to the amount of a quarter of a million dollars, within two years, from his brother General Smith and his connections, and on the face of the accounts it appeared that these were to some extent accommodation bills; in other words, that the government money had been by collusion left in the hands of General Smith's firm until it suited their convenience to remit it to Leghorn. The effect of this operation was to give the firm of Smith & Buchanan the use of public money without obliging them to make the same immediate provision for honoring their bills as would in other cases have been necessary; to give them also the almost exclusive privilege of selling bills on Leghorn, and to throw upon the public the risk arising from protested bills. This affair came to the knowledge of Mr. Gallatin at the time when General Smith was, with the aid of Mr. Giles and Dr. Leib, forcing Mr. Robert Smith upon Mr. Madison as Secretary of State, and in conjunction with his brother-in-law, Mr. Wilson Cary Nicholas, overthrowing Mr. Gallatin's plans of public expenditure. He was very indignant, and expressed his opinions to his friend Joseph H. Nicholson, who made no secret of the story and used it to prevent the re-election of General Smith to the Senate. In the extra session in June, 1809, John Randolph, at the urgent request of Judge Nicholson, procured the appointment of an investigating committee, which published the facts. Mr. Gallatin was called upon for a report, which he made in February, 1811. General Smith on his side made a statement which certainly relieved him to a considerable extent from the weight of some of the most doubtful parts of the transaction. Mr. Gallatin had nothing to do with Judge Nicholson's proceeding, and gave it no encouragement, but his feeling in regard to the scandal was very strong, and after the attacks made upon the Smiths, both by the investigating committee of the House and by the Baltimore press, the following exchange of letters occurred:

GENERAL SAMUEL SMITH TO GALLATIN.

BALTIMORE, 26th June, 1809.

SIR,—I do myself the honor to enclose two papers for your perusal. The editors of the Federal Republican make use of your name to bolster them up in the nefarious charge they have made against me, in the following manner, to wit: " Mr. Gallatin, we understand, spoke of this transaction in terms of great indignation." I will not believe that any of that indignation could have been directed at me. I believe it impossible that any man who has the least pretensions to character would commit an act so base as that charged on me, to wit: " to secure a debt which I considered bad by transferring the same to the Navy Department, and thus involving the United States in the loss." Some time after my house drew the last bill (for I was at Washington), an evil report had been sent from Leghorn relative to Degen, Purviance & Co., in consequence whereof Mr. Oliver (who had a ship ready to sail to their address) sent an agent, who, finding the house in as good credit as any in that city, did put the cargo under their care. I thought the house superior to any in Leghorn.

I am, sir, your obedient servant,

S. SMITH.

GALLATIN TO GENERAL SMITH.

TREASURY DEPARTMENT, 29th June, 1809.

SIR,—I received the day before yesterday your letter of 26th inst., enclosing two Baltimore papers.

I have no other knowledge of the circumstances connected with the naval agency of Degen and Purviance than what is derived from their account as stated by the accountant of the Navy Department. The transaction, such as it appears there, is, under all its aspects, the most extraordinary that has fallen within my knowledge since I have been in this Department. It has certainly left very unfavorable impressions on my mind, and these have on one occasion been communicated verbally to a friend. Yet I hardly need say that I never supposed that the bills had been sold to government for the purpose "of securing a debt which you then considered bad, and of thus throwing the loss on the United States." But I did believe that you had drawn without having previously placed sufficient funds in the hands of Degen and Purviance, and that they had accepted your bills and passed the amount to the credit of the United States, without having at the time in their hands sufficient funds belonging to you. That this was my impression you will perceive by the enclosed extract of a letter to Mr. Armstrong; and Mr. Purviance's statement, which you enclosed to me, shows that I was not mistaken. I do not intend to comment on this and other circumstances of the case. Taking them altogether, I have believed that, if we failed in our endeavors to recover the money from Degen and from Mr. Purviance, we might have recourse against the drawers of the bills.

I am, sir, &c.

Such a letter was not calculated to conciliate the Smiths, and appears to have received no reply. General Smith ultimately secured his re-election to the Senate. As the case stood, therefore, Mr. Gallatin could count with absolute certainty upon the determined personal hostility of General Smith, Mr. Giles, and Dr. Leib, backed by the vigorous tactics of Duane and the Aurora, and he had to decide the very serious question whether he should remain in the Cabinet in the face of so alarming a party defection, or whether he should give way to it and retire. On the 11th May, 1809, he wrote to Judge Nicholson that the ensuing session would decide this point. Judge Nicholson replied in his own impetuous style: "Your retiring from office is a subject upon which I do not like to reflect, because I believe that you will be a great public loss. It will be a loss that Mr. Madison will feel immediately, but the public will not perceive it in its full extent for some years. When the government gets entirely in the possession of those men who are resolved to seize it, and their selfish and mercenary motives and conduct are hereafter exposed, as they must be, the public will then perceive how important it would have been to retain a man who was at once capable and honest. But I think, were I in your situation, I should not continue in the present state of the Cabinet, and I should tell Mr. Madison that it was impossible to serve with Mr. Smith after a development of the late transaction. The most perverse man must acknowledge the absolute dishonesty that is apparent on the face of it. I have never believed that you took as strong ground in the Cabinet as you ought to do, and it is time that you should do more than content yourself with a bare expression of opinion. I should say that Mr. Smith or myself must go out, and Mr. Madison ought to know you too well to believe that this contained anything of a threat. If you are disposed to continue in the Treasury, the Department of State might certainly be filled with an abler and a better man. Our love to Mrs. Gallatin. Tell her I agree with her that vice and corruption do rule everywhere, and it arises entirely from the ill-timed modesty of virtue."

This last paragraph is in reply to the concluding paragraph of Mr. Gallatin's letter: "Mrs. Gallatin says that vice and intrigue are all-powerful here and there [in Baltimore]. I tell her that virtue is its own reward, and she insists that that language is mere affectation."

What Mr. Gallatin's frame of mind now was may be seen from a letter to his old friend Badollet, whom he had sent out to the land-office at Vincennes, in the Indiana Territory, and who, discovering that vice and intrigue ruled even there, was carrying on a fierce and passionate struggle with General W. H. Harrison, the governor, to prevent the introduction of negro slavery.

GALLATIN TO BADOLLET.

WASHINGTON, 12th May, 1809.

I have received your letter of 7th March, and am as desirous as yourself of a refreshing interview. The summer session has prevented my going to Fayette this spring, but I must go there either in August or September. I cannot yet determine the precise week or month, and will not be able to stay more than four or five days, unless I return at that time with my family for the purpose of permanently residing there, which is not impossible, though not yet decided on. The decision, not to induce you into mistake, rests entirely with myself. Will it be prudent for you to incur the expense and trouble of so long a journey merely in order to see me? It was with regret that I saw you go to Vincennes; for I apprehended the climate, and I hated the distance. But there was no option. The Ohio representative claimed for residents there the exclusive right of filling the Federal offices in that State, and it was your express opinion that you could not subsist in Greene County. The same obstacles seem to oppose a change. I see no prospect of your being transferred to a nearer district, and you will find the same difficulty in supporting your family in case you should return to Pennsylvania. Still, I not only feel your situation, but I *think* that your happiness in the eve of life will in part depend on our spending it in the same vicinity. I *know* that it will be the case with me. If you can perceive any means in which I can assist to attain that object, state it fully and in all its details; that we may attempt whatever is practicable, but nothing rashly. What would your little property in Indiana sell for? What would be the expenses of bringing your family up the river? What are the precise ages and capacities of your children? I do not know what you can do yourself without an office, but I will not prejudge, and I earnestly wish that we may discover some means of *reunion.*

As to your squabbles and disappointment, they are matters of course. At what time or in what country did you ever hear that men assumed the privilege of being more honest than the mass of the society in which they lived, without being hated and persecuted? unless they chose to remain in perfect obscurity and to let others and the world take their own course, and in that case they can never have been heard of. All we can do here is to fulfil our duty, without looking at the consequences so far as relates to ourselves. If the love and esteem of others or general popularity follow, so much the better. But it is with these as with all other temporal blessings, such as wealth, health, &c., not to be despised, to be honestly attempted, but never to be considered as under our control or as objects to which a single particle of integrity, a single feeling of conscience should be sacrificed. I need not add that I preach better than I practise.

But I may add that you practise better than I do, your com-
plaining of the result only excepted. The purity with which
you shall have exercised the duties of land-officer may be felt
and continue to operate after you have ceased to act. And if
you have had a share in preventing the establishment of slavery
in Indiana, you will have done more good, to that part of the
country at least, than commonly falls to the share of man. Be
that feeling your reward. When you are tired of struggling
with vice and selfishness, rest yourself, mind your own business, and fight them only when they come directly in your
way.

Give my best and affectionate love to your worthy wife, who
has been your greatest comfort in this world, and on whose
judgment you may rely with great safety in any plan you may
form.

Ever yours.

Mr. Gallatin did not follow the advice of Judge Nicholson.
After the summer session of this year was over, the sudden disavowal by the British government of Mr. Erskine's arrangement threw pressing burdens upon his shoulders. In reply to
his summons to Washington, Mr. Madison wrote from Montpelier that he did not think his presence there necessary. On the
9th August the President's proclamation was issued, accompanied
by a circular from the Treasury reviving the Non-Importation
Act, and the country settled back to its old condition of chronic
complaint and discomfort. Nothing more could be done till the
arrival of the new British envoy, Mr. Jackson, and the meeting
of Congress, nor could energetic action be expected even then.

After the proclamation was issued, Mr. and Mrs. Gallatin
went into Virginia to visit the Madisons, and the whole party,
towards the end of August, arrived at Monticello. While there,
Mr. Gallatin opened his mind fully to his friends, and the triumvirate deliberated solemnly upon the situation. What passed
can only be inferred from the two following letters. No decisive
action was taken or asked. Mr. Gallatin went no further than
to explain his difficulties, leaving Mr. Madison to act as he
pleased.

JEFFERSON TO GALLATIN.

MONTICELLO, October 11, 1809.

DEAR SIR,—. . . I have reflected much and painfully on the change of dispositions which has taken place among the members of the Cabinet since the new arrangement, as you stated to me in the moment of our separation. It would be indeed a great public calamity were it to fix you in the purpose which you seemed to think possible. I consider the fortunes of our Republic as depending in an eminent degree on the extinction of the public debt before we engage in any war; because that done we shall have revenue enough to improve our country in peace and defend it in war without recurring either to new taxes or loans. But if the debt should once more be swelled to a formidable size, its entire discharge will be despaired of, and we shall be committed to the English career of debt, corruption, and rottenness, closing with revolution. The discharge of the debt, therefore, is vital to the destinies of our government, and it hangs on Mr. Madison and yourself alone. We will never see another President and Secretary of the Treasury making all other objects subordinate to this. Were either of you to be lost to the public, that great hope is lost. I had always cherished the idea that you would fix on that object the measure of your fame and of the gratitude which our country will owe you. Nor can I yield up this prospect to the secondary considerations which assail your tranquillity. For sure I am, they never can produce any other serious effect. Your value is too justly estimated by our fellow-citizens at large, as well as their functionaries, to admit any remissness in their support of you. My opinion always was that none of us ever occupied stronger ground in the esteem of Congress than yourself, and I am satisfied there is no one who does not feel your aid to be still as important for the future as it has been for the past. You have nothing, therefore, to apprehend in the dispositions of Congress, and still less of the President, who above all men is the most interested and affectionately disposed to support you. I hope, then, you will abandon entirely the idea you expressed to me, and that you will consider the eight years to come as essential to your political career. I should certainly consider any earlier day of your retirement as the most inauspicious day our new government has ever seen. In addition to the common interest in this question, I feel, particularly for myself, the considerations of gratitude which I personally owe you for your valuable aid during my administration of public affairs, a just sense of the large portion of the public approbation which was earned by your labors and belongs to you, and the sincere friendship and attachment which grew out of our joint exertions to promote the common good, and of which I pray you now to accept the most cordial and respectful assurances.

GALLATIN TO JEFFERSON.

WASHINGTON, November 8, 1809.

DEAR SIR,—I perused your affectionate letter of the 11th ult. with lively sensations of pleasure, excited by that additional evidence of your continued kindness and partiality. To have acquired and preserved your friendship and confidence is more than sufficient to console me for some late personal mortifications, though I will not affect to conceal that these, coming from an unexpected quarter, and being as I thought unmerited, wounded my feelings more deeply than I had at first been aware of. [Had I listened only to those feelings, I would have resigned and probably taken this winter a seat in Congress, which as a personal object would have been much more pleasing than my present situation, and also better calculated to regain the ground which to my surprise I found I had lost at least in one of the branches of the Legislature. After mature consideration I relinquished the idea, at least for that time, in a great degree on account of my personal attachment to Mr. Madison, which is of old standing, I am sure reciprocal, and strengthened from greater intimacy; and also because I mistrusted my own judgment, and doubted whether I was not more useful where I was than I could be as a member of Congress. All this passed in my mind before the last session; and the communication which I made to you at Monticello arose from subsequent circumstances.][1]

---

[1] The passages in brackets were omitted in the final draft.

Yet I can assure you that I will not listen to those feelings in forming a final determination on the subject on which I conversed with you at Monticello. The gratitude and duty I owe to the country which has received me and honored me beyond my deserts, the deep interest I feel in its future welfare and prosperity, the confidence placed by Mr. Madison in me, my personal and sincere attachment for him, the desire of honorably acquiring some share of reputation, every public and private motive would induce me not to abandon my post, if I am permitted to retain it, and if my remaining in office can be of public utility. But in both respects I have strong apprehensions, to which I alluded in our conversation. It has seemed to me from various circumstances that those who thought they had injured were disposed to destroy, and that they were sufficiently skilful and formidable to effect their object. As I may not, however, perhaps see their actions with an unprejudiced eye, nothing but irresistible evidence both of the intention and success will make me yield to that consideration. But if that ground which you have so forcibly presented to my view is deserted; if those principles which we have uniformly asserted and which were successfully supported during your Administration are no longer adhered to, you must agree with me that to continue in the Treasury would be neither useful to the public or honorable to myself.

The reduction of the public debt was certainly the principal object in bringing me into office, and our success in that respect has been due both to the joint and continued efforts of the several branches of government and to the prosperous situation of the country. I am sensible that the work cannot progress under adverse circumstances. If the United States shall be forced into a state of actual war, all the resources of the country must be called forth to make it efficient, and new loans will undoubtedly be wanted. But whilst peace is preserved the revenue will, at all events, be sufficient to pay the interest and to defray necessary expenses. I do not ask that in the present situation of our foreign relations the debt be reduced, but only that it shall not be increased so long as we are not at war. I do not pretend to step out of my own sphere and to control the internal management of other Departments. But it seems to me that, as Secretary of the Treasury, I may ask that whilst peace continues the aggregate of expenditure of those Departments be kept within bounds, such as will preserve the equilibrium between the national revenue and expenditure without recurrence to loans. I cannot, my dear sir, consent to act the part of a mere financier, to become a contriver of taxes, a dealer of loans, a seeker of resources for the purpose of supporting useless baubles, of increasing the number of idle and dissipated members of the community, of fattening contractors, pursers, and agents, and of introducing in all its ramifications that system of patronage, corruption, and rottenness which you so justly execrate. I thought I owed it to candor and friendship to communicate as I did to Mr. Madison and to yourself my fears of a tendency in that direction, arising from the quarter and causes which I pointed out, and the effect such a result must have on my conduct. I earnestly wish that my apprehensions may have been groundless, and it is a question which facts and particularly the approaching session of Congress will decide. No efforts shall be wanted on my part in support of our old principles. But, whatever the result may be, I never can forget either your eminent services to the United States, nor how much I owe to you for having permitted me to take a subordinate part in your labors.

Mr. Jefferson's letter was obviously written not merely to encourage Mr. Gallatin, but to be shown to members of Congress. From it one would suppose that Mr. Gallatin had in the moment of departure merely suggested the possibility of his retirement; from Mr. Gallatin's reply, which has no such semi-official reticence, the real import of the conversation, and the fact that it was addressed to Mr. Madison, are made evident.

"Those who thought they had injured were disposed to destroy, and were sufficiently skilful and formidable to effect their object." Mr. Gallatin's life for the next four years was little more than a commentary on this paragraph. There has, perhaps, never in our history been a personal contest more determined, more ferocious, more mischievous than this between Mr. Gallatin, with the Executive behind him, and the knot of his enemies who controlled the Senate; it is not too much to say that to this struggle, complicating itself with the rising spirit of young nationality, we owe the war of 1812, and some of the most imminent perils the nation ever incurred. It was not unlike the great contest of ten years before between John Adams and a similar group of Senators; it went through a similar phase, and in each case the result was dependent on the question of war or peace. There are few more interesting contrasts of character in our history than that between the New England President, with his intense personality and his overpowering bursts of passion, confronting his enemies with a will that could not control or even mask its features, and "the Genevan," as the Aurora called him, calm, reticent, wary, never vehement, full of resource, ignoring enmity, hating strife. Perhaps a combination of two such characters, if they could have been made to work in harmony, might have proved too much even for the Senate; and, if so, a problem in American history might have been solved, for, as it was, the Senate succeeded in overthrowing both.

As Mr. Gallatin had predicted, the mission of Mr. Jackson proved to be merely one more insult, and our government very soon put an end to its relations with him and sent him away; but, in doing so, Mr. Madison expressly declared the undiminished desire of the United States to establish friendly relations with Great Britain, so that the only effect of this episode was to procure one year more of delay; precisely the object which Mr. Canning had in view. As the country now stood, Mr. Canning's policy had been completely successful; he had taken away the neutral commerce of the United States, and the United States had submitted to his will; he had taken away her seamen, and she forced her seamen to go. Just at this moment Mr. Canning himself was thrown out of office; his dictatorial temper met more resistance from his colleagues than from America, and he found himself a private man, with a duel on his hands, at the instant when his administration of foreign affairs was most triumphant. His successor was the Marquess Wellesley, whose reputation for courtesy and liberality was high, and therefore inspired the United States with a hope of justice, for even Mr. Madison, as his letters show, could never quite persuade himself that the British government meant what its acts proclaimed.

The dismissal of Mr. Jackson immediately preceded the meeting of Congress; the interval was hardly sufficient to supply time for elaborating a new policy. The President's message, sent in on the 29th November, 1809, was very non-committal on the subject of further legislation, and only expressed two opinions as to its character; he was confident that it would be worthy of the nation, and that it would be stamped with unanimity. What ground Mr. Madison had for this confidence, nowhere appears; and if he was honest in expressing this as an opinion rather than as a hope, he was very little aware of the condition of Congress; even Mr. Jefferson never was more mistaken.

As usual, the task of creating and carrying through Congress the Executive policy fell upon Mr. Gallatin, and as usual, bowing to the necessities of the situation, he set himself to invent some scheme that would have a chance of uniting a majority in its support and of giving government solid ground to stand upon. The task was more than difficult, it was impossible. Since the war-policy broke down and the embargo was abandoned, no solid ground was left; Mr. Gallatin, however, had this riddle to solve, and his solution was not wanting in ingenuity.

His report, sent in on December 8, 1809, for the first time announced a deficit. "The expenses of government, exclusively of the payments on account of the principal of the debt, have exceeded the actual receipts into the Treasury by a sum of near $1,300,000." This was a part of the price of the embargo. For the next year authority for a loan of $4,000,000 would be required in case the military and naval expenditure were as large as in 1809; if Congress should resolve on a permanent increase in the military and naval establishments, additional duties would be requisite; if not, a continuation of the Mediterranean Fund would be sufficient.

But the essence of the report lay in its last paragraph. "Whatever may be the decision of Congress in other respects, there is a subject which seems to require immediate attention. The provisions adopted for the purpose of carrying into effect the non-intercourse with England and France, particularly as modified by the act of last session, under an expectation that the orders of council of Great Britain had been revoked, are inefficient and altogether inapplicable to existing circumstances. It will be sufficient to observe that exportation by land is not forbidden, and that no bonds being required from vessels ostensibly employed in the coasting-trade, nor any authority vested by law which will justify detention, those vessels daily sail for British ports without any other remedy but the precarious mode of instituting prosecutions against the apparent owners. It is unnecessary and it would be painful to dwell on all the effects of those violations of the laws. But without any allusion to the efficiency or political object of any system, and merely with a view to its execution, it is incumbent to state that from the experience of the last two years a perfect conviction arises that either the system of restriction, partially abandoned, must be reinstated in all its parts and with all the provisions necessary for its strict and complete execution, or that all the restrictions, so far at least as they affect the commerce and navigation of the citizens of the United States, ought to be removed."

This report, as already said, was sent to Congress on the 8th December, 1809. On the 19th December, Mr. Macon, from the Committee on Foreign Relations, reported a bill which was understood to come from the Treasury Department, and which explained the somewhat obscure suggestion in the last lines of the report. This bill, commonly known as Macon's bill, No. 1, contained twelve sections. The 1st and 2d excluded English and French ships of war from our harbors; the 3d excluded English and French merchant vessels from our harbors; the 4th restricted all importations of English and French goods to vessels owned wholly by United States citizens; the 5th, 6th, 7th, and 8th restricted these importations to such as came directly from England and France; the 9th authorized the President to remove these restrictions whenever either England or France should remove theirs; the 11th repealed the old non-intercourse, and the 12th limited the duration of the act to the 4th March, 1810.

The bill was in short a Navigation Act of the most severe kind, and met the orders in council and the French edicts on their own ground. The Federalists at once pointed out that the measure was a violent one; that it would be immediately met by Great Britain with retaliatory measures, and that the result must amount to a new embargo or to war. To this the supporters of the bill replied that government contemplated such retaliation; that it was intended to throw the burden upon England and compel her to carry it; that Congress had tried an embargo, the principle of which was non-exportation; that it had tried non-intercourse, the principle of which was non-importation; and now, since both these had failed, it must try a navigation law that could only be countervailed by restrictive measures to be carried out by England herself.

The fact soon appeared that this bill was a very difficult one for its opponents to deal with; it did in fact strike out the only policy, short of war, which was likely to bring England to terms, and which, according to Mr. Huskisson's assertion some years later,[1] she has always found herself powerless to meet. The opponents of the bill at once showed their embarrassment in a manner which is always proof of weakness; they adopted in the same breath two contradictory arguments; the bill was too strong, and it was too weak. For the Federalists it was too strong; they wished frankly to take sides with England. For Duane and Leib it was too weak, a mean submission, a futile and disgraceful measure; not that they wished war, for they did not as yet venture to take that ground; not that they suggested any practical measure that would stand a moment's criticism; but that they were decidedly opposed to this special plan. So far as war was concerned, the President was still in advance of Congress, for not only was Macon's bill a stronger measure than the majority relished, but the President was calling upon Congress to fill up the army and the navy, and Mr. Gallatin was steadily pressing for war taxes.

---

[1] Speech of 12th May, 1826.

After more than a month of debate, Macon's bill passed the House by 73 to 52, and went up to the Senate, where it was consigned to the tender mercies of General Smith and Mr. Giles. On the motion of General Smith, February 21, 1810, all the clauses except the 1st, 2d, and 12th were struck out by a vote of 16 to 11. The Senate debates are not reported, but General Smith subsequently made a speech on the bill, which he printed, and in which he took the ground that the measure was feeble, and that it was so strong as to justify England in confiscating all our trade. This was the ground also taken by the Aurora. General Smith proposed to arm our merchant vessels and furnish them convoy, a measure over and over again rejected. By a vote of 17 to 15 the Senate ultimately adhered to its amendments and killed the bill, Gallatin's personal enemies deciding the result.

Throughout all this transaction the Secretary of State had acted a curious part. Silent or assenting in the Cabinet, where, notwithstanding rumors to the contrary, there was always apparent cordiality, Mr. Smith's conversation out-of-doors, and especially with opponents of the Administration, was very free in condemnation of the whole policy which he officially represented.[1] No one, indeed, either in or out of the Cabinet, pretended an enthusiastic admiration of Macon's bill; Mr. Madison, Mr. Gallatin, Mr. Macon himself, only regarded it as "better than nothing," and "nothing" was the alternative. Congress had put the country into a position equally humiliating, ridiculous, and unprofitable; it had for two sessions refused to follow the Administration and had refused to impose any policy of its own. The influence of General Smith, solitary and unsupported except by Leib and the Aurora faction, now barred the path of legislation and held Congress down to its contemptible and crouching attitude of impotent gesticulation and rant. The Secretary of State was a party to his brother's acts, and although too dull a man to have any distinct scheme of his own or any depth of intrigue; although obliged to let the President write his official papers and Mr. Gallatin control both his foreign and his domestic policy, he nevertheless used the liberty thus obtained

---

[1] See Mr. Madison's "Memorandum." Writings, ii. 495–506.

to talk with unreserved freedom both to Federalists and discontented Republicans about the characters of his associates and the contents of his despatches.

Thus the policy of a Navigation Act was defeated, and another year was lost. Only at the very close of the session, when it became apparent that something must be done, Mr. Macon got his bill No. 2 before the House. This was on April 7, and on the 10th he wrote to Nicholson: "I am at a loss to guess what we shall do on the subject of foreign relations. The bill in the enclosed paper, called Macon's No. 2, is not really Macon's, though he reports it as chairman. It is in truth Taylor's. This I only mention to you because when it comes to be debated I shall not act the part of a father but of a step-father." After a violent struggle between the two Houses, a bill was at length passed, on May 1, 1810, which has strong claims to be considered the most disgraceful act on the American statute-book. It surrendered all resistance to the British and French orders and edicts; it repealed the non-importation law; it left our shipping unprotected to the operation of foreign municipal laws; it offered not even a protest against violence and robbery such as few powerful nations had ever endured except at the edge of the sword; and its only proposition towards these two foreign nations, each of which had exhausted upon us every form of insult and robbery, was an offer that if either would repeal its edicts, the United States would prohibit trade with the other.

The imagination can scarcely conceive of any act more undignified, more cowardly, or, as it proved, more mischievous; but in the utter paralysis into which these party quarrels had now brought Congress, this was all the legislation that could be got, although, in justice to Congress, it is but fair to add that even this was universally contemned. The Administration had nothing to do but to execute it, and to make what it could of the policy it established.

In the contest upon Macon's bill, Mr. Gallatin had the President's full support and co-operation. But in another and to him a much more serious struggle he stood quite alone, and all he could obtain from the President was that the Executive influence should not be thrown against him. The charter of the United

States Bank was about to expire. In the present condition of the country, with war always in prospect and public and private finances seriously disordered, the bank was an institution almost if not quite indispensable to the Treasury. To abolish it was to create artificially and unnecessarily a very serious financial embarrassment at the moment when the national existence might turn on financial steadiness. To create a new system that would answer the same purposes would be the work of years, and would require the most careful experiments. The subject had been referred to Mr. Gallatin by the Senate, and he had at the close of the last session sent in a report representing in strong language the advantages derived from the bank. He now drew up a bill by which the existing charter was to be considerably modified; the capital raised to thirty millions, three-fifths of which was to be lent to the government; branch banks to be established in each State, and half the directors appointed by the State; with various other provisions intended to secure the utmost possible advantage to the government. Parties at once divided on this question as on the foreign intercourse question, but with a change of sides. The Federalists favored, the old Republicans resisted, the bank, and General Smith resisted Mr. Gallatin. During this session, however, little more was done than to introduce the bills; the matter was then thrown aside until next year.

These subjects, and a hasty report on domestic manufactures, occupied the session almost exclusively, so far as Mr. Gallatin was concerned. When Congress rose, on the 1st May, 1810, every one was obliged to concede that a more futile session had never been held, and the Aurora fulminated against Mr. Gallatin as the cause of all its shortcomings. More and more the different elements of personal discontent made common cause against the Secretary of the Treasury, and before the end of the year 1810 the Aurora and its allies opened a determined assault upon him with the avowed intention of driving him from office.

It was in reference to these attacks, which incessantly recurred to the old stories of 1806, that Mr. Jefferson wrote to Mr. Gallatin as follows:

JEFFERSON TO GALLATIN.

16 August, 1810.

I have seen with infinite grief the set which is made at you in the public papers, and with the more as my name has been so much used in it. I hope we both know one another too well to receive impression from circumstances of this kind. A twelve years' intimate and friendly intercourse must be better evidence to each of the dispositions of the other than the letters of foreign ministers to their courts, or tortured inferences from facts true or false. I have too thorough a conviction of your cordial good-will towards me, and too strong a sense of the faithful and able assistance I received from you, to relinquish them on any evidence but of my own senses. With entire confidence in your assurance of these truths I shall add those only of my constant affection and high respect.

" The letters of foreign ministers to their courts" were Mr. Erskine's despatches of December, 1808, to Mr. Canning, which had been printed in England, and, on reaching America, compelled Mr. Gallatin very reluctantly to make a public denial of their accuracy.[1] They represented Mr. Gallatin as acquiescing in the belief that Mr. Jefferson was under French influence. Mr. Gallatin, with the aid of Mr. Madison, drew up a paper correcting Mr. Erskine's errors, and of course stimulating the attacks of the Aurora. To Mr. Jefferson's letter Gallatin replied:

GALLATIN TO JEFFERSON.

10th September, 1810.

I need not say how much shocked I was by Mr. Erskine's despatch. However reluctant to a newspaper publication and to a denial on matters of fact, I could not permit my name to be ever hereafter quoted in support of the vile charges of foreign partialities ascribed to you, and I knew that in that respect my disavowal would be decisive, for, if my testimony was believed, they did not exist, and if disbelieved, no faith could be placed

---

[1] See Writings, vol. i. p. 475.

in whatever I might be supposed to have said to Erskine.
Although I never for a moment supposed that either his letter
or any newspaper attack could, after so long and intimate acquaintance, create a doubt in your mind of the sincerity and
warmth of my sentiments towards you, or alter your friendship for me, the assurance was highly acceptable and gratefully
received.   The newspaper publications to which you allude,
I have heard of, but not seen, having not received the papers
south of this place [New York] during my stay here.   But I
had anticipated that from various quarters a combined and malignant attack would be made whenever a favorable opportunity
offered itself.   Of the true causes and real authors I will say
nothing.   And however painful the circumstance and injurious
the effect, the esteem of those who know me and the consciousness
of having exclusively devoted my faculties to the public good,
and of having severely performed public duties without regard
to personal consequences, will, I hope, support me against evils
for which there is no other remedy.   Yet that a diminution of
public confidence should lessen my usefulness will be a subject
of deep regret.

Meanwhile, the situation of affairs abroad was more and more
becoming the measure of American politics, and the question of
war or peace was more and more clearly defined as the turning-
point of Mr. Gallatin's life.   The exhaustion of the Treasury
was alone, for him, a sufficient argument against war.   He began
to believe, and he was right in believing, that the worst had
now passed; that, as America could hardly suffer more humiliation than she had already borne, her objects could perhaps be
attained by peaceful methods; and almost mechanically, as the
government became impressed with this conviction, the opposition, so far as it was personal, tended to the opposite side, and
advocated war.   There was no other ground to stand upon,
unless they went frankly over to the Federalists, which was
rapidly becoming inevitable if they continued their old tactics.
    Curiously enough, the feeble and disgraceful law of May 1,
1810, known as Macon's law, had a more immediate effect on
the situation abroad than any of the stronger measures which

had been tried. Ever since the repeal of the embargo on March 4, 1809, England had been the favored nation; our people, in fact, gave her our commerce on her own terms, and were glad to do so. Macon's law did away with even the pretence of resistance to her authority on the ocean. Disgraceful as such a result doubtless was to the honor and dignity of the United States, it was in its effects on France a very vigorous engine, for it was nothing more nor less than taking active part with England against her; and inasmuch as Bonaparte had within his limited range shown, if possible, somewhat more disposition to rob us, and a still greater latitude of personal insult, than had been displayed even by Mr. Canning, this result might fairly be viewed with indifference, or perhaps with some slight satisfaction, by the people of the United States. Upon the Emperor it acted, as with a man of his temper was not unnatural, in a most decided manner; he was furious; he seized all the American property he could get within his clutches; he stormed at the American minister, and heaped outrage upon insult; but the fatal arrow could not be shaken out; random as the shot had been, it struck a vital spot, and Bonaparte had to submit. The change which he was thus forced to make illustrates his character.

When the Act of May 1, 1810, commonly known as Macon's Act, reached Paris, General Armstrong communicated it inofficially to the minister of foreign affairs, Champagny, Duke de Cadore, who laid it before the Emperor. According to all ordinary theories, the Act of May 1, by which the non-intercourse was repealed, would work against France and against France alone; by it America abandoned even the pretence of resisting the absolute domination of England on the seas, and accepted whatever commercial law she chose to impose. The Emperor, moreover, had no means of counteracting or punishing it. He had already resorted to the strongest measure at his command, and seized all the American vessels he could lay his hands on. These were now waiting condemnation. The next step was war, which would, of course, operate only to the advantage of England. For once Bonaparte was obliged to retrace his steps, or at least affect to do so.

On the 5th August, therefore, the Duke de Cadore wrote to General Armstrong a letter, in which, with the usual effrontery of the imperial government, he took the ground that the Act of May 1 was a concession to France, and that France recognized its obligations. "The Emperor loves the Americans;" the Emperor revoked his decrees of Berlin and Milan, which, after the 1st November next, would cease to have effect, it being understood that, in consequence of this declaration, the English should revoke their orders in council and renounce their new principles of blockade, or that America should carry out the terms of the Act and cause her rights to be respected.

This letter was curious in many ways, but it is to be observed more particularly that while Macon's law required either belligerent to "so revoke or modify her edicts as that they shall cease to violate the neutral commerce of the United States," the Emperor as a matter of fact revoked only the Berlin and Milan decrees, and said nothing of others still more offensive, especially the Rambouillet decree, then only four months old, under which he now held and meant to continue holding possession of all the American property in France,—a decree unknown to Congress when the law of May 1 was passed.

Then came the Emperor's master-stroke, which was to punish the Americans for blundering into success. Long unknown to our government, it was only revealed by accident to Mr. Gallatin when minister to France in 1821, after Napoleon and his decrees had been forgotten by all but the unhappy merchants whom he had plundered. At that time the Duke de Bassano, Napoleon's Minister of State, had been allowed by the government of Louis XVIII. to return to Paris. He had preserved a register of the various acts and decrees of Napoleon, and was more intimate with their nature and bearing than any one even in the government of that time. To him the claimants sometimes applied for copies of documents to support their memorials, and he furnished them. On one occasion they sought the text of an order by which the proceeds of certain cargoes sequestered at Antwerp were transferred to the Treasury. The Duke furnished what he supposed to be the paper, and it was brought to Mr. Gallatin. The following extract from his despatch of 15th September, 1821, to the Department of State explains what this paper was, and what his sensations were in regard to it.

"The enclosed copy of a decree dated at Trianon on the 5th of August, 1810, which has never been published nor, to my knowledge, communicated to our ministers or government, was obtained through a private channel. . . . It bears date the same day on which it was officially communicated to our minister that the Berlin and Milan decrees would be revoked on the first day of the ensuing November, and no one can suppose that if it had been communicated or published at the same time, the United States would, with respect to the promised revocation of the Berlin and Milan decrees, have taken that ground which ultimately led to the war with Great Britain. It is indeed unnecessary to comment on such a glaring act of combined injustice, bad faith, and meanness, as the enactment and concealment of that decree exhibits."

The text of this decree which proved how "His Majesty loves the Americans. Their prosperity and their commerce are within the scope of his policy;" and which was written with the same pen on the same day as that celebrated declaration of Napoleonic affection,—the full text of this decree may be seen attached to Mr. Gallatin's despatch.[1] Under the pretext of reprisals for American confiscations which had never in fact been made,[2] it confiscated into the imperial treasury, without trial or delay, all American property in France, both that which had been already sequestered and sold, subject to final judgment, and that which was still in the form of merchandise or ships brought into France previous to the 1st May, 1810, the date of Macon's Act. And it further provided that until November 1, when the Berlin and Milan decrees were to be conditionally revoked, American ships should be allowed to enter French ports, but not to unload, and presumably not to depart, without a permission from the Emperor.

When Mr. Gallatin, at sixty years of age, used language so strong as that just quoted and characterized an act as one of combined injustice, bad faith, and meanness, the world may very reasonably conclude that he was unusually moved. On another occasion he called it "a mean and perfidious act." There was

---

[1] Writings, vol. ii. p. 198.   [2] Ibid., p. 279.

good reason why he should have been deeply exasperated at the discovery, for of that meanness and perfidy he was a principal victim.

What share Mr. Gallatin now had in deciding the action of the President is unknown. In the absence of evidence to the contrary it is to be presumed that he at least acquiesced in the decision of the Cabinet, yet not only is it clear that the letter of Champagny of August 5 was not a compliance with the terms of Macon's Act; did not revoke or modify Napoleon's edicts so as that "they shall cease to violate the neutral commerce of the United States," and, therefore, that the President had no legal power to act as though it did; but it is clear, from Secretary Smith's letter on the subject to General Armstrong, dated November 2, 1810, that the President was aware of the fact and escaped it only by strange subterfuge. Already on the 5th July Mr. Smith had instructed General Armstrong that "a satisfactory provision for restoring the property lately surprised and seized by the order or at the instance of the French government must be combined with a repeal of the French edicts, with a view to a non-intercourse with Great Britain, such a provision being *an indispensable evidence* of the just purpose of France toward the United States." Yet, on the 2d November, writing to General Armstrong that the President had issued his proclamation against England on the strength of the French revocation of the Berlin and Milan decrees alone, Mr. Smith could only justify this evident abandonment of his former and correct ground by adding: "You will, however, let the French government understand that this has been done *on the ground* that the repeal of these decrees does involve an extinguishment of all the edicts of France actually violating our neutral rights. . . . It is to be remarked, moreover, that in issuing the Proclamation *it has been presumed* that the requisition contained in that letter [of July 5], on the subject of the sequestered property, will have been satisfied ;" and the writer goes on to show on what evidence this presumption rested.

That is to say, President Madison did an act which he recognized as one of doubtful propriety, on the ground of two assumptions of fact, neither of which had the smallest foundation.

These objections and criticisms were made at the time, and they were semi-officially answered by Joel Barlow in the National Intelligencer of July 9, 1811, by drawing a distinction between "belligerent maritime edicts violating our neutral rights, and edicts authorizing other depredations on the property of our citizens." The Berlin and Milan decrees, it appears, were maritime; the Rambouillet decree was municipal, not a violation of our neutral rights contemplated by Macon's Act. Similar British depredations had been disregarded in accepting Erskine's arrangement.

If this were the case in November, Mr. Madison would have done better not to have said in July that a revocation of the Rambouillet decree was an *indispensable* evidence of the Emperor's intentions, and also that he assumed, on the part of the French government, an extinguishment of all its edicts and a restoration of the sequestered property as the ground of his proclamation. Moreover, if this were the case, it is not quite plain why Mr. Gallatin should have declared in 1821 that a knowledge of the secret Trianon decree would have prevented Mr. Madison from issuing that proclamation. The Trianon decree was merely the authority for acts which were notorious.

Although there is not a shadow of evidence to show what Mr. Gallatin's opinions on this question were, yet the result of the decision was so important in its ultimate bearings upon his fortune that the subject could not be left unmentioned. In Mr. Madison's private letters of this time there is a disposition clearly evident to subordinate all other considerations to the object of bringing England to terms, and this doubtless was the tendency of public feeling. Acting on this principle, the Administration decided that Champagny's announcement of the intended revocation of the Berlin and Milan decrees was a sufficient fulfilment of the terms of Macon's Act, and accordingly, on the 1st November, issued the proclamation to that effect. Simultaneously Mr. Gallatin issued a circular to the collectors announcing that after the 2d February, 1811, all intercourse with Great Britain and her dependencies would cease.

In this there was nothing unfair to England. Napoleon had in appearance been compelled to give way, and the United States had a perfect right to make the most of her success. If in doing so she submitted to more robbery, this was no more than she had done when she had attempted similar arrangements with England; it was less than she had done every day for nearly twenty years, in submitting to the impressments of her seamen for the benefit of the British navy. Nevertheless, the ground on which she stood was very weak as regarded argument, for there could be no reasonable doubt then, any more than there was ten years later, that Bonaparte had acted a " mean and perfidious" part, and yet she called upon England to act as though it were an honest one. England rightly enough replied that Napoleon was attempting another fraud to which England would not be a party; thus the situation was rendered more critical than ever, and Napoleon, by a course of conduct which was precisely what Mr. Gallatin described it in 1821, plunged the United States into a war with England on ground that, so far as France was concerned, would not bear examination.

Though there is reason to regret that Mr. Madison should have made himself so eagerly the dupe of Napoleon, and though there seems to be something surprising in the irritation of Mr. Gallatin on discovering only one among the many instruments of the Emperor's duplicity, the good faith of the American government cannot fairly be called in question. The situation of the United States as regarded England was intolerable, and Mr. Madison snatched at any fair expedient to escape it. England alleged that the Berlin and Milan decrees were the cause of her orders in council. The United States, by a lucky stroke of legislation, compelled Napoleon to promise revocation of those decrees on a certain day, and then turned that promise against England. England refused belief in it, which was reasonable enough, but in reality had those decrees been the only cause of the orders in council, the alleged revocation would have afforded ample excuse for England's concession. On both sides the diplomatic veil was transparent. Napoleon, in fact, had not revoked his decrees, as he unblushingly avowed within the next year, while England cared nothing for those decrees, except so far as they were mere municipal regulations; so far as they violated international law on the ocean they were, indeed, quite ineffective. England's real object was to maintain her clutch on American shipping and sailors.

Such was the situation of affairs when Congress met on the 3d December, 1810. One more step had been taken, but no man could certainly say whether it was towards a solution. Meanwhile, Mr. Gallatin was burdened with an undertaking that plunged him deeper into the miserable complications of political warfare, disorganizing his followers and his friends, stimulating personal hostilities, and yet leaving him no choice of action. The question of the bank charter was to be decided this winter before the Congress expired on the 4th March, 1811. As a matter of public welfare, more especially in the situation the country now occupied, Mr. Gallatin was obliged to do his utmost to prevent the destruction of the bank. It was no mere matter of party or of personal feeling; the bank at that moment was essential to public safety; to lose it might be a question of national life.

Every argument which Mr. Gallatin could use was put to the service of the bill. He was its open and earnest advocate both in his special reports and in his conversation, yet even the malignity of the Aurora and the less bitter but perhaps more dangerous hostility of the Richmond Enquirer failed to find in them a single expression that could be made to rouse personal irritation or popular feeling. He conducted his case with all his usual temper, tact, and persistence; it is due also to his opponents in Congress to say that they avoided personal attacks upon him, at least for the most part, and left vituperation to the press. Not the less, however, was it distinctly understood that the bank was the test of Mr. Gallatin's power; that its overthrow was one and the most important step towards driving him from office; and that nothing less than the overshadowing growth of his influence could possibly make the continued existence of the bank even a subject of discussion in the Republican party.

The debate in the House was long and able, but when a vote was reached on January 24, 1811, the numbers stood 65 to 64 in favor of indefinite postponement. Many of Mr. Gallatin's best friends voted with the majority; the Federalists in a mass voted on his side; his personal enemies turned the scale. Whatever

Mr. Gallatin's feelings were at this defeat, he made no display of them even to his intimates. On the 28th January, Mr. Macon wrote to Judge Nicholson: "I was at Gallatin's yesterday; all well. He is, I fear, rather mortified at the indefinite postponement of the bill to renew the charter of the Bank of the United States. I am really sorry that my best judgment compelled me on that question to vote agreeable to what I believe to be the anxious wish of the invisibles. Mr. Madison was at the last session, I am informed, in favor of the renewal; that he considered it, according as my informant gave his words, *res adjudicata*. What cause has produced the change in his mind I have not heard. I have also been told that Mr. Giles was of the same opinion then and that he also has changed. These are natural rights, and ought to be exercised whenever the mind is convinced that opinions are founded in error; but when great men, or rather men in high, responsible stations, change their deliberate opinions it seems to me that they in some way or other ought to give the reason of the change. I incline to think that Mr. Madison's opinion last winter had a good deal of weight, and it is presumed it may have been the means of inducing a few members to take pretty strong hold of the constitutional side of the question. Now that he has changed, they are thrown with Gallatin on the Federal side of the question. I also incline to think that his present opinion has had some weight in the late decision."

Mr. Macon was probably mistaken in thinking that the President had changed his position; the letter is curious as showing what confusion Mr. Madison's course created, but the story itself was apparently a mere rumor set afloat by the enemies of the bank, those "invisibles," as the Smith faction were significantly called by Mr. Macon and his friends, and whose alliance with the Aurora was now complete. A few days later, on the 9th February, Mr. Macon wrote: "It seems to me not very improbable that Mr. Madison's Administration may end something like Mr. Adams's. He may endeavor to go on with the government with men in whom he has not perfect confidence, until they break him down, and then, as John did, turn them out after he has suffered all that they can do to injure him. It is true, if he means ever to turn out, he has now delayed it almost too long, because the senatorial elections are over, while these people retained their influence, if they can be said to have a fixed influence in the nation."

Meanwhile the debate on the bank charter had begun in the Senate, and a curious debate it was. Mr. William H. Crawford. of Georgia, appeared as Mr. Gallatin's champion, and supported the charter with such energy, courage, and ability as earned Mr. Gallatin's lasting gratitude, and made Mr. Crawford the representative of the Administration in the Senate, and the favorite candidate of the Jeffersonian triumvirate for succession to the Presidency. Mr. Giles, on the other hand, spoke judicially. The Legislature of Virginia, like the Legislatures of Pennsylvania and Kentucky, had instructed their Senators to vote against the charter. Mr. Giles declared himself ·a representative of the people of the United States, not a mere agent of the Virginia Legislature, and his speech was an elaborate effort at candid investigation, unaffected, as he .averred, by his personal sentiments towards the Secretary of the Treasury. But he, too, at last concluded that the bank was a British institution, which had not prevented the orders in council or the attack on the Chesapeake, and therefore should be suppressed. He admitted that the time was inauspicious for putting an end to the establishment. but the danger from British influence was greater than the danger from financial confusion. Henry Clay, the young Senator from Kentucky, followed and ridiculed the ponderous Mr. Giles, who had "certainly demonstrated to the satisfaction of all who heard him, both that it was constitutional and unconstitutional, highly proper and improper, to prolong the charter of the bank." Mr. Clay was not disposed to enlist with Mr. Giles in factious opposition to the government, but he was still less disposed to join Mr. Crawford in its support; he hotly denied the constitutionality of the charter, and, like Mr. Giles, he declared that the bank was responsible for not preventing impressments and orders in council. Then General Smith, in a speech covering two days, proved that the whole theory of the usefulness of a national bank was a delusion; that State institutions were better depositaries of the public money; that the Secretary of the Treasury was quite mistaken in all his statements about the convenience of the bank, even in regard to remittances, and knew nothing about foreign exchange; that no possible trouble could arise from abolishing the bank; and that the constitutional objection was final.

On the 20th February, 1811, the Senate reached a vote. It was 17 to 17, and the Vice-President, George Clinton, whose personal hostility to the President was notorious, decided the question in the negative. Among the votes which then settled the fate of the bank, and incidentally the fate of Mr. Gallatin, were those of Joseph Anderson, of Tennessee, Henry Clay, of Kentucky, William B. Giles, of Virginia, Michael Leib, of Pennsylvania, and Samuel Smith, of Maryland. Readers who are curious in matters of biography will naturally ask how the opinions of these men stood the test of time. Less than four years later, after Mr. Gallatin had been fairly driven from the Treasury, his most intimate friend, Alexander J. Dallas, was called to fill the place. Government was bankrupt, the currency in frightful disorder, and loans impracticable. Mr. Dallas, as his last resource, insisted upon a bank, and he got it. Michael Leib was then no longer in the Senate; his political career had come to an untimely end. Gideon Granger, Postmaster-General, and one of the factious number, had exhausted President Madison's patience by appointing Leib postmaster at Philadelphia, and had lost his office in consequence; Leib was removed, and disappeared into political obscurity. Giles was consistent in opposing the bank, and in 1816, so soon as his senatorial term expired, he too subsided into obscurity, from which he only rescued himself by his success in using the same tactics against John Quincy Adams that he had used against Albert Gallatin. Anderson, Clay, and Smith have left their names recorded among the supporters of the new charter.

Thus, in the face of difficulties and dangers such as might well have appalled the wisest head and the stoutest heart, the Legislature deprived the Executive of the only efficient financial agent it had ever had. What the financial consequences of destroying the bank actually were will be seen presently; it is enough to say that Congress acted in this instance with a degree of factious incompetence that cost the nation infinite loss and trouble, and was not far from imperilling its existence. No one knew better than Mr. Giles, General Smith, and George Clinton that whatever the objections to a bank might be, this was no time to destroy it, and even Henry Clay, with all his youthful self-confidence, had intelligence enough to make him inexcusable in refusing to prolong, if only for a very few years, the existence of an agent which the Treasury considered indispensable, in the face of a war which he was, against the will of the Administration, forcing upon its hands.

John Randolph was one of those who saw most clearly through the intrigues that beset the government. Never strong in common sense, Randolph's mind was yielding more and more to those aberrations which marked his later years. Though all intimacy of relation between the two men had long ceased, Randolph had yet preserved as much respect for Gallatin as his universal misanthropy permitted, while at the same time his contempt for "the invisibles" was unbounded. Whatever mistakes Randolph made, he at least never descended so low as to make the Aurora his ally. On the 14th February he wrote to Judge Nicholson: "Giles made this morning the most unintelligible speech on the subject of the Bank of the United States that I ever heard. He spoke upwards of two hours; seemed never to understand himself (except upon one commonplace topic of British influence), and consequently excited in his hearers no other sentiment but pity or disgust. But I shall not be surprised to see him puffed in all the newspapers of a certain faction. The Senate have rejected the nomination of Alex. Wolcott to the bench of the Supreme Court—24 to 9. The President is said to have felt great mortification at this result. The truth seems to be that he is President *de jure* only. Who exercises the office *de facto* I know not, but it seems agreed on all hands that 'there is something behind the throne greater than the throne itself.' I cannot help differing with you respecting [Gallatin]'s resignation. If his principal will not support him by his influence against the cabal *in the ministry itself*, as well as out of it, a sense of self-respect, it would seem to me, ought to impel him to retire from a situation where, with a tremendous responsibility, he is utterly destitute of power. Our Cabinet presents a novel spectacle in the political world; divided against itself, and the most deadly animosity raging between its principal members, what can come of it but confusion, mischief, and ruin? Macon is quite out of heart. I am almost indifferent to any possible result. Is this wisdom or apathy? I fear the latter."

A few hours later he added: "Since I wrote to you to-night, Stanford has shown me the last Aurora,—a paper that I never read, but I could not refrain, at his instance, from casting my eyes over some paragraphs relating to the Secretary of the Treasury. Surely, under such circumstances, Mr. G. can no longer hesitate how to act. It appears to me that only one course is left to him,—to go immediately to the P., and to demand either the dismissal of Mr. [Smith] or his own. No man can doubt by whom this machinery is put in motion. There is no longer room to feign ignorance or to temporize. It is unnecessary to say to you that I am not through you addressing myself to another. My knowledge of the interest which you take not merely in the welfare of Mr. G., but in that of the State, induces me to express myself to you on this subject. I wish you would come up here. There are more things in this world of intrigue than you wot of, and I should like to commune with you upon some of them."

Again, on February 17, Randolph wrote: "I am not convinced by your representations respecting [Gallatin], although they are not without weight. Surely it would not be difficult to point out to the President the impossibility of conducting the affairs of the government with such a counteraction in the very Cabinet itself, without assuming anything like a disposition to dictate. Things as they are cannot go on much longer. The Administration are now in fact aground at the pitch of high tide, and a spring tide too. Nothing, then, remains but to lighten the ship, which a dead calm has hitherto kept from going to pieces. If the cabal succeed in their present projects, and I see nothing but promptitude and decision that can prevent it, the nation is undone. The state of affairs for some time past has been highly favorable to their views, which at this moment are more flattering than ever. I am satisfied that Mr. G., by a timely resistance to their schemes, might have defeated them and rendered the whole cabal as impotent as nature would seem to have intended them to be, for in point of ability (capacity for intrigue excepted) they are utterly contemptible and insignificant."

Randolph did not know that even as early as the autumn of 1809 Mr. Gallatin had strained his influence to the utmost to offer "timely resistance to their schemes;" and even Randolph, on reflection, doubted "whether Madison will be able to meet the shock of the Aurora, Whig, Enquirer, Boston Patriot, &c., &c.; and it is highly probable that, beaten in detail by the superior activity and vigor of the Smiths, he may sink ultimately into their arms, and unquestionably will, in that case, receive the law from them."

In all this confusion one thing was clear,—Mr. Gallatin's usefulness was exhausted. There are moments in politics when great results can be reached only by small men,—a maxim which, however paradoxical, may easily be verified. Especially in a democracy the people are apt to become impatient of rule, and will at times obstinately refuse to move at the call of a leader, when, if left to themselves, they will blunder through all obstacles, blindly enough, it is true, but effectually. Mr. Gallatin was now an impediment to government, even though it was conceded that the Treasury could not go on without him; that the party contained no man who could fill his place; that if he retired, confusion must ensue. To Mr. Madison the loss would of course be extremely embarrassing; for ten years Gallatin had taken from the President's shoulders the main burden of internal administration and a large part of the responsibilities of foreign relations; his immense knowledge, his long practical experience, his tact, his fertility of resource, his patience, his courage, his unselfishness, his personal attachment, his retentive memory, even his reticence, were each and all impossible to replace. The material from which Mr. Madison would have to draw was, in comparison, ridiculously unequal to the draft. For ten years the triumvirate had looked about them to find allies and successors; John Randolph had failed them from sheer inability to follow any straight course; John Breckenridge, of Kentucky, had died at the outset of his career; Monroe had not developed great powers, and had repeatedly disappointed their expectations, yet Monroe was still the best they had; William H. Crawford was a crude Georgian, with abilities not yet tried in administration; as for Giles, General Smith, and the other minor luminaries of the old party, their relations with Mr. Madison were hardly better than Randolph's. Whom, then, could he put in the Treasury? What dozen men in the party could pretend to make good to him the loss of his old companion? How could the Administration stand without him?

All this was urged at the time, and was obvious enough to the great body of Republicans in Congress; and yet, granting all this, it was answered that Mr. Gallatin had better retire. Undoubtedly the business of the Treasury would break down; that is to say, the public interests would for a time be ignorantly, wastefully, and perhaps corruptly managed; undoubtedly Mr. Madison would be left in a most unpleasant situation, and would find his personal difficulties vastly increased; Congress and the press would precipitate themselves upon him instead of upon Mr. Gallatin, and he would inevitably be swept away by the torrent. This, however, would be only temporary; the evil would cure itself; faction would produce force to oppose it, and a generation of younger men would invent its own processes to solve its own problems.

Mr. Gallatin saw the situation as clearly as any disinterested spectator could have done, and fully accepted it. At the close of the bank struggle he recognized that he was defeated and that his power for good was gone. It was at once rumored that he would resign. Judge Nicholson wrote on the 6th March, two days after the session ended: "Randolph is here, and told me that a friend mentioned to him that you would probably resign in September, as it would take you till that time to arrange the matters in the Treasury. He did not say in express terms, but I collected that he alluded to Crawford, and I fear that the joint remonstrances of his friends here have not had their due weight with Mr. M."

The following letter, printed from a first draft without date, was probably written at this time, and delivered on the adjournment of Congress, March 4, or immediately afterwards:

GALLATIN TO MADISON.

[March 4, 1811. ?]

DEAR SIR,—I have long and seriously reflected on the present state of things and on my personal situation. This has for some time been sufficiently unpleasant, and nothing but a sense of public duty and attachment to yourself could have induced me to retain it to this day. But I am convinced that in neither respect can I be any longer useful under existing circumstances.

In a government organized like that of the United States, a government not too strong for effecting its principal object, the protection of national rights against foreign aggressions, and particularly under circumstances as adverse and embarrassing as those under which the United States are now placed, it appears to me that not only capacity and talents in the Administration, but also a perfect, heartfelt cordiality amongst its members, are essentially necessary to command the public confidence and to produce the requisite union of views and action between the several branches of government. In at least one of those points your present Administration is defective, and the effects, already sensibly felt, become every day more extensive and fatal. New subdivisions and personal factions equally hostile to yourself and the general welfare daily acquire additional strength. Measures of vital importance have been and are defeated; every operation, even of the most simple and ordinary nature, is prevented or impeded; the embarrassments of government, great as from foreign causes they already are, are unnecessarily increased; public confidence in the public councils and in the Executive is impaired, and every day seems to increase every one of those evils. Such state of things cannot last; a radical and speedy remedy has become absolutely necessary. What that ought to be, what change would best promote the success of your Administration and the welfare of the United States, is not for me to say. I can only judge for myself, and I clearly perceive that my continuing a member of the present Administration is no longer of any public utility, invigorates the opposition against yourself, and must necessarily be attended with an increased loss of reputation by myself.   Under those impressions, not without reluctance and after having perhaps hesitated too long in hopes of a favorable change, I beg leave to tender you my resignation, to take place at such day within a reasonable time as you will think most consistent with the public service.   I hope that I hardly need add any expressions of my respect and sincere personal attachment to you, of the regret I will feel on leaving you at this critical time, and the grateful sense I ever will retain of your kindness to me.

This letter, backed by the remonstrances of Crawford and others, produced a Cabinet crisis.   Mr. Madison declined to accept it, and appears either to have returned it to Mr. Gallatin or to have burned it, for it is not to be found among his papers. He then took a step necessary in any event; he dismissed his Secretary of State, and authorized Mr. Gallatin to sound James Monroe, then Governor of Virginia, as to his willingness to enter the Cabinet.   Mr. Gallatin applied to Richard Brent, a Senator from Virginia, who appears to have written to Mr. Monroe somewhere about the 7th March, but who did not receive a reply till the 22d.[1]   A portion of this reply is worth quoting.

" You intimate," said Mr. Monroe, " that the situation of the country is such as to leave me no alternative.   I am aware that our public affairs are far from being in a tranquil and secure state.   I may add that there is much reason to fear that a crisis is approaching of a very dangerous tendency ; one which menaces the overthrow of the whole Republican party.   Is the Administration impressed with this sentiment and prepared to act on it ? Are things in such a state as to allow the Administration to take the whole subject into consideration and to provide for the safety of the country and of free government by such measures as circumstances may require and a comprehensive view of them suggest ?   Or are we pledged by what is already done to remain

---

[1] See Gallatin's Writings, vol. i. p. 496.

spectators of the interior movement in the expectation of some change abroad, as the ground on which we are to act? I have no doubt, from my knowledge of the President and Mr. Gallatin, with the former of whom I have been long and intimately connected in friendship, and for both of whom in great and leading points of character I have the highest consideration and respect, that if I came into the government the utmost cordiality would subsist between us, and that any opinions which I might entertain and express respecting our public affairs would receive, so far as circumstances would permit, all the attention to which they might be entitled. But if our course is fixed and the destiny of our country dependent on arrangements already made, on measures already taken, I do not perceive how it would be possible for me to render any service at this time in the general government."

Mr. Monroe received the desired assurances, and assumed the new office on the 1st April, 1811. Mr. Robert Smith went out, and issued a manifesto against the government, in which, among numerous ill-digested and incongruous subjects of complaint, there were one or two which showed how serious a misfortune his incompetence had been. A newspaper war ensued, and curious readers may find in the National Intelligencer all the literature of the Smith controversy which they will need to satisfy their doubts. Mr. Smith had much the same fate as Colonel Pickering ten years before; he found that even his friends showed a certain unwillingness to fight his battles. Before the end of the summer it had become evident that Mr. Smith was reduced to insignificance, and it hardly needed the mild severity of Mr. Madison or the newspaper rhetoric of Joel Barlow to accomplish this; Mr. Smith's own clerk was equal to the task.[1]

The change in the State Department was a great relief to the President, and perhaps he may have asked the question why he had ever allowed himself to be dragooned into the fatal appoint-

---

[1] See, for another account of the struggle between Gallatin and the Smiths, the "Recollections of the Civil History of the War of 1812, by Joseph Gales;" a series of papers printed in the National Intelligencer, numbered from I. to IX., and published between June 9 and September 12, 1857.

ment of Mr. Smith; but Monroe came too late to save Gallatin.
To him the change brought only an increase of annoyance.
Although, as between Mr. Madison and Mr. Smith in the
controversy about the removal, the name of Gallatin was not
mentioned, the public well knew that the dismissal of Mr. Smith
was the work of the Secretary of the Treasury, and the chorus
of newspapers, led by the Aurora, joined in a cry of savage
hostility against him. His course in regard to the bank had
necessarily thrown a considerable portion of the press and the
party into antagonism; Pennsylvania had long since abandoned
him; Virginia now threw him over. The confidence of Mr.
Madison and his own supereminent qualities alone sustained
him. All this was notorious, and was little calculated to diminish
the zeal of personal enmity. Duane's attacks were in themselves
not formidable; his long articles of financial and political criticism were impressive only to the very ignorant; his colossal and
audacious untruthfulness was evident to any intelligent reader,
and had been evident ever since the Aurora had begun its existence; but nevertheless their effect was serious from the fact that
they operated in a way perhaps not intended or fully understood by Duane himself. In discussing the next Presidential
election, for example, the Aurora said:[1] "We are at present
led into these considerations in consequence of the assertions of
certain adherents of Mr. Gallatin, namely, 'that this gentleman
possesses more talents than all the other officers in the Administration put together, including Mr. Madison himself; that Mr.
Madison could not stand, nor the executive functions of the
government be performed, without him.' This is verbatim the
language that is held forth at present. Now, what do these assertions amount to? Why, clearly, that Mr. Gallatin is, to all
intents and purposes, the President, and even more than President of the United States." "This comes from the particular
friends of the Secretary of the Treasury,—can it be true? It is
a fact that the people of the United States, in nominally electing
Mr. Madison President, have in reality placed Mr. Gallatin in
that high station. . . . It is said Mr. Gallatin aspires to the

---

[1] 8th April, 1811.

Presidency himself, but that we do not believe; no man knows better the impracticability of such a desire than himself; but if those assertions of Mr. Gallatin's friends are true, it cannot be so much an object to him, since the salary is very little compared with the profits to be made by the Treasury." Then comes the inevitable "extract of a letter from a gentleman of high standing" in New York to Dr. Leib: "The events at Washington have not at all surprised me; nay, they were such as I had been looking for for some time, knowing the ascendency which Gallatin had acquired over the mind of Mr. Madison, and knowing too the secret and invisible agency which was operating to produce it and to keep this crafty Genevan in place." Under the form of an allegory the same idea is intensified :[1] "He was a man of singular sagacity and penetration; he could read the very thoughts of men in their faces and develop their designs; a man of few words; made no promises but to real favorites that would help him out at a dead lift, and ever sought to enhance his own interest, power, and aggrandizement by the most insatiate avarice on the very vitals of the unsuspecting nation."

The charges of embezzlement and wholesale speculation in public lands, of immense wealth and limitless corruption, were probably harmless; they affected only the groundlings; but the insidious elevation of Mr. Gallatin, the displaying him as an irresistible magician whose touch was superhuman; the ascribing to him every power and every act that emanated from government, and the concentration upon him of the whole blaze of attack, destroyed his usefulness by indirection. No man can afford to stand in this attitude; it creates jealousies, estranges precisely the men of force and character who value their own independence, exposes to the attacks and obstructions of those who wish to be known by the greatness of their enmities, and in a manner stifles direct and warm co-operation. In such cases every newspaper, every Congressman, and every small politician thinks it necessary to protest that he is not under the alleged influence; that he is not afraid to oppose it; and that he holds a position of judicial

---

[1] 3d September, 1811.

neutrality. The Virginians thought it a matter of regret that Mr. Gallatin had not retired with Mr. Smith. Gallatin was fortunate if the men who disavowed him in public did not offer him an additional insult by assuring him in secret of their friendship.

" These repeated attacks are enough to beat down even you," wrote Judge Nicholson. And Mr. Dallas, in a letter dated 21st April, 1811, added : " If Mr. Jefferson and his powerful friends at Washington, in the year 1805, had not given their countenance to the proscriptions of the Aurora, the evils of the present time would not have happened. I do not say this by way of reproach, but to point out the true cause why no man of real character and capacity in the Republican party of Pennsylvania has the power to render any political service to the Administration. It rests with Duane and Binns to knock down and set up whom they delight to destroy or to honor. In the present conflict, so far as you are personally concerned, I see with pride and pleasure that the influence of Duane is at an end."

Even Mr. Jefferson was now obliged to choose sides. It is, perhaps, useless to expect that a public or private man will deal harshly with followers and flatterers ; Duane had served Jefferson well, and Jefferson clung to him as to a wayward child ; but now that Mr. Gallatin had at last forced the issue, Mr. Jefferson came to the President's support, and, stimulated by the blunt response of Wirt and the Richmond Republicans that Duane might go to the Smiths for money but would not get it from them, he wrote Duane a letter to say, with a degree of tenderness that seems to the cold critic not a little amusing, that the Aurora had gone too far and was to be read out of the party. This was well enough ; but the curb, as Mr. Dallas very properly said, should have been applied five years before ; the harm was done, and it made very little difference whether the Aurora were in opposition or not ; perhaps, indeed, it was already more dangerous in friendship than in enmity.

Mr. Gallatin himself was far from exulting over the fall of Robert Smith. There was something humiliating in the mere thought that he should have been pitted against so unsubstantial an opponent: there was a loss of power, an exhaustion of reserved force in the very effort he had been obliged to make. His success, if it were success, deprived him of freedom of action, tied him beyond redemption to the chariot of government, and took away his last means of escape from the humiliations his enemies might inflict. As he wrote to Judge Nicholson on the 30th May, a few weeks after the Cabinet crisis: "Notwithstanding the change, I feel no satisfaction in my present situation, and the less so because that circumstance has made me a slave. Perhaps for that reason I feel an ineffable thirst for retirement and obscurity." Further Cabinet changes were imminent. Dr. Eustis, who had succeeded General Dearborn as Secretary of War, was unequal to the growing responsibilities of the office. Among prominent Republicans the only conspicuous candidate for the place was General Armstrong, just returned from France, one of the Clinton family, whom Mr. Gallatin always disliked, and who cordially returned the sentiment. There could be no real harmony between Mr. Gallatin and General Armstrong. Meanwhile, Justice Chase of the Supreme Court was dead, and the Attorney-General, Rodney, wished to be appointed to the bench. Mr. Madison passed him over to appoint Gabriel Duval, of Maryland; he resigned, and William Pinkney, recently minister to England, took the post of Attorney-General. The following letters of Mr. Dallas show the discontent aroused by these changes:

A. J. DALLAS TO GALLATIN.

24th June, 1811.

DEAR SIR,—I do not know the arrangements to fill the vacancy occasioned by the death of Judge Chase. I do not wish to suggest any name from personal feelings. But perhaps it may be useful that you should know that Mr. Ingersoll would accept the appointment, as far as I can infer from his conversations during the vacancy occasioned by Judge Cushing's death.

Do you not think Pennsylvania entitled to some notice? Everybody else seems to think so.

Private and confidential: if such a thing can be.

24th July, 1811.

DEAR SIR,—I wrote to you respecting the vacancy on the bench of the Supreme Court. I have, perhaps, no right to expect an answer in these times. But reports are so strange upon the succession to Judge Chase that I beg you explicitly to understand the sense of the Pennsylvania profession, Federal, Republican, Quid, and Quadroon. We do not think that the successor named in the public prints is qualified in any respect for the station. I care not who is appointed, provided he is fit in talents, in experience, and in manners; but, for Heaven's sake, do not make a man a judge merely to get rid of him as a statesman.

Poor Pennsylvania! Except yourself, who has been distinguished by Federal favor? Local offices must have local occupants; but from the commencement of the Federal government, and particularly from the commencement of the Republican Administration, what citizen of Pennsylvania has been invited by the Executive to share in Federal honors? There are the exceptions of Judge Wilson and Mr. Bradford, appointed by President Washington; but they are merely exceptions to my remark.

Look at the judiciary establishment! There are seven judges. Four reside on the south of the Potomac. Two reside in Virginia. The Attorney-General resides in Delaware. For the whole region beyond the Potomac, north-east, there are two judges. The report states that another judge is to be taken from Delaware, and an Attorney-General from Maryland!

I am cordially attached to the whole Administration. Of you personally I only think and speak as of a brother. But really, knowing that no confidence has ever been placed in me upon political subjects, and not knowing where your confidence is now placed, I do not understand your measures, nor am I acquainted with your friends. It is not the puff of a toast nor the flattery of a newspaper squib that can maintain the Republican cause or vindicate the Administration from reproach. A free press is an excellent thing, but a newspaper government is the most execrable of all things.   The use of the press is to give information; its abuse is to impose the law upon private feeling and public sentiment.   Do, therefore, think less of the denunciations of Duane and of the blandishments of Binns, and let your friends *know* that you act right, in order that they may *think* so.[1]

This letter I have a strong inclination to address to Mrs. Gallatin; for as men have ceased to keep secrets, I hope it will cease to be a wonder that a lady should keep them.   But I will content myself with requesting you to tell her that if there is a

---

[1] Mr. J. Q. Adams, in the year 1820, commented upon Pennsylvania politics in his Diary (vol. v. p. 112): "Pennsylvania has been for about twenty years governed by two newspapers in succession; one, the Aurora, edited by Duane, an Irishman, and the other, the Democratic Press, edited by John Binns, an Englishman.   Duane had been expelled from British India for sedition, and Binns had been tried in England for high treason. They are both men of considerable talents and profligate principles, always for sale to the highest bidder, and always insupportable burdens, by their insatiable rapacity, to the parties they support.   With the triumph of Jefferson in 1801, Duane, who had contributed to it, came in for his share, and more than his share, of emolument and patronage.   With his printing establishment at Philadelphia he connected one in this city; obtained by extortion almost the whole of the public printing, but, being prodigal and reckless, never could emerge from poverty, and, always wanting more, soon encroached upon the powers of indulgence to his cravings which the heads of Departments possessed, and quarrelled both with Mr. Madison and Mr. Gallatin for staying his hand from public plunder.   In Pennsylvania, too, he contributed to bring in McKean, and then labored for years to run him down; contributed to bring in Snyder, and soon turned against him. Binns in the mean time had come, after his trial, as a fugitive from England, and had commenced editor of a newspaper.   Duane had been made by Mr. Madison a colonel in the army; and as Gibbon the captain of Hampshire militia says he was useful to Gibbon the historian of the Roman Empire, so Duane the colonel was a useful auxiliary to Duane the printer, for fleecing the public by palming upon the army at extravagant prices a worthless compilation upon military discipline that he had published.   But, before the war with England was half over, Duane had so disgusted the army and disgraced himself that he was obliged to resign his commission, and has been these seven years a public defaulter in his accounts to the amount of between four and five thousand dollars, for which he is now under prosecution.   Snyder, assailed by Duane, was defended by Binns, who turned the battery against him, and finally ran down the Aurora so that it lost all influence upon public affairs."

special session of Congress, Mrs. Dallas and M. . . . will visit Washington.

Had Mr. Gallatin controlled the action of the Executive, he would long since have thrown Duane into open opposition, where he would have been harmless. Duane was simply a blackguard, of a type better understood now than then. That he had good qualities is evident from the descendants he left behind him, but these qualities had not been trained to excellence. The only way to deal with him was the direct way, and the only argument he would listen to was the coarse argument of the truth. From the first, however, both Mr. Jefferson and Mr. Madison sacrificed their Secretary of the Treasury to this profligate adventurer, whom they conciliated, flattered, persuaded, argued with, and supported by public and private aid. On this subject Mr. Gallatin never opened his lips; the letter of Mr. Dallas, quoted above, shows that even to him, his oldest and most intimate political friend, he never mentioned it. He even submitted to bear, without reply, the sharp criticisms of Mr. Dallas on his own silence, and reflections manifestly unjust. That the manner of Mr. Jefferson and Mr. Madison towards Duane cut deeply into the susceptibilities of Mr. Gallatin is certain; but, with the exception of one single expression, he never by word or sign intimated his sense of the indignity he felt himself to be receiving at their hands. His loyalty to his chiefs was too entire to be shaken for so mean a cause.

With this wound incessantly smarting at his heart; with all his great schemes and brilliant hopes of administrative success shattered into fragments; with a majority of bitter personal enemies in the Senate eager to obstruct every inch of his path; with a great part of his administrative machinery snatched out of his hands, and utter financial confusion around him; with a war against the richest and most powerful nation in the world staring him in the face, and almost certain domestic treason behind; with his own expedients invariably defeated, and with the most contemptible and shifting experiments in politics forced into his hands, Mr. Gallatin was now called upon to take up his burden again and march. He could not escape. Mr. Madison's friendship.

when forced to the final test, proved true, and Gallatin was fettered by his own act.

Of his whole public life, the next year, which should be the most important, is the most obscure. He wrote none but public letters. He never recurred to the time with pleasure, and he left no notes or memoranda to explain his course. Much, therefore, must be left to inference, something may be drawn from scattered hints, and most must depend on the well-known traits of his character and his habits of thought.

The last Congress had, before adjournment, sanctioned the President's course in reviving the non-intercourse with England on the strength of the supposed revocation of the Berlin and Milan decrees by Napoleon. The Administration party, in doing this, took the ground that the act was the necessary result of a contract with France already carried into effect by her. Thus the United States took one more step towards war with England by precluding herself from acting in any other direction than as the Emperor wished; even the most flagrant deception on his part could not shake the compact so far as America was concerned. For the wholesale robbery committed on American property in Europe by the Emperor's order, the United States mildly asked compensation. At about the same time Russia, then on the friendliest terms with France, directed her minister at Paris to intercede in favor of a similar claim on the part of Denmark. To Count Romanzoff's representation Bonaparte only replied: "Give them a very civil answer: that I will examine the claim, et cetera; mais on ne paye jamais ces choses-là, n'est-ce. pas?"[1] The American claim had small chance of success, but perhaps all that, under the circumstances, it deserved. On the other hand, all the events of the summer tended to war with England. Mr. Foster, the new British minister, instead of lessening the conditions of repeal of the orders in council, increased them. The British Court of Admiralty resumed its sweeping condemnations. The affair of the Chesapeake was at last settled by Mr. Foster, but the British sloop-of-war Little Belt was fired upon and nearly sunk by the United States frigate

---

[1] Gallatin's Writings, ii. 490.

President; and, what was of far more consequence than all this, the people of the United States, more especially in the south and west, and the younger generation, which cared little for old Jeffersonian principles, were at last in advance of their government and ready for war. Henry Clay, John C. Calhoun, Langdon Cheves, William Lowndes, Felix Grundy, the leaders of the new sect, were none of them more than thirty-five years of age at this time, or about the age at which Mr. Gallatin had entered Congress more than fifteen years before.

The President and his Cabinet did not want war, but, if the people demanded it, they were not disposed to resist. Mr. Madison would not allow his Administration to fall behind the public feeling in its assertion and maintenance of national dignity; nevertheless, Mr. Madison seems at this moment to have had only a very vague conception of what he himself did want. Although he had a superfluity of only too good causes for war with Great Britain, he allowed himself to be hoodwinked by France into an untenable statement of his case against the British government. He then called Congress together on the 4th November, which was hardly a peace measure. Possibly he underestimated the temper of that body, for his message, sent in on the 5th November, 1811, though high in tone, did not recommend war; it recommended that "a *system* of more ample provisions for maintaining" national rights should be provided; it recommended Congress to put the country "into an armor and an attitude demanded by the crisis," namely, the filling up the regular army, providing an auxiliary force, volunteer corps and militia detachments, and organizing the militia; but government had urged nearly all this for years past. Yet on the 15th November, only ten days later, Mr. Madison fully understood the situation, for he wrote to Europe that, as between submission and hostilities, Congress favored the latter, though it would probably defer action till the spring.

Mr. Gallatin's report, which was sent in on the 25th November, was equally cautious. For the past year the Treasury showed a surplus of over $5,000,000, owing to the large importations under the system of open trade previous to February, 1810; but for the next year the estimated expense of increased armaments and the diminished receipts under the non-intercourse with England would cause a deficit of over one million dollars and necessitate a loan.

The public debt of the United States extinguished between the 1st April, 1801, and the 31st December, 1811, amounted to the sum of $46,022,810, and there remained on the 1st January, 1812, $45,154,189 of funded debt, bearing an annual interest of $2,222,481. This represents all that was directly accomplished by Mr. Gallatin towards his great object of the extinction of debt. This result had been accompanied by the abandonment of the internal taxes and the salt tax, but also by the imposition of the $2\frac{1}{2}$ per cent. ad valorem duties known as the Mediterranean Fund. "It therefore proves decisively," said the report, "the ability of the United States with their ordinary revenue to discharge in ten years of peace a debt of forty-two millions of dollars; a fact which considerably lessens the weight of the most formidable objection to which that revenue, depending almost solely on commerce, appears to be liable. In time of peace it is almost sufficient to defray the expenses of a war; in time of war it is hardly competent to support the expenses of a peace establishment. Sinking at once under adverse circumstances from fifteen to six or eight millions of dollars, it is only by a persevering application of the surplus which it affords in years of prosperity to the discharge of the debt, that a total change in the system of taxation, or a perpetual accumulation of debt, can be avoided."

The report went on to discuss the provision to be made for ensuing years. The present revenue, under existing circumstances, was estimated at $6,600,000; the expenditure at $9,200,000. To provide for the deficiency an addition of fifty per cent. to the existing duties on imports would be required, and was preferable to any internal tax. "The same amount of revenue would be necessary, and, with the aid of loans, would, it is believed, be sufficient in case of war." By inadvertence, Mr. Gallatin made here an important omission. He was speaking only of "fixed revenue," sufficient to defray the ordinary expenses of government; and, as he was afterwards obliged to explain, this expression was wrongly applied to the case of war. He omitted to add that with each loan, provision to meet its interest must be made by increasing taxation; this fact had already been pointed out in the financial paragraph of the President's message, quoted in a previous part of the report, but the oversight gave rise to subsequent sharp attacks upon the Secretary.

He then came to the question of loans, and expressed the opinion that in case of war " the United States must rely solely on their own resources. These have their natural bounds, but are believed to be fully adequate to the support of all the national force that can be usefully and efficiently employed;" but it was to be understood that if the United States wished to borrow money it must pay for it: " It may be expected that legal interest will not be sufficient to obtain the sums required. In that case the most simple and direct is also the cheapest and safest mode. It appears much more eligible to pay at once the difference, either by a premium in lands or by allowing a higher rate of interest, than to increase the amount of stock created, or to attempt any operation which might injuriously affect the circulating medium of the country;" and he proceeded to show that " even" if forty millions were borrowed, the difference between paying eight and six per cent. would be only $800,000 a year until the principal was reimbursed.

These were the chief points of the report, and taken with the tone of the message they indicate clearly enough that the Administration, now as heretofore, whatever the private feelings of its members might be, was prepared to accept any distinct policy which Congress might lay down. One of the main grounds of attack upon Mr. Gallatin was that he had habitually alarmed the public with the poverty of the Treasury, and by doing so had checked energetic measures of defence. The charge was so far true that Mr. Gallatin had never concealed or attempted to color the accounts of the Treasury. On this occasion he probably aimed, as was always his habit, at furnishing Congress with as favorable an estimate as the truth would permit, with a view to obtaining united and cordial co-operation between the Executive and Congress. His only mistake was in accepting the estimates of war expenditure then current. He himself could not wish for war, and still hoped to avoid it; he knew that the Treasury, in its present situation, could not stand the burden, but he had suffered too much from the charge of attempting to direct legislation, to allow of his again exposing himself to it without necessity.

The President and the Secretary of the Treasury were therefore in perfect accord; they did not recommend war, but they recommended immediate and energetic preparation. The President advised Congress to provide troops; the Secretary recommended increased taxes and a loan of $1,200,000, to pay these troops and support them. This was the extent of their recommendations, and it remained for Congress to act.

Congress did indeed act; within a very short time it was clear that Mr. Madison had no control over its proceedings. To Mr. Gallatin the action of Congress was merely a sign that, as his influence in the Senate had long since vanished, his influence in the House had now followed it, and that for the future he could expect no friendly co-operation from the Legislature. At first, indeed, the proceedings of both bodies were in outward accord with the Executive recommendations; the reports of committees, and the House bill introduced in pursuance of them, were such as Mr. Madison had suggested; the only warlike measure proposed was that of permitting merchant vessels to arm. The Senate, however, very soon returned to its old tactics. Mr. Madison, as was well understood, asked only for an army of ten thousand men, and his recommendations were referred to a committee, of which Mr. Giles was the chairman, who immediately reported a bill for raising twenty-five thousand men, and in a speech on the 17th December fairly took the ground that his principal motive was to annoy the Secretary of the Treasury. Mr. Giles declared himself a friend of peace; no man more deprecated war; but " if war should now come, it would be in consequence of the fatal rejection of the proposed measures of preparation for war." The only reason for rejecting them he averred to be " the decrepit state of the Treasury and the financial fame of the gentleman at the head of that Department." He launched into a bitter attack upon Mr. Gallatin, thoroughly in the spirit of Duane and the Aurora. Considering that he was playing with such tremendous interests, and that the national existence, to say nothing of private life and fortune, was dancing on the edge of this precipice of war at the mercy of Mr. Giles's personal malignity towards Mr. Gallatin, Mr. Madison, and Mr. Monroe, there is actually something dramatic and almost classic in the taunts he now flung out. "Until now the honorable Secretary has had no scope for the demonstration of his splendid financial talents." "If, then, reliance can be placed upon his splendid financial talents, only give them scope for action; apply them to the national ability and will." "All the measures which have dishonored the nation during the last three years are in a great degree attributable to the indisposition of the late and present Administration to press on the Treasury Department and to disturb the popularity and repose of the gentleman at the head of it." In order to give sufficient occupation to the splendid financial talents of the Secretary of the Treasury, Mr. Giles had done all that was in his power to do; he had thwarted every plan of policy; wasted every dollar of money; struck from the hands of government every resource and every financial instrument he could lay hold on; and all this was not enough. The Secretary still had reputation; he had popularity; he had, if not repose, at least dignity. The Senator from Virginia was equal to the occasion; there are few oratorical taunts on record which echo more harshly than this, that as yet "the Secretary has had no scope for the demonstration of his splendid financial talents;" war alone could do those talents justice, and war the Secretary should have.

Mr. Giles carried his bill through the Senate; Clay and Lowndes carried it through the House. The war spirit meanwhile was rapidly rising; resolutions poured in from the State Legislatures; Congress hurried into further measures. What Mr. Madison thought of these is shown in a letter of his to Mr. Jefferson, dated February 7, 1812: "The newspapers give you a sufficient insight into the measures of Congress. With a view to enable the Executive to step at once into Canada, they have provided, after two months' delay, for a regular force, requiring twelve to raise it, on terms not likely to raise it at all for that object. The mixture of good and bad, avowed and disguised

29

motives accounting for these things, is curious enough, but not to be explained in the compass of a letter."

Although Mr. Gallatin had lost his old control in the House, he still preserved his influence with the Committee of Ways and Means and its chairman, Ezekiel Bacon, of Massachusetts. To this committee the annual report of the Secretary of the Treasury was referred, and when it became clear that war was really imminent, the committee, early in December, requested Mr. Gallatin to appear before them to discuss the question of war taxes. Mr. Gallatin at once complied, and gave his opinions explicitly and emphatically: "I do not," said he, "feel myself particularly responsible for the nation being in the position in which it now finds itself; it might perhaps have been avoided by a somewhat different course of measures, or the ultimate issue longer deferred. But, placed as it is, I see not how we can now recede from our position with honor or safety. We must now go on and maintain that position with all the available means we can bring to bear on the enemy whom we have selected, and we should in my judgment resort immediately to a system of taxation commensurate with the objects stated in my annual report and by the President in his message at the opening of the session." [1] Very soon afterwards, on December 9, the committee, through its chairman, wrote Mr. Gallatin a letter asking for a written statement of his views, and a month later Mr. Gallatin sent in a paper, which was to all intents and purposes a war budget.

This was a remarkable—for Mr. Gallatin's calm temper, almost a defiant—document, written, said Mr. Bacon, "to the great disobligement, as we had reason to know, of some of his strong political friends at that time," and intended to force Congress into an honest performance of its financial duties. This intent was marked by a defence of his own course which could not but read as a severe criticism of the course pursued by Congress.

"It was stated," said Mr. Gallatin, "in the annual report of December 10, 1808, that 'no internal taxes, either direct or in-

---

[1] Letter of Ezekiel Bacon, dated 24th October, 1845, published in the New York Courier and Enquirer.

direct, were contemplated even in the case of hostilities carried against the two great belligerent powers;' an assertion which renders it necessary to show that the prospect then held out was not deceptive, and why it has not been realized.

"The balance in the Treasury amounted at that time to near fourteen millions of dollars; but aware that that surplus would in a short time be expended, and having stated that the revenue was daily decreasing, it was in the same report proposed 'that all the existing duties should be doubled on importations subsequent to the 1st day of January, 1809.' . . . If the measure then submitted had been adopted, we should, after making a large deduction for any supposed diminution of consumption arising from the proposed increase, have had at this time about twenty millions of dollars on hand,—a sum greater than the net amount of the proposed internal taxes for four years.

"In proportion as the ability to borrow is diminished, the necessity of resorting to taxation is increased. It is therefore also proper to observe that at that time the subject of the renewal of the charter of the Bank of the United States had been referred by the Senate to the Secretary of the Treasury, nor had any symptom appeared from which its absolute dissolution, without any substitute, could have then been anticipated. The renewal in some shape and on a more extensive scale was confidently relied on; and accordingly, in the report made during the same session to the Senate, the propriety of increasing the capital of the bank to thirty millions of dollars was submitted, with the condition that that institution should, if required, be obliged to lend one-half of its capital to the United States. The amount thus loaned might without any inconvenience have been increased to twenty millions. And with twenty millions of dollars in hand, and loans being secured for twenty millions more, without any increase of the stock of the public debt at market, internal taxation would have been unnecessary for at least four years of war, nor any other resource been wanted than an additional annual loan of five millions, a sum sufficiently moderate to be obtained from individuals and on favorable terms."

Leaving Congress to reflect at its leisure upon the criticisms implied in these remarks, the Secretary went on to lay down the rules now made necessary by the refusal to follow his previous advice. After doubling the imposts and reimposing the duty on salt, he could promise a net revenue of only $6,000,000 for war times. The committee assumed that annual loans of $10,000,000 would be required during the war, which left an annual deficiency, to be provided for by taxation, amounting to $5,000,000, calculated to cover the interest of the first two loans only, after which additional taxes must be imposed to provide for the interest of future loans.

Five millions a year, therefore, must be raised by internal taxes, and Mr. Gallatin proposed to obtain three millions by a direct tax and two millions by excise, stamps, licenses, and duties on refined sugar and carriages. A few remarks on loans and Treasury notes closed the letter.

This communication startled the House, and even produced an excitement of no ordinary nature. Congress suddenly awoke to the fact that the Secretary was in earnest, and that, if war came, Congress must learn to take advice. The faction 'that followed Mr. Giles and General Smith were not quick in learning this lesson, and fairly raved against the Secretary. What so exasperated them may be gathered best from a speech by Mr. Wright, of Maryland, one of the most extreme of the Smith connection. On March 2, 1812, he spoke thus:

"Sir, at the last session, when the question for rechartering the odious British bank was before us, we had to encounter the influence of the Secretary of the Treasury. . . . Now at this session he has told us that, if we had a national bank, we should have no occasion to resort to internal taxes; thereby calling the American people to review the conduct of their representatives in not continuing that bank, and thereby to fix the odium of these odious taxes on the National Legislature. Now a system of taxes is presented truly odious, in my opinion, to the people, to disgust them with their representatives and to chill the war spirit. Yet it is, under Treasury influence, to be impressed on the Committee of Ways and Means, and through them on the House. Sir, I, as a representative of the people, feel it my duty to resist it with all my energies. . . . Sir, is there anything of originality in his system? No! It is treading in the muddy footsteps of his official predecessors in attempting to strap round the necks of the people this odious system of taxation, adopted by them, for which they have been condemned by the people and dismissed from power. . . . And now, sir, with the view of destroying this Administration; with this sentence of a dismissal of our predecessors in office before our eyes, a sentence not only sanctioned, but executed by ourselves, we are to be pressed into a system known to be odious in the sight of the people, and which, on its first presentation in a letter from the Secretary of the Treasury to the Committee of Ways and Means, and by them submitted to us, produced such an excitement in the House."

The "invisibles," however, were not the only class of men upon whom the war-budget fell with startling effect. Mr. Gallatin's old friends with whom he had acted in 1792, when at the unlucky Pittsburg meeting they had united in declaring "that internal taxes upon consumption, from their very nature, never can effectually be carried into operation without vesting the officers appointed to collect them with powers most dangerous to the civil rights of freemen, and must in the end destroy the liberties of every country in which they are introduced;" men like William Findley, his old colleague, were so deeply shocked at the reintroduction of the excise that they would not vote even for the printing of this letter. They looked upon Mr. Gallatin as guilty of flagrant inconsistency. They did not stop to reflect that, if inconsistency there were, it dated as far back as 1796, when, in his "Sketch of the Finances," Mr. Gallatin had taken essentially the same view of the excise as now;[1] and again in 1801, when he had refused to recommend the repeal of the internal taxes.

It was assumed that the Secretary of the Treasury could discover unknown resources; the Aurora dreamed of endless wealth in the national lands; but in point of fact this letter of Mr. Gallatin's erred only in calling for too little. He began by accepting the committee's estimate that loans to the extent

---

[1] See Writings, vol. iii. pp. 90, 91.

of \$50,000,000 would carry on a four years' war. The war lasted two years and a half, and raised the national debt from \$45,000,000 to \$123,000,000, or at the rate of somewhat more than \$30,000,000 a year, nearly three times the estimate. Had Mr. Gallatin foreseen anything like the truth in regard to the coming contest, his demand for resources would have appeared absurd, and he would have lost whatever influence he still had.

For once, however, Gallatin was master of the situation. He could not force his enemies to vote for the taxes, but he could force them to vote for or against, and either alternative was equally unpleasant to them. The honest supporters of war found little difficulty in following Mr. Gallatin's lead, but the mere trimmers, and the men who supported a war policy because the Administration opposed it, were greatly disturbed. Mr. Bacon brought in a report with a long line of resolutions, and seriously proceeded to force them through the House. Nothing, one would think, could have given Mr. Gallatin keener entertainment than to see how his enemies acted under this first turn of the screw which they themselves had set in motion. It was a sign that government was again at work, and that the long period of chaos was coming to an end; but the struggle to escape was desperate, and it was partially successful. At first, indeed, Mr. Gallatin carried his point. On the 4th resolution, for a tax of twenty cents a bushel on salt, the House rebelled, and refused the rate by a vote of 60 to 57, but the next day the whip was freely applied, and Mr. Wright and his friends were overthrown by a vote of 66 to 54. This settled the matter for the time, and the House meekly swallowed the whole list of nauseous taxes, and ordered Mr. Bacon's committee, on the 4th March, 1812, to prepare bills in conformity with the resolutions. This was done, but the bills could not be got before the House till June 26, when there remained but ten days of the session. As it was out of the question to get these taxes adopted by the House and Senate in that short time, Mr. Gallatin was obliged to consent to their going over till November. Congress, however, was quite ready to authorize loans, and promptly began with one of eleven millions, which, small as it was, Mr. Gallatin found difficulty in negotiating, even with the active and valuable assistance of Mr. John Jacob Astor, who now became a considerable power in the state.

The attitude of the Administration towards the war during the winter of 1811–12 seems to have been one of passive acquiescence. Nothing has yet been brought to light, nor do the papers left by Mr. Gallatin contain the smallest evidence, tending to show that Mr. Madison or any of his Cabinet tried to place any obstacle in the way of the war party. That they did not wish for war is a matter of course. Their administrative difficulties even in peace were so great as to paralyze all their efforts, and from war they had nothing to expect but an infinite addition to them. The burden would fall chiefly upon Mr. Gallatin, who knew that the Treasury must break down, and upon the Secretary of War, Eustis, who was notoriously incompetent. Yet even Mr. Gallatin accepted war as inevitable, and wrote in that sense to Mr. Jefferson.

GALLATIN TO JEFFERSON.

WASHINGTON, 10th March, 1812.

DEAR SIR,— . . . You have seen from your retreat that our hopes and endeavors to preserve peace during the present European contest have at last been frustrated. I am satisfied that domestic faction has prevented that happy result. But I hope, nevertheless, that our internal enemies and the ambitious intriguers who still attempt to disunite will ultimately be equally disappointed. I rely with great confidence on the good sense of the mass of the people to support their own government in an unavoidable war, and to check the disordinate ambition of individuals. The discoveries made by Henry will have a salutary effect in annihilating the spirit of the Essex junto, and even on the new focus of opposition at Albany. Pennsylvania never was more firm or united. The South and the West cannot be shaken. With respect to the war, it is my wish, and it will be my endeavor, so far as I may have any agency, that the evils inseparable from it should, as far as practicable, be limited to its duration, and that at its end the United States may be burthened with the smallest possible quantity of debt, perpetual taxation, military establishments, and other corrupting or anti-republican habits or institutions.

Accept the assurances of my sincere and unalterable attachment and respect.

Nevertheless there has always been something mysterious about Mr. Madison's share in causing the final declaration. This letter of Mr. Gallatin, dated March 10, shows that he already considered war to be unavoidable. On the 3d April, only three weeks later, Mr. Madison wrote to Mr. Jefferson that the action of the British government in refusing to repeal the orders in council left us nothing to do but to prepare for war, and that an embargo for sixty days had been recommended. The embargo was accordingly imposed, and on June 1 Mr. Madison finally sent in his message recommending a declaration of war against Great Britain, which took place on June 18.

The Federalist party, however, always maintained that Mr. Madison was dragooned into the war by a committee of Congress. The assertion is that the President, though willing to accept and sign a bill declaring war, was very far from wishing to recommend it, and that to overcome his reluctance a committee headed by Clay waited upon him to announce that he must either recommend the declaration or lose the nomination for the Presidency which was then pending; that he yielded; received the nomination on May 18, and sent in his message on June 1.

This story, openly told in Congress soon afterwards, and as openly and positively denied by Mr. Clay and his friends, has crept into all the principal histories, and in spite of contradiction has acquired much of the force of established fact. It has even been supported by an avowal of James Fisk, a prominent member from Vermont, that he was himself a member of the committee. The charge, such as it is, has been the principal stain on the political history of Mr. Madison, and also by consequence upon that of Mr. Gallatin, who, according to Mr. Hildreth,[1] "clung with tenacity to office" and "did not choose to risk his place by openly opposing what he labored in vain by indirect

---

[1] History, II. Series, iii. 334.

means to prevent," at a time when Mr. Gallatin would probably have been only too happy to find any honorable way of escaping from office.

The papers of Mr. Gallatin, like those of Mr. Madison and Mr. Monroe, are quite silent upon this subject. On the other hand, the papers of Timothy Pickering supply at least the authority on which the charge was made. The two following letters tell their own story, and, although they affect Mr. Gallatin's reputation only indirectly, they have a considerable negative value even for him.

TIMOTHY PICKERING TO ABRAHAM SHEPHERD.

CITY OF WASHINGTON, February 12, 1814.

DEAR SIR,—At the last autumn session, Mr. Hanson, noticing the manner in which the war was produced, in addressing Clay, the Speaker, spoke to this effect: " *You know, sir,* that the President was coerced into the measure; that a committee called upon him and told him that if he did not recommend a declaration of war, he would lose his election. And then he sent his message recommending the declaration."

Now, my dear sir, I learn from Mr. Hanson that Colonel Thomas Worthington, Senator, on his way home to Ohio, gave you the above information, and mentioned the names of Henry Clay, Felix Grundy, and some other or others who composed the committee. This is a very important fact, and I pray you will do me the favor to recollect and state to me all the information you possess on the subject; at what time and from whom you received it.

ABRAHAM SHEPHERD TO TIMOTHY PICKERING.

Near SHEPHERDSTOWN, February 20, 1814.

DEAR SIR,—I received your favor of the 12th instant, and observed the contents. Some time in the beginning of April, 1812, General Worthington came to my house from the city to see Mrs. Worthington and children set out for Ohio; he continued part of two days at my house, within which time we had considerable conversation on the prospect of war. He insisted war was inevitable. I condemned the folly and madness of such a measure. He then told me that Mr. Bayard would first be sent to England to make one effort more to prevent the war; that Mr. Madison had consented to do so; and that Mr. Bayard had agreed to go; that he had used every means in his power with some more of the moderate men of their party to effect this object, and that he had frequent conversations with Mr. Madison and Bayard on this subject before it was effected, and that I might rely upon it that such measures would be adopted. He left my house and returned to the city. After the declaration of war and rising of Congress, General Worthington, on his way home to the State of Ohio, called at my house and stayed a night. I then asked him what had prevented the President from carrying into effect this intended mission to England, and observed I was very sorry it had not been put in execution. He answered he was as sorry as I possibly could be, and that he had never met with any occurrence in his life that had mortified him so much. He said as soon as he returned to the city from my house he was informed of what had taken place by a set of hot-headed, violent men, and he immediately waited on Mr. Madison to know the cause. Mr. Madison told him that his friends had waited upon him and said, if he did send Mr. Bayard to England they would forsake him and be opposed to him, and he was compelled to comply, or bound to comply, with their wishes. I then asked General Worthington who those hot-headed, violent men were. He said Mr. Clay was the principal. I cannot positively say, but think Grundy was mentioned with Clay.

I clearly understood that Clay and Grundy were two of the number that waited on the President. I did not ask him how he got his information. As I understood the business, a caucus was held and Mr. Clay and others appointed, and waited on the President in the absence of Worthington, which will ascertain when this business took place.

Mr. Pickering seems to have thought that this explanation hardly supported the charge, and he discreetly allowed the subject to drop. So far, indeed, as the original charge was concerned, the letter of Mr. Shepherd entirely disposed of it, and proved that Mr. Hanson and Mr. Pickering had no authority for asserting that the President was coerced into sending the message of June 1, or that this message was the price of his re-nomination. On the other hand, Mr. Shepherd's statement raises a new charge against Mr. Madison. In his letter of 24th April, 1812, to Mr. Jefferson, the President said: "You will have noticed that the embargo, as recommended to Congress, was limited to sixty days. Its extension to ninety proceeded from the united votes of those who wished to make it a negotiating instead of a war measure," &c., &c. Of these Senator Worthington was doubtless one, for the substitution of "90" for "60" was made by the Senate on April 3, on motion of Dr. Leib, and Worthington voted for it. There was, then, a party in Congress which wished to use the embargo as a weapon of negotiation. It is not improbable that this party may have wished Mr. Madison to send a special mission to England, and that they may have pressed Mr. Bayard for the place. It is possible that Clay and his friends may have told Mr. Madison that in such a step he must not expect their support. This is all that can be now affirmed in regard to the celebrated charge that Mr. Madison made war in order to obtain a re-election.

Mr. Madison's Administration wanted energy and force. No one who is at all familiar with the private history of this party can escape the confession that the President commanded personal love and esteem in a far higher degree than obedience. Whether Senator Worthington counted Mr. Madison and Mr. Gallatin among the active supporters of his proposed peace mission does not appear, nor is there any clue to the other friends of that policy; but there can be little doubt that this was merely one of many suggestions with which the remnant of the old Jeffersonian democracy struggled in a helpless way to stem the current of the times. Mr. Gallatin's ears were wearied with the complaints and remonstrances of his friends, the Macons, the Worthingtons, the Dallases, the Nicholsons; and the strident tones of John Randolph echoed their complaints to the public. The President heard, but, both by temperament and conviction, followed the path which seemed nearest the general popular movement, without a serious effort to direct it or to provide for its consequences. Even Mr. Worthington believed war to be inevitable. Yet had they known that only the utter disorganization of the British government now prevented a repeal of the orders in council; had there been an American minister in London capable of seeing through the outer shell of politics and of measuring the force of social movements, war might even yet have been avoided. Nay, had Mr. Madison thrown himself at this decisive moment into the arms of the peace party; had he, on the 1st April, 1812, sent to the Senate, together with his embargo message, the nominations of Mr. Bayard and Mr. Monroe or Mr. Gallatin as special commissioners to England, the war could hardly have happened, for the commissioners would have found the orders in council revoked before negotiations could have been seriously begun.

This, however, Mr. Madison did not know, and, perhaps, even had he known it, the fate of John Adams might have seemed to his gentler spirit a warning not to thwart a party policy. His action was founded on the official utterances of the British government and the temper of our own people; it was perfectly consistent from beginning to end, and there was no disagreement in the Cabinet on the subject. It is true that until Congress met he was in doubt what course was best to pursue; his message did not directly recommend war; but from the moment Congress assembled and showed a disposition to support the national dignity, Mr. Madison and his Cabinet accepted the situation and needed no outside compulsion. To use his own words, as written down by a celebrated visitor in the year 1836, " he knew the unprepared state of the country, but he esteemed it necessary to throw forward the flag of the country, sure that the people would press onward and defend it." [1] He had been ready to do this in the winter of 1808–09. He had urged measures almost equivalent to

---

[1] WASHINGTON, 11th April, 1878.

MY DEAR SIR,—In March, 1836, I was the guest of Mr. Madison for several days. He knew the object of my visit, and kept me at his side during many hours of each day, sometimes starting topics, sometimes answering my questions and allowing me to take down his words from his lips in

war in every following session, so far as Congress would allow him to do so.   He had wished to maintain peace, but he had been quite aware that government must have the moral courage to resist outrage, as a condition of maintaining peace.   It is not to be denied that his party was far behind him, and that, as a consequence, the whole foreign policy from February, 1809, to June, 1812, was one long series of blunders and misfortunes.   France made a dupe of him and betrayed him into a diplomatic position which was, as regarded England, untenable.   To use his own words in a letter to Joel Barlow, his minister at Paris, dated August 11, 1812 : " The conduct of the French government . . . will be an everlasting reproach to it. . . . In the event of a pacification with Great Britain, the full tide of indignation with which the public mind here is boiling, will be directed against France, if not obviated by a due reparation of her wrongs.   War will be called for by the nation almost *una voce*."   But the diplomatic mistake did not affect the essential merits of the case, and the factiousness of Congress merely prevented the possibility of a peaceable solution.   Neither the one nor the other offers the smallest evidence of inconsistency in Mr. Madison or in his Cabinet.   Even Mr. Gallatin, to whose success peace was essential, had never wished and did not now wish to obtain it by deprecating war.

The real trouble which weighed upon the mind of Mr. Gallatin was not the war; he accepted this as inevitable.   His difficulty was that the government wanted the faculties necessary for carrying on a war with success, and that Mr. Madison was not the person to supply, by his own energy and will, the

---

his presence.   The memorandum annexed is, for the most part, in his own words, and committed to paper as they were uttered.

Ever yours,
GEORGE BANCROFT.

[Memorandum.]   March, 1836.—Madison was a friend of peace.   But he told me " that the British left no option ; that war was made necessary ; that under the circumstances of the negotiations with England war was unavoidable."   He further said, " he knew the unprepared state of the country, but he esteemed it necessary to throw forward the flag of the country, sure that the people would press onward and defend it."

deficiencies of the system.   Mr. Gallatin knew, what was known to every member of Congress and every newspaper editor in the land, that both the Navy and Army Departments were wholly unequal to the war.   With regard to the navy, this was of the less consequence, because the subordinate material was excellent, and our naval officers were sure to supply the lack of energy in their official head; yet even here the mere fact that Governor Hamilton wanted the qualities necessary to a Secretary of the Navy in war times diminished the confidence of the public and the vigor of the Cabinet.   In regard to Dr. Eustis and the War Department the situation was far worse; this had always been the weak branch of our system, for the army was wanting in very nearly every element of success derived from efficient organization.   Complete collapse was inevitable if the situation were prolonged.

The weight of government now fell almost wholly upon Mr. Monroe and Mr. Gallatin; it is believed that even the Act for the organization of the army at the beginning of the war was drawn up by Mr. Gallatin.   The Cabinet broke down first of all, and this helplessness of the War Secretaries, as they were called, has led to a strange mystification of history in regard to the first achievements of our navy in 1812.   Long afterwards, in the year 1845, Mr. C. J. Ingersoll published a history of the war, in which he dealt his blows very freely upon Mr. Madison and Mr. Gallatin, and charged them, among other things, with having meant to dismantle our frigates and convert them into harbor defences.   This attack drew a paper from Commodore Stewart, who gave another account of the affair.   His statement was that he and Commodore Bainbridge arrived at Washington on the 20th June; that on the 21st they were shown by Mr. Goldsborough, chief clerk of the Navy Department, a paper containing the orders, which had just been drawn, for Commodore Rodgers not to leave the waters of New York with his naval force; that on the same day the Secretary of the Navy informed them that it had been decided by the President and the Cabinet to lay up our vessels of war in the harbor of New York; that they had an interview with the President on the same day, in which the President confirmed this decision;

that on the 22d the two commodores presented a joint remonstrance; and that the subsequent orders, under which the vessels went to sea, were the result of this remonstrance. A letter of Mr. Goldsborough to Commodore Bainbridge, dated May 4, 1825, confirmed the fact of the joint remonstrance, and added some details in regard to the transaction.

This statement of Commodore Stewart drew from Mr. Gallatin a reply, which will be found in his printed Writings.[1] He asserted that he had no recollection of any such scheme for laying up the frigates; that he was confident no such Cabinet council was ever held as was referred to by Commodore Stewart; that the President, under the laws, had no power to make such a disposition of the navy; that Congress had never contemplated anything of the sort; and that the orders previously or simultaneously given contradicted such an idea.

His remarks upon the Secretary of the Navy, however, show the situation as it then existed: "Owing to circumstances irrelevant to any question now at issue, my intercourse with Mr. Hamilton was very limited. He may have been inefficient; he certainly was an amiable, kind-hearted, and honorable gentleman. From his official reports he appears to have been devoted to the cause of the navy, and I never heard him express opinions such as he is stated to have entertained on that subject. Yet his official instructions of 18th June and 3d July, 1812, to Commodore Hull, which I saw for the first time in Mr. Ingersoll's work, evince an anxiety bordering on timidity, a fear to assume any responsibility, and a wish, if any misfortune should happen, to make the officer solely responsible for it."

Mr. Ingersoll and Commodore Stewart, though in different ways, both in effect charged upon Mr. Gallatin this scheme of laying up the navy; it was, according to them, his influence in the Cabinet which had almost deprived the nation of its maritime glories. This is one of those curious echoes of popular notions which so often bias historians, and was founded partly on his old hostility to the navy, partly on his known indisposition towards the war. There was, in fact, no truth in it. Mr.

Gallatin has himself, in the paper quoted above, recorded his feelings about the navy at this time :

" For myself I have no reason to complain. Commodore Stewart, in mentioning my name, only repeats what he heard another say, and he ascribes to me none but honorable motives and opinions, which, as he believed, were generally those of the public at large. He says, indeed, that out of the navy he knew at Philadelphia but one man who thought otherwise. My associations were, however, more fortunate. From my numerous connections and friends in the navy, and particularly from conversations with Commodore Decatur, who had explained to me the various improvements introduced in our public ships, I had become satisfied that our navy would, on equal terms, prove equal to that of Great Britain, and I may aver that this was the opinion not only of Mr. Madison, but of the majority of those in and out of Congress with whom I conversed. The apprehension, as far as I knew, was not on that account, but that by reason of the prodigious numerical superiority of the British there would be little chance for engagements on equal terms, and that within a short time our public ships could afford no protection to our commerce. But this did not apply to the short period immediately subsequent to the declaration of war, when the British naval force in this quarter was hardly superior to that of the United States. The expectation was general, and nowhere more so than in New York, where the immediate capture of the Belvidere was anticipated, that our public ships would sail the moment that war was declared. In keeping them in port at that time the Administration would have acted in direct opposition to the intentions of Congress and to public opinion."

Commodore Stewart replied in rather indifferent temper to Mr. Gallatin's very mild statement,[1] but in doing so he printed the sailing orders of June 22, 1812. An examination of the Madison papers in the State Department at Washington also brings to light the following note, and by placing the note of Mr. Gallatin side by side with the sailing orders sent by the Secretary of the

---

[1] All these papers will be found in Niles's Register for 1845, and in the New York Courier and Enquirer.

Navy to Commodore Rodgers, it will be easily seen who was responsible for sending Rodgers to sea.

GALLATIN TO MADISON.

[No date. June 20 or 21, 1812.]

DEAR SIR,—I believe the weekly arrivals from foreign ports will for the coming four weeks average from one to one and a half million dollars a week. To protect these and our coasting vessels whilst the British have still an inferior force on our coasts, appears to me of primary importance. I think that orders to that effect ordering them to cruise accordingly ought to have been sent yesterday, and that at all events not one day longer ought to be lost.

Respectfully.

SECRETARY HAMILTON TO COMMODORE RODGERS.

NAVY DEPARTMENT, 22d June, 1812.

. . . For the present it has been judged expedient so to employ our public armed vessels as to afford to our returning commerce all possible protection. Nationally and individually the safe return of our commercial vessels is obviously of the highest importance, and, to accomplish this object as far as may be in your power, you will without doubt exert your utmost means and consult your best judgment. . . . Your general cruising ground for the present will be from the Capes of the Chesapeake eastwardly. Commodore Decatur, . . . having the same object in view, will, for the present, cruise from New York southwardly. . . . You are now in possession of the present views of the government in relation to the employment of our vessels of war. . . .

These two documents establish beyond question the curious fact that it was Mr. Gallatin who fixed the policy of the Administration in regard to the navy in 1812; that it was he who urged the President and the Navy Department up to their work; and that it was he who should have had the credit, whatever it may be, of sending Rodgers and Decatur to sea. These orders of June

22 were the actual cruising orders which settled the policy of the navy for the time, and took the place of temporary orders issued to Rodgers on June 18, in which he was directed to make a dash at the British cruisers off Sandy Hook and return immediately to New York.

In the face of these incontrovertible pieces of evidence, one is left to wonder what can have been the foundation for the circumstantial story told by Stewart and Bainbridge that they read on June 21, 1812, in the chief clerk's room at the Navy Department in Washington, orders which had just been drawn at the instance of Mr. Gallatin for Commodore Rodgers not to leave the waters of New York with his naval force; orders issued, as the Secretary of the Navy then and there explained, because it had been decided by the President and Cabinet, also at Mr. Gallatin's suggestion, to dismantle the ships and use them as floating batteries to defend New York harbor; and that the cancelling of these orders and the reversal of this policy were due to the vehement remonstrances of these two gallant naval officers, who won a victory in the President's mind over the blasting and fatal influence of Mr. Gallatin. It is a new illustration of the old jealousy between arms and gowns.

GALLATIN TO JOSEPH H. NICHOLSON.

WASHINGTON, 26th June, 1812.

DEAR SIR,—I am just informed that you are in Baltimore. If it be true that your Legislature has authorized the banks to lend a portion of their capital to the United States, can you ascertain what amount may be obtained from them all either by taking stock or by way of temporary loans reimbursable at the expiration of one or more years? We have not money enough to last till 1st January next, and General Smith is using every endeavor to run us aground by opposing everything, Treasury notes, double duties, &c. The Senate is so nearly divided and the divisions so increased by that on the war question that we can hardly rely on carrying anything. . . .

War being now declared, Mr. Gallatin was condemned to do

that which, of all financial work, he most abhorred; to pile debt upon debt; "to act the part of a mere financier; to become a contriver of taxes, a dealer of loans," and, in the inevitable waste of war, to be the helpless abettor of extravagance and mismanagement. These were not the objects for which he had taken office; they were, in fact, precisely the acts for which he had attacked his predecessors, had driven them from power, and appropriated their offices and honors, and no one felt this inconsistency more severely than Mr. Gallatin himself, although five years of painful effort and constant failure had taught him how feeble were party principles and private convictions in the face of facts. He was compelled to go on and to see worse things still. Every part of the administrative system, except one, collapsed. The war was miserably disastrous. The Act for raising 25,000 men had not become law until the 11th January, 1812; the selection of officers was not completed until the close of the year; the recruiting service was not organized in time; the enlistments fell short of the most moderate calculation, and the total number of recruits was so small as to make impossible any decisive movement on the line of Lake Champlain, although Montreal was almost unprotected. No sufficient naval force was provided on the Lakes, and in consequence an American army at Detroit was surrounded and captured by a mere mob of Canadians and Indians, who, inferior in every other respect to their opponents, had the inestimable advantage of a brave, energetic, and capable leader. Bad as this experience was, it hardly equalled the military performances at Niagara, where the commanding generals showed a degree of incompetence that descended at last to sheer buffoonery. The War Department in all its branches completely broke down, and if it had not been for the exploits of those half-dozen frigates whose construction had been so vehemently resisted by the Republican party under Mr. Gallatin's lead, the Navy Department would have appeared equally poorly. The control of the Lakes was in fact lost, and only partially regained in 1813; the whole gun-boat system, on which millions had been wasted, went to pieces; even the frigates were mostly soon captured or blockaded, and, but for the privateers, England, at the end of the war, had little to fear on the ocean. Amid this general collapse of administration, Mr. Gallatin might have found hope and comfort had Congress shown capacity, but Congress was at least as inefficient as the Executive. Nothing could induce it to face the situation; with the exception of an Act for doubling the duties on importations, it passed no tax law until more than a year after the declaration of war, and it was not till the public credit was ruined and the Treasury notes were dishonored that Mr. Dallas, then Secretary of the Treasury, succeeded in bringing the Legislature to double the direct tax, to increase the rate of the internal duties and add new ones, immediately before the peace.[1]

A thorough reorganization of the Executive Departments was necessary, and should have been undertaken by the President before the war was even declared, but energy in administration was not a characteristic of Mr. Madison. He hesitated, delayed, postponed, and at length, as in the case of Robert Smith, he was dragged at the heels of men and events. Hardly a month had passed since the declaration of war, and Congress had adjourned on July 6 to meet again on the 3d November; Mr. Gallatin had just started for New York to seek for money, and the President had set out for his farm at Montpelier, when an express arrived with the news that General Hull had surrendered Detroit. What Mr. Gallatin thought of this affair may be inferred from the following extract of a letter to his wife:

GALLATIN TO HIS WIFE.

WASHINGTON, 31st August, 1812.

. . . Hull has in unaccountable manner surrendered all his troops (about 1800) prisoners of war to an inferior force. We have no direct accounts from him, but the fear of Indians for himself and the inhabitants is the probable cause of his not having extricated himself by retiring and abandoning the country. Proper measures for repairing the loss will be adopted; but how they will be executed by Eustis, no one can say. . . .

---

[1] Gallatin's Writings, vol. iii. p. 538.

The disaster at Detroit made a change in the War Department inevitable, but the change was not yet made. Mr. Gallatin pressed it as necessary from a financial point of view. When he found that the army and navy estimates would require a loan of $21,000,000 for the year 1813, he wrote to the President as follows: "I think a loan to that amount to be altogether unattainable. From banks we can expect little or nothing, as they have already lent nearly to the full extent of their faculties. All that I could obtain this year from individual subscriptions does not exceed $3,200,000. There are but two practicable ways of diminishing the expenditure: 1, by confining it to necessary objects; 2, by introducing perfect system and suppressing abuses in the necessary branches. 1. In the War Department, to reduce the calls for militia, and, above all, to keep the control over those calls and other contingent expenses; in the Navy, to diminish greatly the number of gun-boats, and to strike off all supernumerary midshipmen, pursers, sailing-masters, and other unnecessary officers. 2. System requires skill in forming and decision in executing. But the preparing and executing such plans must rest almost exclusively with the heads of the Departments. I have no doubt that knowledge and talents would save several millions, and the necessary business be better done."

This letter was written towards the end of October, 1812. Already on the 11th of that month, as appears from a brief note written by Mr. Gallatin to the President,[1] some exchange of places had been suggested by Mr. Madison, perhaps between Eustis and Monroe, but the suggestion was condemned by Gallatin as more open to criticism than almost any other course that could be adopted. So far as can now be guessed, it is probable that Mr. Gallatin and Mr. Monroe wished to reorganize the Cabinet throughout; Mr. Monroe would then have become Secretary of War, Mr. Gallatin would have succeeded him as Secretary of State, and possibly William H. Crawford would have taken the Treasury; an arrangement which would have given great strength to the government and eliminated many

---

[1] Gallatin's Writings, i. 526.

causes of weakness. To this, however, Mr. Madison would not consent, probably from the belief that it would infalliby be defeated in the Senate. In this state of suspense the Administration stumbled on until the end of the year; then Dr. Eustis resigned of his own accord, and Mr. Monroe assumed temporarily the duties of his office, as he easily might, since the war had made the Department of State a sinecure. Governor Hamilton also resigned of his own accord, and immediate action by the President thus became necessary.

GALLATIN TO JEFFERSON.

WASHINGTON, 18th December, 1812.

. . . The series of misfortunes experienced this year in our military land operations exceeds all anticipations made even by those who had least confidence in our inexperienced officers and undisciplined men. I believe that General Dearborn has done all that was in his power. The conduct of Hull, Rensselaer, and Smyth cannot be accounted for on any rational principle. It is to be hoped that Mr. Eustis's resignation will open brighter prospects. For, although those three disasters cannot with justice be ascribed to him, yet his incapacity and the total want of confidence in him were felt through every ramification of the public service. To find a successor qualified, popular, and willing to accept, is extremely difficult.

It was just this moment that Mr. Josiah Quincy, hottest of all Federalists, chose for his once celebrated attack on the Administration: "It is a curious fact," he said, in his speech of 5th January, 1813, "but no less true than curious, that for these twelve years past the whole affairs of this country have been managed, and its fortunes reversed, under the influence of a Cabinet little less than despotic, composed, to all efficient purposes, of two Virginians and a foreigner. . . . I might have said, perhaps with more strict propriety, that it was a Cabinet composed of three Virginians and a foreigner, because once in the course of the twelve years there has been a change in one of the characters. . . . I said that these three men constituted to all efficient purposes the whole Cabinet. This also is notorious. It is true that during this period other individuals have been called into the Cabinet; but they were all of them comparatively minor men, such as had no great weight either of personal talents or of personal influence to support them. They were kept as instruments of the master spirits; and when they failed to answer the purpose, or became restive, they were sacrificed and provided for; the shades were made to play upon the curtain; they entered; they bowed to the audience; they did what they were bidden; they said what was set down for them; when those who pulled the wires saw fit, they passed away. No man knew why they entered; no man knew why they departed; no man could tell whence they came; no man asked whither they were gone."

In this description there was truth as well as oratory; but Mr. Quincy did not add that this despotism had been tempered by faction to an extent which had left in it very little of the despotic. Even while Mr. Quincy was charging the mysterious three with the design of making Mr. Monroe " generalissimo" in order to perpetuate their power, the three were in a quandary, as much perplexed as any of their neighbors, and actually deciding to accept General Armstrong as the least of their evils. Not one of them had any confidence in General Armstrong; they knew him to be no friend of theirs; to belong to a family—the Clintons—which had for twenty years or thereabouts acted without reference to them; one of whose chiefs, George Clinton, had, as Vice-President, given infinite annoyance to the Administration, while another, De Witt Clinton, had, within three months, run a mad race to get himself elected President by the Federalists in opposition to Mr. Madison; they knew that Armstrong had been through life a master of intrigue, and that his ambition was only checked by his indolence; but they knew that he had ability and that he had loyally supported the government. General Armstrong, therefore, became Secretary of War, while the Navy Department was given to William Jones, of Philadelphia, an active merchant and politician, who, in other days, had served as lieutenant under Commodore Truxton.

Meanwhile, Mr. Gallatin had in his own department cares enough to occupy all his energies. When Congress met in November, 1812, the House was still less disposed to support the Secretary than it had been in the spring. Langdon Cheves, of South Carolina, was now chairman of the Committee of Ways and Means. The Presidential election was over and Mr. Madison was secure in his seat, but the House had less appetite for taxation than before; it refused even to support the Secretary in other money measures. The first trial of strength, in which Mr. Gallatin was worsted, came in an embarrassing form. When the British government on June 23, 1812, revoked its orders in council, the declaration of war being then unknown in England, great quantities of British merchandise were at once shipped to America on the faith of the Act of Congress of March 2, 1811, which promised a renewal of intercourse whenever the British orders should be revoked. Even after the declaration of war became known, these shipments continued, protected by British licenses from British cruisers. All these vessels and cargoes were of course seized on arriving in American ports. The next step was to release such property as was owned in good faith by Americans, the Treasury taking bonds to the value of the cargoes, and, owing to the great rise in prices consequent on the war, the owners made very large profits, in some cases even to the whole amount of the bonds. Mr. Gallatin, unwilling to assume the responsibility of remitting or exacting the forfeitures, referred the subject to Congress, and in doing so expressed the opinion that in the peculiar circumstances of the case a reasonable compromise would authorize the remission of one-half the forfeitures, due to the collectors, and the exaction of the other half, or its equivalent, due to the government. The amount of property involved was about $40,000,000, including the importers' profit. Mr. Gallatin's proposition would have assumed a forfeiture to the amount of about $9,000,000. The regular duties, if the forfeitures were wholly remitted, would amount to about $5,000,000.

On this question there arose a sharp battle in the House, and Mr. Cheves led the Federalists in a vigorous assault upon the Secretary. Perhaps this attack was more honest and less spiteful than the attacks of Mr. Giles, but it was hardly less mischievous:

" I would rather see the objects of the war fail; I would rather see the seamen of the country impressed on the ocean and our commerce swept from its bosom, than see the long arm of the Treasury indirectly thrust into the pocket of the citizen through the medium of a penal law.   We might suffer all these disasters and our civil liberties would yet be safe.   That principle of our government would still be preserved which subjects the purse of the citizen to no authority but a law so plain that he who runs may read.   How are the exigencies of the government for the next year to be supplied?   That portion of them which is provided is rather the result of accident than forecast.   Is the deficiency to be derived from taxes?   No!   I will tell gentlemen who are opposed to them, for their comfort, that there will be no taxes imposed for the next year.   It was said last session that you would have time to lay them at this session, but I then said it was a mistake.   You now find this to be the fact.   By your indecision then, when the country was convinced they were necessary, you have set the minds of the people against taxes.   But were it otherwise, you have not time now to lay them for the next year."

Jonathan Roberts, of Pennsylvania, a member of the Committee of Ways and Means, led the debate in defence of Mr. Gallatin, but in the end Mr. Cheves, aided by the Federalists and by Calhoun, Lowndes, Macon, and other very honest men, carried his point, and the forfeitures were entirely remitted, by a very close vote of 63 to 61.   Mr. Gallatin's hold even on the Committee of Ways and Means was now lost.

At this point of the war, within four months of its declaration, the Treasury was threatened with a collapse more fatal than that which had overwhelmed the War Department.   The circulating capital of the United States was concentrated in the large cities chiefly north of the Potomac, and more than one-fourth of this capital belonged to New England.   Not only did New England lend no aid to the Treasury, but her whole influence was thrown to embarrass it.   Of loans to the amount of $41,000,000 paid into the Treasury during the war, she contributed less than three millions.   This was not all.   A large importation of foreign goods into the Eastern States, and an extensive trade in British government bills of exchange, caused a drain of specie through New England to Great Britain. The specie in the vaults of the Massachusetts banks rose from $1,700,000 in June, 1811, to $3,900,000 in June, 1812, and to $7,300,000 in June, 1814, all of which was lost to the government and the Treasury. Even the most prejudiced and meanest intelligence could now understand why the destruction of the United States Bank threatened to decide the fate of the war and of the Union itself. The mere property in the bank, important as this was, counted for comparatively little in the calculation, although seven millions of foreign capital, invested in its stock, were lost to the country by its dissolution and had been remitted to Europe shortly before the war. This was the "British gold" of which Mr. Giles and Mr. Duane were so jealous, and which, had it been allowed to remain, would have probably doubled the resources of the government in fighting British armies and navies, for, setting aside the useless wealth of New England, it is doubtful whether the country contained $7,000,000 in specie in 1812 as the basis of its entire currency system. This, however, was not the most serious loss. The State banks, with a capital of something more than $40,000,000, took up the paper previously discounted by the United States Bank, to the amount of more than $15,000,000. Then came the war, and Mr. Gallatin applied every possible inducement to borrow for government the means of the State banks. Those of New York, Philadelphia, and Baltimore responded to the call; they subscribed directly to the loans, and they enlarged their discounts to such of their customers as subscribed; in doing so they necessarily exceeded their resources and were obliged to enlarge their issues of bank paper. Meanwhile, in order to fill the chasm made by the dissolution of the United States Bank, new banks were created in the States; a bank mania broke out; in four years one hundred and twenty new banks were chartered, doubling the banking capital at a time when commerce was annihilated and banks were less needed than ever. They created no new capital and withdrew what would otherwise have been lent to the government. Governor Snyder, in Pennsylvania, was forced to veto a bill making a wholesale creation of new banks. Finally, since, in the absence of a national bank, the government had no means of controlling the issues, these rapidly increased to an amount greatly in excess of the requirements, until a suspension of specie payments and hopeless confusion of the currency became inevitable. This took place in 1814, and it was Mr. Gallatin's opinion, as it must be the opinion of every financier, that if the United States Bank had been in existence the suspension might have been delayed for a considerable time, while the terrible disorganization of the whole system of internal exchanges, by which the government was very nearly brought to a stand-still, need not have taken place at all.[1]

Had Congress been more tractable, something might perhaps have been done to alleviate the situation; but the Senate was utterly beyond control, and the House was becoming almost equally perverse. The expedient adopted by government fifty years later in the face of similar difficulties, even had it been now thought of, would have had little chance of general acceptance. Mr. Gallatin could get no action from Congress. His tax bills of the preceding session had been postponed on the understanding that they should be adopted before the 1st January, 1813; but, meanwhile, experience proved that these bills, violent as they had at first been thought, were quite unequal to the occasion, and that much stronger measures were needed. The five millions which had luckily fallen in, owing to the enormous British shipments after war was declared, helped to tide the Treasury over its immediate difficulties, but it helped also to encourage the inaction of Congress. Mr. Cheves did not contribute to smooth the path of the Treasury. He wished to force Congress to raise revenue by abandoning the non-importation system, which was still maintained as a coercive measure against Great Britain; this was also Mr. Gallatin's wish, but Congress refused its consent. Meanwhile, the tax bills were untouched. Month after month passed, and still nothing was done until the session closed on March 3, 1813, when, since it was universally conceded that these bills must be taken up, an extra session in May for this express purpose became necessary. All Congress would do, meanwhile, was to authorize loans, the favorite resource of incompetent financiers.

---

[1] See Gallatin's Writings, iii. 283, ff.

Many years later, Mr. Jonathan Roberts, who had been a member of this Congress, writing to Mr. Gallatin in the garrulity of age, recalled his recollections of the war. The letter is dated December 17, 1847, and seems to have been merely a spontaneous expression of old feelings. "When it was first my fortune to have met you," he wrote, "I found you to be a ripe and experienced statesman, possessed of the affectionate confidence of the most eminent and wisest among your compeers. You were only about ten years my senior, but immeasurably advanced above me in capacity for usefulness for that small disparity in years. In a very early period of our intercourse you gave me proofs of your confidence, of which I felt myself not unworthy, but which I had not been taught to look for from one who had so long mixed in state affairs. . . . While I witnessed an admiration of your character among enlightened and liberal minds, abundant evidences were not wanting of envy, jealousy, and even hatred. My sympathies were enlisted in your favor, and my indignation was roused in witnessing ebullitions of these detestable passions. You stood the friend of peace in the crisis pending the last war,—an attitude that called for the exercise of higher moral nerve than the opposite position; while our friends Madison and Macon, feeling with you, each in your places, fulfilled every duty with the honest purpose to seek for peace as the object they most desired.

"You can hardly fail to remember how Mr. Cheves acted towards you as chairman of Ways and Means, and how Colonel Johnson baffled every effort to report the tax bills. These men, too, gave their votes for an extravagant loan bill, which probably [no] man could have raised, even on the predicate of adequate taxes. At your suggestion I hastened to visit Governor Snyder, to give him your views of what would be the effect of the measure of the forty-one new banks on the prospects of raising loans. On meeting him I found he had negatived the bank bill, and it only remained for me to leave with him the views you had charged me with."

Mr. Gallatin's annual report in November, 1812, had been reticent in tone, perhaps because he was unwilling to discourage, and yet had nothing encouraging to say. He simply gave the condition of the Treasury and announced that a loan of twenty millions would be required. Congress authorized a loan of sixteen millions and the issue of five millions in Treasury notes; it would do no more; every other plan or suggestion of Mr. Gallatin or of the President was defeated or ignored.

Such was the situation when Congress adjourned on the 4th March, 1813. Mr. Gallatin then opened his loan. The Treasury was nearly exhausted; so nearly that on the 1st April it was absolutely empty, and must have ceased to meet the requisitions of the War and Navy Departments; the Federalists were in high hope that the loan would fail and government fall to pieces, and they made the most active efforts to force this result. The crisis was serious, and it was in this emergency that Mr. John Jacob Astor rendered to Mr. Gallatin and to the country essential aid; by his assistance Mr. Gallatin was enabled to make his terms with Mr. Parish and Mr. Girard, and thus three foreigners by birth, Mr. Gallatin himself being of foreign birth, saved the United States government for the time from bankruptcy, and perhaps from evils far more fatal; so, at least, the Federalists thought, and they long vented their wrath against these foreigners, as they called them, for an act which was certainly a somewhat bitter satire upon American patriotism.

Just at this moment the Russian minister, Daschkoff, communicated to the Secretary of State an offer of mediation on the part of the Emperor. His note bore date the 8th March, and in the situation of our government not only towards that of Russia, but towards the peace party at home, it had the gravest significance. There could be no hesitation in accepting the offered mediation, but there might be a question whether it were best to accept it before hearing from England. To show overeagerness for peace would weaken our position abroad; but the position abroad was of less consequence than union at home, and sluggishness in meeting peace propositions would stimulate every domestic faction. The President decided not to wait, but to send commissioners at once. Mr. Gallatin had now, by the end of March, disposed of his loan; he could easily arrange the affairs of his Department so as to admit of his absence, and he requested the President to let him go to Russia.

So many and so complicated are the influences which must have acted upon Mr. Gallatin's mind to produce this decision, that they are hardly to be set forth with any certainty of measuring their precise relative weight; yet there can be little possibility of error in assuming, as the most powerful, the conviction which had long weighed upon his mind that his usefulness in his present position was exhausted, and that Congress would do better, at least for a time, without him. So accustomed had Congress become to throwing upon him the burden and the blame of every measure, that nothing short of his retirement would break the spell which bound them, and so ineradicable were the enmities which neutralized all his efforts, that only his self-effacement could extinguish them. This he had long known, but the President's wishes had tied his hands. He could not desert the President or the country if his services were needed; but the situation had now become such as to create a serious doubt whether his services were not really more necessary abroad than at home. A year not yet quite elapsed had already brought the country into a position grave in the extreme; financial collapse and domestic treason were becoming mere questions of time; another campaign was inevitable, and it might fairly be reckoned that, if this were not successful, success was out of our power; diplomacy, therefore, had become the most important point of action next to service in the field, and in diplomacy Mr. Gallatin naturally felt that he had a brilliant future before him. Here he would escape from all his old difficulties and enmities; to Europe the Smiths, Duanes, Gileses, and Leibs would hardly care to follow him. The past was a failure; he might fling it away, and still rescue his country and himself by this change of career.

Mr. Gallatin grew more and more silent with age and experience; he never complained, and never said what was calculated to wound; but he had now stood for five years in a position inconsistent with his principles and grating to his feelings. In deciding to go to St. Petersburg he was well aware that he would be charged with having deserted his post, and charged by the same men who for four years had made it impossible for him to perform the duties of that post, and who still presented an

impenetrable barrier to every attempt on his part at efficient
administration. It is probably true that Mr. Gallatin himself
hoped not to return to the Treasury; if he returned at all, he
would have preferred the dignified ease of the State Department;
but these points he did not and would not attempt to settle in
advance; he left it absolutely in the hands of Mr. Madison to
decide for the public interest what disposition to make of his
services. There were two obvious contingencies; the one, in
case the Senate should insist upon his resignation as Secretary,
and, to obtain this, reject his nomination as commissioner; the
other, the case of diplomatic delays that might prevent his
return and compel the President to fill his vacant place: "Mr.
Bayard asked me," wrote Mr. Dallas in the following February, "whether you had reflected upon the first event as a
probable one, and you merely smiled when I repeated his
question to you." Mr. Dallas seems to have felt a little irritation at this reticence, but a sadder smile than Gallatin's
can hardly be imagined even among the Administration in
these trying times, although it may have been brightened by
a touch of humor at the thought how readily the Senate
would fall into that agreeable occupation, and how willingly
he would throw upon them that responsibility. In any case
it was not for him to direct the President's action; Mr. Madison himself could alone be the judge of what the occasion
required.

Of course it was fully in Mr. Madison's power to retain Mr.
Gallatin at his post. He too seems, however, to have been impressed with the advantages of sending him to Russia, and the
act was carefully considered and was his own. In the case of
negotiations taking place, America afforded no negotiator com-
parable to Gallatin; if he were willing to go, his presence would
be invaluable.

With Mr. Gallatin it was at last decided to associate Mr.
Bayard, of Delaware, so that the mission finally consisted of
Gallatin, J. Q. Adams, then Minister to St. Petersburg, and
James A. Bayard. Of course the most rapid action was neces-
sary; Mr. Bayard's appointment was only decided on the 5th
April, and Mr. Monroe then expected the vessel to sail with Mr.

Gallatin within a fortnight.   Fortunately, the necessary business of the Treasury was well in hand.   On the 17th April, Mr. Gallatin wrote a letter to the Secretaries of War and of the Navy, giving a general view of the fiscal situation for the year and regulating the drafts which these two Departments might make upon the Treasury, to the amount, namely, of $17,820,000, to January 1, 1814.   The tax bills were ready for Congress to act upon; a draft for a new bank charter was prepared and left behind; every contingency, as far as possible, was provided for.   Mrs. Gallatin and the younger children were to pass their summer as usual in New York, while the eldest son, James, accompanied his father as private secretary.

Before closing this part of Mr. Gallatin's history and turning to the new career which was to occupy nearly all his thoughts for sixteen years to come, the results of his sudden departure upon Congress and upon the Treasury shall be briefly told. Another extract from the letter of Jonathan Roberts already quoted will furnish an idea of the immediate effect of Mr. Gallatin's absence.   He sailed on May 9, and Congress met on May 23.   Mr. Roberts proceeds:

" At the called session in May following you had left the seat of government on the mission of peace.   I soon found, however, that you left nothing undone that made your presence necessary to forward the vital measure of adequate taxation.   You promptly responded to a call early made for a scheme of revenue that you deemed to embrace every item that could justify a levy and collection.   This was abundantly confirmed by Mr. Eppes's subsequent trial of watch-tax, &c.   Mr. E. was now made chairman of Ways and Means, but could not attend the committee from ill health, which both Dr. Bibb and myself thought fortunate for the early attainment of the object of the session.   To almost every item in your reported list objections were felt in the committee. Bibb himself disrelished a direct tax, but could not deny its indispensable necessity.   It was soon found there was no alternative.   No new project could be devised, and you were not present to be worried by calls for a modification.   The bills were reported; no opening speech was made, and no debate provoked. Dr. Bibb conducted the deliberations with successful address, but I then felt that your absence placed the tourniquet on Congress. Having finished your duties at home, you accepted the place in which you hoped to be most useful. . . . Your real friends felt the vacancy made by your absence, and hoped for and would have hailed your return to our home councils as a joyful event. Your place never has been, nor, I believe, never will be filled."

Before his departure Mr. Gallatin wrote three or four letters, which contain parting suggestions that, for his calm temper, express unusual feeling. One of these was to Mr. Monroe, dated the day before he sailed, to dissuade him from pushing the military occupation of Florida, for fear of a war with Spain, that would still more exasperate the Northern States. "You will pardon the freedom with which, on the eve of parting with you, I speak on this subject. It is intended as a general caution which I think important, because I know and see every day the extent of geographical feeling and the necessity of prudence, if we mean to preserve and invigorate the Union."

The letter to his brother-in-law, James W. Nicholson, explains the motives that influenced him, at least in part. General Armstrong had been at his old practices during the short three months he had controlled the War Department. The National Intelligencer for April 16 had contained the announcement that William Duane was appointed Adjutant-General in the United States army. All the love and esteem which Mr. Gallatin felt then and ever continued to feel for Mr. Madison could not overcome the disgust with which this last blow was received.

GALLATIN TO BADOLLET.

PHILADELPHIA, May 5, 1813.

DEAR FRIEND,— . . . The newspapers will have informed you of my mission to Russia. Whether we will succeed or not depends on circumstances not under any man's control. But on mature reflection, having provided all the funds for the service of this year, and having nothing to do but current business during the remainder, I have believed that I could be nowhere more usefully employed than in this negotiation. I hope that my absence will be very short, and leave all my family behind, James excepted.

Ever yours.

GALLATIN TO JAMES W. NICHOLSON.

PHILADELPHIA, 5th May, 1813.

DEAR SIR,—You have heard by the papers of my intended mission to Russia; but I have delayed to the last moment writing to you. Having provided all the funds for this year's service, and none but current business to attend to during its remainder, I have made up my mind that I could in no other manner be more usefully employed for the present than on the negotiation of a peace. Peace, at all times desirable, is much more so for two reasons: 1. The great incapacity for conducting the war, which is thereby much less efficient and infinitely more expensive than it ought to have been. 2. The want of union, or rather open hostility to the war and to the Union, which, however disgraceful to the parties concerned, and to the national character, is not less formidable and in its consequences of the most dangerous tendency. But in addition to those considerations I believe that the present opportunity affords a better chance to make an honorable peace than we have any right hereafter to expect. England must be desirous at this critical moment to have it in her power to apply her whole force on the Continent of Europe, and the mediation of Russia saves her pride; whilst both the personal feelings of the sovereign, a common interest on all neutral questions, and other considerations of general policy, give us the best pledge that a nation can obtain that the mediator will support the cause of justice and of the law of nations. Finally, provided we can obtain security with respect to impressments, peace will give us everything we want. Taught by experience, we will apply a part of our resources to such naval preparations and organization of the public force as will within less than five years place us in a commanding situation. This we cannot effect pending the war, and if this continues any length of time it will leave the United States so exhausted that they will not effect the same objects within the same period nor without oppressive taxation. To keep down the Tory faction at home and ultimately to secure in an effectual manner our national rights against England, peace is equally necessary. The Essex-Junto men and other high-toned Federalists of course fear it more than any other event, as they are well aware that a continuation of the war must necessarily place government in their hands before the end of four years.

Whether, however, we will succeed in making peace is another question, which depends on events not under our control. So far as relates to myself, I am well aware that my going to Russia will most probably terminate in the appointment of another Secretary of the Treasury, and in my returning to private life. If I shall have succeeded in making peace, I will be perfectly satisfied; and, at all events, I will acknowledge to you that Duane's last appointment has disgusted me so far as to make me desirous of not being any longer associated with those who have appointed him. . . .

The departure of Mr. Gallatin to Europe did not, however, at once close his career as Secretary of the Treasury, and it was not until a year later, on the 9th February, 1814, that he ceased to hold that office. Meanwhile, the Senate had exercised in its full extent that unrestrained liberty of personal attack which Mr. Gallatin had so contemptuously left to them. By a vote of 20 to 14 they rejected his nomination to Russia, on the ground that it was inconsistent with his station in the Treasury. Their true motive is not a matter of much importance; the oldest and wisest politicians are most apt to warn their younger associates not to search for the motives of public men, and this Christian precept rests on the general fact that human nature often, and nowhere oftener than in politics, opens into abysses of baseness only to be measured by baseness equally profound. The doctrine that the post of Secretary was incompatible with that of treaty commissioner was certainly new and astonishing as coming from a body which had twice confirmed the nomination of the Chief Justice to an identical situation; but, apart from its inconsistency, the new rule was wise and the result good. Perhaps, however, Senators would have shown more dignity in not proclaiming quite so loudly their eagerness to confirm Mr. Gallatin if he could be forced to leave the Treasury.

The following letters tell the story in all its nakedness:

MONROE TO JEFFERSON.

WASHINGTON, June 28, 1813.

DEAR SIR,—From the date of my last letter to you, the President has been ill of a bilious fever, of that kind called the remittent. It has perhaps never left him, even for an hour, and occasionally the symptoms have been unfavorable. This is, I think, the fifteenth day. Elgey, of this place, and Shoaff, of Annapolis, with Dr. Tucker, attend him. They think he will recover. The first mentioned I have just seen, who reports that he had a good night, and is in a state to take the bark, which, indeed, he has done on his best day for nearly a week. I shall see him before I seal this, and note any change, should there be any, from the above statement.

The Federalists, aided by the malcontents, have done and are doing all the mischief they can. The nominations to Russia and Sweden (the latter made on an intimation that the Crown Prince would contribute his good offices to promote peace on fair conditions) they have embarrassed to the utmost of their power. The active partisans are King, Giles, and (as respects the first nomination) Smith. Leib, German, and Gilman are habitually in that interest, active, but useful to their party by their votes only. The two members from Louisiana, Gailliard, Stone, Anderson, and Bledsoe are added to that corps on these questions. They have carried a vote, 20 to 14, that the appointment of Mr. Gallatin to the Russian mission is incompatible with his station in the Treasury, and appointed a committee to communicate the resolution to the President. They have appointed another committee to confer with him on the nomination to Sweden. The object is to usurp the executive power in the hands of a faction in the Senate. To this several mentioned are not parties, particularly the four last. A committee of the Senate ought to confer with a committee of the President through a head of a Department, and not with the Chief Magistrate; for in the latter case a committee of that House is equal to the Executive. To break this measure, and relieve the President from the pressure, at a time when so little able to bear it, indeed when no pressure whatever should be made on him, I wrote the committee on the nomination to Sweden, that I was instructed by him to meet them, to yield all the information they might desire of the Executive. They declined the interview. I had intended to pursue the same course respecting the other nomination had I succeeded in this. Failing, I have declined. The result is withheld from the President. These men have begun to make calculations and plans founded on the presumed death of the President and Vice-President, and it has been suggested to me that Giles is thought of to take the place of President of the Senate as soon as the Vice-President withdraws.

General Dearborn is dangerously ill, and General Lewis doing little. Hampton has gone on to that quarter, but I fear an inactive command. General Wilkinson is expected soon, but I do not know what station will be assigned him. The idea of a commander-in-chief is in circulation, proceeding from the War Department, as I have reason to believe. If so, it will probably take a more decisive form when things are prepared for it. A security for his, the Secretary's, advancement to that station is, I presume, the preparation desired.

Your friend.

I have seen the President, and found him in the state represented by Dr. Elgey.

THE SECRETARY OF STATE TO THE AMERICAN COMMISSIONERS.

DEPARTMENT OF STATE, 5th August, 1813.

GENTLEMEN,—I am very sorry to be under the necessity of communicating to you an event of which there was no anticipation when you left the United States. The event to which I allude is the rejection by the Senate of the nomination of Mr. Gallatin, on the idea that his mission to Russia was incompatible with the office of Secretary of the Treasury. After the appointment of Mr. Jay, when Chief Justice of the United States, by

President Washington, and of Mr. Ellsworth, when holding the same office, by President Adams, by which a member of a separate branch of the government was brought into an office under the Executive, and after the sanction given in practice as well as by law to the appointment of persons during the absence of a head of a Department to perform its duties, it was presumed that there would not be any serious or substantial objection to the employment in a similar service, for a short term and especial occasion, of a member of the Administration itself. Although this nomination was opposed in the Senate as soon as it was acted on, yet it was not believed that it would be rejected until the vote was taken. At an early stage the President was called on by a resolution of the Senate to state whether Mr. Gallatin retained the office of Secretary of the Treasury, and, in case he did, who performed the duties of that Department in his absence. The President replied that the office of Secretary of the Treasury was not vacated by Mr. Gallatin's appointment to Russia, and that the Secretary of the Navy performed its duties in his, Mr. Gallatin's, absence. After this reply, which was given in conformity with the President's own views of the subject, and with those of Mr. Gallatin when he left the United States, it was impossible for the President, without departing from his ideas of propriety in both respects, to have removed Mr. Gallatin from the Treasury to secure the confirmation of his nomination to Russia. It would have been still more improper to have taken that step after the rejection of the nomination. The President resolved, therefore, to leave the mission on the footing on which it was placed by the vote of the Senate by which the nomination of Mr. Adams and Mr. Bayard was confirmed. Whatever has been done jointly under the commission given to the three commissioners by the President when you left the United States in compliance with your instructions, will not be affected by this event.

MONROE TO GALLATIN.

WASHINGTON, 6th August, 1813

DEAR SIR,—To the official communications which you will receive with this I have little to add. Indeed, as I know that the President intends to communicate to you in a private letter all the details which could not be included in a public one, I should not write you this except that I could not permit Mr. Wyer to sail without bearing this testimony of my good wishes towards you.

The Senate has got into a strange and most embarrassing situation, of which the rejection of your nomination and of that of Mr. Russell are proofs; many others were afforded during the session. The attempt to control the President, or at least to influence his conduct by a committee of the Senate authorized to confer with him, thereby placing a committee on a footing with the Chief Magistrate and without limitation as to what it might say or demand, was a very extraordinary measure. It was the more embarrassing as the occurrence took place at a time when the President was confined with a bilious fever which endangered his life. The pressure gave him, as you will readily conceive, the greatest concern, more particularly the rejection of your nomination and the question which grew out of it, your removal from the Treasury to secure your confirmation in the mission to Russia. Among the objections to that step, the sentiments of those friends who supported your nomination were entitled to and had great weight. They thought that your removal from the Treasury would operate as a sanction to the conduct of your opponents and a censure on themselves. Other objections were strong, but this was conclusive.

I presume that the business on which you and Mr. Bayard left this country is settled by this time, or will be before you receive this letter. If Great Britain accepted the mediation with a sincere desire to make peace, the treaty would have been soon concluded. If she rejected it, a very short time would have enabled you to conclude a treaty of commerce with Russia. So that in either event we expect soon to have the pleasure of seeing you here.

With great respect and esteem, I am, &c.

MRS. MADISON TO MRS. GALLATIN.

29th July, 1813.

. . . You have heard no doubt of the illness of my husband, but can have no idea of its extent and the despair in which I attended his bed for nearly five weeks. Even now I watch over him as I would an infant, so precarious is his convalescence. Added to this are the disappointments and vexations heaped upon him by party spirit. Nothing, however, has borne so hard as the conduct of the Senate in regard to Mr. Gallatin. Mr. Astor will tell you many particulars that I ought not to write, of the desertion of some whose support we had a right to expect, and of the manœuvring of others always hostile to superior merit. We console ourselves with the hope of its terminating both in the public good and Mr. Gallatin's honorable triumph. . . .

A. J. DALLAS TO MRS. GALLATIN.

22d July, 1813.

MY DEAR MADAM,—Our friend Mr. Macon has just written to me that Mr. Gallatin's nomination has been rejected by a majority of one vote. I find from another quarter that Mr. Anderson and Mr. Stone voted against it.

I did not choose to tease you with the agitation of the subject while I was at Washington. The question turned upon this; if Mr. Madison would declare the Secretary's office vacant, the Senate would confirm the nomination; but he firmly refused to do so. The Federalists were very busy on the occasion; but the malcontent junto of self-styled Republicans were worse; and Armstrong,—he was the devil from the beginning, is now, and ever will be. In short, every art has been employed to defeat the mission, to ruin the Administration, and to depreciate Mr. Gallatin. In the last object the host of ill-assorted enemies will fail; but the political mischief that has been done and will be done is incalculable. . . .

J. J. ASTOR TO GALLATIN.

NEW YORK, 9th August, 1813.

DEAR SIR,—By this opportunity you will receive an account of the strange, if not wicked, proceedings of the Senate. The President has been led astray by some of its members in the belief of a majority in favor of the nomination and retaining you at same time as Secretary of the Treasury. He made this a point on which they split. I came to Washington some few days after the rejection had passed. It was well understood that if he would re-nominate with an understanding to appoint another Secretary, the nomination should be confirmed. It was evident that he was much at a loss; what from personal attachment to you, not knowing what might be your wish and your feelings, and what in the difference of opinion of your own friends, together with a natural dislike to yield to the Senate, he was in great perplexity and hesitation. My decided opinion was to have a nomination made, for, from a letter which you wrote to Mr. Worthington, I was clearly of opinion that you contemplated what would likely happen in the Senate; but many of your friends being entirely unacquainted with your ideas on this subject, there was a difference of opinion between them. I advised Mr. W. to tell Mr. Madison that he had such a letter from you, and to make it known to your friends, which if he had done in time, I believe the President would not have made it a point as he did. I mentioned to him of the letter, but it was too late, for he began to believe that in consequence of the armistice on the continent there would be no negotiation, and, not willing to part with you or to have you withdrawn from the Administration without your own desire, he determined to hold on as he did. He may be right, but I think I would have done otherwise. He certainly suffered much in mind on your account; but I think I should have let the public good take the lead. He may have many reasons which I know nothing of; your own feelings were certainly of weighty consideration with him. . . .

I wonder that you did not impart your ideas to some of your friends; no one, except Mr. Worthington, seemed to know anything about it. I wish I had known half as much, and I would have made use of it to effect. Though I might have run risk to displease you, I should have done good to the country, unless there be no negotiation, in which case you cannot return too soon. On every account you are wanting at Washington. . . .

W. H. CRAWFORD TO GALLATIN.

PARIS, 20th April, 1814.

DEAR SIR,— . . . The French papers of yesterday state that you are added to the commission to treat at Gottenburg. Mr. Beasley says that Mr. Adams is also of the commission. I cannot believe that all of you are to proceed to Gottenburg. If you are going, I presume it is in consequence of your having vacated your seat in the Cabinet. I hope this conjecture is unfounded. This is the course which your enemies wished to compel you to adopt. I agree that the treatment you have received would justify the measure, but when I know the gratification which Messrs. Giles, Smith, and Leib will feel from your resignation, I cannot reconcile it to my feelings. All this mischief has grown out of Brent's mobility or his thirst. The day before I left Washington I called on a number of the Senators and insisted on the danger of delay and urged them to decide the question before they adjourned. They decided every embarrassing question about 4 P.M., when Mr. Brent, as he says, out of complaisance to Mr. King, consented to let the nomination stand over till the next day. They had a decided majority, and Anderson, who voted against them on all the embarrassing questions, declared he would vote for the nomination. I have no doubt that he voted against it in the end. The desire to get Mr. Cheves into the Treasury had some influence upon two or three Senators. I told Mr. Madison that he would be pressed on that point. . . .

A. J. DALLAS TO GALLATIN.

14th February, 1814.

DEAR SIR,—If you receive this letter in Europe you will have an opportunity to hear from Mr. Clay and Mr. Russell all the public news of this country; and consequently it would be an unnecessary trouble both to you and to me to enter into a written detail. Your absence has embarrassed everybody. It is a subject of lasting regret that you did not confide to some friend your wishes respecting the course to be taken if the Senate should refuse to confirm your nomination as minister while you retained the office of Secretary, or if the business and casualties of the mission should protract your absence so long as to render it impracticable to keep the Treasury Department open for you.   Mr. Bayard asked me whether you had reflected upon the first event as a probable one, and you merely smiled when I repeated his question to you.   However, the arrangement is now made in the best manner to evince the President's attachment and the public confidence by restoring you to the mission when it became indispensable to treat the Treasury Department as vacant.   I do not believe that during any part of your public life you enjoyed more general respect and more valuable popularity than at the present crisis.   Indeed, your name being restored to the mission has revived the hope of its success, which failed when your name was excluded.   I look confidently to your return with additional claims to public gratitude and honors. . . .

Lovers of historical detail may without much difficulty pick from the wreck and ruin of Mr. Gallatin's administrative policy such fragments as survived their originator and became foundation-stones of the ultimate governmental system.   Many such fragments there were, and of the first importance, but it is not by them that Mr. Gallatin is to be measured.   No one has ever seriously questioned his supereminence among American financiers.   No one who has any familiarity with the affairs of our government has failed to be struck with the evidences of his pervading activity and his administrative skill.   His methods were simple, direct, and always economical.   He had little respect for mere financial devices, and he labored painfully to simplify every operation and to render intelligible every detail of business.   It may be doubted whether he ever made a mistake in any of his undertakings, and whether any work done by him has ever been found inefficient; but it is useless to catalogue these undertakings.   His system was not one of detached ideas or of parti-colored design.   As their scheme existed in the minds of Mr. Jefferson, Mr. Gallatin, and Mr. Madison, it was broad as society itself, and aimed at providing for and guiding the moral and material development of a new era,—a fresh race of men.   It was not a mere departmental reform or a mere treasury administration that Mr. Gallatin undertook; it was a theory of democratic government which he and his associates attempted to reduce to practice.   They failed, and although their failure was due partly to accident, it was due chiefly to the fact that they put too high an estimate upon human nature.   They failed as Hamilton and his associates, with a different ideal and equally positive theories, had failed before them.   Yet, whatever may have been the extent of their defeat or of their success, one fact stands out in strong relief on the pages of American history.   Except those theories of government which are popularly represented by the names of Hamilton and Jefferson, no solution of the great problems of American politics has ever been offered to the American people.   Since the day when foreign violence and domestic faction prostrated Mr. Gallatin and his two friends, no statesman has ever appeared with the strength to bend their bow,—to finish their uncompleted task.

BOOK IV.

DIPLOMACY. 1813–1829.

"9TH May, Sunday.—At 3 P.M. sailed from New Castle on board the ship Neptune, of 300 tons, Captain Lloyd Jones. We are in all 34 persons on board, viz., Albert Gallatin and James A. Bayard, ministers of the United States; George M. Dallas, George B. Milligan, John P. Todd, and James Gallatin, their secretaries; Henry Smothers, Peter Brown, and George Shorter, their black servants; Mr. Pflug, a Russian, and his black boy, Peter; Captain Jones, his two mates Tomlinson and Fisher, and William C. Nicholson, midshipman; Dr. Layton, a black steward, a white and a black cook, a boatswain, eleven able and three ordinary seamen. Rodney and Collector McLane accompanied us with the revenue cutter, in which they returned in the evening. Anchored at night near Bombay Hook.

"11th May, Tuesday.—Bore down for a British frigate. Fell to the leeward. She, being at anchor, sent her boat on board with a lieutenant and compliments from the captain to me, and that he would be glad to see me on board. This was perhaps intended as civility, but was of course declined, and we sent Dallas and Milligan on board with our compliments. Captain Jones went at the same time to show to the captain of the frigate Admiral Warren's passport, which the captain endorsed. His name is Braynton; the frigate's, Spartan, a 36 . . . The Spartan is the only armed English vessel here. At 3 P.M. sailed to sea, and in the evening took our departure from Cape Henlopen.

"The incidents of voyage to Gottenburg but few. . . .

"20th June, Sunday.—At 8 o'clock A.M. anchored in the quarantine ground. . . . At 7 in the evening the officer returned from Gottenburg with permission to land. . . . We immediately jumped in the boat and went ashore on the quarantine island,

and scampered amongst the rocks, pulling wild roses and bunches of clover, which grew in small patches of low ground, none containing more than two acres, all the rest of the island consisting of barren rocks. . . . At night we returned on board.

"21st June, Monday.—After breakfast we hired the quarantine and a fisherman's boat to take us to Gottenburg. . . . Our boatmen told us that the current · being very rapid down the river Gotha after we should have passed the castle, and the wind right ahead, we must land at some houses on the main about four miles by land from Gottenburg, where we could get carriages to take us to town. This we accordingly did, on as barren and rocky spot as what we had yet seen, and there we entered the first Swedish houses. They had inside the appearance of Pennsylvania German houses, both as to smell, inhabitants, and furniture. A fat, fair, ugly woman was blowing her nose in her apron. The husband was drinking a dish of very strong coffee. On the table was a large lump of loaf sugar, the only kind used even by poor people. Although their dress and appearance reminded me of the Germans, they are much fairer complexion, and, if tanned, their hair and eyes still discover it. But they did not to me appear as healthy-looking as our Americans. . . . Four wooden open chairs, not better-looking than carts, some with steel and some with wooden springs, were soon brought, each drawn by a small but pretty good horse, harnessed with ropes. The drivers sat at the bottom, and we set off, two in each. . . . At the end of four miles we came in sight of the river Gotha, about three-quarters of a mile wide, and had a view of the suburb of Martagat and of much shipping along its wharves. . . . Knowing nobody, we stopped at the house of a Mr. Dixon, a Scotchman, who had formerly acted as American consul, and requested him to show us the best inn. . . . There we were soon joined by Mr. Fosdick, of Boston. . . . Mr. Lawrence, of Philadelphia, and Mr. Bowie, of Georgetown, came also to see us and to hear from America. We had been delighted to see once more population of any kind, but to meet Americans at such distance from home is a feeling to be understood only by those who have experienced it. I could have pressed every one to my bosom as a brother. . . .

"22d June, Tuesday.—We left Gottenburg after breakfast
. . . and in two hours reached our ship. . . . At night, having
had two sets of pilots, though the distance was but twelve miles,
we reached the sea. . . .

"24th June, Thursday.—. . . At dusk anchored in Copen-
hagen inner roads.

"25th June, Friday.—Landed at 10. Bachalan's hotel. . . .

"1st July, Thursday.—Breakfasted and went on board. . . .
Detained all day by southeast wind. Field of battle of Nelson,
1801. New fortifications and defences. Block ships sunk in
sixteen feet water. Bombardment in September, 1807; 400
houses destroyed, 1500 persons killed. This cause of great
increase of army and expense. Batteries everywhere; armed
population. Norway starved and faithful. Frugality of King
in personal expenses. Ministers serve for nothing (nominal
salary, 8000 old rigs, or about 200 Spanish dollars). Existence
of kingdom at stake. Conduct of Russia and England towards
it unintelligible. They have thrown it in France's hands, much
against their will. Despotism and no oppression. Poverty and
no discontent. Civility and no servile obsequiousness amongst
people. Decency and sobriety. . . .

"8th July, Thursday.—Fair weather; head-wind. We grow
very impatient. We are opposite to Courland. . . .

"12th July, Monday.—Head-wind. . . . Entered Gulf of
Finland."

Here end Mr. Gallatin's memoranda of his voyage, and here
begins the history of his long diplomatic career. He arrived at
St. Petersburg on the 21st July, and set to work with his colleagues to carry out the purposes of the mission.

As now completed, the American commission appointed to
negotiate for peace under the mediation of Russia consisted of
Mr. Gallatin, Mr. J. Q. Adams, then our minister at St. Petersburg, and Mr. James A. Bayard. For the first time Gallatin
was now associated in public business with J. Q. Adams, and
by a curious combination of circumstances this association was
destined to last during all the remainder of Mr. Gallatin's public
life. What each of these men thought of the other will be seen

in the course of the story, for neither of them had anything to conceal. Cast as they were in two absolutely different moulds, it was not in the nature of things that they should ever stand in such close and affectionate intimacy as had existed between Mr. Gallatin and the two Presidents of his own choice, especially since the Virginia triumvirate was even more remarkable for the private than for the public relations of its members, and in this respect stands without a parallel in our history. Although there was little in common between the New England temperament of Mr. Adams and the Virginia geniality of Mr. Jefferson and Mr. Madison; although Mr. Adams, as the younger man and at first the inferior in rank and influence, could under no circumstances stand to Mr. Gallatin in the same light as his older and more confidential friends; although the previous history of both seemed little calculated to inspire confidence or good will in either; there was nevertheless a curious parallelism in the lives and characters of the two men, which, notwithstanding every jar, compelled them to move side by side and to agree in policy and opinion even while persuading themselves that their aims and methods were radically divergent. Mr. Adams was about six years the junior. When young Gallatin took his degree at the College of Geneva in May, 1779, young Adams was arriving with his father at Paris to begin his education as diplomate and scholar in the centre of all that was then most cultivated and stimulating in the world. While Gallatin was wandering with Serre among the Maine woods, Adams was wandering between Paris and St. Petersburg, picking up his education as he went. Had Gallatin remained two years longer at Harvard College, he would have met Adams there. As they grew older they were in opposing ranks as public men. For Gallatin's early political theories Adams felt little respect, and for his eminent share in expelling the Federalists from office the son of the expelled President could hardly have been grateful. A few years, however, brought them together. As Senator the force of circumstances compelled Mr. Adams to support the Administration and the measures of Mr. Jefferson for the same reasons which compelled Mr. Gallatin to support those measures which, abstractly considered, were entirely inconsistent with his

past history and his early convictions. In 1813 there was no
very decided opinion to divide them. They worked cordially
together at St. Petersburg and at Ghent. During nearly twelve
years they continued to work together in the management of our
foreign relations. The irruption of President Jackson and his
political following threw them both out of public life; and when
Mr. Adams returned to it as member of Congress, Mr. Gallatin
remained in retirement. Both were then non-partisan; both
held very strong convictions in regard to the duties and the
short-comings of the day; both died near the same time, the last
relics of the early statesmanship of the republic.

So far as his colleagues in the mission to St. Petersburg were
concerned, although Mr. Adams had been and Mr. Bayard still
was a moderate Federalist, Gallatin found no difficulties in the
way of harmonious action; but almost from the first moment it
became evident that the negotiation itself was destined never to
take place. The English government, though somewhat embarrassed by Russia's offer to mediate, and yet more by the quick
action of President Madison in sending commissioners under that
offer, was clear in its determination not to allow Russia or any
other nation to interpose in what it chose to consider a domestic
quarrel. The questions involved were questions of neutral rights,
and on that ground the position of the Baltic powers had never
been satisfactory to England; accordingly, England had met the
invitation of Russia, if not with a positive refusal, certainly with
decided coldness. Instead of finding everything prepared for
negotiation, Mr. Gallatin found on his arrival that not a single
step had yet been taken by England beyond the communication
of a note which discouraged any arbitration whatever. Unfortunately, too, there were complications beneath the surface;
complications with which the American commissioners were not
familiar, and which no agency of theirs could remove. The
Emperor was not at St. Petersburg; he was with his army,
fighting Napoleon. He had left Count Romanzoff behind him
at St. Petersburg, and was accompanied by Count Nesselrode.
Count Romanzoff had nominal charge of foreign affairs; he
held strong opinions on the subject of neutral and commercial
rights; he was regarded as not peculiarly friendly to England;

32

and he was the author or instigator of the Emperor's offer of mediation. On him alone in the imperial court could the American commissioners rely. On the other hand, every immediate interest dictated to the Emperor the policy of close friendship with England. This policy was apparently represented by Count Nesselrode, and Count Nesselrode now had every advantage in impressing it upon the Emperor. The British government before the arrival of the American commissioners would have preferred that Alexander should quietly abandon his scheme of mediation and that all discussion of the subject should be dropped. The object of Romanzoff was to press the mediation in order to secure in the United States a balance against the overpowering dominion of England on the ocean.

The sudden arrival of the American commissioners was an event which no one expected or wished. Upon Count Romanzoff, already tottering, it brought a new strain, which appears to have been more than he could meet; yet, although his influence was nearly at an end, he still caused no little irritation to the British government before his fall, and the arrival of Mr. Gallatin and Mr. Bayard added greatly to this embarrassment. Lord Castlereagh was obliged to abandon the attempt to smother the Emperor's mediation, and to take a more decided tone.

Nothing could well be more unpleasant than the position of Mr. Gallatin and his colleagues at St. Petersburg. To see plainly that they were not wanted was in itself mortifying, but to feel that they were gravely embarrassing their only real friend was painful. Yet it was impossible to get away; Count Romanzoff was not disposed to retreat from the ground he had taken; without waiting to be pressed,—indeed, immediately on hearing of the arrival of the commissioners at Gottenburg,—he wrote to the Emperor suggesting a renewal of the offer of mediation to England. He did all in his power to make the envoys comfortable in their unpleasant situation, and he set himself to study their case with the aid of a masterly little memoir which Mr. Gallatin prepared at his request.

On the 10th of August the Emperor's reply was communicated to the envoys, and it authorized Romanzoff not only to renew the offer of mediation, but to send it direct to London without further advice from headquarters. On the 24th, the Count summoned Mr. Gallatin and his two colleagues to listen to the reading of his despatches, by which the offer was to be renewed ; and at Mr. Gallatin's suggestion two slight alterations were made in the draft.

The envoys had already waited more than a month at St. Petersburg, and the summer was gone without the accomplishment of a single object. Mr. Gallatin ought soon to be on his way home, if he had any idea of resuming his post at the Treasury, but to escape was now out of the question, while any effective action was even more hopeless. The envoys discussed the subject from every point of view, but their means were slender enough and the power of England was omnipotent about them. For their purposes it was essential to open some private communication with the Emperor Alexander at headquarters ; General Moreau offered himself for this service, and Mr. Gallatin wrote to him at considerable length on the subject.[1] To ascertain directly the views and intentions of the British government was more important, and here Mr. Gallatin was even more fortunate. On his arrival at Gottenburg he had written to his old acquaintance Alexander Baring, announcing his progress towards St. Petersburg, and in this letter he had invited communication of intelligence connected with the mission. Mr. Baring replied on the 22d July, and his letter reached St. Petersburg about the middle of August; it was written with the knowledge and advice of Lord Castlereagh, and showed in every line the embarrassment caused by the Russian offer of mediation. In order to withdraw questions of blockade, contraband, and right of search from the mediation of a Baltic power, the British government was driven to assume the position that this was "a sort of family quarrel, where foreign interference can only do harm and irritate at any time, but more especially in the present state of Europe, when attempts would be made to make a tool of America in a manner which I am sure neither you nor your colleagues would sanction. These, I have good reason to know, are pretty nearly the sentiments of government

---

[1] See both letters in Gallatin's Writings, vol. i. pp. 562, 576.

here on the question of place of negotiation and foreign mediation, and, before this reaches you, you will have been informed
that this mediation has been refused, with expressions of our
desire to treat separately and directly here, or, if more agreeable to you, at Gottenburg."

This was clumsy enough on the part of the British ministry,
whose parental interest in protecting the innocence of America
from contact with the sinfulness of Russia was not calculated
to effect its avowed object, and still less to please the Emperor
and his continental allies, who were here plainly charged with
intending to make a tool of the United States; but at this time
English diplomacy cultivated very few of the arts and none
at all of the graces; there is hardly an important state paper
in the whole correspondence between England and America
from 1806 to 1815, which, if addressed to the United States
government to-day, would not lead to blows. The letter of
Mr. Baring, kindly meant and highly useful as it was, had all
the characteristics of the English Foreign Office, and in the hands
of an indiscreet man would have done more harm than good;
Mr. Gallatin's temper, however, was not irritable; he did not
even show the letter itself to Count Romanzoff, and he answered
Mr. Baring without a trace of sarcasm or irony. His reply is,
indeed, a model of dignified and persuasive address, brief,
straightforward, and comprehensive,[1] and the passage in which
he refers to his own sacrifice throws some light on the nature of
his private feelings: " I would not have given up my political
existence and separated myself from my family unless I had believed an arrangement practicable and that I might be of some
utility in effecting it."

The situation was now more than ever perplexing. On the
one hand, not only Mr. Baring but the British government
maintained that the mediation had been refused and that direct
negotiation had been offered in its place; on the other hand,
Count Romanzoff denied that the mediation had been refused,
and in a manner obliged the three envoys to wait the result of
another application. As a matter of fact, England had made as

---

[1] All this correspondence is printed in Gallatin's Writings, vol. i. p. 545, ff.

yet no offer of direct negotiation; had this offer been made when it was said to have been determined upon, in June, and then transmitted to America, the situation would have been simple; but, as matters now stood, the American envoys were fully justified in thinking that the British government had no other purpose than to mislead them, and their impatience naturally increased.

Under such circumstances, Mr. Gallatin lingered helplessly in St. Petersburg, idle and anxious, while the world seemed convulsed with agony. He wrote a long letter to General Moreau on the 2d September, ignorant that, while he wrote, Moreau was drawing his last breath. With what patience he could command, he amused himself with such resources as St. Petersburg offered. No answer had yet been received from England, when, on the 19th October, letters arrived from the United States, announcing that his nomination as envoy to Russia had been rejected by the Senate, and that consequently he was no longer a member of the mission.

Curiously enough, only one week had elapsed since Mr. Gallatin had been officially recognized as envoy by Count Romanzoff; the difficulty of communicating with the Emperor had caused delays in every detail, so that all Mr. Gallatin's share in the transactions under the mediation was, with the exception of this single week, unofficial. The news of his rejection by the Senate was probably not unexpected, but, like everything else in this unlucky mission, it came in just such a way as to increase complications; no official information of the fact and no instructions were received, nor did these reach Mr. Gallatin until the end of March in the following year, and yet without such official advices it was difficult to get away from St. Petersburg, and Count Romanzoff was strongly of the opinion that he could not go.

Nevertheless, there were some advantages in the situation. The Senate had at least restored to Mr. Gallatin his liberty of action; he was no longer dependent on his colleagues; if not envoy, he was still Secretary of the Treasury, strong in his relations with the President, master of all the threads of the negotiation, and it depended only upon himself to say what measures he should take. Little consideration was needed to show that he could do no good by returning to America. His enemies were there in possession of the field, and his failure in diplomacy would strengthen their hands; his only chance of baffling them was by rescuing the negotiation, and this he set himself to accomplish. Somewhat to the disgust of Mr. Adams, he proceeded, delicately but decidedly, to mark out his own course. Mr. Baring had urged the mission to go to England to treat directly of peace. Mr. Gallatin did, in October, send his secretary, George M. Dallas, to London to make a channel of communication between Lord Castlereagh, Count Lieven, the Russian Ambassador, and Mr. Baring on one side, and himself and Mr. Madison on the other. The news of Mr. Gallatin's rejection by the Senate arrived precisely as young Dallas was starting for London. Thither Gallatin meditated following him, and as for the responsibility thus assumed, he bluntly told Mr. Adams " that *he* was no longer a member of the mission ; he was a private gentleman, and might go home by the way of England or any other way, as he pleased ; that as to the approbation of the government, he should not trouble himself about it; he would not disobey their orders, but if he was right he should not much regard whether they liked it or not. Mr. Baring's letter did indeed speak of the decision of the British government upon the point of impressment in the clearest and strongest terms, but he believed the point might still be presented to them in a manner which would induce them to judge of it otherwise. This, he thought, would be the utility of their going to England. For his purpose was to convince the British ministers that unless they should yield on the article of impressment, there was no possibility of treating at all."[1]

Another scheme of Mr. Gallatin's was to go directly to the Emperor Alexander's headquarters and attempt to stimulate his action; but to effect this object a strong friend was needed, and since Moreau's death there was no individual about the Emperor on whose aid reliance could be put.

The anomalous attitude and independent action of Mr. Galla-

---

[1] Memoirs of J. Q. Adams, ii. 549, 19th November, 1813.

tin naturally annoyed his colleagues and might easily have made a coolness, but he had the tact to follow his own path without giving offence. Meanwhile the curious diplomatic mystification which had perplexed the American envoys all summer, and of which the Emperor was the innocent cause, began to approach an end. As early as July 14, Lord Castlereagh had instructed Lord Cathcart, in the most positive language, to make the Emperor understand that England could not consent to even the *appearance* of foreign intervention in the American dispute,[1] and this final decision seems to have been communicated to the Emperor on the 1st September, at Töplitz, when Alexander had already authorized Romanzoff to renew the offer of mediation; when Romanzoff had indeed already written his despatches to that effect and forwarded them to the Emperor for approval. On the arrival of these despatches at headquarters, Alexander wrote back on September 8, approving the draft for a new offer of mediation notwithstanding the fact that Lord Cathcart, only a week before, had officially announced that under no circumstances could England admit of mediation, but that she meant to negotiate directly. The second proposal to mediate was, therefore, forwarded by Romanzoff to Count Lieven, the Russian ambassador in London, and the Count must have informally notified Lord Castlereagh of its contents, for it seems to have been on the strength of information contained in this despatch that the British note to Mr. Monroe, dated November 4, and offering to negotiate directly, was founded; but Count Lieven never officially communicated the proposal itself to Lord Castlereagh; by the usual diplomatic jugglery this second offer was quietly suppressed at the British minister's hint, and Count Lieven only wrote back that Lord Castlereagh had transmitted directly to the Emperor in person a memoir containing his reasons for declining mediation. The Emperor forgot to communicate this memoir to Romanzoff, and when the latter received Lieven's letter early in November he could only communicate it without explanation to the Americans. This was done on November.3,

---

[1] See Lord Castlereagh's private letter in the Castlereagh Correspondence, 3d Series, vol. i. p. 34.

and by this time another British minister, Lord Walpole, had arrived in St. Petersburg, who irritated the Americans still further by talking openly and bitterly of Count Romanzoff's intrigues. No one knew how to explain the riddle. Even Lord Cathcart, who was with the Emperor, wrote to Lord Castlereagh on the 12th December: "I think Nesselrode knows nothing of the cause of the delay of communicating with the American mission; that it was an intrigue of the Chancellor's, if it is one; and that during the operations of war the Emperor has lost the clue to it, so that something has been unanswered. If it is not cleared up, I will write another note and send a copy to Walpole."[1] Romanzoff himself was deeply mortified, and this evidence of the Emperor's neglect seems to have been the cause of his retirement from office. He now announced to the Americans that he should remain Chancellor a short time longer solely to close the affair of this mission.

All the parties to this imbroglio, confused and irritated by the veil of mystery which surrounded it, suspected intrigue and treachery in their opponents. The Americans naturally believed that England was to blame, and, although this was not the case, there was some reason in the suspicion, for Lord Castlereagh, straightforward and honest in his treatment of Russia, was very slow in dealing with America, and, instead of writing on July 14 to the United States government, he had waited until Count Lieven again jogged his elbow by bringing to his knowledge Count Romanzoff's second offer of mediation. This was the entire advantage gained for America by Russia, and the whole result accomplished by Mr. Gallatin's voyage. On the 4th November, Lord Castlereagh forwarded to America the offer of direct negotiation which he had announced in his instructions to Lord Cathcart of the 14th July. Not until Mr. Baring wrote to Mr. Gallatin on the 14th December did these facts become certainly known to the Americans, and even then Mr. Baring was mistaken in regard to the dates furnished him from the Foreign Office.

All hope of success from the mediation had long vanished;

---

[1] Castlereagh Correspondence, 3d Series, vol. i. p. 94.

the winter had set in; Gallatin was not even a member of the commission; yet he still lingered at St. Petersburg, partly in deference to Count Romanzoff's wish, partly in the hope of receiving the long-expected communication from the Emperor which was to close the mission, partly in expectation of receiving more decisive news from England or of getting instructions from America, partly in order to have the company of Mr. Bayard on his journey. Not until the 25th January, 1814, did they leave St. Petersburg, and still without a word from the Emperor.

They travelled with all the slowness inevitable in the movements of those times from St. Petersburg to Amsterdam. There they arrived on the evening of the 4th March, and there they remained during four weeks. The situation of affairs did not grow better. The complete destruction of France was practically accomplished, and America was now left to oppose alone the whole power of England, which would infallibly be directed against her. On reaching Amsterdam Mr. Gallatin learned that Lord Castlereagh's offer of direct negotiation had been promptly met on the part of Mr. Madison by the appointment of a new commission, of which Mr. Gallatin himself was not one, for the reason that at the time these nominations were made he was supposed to be on his way home to resume his post at the Treasury. When the mistake was discovered, and after it had become evident that the Treasury must no longer be left vacant, the President, on the 8th February, nominated Mr. Gallatin as a member of the new commission, and at the same time appointed Mr. G. W. Campbell Secretary of the Treasury. By this accident Mr. Gallatin, instead of standing first in the commission, was made its last member, and all his colleagues, Mr. Adams, Mr. Bayard, Henry Clay, and Jonathan Russell, took precedence of him.

These proceedings had no effect in changing Mr. Gallatin's movements; whether first or last in the commission, or whether omitted from it entirely, he continued to superintend all the diplomatic operations connected with the proposed peace. Towards the end of March he received from Mr. Baring the necessary permission to visit England, and immediately afterwards he crossed the channel with Mr. Bayard and established himself in

London. Almost at the same moment Mr. Clay and Mr. Russell arrived at Gottenburg, and brought with them Mr. Gallatin's appointment as fifth commissioner. A considerable time necessarily elapsed before all the five envoys could be brought together, and during this interval Mr. Gallatin was quietly employed in smoothing the path of negotiation.

With the British government itself he held no direct communication on the difficult points involved in the future settlement, and if he still hoped to persuade that government to make concessions on the subject of impressment, his hope was altogether disappointed; neither Mr. Baring nor Lord Castlereagh himself would at that moment have dared to suggest the smallest concession on that point in the face of the excited popular feeling of England. Mr. Gallatin appears to have refrained from every attempt to negotiate on his own account, and to have contented himself with removing such obstacles and with setting in motion such influences as it was in his power to affect or control.

The first object he had at heart was the removal of the place of negotiation. Their instructions, not as yet known to Mr. Gallatin, authorized the envoys to treat, and assumed Gottenburg as the place, rejecting the British proposition to treat at London. Mr. Gallatin would have preferred London, because he believed, and with justice, that his chances were better with Lord Castlereagh than with any mere agent of the Foreign Office; but this point was one of pride as well as fear among Americans; to London they would not go, and accordingly Mr. Gallatin contented himself with changing the place of negotiation to Ghent. The following letter explains his motives for this movement.

GALLATIN TO HENRY CLAY.

London, 22d April, 1814.

DEAR SIR,—We have just heard of your arrival, but have received no letters, and I am yet ignorant whether I am one of the new commission to treat of peace. My arrangements must depend on that circumstance, and I wait with impatience for the official account which you must have brought. For that reason

Mr. Bayard addresses you and Mr. Russell in his own name, but I coincide fully with him in the opinion that the negotiations should by all means be opened here, or at least in Holland, if this is not rendered impracticable from the nature of the commission.   If this has unfortunately been limited to treating of peace at Gottenburg, there is no remedy; but if the commission admits of a change of place, I would feel no hesitation in removing them at least to any other neutral place, whatever may be the language of the instructions.   For their spirit would be fully answered by treating in any other friendly country as well as if at Gottenburg.   On that point I feel great anxiety, because, on account of the late great changes in Europe, and of the increased difficulties thence arising in making any treaty, I do believe that it would be utterly impossible to succeed in that corner, removed from every friendly interference in our favor on the part of the European powers, and compelled to act with men clothed with limited authorities, and who might at all times plead a want of instructions.

You are sufficiently aware of the total change in our affairs produced by the late revolution and by the restoration of universal peace in the European world, from which we are alone excluded.   A well-organized and large army is at once liberated from any European employment, and ready, together with a superabundant naval force, to act immediately against us.   How ill prepared we are to meet it in a proper manner no one knows better than yourself; but, above all, our own divisions and the hostile attitude of the Eastern States give room to apprehend that a continuance of the war might prove vitally fatal to the United States.

I understand that the ministers, with whom we have not had any direct intercourse, still profess to be disposed to make an equitable peace.   But the hope, not of ultimate conquest, but of a dissolution of the Union, the convenient pretence which the American war will afford to preserve large military establishments, and, above all, the force of popular feeling, may all unite in inducing the Cabinet in throwing impediments in the way of peace.   They will not certainly be disposed to make concessions, nor probably displeased at a failure of negotiations.   That the war is popular, and that national pride, inflated by the last un-expected success, cannot be satisfied without what they call the chastisement of America, cannot be doubted. The mass of the people here know nothing of American politics but through the medium of Federal speeches and newspapers faithfully tran-scribed in their own journals. They do not even suspect that we have any just cause of complaint, and consider us altogether as the aggressors and as allies of Bonaparte. In those opinions it is understood that the ministers do not participate, but it will really require an effort on their part to act contrary to public opinion, and they must, even if perfectly sincere, use great caution and run some risk of popularity. A direct, or at least a very near, intercourse with them is therefore highly important, as I have no doubt that they would go further themselves than they would be willing to intrust any other person. To this must be added that Lord Castlereagh is, according to the best infor-mation I have been able to collect, the best disposed man in the Cabinet, and that coming from France, and having had inter-course with the Emperor Alexander, it is not improbable that those dispositions may have been increased by the personal ex-pression of the Emperor's wishes in favor of peace with America. Whatever advantages may be derived from that circumstance and from the Emperor's arrival here would be altogether lost at Gottenburg. . . .

HENRY CLAY TO GALLATIN.

GOTTENBURG, 2d May, 1814.

DEAR SIR,—I am rejoiced at finding you in Europe. We had great fears that you would have left it before our arrival and proceeded to America. Your rejection last summer in the Senate was very generally condemned by the people, and pro-duced a reaction highly favorable to you. The total uncertainty in which the government was left as to your movements (for on the 1st February, when I left Washington, not one syllable had been received from either yourself or Mr. Bayard), and the in-creased and complicated concerns of the Treasury, produced a state of things highly embarrassing to the President; so much so that he could no longer resist the pressure to fill the Treasury. After this measure was determined on, it became more than ever desirable that the public should have the benefit of your services here.   Had it not been confidently believed when the new commission was formed that you were on your way to America and would be there shortly, you would have been originally comprehended in it.

I have not time to say what I want to communicate on American affairs.   Peace, necessary to our country before the astonishing events which have recently occurred on this side of the Atlantic, events with which the imagination can scarcely keep pace, will doubtless be now more than ever demanded.   I think, however, you attach more consequence than belongs to the indications in the Eastern States.   I have no doubt that a game of swaggering and gasconade has been played off there, without any serious intention to push matters to extremity.   After a great deal of blustering about raising 20,000 men and declaring the freedom of the port of Boston, a meeting of the malcontents there determined it inexpedient to take any such measure during the last session of the Legislature.   The truth is, they want men, they want money, the principal actors want courage.   Yet I would not despise these appearances.   If the British government should determine to land a considerable force in the Eastern States, avowing friendship to them and an intention only to war with the Southern States, or with the Administration, certainly very serious consequences might ensue, though I believe they would fall far short of conquest or dissolution. . . .

On the point of removing the place of negotiation from Gottenburg to Ghent Mr. Gallatin was successful, and perhaps it was on the whole fortunate that he was disappointed in his wish to negotiate at London, for the delays consequent on the distance of Ghent were an element in the success of the negotiation.

Another point which Mr. Gallatin pertinaciously labored to gain was the active aid of the Emperor Alexander.   What Romanzoff had been unable to effect, and what Moreau had died too soon to accomplish, Mr. Gallatin was bent upon doing by other means.   Fortunately, his former ally, William H. Crawford, had been taken by Mr. Madison from the Senate and sent as minister to Napoleon, after whose fall he remained in Paris, waiting for new credentials and for recognition from Louis XVIII. As a diplomate, Mr. Crawford was not altogether successful; his temper and manners were little suited to the very delicate situation in which he was placed; nevertheless he was a person on whose aid Mr. Gallatin could thoroughly rely, and the assistance of La Fayette and Humboldt went far to supply his deficiencies. Mr. Gallatin, therefore, enrolled him also in the service, and wrote at some length, giving him a sketch of the situation in much the same language used in the letter to Mr. Clay of the next day, but with a different conclusion.

GALLATIN TO W. H. CRAWFORD.

LONDON, 21 April, 1814.

The only external check to those dispositions [of enmity in England] can be found in the friendly interposition of the Emperor Alexander, not as a mediator, but as a common friend, pressing on this government the propriety of an accommodation and expressing his strong wishes for a general restoration of peace to the civilized world. I do not know whether your situation affords you means of approaching him, and can only state my opinion of the great importance that an early opportunity should be taken by you or any other person you may think fitted for the object, to call his attention to the situation in which we are left, and to the great weight which his opinion in favor of peace on liberal conditions, strongly expressed to this government, must necessarily have at this time. Of his friendly disposition for the United States there is no doubt; but we may be forgotten; and it is necessary that he should be apprised of the hostile spirit which prevails here, and which, if not balanced by some other cause, may even carry ministers beyond their own wishes and views. It should also be stated that our government having accepted one year ago the Emperor's mediation, and not having supposed that, considering the political connection between him and Great Britain, she could reject that offer, no other provision was made on our part to obtain peace until our government was apprised, in January last, of the rejection of the mediation by England. Thus was a delay of a year produced, and the opening of our negotiations unfortunately prevented till after England is at peace with the rest of the world, a circumstance which, although it does not give us a positive right to claim the Emperor's interference, affords sufficient ground to present the subject to his consideration. I entreat you to lose no time in taking such steps as may be in your power in that respect, and to write to me whatever you may think important for the success of the mission should be known to us. . . .

On the 13th May, Mr. Crawford replied that he had attempted to carry out Mr. Gallatin's wishes, and had received a polite rebuff from Count Nesselrode and no notice whatever from the Emperor. He added: "After I had failed in obtaining access to the Emperor of Russia and to his minister, I requested General La Fayette to endeavor, through Colonel La Harpe, to have the proper representations made to Nesselrode or to the Emperor. Every effort to effect this object has been abortive. It seems as if there had been a settled determination to prevent the approach of every person who is suspected of an attachment to the United States. The general has, however, come in contact several times with Baron Humboldt, the Prussian minister, who has imbibed already the British misrepresentations."

La Fayette soon succeeded, however, in breaking down these barriers which English influence had raised about the Emperor. On the 25th May he wrote: "Mr. Crawford is better qualified than I am to give you all the information from this quarter which relates to American concerns. The confidence with which he honors my zeal has enabled me to discuss the matter with some influencing characters among the allied generals and diplomates. Two of the latter act a great part in the present negotiations. I found them well acquainted with British arguments and impressed with British prejudices which convinced me that care had been taken to influence their opinion. An opportunity has been sought, which I am bound not to name, for putting directly under the eyes of Emperor Alexander a note of Mr. Crawford. You may depend it has been faithfully delivered, with proper comments, along with a letter, the copy of which Mr. Crawford has desired me to enclose. I expect this evening to meet the Emperor of Russia at a friend's house, and shall try to obtain some conversation on the subject."

On the 26th May, General La Fayette wrote the following letter to Mr. Crawford, who enclosed it on the 28th in a despatch to Mr. Gallatin.

LA FAYETTE TO W. H. CRAWFORD.

26th May, 1814.

MY DEAR SIR,—I passed the last evening in company with the Emperor Alexander, who, however prepossessed in his favor, has surpassed my expectations. He really is a great, good, sensible, noble-minded man, and a sincere friend to the cause of liberty. We have long conversed upon American affairs. It began with his telling me that he had read with much pleasure and interest what I had sent him. I found ideas had been suggested that had excited a fear that the people of the United States had not properly improved their internal situation. My answer was an observation upon the necessity of parties in a commonwealth, and the assertion that they were the happiest and freest people upon earth. The transactions with France and England were explained in the way that, although the United States had to complain of both, the British outrages came nearer home, particularly in the affair of impressments. He spoke of the actual preparation and the hostile dispositions of England. I of course insisted on the rejection of his mediation, the confidence reposed in him by the United States who hastened to send commissioners chosen from both parties, which he very kindly acknowledged. He said he had twice attempted to bring on a peace. " Do, sir," said I, "make a third attempt; it must succeed; ne vous arrêtez pas en si beau chemin. All the objects of a war at an end, and the re-establishment of their old limits can the less be opposed as the Americans have gained more than they have lost. A protraction of the war would betray intentions quite perverse and hostile to the cause of humanity. Your personal influence must carry the point. I am sure your majesty will exert it." "Well,"

says he, "I promise you I will.   My journey to London affords
opportunities, and I will do the best I can."   I told him I had
received a letter from Mr. Gallatin, now in London, and we
spoke of him, Mr. Adams, Mr. Bayard, and the two new commissioners.   I had also other occasions to speak of America; one
afforded me by the Swedish Marshal Stadinck, who mentioned
my first going over to that country; another by a well-inten-
tioned observation of Mme. de Staël that she had received a letter
from my friend Mr. Jefferson, of whom he spoke with great
regard.   This led to observations relative to the United States
and the spirit of monopoly in England extending even to liberty
itself.   The Emperor said they had been more liberal in Sicily
than I supposed them.   I did not deny it, but expressed my
fears of their protecting Ferdinand against the cortes.   His sentiments on the Spanish affairs were noble and patriotic.   The
slave-trade became a topic upon which he spoke with philanthropic warmth.   Its abolition will be an article in the general
peace.

You see, my dear sir, I had fully the opportunity we were
wishing for.   If it has not been well improved, the fault is
mine.   But I think some good has been done.   And upon the
promise of a man so candid and generous I have full dependence.   If you think proper to communicate these details to Mr.
Gallatin, be pleased to have them copied.   He spoke very well
of him, and seemed satisfied with the confidence of the United
States and the choice of their representatives to him.   By his
last accounts Mr. Adams was at St. Petersburg.   The particulars of this conversation ought not, of course, to be published;
but you will probably think it useful to communicate to the
commissioners.

The obstinate determination of England to isolate the United
States and cut off all means of co-operation between her and the
Baltic powers became more and more evident as the season advanced, and stimulated Gallatin's efforts.   On the 2d June he
wrote to Mr. Monroe from London: "I have remained here
waiting for the answers of our colleagues at Gottenburg, and
will depart as soon as I know that they and the British com-

missioners are on their way to the appc'nted place. The definitive treaty of European peace being signed and ratified, Lord Castlereagh is expected here this day, and the Emperor of Russia in the beginning of next week. I enclose copy of an extract of a letter of Mr. Crawford to me. I may add that I have ascertained that the exclusion of all discussions respecting maritime questions and of any interference in the American contest was one of the conditions proposed at the Châtillon conferences, and I have reason to believe that, with respect to the first point, a positive, and in the other at least a tacit, agreement have taken place in the late and final European negotiations at Paris."

Doubtless one of Mr. Gallatin's objects in remaining so long in London was to have a personal interview with the Emperor. La Fayette wrote to him from Paris on the 3d of June, recounting briefly the incidents·of his own interview with the Emperor at the house of Mme. de Staël, and urging Mr. Gallatin to see him : " You may begin the conversation with thanking him for the intention to do so [to serve us] to the best of his power, which he very positively expressed to me. Our friend Humboldt, who has already spoken to him on the subject, would be happy to receive your directions for anything in his power. I hasten to scribble this letter to be forwarded by him."

The Emperor Alexander came to London, and Mr. Gallatin had his interview on the 17th or 18th June. Of this interview Mr. C. J. Ingersoll, in his History of the War of 1812, has given a somewhat dramatic account, derived perhaps from Mr. Levett Harris, who had been secretary to the mission at St. Petersburg, and who, being now in London, accompanied Mr. Gallatin to the audience. Mr. Ingersoll has in that work so seldom succeeded in stating facts with correctness, that to quote him is usually to mislead. All Mr. Gallatin ever recorded on the subject of the interview is contained in his despatch of June 20 to Mr. Monroe: " Mr. Harris and myself had on the 17th an audience from the Emperor of Russia. His friendly dispositions for the United States are unimpaired; he earnestly wishes that peace may be made between them and England; but he does not give or seem to entertain any hope that he can on that subject be of any service. I could not ascertain whether he had touched the subject since he had been here; only he said, ' I have made two—three attempts.' If three, the third must have been now. He added, ' England will not admit a third party to interfere in her disputes with you. This is on account of your former relations to her (the colonial state), which is not yet forgotten.' He also expressed his opinion that, with respect to conditions of peace, the difficulty would be with England and not with us. On the whole, this conversation afforded no reason to alter the opinions expressed in my letter of 13th inst.[1] I yesterday, with his permission, sent him a note, . . . which contains nothing new to you, and which will not probably produce any effect."[2]

To these facts Mr. Ingersoll adds some details. According to him, the interview took place on the 18th, the day when the city of London gave its great banquet to the allied sovereigns at Guildhall. The time appointed by the Emperor for his audience was the hour before he left his residence in Leicesterfields to attend the entertainment; and Mr. Gallatin and Mr. Harris drove in " a mean and solitary hackney-coach, with a permit," through the shouting crowd, unknown and unnoticed, except by an occasional jeer and a hail as " old Blucher" from the throng. The Emperor's words are not given, but the substance was that Mr. Gallatin and his associates should take a high tone and outbrag the British.

The reader may safely assume that the Emperor said nothing of the kind, for Alexander was not a man to indulge in impertinence. He earnestly wished for peace, and he saw how small a chance there was of obtaining it. He doubtless spoke to Mr. Gallatin with perfect sincerity of his wishes and his acts; he may have hinted that America would gain little by showing too great eagerness for peace, but he would certainly have said nothing which, if repeated, could possibly have offended England. Indeed, he had gone to the extreme verge of civility in giving any audience at all to an American agent while he was

---

[1] See Writings, vol. i. p. 627, and below, p. 517.

[2] See this note in Writings, vol. i. p. 629.

himself the guest of the country with which America was then at war.

The result of all Mr. Gallatin's efforts in this direction was, therefore, apparently a complete failure. The power of England was supreme in Europe, and whatever irritation the continental sovereigns may have felt under the extravagant maritime pretensions of Great Britain, not one of them ventured to lisp a word of remonstrance. Yet it is by no means certain that Mr. Gallatin was so unsuccessful as he seemed. The fate of the negotiation at Ghent hung on Lord Castlereagh's nod, and among the many influences which affected Lord Castlereagh's mind, a desire to preserve his friendly relations with Russia was one of the most powerful. The moment came when the British ministry had to decide the question whether to let the treaty fail or to abate British pretensions, and it can hardly be doubted that the repeated remonstrances of Russia had some share of influence in causing England to recoil from a persistent policy of war. At the crisis of the negotiation, on the 27th September, Lord Liverpool wrote to Lord Castlereagh, who was then at Vienna, advising him of the capture of Washington and the state of affairs at Ghent, and adding: "The Americans have assumed hitherto a tone in the negotiation very different from what their situation appears to warrant. In the exercise of your discretion as to how much you may think proper to disclose of what has been passing to the sovereigns and ministers whom you will meet at Vienna, I have no doubt you will see the importance of adverting to this circumstance, and of doing justice to the moderation with which we are disposed to act towards America. I fear the Emperor of Russia is half an American, and it would be very desirable to do away any prejudice which may exist in his mind or in that of Count Nesselrode on this subject."[1]

While Mr. Gallatin was engaged in arranging the preliminaries of negotiation and in bringing to bear on the British ministry such pressure as he was able to command, he did not neglect to act the part of diplomatic agent for the instruction of his own

---

[1] Supplementary Despatches of the Duke of Wellington, vol. ix. pp. 290-291.

government. The time was long gone by when Mr. Gallatin and his party had declaimed against the diplomatic service. Mr. Madison had now sent abroad nearly every man in America whose pretensions to civil distinction were considerable. There were six full ministers between London, Holland, and Paris, and among them were included two Senators, the Speaker of the House, and the Secretary of the Treasury. The position of Mr. Gallatin in London was particularly delicate, since he was in a manner bound not to betray the confidence which Lord Castlereagh had placed in him by permitting his residence in England; but he knew little more of military movements than was known to all the world, and within these limits he might without impropriety correspond with his government. Thus his well-known despatch of June 13 was written.[1] In this letter he gave a sketch of the whole field of diplomatic and military affairs. Beginning with the announcement that England was fitting out an armament which, besides providing for Canada, would enable her to land at least 15,000 to 20,000 men on the Atlantic coast; that the capture of Washington and New York would most gratify them, and the occupation of Norfolk, Baltimore, &c., might be expected; this letter continued:

"Whatever may be the object and duration of the war, America must rely on her resources alone. From Europe no assistance can for some time be expected. British pride begins, indeed, to produce its usual effect. Seeds of dissension are not wanting. Russia and England may at the approaching Congress of Vienna be at variance on important subjects, particularly as relates to the aggrandizement of Austria. But questions of maritime rights are not yet attended to, and America is generally overlooked by the European sovereigns, or viewed with suspicion. Above all, there is nowhere any navy in existence, and years of peace must elapse before the means of resisting with effect the sea-power of Great Britain can be created. In a word, Europe wants peace, and neither will nor can at this time make war against Great Britain. The friendly disposition of the Emperor of Russia, and a just view of the subject, make him sincerely desirous that

---

[1] See Writings, vol. i. p. 627; also Ingersoll's Late War, ii. 293.

peace should be restored to the United States. He may use his endeavors for that purpose; beyond that he will not go, and in that it is not probable he will succeed. I have also the most perfect conviction that, under the existing unpropitious circumstances of the world, America cannot by a continuance of the war compel Great Britain to yield any of the maritime points in dispute, and particularly to agree to any satisfactory arrangement on the subject of impressment; and that the most favorable terms of peace that can be expected are the *status ante bellum*, and a postponement of the questions of blockade, impressment, and all other points which in time of European peace are not particularly injurious; but with firmness and perseverance those terms, though perhaps unattainable at this moment, will ultimately be obtained, provided you can stand the shock of this campaign, and provided the people will remain and show themselves united." . . .

This despatch arrived in Washington only when one part of its advices had been already verified by the capture and destruction of that city. Meanwhile the other American commissioners were beginning to assemble at Ghent, and the British government showed no sign of haste in opening the negotiation. Mr. Gallatin, on the 9th June, attempted to hurry Lord Castlereagh's movements by asking when the British commissioners would be ready. He was told they would start for Ghent on the 1st July, and on the strength of this information he himself left London on June 21, and, after a rapid visit to Paris, arrived at Ghent on July 6.

Nearly three months had Mr. Gallatin thus passed in London, and, after all his efforts, little enough had been attained. His hopes of success were certainly not brighter than when he left America, more than a year before; indeed, it was not easy to deny that there had been actual loss of ground. Mr. Gallatin had undertaken a diplomatic *tour de force*, and thus far his successes had been far from brilliant; his failures had been conspicuous. Nevertheless he persisted with endless patience and with his usual resource. His residence in London could not but be unpleasant, and perhaps the brightest spot in his whole experience there was the meeting with his old friend and school-fellow

Dumont, the Genevan, whom he had once half wished to tempt into the Ohio wilderness, but who had remained in Europe to float on the waves of revolution until they threw him into the arms of Jeremy Bentham, whose friend and interpreter he became. Through him Mr. Gallatin became acquainted with Bentham, but Gallatin had drifted further than his school-mate from the theorizing tastes of his youth, and he now found quite as much satisfaction in discussing finance with Alexander Baring as in reforming mankind with Bentham and Dumont.

From the 6th July till the 6th August the American commissioners waited the arrival of their British colleagues, and amused themselves as they best might. This delay was the more irritating to Mr. Gallatin because his own visit to Paris was said to have been given by Lord Castlereagh in the House of Commons, on the 20th July, as an excuse for the delay of the British commissioners. The conduct of the English government promised ill for the success of the mission, and it was natural that the Americans should believe they were a second time to be made the victims of diplomacy. This inference was not necessarily a fair one; the motives which influenced Lord Castlereagh varied from day to day, and events proved that he acted more shrewdly in the interests of peace than Mr. Gallatin imagined. There was more to be hoped from delay than from haste.

At last the British commissioners arrived: Lord Gambier, Henry Goulburn, and William Adams; none of them very remarkable for genius, and still less for weight of influence; as compared with the American commissioners they were unequal to their task. This again, unpromising as it looked, was not really a misfortune, for the British commissioners, deficient as they were in ability, polish of manners, and even in an honest wish for peace, were the mere puppets of their government, and never ventured to move a hair's-breadth without at once seeking the approval of Lord Castlereagh or Lord Liverpool. Mr. Gallatin had nothing to fear from them; singly or together he was as capable of dealing with them as Benjamin Franklin, under very similar conditions, had proved himself equal to dealing with their predecessors thirty years before. Gallatin's great difficulty was the same with which Dr. Franklin had struggled. The American habit of negotiating by commissions may have its advantages for government, but it enormously increases the labor of the agents, for it compels each envoy to expend more effort in negotiating with his colleagues in the commission than in negotiating with his opponents. Mr. Gallatin had four associates, none of whom was easily managed, and two of whom, Mr. Adams and Mr. Clay, acted upon each other as explosives. To keep the peace between them was no easy matter, and to keep the peace between them and the Englishmen was a task almost beyond hope; indeed, Mr. Gallatin's own temper was severely tried in his conversations with the English envoys, and perhaps a little more roughness on his part would have been better understood and better received by them than his patient forbearance. If Gallatin had a fault, it was that of using the razor when he would have done better with the axe.

If all the preliminaries were calculated to discourage, the opening of the negotiation justified something worse than discouragement. Very unwillingly and with deep mortification the President and his advisers had submitted to the inevitable and consented to offer terms of peace which settled no one principle for which they had fought. They had agreed to what was in fact an armistice; restoration of the *status ante bellum;* a return to the old condition of things when war was always imminent and American rights were always trampled upon. Now that Europe was again at peace, they were willing to leave the theoretical questions of belligerency undetermined, since it was clear that England preferred war to concession. To Mr. Clay, who had made the war, and to Mr. Adams, who fully sympathized with Mr. Clay in his antipathy to the English domination, these concessions seemed enormous; even to Mr. Gallatin, always the friend of peace, they seemed to reach the extreme verge of dignity; but when the English envoys unfolded their demands, the mildest of the Americans was aghast; it is a matter of surprise that there was not an outburst of indignation on the spot, and that negotiation did not end the day it began. In the first interview, which took place on August 8 and was continued the next day, the British commissioners required as a preliminary basis of discussion and a *sine qua non* of the treaty that the United States government should set apart forever for the Indian tribes the whole North-West Territory, as defined by the treaty of Greenville in 1795; that is to say, the whole country now represented by the States of Michigan, Wisconsin, and Illinois, four-fifths of Indiana, and one-third of Ohio; so that an Indian sovereignty should be constituted in that region under the guaranty of Great Britain, for the double purpose of interposing neutral territory between Canada and the United States and curbing the progress of the latter.   Mr. Gallatin suggested that there were probably one hundred thousand American citizens settled within that region, and what was to become of them?   " Undoubtedly they must shift for themselves," was the reply.

In comparison with so enormous a pretension the smaller demands of the British government were of trifling importance, even though they included a " rectification" of the frontier and a cession of Sackett's Harbor and Fort Niagara as a guaranty for the British control of the lakes.[1]

Under such circumstances, the path of the American commissioners was plain.   They had no opportunity to disagree on so simple an issue, and they wanted no better popular argument for unanimity in support of the war than this avowed determination to dismember the United States.   They had merely to draft their rejection of the British *sine qua non*.

The negotiation with the British commissioners was, however, much more simple than the negotiation with one another; of the first the diplomatic notes and protocols give a fair description, but of the last a far more entertaining account is given in the Diary of John Quincy Adams.   The accident which placed Mr. Gallatin at the foot of the commission placed Mr. Adams at its head,—a result peculiarly unfortunate, because, even if the other

---

[1] See Lord Castlereagh's instructions of August 14, 1814, to the British commissioners at Ghent, Castlereagh Correspondence, 3d Series, vol. ii. p. 86 ff.   Also Mr. Goulburn's acknowledgment of these instructions to Lord Bathurst of 21st August, Supplementary Despatches of the Duke of Wellington, vol. ix. p. 188.   Lord Liverpool to Lord Bathurst, 11th September, ibid., p. 240.   Lord Bathurst to the commissioners, 18th and 20th October, Castlereagh Correspondence, 3d Series, vol. ii. pp. 168 and 172.

commissioners had conceded respect to the age, the services, and the tact of Mr. Gallatin, they had no idea of showing any such deference to Mr. Adams. From the outset it was clear that Messrs. Bayard, Clay, and Russell meant to let Mr. Adams understand that though he might be the nominal mouth-piece he was not the autocrat of the commission, and their methods of conveying this information were such as in those days Mr. Clay was celebrated for successfully using. Mr. Adams had little of Mr. Gallatin's capacity for pacifying strife; he was by nature as combative as Mr. Clay, and before the commission separated there were exciting and very amusing scenes of collision, in one of which Mr. Adams plainly intimated his opinion of the conduct of his colleagues, and Mr. Clay broke out upon him with: "You *dare* not, you *cannot*, you SHALL not insinuate that there has been a cabal of three members against you."

In this affair Mr. Gallatin's situation was delicate in the highest degree. All recognized the fact that he was properly head of the mission; his opinion carried most weight; his pen was most in demand; his voice was most patiently heard. The tact with which he steered his way between the shoals that surrounded him is the most remarkable instance in our history of perfect diplomatic skill; even Dr. Franklin, in a very similar situation, had not the same success. In no instance did Mr. Gallatin allow himself to be drawn into the conflicts of his colleagues, and yet he succeeded in sustaining Mr. Adams in every essential point without appearing to do so. When the negotiation was closed, all his four colleagues were united, at least to outward appearance, in cordiality to him, and Mr. Adams had reason to be, and seems in fact always to have been, positively grateful. If Mr. Clay felt differently, as there was afterwards reason to believe, he showed no such feeling at the time. The story as told in Mr. Adams's Diary proves clearly enough that this delicate tact of Mr. Gallatin probably saved the treaty.

The very earliest despatch they had occasion to send showed Mr. Gallatin the delicacy of his ground. As first member of the commission, Mr. Adams drafted this despatch and gave his draft for revision to the other gentlemen, who showed it little mercy; Mr. Bayard used it merely as the foundation for an entirely new draft of his own, which was substituted by the commission for that of Mr. Adams.   Mr. Bayard's essay, however, proved to be little more satisfactory than Mr. Adams's, and at last it was referred to Mr. Gallatin to be put in final shape.   This was done, and the commissioners ended by adopting his work.   The next despatch was drafted at once by him and accepted with little alteration.   Henceforth the duty of drawing up all papers was regularly performed by him.   Mr. Adams's account of the characteristic criticisms of his four colleagues, as well as of his own peculiarities of thought and expression, is very amusing, and probably very exact.   " On the general view of the subject [of the note in reply to the British commissioners] we are unanimous, but, in my exposition of it, one objects to the form and another to the substance of almost every paragraph.   Mr. Gallatin is for striking out every expression that may be offensive to the feelings of the adverse party.   Mr. Clay is displeased with figurative language, which he thinks improper for a state paper.   Mr. Russell, agreeing in the objections of the two other gentlemen, will be further for amending the construction of every sentence; and Mr. Bayard, even when agreeing to say precisely the same thing, chooses to say it only in his own language."

At this moment, that is to say, from the 10th August to the 8th October, it was a matter of little consequence what form these personal annoyances might take, for no doubt was felt by any of the commissioners that negotiation was at an end.   Even Mr. Gallatin abandoned hope.   That the British government was really disposed to make peace seemed to him, as to his colleagues, too improbable to be worth discussion.   On the 20th August he wrote privately to Mr. Monroe: " The negotiations at this place will have the result which I have anticipated.   In one respect, however, I had been mistaken.   I had supposed whilst in England that the British ministry, in continuing the war, yielded to the popular sentiment, and were only desirous of giving some éclat to the termination of hostilities, and, by predatory attacks, of inflicting gratuitous injury on the United States. It appears now certain that they have more serious and dangerous objects in view."   After dwelling at some length on the indications that pointed to New Orleans as the spot where the ultimate struggle for supremacy was to come, he concluded: "I do not expect that we can be detained more than two or three weeks longer for the purpose either of closing the negotiation, of taking every other necessary step connected with it, and of making all the arrangements for our departure." To Mr. Dallas he wrote the same day: "Our negotiations may be considered as at an end. Some official notes may yet pass, but the nature of the demands of the British, made also as a preliminary *sine qua non*, to be admitted as a basis before a discussion, is such that there can be no doubt of a speedy rupture of our conferences, and that we will have no peace. Great Britain wants war in order to cripple us; she wants aggrandizement at our expense; she may have ulterior objects: no resource left but in union and vigorous prosecution of the war. When her terms are known it appears to me impossible that all America should not unite in defence of her rights, of her territory, I may say of her independence. I do not expect to be longer than three weeks in Europe."

Nevertheless, the three weeks passed without bringing the expected rupture. None of the American envoys knew the reasons of this delay; but the letters of the British negotiators, since published, explain the steps in that backward movement which at last brought about an abandonment of every point the British government had begun by declaring essential. Mr. Goulburn, who from the first was strongly inclined to obstruct a settlement and to put forward impossible conditions,[1] announced to his chief on the 23d August: "We are still without any answer to the note which we addressed to the American plenipotentiaries on Friday last. We have, however, met them to-day at dinner at the intendant's, and it is evident from their conversation that they do not mean to continue the negotiations at present. Mr. Clay, whom I sat next to at dinner, gave me clearly to understand that they had decided upon a reference to America for instructions, and that they considered our propositions equivalent to a demand for the cession of Boston or New York; and after dinner Mr. Bayard took me aside and

---

[1] See his letter of August 21 to Earl Bathurst, Wellington Sup. Desp., ix. 188.

requested that I would permit him to have a little private and confidential conversation. Upon my expressing my readiness to hear whatever he might like to say to me, he began a very long speech by saying that the present negotiation could not end in peace, and that he was desirous of privately stating (before we separated) what Great Britain did not appear to understand, viz., that, by proposing terms like those which had been offered, we were not only ruining all prospects of peace, but were sacrificing the party of which he was a member to their political adversaries. He went into a long discussion upon the views and objects of the several parties in America, the grounds upon which they had hitherto proceeded, and the effect which a hostile or conciliatory disposition on our part might have upon them. He inculcated how much it was for our interest to support the Federalists, and that to make peace was the only method of supporting them effectually; that we had nothing to fear for Canada if peace were made, be the terms what they might; that there would have been no difficulty about allegiance, impressment, &c.; but that our present demands were what America never could or would accede to. This was the general tenor of his conversation, to which I did not think it necessary to make much reply, and which I only mention to you in order to let you know at the earliest moment that the negotiation is not likely now to continue. . . . As I find, upon reading over what I have written, that I have drily stated what the American plenipotentiaries said to me, I cannot let it go without adding that it has made not the least impression upon me or upon my colleagues, to whom I have reported it."

If the notes and conversation of the American commissioners made no impression on Mr. Goulburn and his colleagues, the case was very different with their chiefs. A few days before Mr. Goulburn's letter was written, Lord Castlereagh passed through Ghent on his way to Vienna. He found that Goulburn had made a series of blunders, and was obliged to check him abruptly,[1] writing at the same time to Lord Liverpool,

---

[1] See his letter to Goulburn of August 28, 1814, Castlereagh Correspondence, 3d Series, vol. ii. p. 102.

advising a considerable "letting down of the question."[1] Lord
Liverpool replied on the 2d September, saying that his advice
had already been followed: "Our commissioners had certainly
taken a very erroneous view of our policy. If the negotiation
had been allowed to break off upon the two notes already presented, or upon such an answer as they were disposed to return,
I am satisfied the war would have become quite popular in
America."[2] Mr. Goulburn himself became a little nervous;
he wrote on the 2d September of the American commissioners:
"Their only anxiety appears to me to get back to America.
Whenever we meet them they always enter into unofficial discussions, much of the same nature as the conversation with
which Mr. Bayard indulged me; but we have given no encouragement to such conversations, thinking that they are liable
to much misrepresentation and cannot lead to any good purpose.
All that I think I have learnt from them is this: that Mr.
Adams is a very bad arguer, and that the Federalists are quite
as inveterate enemies to us as the Madisonians. Those who
know anything of America or Americans probably knew this
before. We await with some anxiety your note."[3] On the 5th
September, only three days afterwards, Mr. Goulburn's temper,
in view of the awkward position he was in, had become irritable; the American commissioners had never, he thought, had
any intention of making peace: "They gave it out all over the
town (previously even to sending their note) that the negotiations
would end in nothing, and I have never met them anywhere
without hearing their complaints at being detained here, and
their wish to leave the place on the 1st of October at the latest.
Some days since they gave their landlord notice that they meant
to quit their house, and two of their private secretaries set
out to make a tour in England before their note was written,
one of whom openly stated to me that, as they were on the
point of returning to America, he wished, first of all, to see
London."[4]

---

[1] Castlereagh to Liverpool, Correspondence, 3d Series, vol. ii. p. 100.
[2] Wellington Sup. Desp., ix. 214.
[3] Wellington Sup. Desp., ix. 217: Goulburn to Lord Bathurst.
[4] Ibid., p. 222.

The result of the first round in this encounter was clearly in favor of the American champions. The unfortunate Goulburn was worsted, and forced, with very bad grace, to accept the admonitions of his chiefs and to endure the triumph of his opponents.

Lord Bathurst accordingly undertook to correct the mistakes of his envoys, and forwarded on the 1st September an argumentative note calculated to persuade the Americans that nothing could be more becoming in them than to surrender the lakes to Great Britain and the North-West Territory to the Indians. The long reply of the American commissioners, delivered on the 9th September, was mostly written by Mr. Gallatin, and Mr. Adams candidly says in his Diary : " I struck out the greatest part of my own previous draft, preferring that of Mr. Gallatin upon the same points." Its contents were briefly characterized in a short note from the Foreign Office to the Duke of Wellington, dated September 13 : " It rejects all our proposals respecting the boundary and the military flag on the lakes, and refuses even to refer them to their government, offering at the same time to pursue the negotiation on the other points ;" and on the 16th the Duke was notified that : " We mean in our reply to admit that we do not intend to make the *exclusive military possession of the lakes a sine qua non of the negotiation.*" This was, however, not the only concession ; the new ground which Lord Bathurst now marked out for his negotiators was still further in the rear of Mr. Goulburn's first position, and abandoned not only the lakes but also the attempt to create an Indian sovereignty. The British note was sent in on the 19th September, and Mr. Adams gives in his Diary a graphic account of the conflicting feelings it aroused : " The effect of these notes upon us when they first come is to deject us all. We so fondly cling to the vain hope of peace that every new proof of its impossibility operates upon us as a disappointment. We had a desultory and general conversation upon this note, in which I thought both Mr. Gallatin and Mr. Bayard showed symptoms of despondency. In discussing with them I cannot always restrain the irritability of my temper. Mr. Bayard meets it with more of accommodation than heretofore, and sometimes with more compliance than I expect. Mr. Gallatin, having more pliability of character and more playfulness of disposition, throws off my heat with a joke.   Mr. Clay and Mr. Russell are perfectly firm themselves, but sometimes partake of the staggers of the two other gentlemen.   Mr. Gallatin said this day that the *sine qua non* now presented—that the Indians should be positively included in the peace, and placed in the state they were in before the war—would undoubtedly be rejected by our government if it was now presented to them, but that it was a bad point for us to break off the negotiation upon; that the difficulty of carrying on the war might compel us to admit the principle at last, for now the British had so committed themselves with regard to the Indians that it was impossible for them further to retreat. Mr. Bayard was of the same opinion, and recurred to the fundamental idea of breaking off upon some point which shall unite our own people in the support of the war. . . . I said . . . that if the point of the Indians was a bad point to break upon, I was very sure we should never find a good one; if that would not unite our people, it was a hopeless pursuit.   Mr. Gallatin repeated, with a very earnest look, that it was a bad point to break upon. 'Then,' said I, with a movement of impatience and an angry tone, 'it is a good point to admit the British as the sovereigns and protectors of our Indians.'   Gallatin's countenance brightened, and he said in a tone of perfect good humor, 'That's a non-sequitur.'   This turned the edge of the argument into mere jocularity.   I laughed, and insisted that it was a sequitur, and the conversation easily changed to another point."

Mr. Gallatin was right, and he drafted the reply to the British note accordingly.   There was a somewhat warm discussion over his draft, but his influence was now so decisive that Mr. Adams declares opposition useless; unless Gallatin voluntarily abandoned his point, he was uniformly sustained.   This note, while refusing to admit the Indians into the treaty in any manner that would recognize them as independent nations, offered a stipulation that they should retain all their old rights, privileges, and possessions. It was signed and sent on the 26th September; on October 1 the news of the capture of Washington arrived.

The following letters give some conception of what was passing in the United States while the American commissioners

were forcing Great Britain to abandon one position after
another:

MRS. MADISON TO MRS. GALLATIN.

28th July, 1814.

. . . We have been in a state of perturbation here for a long
time. The depredations of the enemy approaching within twenty
miles of the city, and the disaffected making incessant difficulties
for the government. Such a place as this has become! I cannot describe it. I wish for my own part we were at Philadelphia. The people here do not deserve that I should prefer it.
Among other exclamations and threats, they say, if Mr. M. attempts to move from this house, in case of an attack, they will
stop him, and that he shall *fall with it.* I am not the least
alarmed at these things, but entirely disgusted, and determined
to stay with him. Our preparation for defence, by some means
or other, is constantly retarded, but the small force the British
have on the bay will never venture nearer than at present,
twenty-three miles. . . .

JOSEPH H. NICHOLSON TO MRS. GALLATIN.

BALTIMORE, 4th September, 1814.

MY DEAR MADAM,— . . . You have of course heard of and
grieved over our disasters at Washington. You have heard, too,
of the disgraceful capitulation of Alexandria. Baltimore was
at one time certainly prepared to pursue the baneful example,
but the arrival of Rodgers, Porter, and Perry, the manly language which they held to our generals, and the great number of
troops which are now here, have inspired more confidence. If
the enemy had acted wisely they would have marched directly
from Washington to this place, and would have found it an easy
prey. If they come now, which we look for daily, or rather
nightly, they will have a fight, but I am not quite sure that it
will be a hard one. Our militia are so raw and so totally undisciplined, and our commanding generals so entirely unqualified
to organize them, that I have very little confidence of success.
The command has been taken from General Winder and given

to General Smith. The latter assumed it in the first instance without authority at the request of some of our citizens, and the usurpation has since been confirmed at Washington. There is some derangement of the Administration which I do not understand. General Armstrong is here, and says he is no longer Secretary of War; but every one who comes from the city says he is still considered so there. He explained the thing to me in this way. Mr. Madison had been waited on by a deputation from Georgetown, of whom A. C. Hanson was one, who told him that they would not agree to defend the place or to make any resistance if General Armstrong was to have any control over them. That Mr. Madison, in consequence of this and much other remonstrance of a similar nature, proposed to Armstrong that he should do all the business of the War Department except that which related to the District; that Armstrong immediately answered that he must do the whole business or none, and tendered his resignation, which was not accepted. He added, however, in his conversation with me: "I am here, and the President is in Washington." He said, too, he was going immediately to New York; but he has remained several days, and is here yet. I had thought it probable he was waiting for a recall, but he said yesterday he should go to-day, and expressed some satisfaction at being again in private life. This seemed to relate altogether to his pecuniary concerns. He speaks with no irritation of the Administration, and it is certain that either he or Mr. Madison, or possibly both, have yielded to a contemptible faction in a contemptible village, at a most critical moment for our country. This is the precise language in which I expressed myself to him, but he said he washed his hands of it.

The loan is taken *in part* only at $80 for $100, and, I believe, a small part. If Congress do not act immediately with vigor, the nation, I fear, is lost.

Did you feel very, very sorry at hearing that your old house was burnt? I did, really, I had spent so many happy hours in it.

A short correspondence with Mme. de Staël, then a power in diplomacy, claims also a place here.

MADAME DE STAËL TO GALLATIN.

Ce 31 juillet, 1814.
COPPET, SUISSE, PAYS DE VAUD.

Vous m'avez permis de vous demander si nous avons quelque succès heureux à espérer de votre mission. Mandez-moi à cet égard, my dear sir, tout ce qu'il vous est permis de me dire. Je suis inquiète d'un mot de Lord Castlereagh sur la durée de la guerre, et je ne m'explique pas pourquoi il a dit qu'il était de l'intérêt de l'Angleterre que le congrès de Vienne s'ouvrît plus tard. C'est vous Amérique qui m'intéressez avant tout maintenant, à part de mes affaires pécuniaires. Je vous trouve à présent les opprimés du parti de la liberté et je vois en vous la cause qui m'attachait à l'Angleterre il y a un an. On souhaite beaucoup de vous voir à Genève et vous y trouverez la république telle que vous l'avez laissée, seulement elle est moins libérale, car la mode est ainsi maintenant en Suisse. Aussi les vieux aristocrates se relèvent et se remettent à combattre, en oubliant, comme les géants de l'Arioste, qu'ils sont déjà morts. J'espère que la raison triomphera, et quand on vous connaît, on trouve cette raison si spirituelle qu'elle semble la plus forte. Soyez pacifique cependant et sacrifiez aux circonstances. Vous devez vous ennuyer à Gand, et je voudrais profiter pour causer avec vous de tout le temps que vous y perdez. Avez-vous quelques commissions à faire à Genève et voulez-vous me donner le plaisir de vous y être utile en quelque chose?

Mille compliments empressés.

Vous savez que M. Sismondi vous a loué dans son discours à St. Pierre.

MADAME DE STAËL TO GALLATIN.

Ce 30 septembre.
PARIS, RUE DE GRENELLE ST. GERMAIN, No. 105.

Je vous ai écrit de Coppet, my dear sir, et je n'ai point eu de réponse de vous. Je crains que ma lettre ne vous soit pas parvenue. Soyez assez bon pour me dire ce que vous pouvez me dire sur la vente de mes fonds en Amérique. Je suis si inquiète

que l'idée me venait d'envoyer mon fils en Amérique pour tirer
ma fortune de là.   Songez qu'elle y est presque toute entière,
c'est à dire que j'y ai quinze cents mille francs, soit en terres,
soit en fonds publics, soit chez les banquiers.   Soyez aussi assez
bon pour me dire si vous restez à Gand.   Mon fils en allant en
Angleterre pourrait passer par chez vous et vous donner des
nouvelles de Paris.   Enfin je vous prie de m'accorder quelques
lignes sur tout ce qui m'intéresse.   Vous pouvez compter sur
ma discrétion et sur ma reconnaissance,—et je mérite peut-être
quelque bienveillance par mes efforts pour vous servir.   Lord
Wellington prétend que je ne le vois jamais sans le prêcher sur
l'Amérique.   Vous savez de quelle haute considération je suis
pénétrée pour votre esprit et votre caractère.

Mille compliments.

GALLATIN TO MADAME DE STAËL-HOLSTEIN.

GAND, 4 octobre, 1814.

Ce n'est que hier, my dear madam, que j'ai reçu votre lettre
du 23 septembre; celle que vous m'aviez fait le plaisir de m'écrire
de Coppet m'était bien parvenue; mais malgré la parfaite confiance que vous m'avez inspirée, il était de mon devoir de ne rien
laisser transpirer de nos négociations; et j'espérais tous les jours
pouvoir vous annoncer le lendemain quelque chose de positif.
Nous sommes toujours dans le même état d'incertitude, mais il me
paraît impossible que cela puisse durer longtemps, et je vous pro-
mets que vous serez la première instruite du résultat.   Malgré les
fâcheux auspices sous lesquels nous avions commencé à traiter, je
n'avais point perdu l'espérance de pouvoir réussir.   Il faut cependant convenir que ce qui s'est passé à la prise de Washington
peut faire naître de nouveaux obstacles à la paix.   Une incur-
sion momentanée et la destruction d'un arsenal et d'une frégate
ne sont qu'une bagatelle; mais faire sauter ou brûler les palais
du Congrès et du Président, et les bureaux des différents départe-
ments, c'est un acte de vandalisme dont la guerre de vingt ans
en Europe, depuis les frontières de la Russie jusques à Paris et
de celles du Danemarc jusqu'à Naples, n'offre aucun exemple, et
qui doit nécessairement exaspérer les esprits.   Est-ce parceque à

l'exception de quelques cathédrales, l'Angleterre n'avoit aucun édifice public qui pût leur être comparé? Ou serait-ce pour consoler la populace de la cité de Londres de ce que Paris n'a été ni pillé ni brûlé?

Tout en vous disant cela, je ne me plains point de la conduite des Anglais, qui, si la guerre continue, loin de nous nuire, n'aura servi qu'à unir et animer la nation. Sous ce point de vue, la manière dont on nous fait la guerre doit pleinement rassurer ceux qui avaient des craintes mal fondées sur la permanence de notre union et de notre gouvernement fédératif. Et il n'y a qu'une dissolution totale qui puisse renverser nos finances et nous faire manquer à nos engagements. Je comprends cependant fort bien que lorsqu'on n'est pas Américain, l'on désirerait dans ce moment avoir sa fortune ailleurs que dans ce pays là; je puis avoir des préjugés trop favorables et ne voudrais aucunement vous induire en erreur. Mais il me semble que vendre vos fonds à 15 ou 20 pour cent de perte serait un sacrifice inutile. Ils tomberont probablement encore plus si la guerre continue, mais les intérêts seront toujours fidèlement payés et le capital sera au pair six mois après la paix. Nous nous sommes tirés d'une bien plus mauvaise situation. À la fin de la guerre de l'indépendance nous n'avions ni finances ni gouvernement; notre population ne s'élevait qu'à environ trois millions et demi, la nation était extrêmement pauvre, la dette publique était presqu'égale à ce qu'elle est actuellement; les fonds perdaient de 80 à 85 pour cent. Nous n'avons cependant pas fait faillite; nous n'avons pas réduit la dette à un tiers par un trait de plume; avec de l'économie et surtout de la probité, nous avons fait face à tout, remis tout au pair, et pendant les dix années qui avaient précédé la guerre actuelle nous avions payé la moitié du capital de notre ancienne dette. Au milieu de toutes nos factions, n'importe quel parti ait gouverné, le même esprit les a toujours animés à cet égard. Le même esprit règne encore; nous sommes très-riches; nous étions huit millions d'âmes au commencement de la guerre, et la population augmente de deux cent cinquante mille âmes par an. Si je n'ai pas entièrement méconnu l'Amérique, ses ressources et la moralité de sa politique, je ne me trompe pas en croyant ses fonds publics plus solides que ceux de toutes les puissances européennes.

Si cependant vous avez peur, attendez du moins la conclusion de nos négociations; vous n'avez pas le temps de faire vendre avant cette époque. Je serai au reste encore quinze jours au moins à Gand et donnerai avec grand plaisir à M. votre fils tous les renseignements en mon pouvoir s'il passe par ici en allant en Angleterre. Je suis très-sensible à tout ce que vous avez fait pour être utile à l'Amérique; je sens encore plus combien je vous dois; vous m'avez reçu et accueilli comme si j'eusse été une ancienne connaissance. Avant de vous connaître je respectais en vous Madame de Staël et la fille de Madame Necker, aux écrits et à l'exemple de qui j'ai plus d'obligation que je ne puis exprimer. Mais je vous avouerai que j'avais grand peur de vous; une femme très élégante et aimable et le premier génie de son sexe; l'on tremblerait à moins; vous eûtes à peine ouvert les lèvres que je fus rassuré, et en moins de cinq minutes je me sentis auprès de vous comme avec une amie de vingt ans. Je n'aurais fait que vous admirer, mais votre bonté égale vos talents et c'est pour cela que je vous aime. Agréez-en, je vous prie, l'assurance et soyez sûre du plaisir que me procurerait l'occasion de pouvoir vous être bon à quelque chose.

Mr. Goulburn, meanwhile, under the instructions of his government, was condescending to what had some remote resemblance to diplomacy. On the 23d September he wrote to Lord Bathurst acknowledging the receipt of two private letters, and adding: "You may depend upon our governing ourselves entirely by the instructions which they contain, and upon my continuing to represent to the Americans, as I always have done whenever an opportunity has offered, the very strong opinion which prevails in England against an unsatisfactory peace with America. Of this Mr. Gallatin appears to be the only American in any degree sensible, and this perhaps arises from his being less like an American than any of his colleagues."[1]

Evidently Mr. Gallatin was doing his utmost to keep the peace, and all he could do was hardly enough. When the American note of September 26 was received, Mr. Goulburn

---

[1] Wellington Sup. Desp., ix. 278.

wrote to his government that he considered it a rejection of their proposition *sine qua non*, and that to admit the American offer would be to abandon the principle on which the whole argument had been founded. He accused the American commissioners of irritating and unfounded accusations, of falsehood, of misstatement, and of fraud.[1] Lord Liverpool, however, was in a better temper, and, after consultation with his colleague, Earl Bathurst, framed an article which, in effect, accepted the offer of Indian amnesty proposed by the American envoys; yet so curiously ungracious was the mode of this concession that the Americans were by no means reassured. Instead of pacifying Mr. Adams, it irritated him. Mr. Gallatin had still to act as peacemaker. "The tone of all the British notes," says Mr. Adams, "is arrogant, overbearing, and offensive. The tone of ours is neither so bold nor so spirited as I think it should be. It is too much on the defensive, and too excessive in the caution to say nothing irritating. I have seldom been able to prevail upon my colleagues to insert anything in the style of retort upon the harsh and reproachful matter which we receive." The candid reader of these papers must admit that there is no apparent want of tartness in the American notes, and occasionally the retort is perhaps a little too much in the British style; but in any case the moment when England had yielded, however ungraciously, was justly thought by all Mr. Adams's colleagues to be not the most appropriate occasion for reproach. Even Mr. Clay was earnest on this point, and insisted upon drafting the American reply himself, and thus disposing of the Indian question. This done, the next step was to call for the projet of a treaty.

On the 18th October, Lord Bathurst accordingly sent the sketch for such a projet to Mr. Goulburn. Its most important point was an offer to treat in regard to boundaries on the basis of *uti possidetis*, an offer not in itself unfair, but startling in the application which Lord Bathurst gave to it. He proposed to exchange Castine and Machias, which were held by the British, for Forts Erie and Amherstburg, held by the Americans, while Michilimackinac, Fort Niagara with five miles circuit, and the northern

---

[1] Letter to Lord Bathurst, 26th September, Wellington Sup. Desp., ix. 287.

angle of Maine were to become British territory.[1] The details of this cession were, however, not to be put forward until the American commissioners had admitted the basis of *uti possidetis*, and accordingly the British commissioners, on the 21st October, sent a note to the Americans offering to treat on this ground, and adding that "they trust that the American plenipotentiaries will show, by their ready acceptance of this basis, that they duly appreciate the moderation of His Majesty's government in so far consulting the honor and fair pretensions of the United States, as, in the relative situation of the two countries, to authorize such a proposition."

Three days later, on the 24th October, the Americans sent back a very brief note bluntly refusing to treat on the basis of *uti possidetis*, or on any other basis than the *status quo ante bellum* in respect to territory, and calling for the British projet.

Of all the notes sent by the American negotiators, this, which they seem to have considered a matter of course and to which they gave not even a second thought, produced the liveliest emotions in the British government. Lord Liverpool, on receiving it, wrote at once to the Duke of Wellington: "The last note of the American plenipotentiaries puts an end, I think, to any hopes we might have entertained of our being able to bring the war with America at this time to a conclusion. . . . The doctrine of the American government is a very convenient one; that they will always be ready to keep what they acquire, but never to give up what they lose. . . . We still think it desirable to gain a little more time before the negotiation is brought to a close, and we shall therefore call upon them to deliver in a full projet of all the conditions on which they are ready to make peace before we enter into discussion on any of the points contained in our last note."[2] Mr. Goulburn assumed that everything was over, and merely wished to know whether they had best break off on this point or on that of the fisheries, and he showed almost his only trace of common sense by advising government to select the fisheries.[3] On the British side it

---

[1] Castlereagh Correspondence, 3d Series, ii. 168, 172.

[2] Wellington Sup. Desp., ix. 384.

[3] Goulburn to Bathurst, 14th November, 1814, ibid., p. 432.

was formally, though secretly, announced through the interior official circle, that the American war was to go on, and for a time the only apparent question was how to carry it on most effectively.

Unluckily, however, the more the British government looked at the subject from this point of view the less satisfaction they found in it. Mr. Vansittart, the Chancellor of the Exchequer, was very uncomfortable. Lord Liverpool was quite as uneasy as Mr. Vansittart. On the 28th October, the same day on which he wrote to the Duke of Wellington, he sent a letter to Lord Castlereagh, at Vienna: " I think it very material that we should likewise consider that our war with America will probably now be of some duration. We owe it therefore to ourselves not to make enemies in other quarters, if we can avoid it, for I cannot but feel apprehensive that some of our European allies will not be indisposed to favor the Americans; and if the Emperor of Russia should be desirous of taking up their cause, we are well aware, from some of Lord Walpole's late communications, that there is a most powerful party in Russia to support him. . . . Looking to a continuance of the American war, our financial state is far from satisfactory. Without taking into the account any compensation to foreign powers on the subject of the slave-trade, we shall want a loan for the service of the year of £27,000,000 or £28,000,000. The American war will not cost us less than £10,000,000 in addition to our peace establishment and other expenses. We must expect, therefore, to hear it said that the property tax is continued for the purpose of securing a better frontier for Canada."[1] A week later Lord Liverpool wrote again to Lord Castlereagh in a still lower tone: " I see little prospect of our negotiations at Ghent ending in peace. . . . The continuance of the American war will entail upon us a prodigious expense, much more than we had any idea of. . . . All our colleagues are coming to town, and we are to have a Cabinet on the speech to-morrow. Many of them have not yet seen the American correspondence; but we have got the question into that state that the government is not absolutely committed, and

---

[1] Wellington Sup. Desp., ix. 382.

there will be an opportunity therefore of reviewing in a full Cabinet the whole course of our policy as to America."[1]

This Cabinet council hit upon a brilliant idea to extricate them from their difficulties: the Duke of Wellington should go to America, with full powers to make peace or to fight, and in either case to take the entire responsibility on his own shoulders. This scheme was immediately communicated to the Duke by Lord Liverpool, in a letter dated November 4, the day after the council, and in communicating it the Earl frankly said: "The more we contemplate the character of the American war the more satisfied we are of the many inconveniences which may grow out of the continuation of it. We desire to bring it to an honorable conclusion."

The Duke of Wellington had some experience in acting as scape-goat for the blunders of his government; he was a man immeasurably superior to his civil chiefs, and even his common sense at times amounted to what in other men was genius. He wrote back, on the 9th November, a letter which would alone stamp him as the ablest English statesman of his day. He did not refuse to go to America, but he pointed out the mistakes that had been made there, and which must be remedied before he could do any good service; he then told Lord Liverpool very civilly but very decidedly that he had made a great blunder in requiring territorial concessions: "I confess that I think you have no right, from the state of the war, to demand any concession of territory from America. Considering everything, it is my opinion that the war has been a most successful one, and highly honorable to the British arms; but from particular circumstances, such as the want of the naval superiority on the lakes, you have not been able to carry it into the enemy's territory, notwithstanding your military success and now undoubted military superiority, and have not even cleared your own territory of the enemy on the point of attack. You cannot, then, on any principle of equality in negotiation, claim a cession of territory excepting in exchange for other advantages which you have in your power. I put out of the question the possession taken

---

by Sir John Sherbrooke between the Penobscot and Passamaquoddy Bay. It is evidently only temporary and till a larger
force will drive away the few companies he has left there; and
an officer might as well claim the sovereignty of the ground on
which his piquets stand or over which his patrols pass. Then,
if this reasoning be true, why stipulate for the *uti possidetis?*
You can get no territory; indeed, the state of your military
operations, however creditable, does not entitle you to demand
any; and you only afford the Americans a popular and creditable
ground, which, I believe, their government are looking for, not
to break off the negotiations, but to avoid to make peace. If
you had territory, as I hope you soon will have New Orleans,
I should prefer to insist upon the cession of that province as a
separate article than upon the *uti possidetis* as a principle of
negotiation."[1]

This was plain speaking. The whole British scheme of
negotiation had, moreover, been fatally shaken by the disastrous
failure of Sir George Prevost's attack on Plattsburg. Lord
Liverpool immediately wrote back to the Duke that the question
was still open and the Cabinet was disposed to meet his views on
the subject.[2] A few days later, on the 18th November, he wrote
to Lord Castlereagh announcing that government had at last
decided to recede: " We have under our consideration at present
the last American note of their projet of treaty, and I think we
have determined, if all other points can be satisfactorily settled,
not to continue the war for the purpose of obtaining or securing
any acquisition of territory. We have been led to this determination by the consideration of the unsatisfactory state of the
negotiations at Vienna, and by that of the alarming situation of
the interior of France. We have also been obliged to pay serious
attention to the state of our finances and to the difficulties we
shall have in continuing the property tax. Considering the
general depression of rents, which, even under any corn law that
is likely to meet with the approbation of Parliament, must be
expected to take place under such circumstances, it has appeared

---

[1] Wellington Sup. Desp., ix. 426.   Castlereagh Corr., 3d Series, ii. 186.
[2] Wellington Sup. Desp., ix. 430.

to us desirable to bring the American war, if possible, to a conclusion."[1]

Thus the second round in this diplomatic encounter closed with the British government fairly discomfited; Lord Bathurst and Lord Liverpool had succeeded no better than Mr. Goulburn in dealing with the American envoys, and had received a sharp lesson from the Duke of Wellington into the bargain. When the unfortunate Mr. Goulburn received the despatches containing his new instructions, he was deeply depressed. "I need not trouble you," he wrote on the 25th November to Lord Bathurst, "with the expression of my sincere regret at the alternative which the government feels itself compelled, by the present state of affairs in Europe, to adopt with respect to America. You know that I was never much inclined to give way to the Americans; I am still less inclined to do so after the statement of our demands with which the negotiation opened, and which has in every point of view proved most unfortunate."[2] The draught was a bitter one, but he swallowed it.

Meanwhile, the American commissioners, ignorant of all this secret correspondence and consultation, were busy in framing their projet, and in disputing among themselves in regard to the extension they should give to the principle of the *status quo ante bellum* as applied to other than territorial questions, and especially to the fisheries and the Mississippi.

The task of preparing articles on impressment, blockade, and indemnities was assigned to Mr. Adams; but as these articles were at once declared inadmissible by the British, and were abandoned in consequence, the whole stress of negotiation fell upon those respecting boundaries and the fisheries, which Mr. Gallatin undertook to prepare. On this point local jealousies were involved, which not only troubled the harmony of the mission, but left seeds that afterwards developed into a ferocious controversy between some of its members. This was owing to the fact that the treaty of 1783 had to a certain extent coupled the American right to fish in British waters with a British right to navigate the Mississippi. The British now proposed to put

---

[1] Wellington Sup. Desp., ix. 438.   [2] Ibid., 452.

an abrupt end to the American fisheries, but seemed disposed to retain the navigation of the Mississippi. To settle the question, Mr. Gallatin drew up an article by which the two articles of the treaty of 1783 on these points were recognized and confirmed.[1] To this Mr. Clay energetically objected, and a prolonged discussion took place. The question what the fisheries were worth was a question of fact, which was susceptible of answer, but no human being could say what the navigation of the Mississippi was worth, and for this very reason there could be no agreement. Whatever the right of navigation might amount to in national interest, it was very likely to equal the whole value of Mr. Clay's personal popularity; and whatever the fisheries might be worth to New England, their loss was certain to bankrupt Mr. Adams's political fortunes. Mr. Gallatin acted here not merely the part of a peacemaker, but that of an economist. He took upon himself the burden of saving the fisheries, and not only drafted the article which offered to renew the treaty stipulations of 1783, and thus set off the fisheries against the Mississippi, but assumed the brunt of the argument against Mr. Clay, who would listen to no suggestion of a return in this respect to the old status. On the 5th November the commissioners came to a vote on Mr. Gallatin's proposed article; Mr. Clay and Mr. Russell opposed it; Mr. Gallatin, Mr. Adams, and Mr. Bayard approved it, and it was voted that the article should be inserted in the American projet. Mr. Clay declared that he would not put his name to the note, though he should not go so far as to refuse his signature to the treaty.

The next day, however, a compromise was made. Mr. Clay proposed that Mr. Gallatin's article should be laid aside, and that, instead of a provision expressly inserted in the projet, a paragraph should be inserted in the note which was to accompany the projet. The idea suggested in this paragraph was that the commissioners were not authorized to bring the fisheries into discussion, because the treaty of 1783 was by its peculiar nature a permanent arrangement, and the United States could not con-

[1] See "The Duplicate Letters, the Fisheries, and the Mississippi," p. 126.

cede its abrogation.   True, the right to the Mississippi was thus made permanent, as well as the right to the fisheries, but Mr. Clay conceived that this right could be valid only so far as it was independent of the acquisition of Louisiana.

The reasoning seemed somewhat casuistic; Mr. Gallatin hesitated; he much doubted whether the provisions of 1783 about the fisheries and the Mississippi were in their nature permanent; on this point he believed the British to have the best of the argument; but the advantages of unanimity and of obedience to instructions outweighed his doubts.   Mr. Clay's compromise was accordingly adopted, but at the same time Mr. Adams, with the strong support of Mr. Gallatin, succeeded in adding the declaration that the commissioners were ready to sign a treaty which should apply the principle of the *status quo ante bellum* to all the subjects of difference.   Mr. Clay resisted as long as he could, but at last signed with his colleagues, and the projet sent in on November 10 accordingly contained no allusion to the fisheries or the Mississippi.

This note and projet of November 10 found the British commissioners still in a belligerent temper, for the effect of Mr. Vansittart's remonstrances and of the Duke of Wellington's advice had not yet made itself felt.   Mr. Goulburn wrote on the same day to Lord Bathurst that the greater part of the American projet was by far too extravagant to leave any doubt in his mind and that of his colleagues as to the mode in which it could be combated.[1]   An entire fortnight passed before his government startled him with the announcement that he must again give way, and it was only then, on November 25, that the fishery question was seriously taken up on the British side.

In Lord Castlereagh's original instructions of July 28,[2] the British commissioners had been told that the provisions of the treaty of 1783 in respect to the in-shore fisheries on the coast of Newfoundland had been productive of so much inconvenience as to determine the government not to renew them in their present form or to concede any accommodation to the Americans in this

---

[1] Wellington Sup. Desp., ix. 427.

[2] Castlereagh Correspondence, 3d Series, ii. 67.

respect except on the principle of an equivalent in frontier or otherwise. Supplementary instructions, dated August 14,[1] had also declared that the free navigation of the Mississippi must be provided for. Lord Bathurst had now to settle his policy on these points, and he seems to have instructed Mr. Goulburn, in letters dated the 21st and 22d November, that the treaty might be concluded without noticing the fishery question, since the crown lawyers were of the opinion, although he himself thought otherwise, that the American rights, unless expressly renewed, would necessarily terminate. These letters of Lord Bathurst, however, have not been printed, and their tenor can only be inferred from Mr. Goulburn's reply on the 25th November, from which it appears that the British were almost as much in doubt as the Americans in regard to the fishery rights: "Had we never mentioned the subject of the fisheries at all," said Mr. Goulburn, "I think that we might have argued the exclusion of the Americans from them on the general principle stated by Sir W. Scott and Sir C. Robinson; but having once brought forward the subject, having thus implied that we had (what Lord Castlereagh seemed really to have) a doubt of this principle; having received from the American plenipotentiaries a declaration of what they consider to be their right in this particular, and having left that declaration without an answer, I entirely concur in your opinion that we do practically admit the Americans to the fisheries as they enjoyed them before the war, and shall not, without a new war, be able to exclude them. I ought to add, however, that Dr. Adams and Lord Gambier do not agree in this opinion. You do us but justice in supposing that, without positive instructions, we shall not admit any article in favor of the American fishery even if any such should be brought forward by them; indeed, we did not at all understand your letter, either public or private, as implying any such concession."

The British counter-projet, sent in on November 26, contained accordingly no allusion to the fisheries and took no notice of Mr. Clay's paragraph in regard to the treaty of 1783, but, on the other hand, contained a clause stipulating for the free navigation

---

[1] Castlereagh Correspondence, 3d Series, ii. 86.

of the Mississippi. When this counter-projet came up for discussion in the American commission on the 28th November, another hot dispute arose. Mr. Gallatin proposed to accept the British clause in regard to the Mississippi, and to add another clause to continue the liberty of taking, drying, and curing fish, "as secured by the former treaty of peace." To this proposition Mr. Clay offered a stout resistance; he maintained that the fisheries were of little or no value, while the Mississippi was of immense importance, and he could see no sort of reason in treating them as equivalent. Mr. Adams maintained just the opposite view, and after the dispute had lasted the better part of two days, "Mr. Gallatin brought us all to unison again by a joke. He said he perceived that Mr. Adams cared nothing at all about the navigation of the Mississippi and thought of nothing but the fisheries. Mr. Clay cared nothing at all about the fisheries and thought of nothing but the Mississippi. The East was perfectly willing to sacrifice the West, and the West equally ready to sacrifice the East. Now he was a Western man, and would give the navigation of the river for the fisheries. Mr. Russell was an Eastern man, and was ready to do the same."

The proposition was accordingly made, and met with a prompt refusal from the British government, which proposed to adopt a new article by which both subjects should be referred to a future negotiation. This offer gave rise among the commissioners to a fresh contest, waged hotly about the point whether or not the United States should concede that a right fixed by the treaty of 1783 was open to negotiation. Here Mr. Gallatin parted company with Mr. Adams. He was unwilling to pledge the government to the doctrine that liberties granted by the treaty of 1783 could not be discussed, and he carried all his colleagues with him, Mr. Adams only excepted, in favor of a qualified acceptance of the British proposition, provided the engagement to negotiate applied to all the subjects of difference not yet adjusted, and provided it involved no abandonment of any right in the fisheries claimed by the United States.

Mr. Goulburn had flattered himself upon having at length gained a point. On the 10th December he had written to Lord Bathurst: "I confess my own opinion to be that the question

of the fisheries stood as well upon the result of the last conference as it can do upon any reply which they may make to our
proposition of this day. The arguments which they used at the
time will certainly be to be learnt only from the *ex parte* statements of the negotiators; but the fact of their having attempted
to purchase the fisheries is recorded, and is an evidence (to say
the least of it) that they doubt their right to enjoy them without a stipulation. If they receive our proposition, all will be
well; but if they reject it, they may derive from that rejection an argument against what we wish to deduce from the
protocol." [1]

Even the poor consolation which Mr. Goulburn thus hugged
was disappointed, for Mr. Gallatin's note neither accepted nor
rejected the British offer to negotiate, but expressed a willingness
to agree to do so only with the most emphatic reservation of all
rights claimed by the United States. Mr. Goulburn was obliged
to contemplate the abandonment of his last stronghold; he mildly
wrote to Lord Bathurst, suggesting that all stipulations respecting
the Mississippi and the fisheries should be omitted. [2]

After Mr. Gallatin had, with no little difficulty, succeeded in
carrying his point, and after the usual delay consequent on the
inevitable reference to London, an answer was returned on the
22d December. Somewhat to the discomfiture of both Mr. Clay
and Mr. Adams, the Eastern and Western belligerents, this reply
suddenly drew their war-chariots from under them. The British
government was now more eager for peace than the American
commissioners; it declared that it cared nothing about its proposed article by which the fisheries and the Mississippi were to be
referred to negotiation, and would withdraw it with pleasure, so
that the treaty might be silent on the subject. The practical
result was that Mr. Adams's view of the treaty of 1783 inevitably became the doctrine of his government, and that Mr. Clay
was overset. Mr. Clay saw this, and was nettled by it; but
Mr. Gallatin's very delicate management, and the now clearly
avowed desire of the British government to make peace, had
clinched the settlement; further discussion or delay was out of

---

[1] Wellington Sup. Desp., ix. 472.   [2] Ibid., p. 479.

the question, and three days later, on Christmas-Day, the treaty was signed.

Far more than contemporaries ever supposed or than is now imagined, the treaty of Ghent was the special work and the peculiar triumph of Mr. Gallatin. From what a fearful collapse it rescued the government, every reader knows. How bitterly it irritated the war-party in England, and what clamors were raised against it by the powerful interests that were bent on "punishing" the United States, can be seen in the old leaders of the London Times. What Lord Castlereagh at Vienna thought of it may be read in his letter of January 2, 1815, to Lord Liverpool : "The courier from Ghent with the news of the peace arrived yesterday morning. It has produced the greatest possible sensation here, and will, I have no doubt, enter largely into the calculations of our opponents. It is a most auspicious and seasonable event. I wish you joy of being released from the millstone of an American war."[1] The peace was due primarily to the good sense of Lord Castlereagh, Lord Liverpool, and the Duke of Wellington ; but there is fair room to doubt whether that good sense would have been kept steady to its purpose, and whether the American negotiators could have been held together in theirs, without the controlling influence of Mr. Gallatin's resource, tact, and authority ; whether, indeed, any negotiation at all could have been brought about except through Mr. Gallatin's personal efforts, from the time he supported the mission in the Cabinet to the time when he took the responsibility of going to England. Sooner or later peace must have come, but there may be fair reason to think that, without Mr. Gallatin, the United States must have fought another campaign, and, Mr. Clay to the contrary notwithstanding, the position of New England and of the finances made peace vitally necessary. On that subject Mr. Gallatin's knowledge of New England and of finance made him a wiser counsellor than Mr. Clay. Yet if Mr. Clay really had thought as he talked, he would not have crossed the ocean to assist in doing precisely what Mr. Gallatin's policy dictated ; he well knew that the United States could possibly win in the field

---

[1] Castlereagh Corr., 3d Series, ii. 523.

no advantages to compensate for the inevitable mischief that
another year of war must have caused to the government.

Be this as it may, the task done was done in the true spirit of
Mr. Gallatin's political philosophy and in the fullest sympathy
with his old convictions. Stress of circumstances had wrested
control from his hands, had blocked. his path as Secretary of the
Treasury, and had plunged the country headlong into difficulties
it was not yet competent to manage. Gallatin had abandoned
place and power, had thrown himself with all his energy upon
the only point where he could make his strength effective, and
had actually succeeded, by skill and persistence, in guiding the
country back to safe and solid ground. He was not a man to
boast of his exploits, and he never claimed peculiar credit in any
of these transactions, but as he signed the treaty of Ghent he
could fairly say that no one had done more than himself to
serve his country, and no one had acted a more unselfish part.

After a furious parting quarrel between Mr. Clay and Mr.
Adams, in which Mr. Gallatin again exercised all his tact to
soothe the angry feelings of the two combatants, while he quietly
threw his weight on Mr. Adams's side, the commissioners separated, and he found himself free to follow his own fancy. As
might be expected, his first act was to revisit his family and his
birthplace; he took the road to Geneva.

Of this visit very little can be said. His letters to his wife
during all the period of this stay in Europe have been lost, and
their place cannot be supplied. No man, however, can go through
the experience of returning to the associations of his youth, after
more than thirty years of struggle like his, without sensations
such as he would not care to express in words. He left only one
allusion to the subject: he said that, as he approached Geneva,
calm as his nature was, his calmness deserted him.

The citizens of his native town received him with the most
cordial welcome; they were proud of him, and he was greeted
with all the distinction he could have expected or wished. He
passed a short time in renewing his relations with the surviving
members of his family and with his old friends; then, departing
again for Paris, he arrived there in season to witness the return
of Napoleon from Elba, and to receive the information of his own

appointment as minister to France in place of Mr. Crawford, who had decided to return home.   In April he crossed the channel to England.   He had not yet determined to accept the French mission, and in any case his family and his private affairs made a return to America necessary; meanwhile, he and his colleagues lingered, hoping to effect still further negotiation under their powers for a commercial treaty.

The following letter is a memento of his stay in Paris.

ALEXANDER VON HUMBOLDT TO GALLATIN.

Je n'ai pas été assez heureux pour vous trouver ce matin, mon illustre ami.   J'aurais bien désiré cependant vous parler de mon attachement constant et tendre, de mon vif intérêt pour la paix que vous avez eu la gloire de conclure dans des circonstances difficiles. J'aurais aussi voulu vous féliciter sur cette belle et noble défense de la Nouvelle-Orléans qui fera respecter les armées de la Liberté, comme les flottes qui voguent sous votre pavillon se sont couvertes de gloire depuis longtemps.   Que dans ces temps malheureux mes yeux se fixent avec attendrissement sur ces contrées qui seront bientôt le centre de la civilisation humaine! Je ferai d'autres tentatives pour vous trouver et vous recommander de nouveau Mr. Warden, mon ami et celui de Messrs. Berthollet, Thenard, Gay Lussac, et de tout ce qui aime les sciences.   Je ne puis croire qu'un homme aussi instruit, aussi doux, aussi honnête, aussi attaché aux États-Unis, à M. Jefferson et aux doctrines vertueuses puisse etre rejetté par votre gouvernement.   Je supplie Madame Gallatin d'agréer l'hommage de mon respectueux dévouement. Quel contraste entre cette époque et celle où vous me vîtes à Londres ennuyé des " magnanimous Soverains" et de la croisade des héros !

HUMBOLDT.

Quai Malaquais, No. 3.
Jeudi.

Mr. Gallatin and Mr. Clay arrived in London early in April and began negotiations with Lord Castlereagh.   Mr. Adams, now appointed minister to England, joined his colleagues in the fol-

lowing month, but Mr. Bayard remained in Paris or on ship-
board. The President had appointed him minister to Russia,
but he was not in a condition to accept the post even if he had
cared to take it; broken down by illness, he was destined to
reach home only to die. The negotiation with Lord Castlereagh
was carried on almost entirely by Mr. Gallatin, and was the first
of a long series of similar negotiations mainly conducted by him
during the next fifteen years.

So far as England was concerned, excepting the questions of
the fisheries, impressment, and boundary, the only source of
serious difficulty arose in her colonial policy and the complications necessarily springing from it. These complications were
numerous, but became threatening only when England was
engaged in maritime war; at other times they were merely annoying, and kept our government incessantly employed in efforts
to obtain the relaxation or abandonment of vexatious commercial
restrictions. To obtain this result, however, the United States
had left herself no inducements to offer. Most of the maritime
powers in Europe had colonies, which they regarded as mere
farms of the State; private property with regard to other nations;
industrial speculations with which foreigners had no more to do
than with their arsenals and dock-yards; places where they were
admitted only on tolerance, and where they dealt not with the
colonist, but with the imperial government. England especially
had created a great system of this kind, and, to protect it, she had
enacted a long series of navigation laws whose object was to secure
all her own colonial trade to her own ships, and as much of her
neighbors' trade as she could gather into her ubiquitous hands.
Between European nations there was a sort of colonial compact;
they bargained one colonial trade against another, and admitted
one another's ships into their colonial ports provided their own
ships were admitted in return; but when the United States
claimed the same privilege, the European governments, with the
spirit and in the language of so many small hucksters, asked what
equivalent the United States could offer; where were the American colonies whose trade could be exchanged for that of the
European? Mr. Gallatin pointed out where the American colonies lay, a long uninterrupted succession stretching from Lake Erie

and Lake Superior to Mobile and New Orleans,—colonies whose growth surpassed that of the most prosperous European settlement as absolutely as the American continent surpassed in size and wealth the largest and richest island of either Indies. To this there was but one reply. The United States had already thrown the trade of her colonies open to the world; she could not now bargain for an equivalent. Even retaliation was precluded, for her own constitution would neither permit her to close any of her ports without closing all, nor to lay a duty on exports.

The English colonial system was the most difficult to deal with, since it was not only the most extensive, the most valuable, and the English colonies among the nearest to the United States, but its complications and inconsistencies were the most elaborate and perplexing, while to the British nation there was no absurdity in the whole mass that was not twisted deeply about some strong moneyed interest and that was not sanctified by age and English blood. To the United States there were three groups of questions involved in commercial relations with the British colonies. The first group included Canada and the whole trade with the provinces on our northern frontier, and was further complicated by our claim to the right of navigating the St. Lawrence. The second group included the British West India islands and their indirect trade with the United States through Nova Scotia. The third group consisted of the East Indies, and involved the trade between Calcutta, Europe, and the United States. These were the subjects which Mr. Gallatin attempted to settle by a commercial convention in the summer of 1815, and which detained him, much against his will, in England at a time when he was extremely anxious to be again at home.

Lord Castlereagh was friendly, and did what he could to smooth negotiation. Mr. Goulburn and Dr. Adams were continued in the British commission; but, in place of Lord Gambier, the American commissioners had a man to deal with whose qualifications and temper were of a very different kind. This was Frederic Robinson, afterwards Lord Goderich and Earl Ripon, who played a distinguished part in reforming the worst faults of the English commercial system. He was now vice-president of the Board of Trade, and treated the American ministers with courtesy and kindness, although able to do little more. Mr. Gallatin succeeded in disposing of none of the more difficult points in dispute. Not only did the British government politely decline to open the questions of impressment, blockade, and the trade with enemies' colonies in time of war, but it withdrew the whole subject of the West India trade from discussion, and refused to listen to the American proposition for regulating the traffic with Canada and opening the river St. Lawrence. There remained only the East Indies, and a convention was ultimately signed which secured the Americans for four years in the enjoyment of this branch of commerce. In discussing with the Secretary of State the merits of this commercial convention of 1815, Mr. Gallatin afterwards declared that the only portion of it which appeared to him truly valuable was that which abolished discriminating duties, "a policy which, removing some grounds of irritation, and preventing in that respect a species of commercial warfare, may have a tendency to lay the foundation of a better understanding between the two nations on other points."[1] This result of three months' labor was small enough, but Mr. Gallatin might derive some encouragement from the fact that the British government looked upon itself as having done a very generous act, since, in the words of its last note, "it considers itself as granting to the United States a privilege in regard to the East Indies for which it is entitled to require an equivalent."

The negotiation did not close without its inevitable accompaniment of discord.[2] Mr. Adams, who commonly recorded all his own sins of temper with conscientious self-reproach, seems in this case to have thought Mr. Gallatin at fault, and accuses him of speaking in a peremptory and somewhat petulant manner against a point of form in which Mr. Adams was undoubtedly right. The charge may very possibly be in this instance correct. The whole matter was trivial, so far as the dispute was concerned, and, like all these diplomatic irritations, had no

---

[1] Gallatin to Monroe, 25th November, 1815. Writings, i. 665.
[2] Memoirs of J. Q. Adams, iii. 242.

lasting effect except to associate in Mr. Gallatin's mind the recollection of Mr. Adams with ideas of deplorable wrong-headedness. This was not necessarily a correct conclusion, and Mr. Adams was naturally led to retaliate by thinking Mr. Gallatin tortuous. In point of fact, Mr. Adams was but one representative of a common New England type, little understood beyond the borders of that province; a type which, with an indurated exterior, was sinewy and supple to the core. The true Yankee wrested from man and from nature all he could get by force, but when force was exhausted he could be as pliable as his neighbors. In the present case, Mr. Adams attempted an experiment of this kind at the risk of some personal inconvenience to Mr. Gallatin. The nearly futile negotiation had detained Gallatin and Clay in England much beyond their intention; meanwhile, Bayard and Crawford, on June 18, had sailed in the Neptune, leaving their two companions to get home as they best could. It was now the 2d of July, and the treaty was waiting to be signed, when Mr. Adams made in the final draft some changes of form, which were certainly proper as a matter of national dignity, but which threatened to create further delay. This appears for a moment to have disturbed Gallatin's equanimity; but Mr. Adams carried his point, Mr. Robinson made no difficulty, and the disagreement ended by Gallatin saying to Adams: "Well, they got over the transpositions very easily; but you would not have found it so if Dr. Adams had had the reading of your copy instead of Robinson." "I said, that might be," was Mr. Adams's final entry.

That evening Mr. Gallatin dined for the last time during these negotiations with Mr. Alexander Baring, now and ever afterwards his warm friend, who had done more than any other man in England, or perhaps, with one exception, even in America, to hasten the peace, and who had, with the knowledge and consent of his own government, rendered very important financial assistance even while the war was going on. There had been much social entertainment in London, part of which is recorded in Mr. Adams's Diary; but the only English friend Mr. Gallatin ever made whose society he greatly enjoyed, and whose character he deeply respected, was Mr. Baring.

On July 4, Mr. Gallatin began his homeward journey, and, after the usual delays, he reached America early in September. On the 4th of that month he wrote from New York to President Madison: "I received the account of my appointment to France with pleasure and gratitude, as an evidence of your undiminished friendship and of public satisfaction for my services. Whether I can or will accept, I have not yet determined. The season will be far advanced for taking Mrs. Gallatin across the Atlantic, and I have had no time to ascertain what arrangements, if any, I can make for my children and private business during a second absence. The delay has been rather advantageous to the public, as it was best to have no minister at Paris during the late events."

GALLATIN TO JEFFERSON.

6th September, 1815.

I was much gratified by the receipt of your kind letter of March last, brought by Mr. Ticknor. Your usual partiality to me is evinced by the belief that our finances might have been better directed if I had remained in the Treasury. But I always thought that our war expenses were so great; perhaps necessarily so in proportion to the ordinary resources of the country; and the opposition of the moneyed men so inveterate, that it was impossible to avoid falling into a paper system if the war should be much longer protracted. I only regret that specie payments were not resumed on the return of peace. Whatever difficulties may be in the way, they cannot be insuperable, provided the subject be immediately attended to. If delayed, private interest will operate here as in England, and lay us under the curse of a depreciated and fluctuating currency. In every other respect I must acknowledge that the war has been useful. The character of America stands now as high as ever on the European Continent, and higher than ever it did in Great Britain. I may say that we are favorites everywhere except at courts, and even there, although the Emperor of Russia is perhaps the only sovereign who likes us, we are generally respected and considered as the nation designed to check the naval despotism of England. France, which alone can have a navy, will, under her present dynasty, be for some years a vassal of her great rival, and the mission with which I have been honored is in a political view unimportant. The revolution has not, however, been altogether useless. There is a visible improvement in the agriculture of the country and the situation of the peasantry. The new generation belonging to that class, freed from the petty despotism of nobles and priests, and made more easy in their circumstances by the abolition of tithes and by the equalization of taxes, have acquired an independent spirit, and are far superior to their fathers in intellect and information. They are not republicans, and are still too much dazzled by military glory, but I think that no monarch or ex-nobles can hereafter oppress them long with impunity.

The first question that pressed for an answer regarded the mission to France, but behind this a more serious subject presented itself; Mr. Gallatin must now decide what provision he could make for his children. This anxiety weighed upon his mind and caused much anxious thought and much hesitation in his conclusions. Fortunately, he had but the trouble of choice. In the course of a few months, one by one, the doors of every avenue to distinction or wealth were thrown open to him. The mission to France came first, and this, on the 23d November, he declined, alleging as his reason the private duties which required his attention to the interests of his children. Meanwhile, on the 23d September, 1815, Richard Bache wrote to him from Philadelphia, as follows: "A number of the conferees appointed to nominate a Democratic candidate to represent this district in the next Congress having met together last evening, it was unanimously agreed to nominate you, should you consent to serve. . . . We all anxiously hope that it will be consistent with your views to stand as a candidate, and we assure you that we are confident of success."

If ambition were his object, this invitation opened to Mr. Gallatin the path to Congress, and a seat in the Senate might reasonably be assumed as standing not far in the distance. Mr. Gallatin's reply was written the next day: "I am more gratified by the mark of confidence given me by the Republican conferees of the Philadelphia district than I can express. But I cannot serve them in the station with which they would honor me. My property is not half sufficient to support me anywhere but in the western country. To my private business and to making arrangements for entering into some active business I must necessarily and immediately attend. It is a duty I owe to my family."

A few days later, on the 9th October, his friend Mr. John Jacob Astor wrote him a long letter proposing that he should become a partner in Mr. Astor's commercial house. He had, he said, at that time a capital of about $800,000 engaged in trade. He estimated his probable profits at from $50,000 to $100,000 per annum, interest and all expenses deducted. " I propose to give you an interest of one-fifth, on which I mean to charge you the legal interest; if you put any funds to the stock, interest will be allowed to you of course."

On the 4th December, Mr. Monroe wrote to him : " To your other letter I have felt a repugnance to give a reply. We have been long in the public service together, engaged in support of the same great cause, have acted in harmony, and it is distressing to me to see you withdraw. I will write you again on this subject soon." He did write again, on the 16th, urging new reasons why Mr. Gallatin should accept the French mission. To this letter Mr. Gallatin made the following reply :

GALLATIN TO MONROE.

NEW YORK, 26th December, 1815.

DEAR SIR,—I have received your friendly letters of 4th and 16th instant, and have a grateful sense of the motives which dictated them. I can assure you that I feel a great reluctance to part with my personal and political friends, and that every consideration merely personal to myself and detached from my family urges a continuance in public life. My habits are formed and cannot be altered. I feel alive to everything connected with the interest, happiness, and reputation of the United States. Whatever affects unfavorably either of them makes me more unhappy than any private loss or inconvenience. Although I have nothing to do with it, the continued suspension of specie payments, which I consider as a continued unnecessary violation of the public faith, occupies my thoughts more than any other subject. I feel as a passenger in a storm,—vexed that I cannot assist. This I understand to be very generally the feeling of every statesman out of place. Be this as it may, although I did and do believe that for the present at least I could not be of much public utility in France, I did in my private letter to the President place my declining on the ground of private considerations. In that respect my views are limited to the mere means of existence without falling in debt. I do not wish to accumulate any property. I will not do my family the injury of impairing the little I have. My health is frail; they may soon lose me, and I will not leave them dependent on the bounty of others. Was I to go to France, and my compensation and private income (this last does not exceed $2500 a year) did not enable me to live as I ought, I must live as I can. I ask your forgiveness for entering in those details, but you have treated me as a friend, and I write to you as such. You have from friendship wished that I would reconsider my first decision, and I will avail myself of the permission. It will be understood that in the mean while, if the delay is attended with any public inconvenience, a new appointment may immediately take place. My motive for writing when I did was a fear that, specially with respect to other missions, the belief that I would go to France might induce the President to make different arrangements from those he would have adopted on a contrary supposition.

On the 27th January, 1816, Mr. Monroe replied by again urging Mr. Gallatin to accept, and pressing for a quick decision. On the 2d February Mr. Gallatin wrote his final acceptance.

GALLATIN TO JEFFERSON.

WASHINGTON, 1st April, 1816.

. . . After what I had written to you you could hardly have expected that I would have accepted the French mission. It was again offered to me in so friendly a manner and from so friendly motives that I was induced to accept. Nor will I conceal that I did not feel yet old enough, or had I philosophy enough, to go into retirement and abstract myself altogether from public affairs. I have no expectation, however, that in the present state of France I can be of any utility there, and hope that I will not make a long stay in that country. . . .

Mr. Gallatin, like most men, had the faculty of deceiving himself. In writing these lines, he was so inconsistent as to ignore the fact that he had already refused to return to public life on the ground that he must provide for his family. He was driven into still greater inconsistencies a few days later.

MADISON TO GALLATIN.

WASHINGTON, April 12, 1816.

DEAR SIR,—Mr. Dallas has signified to me that, it being his intention not to pass another winter in Washington, he has thought it his duty to give me an opportunity of selecting a successor during the present session of Congress; intimating a willingness, however, to remain, if desired, in order to put the National Bank in motion.

Will it be most agreeable to you to proceed on your mission to France, or are you willing again to take charge of a department heretofore conducted by you with so much reputation and usefulness, on the resignation of Mr. Dallas, which will, it is presumed, take effect about the 1st of October? In the latter case it will be proper that a nomination be forthwith made for the foreign appointment. Favor me with your determination as soon as you can make it convenient, accepting in the mean time my affectionate respects.

There could be no possible doubt that in this case ambition and public duty went hand in hand. If Mr. Gallatin still felt a passion for power, or still thought himself able to do good, this was his opportunity. His warm friend Joseph H. Nicholson wrote at once with all his old impetuosity to urge his acceptance.

JOSEPH H. NICHOLSON TO GALLATIN.

13th April, 1816.

MY DEAR SIR,—I have this moment learned that Dallas is certainly going out. For God's sake come into the Treasury again. I think you must be satisfied that you *can* if you will; and *I* am satisfied, and so is all the world, that you can be infinitely more useful there than in France, where you have nothing to gain and may lose. I think you will be looked to for the Treasury by all parties except Duane's.

GALLATIN TO MADISON.

NEW YORK, April 18, 1816.

DEAR SIR,—Your letter of the 12th reached me only the day before yesterday, and, not willing to make a hasty decision, I have delayed an answer till to-day. I feel very grateful for your kind offer, which I know to have been equally owing to your friendship for me and to your views of public utility. I decline it with some reluctance, because I think I would be more useful at home than abroad, and I had much rather be in America than in Europe. The reasons which induce me nevertheless to decline, under existing circumstances, preponderate. With these I do not mean to trouble you, and will only mention that, although competent as I think to the higher duties of office, there is for what I conceive a proper management of the Treasury a necessity for a mass of mechanical labor connected with details, forms, calculations, &c., which, having now lost sight of the thread and routine, I cannot think of again learning and going through. I know that in that respect there is now much confusion due to the changes of office and the state of the currency, and I believe that an active young man can alone reinstate and direct properly that department. I may add that I have made a number of arrangements founded on the expectation of the French mission, of a short residence there, and of a last visit to my Geneva relations, which could not be undone without causing inconvenience to me and disappointment to others. Accept my grateful thanks and the assurance of my constant and sincere attachment and respect.

Your obedient servant.

This letter shows rather a wish to find excuses than a faith in the weight of those alleged.   There was clearly no weight in them such as could justify Mr. Gallatin's refusal; had he accepted the Treasury he would probably have held it twelve years, unless he had himself chosen to retire, for although he appears rather to have favored the candidacy of Mr. Tompkins, of New York, than of Mr. Monroe, for the succession to President Madison, this probably indicated merely his unwillingness to exhaust public patience with indefinite Virginia supremacy, and did not imply hostility to Monroe, who would doubtless have retained him in the Cabinet, and to whom he would have been far more acceptable than the actual Secretary, William H. Crawford.   Gallatin, too, would have made a much better Secretary than Crawford, and Mr. Monroe would have been spared most of the political intrigue in his Cabinet that caused him such incessant vexation; the national finances would have been better managed, and Mr. Gallatin would have enjoyed the triumph of restoring specie payments, practically extinguishing the national debt, and possibly carrying out his schemes for internal improvement.

On the other hand, one evident fact sufficiently explains why he was unwilling to resume his old post.   The signature of the treaty of Ghent, on the 25th December, 1814, had closed one great epoch in his life, and, looking back from that standpoint upon the events of his political career, he could not avoid some very unpleasant conclusions.   Riper, wiser, and infinitely more experienced than in 1800, Gallatin had still lost qualities which, to a politician, were more important than either experience, wisdom, or maturity.   He had outgrown the convictions which had made his strength; he had not, indeed, lost confidence in himself, for, throughout all his trials and disappointments, the tone of his mind had remained as pure as when he began life, and he had never forfeited his self-respect; but he had lost something which, to his political success, was even more necessary ; that sublime confidence in human nature which had given to Mr. Jefferson and his party their single irresistible claim to popular devotion. His statesmanship had become, what practical statesmanship always has and must become, a mere struggle to deal with concrete facts at the cost of philosophic and *a priori* principles. Gallatin, like Madison and Monroe, like Clay and Calhoun, had outgrown the Jeffersonian dogmas. There was no longer any great unrealized conviction on which to build enthusiasm; and even on those questions which were likely to arise, Mr. Gallatin was rather in sympathy with his old opponents than with his old friends or his old self. The following letter could hardly have been written in 1801 by Mr. Gallatin or received by Matthew Lyon.

GALLATIN TO MATTHEW LYON.

New York, May 7, 1816.

 . . . The war has been productive of evil and good, but I think the good preponderates. Independent of the loss of lives and of the losses in property by individuals, the war has laid the foundation of permanent taxes and military establishments which the Republicans had deemed unfavorable to the happiness and free institutions of the country. But under our former system we were becoming too selfish, too much attached exclusively to the acquisition of wealth, above all, too much confined in our political feelings to local and State objects. The war has renewed and reinstated the national feelings and character which the Revolution had given, and which were daily lessened. The people have now more general objects of attachment with which their pride and political opinions are connected. They are more Americans; they feel and act more as a nation, and I hope that the permanency of the Union is thereby better secured. . . . I have lost three old friends: Mr. Savary, Thomas Clare, and Mr. Smilie.

He had come into office in 1801, with power more complete than he could ever hope to enjoy again ; his aims and his methods had been pure, unselfish, and noble; yet he had been the sport of faction and the victim of bitter personal hatred. He had no fancy for repeating the experience. Moreover, there was no longer any essential disagreement among the people in regard to political dogmas. Federalists and Republicans had fused their theories into a curious compound, of which this letter to Matthew Lyon gives an idea, and upon the ground thus formed all parties were now glad to unite, at least for a time. There remained no sufficient force, perhaps no sufficient prejudice, to overbalance the natural tendency of Mr. Gallatin's mind towards science and repose.

The seven years he passed in Paris were the most agreeable years of his life. Far the best diplomatist in the service, he was indispensable to his government, and was incessantly employed in all its most difficult negotiations, so far as they could be brought within his reach. Conscious of his peculiar fitness for diplomacy, weary of domestic intrigue, and indifferent to the possession of power, he dismissed his early ambitions and political projects not only without regret, but with positive relief.

GALLATIN TO MADISON.

NEW YORK, 7th June, 1816.

. . . I am urging the captain of the Peacock, and still hope that he will be ready to sail the day after to-morrow. I almost envy you the happy time which you will spend this summer in Orange, and which will not, I hope, be disturbed by any untoward change in our affairs. I think that, upon the whole, we have nothing to apprehend at this time from any foreign quarter. You already know how thoroughly impressed I am with the necessity of restoring specie payments. This subject will not disturb you in the country, but the present state of the currency is the only evil of any magnitude entailed by the war, and which it seems incumbent on us (pardon the expression) to cure radically. Public credit, private convenience, the sanctity of contracts, the moral character of the country, appear all to be involved in that question, and I feel the most perfect conviction that nothing but the will of government is wanted to reinstate us in that respect. The choice of the Secretary of the Treasury is, under those circumstances, important, and I am sorry that Mr. Crawford, as I am informed, has declined the appointment. I wish it may fall on Mr. Lowndes or on Mr. Calhoun. Our Maryland and Pennsylvania politicians, without excepting some of the most virtuous and whom I count amongst my best friends, are paper-tainted. The disease extends, though more particularly to this State.

I beg you to forgive this digression on a subject which I had no intention to touch when I began this letter.

On the 9th July, Mr. Gallatin, now accompanied by all his family, arrived in Paris. There he remained until June, 1823. During these seven years his connection with American politics was almost absolutely severed. His only political correspondent was Mr. Crawford, Secretary of the Treasury, who wrote him long and confidential letters, little calculated to excite in Mr. Gallatin the slightest desire to share in the political game. Indeed, politics had now become so exclusively a game in the United States, all vestige of party principles and all trace of deep convictions had so entirely vanished, that a statesman of the old school had no longer a place in public life. Petty factions grouped themselves about Crawford, Clay, Adams, Calhoun, De Witt Clinton, and General Jackson, and political action was regulated by antipathies rather than by public interest. If any one of these leaders seemed to be gaining an advantage, the followers of all the others combined to pull him down. Mr. Crawford's correspondence dealt largely in matters of this sort, and Mr. Gallatin was familiar enough with the style of intrigue to feel himself happy in escaping it.

If there was little to regret at Washington, there was much to enjoy in Paris. There Mr. Gallatin's position was peculiarly enviable. The United States, though a republic, was, in the royalist jargon of the French Court, a " legitimate" government. Its minister held a position which in itself was neither good nor bad, but which was capable of becoming the one or the other, according to the character of the man. In Gallatin's hands it was excellent. Not only was Mr. Gallatin a man of refinement in manners, tastes, and expression, a man of dignified and persuasive address, such as suited the highly exacting society of Paris under Louis XVIII.; he had a passport much more effective than this to the heart of French society. By family he was one of themselves. In Geneva, indeed, where republican institutions prevailed, there were no titles and no privileges attached to the name of Gallatin; but in France the family had been received as noble centuries since, and Mr. Gallatin had presumedly the right to appear before Louis XVIII. as the Comte de Gallatin, had he chosen to do so. His distant cousin, then minister of the King of Würtemberg at Paris, was, in fact, known as Comte de Gallatin, a royalist and conservative of the purest breed, but closely intimate with and attached to his democratic relative. This accident of noblesse was a matter of peculiar and exceptional importance at this Court, which was itself an accident and an anomaly, a curious fragment of the eighteenth century, floating, a mere wreck, on the turbulent ocean of French democracy. As one of an ancient family whom the Kings of France had from time immemorial recognized as noble, Mr. Gallatin was kindly received at Court; he was somewhat a favorite with the King and the royal family, and it is said that on one occasion Louis, in complimenting him upon his French, maliciously added, "but I think my English is better than yours;" a remark which must have called up in the minds of both a curious instantaneous retrospect and comparison of the circumstances under which they had learned that language,—a retrospect less agreeable to the King, one might suppose, than to Mr. Gallatin. There was another aristocratic tie between the minister and Parisian society. As already shown, Mme. de Staël had established relations with Mr. Gallatin on his first visit to Paris before the negotiations at Ghent. She had been very useful in bringing the Emperor Alexander in contact with American influences. She was herself by birth and residence a Genevan, and a distant relative of the Gallatins. Her daughter was married to the Duke de Broglie in February, 1816, and as a consequence Mr. Gallatin found a new intimacy ready to his hand. American readers of the Memoirs of George Ticknor will remember how much the Spanish historian owed to that intimacy with the Broglies, which he obtained through Mr. Gallatin's introduction, among others, to Mme. de Staël.

But the charm of Parisian society in Mr. Gallatin's eyes did not consist in his aristocratic affiliations. These indeed smoothed his path and relieved him from that sense of awkward strangeness which was the lot of most American diplomates in European society; but his sympathies lay with another class of men. "There is Talleyrand," said he to Benjamin Ogle Tayloe, when introducing him at court; "he is a humbug, unworthy of his reputation, but the world thinks otherwise, and you must not speak of my opinion." The apostles of legitimacy and the oracles of the Faubourg St. Germain were never favorites with him, and his old republican principles were rather revived than weakened by this contact with the essence of all he had most disliked in his younger and more ardent days. His real sympathies lay with the men of science; with Humboldt, with La Place, or with pure diplomatists like Pozzo di Borgo, the brilliant Russian ambassador at Paris, with whom his relations were close and confidential; or, finally, with French liberals like La Fayette, between whom and all Americans the kindest exchange of friendly civilities was incessant. Insufficient as the salary of American minister was, Mr. Gallatin had a handsome establishment and entertained as freely as his position required. The company he selected as a matter of personal choice may be partly inferred from a dinner at which Mr. Ogle Tayloe was present in 1819; La Fayette, the Duke de Broglie, his brother-in-law, De Staël, Lord and Lady Ashburton (Alexander Baring), and Baron Humboldt. "Humboldt talked nearly all the time in good English." French society was, however, in a very disturbed condition, and Mr. Gallatin did not always find it easy to avoid embarrassments. One example of such difficulties occurred in the case of La Place, who was somewhat sensitive in regard to his relations with the reigning family, and who, on finding himself about to be seated at Mr. Gallatin's table in company with so obnoxious a Republican as La Fayette, was seized with a sudden illness and obliged to return home.

Social amusements, however, Mr. Gallatin regarded very much as he did good wine or good cooking,—things desirable in them-

selves, but ending with the momentary gratification. He made
no record of this evanescent intellectual flavor. He wrote almost
nothing except his official letters. During no period of his life
are his memoranda and his correspondence so meagre and uninteresting as now. He had little to occupy him so far as official
work was concerned, except at intervals when some emergency
arose, and at first he chafed at this want of interest. He was
indeed always possessed with the idea that he would rather be at
home, and he averred every year with great regularity that he
expected to return in the following summer. This is, however,
a very common if not universal rule among American diplomatists of the active type. In reality, Mr. Gallatin never was
so happy and never so thoroughly in his proper social sphere as
when he lived in Paris and talked of Indian antiquities with
Humboldt, of bi-metallic currency with Baring, and of Spanish
diplomacy with Pozzo di Borgo.

Even his letters to Jefferson show his self-reproachful idleness :

GALLATIN TO JEFFERSON.

PARIS, 17th July, 1817.

DEAR SIR,— . . . The growing prosperity of the United
States is an object of admiration for all the friends of liberty
in Europe, a reproach on almost all the European governments.
At no period has America stood on higher ground abroad than
now, and every one who represents her may feel a just pride in
the contrast between her situation and that of all other countries,
and in the feeling of her perfect independence from all foreign
powers. This last sentiment acquires new force here in seeing
the situation of France, under the guardianship of the four great
potentates. That this state of things should cease is in every
respect highly desirable. Although not immediately affected by
it, we cannot but wish to see the ancient natural check of England resume its place in the system of the civilized world ; and
it can hardly be borne in the present state of knowledge, that
Austria or Russia should in the great scale stand before France.
Indeed, it is only physical power that now prevails, and as I had
most sincerely wished that France, when oppressing others, should

be driven back within her own bounds, I may be allowed to sigh for her emancipation from foreign yoke. I cannot view the arrangements made at Vienna as calculated to ensure even tranquillity. There is now a kind of torpid breathing-spell; but the fire is not extinct. The political institutions do not either here, in Italy, or even in Germany, harmonize with the state of knowledge, with the feelings and wishes of the people. What must be the consequence? New conflicts whenever opportunity will offer, and bloody revolutions effected or attempted, instead of that happy, peaceable, and gradual improvement which philanthropists had anticipated, and which seems to be exclusively the portion of our happy country.

We have lately lost Mme. de Staël, and she is a public loss. Her mind improved with her years without any diminution of her fine and brilliant genius. She was a power by herself, and had more influence on public opinion, and even on the acts of government, than any other person not in the ministry. I may add that she was one of your most sincere admirers.

I thirst for America, and I hope that the time is not distant when I may again see her shores and enjoy the blessings which are found only there. There I also hope of once more meeting with you.

Nevertheless, Mr. Gallatin was far from idle during these seven years. The wars in Europe had left a long train of diplomatic disputes behind them. Commercial treaties were necessary for the protection of American commerce. The old difficulties with England were still unsettled, and were pressing for settlement. Spain was always on the verge of war with the United States, both in respect to her undecided Florida boundary and the status of her revolted American colonies. Mr. Gallatin was at the head of the diplomatic service, highly valued both by Mr. Monroe, by Mr. Adams, who, in 1817, succeeded Mr. Monroe as Secretary of State, and by Mr. Crawford, who, as Secretary of the Treasury, had much to say in regard to questions of foreign commerce. Perhaps there was more unanimity among these three gentlemen, in their opinions of Mr. Gallatin, than there was on any other political subject. In fact, since the time of Dr. Franklin, the United States had never sent a minister abroad with qualifications equal to his, and it will never be possible to find a minister to France who approaches more nearly the highest ideal; accordingly, the government mainly depended upon him for its work, and economized his services by employing him freely in all its foreign relations.

The immediate object of sending a minister to France was to press for a settlement of American claims. These claims ran back ten years or more, to the time of the Berlin and Milan decrees, when large numbers of American ships with their cargoes were seized and confiscated, or destroyed at sea, by order of the Emperor Napoleon, in violation of every principle of decency, equity, and law. To exact a settlement of these claims was one of the points on which our country was most determined; to elude a settlement was a matter of equal determination with the government of Louis XVIII. No one, least of all the French ministries of the restoration, denied the indignity and the outrage of the robberies committed by Napoleon, nor did they quite venture to assert that Louis was not responsible for the acts of his predecessor; indeed, in Mr. Gallatin's first interview with the Duke de Richelieu, that minister frankly admitted the justice of the demand, and only asked some consideration for the helpless condition of France, weighed to the ground by indemnities exacted from her by the great European powers. But this was only a temporary weakness; Mr. Gallatin very soon found that there was little hope of obtaining any formal recognition, much less any settlement, of his claims, and he saw with some irritation and some amusement a host of difficulties, side-issues, petty complaints, and assumed quarrels, started by one French minister after another to distract his attention and check his pressure, until year after year elapsed without his gaining a single step, and at last the minister in 1823, M. de Chateaubriand, ceased to pay his notes any attention at all, and contented himself with replying that they did not alter his view of the subject. This exhausted Mr. Gallatin's patience, and he roundly told M. de Chateaubriand that if France meant to remain friends with America, her conduct must be changed. Simple as the case was, Mr. Gallatin gained nothing in seven years of patient effort; his elaborate and admirable notes were utterly thrown away; and he left the whole question at last, to all appearance, precisely where he found it.

During the first year of his residence abroad, this subject of the French claims was the only one which occupied his attention, and when it became clear that the French government would do nothing about these, he complained that he was absolutely without occupation. In July, 1817, he was sent to the Hague to assist Dr. Eustis, then minister there, in negotiating a commercial treaty with the Netherlands. This negotiation occupied two months and was also a failure. The Dutch insisted even more pertinaciously than the English on what Mr. Gallatin called the "preposterous ground" of colonial equivalents. It was found impossible even to stipulate for the mutual abandonment of discriminating duties, a stipulation which Mr. Gallatin regarded as the most valuable part of his convention with England in 1815. The Dutch insisted that a repeal of discriminating duties must not be limited merely to importations of the produce and manufactures of the two countries, and argued with great force that the geographical position of Holland and Belgium made it impossible to distinguish between their own produce and that brought down the Rhine or from across their border. To this Mr. Gallatin could only reply that his government could not offer more than fair reciprocity, and that the abolition of discriminating duties such as the Dutch claimed, would be wholly to the disadvantage of the American merchant and equally so to that of the American government in its negotiations with other powers. Yet, if the Dutch would have conceded the first point of admitting American vessels on favorable terms to their East India colonies, some compromise might have been effected in regard to the discriminating duties; in the inability to effect any transaction of this sort, the negotiation was in a friendly way adjourned.

In the following year Mr. Gallatin was employed on a more serious mission. The commercial convention of July 3, 1815, which he had negotiated in London after the Treaty of Ghent, would expire by limitation in July, 1819, and a timely agreement with the British government in regard to its renewal was very desirable. The opportunity was taken by the President to reopen negotiations on the whole range of disputed points left unsettled by the Treaty of Ghent, or arising under that treaty. As for impressment, indeed, Lord Castlereagh had very recently again declined the American proposals for a settlement, and the subject was therefore not pressed; but the fisheries, the commercial intercourse with Canada and the West Indies, and the boundary from Lake Superior to the Rocky Mountains, were all added to the negotiation; indemnity for slaves carried away under the Treaty of Ghent was to be urged; and the serious character of the dispute over the North-West boundary was just beginning to make itself evident in connection with Mr. Astor's trading settlement on the Columbia River.

Mr. Richard Rush was then the American minister in England; he had been called into public life by Gallatin, who made him Comptroller of the Treasury and presumably urged him for the place of Attorney-General, to which post he had been appointed on the retirement of William Pinkney in 1811. With him Mr. Gallatin was on most friendly terms, and Mr. Rush welcomed with great pleasure, what is always a somewhat delicate act, the intrusion of a third person in his relations with the government to which he was accredited. Mr. Gallatin was ordered to England, where he arrived August 16, 1818, and was occupied till the end of October, his "necessary and reasonable expenses" being, as usual, his only remuneration.

The negotiation with England of 1818 was not very much more fruitful in result than that of 1815; nevertheless the two countries had made some progress. On the one hand, Lord Castlereagh was still far in advance of public sentiment and had done something towards breaking down the insular arrogance of the colonial and navigation system; on the other hand, the United States government had plucked up courage to hasten the rapidity of British movements by retaliatory legislation of its own. Early in 1817 Congress passed two acts, by one of which British vessels were prohibited from importing into the United States any articles other than those which were produced or manufactured within the British dominions; by the other a tonnage duty of two dollars a ton was levied on all foreign vessels entering the

United States from any foreign port with which vessels of the United States were not ordinarily permitted to trade. A year later, shortly before Mr. Gallatin was sent to England, Congress had gone one step further, and had absolutely closed the ports of the United States against every British vessel coming from ports ordinarily closed against vessels of the United States.

This was the condition of affairs with which Mr. Gallatin and Mr. Rush had to deal. As in 1815, the British government was represented by Mr. Frederic Robinson, now president of the Board of Trade, assisted by Mr. Goulburn. The American commissioners offered five articles, covering the fisheries, the boundary, the West India trade, that with Nova Scotia and New Brunswick, and the captured slaves. The English plenipotentiaries offered a scheme for regulating impressment. Finally, the Americans proposed a series of rules in regard to contraband and maritime points.

The result of repeated conferences was to throw out the articles on maritime rights and impressment, and to refer the West India article to the President. A convention limited to ten years was then signed covering the fisheries, the boundary between the Lake of the Woods and the Rocky Mountains, the joint use of the Columbia River, the slave indemnity, and finally the renewal of the commercial convention of 1815. On the whole, there was certainly a considerable improvement in the relations of the two countries; even in the matter of impressments, Lord Castlereagh was ready to concede very nearly all that was required; the navigation of the Mississippi was definitively set at rest; even in regard to the West India trade, Mr. Robinson made very liberal concessions, and accepted in full the principle that this trade should be thrown open on principles of perfect reciprocity. That the British should have got so far as to admit that they were ready to open this trade at all on principles of reciprocity was no small step, but when Mr. Gallatin undertook to put upon paper his ideas of perfect reciprocity, it was found that agreement was still out of the question. He required that the vessels and their cargoes should on either side be subject to no charges to which both parties should not be equally liable, while the British insisted upon reserving the right to impose discriminating duties in favor of the trade of Nova Scotia and New Brunswick. Mr. Robinson did not, however, attempt to defend the dogmas of the British colonial and navigation laws; he only urged the impossibility of breaking them down at once. To the American argument of reciprocity he opposed the powerful interests he was obliged to humor,—the fish and the lumber of Nova Scotia and New Brunswick; the salted provisions and the flour of Ireland; the shipping of England; and the influence of the West India planters who sat in Parliament or moved in the business circles of the city.

There could be little doubt that the new retaliatory legislation of the United States would sooner or later bring the two countries into collision on this old subject of controversy; for the United States government was by no means inclined to look back with pleasure or with pride upon the humiliations which it had endured, ever since the peace of 1783, on this point of the colonial trade. Perhaps it had now a tendency to assert its rights and its dignity in a tone somewhat too abrupt, and even unnecessarily irritating to European ears. The new-born sense of nationality with which, since the peace of Ghent, every American citizen was swelling would tolerate from the national government nothing short of the fullest assertion of the national pride; and political parties no longer, as in the days of Mr. Jefferson, shrank from supporting their rights by force. Mr. Gallatin had done what he could to prevent mischief, and it remained to be seen whether his efforts were to be successful. His despatches dwelt repeatedly on the intimation of Mr. Robinson that Great Britain was certain to recede if she were allowed time to prepare, and that unlimited intercourse with the colonies would be the sure result of such a partial intercourse as he offered. On the other hand, however, the United States were still better aware that English diplomacy was inclined to respect very little except strength.

While the colonial dispute was thus left open, another serious question was only partially closed. On the subject of the fisheries, Mr. Gallatin effected a compromise not altogether satisfactory even to himself; he obtained an express recognition of the permanent right, but he was obliged to concede essential limitations of the practice. Perhaps, indeed, this question is one of those which admits of no complete settlement; as Mr. Gallatin wrote on November 6 to Mr. Adams: "The right of taking and drying fish in harbors within the exclusive jurisdiction of Great Britain, particularly on coasts now inhabited, was extremely obnoxious to her, and was considered as what the French civilians call a servitude. . . . I am satisfied that we could have obtained additional fishing-ground in exchange of the words 'for ever.' . . . Yet I will not conceal that this subject caused me more anxiety than any other branch of the negotiations, and that, after having participated in the Treaty of Ghent, it was a matter of regret to be obliged to sign an agreement which left the United States in any respect in a worse situation than before the war. . . . But . . . if a compromise was to take place, the present time and the terms proposed appeared more eligible than the chance of future contingencies. . . . With much reluctance I yielded to those considerations, rendered more powerful by our critical situation with Spain, and used my best endeavors to make the compromise on the most advantageous terms that could be obtained."[1]

On his return to Paris in October, 1818, an entirely different class of objects forced themselves on Mr. Gallatin's attention. This was the period when Spain's American colonies were in revolt, and it was of the highest importance to the United States that Europe should intervene in no way in the quarrel. Mr. Gallatin's business was to obtain early information of whatever concerned this subject, and to prepare the European powers for the recognition by the United States of the South American republics. The Congress of Aix-la-Chapelle was then sitting, and its proceedings were an object of intense curiosity throughout the world. So far as the policy of the United States was concerned, the result of this congress was very favorable; for Spain, finding herself abandoned by Europe, was driven into a treaty for the sale of Florida. This treaty was made, but its ratification was refused by the Spanish government on various pretexts, until a new revolution in Spain brought about a change

---

[1] Writings, ii. 83, 84.

of policy. In all these transactions Mr. Gallatin was deeply interested, and his advices to the home government furnished much of its best information.

Meanwhile, his powers to negotiate a commercial convention with France had lain nearly dormant, until in 1819 they were called out by a complication which soon brought the two countries to the verge of a commercial war. The French commercial system had never been a very enlightened one, but so long as her shipping remained in the state of nullity in which the long wars left it, American commerce had hardly perceived the fact that American ships were loaded with extra charges and discriminating duties such as made quite impossible all effective competition with the vessels of France. When at last the French commercial marine revived, complaints of the excessive burden of these discriminating duties and charges began to pour in from American consuls and merchants. The question was one of time only, when all commerce between the United States and France would be carried on exclusively in French ships. Well aware that the French government was entirely controlled in its commercial policy by the spirit of monopoly and narrow interests, Mr. Gallatin, while remonstrating to the minister of foreign affairs, warned the President that mere remonstrance would have no effect and that stronger measures must be used. He would have preferred an amendment to the Constitution authorizing Congress to lay an export duty on American produce when exported in foreign vessels; but, rather than wait for so distant and uncertain a remedy, he recommended that Congress should at once impose a countervailing tonnage duty of $12.50 per ton on French ships. This despatch was written on the 25th October, 1819. The rest of the story may be found recorded in Mr. Adams's Diary:

"May 15, 1820.— . . . Mr. Hyde de Neuville, the French minister, was there [at the Capitol] much fretted at the passage of a bill for levying a tonnage duty of $18 a ton upon French vessels, to commence the 1st July next. It is merely a countervailing duty to balance discriminating duties in France upon the same articles as imported in French or American vessels. It passes on the earnest recommendation of Mr. Gallatin after a neglect of three years by the French government of our repeated proposals to negotiate a commercial treaty, and after full warning given by Mr. Gallatin that, if they did not come to some arrangement with us, countervailing measures would be taken at the present session of Congress. The bill has been before Congress half the session, and De Neuville had never mentioned it to me. He probably had flattered himself that it would not pass. Now, after it had passed both Houses, he was in great agitation about it, and entreated me to ask the President to object to its passage, at least to postpone its commencement till the 1st of October. He said the 1st of July was only six weeks off, and would not even give the French merchants notice of what was awaiting them. . . . I told him it was now too late to make the amendment. I mentioned, however, his request to the President, who said it could not be complied with."

"September 5, 1820.—I received a despatch of 14th July from A. Gallatin, after Mr. Hyde de Neuville had arrived in Paris. Gallatin encloses a copy of a very able note that he had sent to Baron Pasquier, the French Minister of Foreign Affairs, concerning the tonnage duty upon French vessels coming into the ports of the United States, laid at the last session of Congress, but he complains that the measures of Congress, which he had recommended, were not adopted, but others more irritating to France, and also that his letters were published. The law of Congress was certainly a blister, and his letters were not oil to soften its application. The commencement of the law was fixed too soon, and the duty was too high. But France had been so sluggish and so deaf to friendly representations that it was necessary to awaken her by acts of another tone."

Certainly government was much to blame in this matter. Mr. Gallatin sent over a careful outline of the bill he wished to pass, fixing the duty at $12.50 and arranging the details so as to facilitate negotiation. Government proceeded to enact an unjust and extravagant bill, and then threw the responsibility on Mr. Gallatin. This is the special annoyance to which diplomatic agents are most frequently subjected. Mr. Gallatin remonstrated to his government and maintained his position stoutly against the French minister, who, after at once doubling the

French discriminating duties, at last transferred the negotiation to Washington, where Mr. Adams was obliged to take it up.

"February 24, 1821.—I called at the President's with a note received of yesterday's date from the French minister, Hyde de Neuville. I sent him two or three days since the copy of a full power, made out by the President's direction, authorizing me to treat with him upon commercial arrangements. The note of yesterday was introductory to the negotiation. Its principal object was to ask an answer to a long letter which De Neuville had written to me the 16th of June, 1818, upon a claim raised by the French government upon the 8th article of the Louisiana cession treaty. I had already answered one long note of his upon the subject, and had left his reply unanswered only to avoid altercation upon a claim which had no substance and upon which my answer to his first letter was of itself a sufficient answer to his reply. But when after the Act of Congress of 15th May last, and the retaliatory ordinances of the King of France of 26th July, the French government had been dragged into this negotiation, finding themselves unanswerably pressed by notes of great ability from Gallatin, they started from the course by setting up again this Louisiana claim and declaring it indispensably connected with the arrangement of the question upon discriminating duties. And as Mr. Gallatin was not instructed upon the Louisiana claim, they made this a pretext for transferring the negotiation here, and sending De Neuville back here to finish it, with an ulterior destination to Brazil, held out to our cotton-planters 'in terrorem.'"

But if Mr. Adams irritated Mr. Gallatin by the manner of carrying out his recommendation of retaliatory laws against France, Mr. Gallatin irritated Mr. Adams by his treatment of another diplomatic difficulty still more delicate. A French ship, the Apollon, had been seized by order of our government in the river St. Mary's, on the Spanish side, for infringing and evading our navigation laws. The seizure was a high-handed act, hardly defensible in law, and of the same class with many acts rendered, or supposed to be rendered, necessary by the inefficiency of the Spanish administration in Florida. Mr. Adams, who rarely allowed himself to be hindered by merely technical impediments in carrying out a correct policy, defended this act much as he defended the far more unjustifiable execution of Arbuthnot and Ambrister by General Jackson; that is, he made the best defence he could, and carried it off with a high hand. Mr. Gallatin, however, tried to justify the seizure by proving that it took place in American waters, and in discussing the subject in correspondence with Mr. Adams he added the remark which was, to any one who knew his mode of thought, quite inevitable as his summing up, that the tenor of Mr. Adams's argument was dangerous and would not find acceptance in Europe. This seems to have extremely irritated the Secretary, and called out the following entry in his Diary:

"8th November, 1821.—The most extraordinary part of Gallatin's conduct is that after a long argument to the French government upon grounds entirely new and different from those we had taken here, he gives us distinctly to understand that he considers all these grounds, ours and his own, as not worth a straw. I asked Calhoun to-day what he thought it could mean. He said perhaps it was the pride of opinion. I think it lies deeper. Gallatin is a man of first-rate talents, conscious and vain of them, and mortified in his ambition, checked, as it has been, after attaining the last step to the summit; timid in great perils, tortuous in his paths; born in Europe, disguising and yet betraying a supercilious prejudice of European superiority of intellect, and holding principles pliable to circumstances, occasionally mistaking the left for the right-handed wisdom."

The character thus drawn by Mr. Adams is very interesting as a study of something more than Mr. Gallatin only Mr. Gallatin certainly was a man of first-rate talents and was no doubt conscious of them; he would have been more than human had he not felt the injustice of that prejudice which had shut the door of the Presidency in his face because he was born in another republic; he certainly had the faculty of keeping his opinions, whatever they were, to himself, which is always an assumption of superiority; he was moreover an extremely adroit politician, full of resource, conciliatory and pliable in a remarkable degree; possibly, too, he may have at times mistaken his path. Timid he was not, but his courage was of a kind so perfectly self-assured

that it often disregarded imputations of timidity which would
have been intolerable to more sensitive men.   Mr. Adams himself
long afterwards and in the most public manner paid a tribute to
his absolute honesty such as he would have been willing to pay
hardly any other very prominent man of the time, unless it were
Madison and Monroe.   The character may, therefore, be admitted
as at least half true, and as throwing much light on its subject;
but it was very amusing as coming from the sources that produced it.   Ambition is not, within reasonable limits, a deadly
sin, but if it were, there was not a leading man of that time,
from Thomas Jefferson to De Witt Clinton, whose chance of
salvation was better than Mr. Gallatin's.   Vanity is a pardon-
able weakness, but the virtue of extreme modesty was not among
those merits which most characterized the American statesmen
of President Monroe's day.   Pliability in politics, if accompanied by honesty, is a virtue; business can be conducted in no
other way; but in all Mr. Gallatin's long career there was and
was to be no parallel to the political pliability to be found among
the Cabinet officers of President Monroe.   Human nature is only
relatively perfect; absolute perfection is a higher standard than
statesmen are required to attain; but even as regards relative
perfection, there is a curious suggestiveness in finding Mr. Gallatin singled out for pride of opinion, vanity, timidity, and tortu-
ousness, pliability, superciliousness, and mistakes of judgment,
among Mr. Calhoun and Mr. Adams, Mr. Crawford and Mr.
Clay.

This, however, was merely one of those diplomatic quarrels
which, like those at Ghent, have no real significance.   Mr. Gallatin was probably right in the opinion which vexed his chief.   At
all events, the French negotiation went on undisturbed, and even
after its transfer to Washington, which a very sensitive man
would have felt as a slight, Mr. Gallatin continued his active
assistance to Mr. Adams and pressed upon the French government with all his weight.   Ultimately an agreement was effected
and a treaty signed at Washington which, as Mr. Gallatin seems
to have thought, conceded somewhat more than was necessary,
but which at least put an end to the commercial war.

The conclusion of this treaty had been the principal object of

Mr. Gallatin's continuance at Paris, but this affair, the anxious condition of our relations with Spain, and his own increasing sense of satisfaction in diplomatic life, made him contented and even happy to remain over the year 1822. Mr. Crawford, whose candidacy for the succession to Mr. Monroe was then likely to prove successful, took pains to maintain close relations with Mr. Gallatin, and was especially anxious for his early return in order that his influence might be felt in the important State of Pennsylvania. This duty seems, however, to have little suited Mr. Gallatin's taste. He remained of his own accord in Paris, his opinion agreeing with that of the President that his presence there was desirable. At the same time he declined the office of president of the Bank of the United States. While thus holding himself aloof from public interests in America, he took a resolution which seems to show how little he understood the change that time and experience had worked in his circumstances. He sent his younger son to New Geneva with directions to build a stone house in extension of the brick building he had constructed thirty years before; here he proposed to return with his family and to pass the remainder of his life.

One of Sir Walter Scott's favorite sayings was that the wisest of our race often reserve the average stock of folly to be all expended upon some one flagrant absurdity. He might have added that when a shrewd and cautious man once commits such a folly there is more than a fair probability of his repeating it. Mr. Calhoun, who should have had some sympathy with this trait, may have been right in seeking for the source of unusual acts in "pride of opinion;" or a wider philosophy might trace such eccentricities to the peculiar structure of individual minds and to ineradicable habits of thought. Mr. Gallatin had in the pride of youth and the full fervor of fresh enthusiasm committed the folly of burying himself in the wilderness, and now, when more than sixty years old, after an active life of constant excitement, with a family of children almost entirely educated in Paris, and a wife who even thirty years before had found the western country intolerable, he proposed to return there and end his life. Had the great wave of western improvement swept New Geneva before it in its course, there might have been an excuse for Mr. Gallatin's determination; but New Geneva remained what he had left it, a beautiful and peaceful mountain valley, where no human being could find other employment than that of cultivating the soil with his own hands. There Mr. Gallatin decided to go, on the extraordinary plea that he could afford to live nowhere else, and the loss of a part of his private income in 1823 only fixed him more firmly in his determination.

Had he wished to return to Congress or to political life, there might have been reason in his course; but the only political position he cared to hold was that of minister in Paris, and this he relinquished in order to live on the banks of the Mononga-hela. The following letters will show what his friends wished and expected him to do, and what he did. His own letters from Paris, in reply to Mr. Crawford and Mr. Astor, are lost or destroyed; but it is clear that he paid very little attention to their suggestions. His own preference would have been to take only a leave of absence in 1823, to arrange his affairs and settle his sons in business; then to return himself to Paris.

CRAWFORD TO GALLATIN.

WASHINGTON, 13th May, 1822.

MY DEAR SIR,—It is now nearly two years since I have received a letter from you. Your last was dated about the 30th August, 1820.

The negotiation between France and the United States which has been carried on here for two years past, concerning our commercial relations, is likely to terminate successfully. I know of nothing which will probably prevent it, unless our determination to support every officer of the government in violating the orders, laws, and Constitution of the government and nation should oppose an insurmountable obstacle to it. Captain Stockton, of the Alligator, has seized a number of French vessels under the French flag, with French papers and French officers, and crews at least not composed of American citizens; yet we have tendered no satisfaction to the French government for this outrage upon their flag and upon the principles which we stoutly defend against England. A disposition to discuss has always characterized our government, but until recently an appearance of moderation has marked our discussions. Now our disposition to discuss seems to have augmented, and the spirit of conciliation has manifestly been abandoned by our councils. We are determined to say harsher things than are said to us, and to have the last word. Where this temper will lead us cannot be distinctly foreseen. We are now upon bad terms with the principal maritime states, and perhaps on the brink of a rupture with Russia on account of the prohibition to trade with the north-west coast beyond the 51st degree of north latitude and to approach within 100 Italian miles of the islands on the Asiatic side. I have labored to restrain this predominant disposition of the government, but have succeeded only partially in softening the asperities which invariably predominate in the official notes of the State Department. If these notes had been permitted to remain as originally drafted, we should, I believe, have before this time been unembarrassed by diplomatic relations with more than one power. The tendency to estrange us from all foreign powers, which the style of the notes of the State Department has uniformly had, has been so often demonstrated, yet so often permitted, that I have almost given up the idea of maintaining friendly relations with those powers; but of late another embarrassment no less perplexing in its tendency has arisen. Our Mars[1] has intuitive perceptions not only upon military organization, but upon fortifications and other military subjects. These intuitions of his have involved the President in contests with both Houses of Congress. He has contrived to make them those of the President instead of his own. A state of irritation prevails which greatly exceeds anything which has occurred in the history of this government. The Secretary of War is now, in the estimation of the public, lord of the ascendant. Certain it is that every appointment in Florida was made without my knowledge, and even the appointments connected with my own Department have been made without regard to my wishes, or rather without ascertaining what they were.

It is understood that an impression has been made on the mind

---

[1] Mr. Calhoun, Secretary of War.

of the President that the rejection of the military nominations by the Senate has been effected by my influence.

I have known this for nearly two months, but have taken no step to counteract it, and shall take none, because I think it will not be injurious to me to remain in this state or even to be removed from office.

The latter, however, is an honor which I shall not solicit, although I do not believe it would be injurious to me in a political point of view.

You will perceive by the newspapers that much agitation has already prevailed as to the election of the next President. The war candidate, as Mr. Randolph calls him, is understood to be extremely active in his operations, and, as it has been said by religious zealots, appears to be determined to take the citadel by storm.

An impression prevails that Mr. Adams's friends, in despair of his success, have thrown themselves into the scale of his more youthful friend, lately converted into a competitor. You will have seen that Mr. Lowndes has been nominated by the South Carolina Legislature, or rather by a portion of it. This event, as well as the present course of the Secretary of War, it is believed may be traced to the election of Governor Clark, of Georgia. This gentleman is personally my enemy. He was elected in 1819 in opposition to Colonel Troup by a majority of 13 votes. In 1821 he was opposed by the same gentleman. Mr. Calhoun, Mr. Adams, and Mr. Lowndes had conceived the idea that, if he should be re-elected, the electoral vote of Georgia would be against me. He was re-elected by a majority of 2 votes. Calhoun and Lowndes had through the year favored Mr. Adams's pretensions; they found, however, that it was an up-hill work. Considering me *hors du combat,* and finding Mr. A. unacceptable to the South, each of them supposed that the Southern interest would become the property of the first adventurer. Mr. C. had made a tour of observation in Pennsylvania, whilst Mr. L. kept watch at home. When the result of the Georgia election was known, Mr. C. threw himself upon Pennsylvania, and Mr. L., who had remained in South Carolina until after the meeting of its Legislature, was nominated by a portion of it to the Presidency.

A conference took place between them, but no adjustment was effected, as each determined to hold the vantage-ground which he was supposed to have gained. The delusion as to Georgia has passed away, but Mr. C. cannot now recede, and entertains confident hopes of success. Pennsylvania he calculates upon, as well as upon many other States. Mr. Clay is held up by his friends, but has not taken any decided measure. I consider everything that has passed as deciding nothing. Everything will depend on the election of Congress, which takes place this year in all the States except Virginia, North Carolina, and Tennessee. My own impression is that Mr. C. will be the Federal candidate if his name is kept up. If he should be put down, and I think he will be, especially if Pennsylvania should declare against him, Mr. Adams will be the Federal candidate. Mr. Clay will be up if Pennsylvania, Virginia, or New York will declare for him. At present there is not much prospect of either.

The stockholders of the Bank of the United States are becoming restive under the low dividends which they receive. A decided opposition to Mr. Cheves will be made the next year. I understand that many of the stockholders are for placing you at the head of that institution. I know not whether you wish such an appointment. The election of governor comes on next year. Many persons are spoken of for that office. Bryan, Ingham, Lowrie, and Lacock are among the number, and some intimations have reached me that, if you were here, you might be selected. Ingham is connected with Mr. Calhoun. The others are unfavorable to his views.

Present my respects to Mrs. Gallatin and every member of your family.

I remain, dear sir, your sincere friend.

CRAWFORD TO GALLATIN.

WASHINGTON, 26th June, 1822.

MY DEAR SIR,—On the 24th inst. a commercial convention was signed by Mr. Adams and Mr. De Neuville. It is published in the Intelligencer of this day. If it is permitted to operate a few years, all discriminating duties will cease. I am, however, apprehensive that it will not be permitted to produce this effect. . . .

In my last letter I suggested the probability that the presidency of the Bank of the United States might be offered to you if you were in the United States at the time of the next election. Mr. Cheves has informed me confidentially that he will resign his office about the latter end of this year. He will declare this intention when the next dividend shall be declared.

As the commercial convention with France has been agreed upon, and as I understand that all the indemnity which will probably ever be obtained will have been obtained before you receive this letter, all inducement to a longer residence in France is at an end. Independent of the office to which I have referred, that of Governor of Pennsylvania will be disposed of next year. If you intend to engage in any way whatever in the concerns of this country after your return, I think you ought to be here during the next autumn. I believe there is no disposition in any party to re-elect Heister. The schismatics, who, with Binns, opposed Finley at the last election, are desirous of uniting with their former friends in the next election. It is understood that they are desirous of bringing you forward, and I presume the great body of the party will meet them upon this subject. Ingham will be supported in caucus by those devoted to F., but that, I believe, is only a small part of those who supported him in his last effort. Bryan, the late auditor, Lowrie, and Lacock are spoken of, but no commitment has taken place except by Ingham and his friends, who, it is understood, wish to connect that question with the election of Mr. Calhoun as President. The other gentlemen are understood to be decidedly opposed to the pretensions of the latter gentleman.

Mr. De Neuville will be able to give you many details upon our local politics, with which he is pretty well acquainted.

The collision between the President and Senate upon certain military nominations has very much soured his mind and given a direction to his actions which I conceive to be unfortunate for the nation as well as for himself. I hope, however, that a better state of feeling will, after the first irritation has passed off, be restored and cherished on both sides. The public seems to have taken less interest in this affair than I had expected. Two or three criticisms have appeared in the Intelligencer upon the conduct of the Senate, but they have attracted but little attention in any part of the Union.

The controversy which is going on between Mr. Adams and Mr. Russell, in which you are made a party, has attracted considerable notice, and will probably continue to command attention. You will readily perceive that the object of the party was less to injure Mr. Adams than to benefit another by placing him in a conspicuous point of view, and especially by showing that Western interests could not be safely trusted to persons residing in the Atlantic States. . . .

J. J. ASTOR TO GALLATIN.

NEW YORK, 18th October, 1822.

. . . Your leaving Paris will be a great loss to me, if I go, as I expect to. I really think you will not like it so much in this country as you did, and I believe you had better remain where you are. For the interest of the United States Bank I am sorry that you will not take it. For your own sake I am glad. It is, as you say, a troublesome situation, and I doubt if much credit is to be got by it. I have been to-day spoken to about your taking the situation, but I stated that you decline it, and I think you are right. Matters here go on irregular enough. It's all the while up and down. So soon as people have a little money they run into extravagancy, get in debt, and down it goes. Exchange is again 12½ to 13, and people will again ship specie, the banks again curtail discounts, bankruptcy ensues, exchange will fall for a short time, and then we have the same scene over again. You know so well this country and character of the people that I need say no more. We have plenty candidates for President; Mr. Clay, Mr. Calhoun, and Crawford are the most prominent. Mr. Crawford, I think, will get it. . . .

GALLATIN TO MONROE.

PARIS, 13th November, 1822.

With respect to my longer stay here I entertain a just sense of your partiality and kind feelings towards me; and I may add that, so far as I am personally concerned, the station is not only highly honorable, but more agreeable than any other public employment which [I] might fill. But considerations connected with my children and with my private affairs imperiously require my presence in America, at least for some months. Under those circumstances I will, with your permission, return next spring, but take leave here as only going with leave of absence. I would probably be ready to return here in the autumn, and take care that the public interest should not in the mean while suffer. Mr. Sheldon is indeed fully equal to the task of managing all the current affairs of the mission; and France has given us the example of leaving a chargé for a short time. But this must not by any means prevent you from filling the place at once on my return, if you think it proper. I will only thank you to let me know your intention in that respect as soon as possible after the receipt of this letter.

GALLATIN TO J. Q. ADAMS.

PARIS, 28th February, 1823.

DEAR SIR,—There not being at this time the least prospect of a settlement of our claims, I do not perceive any reason connected with the public service for protracting my stay in this country. I will terminate, as far as this government will allow, what relates to the fisheries, although I would have wished to hear from you on the subject; and some heavy losses I have experienced at home, as well as certain family circumstances, imperiously requiring my presence there, it is my intention, if nothing new and important of a public nature shall take place, to take my departure in the course of the spring. I had already written a private letter on that subject to the President, to which I had hoped to have received an answer before this time, and in which I had asked only for leave of absence. But, this being an unusual course, it may be better at once to appoint a successor, and I wish it to be done. If the President shall think it more eligible to wait for the meeting of the Senate, you know that Mr. Sheldon is fully competent to carry on the current business; and I believe him equally so to act on any incident that may arise.   As to the still uncertain war with Spain, nothing can possibly be necessary here on our part than perhaps some remonstrance in case of infractions of our neutral rights.   There is no disposition on the part of France to commit acts of that kind, and that subject is also quite familiar to Mr. Sheldon.

GALLATIN TO J. Q. ADAMS.

PARIS, 18th April, 1823.

SIR,—I had the honor to receive your despatch No. 55, and intend to avail myself of the leave of absence granted by the President, and to take my departure in about a month, leaving Mr. Sheldon as chargé d'affaires.

I beg you to express my thanks to the President, but to repeat that it is not my wish that another appointment should be delayed on my account, if deemed useful.

Mr. Gallatin accordingly left Paris with his family about the middle of May, 1823, and arrived in New York on the 24th June.   The following letter, the last which Mr. Crawford wrote him, was not received by Mr. Gallatin in Europe.   Whether the intensity of that struggle for the Presidency in which Mr. Crawford was now engaged had embittered his mind, or whether the paralysis which struck him down only a short time afterwards was casting its shadow before it, this letter shows a peculiar irritation which seems almost ready to make Mr. Gallatin himself its victim.

CRAWFORD TO GALLATIN.

WASHINGTON, 26th May, 1823.

MY DEAR SIR,—Your letter of the 27th of September last was received some time in December thereafter, and is the last letter I have had from you.

Some time in December I understood you had applied for leave of absence, and shortly after was informed that it had been granted.

In the latter end of April the President showed me a private letter from you dated in the early part of March, in which you declare your determination to leave France the 10th of this month, and a few days afterwards I was informed that Mr. Adams had requested you to remain. I understand that this request had been made in consequence of the expected rupture between France and Spain. It would therefore appear that the reasons you assigned for believing your presence at Paris would be useless have not been considered good by the Secretary of State. To me they appeared conclusive when I read the letter, and reflection has only confirmed my first impressions. It is not pretended that the war with Spain will favor the efforts which have for twelve years past been made without success to procure indemnity for unjust spoliations committed upon our merchants. Infractions of our neutral rights must then be apprehended before a successor could be sent. The interest of France to strip Great Britain of an excuse to interfere in the war is the best guaranty that can be offered for her scrupulous respect for neutral rights. All that an American minister can do during the present year at Paris will be to give information of what is going on and speculate upon what may possibly be done in the progress of the war. If the Secretary was at Paris, or if his protégé, Mr. [Alexander] Everett, was there, the curiosity of the government to grasp at future events would have ample gratification. I do not know Mr. Sheldon well enough to form an opinion of his capacity to minister to this propensity of man, but I presume he would supply it with as much, if not as delicate, food as it would receive from you.

Some of the little people who buzz about the government have, I understand, been very busy in the expression of their opinions that the change of relations between France and Spain renders highly important that you should remain. The people have had their cue, and repeat their lesson by rote, for if they were capable of reasoning themselves they would see the folly of their declarations. It is impossible that reflecting men whose judgments are not led astray by some strong impression resulting from selfish purposes, can believe that it is of any importance to have a minister at Paris at this moment.

The reason then assigned for this request is not the true one.

That must be sought not in Paris but in the United States. You will understand it as well as I do upon a moment's reflection. Your presence in the United States during the present year may not suit the views and projects of certain gentlemen; it is, therefore, necessary to devise some cause for keeping you at Paris. It is possible that if Mr. Rush was disposed to return, some cause connected with the rupture between France and Spain would be discovered to render his stay in London necessary. As that gentleman, however, has written a number of letters to his friends in Pennsylvania which may have an effect somewhat similar to that which was apprehended from your return, it is possible that it may facilitate his return.

I have written this letter under an impression that the request of Mr. Adams may arrive at Paris before you leave it. Your friends are desirous of your return, and will be disappointed if you do not. I have understood that Mr. Astor has received a letter from you as late as the 17th ult. which is indicative of your intention to return, but Mr. Astor thinks that you will not, and that you ought not. He is probably governed in this opinion by his interests and wishes. If you do not return in the Montano, which it is now said will not sail before the 20th of this month, he will see you before this letter reaches you, as I shall confide it to the care of Mr. Erving, who, it is understood, will not sail until the arrival of the Montano.

Your friends Lacock and Roberts are very decided on the question which now attracts the attention of the nation. Indeed, there are but few exceptions among your old political associates. Many of them, unfortunately, are no more, and new men have filled their places; the new-comers, however, have a high respect for your character, talents, and opinions, and wish to see and converse with you upon this question. . . .

Mr. Crawford had his wish. Gallatin returned, and was drawn reluctantly but inevitably into the Presidential contest. No true friend of his could have desired it, for he had nothing to gain by returning into public life at a moment when there was not a single element of principle or dignity involved in the election. Never in the whole course of our history has any

Presidential election turned so exclusively on purely personal considerations; never has there been one in which all parties were so helpless. Old association, the prestige of high reputation, and the long control of Treasury patronage combined to make Mr. Crawford the first candidate; he had been the selected favorite of the old triumvirate for many years, and by Mr. Jefferson and Mr. Madison he was regarded as the best representative of the Republican party. The same view was held by Mr. Gallatin, and, on the other hand, Mr. Crawford needed Mr. Gallatin's active support; thus it was that Mr. Gallatin became in a manner compelled to allow his supposed influence to be used for the election of Mr. Crawford as President, and was buffeted about upon the waves of this stormy and unclean ocean until at length he was glad to find even a mortifying means of escape.

His first step was to visit Washington, and thence he went to inspect his new house at Friendship Hill.

GALLATIN TO HIS DAUGHTER.

New Geneva, 17th September, 1823.

. . . Notwithstanding all my exertions, you will find it hard enough when you come next spring to accommodate yourself to the privations and wildness of the country. Our house has been built by a new Irish carpenter, who was always head over heels and added much to the disorder inseparable from building. Being unacquainted with the Grecian architecture, he adopted an Hyberno-teutonic style, so that the outside of the house, with its port-hole-looking windows, has the appearance of Irish barracks, whilst the inside ornaments are similar to those of a Dutch tavern, and I must acknowledge that these form a singular contrast with the French marble chimney-pieces, paper, and mirrors. On one side of that mass of stones which Lucien calls "le château," and in full view as you approach it, is a wing consisting of the gable-end of a log house, with its chimney in front, and I could not pull it down, as it is the kitchen and dining-room where are daily fed two masons and plasterers, two attendants, two stone-quarriers, two painters, a carpenter (besides three who board themselves), Lucien, Albert's black Peter, and M^r, Mad^e,

Mesd^{lles} et les petits Buffle. The grounds are overgrown with elders, iron-weeds, stinking weeds, laurel, several varieties of briers, impenetrable thickets of brush, vines, and underwood, amongst which are discovered vestiges of old asparagus and new artichoke-beds, and now and then a spontaneous apple or peach tree. As to Albert, he has four guns, a pointer, three boats, two riding-horses, and a pet colt, smaller than a jackass, who feeds on the fragments of my old lilacs and *althea frutex*. His own clothes adorn our parlor and only sitting-room in the old brick house; for the frame house is partly occupied by the Buffle family and partly encumbered by various boxes and Albert's billiard-table, the pockets of which are made with his stockings. . . .

NEW GENEVA, 15th October, 1823.

. . . Notwithstanding all my endeavors, more will remain to be done after our arrival next spring than I would have wished. It was impossible for me to attend to anything else for the improvement either of mills, farm, plantation, &c., all of which are in a most deplorable state. . . . Amidst those cares I have been disturbed by political struggles in which I felt but little interested; but the Federalists, by their repeated assertions in all the papers of the State that I supported their candidate, have compelled me, much against my inclination, to come out with a public declaration intended to show that notwithstanding the occasional aberrations of democracy and the abuse sometimes poured on me from that quarter, it was impossible that I should abandon a cause to the support of which my life has been devoted, and which I think inseparably connected with that of the liberty and amelioration of mankind in every quarter of the globe. . . .

Private reasons led Mr. Gallatin to pass the winter in Baltimore. Here he again met his old enemies the Smiths, and resumed relations with them, not, perhaps, so cordial as in early days, but at least externally friendly. The main interest of the winter, however, turned on the Presidential election. Mr. Crawford had been dangerously affected by a stroke of paralysis, and his friends found themselves obliged to put by his side a candi-

date for the Vice-Presidency who would disarm opposition and
command confidence in case of his chief's death; they fixed upon
Mr. Gallatin, who thus became, in the failure of Mr. Crawford,
their leader. From the time this point was decided, Gallatin had
no choice but to obey the wishes of his party in other respects;
and, as it happened that all Mr. Crawford's chances turned upon
the weight of a nomination by a Congressional caucus, Gallatin
was called upon to take a direct share in urging his friends to
the work. Thus he was in a manner forced to write a letter
urging his old friend Macon to give his support to the caucus;
he was also obliged to make a short stay in Washington.

JEFFERSON TO GALLATIN.

MONTICELLO, October 29, 1823.

DEAR SIR,— . . . You have seen in our papers how prema-
turely they are agitating the question of the next President.
This proceeds from some uneasiness at the present state of things.
There is considerable dissatisfaction with the increase of the
public expenses, and especially with the necessity of borrowing
money in time of peace. This was much arraigned at the last
session of Congress, and will be more so at the next. The misfortune is that the persons looked to as successors in the government are of the President's Cabinet, and their partisans in
Congress are making a handle of these things to help or hurt
those for or against whom they are. The candidates, ins and
outs, seem at present to be many, but they will be reduced to
two, a Northern and Southern one, as usual. To judge of the
event, the state of parties must be understood. You are told,
indeed, that there are no longer parties among us; that they are
all now amalgamated; the lion and the lamb lie down together
in peace. Do not believe a word of it. The same parties exist
now as ever did; no longer, indeed, under the name of Republicans and Federalists; the latter name was extinguished in the
battle of New Orleans; those who wore it, finding monarchism
a desperate wish in this country, are rallying to what they deem
the next best point, a consolidated government. Although this is
not yet avowed (as that of monarchism, you know, never was),

it exists decidedly, and is the true key to the debates in Congress, wherein you see many calling themselves Republicans and preaching the rankest doctrines of the old Federalists. One of the prominent candidates is presumed to be of this party; the other, a Republican of the old school, and a friend to the barrier of State rights as provided by the Constitution against the danger of consolidation, which danger was the principal ground of opposition to it at its birth. Pennsylvania and New York will decide this question. If the Missouri principle mixes itself in the question, it will go one way; if not, it may go the other. Among the smaller motives, hereditary fears may alarm on one side, and the long line of local nativities on the other. In this division of parties the judges are true to their ancient vocation of sappers and miners. . . .

J. B. THOMAS[1] TO GALLATIN.

WASHINGTON CITY, 5th January, 1824.

DEAR SIR,—Mr. Lowrie returned from Philadelphia three days ago with the pleasing intelligence that a large majority of both branches of the Pennsylvania Legislature are in favor of a Congressional caucus, and that the measure is daily becoming much more popular in Philadelphia.

. . . Mr. Ingham has lately returned from Pennsylvania, and, finding public opinion there averse to his wishes, he or some one of the party has prepared an address to the people of Pennsylvania, for the delegation from that State to sign, stating that a partial caucus only could be gotten up, and asking instructions from their constituents. I understand that the address is ingeniously written, and that it has been signed by eleven of the Democratic members of Congress. After this address was signed by all who would act without consulting Mr. Lowrie, a meeting of the delegation was called to deliberate upon the subject. Mr. L. attended, and after endeavoring to operate upon the fears of some who had signed the paper, had the meeting adjourned over till to-morrow (Monday). He will, if possible, procure a further postponement, in the hope that you will be here in a few days.

---

[1] U. S. Senator from Illinois.

Many of your friends are exceedingly anxious to see you here, and amongst the rest Mr. Lowrie and Mr. Van Buren, who are both efficient men.

Since my return to Washington I mentioned to those gentlemen the conversation I had with you in Baltimore, and had the satisfaction to learn that they approved of all I said.

They are impressed with a belief that your immediate presence here at the present crisis is all-important. I am convinced that nothing could be more gratifying to the prominent men of the Republican party than to receive a visit from you at this time. Mr. Crawford would be delighted to see you. His physicians, four or five in number, have had a consultation to-day, and have pronounced him quite out of danger.

. . . We have not yet been able to devise a plan by which Mr. Jefferson can be drawn out, nor is it probable that any could be adopted which would be as likely to succeed as that of your addressing him on the subject. If nothing more can be obtained, the letter he has already written you may be of great importance.

In haste, I am, etc.

NATHANIEL MACON TO GALLATIN.

WASHINGTON, 16th January, 1824.

SIR,—The enclosed has been handed to me by Mr. Cobb, a member of the House of Representatives from Georgia. It is sent to you as the best mode of communicating its contents. I know not to what it relates.

Tender my good-will to Mrs. Gallatin and to any of your children who may be with you.

Mr. Crawford is mending slowly; not yet in a condition to write.

God preserve you and all that are near and dear to you many years, is the sincere wish of

Your old friend.

[Enclosure.]

MR. MACON,—Mr. Crawford requests me to say to you that he wished you would write to Mr. Gallatin and tell him that it was necessary he should come on to this city, for that *his* (Mr. Gallatin's) interests, as well as those of *others*, were suffering in consequence of his absence.

THOS. W. COBB.

GALLATIN TO HIS WIFE.

WASHINGTON, 24th January, 1824.

. . . I have been working hard in order to be released as soon as possible; this morning I terminated the revision and selection of my correspondence, and hope that my final account will be settled on Monday. . . . The idea of sending a special mission to England, which is indeed quite unnecessary, has been given up. . . . I was on Wednesday evening at Mrs. Monroe's evening, where she appeared for the first time this season. It was as crowded as any Paris rout, and there were several handsome ladies, but most faces of both sexes were new to me. Ten years is an age in Washington; the place seems dull to me. . . . I hear nothing but election politics, and you know how unpleasant the subject is to me. . . . Mr. Crawford is mending slowly. His friends are not perfectly easy about his final recovery, and Early adduced this to me as a reason why I should be made Vice-President. My answer was that I did not want the office, and would dislike to be proposed and not elected.

A. STEWART[1] TO GALLATIN.

WASHINGTON, 6th February, 1824.

DEAR SIR,—A caucus will be held here on the 14th instant to recommend candidates for President and Vice-President.

About 100 Republican members, it is understood, will attend. Mr. Crawford and yourself will be unanimously nominated. I know of but one gentleman unfriendly to your nomination, and he will readily acquiesce in whatever is done.

The election of the Vice-President nominated is considered certain, be the fate of the President what it may.

Very respectfully, your obedient servant.

---

[1] Member of Congress from Pennsylvania.

WALTER LOWRIE TO GALLATIN.

WASHINGTON, 10th February, 1824.

DEAR SIR,—I have delayed writing till I could write with certainty on the point we had under discussion when we last parted. You will now be nominated for the situation contemplated, and with the information and facts in our possession it does not require the spirit of prophecy to predict that final success will be the result. In the other office more uncertainty prevails. We have a hard and arduous struggle to go through, involving the very existence of the Republican party.

It will be necessary that we should see you before long. At present let me call your attention to one point in which we want your assistance. We are very desirous that Mr. Macon should attend the caucus. He has hitherto resisted all our efforts. A personal interview with you, it is believed, would have been conclusive; that is now too late; but I submit to you whether you could not write him a letter. You will receive this letter to-morrow, Thursday, and on Friday he could receive yours. I know you have more influence with him than any other man except Mr. Jefferson. His long course of public life gives him an importance which he is not otherwise entitled to. The opposition papers boast that he will not attend. In the present crisis if he do not, he will lose the respect and esteem of his friends, and instead of doing his friends a service, he will do himself an injury.

With sincere esteem, yours.

NATHANIEL MACON TO GALLATIN.

WASHINGTON, 13th February, 1824.

SIR,—I have your letter of yesterday; it is received with as much good-will and kindness as it was written. The fatal night which you mention, and which produced in the end the divisions among the three Republicans who were so both in theory and practice, I stated to the meeting they had beaten me by having the cards packed, and that I never would attend another caucus, nor have I unto this day; and would you now, my old and much esteemed friend, have me to appear in a company when and where any person could tell the truth and say, you are not a man of your word? if I go to the caucus, it would be the first time that it could be said truly to me in my whole life.

No party, as I have often told you, and as I stated at the caucus at Marache's, can last unless founded on pure principles; and the minute a party begins to intrigue within itself is the minute when the seed of division is sown and its purity begins to decline. There are not, I imagine, five members of Congress who entertain the opinions which those did who brought Mr. Jefferson into power, and they are yet mine. Principles can never change, and what has lately been called the law of circumstances is an abandonment of principle, and has been the ruin of all free governments, and if the Republican party fall in the United States, it is owing to the same cause.

I verily believe that I can render more service toward electing Crawford by not going to the caucus than by going, but I do not believe that I have the influence you suppose; but if you are right, what has produced it? the belief that I follow my own notions.

Two of my friends are here to advise me to attend, and have stopped my writing. I must conclude to you as I do to them; I cannot go.

I would much rather have talked with you on the subject. Remember me to Mrs. Gallatin and all your family, and believe me

Truly and sincerely your friend.

Written in great haste for the mail.

NATHANIEL MACON TO GALLATIN.

WASHINGTON, 14th February, 1824.

SIR,—Your letter of the 12th instant was yesterday in great haste acknowledged. For some time past my situation has been unpleasant indeed; so much so that I have a thousand times or oftener wished myself at home. What situation can be more disagreeable than to have repeatedly to say no to the best friends, and that, too, to the same question! To me it has been painful in the extreme; no one who has not felt the sensation can imagine the distress it produces,—the day is tiresome, and the night tedious; in the morning I desire night, and at night am anxious for the morning,—and to-day is the most perplexing of all; a something, I know not what, oppresses my mind, and yet I am certain that my determination not to attend the caucus is right, and what I ought to do and must do. The great charge against Crawford is intrigue; add to what was written yesterday, that if I go the charge will be renewed, and he said to be the only man who had touched the cord which could move me; and probably the wicked and false adage applied, that every man has his price. Time, I know, would prove the application false as regards us both; but the election might be over first, and the injury done.

Every generation, like a single person, has opinions of its own; as much so in politics as anything else. This opinion is elegantly expressed in the book of Judges, 2d chapter. The opinions of Jefferson and those who were with him are forgot. On reading the chapter the proper and intended inference will be easily made; I hope, however, we shall not suffer as did the children of Israel after the death of Joshua.

Tender in your best manner my respects and regard to Mrs. Gallatin and your family, and believe me

Your unfeigned friend.

GALLATIN TO BADOLLET.

New Geneva, Pennsylvania, 29th July, 1824.

My dear and old Friend,—I have delayed much too long answering your letter of last year. I have ever since been on the wing, uncertain where I would fix myself. The habits of my wife and children, Albert's excepted, render this a very ineligible place of residence to them; but the impossibility of subsisting on my scanty income in one of our cities, and the necessity of attending to a valuable but mismanaged and unproductive property, have left me no choice; and we are all now here, including James's wife. My health and that of my daughter are delicate; the other members of the family are well. With the exception of James Nicholson, all my old friends are dead or confined by old age to their homes; there is not in this quarter the slightest improvement in the state of society, or indeed of any kind; but my children are good and very affectionate; neither of my sons, unfortunately, brought up to business. Albert, with considerable and varied talents and acquired knowledge, but as yet wanting perseverance and steadiness.; James and Francis more fitted for a court than a wilderness; my wife just as she was twenty-four years ago.

The last seven years I spent in Europe, though not the most useful, were the most pleasant, of my life, both on account of my reception in Geneva, where I found many old and affectionate friends (Hentsch, Dumont, the Tronchins, Butiri, &c.), and from my standing with the first statesmen and men of merit in France and England. Where you do not stand in the way of anybody, instead of collision and envy, you meet with much indulgence if you can fill with credit the place you occupy; and this was a disposition to which I had not been accustomed towards me, and the want of which I now on that account feel, perhaps, more than formerly. These feelings would and ought naturally to have induced me, and you expressed the same wish, to withdraw altogether from public life; and my wife, irksome to her as is her residence here, was of the same opinion. I will briefly state what has brought my name before the people for the office of Vice-President.

During the twelve years I was in the Treasury, I was anxiously looking for some man that could fill my place there and in the general direction of the national concerns, for one indeed that could replace Mr. Jefferson, Mr. Madison, and myself. Breckenridge, of Kentucky, only appeared and died; the eccentricities and temper of J. Randolph soon destroyed his usefulness, and only one man at last appeared who filled my expectations. This was Mr. Crawford, who united to a powerful mind a most correct judgment and an inflexible integrity; which last quality, not sufficiently tempered by indulgence and civility, has prevented his acquiring general popularity; but, notwithstanding this defect (for it is one), I know so well his great superiority over the other candidates for the office of President, that I was anxious for his election and openly expressed my opinion. I would not even compare Jackson or Calhoun to him, the first an honest man and the idol of the worshippers of military glory, but from incapacity, military habits, and habitual disregard of laws and constitutional provisions, altogether unfit for the office; the other a smart fellow, one of the first amongst second-rate men, but of lax political principles and a disordinate ambition not over-delicate in the means of satisfying itself. John Q. Adams is a virtuous man, whose temper, which is not the best, might be overlooked; he has very great and miscellaneous knowledge, and he is with his pen a powerful debater; but he wants to a deplorable degree that most essential quality, a sound and correct judgment. Of this I have had in my official connection and intercourse with him complete and repeated proofs, and, although he may be useful when controlled and checked by others, he ought never to be trusted with a place where unrestrained his errors might be fatal to the country. Mr. Clay has his faults, but splendid talents and a generous mind. I certainly prefer Mr. Crawford to him, although he is far more popular; and yet, notwithstanding that popularity, I believe that, particularly since the West is split between him and Jackson, it is impossible that he should be elected, and that the contest is in fact between Crawford and Adams. Almost all the old Republicans (Mr. Jefferson and Mr. Madison amongst them) think as I do; but they were aware that Mr. Crawford was not very popular, and that the bond of party, which had with great many produced the effect of patriotism and knowledge, being nearly dissolved, neither of the other candidates would withdraw, and they were at a loss whom to unite to him as Vice-President. I advised to nominate nobody for that office, or, if anybody, some person from New York or New England. The last was attached to Adams; there were contentions in New York. The friends of Mr. Crawford thought the persons proposed there too obscure, and that my name would serve as a banner and show their nomination to be that of the old Republican party. I thought and still think that they were mistaken; that as a foreigner, as residuary legatee of the Federal hatred, and as one whose old services were forgotten and more recent ones though more useful were but little known, my name could be of no service to the cause. They insisted, and, being nominated both by the members of Congress and by the Legislature of Virginia, I could not honorably withdraw, though my reluctance was much increased by the dead opposition of Pennsylvania, which is, and nowhere more than in this vicinity, Jackson mad. From all I can collect, I think Mr. Crawford's election (notwithstanding this mistake) nearly certain, and mine improbable. So much for my apology, which I could not make shorter. I have now said everything, I believe, respecting me which could interest you ; and I have only to entreat you not to disappoint the hope you gave me, and to come and spend these unhealthy summer and autumnal months with us, where at least fevers have not yet penetrated, although they prevailed last year everywhere east of Cumberland and west of Wheeling. In summer I must necessarily to preserve health be at rest, and if to effect an interview, probably the last, so dear to both, it is necessary that you should have the trouble and fatigue of the journey, it is but strict justice (if that was any object between us) that the expense should be defrayed by me. Let not that, therefore, stop you, and come once more to see your old friend and refresh your old age by recollections of ancient times. I will add to the stock much that is pleasing from Geneva. Seventeen years of French yoke have united the parties as far as union is practicable in a free country. If there are differences of opinion, they apply to details of administration ; the old distinctions, so odious to the people, are done away. To the general council and to that of Two Hundred has been substituted a large elective representative council, where, as far as I could judge, virtue and talents are almost the only titles for admission, where the most obscure and newest names are mixed with the oldest of the Republic, where Dumont, Bellamy, and two Pictets are in opposition to Desarts, D'Yvernois, and most of the old wigs (which have been, however, set aside). But what kind of opposition ? I have read many of their debates ; and, independent of the interest I felt for questions to others of small and local importance, any one may admire the train of close and logical reasoning they display, and must be delighted with the candor and mutual forbearance which characterize them. They are like discussions conducted amicably but with perfect freedom by members of the same family respecting their common concerns. Nor are the ancient manners much altered. A few amongst the most ignorant and vicious, the remnant of those who disgraced Geneva in 1794, not above three or four hundred, hardly any of the old bourgeoisie, have, I am told, been corrupted by the French whilst in power and their morals have been affected; but those of the great bulk are better than before the revolutions, and they are as pure Genevans, as little Frenchified, as you could desire. Speaking of old bourgeoisie, the distinction does not exist; citoyens, bourgeois and natifs are in every respect, civil and political, on the same footing. And here let me observe how powerful is the moral effect of virtue and knowledge. Whilst Venice, Genoa, Belgium, &c., &c., have been bartered away without scruple or regard to the wishes of the people, not only have Holland and Switzerland escaped unhurt, because they had both a national character and were truly nations, but even little Geneva has been respected and restored to its independence, whilst more than forty imperial cities have been left in the possession of the princes who had usurped them with the permission of Bonaparte. I might say much more, but must reserve it for the time when we meet. In that hope, and with my love to all the members of your family, I remain ever yours.

My wife and James Nicholson send their best compliments.

By the by, you owe me nothing. Your sister was too proud to permit me to join in the support of your father, and your brother's return in 1818 relieved her difficulties. I have not heard from them since that time, and was not in Geneva subsequent to 1817.

Unfortunately for Mr. Gallatin's candidacy, the rapid spread of General Jackson's party overthrew all ordinary calculation. Mr. Calhoun's friends, finding their candidate pressed out of the course, made terms with the Jackson managers, by which Mr. Calhoun received the combined support of both bodies for the Vice-Presidency. This suggested a brilliant stroke of political genius to the fertile brain of Martin Van Buren, who, in those days, was not one of Jackson's followers. As Jackson's chances were improved by coalescing with Calhoun, who reduced his claims accordingly, so Mr. Crawford's chances might be improved by coalescing with Mr. Clay, provided the latter could also be persuaded to accept the position of candidate for the Vice-Presidency. Mr. Clay was sounded on this subject early in September, as appears from his private correspondence, and his reply, dated September 10,[1] seems to have been considered as not discouraging, for, on the 25th September, Mr. Van Buren approached Mr. Gallatin with a formal recommendation that he should withdraw. Mr. Gallatin felt relieved at being permitted to escape even in this manner. He withdrew from the canvass. The result was that Calhoun was elected Vice-President by the people; that Jackson, Adams, and Crawford went before the House of Representatives, and that Mr. Clay caused the election of Mr. Adams to the Presidency.

WALTER LOWRIE TO GALLATIN.

BUTLER, 25th September, 1824.

MY DEAR SIR,—The subject of which this letter treats has given me the most severe pain of mind. The bearer, our mutual friend General Lacock, will inform you of the situation of my family which has prevented me from accompanying him to see you.

From the most authentic information communicated to me by your friends in North Carolina, Virginia, Maryland, Delaware, New Jersey, and New York, the most serious fears are entertained that Mr. Calhoun will be elected by the electors. Or if he should not, his vote will be so great that his chance in the Senate will be almost conclusive in his favor. On this subject I have not a feeling I would not be desirous that you should know. No man can desire your success more than I do. Still, my dear sir, I believe your chance of success is now almost hopeless, and, assuming that as a fact, what is to be done? The question has been met by a number of our friends, and they have

[1] See Private Correspondence of Henry Clay, p. 103.

suggested the arrangement which Mr. Lacock will make known to you. This plan has the approbation of as many of our friends as it was possible to consult, all of them your most decided friends. They are, however, afraid of your success, and wish, if possible, to have an arrangement made with Mr. Clay, to which if he would consent, it would go far to secure the election of Mr. Crawford.

After the most deep and anxious reflection I have been able to bestow on the subject, I would advise you to withdraw from the contest. How that should be done, in case you approve of it, I do not know. Your feelings and views of the best manner of doing it would be conclusive with me. The arrangement submitted to Mr. Lacock and myself contemplated your remaining on the ticket till near the election, in case Mr. Clay would consent; and if he would not consent, then for you to remain on the ticket to the last. I confess I do not like this conditional arrangement, and the letter of Mr. Dickinson makes me dislike it more. These points are all open, and I was most desirous of seeing you and getting your views upon them. In case you approve of having your name withdrawn, it occurs to me that the best manner would be in a letter to Judge Ruggles, which might be published a few days after Mr. Lacock's departure. In that case Clay would not be informed of it till Mr. Lacock would have seen him, and his decision might have been different than if he knew absolutely that you had withdrawn. If you prefer the other, however, that is, to place your withdrawing on the contingency of Mr. Clay's co-operation, I am perfectly satisfied. Indeed, I feel quite at a loss how to advise in the case. Indeed, in this whole communication I write under the greatest pain and embarrassment. Every step I have taken in regard to your name being placed before the nation was dictated by the purest friendship to you and the clearest sense of duty to my country. To have had any agency in placing you in a situation at all calculated to wound your feelings or give pain to your mind, is to me a source of painful reflection. This, added to the perplexed state of public opinion and the uncertainty of the final result, brings with it a distress of mind I have never heretofore experienced.

I am, my dear sir, with sincere esteem, your friend.

FAYETTE COUNTY, PENNSYLVANIA, October 2, 1824.

DEAR SIR,—Your letter of the 25th of September, received on the 29th, has caused me much perplexity, not from any hesitation as to the principles which should govern my conduct, but from want of sufficient knowledge of the facts.

It is evident that I ought not to decline from mere personal motives and in order to avoid the mortification of a defeat, especially if this should be in any degree injurious to the public cause. There is in a nomination a mutual though tacit pledge of support, on the part of those who nominate, of standing a candidate on the part of the person nominated.

But my withdrawing would be proper in case my continuing to stand should either appear injurious to the election of Mr. Crawford or prevent the election of a proper person to the office of Vice-President. On either the one or the other of those grounds I consider your communications decisive so far as relates to New Jersey and New York. There may be no difficulty with respect to Georgia and any other State where the choice of electors remains with the Legislature. The embarrassment is principally in relation to Virginia and North Carolina. I am sensible that my name is in itself of no weight anywhere; but it is not for me, consulting only my feelings, to decide whether, after the active exertions of committees and individuals in favor of the two candidates nominated at Washington, the withdrawing the name of one on the eve of a popular election and without substituting another in his place, may prove favorable or injurious to the success of the Republican tickets.

With that view of the subject, my answer to Mr. Lacock was that I would leave the decision with the central committee of correspondence for the State of Virginia. To that State I am more particularly bound, as the only one where, to my knowledge, the nomination of Washington was confirmed in full by the Republican members of the Legislature. The committee is their legitimate organ; and from their local situation they also are best able to form an opinion concerning North Carolina, with which last State there was hardly time to consult, and whose arrangements on the subject of the election are not known to me. Our friends in those districts of Maryland which may be favorable to us might also be consulted.

I am still of the same opinion; but considering how little time remains and how much would be lost by corresponding with me, I enclose my declaration that I wish my name to be withdrawn, not directed to Mr. Ruggles, since he is not to judge whether and when it must be used, but intended for publication in the newspapers at the discretion of the committee for Virginia, who will of course consult, if necessary, with Mr. Van Buren on the subject.

There will be no necessity for that consultation if they think it advantageous in the Southern States that my name should be withdrawn prior to the election of electors. They may at once in that case publish my declaration, since it is ascertained that the effect will be favorable in the North. To me that course would be the most agreeable. The publication must at all events be made before the result of the election of electors is ascertained, and prior to their being elected by the Legislature of New York.

In order to avoid delays as far as depends on me, I will enclose copies of my declining and of the substance of this letter both to Mr. Van Buren at Albany and to Mr. Stephenson at Richmond, to be communicated by him to the committee of correspondence, as I do not know their names. But he may be absent, and it will be necessary for you to write not only to Mr. Van Buren, but also to Richmond, enclosing copy of my declining and of such parts of this letter as will put them in full possession of the subject.

The publication of my declining should be made, as far as practicable, simultaneously in the National Intelligencer and principal State papers.

I advised Mr. Lacock against negotiating in person with Mr. Clay, as I thought that it would only encourage him to advise his friends in New York to make no compromise that would not secure him a part, at least, of the votes of that State for President. The only way, it seemed to me, was to convince him, by the choice of the electors there, that he had no chance for that office. This, however, was an opinion on a subject in which I can have nothing more to say.

Of your friendship, sincerity, and patriotic motives I am most perfectly satisfied. My nomination has been a miscalculation, and however painful the results may be to our feelings, having nothing to reproach ourselves with throughout the whole transaction, there is nothing in it save the effect it may have on the public cause that can give us any permanent uneasiness.

I have but one observation to add. From my experience, both when Mr. Jefferson was made Vice-President and when, in 1808, Mr. Clinton was re-elected to the same office, I know that nothing can be more injurious to an Administration than to have in that office a man in hostility with that Administration, as he will always become the most formidable rallying-point for the opposition.

I remain, respectfully and sincerely, your friend and obedient servant.

This chapter of secret political history will hardly stand comparison with what were at least the earnest phases of party politics in the days when Mr. Gallatin was really a leader. Parties had no longer a principle, and it was clearly time for Mr. Gallatin to retire. On the 3d December, when it was certain that no choice had been made by the people, he wrote from New Geneva to his son : " The Republican party seems to me to be fairly defunct. Our principal misfortune was perhaps the want of a popular candidate. The great defect of our system is the monarchical principle admitted in our Constitution."

The election of Mr. Adams took place on February 9, 1825. Rumors in regard to the new Cabinet were communicated by Mr. Stewart, the representative of Fayette County, to James Gallatin, at Baltimore, who wrote them to his father. Mr. Gallatin replied in a letter of February 19. Mr. James Gallatin, who, as a boy at Ghent, had been a favorite of Mr. Adams, enclosed this letter to the new President without his father's knowledge. Mr. Adams replied at once, and the correspondence will serve to close this account of the election of 1824–25, disappointing and unsatisfactory to every one who shared in it.

ANDREW STEWART TO JAMES GALLATIN.

WASHINGTON, 15th February, 1825.

. . . Many rumors are afloat on the subject of the new Cabinet. The Treasury Department has been offered to Mr. Crawford in the most flattering terms, which he has, however, declined. It is confidently asserted that it has been or will be offered to your father. Whether he will be disposed to accept you know best. There is evidently a strong wish to conciliate the friends of Mr. Crawford to the new Administration. . . .

ALBERT GALLATIN TO JAMES GALLATIN.

NEW GENEVA, PENNSYLVANIA, 19th February, 1825.

MY DEAR JAMES,—Young Ebert has brought me this evening your letter of the 16th. I have heard nothing on the subject either from Mr. Adams or from any other person. The Washington mail for this place, which may have arrived to-day at Union, will not reach New Geneva before Thursday.

I am sorry to find that you feel so much for me on account of the late political disappointments. There is much consolation in the reflection that, having served the country with entire devotion, perfect fidelity, and to the best of my abilities, the loss of my popularity is not owing to any improper conduct on my part. We must cheerfully submit to what we cannot prevent, enjoy with thanks the blessings within our reach, and not make ourselves unhappy by unavailing regrets. This I mean as advice to you; for I really do not want it for myself.

As to my accepting the Treasury Department, it is out of question. I refused it in 1816, when offered by Mr. Madison. To fill that office in the manner I did, and as it ought to be filled, is a most laborious task and labor of the most tedious kind. To fit myself for it, to be able to understand thoroughly, to embrace and to control all its details, took from me, during the two first years I held it, every hour of the day and many of the night, and had nearly brought a pulmonary complaint. I filled the office twelve years, and was fairly worn out. Having lost sight of the details during the last twelve years would require a new effort, which, at this time, it would be unjust and cruel to require of me.

But even with respect to the Department of State, for which I am better calculated than any other, and as fit as any other person, it appears to me, considering the situation in which I have been placed, that unless Mr. Crawford had remained in the Administration, it would not be proper for me to become a member of it. This is much strengthened by the surmises to which Mr. Clay's conduct has given birth, and by the circumstance of his accepting one of the Departments. I must and will at all events remain above the reach of suspicion.

I do not wish to be understood as speaking or wishing to act in opposition to Mr. Adams or to his Administration. I wish, on the contrary, that it may redound to his honor and be beneficial to his country. I had always stated to Mr. Crawford himself and to our friends that, next to him, Mr. Adams was my choice among the other candidates. To receive our support he has only to act in conformity with our principles.

If you should write to Stewart, enter into no details, and only say that you are satisfied, from the general tenor of my correspondence, that I had not as late as this day received the offer of the Treasury Department, and that, if offered, I could not accept it.

25th February.

I received yours of 19th inst. The information given you by A. Stewart appears to have been erroneous, as I have received nothing from Mr. Adams. I am glad of it, as I like better not to be appointed than to have to decline the appointment. . . .

J. Q. ADAMS TO JAMES GALLATIN.

WASHINGTON, 26th February, 1825.

DEAR SIR,—Conformably to your desire, I return herewith your father's letter, with my thanks for the perusal of it. I have always entertained a very high opinion of your father's character and public services, and am much gratified with the sentiments personal towards me expressed in his letter. That he will support the Administration so far as its conduct shall be conformable to the principles which he approves is what I should have expected from his sense of justice.

My personal feelings towards your father, particularly since we were associated together in the negotiations for peace and commerce with Great Britain, have been eminently friendly. They are so still, and it would have been gratifying to me to have had the benefit of his assistance in the Administration about to commence. The reasons assigned in his letter for his declining the Treasury Department were chiefly those which deterred me from offering him a nomination to it; and those of them founded upon objections to oppressively laborious duties applying more forcibly still to the Department of State than to that of the Treasury contributed to my conclusion that neither of them would have been acceptable to him. Had I been aware that his acceptance of the Department of State would have been conditional either upon Mr. Crawford's remaining in the Administration or upon Mr. Clay's exclusion from it, or upon both, it would have been to me an additional motive to refrain from making the offer. Approving altogether of your father's determination to remain above the reach of suspicion, I should never make him a proposal by the acceptance of which, even in his own imagination, a taint of suspicion could attach to his character. It is my earnest wish that he may to the end of his days remain above the reach of suspicion; but, as that does not always depend upon ourselves, if it should prove otherwise I can only hope that every suspicion which may befall him should be as unjust and groundless as the surmises to which Mr. Clay's conduct has given birth.

The parental advice in your father's letter is worthy of his firmness and conscious integrity. These are never-failing supports under the loss of public favor. This, however, has not been sustained by him to the extent which he appears to apprehend. The respect for his character and services continues unimpaired; in my mind at least it remains as strong as ever, unaffected even by the distrust which I regret to see entertained by him, of the error of which I have no doubt he will live to be convinced.

I am, with great regard and esteem, dear sir, &c.

GALLATIN TO BADOLLET.

NEW GENEVA, PENNSYLVANIA, 18th March, 1825.

Your good letter afforded me, my dear friend, great satisfaction, and would have been long ago answered had it not been for the uncertainty of my movements this spring. You had designated the month of April as the time of your intended visit here, and I had made arrangements to be absent during that and the ensuing month on a visit which I had believed indispensable to my lands in Ohio and on Kanawha. It has at last been agreed that James will go in my place, so that I will be here from this time to the month of October. I expect you, therefore, this spring, and hope that nothing will intervene to prevent the mutual pleasure of this meeting.

I see by your letter that you are not perfectly satisfied either with yourself or the world. As to the first, I may say with truth that you have less to reproach yourself with than any other person within my knowledge. But I believe emigration, when not compulsory, to be always an error, and you are the only person that I ever induced to take that step; so that even in that respect the blame must at least be shared between us. As to the world, I have been, like you, disappointed in the estimate I had formed of the virtue of mankind and of its influence over others. Every day's experience convinces us that most unprincipled men are often most successful. In this country there is much more morality and less of integrity than on the continent of Europe. This we cannot help; and as to myself, taking everything into consideration, I have had so much greater share of all that appears desirable than I had any right to expect, that I have none to complain. Yours has been a harder lot, yet I doubt whether not as happy. . . .

My general health is good, and I do not look older than I am; but I am weak and cannot bear any fatigue. This, indeed, is the reason why my family insisted that I should not take my intended journey. . . . My old friends in this country are almost all dead; the few survivors . . . quite superannuated. . . .

The experiment of living at Friendship Hill did not succeed.

Not only was New Geneva an unsuitable place for the advancement of children, but it was beyond question intolerably dull for
Mr. Gallatin himself. He made the experiment during one winter,
and then abandoned it, as it proved, forever. The Governor of
Pennsylvania offered him in May, 1825, the appointment of
Canal Commissioner, a compliment to his well-known interest in
internal improvements, which he declined. America was now
convulsed by the visit of La Fayette, almost the first occasion on
which the people of the United States showed their capacity for
a genuine national enthusiasm. In his triumphal progress, La
Fayette passed through Western Pennsylvania and was publicly
welcomed by Mr. Gallatin in an address delivered before the
court-house at Uniontown, in which he touched with much skill
upon the subjects which were then most deeply interesting the
liberals of all nations,—the emancipation of the Spanish colonies
and of Greece. La Fayette was a propagandist of the Greek
cause in America, and Mr. Gallatin had always sympathized
with him on this point, even to the extent of meriting the thanks
of the Greek government while he was minister in Paris.   In
the address to La Fayette at Uniontown he spoke with extraordinary earnestness of the critical situation of the Greeks:

"The cause is not yet won! An almost miraculous resistance
may yet perhaps be overwhelmed by the tremendous superiority
of numbers. And will the civilized, the Christian world,—for
those words are synonymous,—will they look with apathy on the
dreadful catastrophe that would ensue? A catastrophe which
they, which even we alone could prevent with so much facility
and almost without danger? I am carried beyond what I intended to say. It is due to your presence,—do I not know that
wherever man, struggling for liberty, for existence, is most in
danger, there is your heart?"

The address to La Fayette was a last revival of the old flame
of eloquence and of republican feeling which had controlled and
inspired the opposition to Washington and John Adams. It
should be read after reading the great speech on foreign intercourse delivered in 1798, and taken in that connection it will
offer a curious standard for comparing the movement of parties
and of men.

La Fayette was received at Uniontown on the 26th May, 1825, and the next day he drove with Mr. Gallatin to Friendship Hill, where he passed the night and resumed his journey on the 28th. His mind was full of his triumphal progress, and of the fortunes of Greece, but he was allowed little rest even in the retirement of New Geneva. Crowds of people thronged Mr. Gallatin's house, and there could be little sensible or connected conversation in the midst of such excitement.

On the 10th June, Mr. Gallatin wrote to a friend: "We are here very retired, which suits me and my sons, but is not so agreeable to the ladies. . . . The uniformity of our life has been enlivened by the visit of our friend La Fayette; but he was in great hurry, and the Nation's Guest had but little time to give to his personal friends, that, too, encumbered even in my house with a prodigious crowd."

After a summer on the Monongahela, Mr. Gallatin took his family to Baltimore for the winter. Early in November he received a letter from Mr. Clay, then Secretary of State, offering him the position of representative of the United States at the proposed Congress of American republics at Panama. When Mr. Gallatin declined the post, on account of the climate and the language, Mr. Clay wrote again urging reconsideration. He said: "I think the mission the most important ever sent from this country, those only excepted which related to its independence and the termination of the late war. It will have objects which cannot fail to redound to the lasting fame of our negotiators, if they should be accomplished, as I think there is much reason to believe they may be." Mr. Gallatin thoroughly sympathized in the policy of strengthening the relations between the American republics, but persisted in declining the appointment. The opposition of his family seems to have been his principal difficulty.

Towards the spring of 1826, a new demand was made on his services. President Adams had on assuming office recalled Mr. Rush from England to take charge of the Treasury Department, and had sent Mr. Rufus King to London. Mr. King's health gave way immediately after his arrival, and he was incapacitated for business. The Administration at once summoned Mr. Gallatin to Washington. The story is told in his own words, in a letter written on the 12th May, 1826:

" You will have seen by the newspapers that I was appointed minister to England. There are important negotiations now pending between that country and the United States, and the state of Mr. King's health was such that he had requested that, for that purpose, an extraordinary minister might be united to him. Under those circumstances I was requested and agreed to go as special minister. Before my nomination was sent to the Senate, Mr. King resigned altogether his place, and his resignation arrived to this country and was accepted. The President, wishing to entrust me alone with the negotiation, and unwilling to nominate at once a special minister for that purpose and an ordinary minister as successor to Mr. King, requested that I should go in the latter character, but with powers to negotiate, and with the understanding that I should be at liberty to return as soon as the negotiation was terminated, in same manner as if I had been appointed on a special mission. With that express understanding I have accepted. But my nomination has been made merely as successor to Mr. King, and the circumstances above mentioned are not publicly known. I now mention them to you in confidence in order to remove your apprehension of another long absence. This cannot last longer than a twelve-month."

The President appears to have intended that Mr. Gallatin should have ample discretionary power to act according to his best judgment in the negotiation; but when the instructions arrived, whether Mr. Clay was not inclined to allow such latitude, or whether Mr. Adams's ideas of discretionary power were different from Mr. Gallatin's, the latter found his position not satisfactory, and before sailing he wrote both to the President and to Mr. Clay letters of warm remonstrance, with suggestions of the changes needed to allow of freer action on his part. This done, he took his departure from New York, on July 1, 1826, accompanied by his wife and daughter, and arrived in London on the 7th August.

The negotiation now to take place was probably the most complicated and arduous ever trusted by the United States government in the hands of a single agent. It embraced not only those commercial questions which had been so often and so fruitlessly discussed, and which involved the whole system of British colonial and navigation laws, but also the troublesome disputes of boundary on our extreme north-eastern and north-western frontier, in Maine and Oregon; the settlement of a long outstanding claim for slaves carried away by British troops in contravention of the First Article of the Treaty of Ghent; and the continuance of the commercial convention negotiated by Mr. Gallatin in 1815 and extended in 1818 for ten years by him and Mr. Rush. All the principal notes and despatches which record from day to day the progress of the various negotiations have been published, and are to be found in the great collection of American State Papers; to them, students must refer for details, which belong to the region of history rather than to biography; here it is enough to describe some of the leading points of the situation and to give some slight idea of the manner in which Mr. Gallatin dealt with his difficulties.

Of these difficulties perhaps the greatest was that Lord Castlereagh was no longer head of the Foreign Office. Lord Castlereagh's political sins may have been many and dark, but towards the United States he was a wise and fair man. No one asked or expected friendship from a British minister of that day; all that America wished was to be treated by the English government with some degree of respect. Lord Castlereagh humored this weakness; his manners and his temper were excellent; his commercial views were much in advance of his time; he conceded with grace, and his refusals left no sting. When in 1822 he put an end to his own career, he was succeeded in the Foreign Office by George Canning, doubtless a greater man, but one whose temper was not gentle towards opposition, and whose old triumphs over embargo and non-intercourse had not left upon his imagination any profound respect for American character. Mr. Canning liked brilliant and aggressive statesmanship. He was not inclined to admit the new doctrines which had been announced by President Monroe in regard to the future exclusion of Europe from America; he felt that the power of the United States was a danger and a threat to England, and he would have been glad to strike out some new path which should relieve the commerce of England from its increasing dependence on America. Unfortunately for Mr. Gallatin, the very moment which Mr. Canning chose for experimenting on this subject was the moment when Gallatin was on his way to England in the summer of 1826. The object which he selected for experiment was the West India trade.

As has been already shown, the British government both in 1815 and in 1818 had declined to accept the American propositions on this subject. The trade between the United States and the West Indies was therefore left to be regulated by legislation as suited the interests of the parties. In proportion as England opened her colonial ports to American vessels, Congress relaxed the severity of its navigation law, and, in spite of incessant dispute about details, this process went on with favorable results as fast as public opinion in England would allow. There was only one drawback to the policy. In the multiplication of restrictive and retaliatory laws the intercourse became so embarrassed that no man could pretend to say what was and what was not permitted or forbidden.

In 1825 Parliament had undertaken a general revision of the colonial and navigation system, and several laws were adopted by which considerable changes had been made and liberal privileges granted to foreign nations on certain conditions. So far as applied to the United States, the condition was that she should place British shipping on the footing of the most favored nation.

The laws were intricate and impossible to understand without authoritative explanation. Mr. Clay and the committees of Congress considered the subject with care. The result was a decision to attempt nothing by way of legislation, but to give Mr. Gallatin authority to make such concessions as would probably secure a satisfactory arrangement by treaty. With these powers in his hand, not doubting that at length this annoying contest would be closed, Mr. Gallatin landed in England, and was met by the announcement that the British government, in consequence of the failure of Congress to fulfil the conditions of the Act of Parliament of July 5, 1825, had withdrawn the privileges conferred by that act; had prohibited, by order in council, all intercourse in American vessels between the British West Indies and the United States; and refused even to discuss the subject further.

In a small way this proceeding was only a repetition of Mr. Canning's abrupt rupture of negotiation in the case of Mr. Monroe's unratified treaty twenty years before. Orders in council had a peculiarly irritating meaning to American ears, and any negotiator would have had some excuse for losing his temper in such a case, but it must be agreed that on this occasion the American government in all its branches appeared with dignity and composure. Mr. Gallatin's notes were excellent in tone, forbearing in temper, and conclusive in argument; Mr. Clay was not less quiet and temperate. Between the two Mr. Canning did not appear equally well. He resorted to what was little better than hair-splitting on the meaning of the words "right" and "claim" as applied to the American trade with the colonies. "When it is contended," said he in a note of November 13, 1826, "that the 'right' by which Great Britain prohibits foreign nations from trading with her colonies is the same 'right' with that by which she might (if she thought fit) prohibit them from trading with herself, this argument (which is employed by the United States alone) implies that the special prohibition is a grievance to the United States, if not of the same amount, of the same kind, as the general prohibition would be. This is a doctrine which Great Britain explicitly denies."

In short, Mr. Canning was determined upon making one more effort to save the colonial system, and he preferred to do it in a way that would be remembered. Possibly his policy was sound; at all events he obtained by its means for England a very degrading apology from the next American Administration, although the number of his diplomatic triumphs over America was by that time no longer a matter of concern to him, and he and his ambition were then things of the past. His motives, in this instance, were not quite clear; what he avowed was the determination to ascertain by experiment whether the West Indies could be made independent of the United States by opening the colonial trade to all the rest of the world and prohibiting it to the United States alone. In the face of this attempt the American government had only one course to pursue: it must acquiesce and resume its retaliatory prohibition. This was accordingly done, without irritating language, and in excellent temper and taste. In regard to this branch of his negotiation, Mr. Gallatin's task therefore became simple; he had merely to obtain from the British government a distinct avowal of its determination to maintain this new policy against a direct offer of negotiation. He reserved this step until the very close of his mission, and his last words to Earl Dudley on the subject are worth quoting:

"The right of Great Britain to regulate the intercourse with her colonies is not questioned, and it is not usual for nations to make any great sacrifice for the sake of asserting abstract principles which are not contested. She is undoubtedly the only proper judge of what should be her commercial policy. The undersigned has not been fortunate enough to be able to discover what actual advantages she derives from the measures in which she perseveres in regard to the colonial intercourse. He has apprehended that considerations foreign to the question might continue to oppose obstacles to a proper understanding. Nothing has been omitted to remove those which might have arisen from misconceptions of the views and proceedings of the American government. It is gratifying to have received assurances that the decision of Great Britain was not influenced by any unfriendly feelings towards the United States. Their sentiments for Great Britain are those of amity and good-will; and their government is animated by a sincere desire to improve and strengthen the friendly relations of the two countries."

This sudden and unexpected blow, which instantly put an end to the most hopeful branch of Mr. Gallatin's intended negotiation, had a very mischievous effect upon the negotiation as a whole; practically and for the moment it annulled all his instructions. He had to act for himself, and he was much perplexed to form any theory of British motives which would serve to guide his course. He attempted to look at the matter from the British point of view, and wrote his first impressions to Mr. Clay on the 22d September, 1826:

"On three points we were perhaps vulnerable. 1. The delay in renewing the negotiation. 2. The omission of having revoked the restriction on the indirect intercourse when that of Great

Britain had ceased. 3. Too long an adherence to the opposition to her right of laying protecting duties. This might have been given up as soon as the Act of 1825 had passed. These are the causes assigned for the late measures adopted towards the United States on that subject, and they have undoubtedly had a decisive effect as far as relates to the order in council, assisted as they were by the belief that our object was to compel this country to regulate the trade upon our own terms. But even this will not account for the refusal to negotiate and the apparent determination to exclude us altogether hereafter from a participation in the trade of the colonies. There is certainly an alteration in the disposition of this government since the year 1818, when I was last here. Lord Castlereagh and Mr. Robinson had it more at heart to cherish friendly relations than Mr. Canning and Mr. Huskisson. The difference may, however, be in the times rather than in the men. Treated in general with considerable arrogance till the last war, with great attention, if not respect, during the years that followed it, the United States are now an object of jealousy; and a policy founded on that feeling has been avowed."[1]

The first part of the above paragraph, down to the words "upon our own terms," was afterwards paraphrased by Mr. Van Buren as the ground of his celebrated deprecation to Great Britain, when giving his instructions, as Secretary of State, to Mr. McLane, as Minister to England. This fact was discovered by Mr. Benton, who has, in his "Thirty Years' View,"[2] printed that portion of the above despatch of 22d September, 1826, at the same time judiciously omitting the remainder, as had been done by Mr. Van Buren himself. This is not the place for making any comment either upon Mr. Van Buren's statesmanship or Mr. Benton's merits as a historian; but it is proper to point out that nothing in Mr. Gallatin's despatch could honestly be made to support the credit of either the one or the other.[3]

[1] See Writings, vol. ii. p. 324.   [2] Vol. i. p. 216.

[3] The objectionable passages in Mr. Van Buren's instructions to Mr. McLane were the following:

" In reviewing the events which have preceded and more or less contributed to a result so much to be regretted, there will be found three grounds upon which we are most assailable. 1st. In our too long and too

But Mr. Gallatin's remarks of September 22 were written before receiving the explanations of his own government, and they did not express a matured opinion. He was greatly per-

---

tenaciously resisting the right of Great Britain to impose protecting duties in her colonies. 2d. In not relieving her vessels from the restriction of returning direct from the United States, after permission had been given by Great Britain to our vessels to clear out from the colonies to any other than a British port; and, 3d. In omitting to accept the terms offered by the Act of Parliament of July, 1825, after the subject had been brought before Congress and deliberately acted upon by our government. It is, without doubt, to the combined operation of these (three) causes that we are to attribute the British interdict; you will therefore see the propriety of possessing yourself fully of all the explanatory and mitigating circumstances connected with them, that you may be able to obviate, as far as practicable, the unfavorable impression which they have produced.

"The opportunities which you have derived from a participation in our public counsels, as well as other sources of information, will enable you to speak with confidence (as far as you may deem it proper and useful so to do) of the respective parts taken by those to whom the administration of this government is now committed, in relation to the course heretofore pursued upon the subject of the colonial trade. Their views upon that point have been submitted to the people of the United States; and the counsels by which your conduct is now directed are the result of the judgment expressed by the only earthly tribunal to which the late Administration was amenable for its acts. It should be sufficient that the claims set up by them, and which caused the interruption of the trade in question, have been explicitly abandoned by those who first asserted them, and are not revived by their successors. If Great Britain deems it adverse to her interests to allow us to participate in the trade with her colonies, and finds nothing in the extension of it to others to induce her to apply the same rule to us, she will, we hope, be sensible of the propriety of placing her refusal on those grounds. To set up the acts of the late Administration as the cause of forfeiture of privileges which would otherwise be extended to the people of the United States, would, under existing circumstances, be unjust in itself, and could not fail to excite their deepest sensibility. The tone of feeling which a course so unwise and untenable is calculated to produce would doubtless be greatly aggravated by the consciousness that Great Britain has, by order in council, opened her colonial ports to Russia and France, notwithstanding a similar omission on their part to accept the terms offered by the Act of July, 1825. You cannot press this view of the subject too earnestly upon the consideration of the British ministry. It has bearings and relations that reach beyond the immediate question under discussion.

"I will add nothing as to the impropriety of suffering any feelings that find their origin in the past pretensions of this government to have an adverse influence upon the present conduct of Great Britain."

plexed to understand the real motives of Mr. Canning. On the 18th October, not one month after this despatch to Mr. Clay, he wrote a private letter to the President, giving some interesting information he had obtained on a short visit to Paris.[1] In this letter he mentioned having received information from a respectable quarter that "a few days before the publication of the order in council of July last, one of the King's ministers had complained to a confidential friend of the general tone of the American diplomacy towards England, still more as respected manner than matter, and added that it was time to show that this was felt and resented." Puzzled to know what could have caused such displeasure, Mr. Gallatin adds that he had looked through all the published correspondence and could find nothing with which the British government could have taken offence, unless it were Mr. Adams's instructions to Mr. Rush, with which that government had no concern. Even in this supposition, however, it soon appeared that he was mistaken; for on the 27th November he wrote to Mr. Clay that he had further ascertained the name of the "King's minister" before mentioned. It was no less a person than Mr. Canning himself; he had said that the language used by America was almost tantamount to a declaration of war; he had used the same language to Mr. Gallatin, and his grievance was not at all against the President or his officers, but against a certain Mr. Baylies, a member of Congress from Massachusetts, who, as chairman of a committee, had made a belligerent report to the House, which had never even been taken into consideration. "It is most undoubtedly that report which has given great offence, and I am apt to think that, though not the remote, or only, it was the immediate cause of the order in council."

Feeling his way in this tentative manner, always the most difficult task of a new minister in critical times, Mr. Gallatin approached the other subjects of negotiation. At the close of the year he wrote to the President, sketching the state of each disputed point and earnestly pressing for instructions. This letter closes with the following unusually severe remarks:

---

[1] Writings, vol. ii. p. 827.

"Although all my faculties are exerted, and it is far from being the first time, in trying to accommodate differences and to remove causes of rupture, it is impossible for me not to see and feel the temper that prevails here towards us. It is perceptible in every quarter and on every occasion, quite changed from what it was in 1815–1821; nearly as bad as before the last war, only they hate more and despise less, though they still affect to conceal hatred under the appearance of contempt. I would not say this to any but to you and your confidential advisers, and I say it not in order to excite· corresponding feelings, but because I think that we must look forward and make those gradual preparations which will make us ready for any emergency, and which may be sufficient to preserve us from the apprehended danger. . . . I must say, after my remarks on the temper here, that I have been personally treated with great, by Mr. Canning with marked, civility."

Thus difficulties thickened round him as he advanced. The West India negotiation could not take place; there was no hope for the navigation of the St. Lawrence; there was no chance of fixing a definitive boundary in Oregon; even to make the preliminary arrangements for compromising the dispute about the Maine boundary would be laborious and arduous; the only point settled was that of payment in a gross sum for captured slaves.

ALBERT GALLATIN TO JAMES GALLATIN.

LONDON, 13th January, 1827.

. . . We continue all well, and I anticipate nothing that can prevent our taking our departure about the middle of June. All that I can possibly do here must be terminated by that time, provided the instructions I have asked on some points be such as not to render another reference to Washington necessary. I have written to the Department of State accordingly, and asked for leave to return by that time, to which I presume no objection will be made, as it was explicitly understood that I should remain no longer than the pending negotiations required, and Mr. Adams's conjecture that they would occupy about twelve months is confirmed. I have written to him a private letter by the last packet, most earnestly entreating him both to direct the necessary instructions to be sent and to grant me leave to return. As you know him, and he has always shown kindness to you, I wish you would join your solicitations to mine, either in writing or by waiting in person on him. There are many things which you may say or explain showing the importance of my return to my family. As to myself, whether it is the result of age (you know that in a fortnight I will enter my sixty-seventh year) or increased anxiety about you and your brother, my mind is enervated, and I feel that a longer absence would have a most serious effect upon me. As it is, though my health is tolerable, I hardly dare to hope that I will see you again. Nor will my return be any public loss. The United States want here a man of considerable talent, but he must be younger than I am and capable of going through great labor with more facility than I now possess. This is at all times the most laborious foreign mission. It is at this time, owing to the negotiations, one of the most laborious public offices. I cannot work neither as long nor do as much work in the same time as formerly. To think and to write, to see the true state of the question, and to state it, not with eloquence, but with perspicuity, all that formerly was done instantaneously and with ease is now attended with labor, requires time, and is not performed to my satisfaction. I believe that Mr. Lawrence will prove a useful public servant. Yet I have missed and do miss your assistance every day. I did not like French diplomacy; I cannot say that I admire that of this country. Some of the French statesmen occasionally say what is not true (cordon sanitaire); here they conceal the truth. The temper also towards us is bad. After all, though it is necessary to argue well, you may argue forever in vain; strength and the opinion of your strength are the only efficient weapons. We must either shut ourselves in our shell, as was attempted during the Jefferson policy, and I might say mine, or we must support our rights and pretensions by assuming at home a different attitude. I think that we are now sufficiently numerous and rich for that purpose, and that with skill our resources would be found adequate. But that is a subject requiring more discussion than can be encompassed in a letter. I fear that you will find this written in a too desponding mood; and I do not wish you to despond as relates to yourself. . . . What you may, or rather ought to, do about our lands, it belongs to you to decide. They are yours and Albert's, and you must consider them as such, keep or sacrifice, since there is no chance of a favorable sale at present, as you shall think best. It is a troublesome and unproductive property, which has plagued me all my life. I could not have vested my patrimony in a more unprofitable manner. . . .

ALBERT GALLATIN TO JAMES GALLATIN.

LONDON, 29th January, 1827.

. . . I do not understand [in your letter] what relates to Mr. Clay's letter and mine on colonial intercourse, and why they should be brought in competition. They were written for different purposes, mine in defence of the general ground taken by America and of her claims on that subject, addressed, too, to Mr. Canning, and on that account more guarded and cautious; that of Mr. Clay principally in defence of the conduct of the Administration on the subject since he came in office, and written without apprehension that it might be answered. I was but indifferently satisfied with my own or with the cause I had to contend for; and that of Mr. Clay, though too long and too hastily written, was better than I had expected. He has great talent, and has vastly improved since 1814. His fault is that he is devoured with ambition, and in all his acts never can detach himself and their effect on his popularity from the subject on which he is called to act. But whilst serving in his Department it is unpleasant to be placed in opposition to him.

J. Q. ADAMS TO GALLATIN.[1]

WASHINGTON, 20th March, 1827.

DEAR SIR,—I have received from you several very kind and friendly letters, for which the unremitted pressure of public business during the session of Congress has not permitted me to

---

[1] Gallatin's Writings, ii. 364.

make the due return of acknowledgment.   The march of time, which stays not for the convenience or the humors of men, has closed the existence of that body for the present, and they have left our relations with Great Britain precisely where they were.

The sudden and unexpected determination of the British government to break off all negotiation concerning the colonial trade, and the contemporaneous measure of interdicting the vessels of the United States from all their ports in the West Indies, as well as many others, has taken us so much by surprise that a single short session of Congress has not been sufficient to mature the system by which we may most effectively meet this new position assumed by the colonial monopoly of Great Britain. . . .

From the state of your negotiation upon the other subjects of interest in discussion between the two governments, as exhibited in your latest despatches and letters, there is little encouragement to expect a satisfactory result regarding them.   There are difficulties in the questions themselves,—difficulties still more serious in the exorbitant pretensions of Great Britain upon every point, —difficulties, to all appearances, insuperable in the *temper* which Great Britain now brings into the management of the controversy.   For the causes of this present soreness of feeling we must doubtless look deeper than to the report of a committee of our House of Representatives or to the assertion by the late President that the American continents were no more subject to future colonization from Europe.   As the assertion of this principle is an attitude which the American hemisphere must assume, it is one which no European has the right to question; and if the inference drawn from it of danger to *existing* colonies has any foundation, it can only be on the contingency of a war, which we shall by all possible means avoid.   As to the report of Mr. Baylies, if Mr. Canning has not enough upon his hands to soothe the feelings of foreign nations for what he says in Parliament himself, he would think it passing strange to be called to account for offences of that character committed by Mr. Brougham or Mr. Hume.   He surely cannot be so ill informed of the state of things existing here as not to know that Mr. Baylies is not the man by whom the sentiments or opinions of this or of the last Administration of the government of the United States were or are wont to be expressed.   The origin, rise, and progress of this "Oregon Territory Committee," of which Mr. Baylies became at last the chairman, is perhaps not known even to you; but you may remember it was the engine by means of which Mr. Jonathan Russell's famous duplicate letter was brought before the House of Representatives and the nation, and that incident will give you a clue to the real purposes for which that committee was raised and to the spirit manifested in the report of Mr. Baylies.

Upon the whole, if the same inflexible disposition which you have found prevailing upon the subject of the colonial trade, and of which indications so distinct have been given upon the boundary questions and the navigation of the St. Lawrence, should continue unabated, our last resource must be to agree upon the renewal for ten years of the Convention of 1818.   This would probably *now* obtain the advice and consent of the Senate for ratification.   On the colonial trade question the opposition here have taken the British side, and their bill in the Senate was concession unqualified but by a deceptive show of future resistance. But you must not conclude that the same spirit would be extended to anything in the shape of concession which you might send to us in a treaty.   One inch of ground yielded on the northwest coast,—one step backward from the claim to the navigation of the St. Lawrence,—one hair's-breadth of compromise upon the article of impressment, would be certain to meet the reprobation of the Senate.   In this temper of the parties, all we can hope to accomplish will be to adjourn controversies which we cannot adjust, and say to Britain, as the Abbé Bernis said to Cardinal Fleuri: Monseigneur, j'attendrai.

Your instructions will be forwarded in season that you may be subjected to no delay in bringing the negotiation to an issue; but I regret exceedingly the loss to the public of your continued services.   The political and commercial system of Great Britain is undergoing great changes.   It will certainly not stop at the stage where it now stands.   The interdicting order in council of last July itself has the air of a start backwards by Mr. Huskisson from his own system to the old navigation laws.   His whole system is experimental against deep-rooted prejudice and a delusion of past experience.   I could earnestly have wished that it might have been consistent with your views to remain a year or two longer in England, and I should have indulged a hope that in the course of that time some turn in the tide of affairs might have occurred which would have enabled us, with your conciliatory management of debatable concerns, to place our relations with Great Britain upon a more stable and friendly foundation.

As though to annoy Mr. Gallatin with indefinite difficulties and delays, a prolonged Cabinet crisis now occurred. Lord Liverpool died suddenly in February, 1827, and the King had to decide whether his authority was sufficient to sustain Mr. Canning as Prime Minister against the personal isolation in which the temper, rather than the social position, of that remarkable man placed him. On the 28th April, Mr. Gallatin wrote to Mr. Clay: "At the dinner of the 23d, Mr. Canning came near Baron Humboldt and me, and told us, ' You see that the opinion universally entertained abroad, and very generally indeed in England, that this government is an Aristocracy, is not true. *It is,*' said he, emphatically, ' *a Monarchy*. The Whigs had found it out in 1784, when they tried to oppose the King's prerogative of choosing his Prime Minister. The Tories have now repeated the same experiment, and with no greater success.' He appears certainly very confident, and speaks of any intended opposition in Parliament as if he had no fear of it." Then Mr. Huskisson, who was the chief commissioner on the English side, was forced to go abroad for his health. Mr. Grant took Mr. Huskisson's place. Under the steady influence of Mr. Gallatin's conciliatory course and of his strong arguments, the British Ministry, pressed as they were by absorbing contests at home, tended towards a better disposition, and, although they still adhered with determination to those points upon which they had committed themselves, they proved more compliant upon others. This tendency was rather hastened than retarded by the death of Mr. Canning in August, and the elevation of Lord Goderich to the post of Prime Minister. The tone of Mr. Gallatin's letters to Mr. Clay became more cheerful. On the 6th August, after much discussion, a treaty was signed which continued the commercial convention of 1815 indefinitely, leaving either party at liberty to abrogate it at twelve months' notice. On the same day another convention was signed by which the joint use of the disputed Oregon territory, as defined in the 3d Article of the convention of 1818, was also indefinitely continued, subject likewise to abrogation at twelve months' notice. Finally, on the 29th September, a new convention was signed providing for the reference of the disputed Maine boundary to a friendly sovereign.

This accomplished, Mr. Gallatin hastened homewards, and, after a passage of fifty-two days, arrived in New York on the 30th November.

J. Q. ADAMS TO GALLATIN.

WASHINGTON, December 12, 1827.

DEAR SIR,—I have received your obliging letter from New York, and, although it would give me great pleasure to see you here, I know not that any material public interest will require your presence. Your three conventions were sent yesterday to the Senate for their consideration. In what light they will view them I cannot yet foresee. I wish they may prove as satisfactory to them as they are to me.

I regret exceedingly for the public interest that you found yourself under the necessity of coming home. At the time of your arrival in England, although I do not believe they had a deliberate purpose of coming to a rupture with us, they were undoubtedly in a waspish temper, and Mr. Canning had determined to play off upon us one of his flourishes for effect. He had been laying up a stock of resentments, for which he was hoping to expose us to public and open humiliation. I believe that which most rankled in his mind was the disappointment of the slave-trade convention, though he said perhaps not a word to you about it.

But, whatever it was, your convention upon the slave indemnities first turned the tide of feeling and soothed irritations on both sides. You gained an ascendency over him by suffering him to fancy himself victorious on some points, by the forbearance to expose too glaringly his absurdities, and his position, from the time of Lord Liverpool's political demise, warned him that he had enemies enough upon his hands without seeking this *querelle d'Allemand* with us.

Nothing can be more preposterous than their obstinacy upon this colonial trade squabble; and you had not set your foot on board ship before they began to grow sick of it. A hurricane had already burst upon the island of St. Kitts and the Virgin Isles. They have now by proclamation opened the Bahama Islands, for vessels in ballast to go and take salt and fruit, and on the 31st of October Mr. Grant told Mr. Lawrence that *he regretted* you had not settled this affair as satisfactorily as the others. Lord Dudley also admires the great ability of your *last* note on the subject. These are among the indications not only that their experiment of supplying their islands without us is failing, but that they begin to feel it. I believe had you stayed over the winter, they would have come to our terms upon this affair before another summer. Whether they would promote our own interest so well as the present condition of things, remains, as it always has been, a more doubtful point to me.

The North-Eastern boundary question is far otherwise important to us than that of the colonial trade,—so important as to give me the deepest concern. I hope your convention will have the approbation of the Senate, and that the sequel will be satisfactory to us. We shall want the benefit of your information and of your advice.

There are so many of these breakers close aboard of us that I have lost some of my concern for the distant danger of impressment. Mr. Canning was so fond of creating worlds that, under his administration, the turn of a straw would have plunged Great Britain into a war with any nation upon earth. His successors will be more prudent, and I hope more pacific. If they should engage in a war to which we shall be in the first instance neutral, I doubt whether they will authorize their officers to impress beyond their own territorial jurisdiction. I would not lose any opportunity of coming to an arrangement with them to abolish this odious practice, but I am weary of renewing with them desperate discussions upon it.

Altogether, if your conventions are ratified, I shall indulge a strong hope that our relations with Great Britain generally will become more friendly than they have lately been.   But I know only that I shall feel most sensibly the loss of your presence at London, and can form no more earnest wish than that your successor may acquire the same influence of reason and good temper which you did exercise, and that it may be applied with as salutary effect to the future discussions between the two governments.

I remain, with great respect and attachment, your friend.

With this letter of President Adams the story of Mr. Gallatin's diplomatic career may fitly close.   Such evidence leaves nothing to be said in regard to his qualities as a diplomate.   In that career he stood first among the men of his time.   He never again returned to Europe, and henceforward his public life may be considered as ended.

He had, however, still one duty to perform.   The President, unable to persuade him to remain in London, requested him to prepare on the part of the United States government the argument in regard to the North-Eastern boundary, which was to be submitted to the King of the Netherlands as arbitrator.   This excessively tedious and laborious duty occupied all his time for the next two years, and resulted in a bulky volume, which may be found among our public documents.   While preparing it he was obliged to pass a portion of his time in Washington, where he found politics less and less to his taste.   The election of 1828 terminated the long sway of the old Republican party, and if what he saw about him had not convinced Mr. Gallatin that his opinions and methods belonged to a past era, instinct must have taught him that his career and that of his party had best close together.

GALLATIN TO HIS WIFE.

WASHINGTON, 16th December, 1828.

. . . I have used every possible endeavor to terminate our business earlier than the day on which it must necessarily be concluded; I have attended to nothing else, and owe now thirty and more visits, yet I do not expect to have done before the 1st of January.   I cannot rise early, the days are short, the details very complex, new materials coming in to the last moment, a

great mass of papers to read, selections to make, several tran-
scribers and draughtsmen to direct, and, independent of age, the
whole much retarded by my being obliged to abstain from
writing. Yet, though I have not worked so hard, the use of the
pen excepted, since I was in the Treasury, I continue to enjoy
perfect health. . . . Notwithstanding their triumphant majority,
the prospect of the conquering party is not very flattering. The
object which alone united them is accomplished, and they dare
not now approach the tariff or any other measure of importance
on which they would immediately divide and break off. Nor is
there any man around whom they can rally, the pretensions
being numerous and discordant. The state of politics is better
in reference to the external relations of the country than during
the existence of the Federal and Republican parties; but it is
truly deplorable with respect to the internal concerns of the
nation. . . .

GALLATIN TO BADOLLET.

NEW YORK, March 26, 1829.

I duly received, my dear friend, your letter of 10th January
last, and it would have been immediately answered had not
an accident deprived me of the use of my right hand. Rest
has now partly restored it; but I am compelled to employ
generally an amanuensis, and to write myself only on special
occasions. . . .

I hope that, with your moderate wants, you find yourself now
comparatively at ease. After much anxiety, I find that our
children must be left to cut their own way and to provide for
themselves; and I have no other uneasiness respecting them
than so far as concerns their health, that of Albert and Frances
being extremely delicate, so much so, indeed, as may perhaps
compel me to change once more my place of residence for one
more southerly and favorable to their lungs. With great indolence and an anxious wish to be rooted somewhere, I was destined
to be always on the wing. It was an ill-contrived plan to think
that the banks of the Monongahela, where I was perfectly satisfied to live and die in retirement, could be borne by the female
part of my family or by children brought up at Washington

and Paris, and, unfortunately for them, in an artificial situation which has produced expectations that can never be realized. Albert was the only one who was happy, and I was obliged to break up a comfortable establishment and to attempt a new one in one of our seaports with means inadequate to our support. Particular circumstances have made Baltimore, which was my choice, objectionable in some respects; and on my return from England, in conformity with the natural wishes of my wife, whose respectable mother, aged eighty-five, is still alive, I settled here. What I may now do is quite uncertain. To Washington I must proceed in a few days on the business of the North-East boundary, which is committed to my care, and will be detained there till the 1st of July. I must add that my public engagements in relation to that important question will cease with the end of this year.

I am not pleased with the present aspect of public affairs, still less with that of the public mind. Perhaps old age makes me querulous. I care little what party and who is in power; but it seems to me that now and for the last eight years people and leaders have been much less anxious about the public service and the manner in which it should be performed than by whom the country should be governed. This feeling appears to me to be growing; and at this moment every movement seems already to be directed towards the next Presidential election, and that not on account of any preference of a system of public measures over another, but solely in relation to persons, or at best to sectional feelings. Amongst other symptoms displeasing to me, I may count the attempt of the West, and particularly of your State, to claim the sovereignty and exclusive right to the public lands. I wish they did of right belong to the several States and not to the United States. But the claim is contrary to positive compact and to common justice, any departure from which, either in our domestic or external policy, is the most fatal injury that can be inflicted on our political institutions, on the reputation of the country, and indeed on the preservation of the Union. But we are going off the scene; I think that we have discharged our duties honestly, and the next generation must provide for itself. . . .

For one moment, however, it seemed possible that Mr. Gallatin might again be employed abroad. The King of the Netherlands could not be expected to arbitrate without assistance and advice, and it was peculiarly important that Mr. Gallatin should be at hand for that purpose. Mr. Van Buren's conscience appears to have been somewhat tender on the subject of Mr. Gallatin since the secret manipulation of the Vice-Presidency in 1824; and after General Jackson had been chosen President in November, 1828, and events had marked out Mr. Van Buren as highly influential with him, that gentleman seems to have intimated that he considered Mr. Gallatin to have claims upon his good-will. Mr. Gallatin's eldest son was then eager for a diplomatic position, and his father authorized him to tell Mr. Van Buren, and later wrote himself to say, that he would accept the mission to France, if offered to him, although he was not willing to return to England or even to be Secretary of State. Unfortunately, Mr. Van Buren soon found that he had no power to dispose of his patronage as Secretary, and in the frightful chaos which followed the inauguration of General Jackson the old servants of the government instantly saw that new principles and new practices left no place for them in the national service.

GALLATIN TO HIS WIFE.

WASHINGTON, 2d May, 1829.

. . . I have made more progress this week than all the time since my arrival. I was not very well, and felt dispirited. My cold has now entirely left me, and I can see as through a vista the end of my labors. . . . After next week most of the writing will be over and my hand may rest; but there will be correcting, altering, collating maps and evidence, &c. You call me a pack-horse, but I am used to it, and might, as relates to the public, have taken for my motto, *Sic vos non vobis*. . . . I will be more than delighted to see Frances, if she can come. . . . As to beaux, I know of none but Van Buren, and he is, I think, a little crest-fallen. . . .

16th May, 1829.

. . . I have this day finished dictating to Albert our argu-

ment,—two hundred pages of his writing.	Mr. Preble promises
to return the whole to me on Monday with his proposed emen-
dations, which will not be either long or important; and I hope
to have it ready for the President's inspection by Tuesday.
. . . In giving my love to Maria, tell her that she and Miss
Harrison must be out of their senses to think that I can have any
influence in placing a clerk or do anything else here; but . . .
upon every occasion I have freely expressed my entire disapproba-
tion of the system of removal for political opinions, particularly
as applied to clerks, inspectors, &c., of which there had been no
instance since the commencement of this government. . . .

23d May, 1829.

. . . Our argument is in the press, and I have every reason to
believe that we will have terminated all that remains to be done
for the present by the 1st of next month.	I am well, though
weak, and you need not fear for me the effect of the Washington
climate either physically or politically.	There are some things
to which I am used, and which do not affect me much or long.
Was I not postponed to make room for Robert Smith, even when
in my prime and with Mr. Jefferson and Mr. Madison to sustain
me?	And most certainly, whatever may be the claims of age and
services, I had none whatever on the present Administration.
Age, also, so advanced as mine, is not a recommendation; and
we must make room for younger men. . . .

WASHINGTON, 8th November, 1829.

. . . We came here without accident. . . . I work as much
as, but not more than, I can well go through, but my progress is
slow; our statement will be nearly as long as one volume of
Frances's novels, and it is no trifling task to execute a piece of
close reasoning and condensed facts of that length, which is ultimately intended for the public eye and will be a national and
perhaps a public European paper.	I do not mean to let it go to
the press till corrected and made as faultless as I can, and am
more afraid of a failure in the style than in the matter. . . .
We dined yesterday at the President's.	He is very cordial, and
did unbend himself entirely.	I have avoided every allusion to

myself, his Cabinet, and the removals. I am told, by one who ought to know, that the Cabinet is divided, Ingham, Branch, and Berrien being the moderate party. I suppose that the division at present is only as to removals, but with an eye to the next Presidential election; and I do not know whether we must not become Jacksonites in preference to intended successors. Van Buren is gone to Richmond to court Virginia. . . .

29th November, 1829.

. . . I got a cold last Tuesday. . . . The weather was so bad that I thought it best to keep in the house. . . . I have lost two dinners by my confinement, one at Mr. —— and the other at the President's, where Albert went. This was a splendid affair; the East room, which, notwithstanding the abuse of Mr. Adams, was but an unfurnished barn, is, under our more Republican Administration, besides the Brussels carpeting and silk curtains, &c., adorned with four immense French looking-glasses, the largest Albert ever saw, and, by the by, not necessary in a dining-room; three splendid English crystal chandeliers, &c. Fifty guests sitting at dinner, one hundred candles and lamps, silver plate of every description, &c., and for a queen, Peggy O'Neal,[1] led in by Mr. Vaughan as the head of the Diplomatic Corps, and sitting between him and the President. All which I mention that, having had with me your share of the vanities and grandeurs of this world, you may be quite satisfied that we were not indebted for them to any particular merit of ours; and that the loss of popularity, which we perhaps regret too much (for as to the vanities I know that you care no more about them than I do), is no more an object of astonishment than the manner in which it is acquired. . . .

---

[1] See Parton's Life of Andrew Jackson, vol. iii. chap. xvii.

Albert Gallatin

BOOK V.

AGE. 1830-1849.

WHATEVER Mr. Gallatin may have thought or said of his physical or intellectual powers, he was from 1830 to 1840 in the prime of life. Never had his mind been more clear, his judgment more keen, or his experience and knowledge so valuable as when the United States government dispensed with his further services at the close of the year 1829. Intellectually, the next fifteen years were the most fruitful of his whole long and laborious career. His case was a singular illustration of the intellectual movement of his time. Had he now been entering instead of quitting the world, he would have found himself drawn, both by temperament, by cast of mind, and by education, into science or business or literature; for the United States of 1830 was no longer the same country as the United States of 1790; it had found a solution of its most serious political problems, and its more active intellectual life was turning to the study of social and economical principles, to purely scientific methods and objects, to practical commerce and the means of obtaining wealth. Old though Mr. Gallatin might think himself, it was to this new society that he and his mental processes belonged, and he found it a pleasure rather than a pain to turn away from that public life which no longer represented a single great political conception, and to grapple with the ideas and methods of the coming generation. In fact, the politics of the United States from 1830 to 1849 offered as melancholy a spectacle as satirists ever held up to derision. Of all the parties that have existed in the United States, the famous Whig party was the most feeble in ideas and the most blundering in management; the Jacksonian Democracy was corrupt in its methods; and both, as well as society itself, were deeply cankered with two desperate sores: the enormous increase of easily acquired wealth, and the terribly rapid growth of slavery and the slave power. In such a spectacle there was to Mr. Gallatin no pleasure and deep pain. He did not, like his old colleague J. Q. Adams, return into public life to offer a violent protest against the degradation of the time, and he did not, like Mr. Adams, pour out his contempt and indignation in the bitterest and most savage comments on men and measures; but he felt quite as strongly, and his thoughts were expressed, whenever they were expressed at all, in language that meant as much. Few Americans can now look back upon that time and remember how the whole country writhed with pain and rage under the lash of Charles Dickens's satire, without feeling that this satire was in the main deserved. Indeed, there can be no philosophy of history that would not require some vast derangement of the national health to account for the mortal convulsion with which that health was at last in part restored.

Although Mr. Gallatin was no longer in office, he was still deeply interested in public affairs. Members of the Cabinet, Senators, and members of Congress, incessantly applied to him for information and advice. Like Mr. Jefferson and Mr. Madison in their retirement, he was consulted as an oracle. His replies were oracular neither in brevity nor in doubtfulness of meaning. He never refused to assist persons, though quite unknown to him, who asked for such counsel. For a considerable time, so long as financial and economical legislation was especially. prominent, in the days of tariffs, nullification, national bank, and sub-treasury, he was still a political power and made his influence deeply felt.

The first occasion for his active interference in politics under the new régime was somewhat accidental. In the early part of General Jackson's Administration the question of renewing the charter of the Bank of the United States was not yet a prominent party issue; that the President would make a bitter personal contest for the destruction of the bank was not suspected, and the tendency of public opinion seemed to favor a renewal of the charter. In April, 1830, soon after the argument on the North-East boundary was disposed of, Mr. Gallatin received a

letter from Robert Walsh, Jr., editor of the American Quarterly
Review in Philadelphia, requesting an article on currency, in
connection with Mr. McDuffie's recent Congressional report on
the Bank of the United States. Mr. Gallatin replied that he
would be disposed to comply if he thought he could add anything to what had been done by others. He described himself
as an "ultra-bullionist," favoring the restriction of paper issues
to notes of $100, to be issued only by the Bank of the United
States, and a bi-metallic currency of gold and silver. This was
essentially the French system, and Mr. Gallatin had, during his
residence in France, become prepossessed in its favor. In reply
to his request for statistical information, Mr. Walsh put him in
communication with Nicholas Biddle, President of the United
States Bank, and an animated correspondence was carried on for
some months between the two gentlemen. Early in August,
Mr. Gallatin was called upon for his paper, and wrote to say
that he was not ready. He excused his apparent sluggishness
by describing his method of work : "I can lay no claim to either
originality of thinking or felicity of expression. If I have met
with any success either in public bodies, as an executive officer,
or in foreign negotiations, it has been exclusively through a
patient and most thorough investigation of all the attainable
facts, and a cautious application of these to the questions under
discussion. . . . Long habit has given me great facility in collating, digesting, and extracting complex documents, but I am
not hasty in drawing inferences ; the arrangement of the facts
and arguments is always to me a work of considerable labor ;
and though aiming at nothing more than perspicuity and brevity,
I am a very slow writer." This assertion must probably be
received with some qualifications ; at least it is clear that much
of Mr. Gallatin's diplomatic work must have been done with
rapidity and ease.

In his correspondence with Mr. Biddle he gave the reasons
which had produced his strong faith in a bi-metallic currency, and
since these reasons are interesting as a part of his experience, they
are worth quoting here : "The most skilfully administered bank
can only be prepared to meet ordinary commercial fluctuations.
But when a real and severe crisis occurs, you are perfectly aware

that moral causes may increase the pressure to an extent which will baffle every calculation, for the very reason that those causes are beyond the reach of calculation. On the other hand, the example of France under the united pressure of a double invasion, a failure of crops, large indemnities to foreign countries, a vast portion of which was paid by the exportation of specie, an unsettled government, and wild stock speculations, is decisive to prove with what facility a crisis is met with an abundant circulating metallic currency. We were, Mr. Baring and myself, spectators of the crisis, of which I could only see the external appearances and results, whilst he was behind the scenes and deeply interested in the event. We conferred often on the subject, and came to the same conclusions. He has ever since been an advocate in England of the simultaneous use of the two metals for the sole purpose of enlarging the basis of the metallic currency."

The "Considerations on the Currency and Banking System of the United States" appeared in December, 1830, and was republished in a separate form, with some further changes and tabular statements, in 1831.[1] As a model for clearness of statement and thorough investigation it then stood alone among American works, and even in Europe it might be difficult to find anything much superior. Nearly half a century has elapsed since this essay was written; finance has made great progress, particularly in the United States, where, under peculiar circumstances, a succession of violent convulsions ended in building up a completely new system of currency and banking; yet even to-day Mr. Gallatin's essay is indispensable to the American student of finance. There is no other work which will guide him so surely through the intricacies of our early financial history.

The essay had, however, one effect which its author did not foresee. He wrote as an economist and financier, whereas the bank charter was a political question. As a matter of finance he argued, as every man who was not a politician and who knew anything of finance then argued, in favor of the bank. That he was perfectly right can hardly be made a matter of question;

---

[1] Reprinted in Gallatin's Writings, vol. iii.

the value of the bank as a financial instrument was very great; the consequences of destroying it were disastrous in the extreme, and were acutely felt during at least five-and-twenty years. The popular fear of its hostility to our liberties was one of those delusions which characterize ignorant stages of society, and which would have had no importance unless politicians had found it a convenient ally. The kindred theory of its unconstitutionality was even then untenable, and is now ridiculous. The people of the United States have learned since that time many lessons in regard to their Constitution, and they have also learned that they hold all corporations at their mercy, and that if there is any danger to liberty it is quite as likely to be the liberties of corporations as those of the people which suffer. All this was even then plain enough to a man like Mr. Gallatin, who had in forty years of experience studied these subjects from every point of view; but there was another question, the answer to which was not so clear. Supposing the bank to be destroyed, was it worth while to attempt its reconstruction? Setting aside the financial question, was it not better to accept the pecuniary loss, even indefinitely, until some new remedy should be found, rather than convulse all economical interests with this perpetually recurring political contest? Most men would now agree with Mr. Gallatin that, under those circumstances, it was better to abandon the struggle and to seek new means for answering the same ends; but this was not the opinion of the Whig party.

Mr. Gallatin's pamphlet was circulated as a campaign document by the bank. He became by this means its spokesman and one of its most influential allies, subjected to suspicion and attack on its account, although it need hardly be said that he not only received no compensation from the bank, but declined the ordinary pay of contributors to the Review. This attitude he was probably prepared to maintain so long as the bank charter was undecided; but after President Jackson had carried his point and the bank perished, after the independent Treasury was organized, and the Whig party was setting everything at stake upon success in effecting a counter-revolution and restoring the bank, there was naturally some irritation against Mr. Gallatin because he took very cautious ground and preferred to accept the situation.

The bank charter was, however, a subordinate and comparatively uninteresting question in the politics of 1831. Another and a more serious political issue was threatening the existence of the Union and entering into all the most earnest discussions of the Presidential election of 1832. This was the protective system, the American system of Mr. Clay, who, always true to his deep feeling for nationality, was himself the best product of the war of 1812, in its character of national self-assertion. All Mr. Gallatin's feelings and education were opposed to protection; his voice had been, as he took pride in thinking, the first in America to make a public assertion of free-trade principles, and now, in 1831, his advocacy of tariff reduction was stimulated by the threatening attitude of South Carolina. That political theory which he had always made his cardinal principle, and which, in its practical form, consisted simply in avoiding issues that were likely to endanger the Union, led him now to urge timely concession. In September, 1831, a convention of the friends of free trade was held in Philadelphia, and delegated to a committee, of which Mr. Gallatin was chairman, the task of preparing a memorial to be presented to both Houses of Congress. This memorial forms a pamphlet of nearly ninety pages, and was such a document as he might have sent to Congress had he been still Secretary of the Treasury; it was, in fact, a Secretary's report, and it probably had as much effect, for it became the text-book of the free-traders of that day.

The memorial began by ascertaining the annual expenditure of the government and the annual value of imports; from these data it concluded that an average duty of 25 per cent. ad valorem on the taxed imports would answer all requirements and should be assumed as the normal standard of taxation; after an argument on the general theory of free trade, the paper went on to examine and criticise the existing tariff and to show the propriety of the proposed reform.

When the memorial was presented to Congress, it called down upon Mr. Gallatin's head a storm of denunciation. For this he was of course prepared, and he could not have expected to escape

blows when, at a time of intense excitement, he voluntarily
placed himself in the thickest of the mêlée. It was then, on the
2d February, 1832, that Mr. Clay made a famous speech in
the Senate in defence of his American system, and into this
carefully prepared oration he introduced the following remarks
upon Mr. Gallatin :

"The gentleman to whom I am about to allude, although
long a resident of this country, has no feelings, no attachments,
no sympathies, no principles in common with our people.   Near
fifty years ago Pennsylvania took him to her bosom, and warmed
and cherished and honored him ; and how does he manifest his
gratitude ?   By aiming a vital blow at a system endeared to her
by a thorough conviction that it is indispensable to her prosperity.
He has filled, at home and abroad, some of the highest offices
under this government during thirty years, and he is still at heart
an alien.   The authority of his name has been invoked, and the
labors of his pen, in the form of a memorial to Congress, have
been engaged, to overthrow the American system and to substitute the foreign.   Go home to your native Europe, and there
inculcate upon her sovereigns your Utopian doctrines of free
trade, and when you have prevailed upon them to unseal their
ports and freely admit the produce of Pennsylvania and other
States, come back, and we shall be prepared to become converts
and to adopt your faith !"

Mr. Clay, in the course of his career, uttered a vast number
of rhetorical periods as defective as this in logic, taste, and judgment ; but he very rarely succeeded in accumulating so many
blunders as in this attack on Mr. Gallatin.   The bad taste of
vilifying an old associate, in a place where he cannot reply ; the
bad logic of answering arguments on the proper rates of impost
duties by remarks on the birthplace of any given individual ;
the bad temper of raising mean and bitter local prejudices against
an honorable and candid opponent, who had never, under any
provocation, condescended to use such weapons against others ;
all these faults are excusable, or, at least, are so common among
orators and debaters as to pass almost unnoticed and unreproved.
It is not these rhetorical flourishes which raise a smile in reading
Mr. Clay's remarks, nor even the adjuration to "Go home to

your native Europe," although this has a startling resemblance to the rhetoric which Charles Dickens, at about this time, attributed to Elijah Pogram. All these are faults, but this paragraph on Mr. Gallatin was worse than a fault: it contained two gross political blunders. One was the pledge that if Europe would adopt free trade America would be prepared to imitate her; a pledge which no sound or well-informed protectionist could, even by inadvertence, have let slip. The other was still more fatal. One principal motive that influenced Mr. Gallatin in pressing at this time his proposition of reducing duties below a maximum of 25 per cent. ad valorem, was the hope that by such a compromise the disunionist propaganda of South Carolina might be paralyzed and the national government might escape with dignity from its embarrassments, without really sacrificing Northern industry. The policy was wise and statesmanlike; in fact, the only solid ground, short of armed compulsion, which could claim logical coherence. Mr. Clay, however, characterized it in terms that cut him entirely away from all consistent recourse to it; yet within twelve months Mr. Clay actually assumed this same ground and went beyond Mr. Gallatin in his abandonment of the protective system. In fact, the difficulty with Gallatin's scheme was that it did not go far enough to please South Carolina, as appears very clearly in a letter written by Gallatin on the 7th April, 1832, to William Drayton, one of the South Carolina representatives, in reply to his request for the sketch of a bill which should reduce the duties to an average of 10 per cent.[1] Mr. Clay's compromise conceded everything, and that too in a worse form and with deplorable consequences. His reputation suffered, and deservedly suffered, in proportion to his previous dogmatism.

Meanwhile, Mr. Gallatin had at last fairly adopted a new career. Certain persons had obtained from the New York Legislature in April, 1829, the charter for a new bank, and finding themselves, after three successive attempts, unable to induce capitalists to subscribe for the stock, they applied to Mr. J. J. Astor for assistance, and Mr. Astor agreed to furnish the

---

[1] See Writings, vol. ii. p. 450.

necessary capital on condition that Mr. Gallatin should be president of the bank. Thus the National (afterwards the Gallatin) Bank came into existence; a small corporation with a capital of only $750,000, and certainly not an institution calculated to inspire or gratify any ambitious thoughts or hopes. Mr. Gallatin drew from it the very modest compensation of $2000 a year, that being the sum which he considered necessary, in addition to his own income, to enable him to live in New York. He never wanted wealth, and was, to his dying day, perfectly consistent on this point with his early declarations. Indeed, his views were far more ambitious when he was surveying the Ohio wilderness with Savary than when he returned to America after nearly fifteen years passed at the most magnificent capitals and courts of the world. What he aimed at and enjoyed was the respect and consideration of his fellow-citizens. In this he was fully gratified. His acquaintance was sought by almost every person of any prominence who visited the city. He was exempted more and more from hostile attack and criticism, and his occupations were such as to keep him always agreeably employed and to bring him in contact with numbers of intelligent and educated men. One by one his old associates passed from the stage,—Jefferson, Monroe, Madison, La Fayette, Badollet,—but a younger generation had already supplied their places. His conversation was, perhaps, freer than when he was forced to weigh his words. His domestic relations were peculiarly happy, and in this respect his good fortune lasted till his death.

Under these pleasant conditions, Mr. Gallatin's active mind turned to those scientific pursuits for which it was so well fitted and in which it took most delight. Perhaps one might not wander very far from the truth if one added that these pursuits were, on the whole, his most permanent claim to distinction. The first debater and parliamentarian of his day, his fame as a leader of Congress has long since ceased to give an echo, and his most brilliant speeches are hardly known even by name to the orators of the present generation. The first of all American financiers, his theories, his methods, and his achievements as Secretary of the Treasury are as completely forgotten by politicians as his speeches in Congress. First among the diplomatists of his time, his reputation as a diplomate has passed out of men's minds. First as a writer and an authority on political economy in America, very few economists can now remember the titles of his writings or the consequences of his action. But he was the father of American ethnology, and there has been no time since his death when the little band of his followers have forgotten him; there never can come a time when students of that subject can venture to discard his work.

The reason of this steadiness in the estimate of his scientific reputation is simply that his method was sound and his execution accurate; having set to himself the task of constructing a large system of American ethnology, he laid its foundations broadly and firmly in an adequate study of comparative philology. Abstaining with his usual caution from all hazardous speculation and unripe theorizing, he devoted immense labor and many years of life to the routine work of collecting and sifting vocabularies, studying the grammatical structure of languages, and classifying the groups and families of our American Indians on the principles thus worked out. Thus it was he who first established the linguistic groups of the North American Indians on a large scale, and made the first ethnographical map of North America which had real merit.

Geography was always one of his favorite studies; but the influence which decided the bent of his mind towards ethnological investigation seems to have come chiefly from Alexander von Humboldt, at whose request he made, in 1823, a first attempt in the shape of an essay, which was not printed, but was quoted with praise in the Introduction to the "Atlas Éthnographique" of M. Balbi. Following up the line of inquiry, he set himself actively to work in the winter of 1825–26 to obtain Indian vocabularies, and the presence of a numerous delegation of Southern Indians at Washington in the course of that winter enabled him to make rapid progress. He was further aided by the War Department, which circulated, at his request, printed forms of a vocabulary containing six hundred words. He then published a table of all the existing tribes in the United States. In 1835, at the request of the American Antiquarian Society of Worcester, Massachusetts, he prepared an essay, which was printed the following year in the second volume of the Society's Transactions, under the title, "A Synopsis of the Indian Tribes within the United States east of the Rocky Mountains and in the British and Russian Possessions in North America." This paper was accompanied by an ethnological map and numerous vocabularies. It was successful in its main object of giving a solid structure to the science, and it was received with applause by American and European ethnologists. Mr. Gallatin was encouraged to go on, and under his influence the American Ethnological Society of New York was organized, which held its first meeting on the 19th November, 1842, and in 1845 published its first volume of Transactions, three hundred pages of which are devoted to Mr. Gallatin's "Notes on the Semi-Civilized Nations of Mexico, Yucatan, and Central America." The second volume appeared in 1848, and contained another essay by Mr. Gallatin on the geography, philology, and civilization of the Indians, printed as an Introduction to a republication of Hale's "Indians of Northwest America."

These three essays, with their vocabularies and maps, may be said to have created the science of American ethnology, which had until that time existed only in a fragmentary shape. So far as they were philological they still form the groundwork of whatever progress is made in the study, and the men who have rendered and are now rendering the highest services in this science are, of all Americans, those who have the keenest sense and speak in the warmest terms of Gallatin's greatness. So far as the papers were general and descriptive, although forty years of investigation have greatly increased our knowledge and modified our opinions, they are still held in high esteem, and show in numerous places the touch of careful and discreet investigation.

GALLATIN TO JOHN BADOLLET.

NEW YORK, February 7, 1833.

I am deeply and most sadly affected by your letter of 20th ult. It has indeed, my dearest friend, been a source of constant regret and the embittering circumstance of my life that not only we should have been separated during the greater part of our existence, but that your lot should have been cast in the comparatively unhealthy climate to which your repeated bilious attacks and their sad consequences must be ascribed. But what else could be done? The necessity of bringing up a family and of an independent existence is imposed upon us. And although I should have been contented to live and die amongst the Monongahela hills, it must be acknowledged that, beyond the invaluable advantage of health, they afforded either to you or me but few intellectual or physical resources. Indeed, I must say that I do not know in the United States any spot which afforded less means to earn a bare subsistence for those who could not live by manual labor than the sequestered corner in which accident had first placed us. We can but resign ourselves to what was unavoidable. And yet I have often thought that we boasted too much of the immense extent of our territory, which, if it makes us more powerful as a nation and offers so large a field for enterprise, carries within itself the seeds of dissolution, by expanding weakens the bonds of union and the devotedness of genuine patriotism, and in the mean while destroys the charm of local attachment, separates friends and disperses to most distant quarters the members of the same family. In your remote situation, thrown at the age of forty-five amongst entire strangers, and amidst the afflictions by which you have been visited, two great comforts have still been left to you,—the excellent wife with which you have been blessed, that bosom friend for whom there are no secrets, that faithful partner of all your joys and sorrows, that being who had your and gave you her undivided affections with tender feelings, without the least affectation, gentle and prudent, such, indeed, as seems to have been a special gift of Heaven intended for you. Add to this the consciousness not only of a life of integrity, but of a pure life, of one which either as private or public should satisfy you and has gained you general consideration and the respect of all that have simply known you. And as to those who have been more intimately acquainted with you, who has been more generally beloved and could always count more sincere friends than yourself?

My dear friend, you judge yourself with too much severity.

For want of greater offences you seek for specks, and your extreme susceptibility magnifies them into unpardonable errors. I tell you the truth, Badollet, when I assure you that in the course of a life which has brought me in contact with men of all ranks and of many nations, I have not known a more virtuous and pure man than yourself. Your education, that of a student, and your simplicity and your unsuspecting integrity, unfitted you for that active life of enterprise which is the characteristic of this nation, and made you unable to cope with the shrewdness of those by whom you were surrounded. Still, you have to the last resisted every temptation and struggled for existence by honorable means. Yet it is true that both you and I, during the years of youthful hopes and those which succeeded of arduous labors, identified with our new country and surrounded by new and dearest objects of domestic affection, it is true that we both neglected to correspond with the friends of our youth and to preserve ties which could not be replaced. The penalty for that offence we have paid, and have been the greatest sufferers. I have been far more to blame in that respect; and yet please to God that I had nothing worse to reproach myself with.

We all went to Greenfield, Connecticut, during the cholera and escaped that calamity; but during our absence we lost Mrs. Nicholson, who died in August of old age (88). It was principally on her account that Mrs. Gallatin wished, on our return from England, to settle here. I found after a while that my income was not sufficient for this conspicuous and expensive city, and this induced me to accept the place of president of a new bank (the National Bank of New York), which I have now filled for near two years, with a salary of 2000 dollars. I might now give it up so far as concerns myself, as the additional income derived from my wife's property is sufficient for us; but whilst my health permits I may remain in it, as it gives me opportunities of introducing my sons in business. Although I neither suffer pain or can complain of serious illness, I grow gradually weaker, thinner, and more and more liable to severe colds and derangement of the bowels. My faculties, memory of recent events or reading excepted, are wonderfully preserved, and my two last essays on Currency and on the Tariff have received the approbation of the best judges here and in Europe. I had another favorite object in view, in which I have failed. My wish was to devote what may remain of life to the establishment, in this immense and fast-growing city, of a general system of rational and practical education fitted for all and gratuitously opened to all. For it appeared to me impossible to preserve our democratic institutions and the right of universal suffrage unless we could raise the standard of *general* education and the mind of the laboring classes nearer to a level with those born under more favorable circumstances. I became accordingly the president of the council of a new university, originally established on the most liberal principles. But finding that the object was no longer the same, that a certain portion of the clergy had obtained the control, and that their object, though laudable, was special and quite distinct from mine, I resigned at the end of one year rather than to struggle, probably in vain, for what was nearly unattainable.

The present aspect of our national politics is extremely discouraging; yet, having heretofore always seen the good sense of this nation ultimately prevailing against the excesses of party spirit and the still more dangerous efforts of disappointed ambition, I do not despair. But although I hope the dangers which threaten us may for the present be averted, the discussions and the acts which have already taken place have revealed the secret of our vulnerable points, dissolved the charm which made our Constitution and our Union a sacred object, and will render the preservation of both much more difficult than heretofore. I have always thought that the dangerous questions arising from the conflicting and, in our complex, half-consolidated, half-federative form of government, doubtful rights of individual States and United States should, if possible, be avoided; that the bond of union, if made too tight, would snap; and that great moderation in the exercise even of its most legitimate powers was, in our extensive country, with all its diversified and often opposite interests, absolutely necessary on the part of the general government.

This is a general observation, and more applicable to futurity than to the present. The acts of South Carolina are outrageous

and unjustifiable.   The difficult part for our government is how
to nullify nullification and yet to avoid a civil war.   A difficult
task, but, in my humble opinion, not impossible to perform.

Do not write to me long letters which tire you; but now and
then drop me three or four lines.   All my family unite in affectionate remembrance and sympathy.   Give my love to your wife
and tell her that, whilst I live, she has a friend to whom she may
apply under any circumstances. Farewell, my dear friend.   May
God throw comfort on your last years!

Ever your own faithful friend.

GALLATIN TO BADOLLET.

NEW YORK, 3d February, 1834.

MY DEAR FRIEND,—. . . I sympathized most truly and
deeply with you in the irreparable loss with which you have
been afflicted.   I had no consolation to offer you, and felt so
painfully, that very wrongfully and shamefully I postponed and
postponed writing to you.   Even now what can I say but what
must renew and embitter your grief?   For no one knew more
thoroughly, appreciated more highly than I did, the merits of
your beloved partner.   She was the solace of your checkered
and in many respects troubled life, a singular blessing bestowed
on you and long preserved.   With heartfelt thanks to Him who
gave it, resignation to his will is a duty, but this does not lessen
the loss or the pain.   May-be it was best that of the two you
should have been the survivor.   Do you now live with any of
your children, and with which of them?   I hardly dare ask
how your health stands.

I have no other infirmities but a derangement of the functions of the stomach, which I manage without medicine, and an
annually increasing debility which none could cure.   It is only
within the last year that I have discovered a sensible diminution
in the facility of thinking and committing thoughts to writing.
But this and other symptoms advise me that my active career is
at an end, and that I cannot continue to vegetate very long. . . .
My daughter has already three children, who engross the attention of my wife.   Mine has for some time been turned, and

will be still more devoted, to the education of James's son, who has tolerable talents and a most engaging disposition. He is the only young male of my name, and I have hesitated whether, with a view to his happiness, I had not better take him to live and die quietly at Geneva, rather than to leave him to struggle in this most energetic country, where the strong in mind and character overset everybody else, and where consideration and respectability are not at all in proportion to virtue and modest merit. Yet I am so identified with the country which I served so long that I cannot detach myself from it. I find no one who suffers in mind as I do at the corruption and degeneracy of our government. But I do not despair, and cannot believe that we have lived under a perpetual delusion, and that the people will not themselves ultimately cure the evils under which we labor. There is something more wanted than improved forms of government. There is something wrong in the social state. Moral still more than intellectual education and habits are wanted. Had I another life before me, my faculties would be turned towards that object much rather than to political pursuits. But all this is for our posterity. Farewell, my dear friend.

Ever most affectionately yours.

The only specimen of Mr. Gallatin's conversation which seems to claim a place in his biography is that recorded by Miss Martineau in her journal. Concise as it is, it has the merits of both the speaker and the listener.

MISS MARTINEAU'S JOURNAL. 1834.

New York, 24th September.—Mr. Gallatin called. Old man. Began his career in 1787. Has been three times in England. Twice as minister. Found George IV. a cipher. Louis Philippe very different. Will manage all himself and *keep* what he has. William IV. silly as Duke of Clarence. Gallatin would have the President a cipher too, if he could,—*i.e.*, would have him *annual*, so that all would be done by the ministry. As this cannot yet be, he prefers four years' term without renewal to the present plan, or to six years. The office was made for the man,—Washington, who was *wanted* (as well as fit) to reconcile all parties. Bad office, but well filled till now. Too much power for one man; therefore it fills all men's thoughts to the detriment of better things. Jackson "a pugnacious animal." This the reason (in the absence of interested motives) of his present bad conduct.

New Englanders the best people, perhaps, in the world. Prejudiced, but able, honest and homogeneous. Compounds elsewhere. In Pennsylvania the German settlers the most ignorant, but the best political economists. Give any price for the best land and hold it all. Compound in New York. Emigrants a sad drawback. Slaves and gentry in the South. In Gallatin's recollection, Ohio, Illinois, and Indiana had not a white, except a French station or two; now a million and a half of flourishing whites. *Maize* the cause of rapid accumulation, and makes a white a capitalist between February and November, while the Indian remains *in statu quo*, and when accumulation begins, government cannot reserve land. The people are the government and will have all the lands. Drew up a plan for selling lands. Would have sold at two dollars. Was soon brought down to one dollar and a quarter with credit. Then, as it is bad for subjects to be debtors to a democratic government, reduction supplied the place of credit, and the price was brought down to one-quarter of a dollar.

All great changes have been effected by the Democratic party, from the first up to the universal suffrage which practically exists.

Aristocracy must arise. Traders rise. Some few fail, but most retain with pains their elevation. Bad trait here, fraudulent bankruptcies, though dealing is generally fair. Reason, that enterprise must be encouraged, must exist to such a degree as to be liable to be carried too far.

Would have no United States Bank. Would have free banking as soon as practicable. It cannot be yet. Thinks Jackson all wrong about the bank, but has changed his opinion as to its powers. It has no political powers, but prodigious commercial. If the bank be not necessary, better avoid allowing this power. Bank has not overpapered the country.

Gallatin is tall, bald, toothless, speaks with burr, looks venerable and courteous. Opened out and apologized for his full communication. Kissed my hand.

GALLATIN TO BADOLLET.

NEW YORK, 3d September, 1836.

MY DEAR FRIEND,—Your grandson Gillem arrived here safely, and with great propriety remained but two days and proceeded at once to West Point. . . . I had intended to go myself to West Point, but chronical infirmities, always aggravated by travelling, have kept me the whole summer in the city.

It is not that I have any right to complain, . . . feeling sensibly the gradual and lately rapid decay of strength both of body and mind. The last affects me most; memory is greatly impaired, and that great facility of labor with which I was blessed has disappeared. It takes me a day to write a letter of any length, and unfortunately the excessive increase of expenses in this city and a heavy loss by last winter's fire (in fire insurance stock) compel me, for the sake of the salary, to continue the irksome and mechanical labors of president of a bank. . . . Neither I nor my children have the talent of making money any more than yourself, though the Genevese are rather celebrated for it. Mrs. Gallatin enjoys excellent health, and so does the family generally. Your grandson gave me a more favorable account of yours than I had hoped to hear. And I was also much gratified by the appointment of your son as your successor in the land office.

My last work, written in 1835, at the request of the Antiquarian Society of Massachusetts, is a synopsis of the Indian tribes of the United States east of the Rocky Mountains and of those of British and Russian America north of the United States. It will contain, besides an explanatory map, about two hundred pages of text and three hundred of comparative vocabularies and grammatical notices. I had expected to have sent you a copy before now, but the printing has been unaccountably delayed by the publisher employed by the society. I have materials for supplementary considerations on banking and currency, but I have not courage to reduce them to order, and, though they might perhaps be of some use, the bank-paper mania has extended itself so widely that I despair of its being corrected otherwise than by a catastrophe. The energy of this nation is not to be controlled; it is at present exclusively applied to the acquisition of wealth and to improvements of stupendous magnitude. Whatever has that tendency, and of course an immoderate expansion of credit, receives favor. The apparent prosperity and the progress of cultivation, population, commerce, and improvement are beyond expectation. But it seems to me as if general demoralization was the consequence; I doubt whether general happiness is increased; and I would have preferred a gradual, slower, and more secure progress. I am, however, an old man, and the young generation has a right to govern itself. . . .

I had expected to write only a few lines, and have fallen into digressions of little personal interest to you. The fact is that as I grow less capable of thinking, I have become quite garrulous. I only wish I could enjoy once more the pleasure of practising in that respect with my old friend, as talking is not at all and writing is quite a labor to me. Fare you well, and, whether silent or writing, believe me, ever, whilst I still breathe,

Your old and faithful friend.

. . . I was rather astonished to hear that Harrison had a majority in Indiana. In the Presidential election I will take no part. . . .

GALLATIN TO MADAME DE BUDÉ, NÉE ROLAZ.

NEW YORK, 1st May, 1845.

. . . Rappelez-moi au souvenir de vos fils et de votre frère. . . . J'espère qu'il laisse faire les gouvernements et qu'il ne se mêle plus de politique; ce qui est, comme je le sais, fort inutile lorsqu'on n'a point d'influence. Et je puis ajouter que mes quatorze dernières années, c'est-à-dire depuis que j'ai été étranger aux affaires publiques, ont été, à tout prendre, les plus heureuses de ma vie. Mes plus belles années avaient été dévouées, je puis dire, exclusivement au service de ma patrie d'adoption; celles-ci l'ont été à mes enfants et aux affections domestiques. De plus,

n'étant plus sur la route de personne, l'envie a disparu.   On ne
m'écoute pas du tout, mais on me considère et personne ne dit du
mal de moi. . . .

His opinions on the practical working of our government,
especially with reference to taxation, were given at considerable
length in a letter written to La Fayette in the year 1833.   One
portion of this letter is worth quoting, coming as it does from an
original Republican of the Jeffersonian school :

"The local taxes in the country, at least where I am acquainted,
amount to at least one-sixth of the income, and that on houses
here [in New York City] to not more than one-twelfth part.
This, merely for local disbursements, is certainly a heavy charge,
particularly in the country, and arises partly from local wants,
which for some objects, such as roads, are very great in proportion to our wealth.   But it is also due in a great degree to our
democratic institutions ; and the burden, which was extremely
light, especially in the country, fifty years ago, has been gradually
and is still increasing.   The reason appears to me obvious enough.
Government is in the hands of the people at large.   They are
an excellent check against high salaries, extravagant establishments, and every species of expenditure which they do not see or
in which they do not participate.   But they receive an immediate benefit from the money expended amongst themselves,
either as being employed in opening roads, the erection of
buildings, &c., or as being more interested in the application of
public money to schools, the payment of jurors and other petty
offices, and even prospectively in the provision for the poor.
They, in fact, pay little or no portion of the direct tax (occasionally enough in towns, but indirectly, by the increase of rents),
and receive the greater part of its proceeds.   You perceive that
I do not disguise what I think to be the defects, and I know no
other of any importance, in our system of taxation.   I do not
know any remedy for it here but in the exertions to obtain the
best men we can for our municipal officers.   But where institutions are yet to be formed, I may say that I have not discovered any evil to arise from universal suffrage in the choice of
representatives to our legislative bodies ; but that for municipal

officers, who have no power over persons, but only that of applying the proceeds of taxes, those who contribute to such payment
ought alone to have the privilege of being electors."

The threatened rupture with France in 1835, when President
Jackson nearly brought on a war on account of the failure of the
French Chambers to appropriate money in pursuance of a treaty
for the settlement of our claims, disturbed Mr. Gallatin greatly,
and at the request of Edward Everett, then a member of Congress, he wrote two very elaborate letters for the use of the Committee of Foreign Relations.[1] The following acknowledgment
has a certain characteristic interest:

JOHN C. CALHOUN TO GALLATIN.

WASHINGTON, 23d February, 1835.

DEAR SIR,—I am obliged to you for putting me in possession
of your views on a French war. They are such as I entertain.
I know of no greater calamity that could befall the country at
this time than a French war. I do not believe the Union would
survive it. My course is taken. So long as France abstains
from force I shall be opposed to war, and I am of the impression
that such will prove to be the sentiment of the entire South. . . .

The time was now coming for one more great effort on the
part of Mr. Gallatin to control the course of public events, an
effort which, considering all the circumstances, was as remarkable
as any struggle of his life. It was his last prolonged attempt,
and singularly characteristic.

Time had at length brought the realization of his most ardent
hopes as Secretary of the Treasury, and the national debt was
paid; all the advantages of that millennium were attained, whatever they might be, and Mr. Gallatin could esteem himself happy
that he had lived to see his vision made fact. It was not to be
denied that the establishment of republicanism, and even of
democracy, had been long antecedent to the discharge of the
debt; had proved to be noways dependent on the debt; had,

---

[1] Writings, vol. ii. p. 474.

indeed, been most rapid and most irresistible under the influence of a war which his own party had made, and under the burden of a heavy additional debt which he had himself helped to accumulate. This, however, was of little consequence; the results were gained, and the time had long passed when Mr. Gallatin would have been inclined to claim exclusive credit for them.

Unfortunately, the fact became immediately obvious that, whatever were the ultimate and permanent advantages gained by the extinction of the debt, the immediate consequences were disastrous and alarming in the extreme. Nullification and imminent civil war were at the head of the list, but were neither the most serious nor the most corrupting. Perhaps a worse result than civil war was the rapid decline in public economy and morality; the shameless scramble for public money; the wild mania for speculation; the outburst of every one of the least creditable passions of American character. At this revelation of the consequences of his own favorite political dogma, Mr. Gallatin stood positively appalled. "I find no one who suffers in mind as I do at the corruption and degeneracy of our government. But I do not despair, and cannot believe that we have lived under a perpetual delusion." So he wrote to his oldest friend. To his alarm he found that extinction of the national debt was a signal for an astonishing increase in the indebtedness of the community at large, one significant sign of which was that the individual States contracted, between 1830 and 1838, new debts to the amount of nearly one hundred and fifty millions, that is to say, very nearly as much as had been discharged by the national government since 1789. Under any circumstances this tendency to extravagance would have been dangerous, but when the President seized this moment for his attack upon the bank, he immensely aggravated the evil. From 1830 to 1837, in anticipation of the failure to renew the bank charter, three hundred new banks were created, with a capital of one hundred and forty-five millions of dollars, precisely doubling the banking capital of the country. Meanwhile, after the discharge of the last instalment of national debt, an alarming surplus rapidly accumulated in the hands of the Treasury officials, until forty millions had been deposited by them in State banks and had become the means of an excessive expansion of credit, acting as a violent stimulus to the wild extravagance of the time.

All these causes produced five or six years of intoxication, during which the public morality was permanently lowered and the seeds of future defalcations, public and private, rapidly matured. Then the tide turned; England stopped lending money and called for payment; the President and Congress attacked the resources and credit of the State banks as earnestly as they had previously helped to create and extend both; the New York banks stopped discounting; a terrible crisis came on; and on the 10th May, 1837, the New York banks suspended specie payments. The universal suspension of all banks throughout the country instantly followed.

Mr. Gallatin's bank suspended with the rest, not because it was obliged to do so, for it might perhaps have held out, but this would have answered no special object and would have produced considerable inconvenience. Mr. Gallatin himself, therefore, was personally involved in, and partially responsible for, an act of bankruptcy which was to him the substance of everything most galling and reproachful. He could not but remember how, in 1815, he had urged on the government the necessity of specie payments after the war, and how there had arisen almost a coldness between him and his friend Dallas, then Secretary of the Treasury, on the subject; how he had remonstrated against waiting for the restoration of the bank, and had pressed the Treasury to resume at once, by funding the excess of Treasury notes, and rejecting the notes of suspended banks when offered in payments to the government. That he should himself now belie his old teachings and become in practice if not in theory an advocate and supporter of an irredeemable paper currency, was intolerable. He had made every effort to prevent the necessity of suspension. He was now called upon by every feeling of self-respect to bring about resumption.

The State law required that a suspended bank, which did not resume its payments before the expiration of one year from the date of suspension, should be deemed to have surrendered its rights, and should be adjudged to be dissolved. This was the principal lever with which Mr. Gallatin could work.   He represented an institution which of itself had very little weight; but, although his only means of interfering at all was in the character of president of a new and unimportant bank, his real authority was wholly personal, and it was fortunate for him that the want of capital behind him was supplied by the active and able co-operation of other bank officers, especially by Mr. George Newbold, of the Bank of America, and by Mr. Cornelius W. Lawrence, of the Bank of the State of New York.

On the 15th August a general meeting was held by the officers of the city banks.   A resolution was adopted appointing a committee to correspond with the leading State banks throughout the Union, for the purpose of agreeing on the time and the measures for resumption.   This committee consisted of Mr. Gallatin, Mr. Newbold, and Mr. Lawrence, and proceeded almost immediately to carry out its instructions.   Three days afterwards, on August 18, a circular-letter was despatched, inviting the other banks to a conference, and laying down in very energetic language the rules which should guide their action: " By accepting their charters the banks contracted the obligation of redeeming their issues at all times and under any circumstances whatever; they have not been able to perform that engagement; and a depreciated paper, differing in value at different places and subject to daily fluctuations in the same place, has thus been substituted for the currency, equivalent to gold or silver, which, and no other, they were authorized and had the exclusive right to issue.   Such a state of things cannot and ought not to be tolerated any longer than an absolute necessity requires it. . . . As relates to the banks of this city, we are of opinion that, provided the co-operation of the other banks is obtained, they may and ought to, we should perhaps say that they must, resume specie payments before next spring."

This circular had one immediate effect: it developed the force and character of the opposition; it brought out the fact that the real point of resistance was to be in Pennsylvania, and that of this resistance the old Bank of the United States was to be the main stay; it showed that politics had been dragged into alliance with the less solvent banking institutions, and that the party opposed to President Van Buren's Administration had hopes of forcing the re-establishment of a national bank by making this the condition of resumption. Mr. Gallatin had no great sympathy with the Administration and no favors to ask from it, but he was not at all disposed to allow his ideas of public duty to be subordinated to the political purposes of the opposition.

On the expiration of the bank charter in March, 1836, the old Bank of the United States had accepted a new charter from the State of Pennsylvania, and had attempted to carry on its business. Bad management, want of confidence, and the universal financial pressure soon reduced it to such a condition that the general suspension of specie payments alone concealed its insolvency; yet its controlling influence over the other Pennsylvania banks was such that they still followed its lead, and all united in replying to Mr. Gallatin's circular, that they deemed it inexpedient to appoint delegates to the proposed meeting of bank officers, for the reason that general resumption depended mainly, if not exclusively, on the action of Congress; thereby implying that no permanent resumption was possible without the adoption of their policy of renewing the charter of the United States Bank. The Baltimore banks followed their example, and those of Boston returned no positive answer.

Unsatisfactory as this result was, the New York banks, with Mr. Gallatin at their head, resolutely pursued their object. On the 20th October the committee issued another circular, in pursuance of a resolution passed at a general meeting on the 10th, and formally invited the other State banks over the whole Union to meet in convention at New York on November 27. This step compelled both Philadelphia and Boston to accede, for fear of the consequences in case New York should act alone. The convention met, and Mr. Gallatin acted in it the prominent part which naturally fell to his share as chairman of the New York committee. His opponents did not, however, press the political argument, but rested their case principally on the injury that would be caused by a premature resumption. Mr. Gallatin met this objection with that direct assertion of moral obligation always so fatal as an argument, raising disputes, as it does, above the ordinary level of expediency, and throwing opposition into an apologetic defensive. He said it was monstrous to suppose that, if the banks were able to resume and to sustain specie payments, they should have any discretionary right to discuss the question whether a more or less protracted suspension was consistent with their views of "the condition and circumstances of the country." There would be no limit to such supposed discretion. The evidence was irresistible that the banks were able to resume. Exchange was favorable. No known cause existed which could prevent a general resumption. The arguments and objections of the United States Bank of Pennsylvania were neither more nor less than excuses for an intended protracted suspension for an indefinite period of time, which was shown by the fact that this bank had actually put in circulation, since the suspension, a large amount of the notes of the dead and irresponsible Bank of the United States.

The situation was thus narrowed down to a local contest between the New York banks, represented by Mr. Gallatin, and the United States Bank of Pennsylvania, directed by Mr. Biddle. The influence of party sympathy led the Boston banks to sustain Mr. Biddle to the last against Mr. Gallatin; Baltimore followed the same course; outside of New York Mr. Gallatin found support only in the North-West and South. Yet, although the convention was nearly equally divided and nothing more than general professions could be obtained from it, the contest was really unequal, and there could be no question that Mr. Gallatin was master of the situation. The New York banks, actively supported by the comptroller and the State government, proceeded to take such measures as would enable them to resume at almost any moment, but they waited still some length of time in the hope of obtaining co-operation. The convention had adjourned to meet again on the 11th April, 1838. Mr. Gallatin and his colleagues, who represented the New York banks in the convention, made a report on the 15th December, 1837, representing in strong language the evils of the situation and pressing for combined action. On the 28th February the same gentlemen

made another report on measures, "in contemplation of the resumption of specie payments by the banks of the city of New
York, on or before the 10th day of May next." Nothing was
omitted that could tend to secure the banks from accident or
designed attack, and even the popular feeling was enlisted on
their side.

When the adjourned convention met on the 11th April, a
letter was presented from the Philadelphia banks declining to
attend, on the ground that the banks and citizens of New York
had already acted independently in announcing their intention
to resume on the 10th May, and that the banks of Philadelphia
" do not wish to give any advice in regard to the course which
the banks of the city of New York have resolved to pursue;
they do not wish to receive any from those banks touching their
own course." One might have supposed that after this defection
of Pennsylvania there would have been no difficulty in controlling the action of the adjourned convention when it met on
the 11th April; but this proved no easier matter than before.
Mr. Gallatin's object was to fix the earliest possible day for general resumption, since New York placed herself in a very critical
position so long as she stood alone. But the convention could
not even be persuaded to fix the first Monday in October for the
day. The utmost that could be got from New England was to
name the 1st January, 1839.

Left thus isolated, Mr. Gallatin and his associates went directly
on their course alone. The New York banks resumed specie
payments on the 10th May, as they had pledged themselves to
do. They resumed in good faith and in full; the resumption
was effected without the slightest difficulty; and it is but just
to add that the other banks made no attempt to impede it.
Then came the inevitable struggle between the solvent and the
insolvent institutions. Boston acted better than she talked, and
all New England resumed in July. Public opinion, operating
first on the Governor of Pennsylvania, compelled the United
States Bank to resume in the course of the same month. The
South and West followed the example. For something more
than a year the insolvent banks managed to crawl on, and then
at last, in October, 1839, the United States Bank went to pieces

in one tremendous ruin, and carried the South and West with it to the ground. A long and miserable period of liquidation generally followed, but New England and New York maintained payments, and Mr. Gallatin had once more, almost by the sheer force of his own will and character, guided the country back to safe and solid ground.

In the year following, on June 7, 1839, he at length resigned his post as president of the National Bank of New York, and retired from all forms of business. His last considerable effort as a financier and economist was the publication of a pamphlet supplementary to his " Considerations on Currency." This essay of one hundred pages, entitled " Suggestions on the Banks and Currency of the several United States," was printed in 1841. Its value is principally that of continuing the history of our financial condition, more particularly as respects currency and banks; and, taken in connection with the earlier essay, it forms a hand-book of American finance down to the year 1840.[1]

Doubtless the students of to-day, who turn their attention to these papers upon which the reputation of Mr. Gallatin, as an author and theorist in finance, principally rests, will find that the point of view has considerably changed, and that a wider treatment of the subject has become necessary. Not less the circumstances than the thought of that generation naturally tended to attribute peculiar and intrinsic powers to currency; a tendency quite as prominent among the English as among the American economists. Mr. Gallatin's writings dealt mainly and avowedly with the currency, because he believed that the condition of the currency was the responsible cause of much if not most of the moral degradation of his time, and that a return to a sound metallic medium of exchange was a means of purifying society. The later school of economists would perhaps lay somewhat less stress upon currency as in itself an active cause, and they would rather treat it as a symptom, an instrument operating mechanically and incapable in itself of producing either all the evil or all the good then attributed to it. The following letter, at all events, shows Mr. Gallatin's opinions on the subject:

---

[1] Reprinted in Gallatin's Writings, vol. iii.

GALLATIN TO JONATHAN ROBERTS.

NEW YORK, 3d June, 1841.

RESPECTED FRIEND,—I received your welcome letter of the 27th May, and return in answer my essay on currency.

I sometimes flatter myself that we old men labor under the disease incident to our age, and that we think that the world has grown worse than it was in former days, because, when young, the vices of the times had become familiar to us, and that we are shocked by those of new growth. Thus, for instance, though you and I were temperate, we were less severe towards drunkards than the present generation.

Yet so far at least as respects political corruption, it is impossible that we should be mistaken. I was twelve years a member either of the Legislature of Pennsylvania or of Congress, the greater part of those in hot party times and conflicts. And I may safely affirm that, without distinction of party, a purer assemblage, in both bodies, of men honest, honorable, and inaccessible to corruption could not be found. I never was tempted; for during my forty years of public life a corrupt offer never approached me.

Now, although I am not so happy as Mr. Calhoun in always finding a cause for every effect, I will venture to assign two reasons for the deterioration we lament.

The American Independence was an event of immense magnitude, and, though not altogether irreproachable in that respect, yet comparatively unsullied by those convulsions, excesses, and crimes which have almost always attended similar revolutions. The greater part of the men employed in the public service during the thirty following years had taken an active part in that event. The objects to which our faculties are applied have a necessary influence over our minds. How diminutive, nay, pitiful, those appear which now engross public attention and for which parties contend, when compared with those for which the founders of the republic staked their fortunes and their lives!— the creation of a great independent nation and the organization of a national yet restricted government. I do believe that the minds, the moral feeling of those thus engaged, were raised above the ordinary standard and elevated to one somewhat proportionate to the magnitude of the objects which they did accomplish.

And those men had been educated at a time when the American people, blessed with an abundant supply of all the necessaries of life, were still frugal and had preserved a great simplicity of manners. Here is the other cause which may be assigned for the present depraved state of public opinion and feeling. We have rioted in liberty and revel in luxury. As we have increased in wealth and power the sense of integrity and justice has been weakened. The love of power, for the sake of its petty present enjoyments, has been substituted for that of country and of permanent fame, and the thirst of gold for the honest endeavors to acquire by industry and frugality a modest independence.

Where is the remedy? We cannot and ought not to restrain by legislative enactments the marvellous energy of this nation and the natural course of things; but we ought not to administer an artificial stimulus. This stimulus is the paper currency; and you will perceive by my letter of 1830 to Mr. Walsh, which I have published for that purpose in the Appendix, that my ultimate object has been, as [it] still is, to annihilate almost altogether that dangerous instrument. I admit its utility and convenience when used with great sobriety. But its irresistible tendency to degenerate into a depreciated and irredeemable currency, and the lamentable effect this produces, not as a mere matter of dollars and cents, but on the moral feeling and habits of the whole community, are such that I am quite convinced that it is far preferable to do without it.

But we must take men and things as they are; a sudden transition would cause great injury and is impracticable. And without ever losing sight of the ultimate object, I formerly proposed, and now suggest, that only such measures [be adopted] as may, it seems to me, be easily carried into effect; as would greatly lessen present evils; and as have a tendency to improve and elevate public opinion, and may assist in gradually preparing a better state of things. With that explanation you will understand more clearly the object of my essay.

In the mean while, as individuals and each in our sphere, we have only to perform our appropriate duties and sustain our precepts by our example. You may be annoyed in your new office;[1] but there is this advantage in an executive office : that it imposes certain specific and clearly-defined duties, to be performed day after day, with unremitted industry and constant respect for law and justice; and this honestly done affords the consciousness of being a useful member of society.

We would indeed be much gratified by your contemplated visit to New York. Left almost alone of my contemporaries, the meeting with an old friend is highly refreshing to me. And you may see, by the general tenor of this letter, that I consider you as one, and one of those I most respect. Mrs. G. requests to be kindly remembered to you, and I pray you to rely on my constant attachment. I am altogether unacquainted with our new President. He has made some sad appointments in this city. That of marshal[1] is too bad.

Respectfully, your friend and servant.

GALLATIN TO JOHN M. BOTTS, M.C.

NEW YORK, 14th June, 1841.

SIR,—I had duly received the letter you addressed to me last winter, and had hoped that my declining to answer it would satisfy you that I had an insurmountable objection to any use whatever being made of any conversation that may have taken place between Mr. Jefferson and myself on the subject of the Bank of the United States. I will only say that the report which reached you was imperfect and incorrect, and that he lived and died a decided enemy to our banking system generally, and specially to a bank of the United States.

My last essay, the receipt of which you do me the honor to acknowledge, was written without reference not only to parties, but even to any general political views, other than the restoration and maintenance of a sound currency. Except in its character of fiscal agent of the general government, I attach much less importance to a national bank than several of those who are in favor of it; and perhaps on that account it is a matter of regret

---

[1] Collector of the port of Philadelphia, appointed by President Harrison.

to me that it should continue to be, as it has been since General Jackson's accession to the Presidency and not before, a subject of warm contention and the pivot on which the politics of the country are to turn.   I am quite sure that if this take place and the issue before the people be bank or no bank, those who shall have succeeded in establishing that institution will be crushed. I do not doubt your sincerity and bravery, but the cause is really not worth dying for.   Did I believe that a bank of the United States would effectually secure us a sound currency, I would think it a duty at all hazards to promote the object.   As the question now stands, I would at least wait till the wishes of the people were better ascertained.   So far as I know, the opponents are most active, virulent, and extremely desirous that the great contest should turn on that point: the friends, speculators and bankrupts excepted, are disinterested and not over-zealous.

I have the honor, &c.

Before dismissing the subject of finance, the following curious correspondence may properly find a place here.   Albert Davy was United States consul at Leeds, England, and happened to be now in Washington obtaining a renewal of his commission:

ALBERT DAVY TO JAMES GALLATIN.

Very *confidential*.

WASHINGTON, 25th December, 1843.

MY DEAR SIR,—I am induced to write you a few lines this evening very confidentially to state that Mr. Robert Tyler has just called on me to ask if I thought Mr. Gallatin would accept the Secretaryship of the Treasury for the remaining Presidential term, or, rather, whether his health would permit him to change his residence.   He told me the President mentioned Mr. Gallatin's name the first to fill that important post, which, I dare say, would be made very easy to him.   This movement is of course in anticipation of Mr. Spencer's leaving.   As no one as yet is aware of it out of the President's immediate circle but myself, I am sure you will see the necessity of not communicating this to any one but to Mr. Gallatin. . . .

NEW YORK, 28th December, 1843.

DEAR SIR,—My son James has shown to me your letter to
him of 25th of this month, received yesterday. It seems hardly
necessary to make a serious answer to it. Yet, as silence might
be misconstrued, I have only to say that I want no office, and
that to accept at my age that of Secretary of the Treasury would
be an act of insanity. I cannot indeed believe that this has
been seriously contemplated by anybody : you must have misunderstood the person who spoke to you. I might give conclusive reasons why, even if I was young and able, I would
not at this time be fit for the office, nor the office at all suit me ;
but this is not called for.

I remain, with great regard, dear sir,

Your obedient servant.

WASHINGTON, January 24, 1844.

MY DEAR SIR,—I have been applied to by one of the President's family to know if you would accept the Treasury Department. If you would, I am assured that it will be tendered to
you so soon as vacated by the confirmation of Mr. Spencer.

This last letter is tersely endorsed by Mr. Gallatin: "Folly, of
which no notice taken."

Finance was, however, only one of the numerous subjects in
which Mr. Gallatin took an active interest. Diplomacy was
another. Our relations with Great Britain, though in some
respects better, were in others worse than before; the postponed
questions of boundary became serious, and especially that of the
North-Eastern or Maine boundary assumed a very threatening
aspect. The arbitration of the King of the Netherlands had
proved a failure, owing perhaps to the fact that our government
failed to take proper measures for supporting its case diplo-
matically. Had Mr. Gallatin been on the spot he would probably have brought about a different result; but Mr. Van Buren's

diplomacy was not so successful in Europe as in the United States, and he had more need of it in Washington than elsewhere. The question between England and America was thus kept open until both countries became seriously anxious. In 1840, Mr. Gallatin revised and reprinted his statement of the North-Eastern boundary argument as laid before the King of the Netherlands in 1830. In 1842 the British ministry sent Lord Ashburton to negotiate a treaty at Washington, and thus Alexander Baring came again to interpose his ever-friendly and ever-generous temper between the fretful jarring of the two great nations. The time had been when the British government and people treated Mr. Baring's warning advice with such contempt as only George Canning could fully embody and express; but that time was now long passed. They had learned to lean upon him, and the American government readily met him in the same spirit.

LORD ASHBURTON TO ALBERT GALLATIN.

WASHINGTON, 12th April, 1842.

DEAR MR. GALLATIN,—My first destination was to approach America through New York, but the winds decided otherwise, and I was landed at Annapolis. In one respect only this was a disappointment, and a serious one. I should have much wished to seek you out in your retreat to renew an old and highly-valued acquaintance and, I believe and hope I may add, friendship; to talk over with you the Old and the New World, their follies and their wisdom, their present and by-gone actors, all which nobody understands so well as you do, and, what is more rare, nobody that has crossed my passage in life has appeared to me to judge with the same candid impartiality. This pleasure of meeting you is, I trust, only deferred. I shall, if I live to accomplish my work here, certainly not leave the country without an attempt to find you out and to draw a little wisdom from the best well, though it may be too late for my use in the work I have in hand and very much at heart.

You will probably be surprised at my undertaking this task at my period of life, and when I am left to my own thoughts I am sometimes surprised myself at my rashness. People here stare when I tell them that I listened to the debates in Congress on Mr. Jay's treaty in 1795, and seem to think that some antediluvian has come among them out of his grave. The truth is that I was tempted by my great anxiety in the cause, and the extreme importance which I have always attached to the maintenance of peace between our countries. The latter circumstance induced my political friends to press this appointment upon me, and with much hesitation, founded solely upon my health and age, I yielded. In short, here I am. My reception has been everything I could expect or wish; but your experience will tell you that little can be inferred from this until real business is entered upon. I can only say that it shall not be my fault if we do not continue to live on better terms than we have lately done, and, if I do not misunderstand the present very anomalous state of parties here, or misinterpret public opinion generally, there appears to be no class of politicians of any respectable character indisposed to peace with us on reasonable terms. I expect and desire to obtain no other, and my present character of a diplomatist is so new to me that I know no other course but candor and plain-dealing. The most inexpert protocolist would beat me hollow at such work. I rely on your good wishes, my dear sir, though I can have nothing else, and that you will believe me unfeignedly yours.

GALLATIN TO LORD ASHBURTON.

NEW YORK, 20th April, 1842.

DEAR LORD ASHBURTON,—Your not landing here was as great disappointment to me as to you. I have survived all my early friends, all my political associates; and out of my own family no one remains for whom I have a higher regard or feel a more sincere attachment than yourself. If you cannot come here, I will make an effort and see you at Washington. Your mission is in every respect a most auspicious event. To all those who know you it affords a decisive proof of the sincere wish on the part of your government to attempt a settlement of our differences as far as practicable; at all events, to prevent an unnatural, and on both sides absurd and disgraceful, war. There are but few intrinsic difficulties of any magnitude in the way. Incautious commitments, pride, prejudices, selfish or party feelings present more serious obstacles. You have one of a peculiar kind to encounter. Our President is supported by neither of the two great political parties of the country, and is hated by that which elected him, and which has gained a temporary ascendency. He must, in fact, negotiate with the Senate before he can agree with you on any subject. It is the first time that we have been in that situation, which is somewhat similar to that of France; witness your late treaty, which the French Administration concluded and dared not ratify. It may be that under those circumstances our government may think it more eligible to make separate conventions for each of the subjects on which you may agree than to blend them in one instrument.

The greatest difficulties may be found in settling the two questions in which both parties have in my humble opinion the least personal or separate interest, viz., the right of visitation on the African seas for the purpose only of ascertaining the nationality of the vessel; and the North-Western boundary. I have no reason, however, to believe that the Administration, left to itself, will be intractable on any subject whatever; I hope that higher motives will prevail over too sensitive or local feelings, and I place the greatest reliance on your sound judgment, thorough knowledge of the subject, straightforwardness, and ardent desire to preserve peace and cement friendship between the two kindred nations. You cannot apply your faculties to a more useful or nobler purpose. I am now in my 82d year, and on taking a retrospective view of my long career I derive the greatest consolation for my many faults and errors from the consciousness that I ever was a minister of peace, from the fact that the twenty last years of my political life were almost exclusively employed in preventing the war as long as I could, in assisting in a speedy restoration of peace, and in settling subsequently as many of the points of difference as was at the time practicable. May God prosper your efforts and enable you to consummate the holy work!

After successfully negotiating his treaty, Lord Ashburton came to New York, and the two men met once more.

There remained the question of the North-Western boundary to fester into a sore. This did not fail to happen, and in 1846 the two nations again stood on the verge of war. On this subject, too, Mr. Gallatin published a pamphlet which took a characteristic view of the dispute.[1] He did not hesitate to concede that the American title to the contested territory was defective; that neither nation could show an indisputable right in the premises; but that America had all the chances in her favor, and that, in any possible event, war was the least effective policy; "the certain consequence, independent of all the direct calamities and miseries of war, will be a mutual increase of debt and taxation, and the ultimate fate of Oregon will be the same as if the war had not taken place." This thoroughly common-sense view was so obvious that neither government could long resist it. The Oregon question, too, was in the end peaceably settled.

There was, however, one political difficulty of far deeper consequence than currency or boundary, and offering a problem to which no such simple· reasoning applied; this was the growth of slavery and the slave power. Here two great principles clashed. The practical rule of politics which had guided Mr. Gallatin through life, to avoid all issues which might endanger the Union, was here more directly applicable than elsewhere, for Mr. Gallatin knew better than most men the dangers involved in this issue. He had found even the liberal mind of Mr. Jefferson impervious to argument on the consequences of extending the slave power. Not only was he no sympathizer with slavery; he was in principle an abolitionist; he never changed that opinion, which he had incorporated so early as 1793 in a draft of an act, declaring that "slavery was inconsistent with every principle of humanity, justice, and right." In 1843, when Maria Chapman urged him to write for her anti-slavery Annual, he declined. "I would not for any consideration say anything that might injure the holy cause in which you are engaged, and yet I must tell the truth, or what appears to me to be the truth." Determined to respect the constitutional compact, he carefully abstained from taking any part in the slavery agitation. Never-

---

[1] Reprinted in Writings, vol. iii.

theless the time came when he could no longer be silent. On the 24th April, 1844, a popular meeting was held in New York to protest against the annexation of Texas; Mr. Gallatin was asked to preside, and one of the most courageous acts of his life was to take the chair and address this great and turbulent assembly:

SPEECH ON THE ANNEXATION OF TEXAS.

At my advanced age and period of life, withdrawn as I am from the politics of the day, desirous of quiet, nothing could have induced me to attend this meeting but the magnitude of the subject. I will simply indicate the points involved in the question which has called us together, leaving to others abler than myself to discuss them at length. Till this day the United States have preserved the highest reputation amongst the nations of the earth for the fidelity with which they have fulfilled all their engagements and generally carried on all their relations with foreign nations. They have never engaged in a war for the sake of conquest, never but in self-defence and for the purpose of repelling aggression against their most sacred rights. They have never acquired any territory by conquest or violence, nor in any other way but by fair treaties, fairly negotiated, with the consent of all the parties that might have any claim to the territory in question. What now is the nature of the question which has been proclaimed lately,—the annexation of Texas? By the most solemn treaties between us and foreign nations Texas has been adjudged as being within the limits of Mexico. If there was any claim on the part of the United States to that country, it was expressly renounced by these treaties. It is perfectly clear then that the attempt now made is a direct and positive violation of treaty stipulations. I have heard it stated that there was danger that it would also lead us into war. I think this but a very partial and erroneous view of the subject. I do assert, without fear of contradiction, that the annexation of Texas under existing circumstances is a positive declaration of war against Mexico. I will say that even if the independence of Texas had been acknowledged by Mexico, it would be still war, for Texas is at war with Mexico, and in such a state of things to annex it to this country is to make us a party to that war. But in existing circumstances and while Texas continues at war with Mexico and her independence is not acknowledged by the latter power, I will say that, according to the universally acknowledged laws of nations and universal usage of all Christian nations, to annex Texas is war; and in that assertion I will be sustained by every publicist and jurist in the Christian world. This war would be a war founded on injustice, and a war of conquest. I will not stop to inquire what Mexico may do or ought to do in such circumstances. It is enough that the war would be unjust. I know nothing of the ability or desire of Mexico to injure us. It is enough to say that an unjust war, founded upon the violation of solemn treaty stipulations, would disgrace the national character, which till this day has been unsullied.

There is another view of this subject, more complex, more delicate, but I do think it is both better and fairer to meet it in the face. I allude to the effect that this measure would have on the question of slavery. The Constitution of the United States was from the beginning founded upon mutual concessions and compromise. When that Constitution was passed it appears that the Southern States, alarmed by the difference of their social state and institutions from ours in the North, required some guarantees. They may have been granted with reluctance, but they are consecrated by the Constitution. The surrender of fugitive slaves and the non-equal principle of representation have been granted, and, however repugnant to our feelings or principles, we must carry out the provisions into effect faithfully and inviolate. But it ought to be observed that these provisions applied only to the territory then within the limits of the United States, and to none other. In the course of events we acquired Louisiana and Florida, and, without making any observations on these precedents, it so happened that, in the course of events, three new States have been added out of territories not, when the Constitution was adopted, within the limits of the United States; and more, eventually Florida was added to the slave-holding States. Thus it has happened that additional security and additional guarantee have been given to the South. With those I think they ought to be satisfied. Nothing is more true than that if we wish to preserve the Union, it must be by mutual respect to the feelings of others, but these concessions must be altogether mutual and not all on one side. If it be asked what we do require from the South, I will answer,—nothing whatever. We do not require from the South any new measure that should be repugnant either to their opinions or feelings. Nor do we interfere with the question of slavery in Texas. We have taken no measures, we do not mean to take any measures, either to prevent or induce them to admit slavery. It is a free, independent State, and we wish them to do precisely what they please. All we ask is to preserve the present state of things. All we ask is that no such plan as shall again agitate that question shall be attempted to be carried into effect. It is too much to ask from us that we should take an active part in permitting the accession of a foreign state, and a foreign slave-holding state, to the Union ; and that we should consent that new States should again be added to those upon an equal basis of representation. This is all we ask. The discussion of these questions does not originate with us. It originates with those who have fostered this plan. We wish every discussion of this question to be avoided. But if it be forced upon us we will be forced to meet it.

There are other considerations and most momentous questions which depend upon this. In the first place, does the treaty-making power imply a power to annul existing treaties? Does that power embrace the right of declaring war? Can the President or Senate, in making a treaty with another power, disregard the stipulations of a treaty with a third party? Again, can a foreign state be admitted in the Union without the unanimous consent of all the parties to the compact? I know that the precedents of Louisiana and Florida may be adduced; but let us see how far they go. Their validity depends solely on the fact that there was universal acquiescence. Not one State in the Union protested against the proceeding, and if upon this occasion the same should occur, I will say that without adverting to forms we might consider it proper to admit that there is a right. But the precedent goes no farther. It does not go to the point that the power does or does not exist.

These, I have said, are momentous questions, such as would necessarily shake the Union to its very centre, and such as I wish to see forever avoided.   Another point.   This measure will bring indelible disgrace upon our democratic institutions; it will bring them into discredit; it will excite the hopes of their enemies; it will check the hopes of the friends of mankind. We had hoped that, when the people of the United States had resumed their rights and the government was in their hands, there would be a gradual amelioration of legislation, of the social state, of the intercourse between men.   All this is checked by a measure on which treaties are violated and an unjust war undertaken.

Still, I do not despair.   My confidence is in the people.   But we must give them time to make, to form, and to express their opinions; and therefore it is that I do strongly reprobate the secret, the insidious manner in which that plot has been conducted, so as to debar the people of the Union from the right of expressing an opinion on the subject.

Gentlemen, I have done.   I thank you for the indulgence with which you have been pleased to listen to me.   I am highly gratified that the last public act of a long life should have been that of bearing testimony against this outrageous attempt.   It is indeed a consolation that my almost extinguished voice has been on this occasion raised in defence of liberty, of justice, and of our country.

Repeatedly interrupted; at moments absolutely stopped by uproar and rioting; able to make his feeble voice heard only by those immediately around him, he still resolutely maintained his ground and persisted to the end.   Mr. Gallatin was at that time in his eighty-fourth year; nothing but the most conscientious sense of duty could possibly have induced him to appear again in public, especially on an occasion when it was well known that the worst passions of the worst populace in the city of New York would be aroused against him.   Not even when he risked his life before the rifles of the backwoodsmen at Redstone Old Fort had he given so striking proof of his moral courage.

Perhaps it was this final proof that gave point to a short

speech of Mr. J. Q. Adams, which has been already alluded to. In the month of November following the annexation meeting, the New York Historical Society, of which Mr. Gallatin was now president, held a celebration, followed by a dinner, given in his honor. Mr. J. Q. Adams was one of the invited guests, and took the occasion to make the following remarks. Readers of his Diary will appreciate how much his concluding words meant to him; honesty, as both Mr. Gallatin and himself had found, was not only the highest, but one of the rarest, public virtues:

"To the letter," said Mr. Adams, "which was sent me, your honorable president added a line, saying, 'I shall be glad to shake hands with you once more in this world.' Sir, if nothing else could have induced me, these words would have compelled my attendance here, and I can conceive of nothing that would have prevented me. I have lived long, sir, in this world, and I have been connected with all sorts of men, of all sects and descriptions. I have been in the public service for a great part of my life, and filled various offices of trust in conjunction with that venerable gentleman, Albert Gallatin. I have known him half a century. In many things we differed; on many questions of public interest and policy we were divided, and in the history of parties in this country there is no man from whom I have so widely differed as from him. But on other things we have harmonized; and now there is no man with whom I more thoroughly agree on all points than I do with him. But one word more. Let me say, before I leave you and him,—birds of passage as we are, bound to a warmer and more congenial clime,—that among all the public men with whom I have been associated in the course of my political life, whether agreeing or differing in opinion with him, I have always found him to be an honest and honorable man."

In spite of all the opposition of the North, the war with Mexico took place. Every moral conviction and every life-long hope of Mr. Gallatin were outraged by this act of our government. The weight of national immorality rested incessantly on his mind. He would not abandon his faith in human nature; he determined to make an appeal to the moral sense of the American public, and to scatter this appeal broadcast by the hundred thousand copies over the country. With this view he wrote his pamphlet on "Peace with Mexico,"[1] yet accompanying it with another on "War Expenses," which invoked more worldly interests. His object was to urge the conclusion of a peace on moral and equitable principles, and, feeling that time was short, he pressed forward with feverish haste. On the 15th February, 1848, he said, "I write with great difficulty, and I become exhausted when I work more than four or five hours a day. Ever since the end of October all my faculties, impaired as they are, were absorbed in one subject; not only my faculties, but I may say all my feelings. I thought of nothing else: Age quod agis! I postponed everything else, even a volume of ethnography which was in the press; even answering the letters which did not absolutely require immediate attention."

The warnings to be quick came thick and fast. Only a week after he wrote this letter, his old associate, J. Q. Adams, breathed his last on the floor of Congress. A few weeks more brought the news that Alexander Baring was dead. In Europe society itself seemed about to break in pieces, and everything old was passing away with a rapidity that recalled the days of the first French revolution. Mr. Gallatin might well think it necessary to press his pace and to economize every instant that remained; and yet in that eventful year the world moved more rapidly still, and he had time—though not much—to spare. His pamphlets were sent in great numbers over the North and East, and certainly had their share in leading the government to accept the treaty of peace which was negotiated by Mr. Trist, notwithstanding instructions to leave Mexico, and signed by him at Guadalupe Hidalgo on the 2d of February.

These pamphlets were his last intellectual effort. As the year advanced, symptoms of decline became more and more evident. His memory began to fail. When alone, he caught himself talking in French as when a boy. His mind recurred much to his early youth, to Geneva, to his school, to Mlle. Pictet, and undoubtedly to that self-reproach for his neglect of her and of

---

[1] Reprinted in Writings, vol. iii.

his family which seems to have weighed upon him throughout life. The Presidential election of 1848 was a great satisfaction to him; but he thought more frequently and naturally of his own past political contests and of the Presidents whom he had helped to make. His mind became more excitable as his strength declined. There was, however, little to be done or desired by him in the way of preparation; his life had left no traces to be erased, and his death would create no confusion and required no long or laborious forethought. He had felt a certain pride in his modest means; his avowed principle had been that a Secretary of the Treasury should not acquire wealth. He had no enemies to forgive. "'I cannot charge myself with malignity of temper,'" he said; "'indeed, I have been regarded as mild and amiable. But now, approaching the confines of the eternal world, I desire to examine myself with the utmost rigor to see whether I am in charity with all mankind. On this retrospect I cannot remember any adversary whom I have not forgiven, or to whom I have failed to make known my forgiveness, except one, and he is no longer living.' Here he named a late eminent politician of Virginia"; doubtless William B. Giles.

During the last months of his life he turned with great earnestness to the promises and hopes of religion. His clergyman, Dr. Alexander, kept memoranda of his conversation on this subject. "I never was an infidel," he said; "though I have had my doubts, and the habit of my thinking has been to push discoveries to their utmost consequences without fear. . . . I have always leaned towards Arminianism; but the points are very difficult. I am a bold speculator. Such has been the habit of my mind all my life long."

He failed slowly as the winter of 1848–49 passed, and was for the most part confined to his room and his bed. In the month of May, 1849, while he thus lay helpless, his wife died in the adjoining room, leaving him deeply overcome and shaken by agitation and grief. Nevertheless, he survived to be taken, as the summer came on, to his daughter's house at Astoria. There, on the 12th August, 1849, his life ended.

INDEX.

A.

Adams, John, 310, 372, 399, 411, 427, 460; Vice-President of the United States, favors Gallatin's claim to eligibility for the Senate, 120, 121; elected President, 178; suspects intrigue, 178; his first speech to Congress, 183; his second speech, 188; declines invitation to birthday ball, 194; nominates William Vans Murray to France, 220, 221; remark on mediation, 223; his third speech to Congress, 223; ostensibly renominated for the Presidency, 241; his conduct in 1801, 258, 265, 266; calls the Senate, 260, 263.

Adams, Mrs. John, 185.

Adams, John Quincy, 429, 502, 634; rejected by the Senate as minister to Russia, 389; his account of the conduct of the Senate in 1809, 389–391; his account of Duane and Binns, 442; commissioner under the mediation, 479; parallelism of his career with Gallatin's, 495–497; his antagonism to Mr. Clay, 520, 522; his account of his colleagues at Ghent, 523, 527, 528; prepares articles, 540; his struggle to secure the fisheries, 540–545; minister to England, 548; joined in negotiating commercial convention, 548; his character, 552, 592, 599; Secretary of State, 562, 566; his negotiation with France in 1819–1822, 573–575, 579; his character of Gallatin, 576, 626, 629, 676; W. H. Crawford's comments on, 580, 584, 586, 588; Gallatin's character of, 599; chosen President, 602, 606; his

reasons for not offering the Treasury to Gallatin, 609; on the distrust of Mr. Clay, 609; on relations with England in 1827, 624, 625, 627, 628; his comments on Mr. Canning, 624, 627, 628; his comments on men and measures, 636; his death, 677.

Adams, William, British commissioner at Ghent, 519, 543; negotiator of the commercial convention, 552.

Addison, Alexander, 177, 223.

Aix-la-Chapelle, Congress of, 572.

Alexander, Emperor of Russia, invites diplomatic relations in 1808, 390; offers mediation, 477, 498; renews the offer, 498, 503; causes misunderstanding, 503, 510, 511; receives a note from Mr. Crawford, 511; his conversation with La Fayette at the house of Madame de Staël, 512, 514; his visit to London, 514; his interview with Gallatin, 514, 515; his influence on the negotiation, 516, 518, 537; his friendliness, 553.

Alien laws, 202, 204, 206, 274, 320.

Algerine powers, war with, 300, 306, 307, 349.

Allegre, Sophia, Gallatin's first wife, her family, 69; her engagement, 70; her mother, 70, 71; her marriage, 71, 72; her death, 72, 75, 80, 83.

Allen, John, M.C. from Connecticut, on the sedition law, 207.

Alston, Joseph, reports of his character, 244, 245.

Ames, Fisher, 154; his speech on Jay's treaty, 155, 165, 198; his opinion on the use of the army in domestic poli-

THE END.